The Ultimate

Spanish Review and Practice

PREMIUM FIFTH EDITION

Ronni L. Gordon, PhD
David M. Stillman, PhD

New York Chicago San Francisco Athens London Madrid
Mexico City Milan New Delhi Singapore Sydney Toronto

1 2 3 4 5 6 7 8 9   LON   28 27 26 25 24 23

ISBN   978-1-265-39422-6
MHID   1-265-39422-9

e-ISBN   978-1-265-39423-3
e-MHID   1-265-39423-7

McGraw Hill books are available at special quantity discounts to use as premiums and sales promotions or for use in corporate training programs. To contact a representative, please visit the Contact Us pages at www.mhprofessional.com.

McGraw Hill is committed to making our products accessible to all learners. To learn more about the available support and accommodations we offer, please contact us at accessibility@mheducation.com. We also participate in the Access Text Network (www.accesstext.org), and ATN members may submit requests through ATN.

McGraw Hill Language Lab App

Extensive materials, including audio recordings, exercises, and flashcards, supplement this book in the McGraw Hill Language Lab app. This is freely available in the Apple App Store (for iPhone and iPad) and the Google Play store (for Android devices). A web version is also available at mhlanguagelab.com. Note: Internet access required for streaming audio.

By the same authors

The Ultimate Spanish Verb Review and Practice: Mastering Verbs and Sentence Building for Confident Communication, Second Edition
The Big Red Book of Spanish Verbs, Second Edition
Spanish Vocabulary Drills
The Ultimate Spanish 101: A Complete First-Year Course, Second Edition

The Ultimate French Review and Practice, Fifth Edition
The Ultimate French Verb Review and Practice: Mastering Verbs and Sentence Building for Confident Communication, Second Edition
The Big Blue Book of French Verbs, Second Edition
French Vocabulary Drills

For Alex and Mimi, whose brilliance, talents, and love illuminate and inspire every word we write

RLG and DMS

Preface

Almost seventy years later, I remember clearly how the magic of translating the words in books into images enriched my life, breaking the barriers of time and space.
—Mario Vargas Llosa, Nobel Prize in Literature 2010

Anyone who really knows two or more tongues realizes that even that small enlargement of liberty gives him new perspectives, exercises his soul anew.
—Benjamin Lee Whorf

The Ultimate Spanish Review and Practice, Premium Fifth Edition, provides English-speaking learners of Spanish with a uniquely comprehensive, integrated, and engaging review book that, accompanied by an expanded and redesigned supplementary app, provides learners with the solid knowledge and essential practice to increase their confidence in using Spanish to express their own thoughts, to comprehend speakers of Spanish from all over the Spanish-speaking world, and to communicate in both speaking and writing in a wide variety of situations.

New to this fifth edition, and a logical outgrowth of our goal to provide learners with a path to mastery of both written and spoken Spanish, is an enhanced and extensive listening comprehension program on the app that will set you on a fast track to mastery of the Spanish language. Listening comprehension is especially important because if you increase your understanding of Spanish, you will also increase your ability to express yourself more accurately in the language.

Grammar presentation

Designed to provide advanced beginners and intermediate and advanced learners of Spanish with a powerful tool for review and progress in the language, *The Ultimate Spanish Review and Practice*, Premium Fifth Edition, presents clear, concise, and well-organized grammar explanations with examples that reflect everyday usage, most often in the form of conversational exchanges. The presentations of structure are easy to understand, and the examples will encourage learners to see the study of grammar as a stepping stone to communication.

Exercise program

The exercise program of this fifth edition of *The Ultimate Spanish Review and Practice* provides extensive practice to ensure mastery of all the grammar topics and sentence patterns that learners of Spanish at this level should know and be able to use. These engaging exercises are contextualized, and the instructions in Spanish help set the scene and prepare you for the task at hand. Vocabulary lists provide a review of the vocabulary common to most first- and second-year Spanish textbooks, as well as new words and phrases essential for particular exercises, thus increasing your vocabulary and enhancing your ability to express yourself on a variety of topics. Vocabulary presentations are grouped by theme and are integrated with the exercises, which reflect authentic, everyday language usage and touch on all areas of modern life, from family and food to business and technology.

Self-expression exercises are included to encourage you to use the target grammar and vocabulary presented to express your own ideas. The **Ejercicio oral** at the end of each chapter of Parts I through III is a motivating culmination exercise in which you and a friend or colleague can practice the grammatical structures and topics presented in the chapter by exchanging information with each other.

Review

The chapter of **Review Exercises** includes 26 exercises keyed to the chapters of the book. The Review section enables you to check your progress, find your strengths and weaknesses, and revisit grammatical topics in the textbook that require additional practice.

Structure

The Ultimate Spanish Review and Practice, Premium Fifth Edition, has 29 chapters divided into five parts:

I   Verbs—Forms and Uses
II   Nouns and Their Modifiers; Pronouns
III   Other Elements of the Sentence
IV   Idiomatic Usage
V   Review

To further your progress and enhance your competence in Spanish, we have included a chapter of useful **idioms, expressions, and proverbs** and a chapter designed to help you avoid some of the most **common errors and pitfalls** that English-speaking learners of Spanish encounter. Updated **Notas culturales**, featured throughout the book, provide interesting and important information about the Spanish language and Spanish-speaking countries and people—including history, geography, politics, art, music, literature, film, and local customs—thereby enhancing the effectiveness of the grammar exercises by providing an authentic context in which to practice.

For convenient learner reference, the appendices of *The Ultimate Spanish Review and Practice,* Premium Fifth Edition, include easy-to-read verb charts and a section on written conventions that explains Spanish rules of spelling and punctuation. The Answer Key at the end of the book allows you to check your work.

App

The Ultimate Spanish Review and Practice, Premium Fifth Edition, is accompanied by an extensive app that contains an innovative variety of exercises, audio recordings, and flashcards. There are hundreds of multiple-choice exercises that allow you to practice verb tenses, grammatical structures, and idiomatic usage included in the first four parts of the book—conveniently available for study on your computer, tablet, or smartphone. All listening work is recorded by native speakers of Spanish and is accompanied by listening comprehension exercises. The **Diagnostic Test** and **Review Test** provide you with excellent tools to assess your progress. To improve your comprehension and pronunciation, the **Listening for Key Contrasts** drills help you distinguish verb forms that may sound similar to English speakers but are very different in meaning. This section targets some of the most important sound contrasts in the Spanish verb system. To understand native Spanish speakers and make yourself understood by them, it is important that you master the phonetics of the language.

The **Audio Modules**, recorded by native speakers of Spanish, consist of engaging narratives and dialogues designed to improve your listening comprehension and pronunciation. The narrators and interlocutors tell interesting stories that reflect aspects of their daily lives, including family and friends, life goals, work, business and the office, education, entertainment, travel, shopping, house and home, and food and restaurants. The passages contain useful, authentic vocabulary that will serve you well in your communication with native speakers of Spanish. Preceding each passage is a list of **Ten Key Words and Expressions** that help you prepare for listening to the passage. You can read a **Transcription** of the audio passage after listening to it; we recommend listening to the passage a second time before reading the transcription. A **Glossary** of words and expressions can be activated to check meaning. All online exercises offer instant feedback, so you can check your progress anywhere, anytime. You will be amazed at how much you will understand and be able to say after you have worked through the app!

The Ultimate Spanish Review and Practice, Premium Fifth Edition, retains the highly effective pedagogy and most important features that made the earlier editions so successful and popular with learners; it offers, in addition, an easily accessible online program of practice. Book and app make an ideal program for learners working on their own and an ideal ancillary for students using a textbook in a classroom setting. It is compatible with all textbooks, types of curricula, and classroom approaches. Chapters may be studied in any order, allowing learners and teachers to individualize grammar practice.

As veteran language teachers, we guide you in developing your skills of listening, speaking, reading, and writing with accuracy, confidence, and joy. It is our expectation that with a sound knowledge of the language, you will feel empowered to continue learning and communicating in Spanish, giving you an exciting new perspective as you acquire a deeper understanding and appreciation of the Spanish-speaking world.

Our heartfelt gratitude to Christopher Brown, our publisher par excellence at McGraw Hill, and esteemed colleague and friend, for his vision, wisdom, and guidance in the creation and success of the *Ultimate* family of language learning textbooks over these 26 years.

Our deepest appreciation to Terry Yokota and Daniel Franklin, principals of Village Bookworks, for their impressive expertise, personalized attention, and consistently valuable assistance in all aspects of the production of the *Ultimate* textbooks.

Ronni L. Gordon, PhD
David M. Stillman, PhD

Contents

III Other Elements of the Sentence

IV Idiomatic Usage

V Review

1

Verbs—Forms and Uses

The Present Tense

The Present Tense of Regular -ar, -er, and -ir Verbs

Verbs are presented in conjugation paradigms that summarize the forms of a verb in each tense. Spanish verbs change their form for person and number. Verbs are said to have three persons: the speaker, the person spoken to, and the third person, referring to neither the speaker nor the person spoken to. Spanish, like English, has two numbers: singular and plural.

Here are the persons of the verb and their corresponding subject pronouns in English.

	SINGULAR	PLURAL
FIRST PERSON	I	we
SECOND PERSON	you	you
THIRD PERSON	he/she/it	they

Here are the persons of the verb and their corresponding subject pronouns in Spanish.

	SINGULAR	PLURAL
FIRST PERSON	yo	nosotros/nosotras
SECOND PERSON	tú	vosotros/vosotras
THIRD PERSON	él/ella	ellos/ellas
THIRD PERSON (you)	usted	ustedes

Differences Between English and Spanish

1 · In English, subject pronouns are required to show who the subject of the verb is, since verbs have only two forms in the present tense. In Spanish, however, verb forms are complete in themselves. Subject pronouns are added for emphasis or contrast.

Él navega en la red y **ella** manda correos electrónicos.

*He surfs the web and **she** sends emails.*

Ellos entran cuando **nosotros** salimos.

*They are coming in when **we** are going out.*

2 · English has only one form for *you*; Spanish has four. **Tú** is a singular form, and is informal. The **tú** form of the verb is used to address one person with whom you have an informal relationship: a family member, a close friend, a fellow student, etc. In Spain, **vosotros** is the plural of **tú**, and the **vosotros** form of the verb is used to address two or more people with whom you have an informal relationship.

tú-vosotros (informal address)

Felipe, ¿adónde vas?	*Felipe, where are you going?*
Mamá, papá, ¿adónde vais?	*Mom, Dad, where are you going?*

Usted is used to address one person with whom you have a formal relationship: a stranger, a customer, a superior at work, etc. **Ustedes** is the plural of **usted**. It is used to address two or more people with whom you have a formal relationship. **Usted** is used with the third person singular forms of the verb. **Ustedes** is used with the third person plural forms of the verb. **Usted** and **ustedes** are often abbreviated as **Ud.** and **Uds.** Other forms of abbreviation are **Vd.** and **Vds.**

usted-ustedes (formal address)

Usted puede esperar aquí, señor.	*You can wait here, sir.*
Ustedes pueden esperar aquí, señores.	*You can wait here, gentlemen* (OR *ladies and gentlemen*).

In Spanish America, **ustedes** is also the plural of **tú**—**vosotros** is not used. Thus, all groups of two or more people are addressed as **ustedes**, whether the relationship is formal or informal.

Mamá, papá, ¿adónde van?	*Mom, Dad, where are you going?*

All Spanish verbs belong to one of three different classes, or conjugations, according to the ending of the infinitive, the verb form ending in **-ar**, **-er**, or **-ir**.

- First-conjugation **-ar** verbs like **hablar** (*to speak*)
- Second-conjugation **-er** verbs like **aprender** (*to learn*)
- Third-conjugation **-ir** verbs like **escribir** (*to write*)

Each conjugation has its own set of endings that are added to the stem for the different persons of the verb. Verbs conjugated according to the patterns below are called *regular* verbs.

Verbs of the first conjugation (**-ar** verbs) are conjugated like **hablar** (*to speak*).

	SINGULAR		PLURAL	
FIRST PERSON	**yo**	hablo	**nosotros**	hablamos
SECOND PERSON	**tú**	hablas	**vosotros**	habláis
THIRD PERSON	**él**		**ellos**	
	ella	habla	**ellas**	hablan
	Ud.		**Uds.**	

Verbs of the second conjugation (-**er** verbs) are conjugated like **aprender** (*to learn*).

	SINGULAR		PLURAL	
FIRST PERSON	**yo**	aprend**o**	**nosotros**	aprend**emos**
SECOND PERSON	**tú**	aprend**es**	**vosotros**	aprend**éis**
THIRD PERSON	**él**		**ellos**	
	ella }	aprend**e**	**ellas** }	aprend**en**
	Ud.		**Uds.**	

Verbs of the third conjugation (-**ir** verbs) are conjugated like **escribir** (*to write*).

	SINGULAR		PLURAL	
FIRST PERSON	**yo**	escrib**o**	**nosotros**	escrib**imos**
SECOND PERSON	**tú**	escrib**es**	**vosotros**	escrib**ís**
THIRD PERSON	**él**		**ellos**	
	ella }	escrib**e**	**ellas** }	escrib**en**
	Ud.		**Uds.**	

NOTES

1 · First-conjugation -**ar** verbs have the vowel **a** in all the endings except the **yo** form.

2 · Second-conjugation -**er** verbs and third-conjugation -**ir** verbs are conjugated alike, except for a difference in the vowel (**e** for -**er** verbs, **i** for -**ir** verbs) of the **nosotros** and **vosotros** endings: **aprendemos**, **aprendéis**, **escribimos**, **escribís**.

3 · The vowel of the infinitive of -**ir** verbs (**i**) appears only in those forms where the ending is stressed (vivímos, vivís). With the exception of the **yo** form, the vowel **e** appears in all other present tense endings of -**ir** verbs.

4 · Stress is a very important feature of the Spanish verb system. The forms of -**ar**, -**er**, and -**ir** verbs are stressed on the stem in the singular and the third person plural (**ellos/ellas/ustedes**) forms, and on the ending in the **nosotros** and **vosotros** forms.

hablo, hablas, habla, hablan, hablamos, habláis
aprendo, aprendes, aprende, aprenden, aprendemos, aprendéis
escribo, escribes, escribe, escriben, escribimos, escribís

Uses of the Present Tense

The present tense forms of Spanish verbs express both the English simple present (*I walk*) and the English present progressive (*I'm walking*).

Tocas el piano.   { *You play* the piano.
                       { *You're playing* the piano.

¿**Comen** Uds. torta?   { *Do you eat* cake?
                          { *Are you eating* cake?

Questions can be formed in Spanish by inverting the subject and the verb or by changing intonation.

¿**Trabajan** Uds. aquí? ⎫
¿Uds. **trabajan** aquí? ⎭   *Do you **work** here?*

The present tense can be used to ask for instructions.

¿**Hablamos** del tema ahora?   ***Shall we talk** about the topic now?*

¿**Entrego** el informe?   ***Shall I hand in** the report?*

The present tense can refer to the future if another element of the sentence expresses future time. English often uses the present progressive to indicate future time if another element of the sentence expresses future time.

Mando el email mañana.   ***I'll send** the email tomorrow.*

Vera **cena** conmigo mañana.   *Vera's **having dinner** with me tomorrow.*

The construction **hace** + expression of time + **que** + verb in the present tense is used to designate actions that began in the past but that continue into the present. The question form of this construction is ¿**Cuánto tiempo hace que...?** The word **tiempo** is optional.

—¿**Cuánto (tiempo) hace que viven**   *How long have you been living*
  en esta casa?   *in this house?*
—**Hace ocho años que vivimos** aquí.   *We've been living here **for eight years**.*

Hace + expression of time may also appear at the end of the sentence; **que** is omitted in this case.

Vivimos aquí **hace ocho años**.   *We've been living here **for eight years**.*

Another construction used to designate actions that began in the past and continue into the present is verb in present tense + **desde hace** + expression of time. To form a question, ¿**Desde cuándo...?** is used.

—¿**Desde cuándo** buscas trabajo?   *How long have you been looking for a job?*
—Busco trabajo **desde hace un mes**.   *I've been looking for a job **for a month**.*

Spanish often uses the verb **llevar** to express *have been/has been* with expressions of time.

—¿Cuánto tiempo **llevas** en Chile?   *How long **have you been** in Chile?*
—**Llevo tres meses** en el país.   ***I have been** in the country **for three months**.*

Llevamos cinco años con esta empresa.   ***We have been** with this company **for five years**.*

Common -ar Verbs

acabar *to finish*   **ahorrar** *to save*
aceptar *to accept*   **alcanzar** *to reach, overtake*
acompañar *to go with, accompany*   **almacenar** *to store*
aconsejar *to advise*   **alquilar** *to rent*
administrar *to manage, administer, run*   **analizar** *to analyze*
aguantar *to put up with, stand, tolerate*   **apagar** *to turn off, shut off*

aparcar *to park*
aprovechar *to take advantage of*
archivar *to file*
armar *to set up, put together*
arrastrar *to drag*
arreglar *to arrange, fix up*
aumentar *to increase*
averiguar *to find out*
avisar *to let know, tell, notify*
ayudar *to help*
bailar *to dance*
bajar *to go down; to lower, turn down; to download*
besar *to kiss*
borrar *to erase*
brindar (por) *to drink a toast (to); to toast*
buscar *to look for*
calcular *to calculate, work out*
cambiar *to change*
caminar *to walk*
cantar *to sing*
cargar *to load; to upload*
celebrar *to celebrate*
cenar *to have dinner*
charlar *to chat*
cobrar *to cash, charge*
cocinar *to cook*
colocar *to put, place*
comprar *to buy*
contestar *to answer*
cortar *to cut*
crear *to create*
cruzar *to cross*
cursar *to take a course/class*
dejar *to let, leave*
desarrollar *to develop*
desayunar *to have breakfast*
descansar *to rest*
descargar *to download*
desear *to want*
dibujar *to draw*
diseñar *to design*
disfrutar (de) *to enjoy*
doblar *to turn (change direction); to dub (film)*
durar *to last*
echar *to throw*
elaborar *to draw up, prepare, write*
empujar *to push*

encargar *to order*
ensayar *to test, try out; to rehearse*
enseñar *to teach; to show*
entrar (en, a) *to go/come in, enter;* **entrar** + (data) *to input (data)*
entregar *to hand in/over*
escanear *to scan*
escuchar *to listen to*
esperar *to wait, hope, expect*
estacionar *to park*
estornudar *to sneeze*
estudiar *to study*
experimentar *to experience*
explicar *to explain*
felicitar *to congratulate*
firmar *to sign*
formatear *to format*
funcionar *to work, function* (of a machine)
ganar *to earn, win*
gastar *to spend, waste*
grabar *to record*
gritar *to shout*
guardar *to keep; to put away; to save (a computer file)*
hablar *to speak*
instalar *to install*
interactuar *to interact*
invitar *to invite*
llamar *to call*
llegar *to arrive*
llevar *to carry; to wear*
llorar *to cry*
luchar *to fight*
mandar *to send, order*
manejar *to drive*
marcar *to dial; to mark*
mascar *to chew*
mirar *to look at*
nadar *to swim*
navegar (en/por) Internet/la red *to surf/browse the Internet/web*
necesitar *to need*
pagar *to pay*
parar *to stop*
pasar *to spend (time); to pass*
patinar *to skate*
pegar *to stick, glue; to hit*
pintar *to paint*

pisar *to stand on, step on*
planear *to plan*
planificar *to plan, design*
practicar *to practice; to go in for, play (a sport)*
preguntar *to ask (a question)*
preparar *to prepare*
presentar *to present, introduce*
programar *to program*
pulsar *to press, push (a button)*
quitar *to take away, remove*
reciclar *to recycle*
regresar *to come back, return*
reparar *to repair, fix*
repasar *to review*
sacar *to take out*
saludar *to greet, say hello to*

tardar (en) *to take/be a long time (in)*
telecargar *to load; to upload*
telefonear *to telephone*
terminar *to finish, end*
textear *to text, send a text*
tirar *to throw*
tocar *to play a musical instrument; to touch*
tomar *to take; to drink*
trabajar *to work*
tratar *to try, treat;* tratar de + *infinitive to try to (do something)*
trotar *to jog*
usar *to use; to wear*
utilizar *to use, utilize*
viajar *to travel*
visitar *to visit*

Common -er Verbs

aprender *to learn*
beber *to drink*
comer *to eat*
comprender *to understand*
correr *to run*
coser *to sew*
creer *to believe, think*

deber *ought, must, to be supposed to; to owe*
leer *to read*
meter *to put in, insert*
prender *to turn on (an appliance)*
romper *to break*
toser *to cough*
vender *to sell*

Common -ir Verbs

abrir *to open*
añadir *to add*
aplaudir *to applaud*
asistir a *to attend*
compartir *to share*
cumplir *to fulfill, carry out; to keep one's word; to turn _____ years old*
describir *to describe*
difundir *to publicize, broadcast, spread*
discutir *to discuss, argue*
escribir *to write*

imprimir *to print*
insistir (en) *to insist (on)*
interrumpir *to interrupt*
ocurrir *to happen*
permitir *to permit, allow*
recibir *to receive*
resistir *to resist, stand, endure*
subir *to go up, raise; to upload*
sufrir *to suffer*
transmitir *to transmit, broadcast*
vivir *to live*

A *En la oficina. Describa lo que hacen estas personas en la oficina hoy. Siga el modelo.*

MODELO   (terminar) Ellos __*terminan*__ su trabajo.

En la oficina
la app de inteligencia artificial *AI (artificial intelligence) app*
la base de datos *database*
el consultor *consultant*
el correo electrónico *email*
los datos *data*

el informe *report*
el plan de negocios *business plan*
el presupuesto *budget*
el proyecto *project*
el sitio web *website*
el técnico *technician*

1. (navegar) Yo _____ por Internet.

2. (leer) Uds. _____ los contratos.

3. (administrar) Nosotros _____ el proyecto.

4. (reparar) El técnico _____ las computadoras.

5. (analizar) Tú _____ los datos.

6. (escribir) La directora _____ un informe.

7. (trabajar) Los jefes _____ en un plan de negocios.

8. (imprimir) Mi colega y yo _____ un documento.

9. (diseñar) Vosotros _____ un sitio web.

10. (mandar) El consultor _____ los documentos.

11. (crear) Los analistas _____ una base de datos.

12. (usar) Ud. _____ una app de inteligencia artificial.

13. (elaborar) Uds. _____ un presupuesto.

14. (compartir) Yo _____ mis ideas con mis colegas.

B *¿Qué hacemos esta noche?* *Describa lo que Ud. y sus amigos hacen esta noche. Siga el modelo.*

> MODELO (asistir) Ellos __*asisten*__ a un concierto.

1. (escuchar) Nosotros _____ música clásica.

2. (tocar) Yo _____ la flauta.

3. (encargar) Ud. _____ una pizza.

4. (caminar) Rodrigo y Sofía _____ por el centro.

5. (comer) Tú _____ comida mexicana.

6. (leer) Uds. _____ unos textos.

7. (beber) Vosotros _____ vino.

8. (mirar) Pablo _____ televisión.

C *En la clase de español.* *Describa lo que pasa en la clase de español del profesor Sierra. Escriba oraciones usando el presente. Siga el modelo.*

> MODELO los estudiantes / hablar español
> → Los estudiantes hablan español.

En la clase de español
aprender de memoria *to memorize*
el equipo *team*
el libro de texto *textbook*
el modismo *idiom*
repasar los tiempos verbales *to review the verb tenses*
el sonido *sound*

1. yo / repasar los tiempos verbales

2. nosotros / trabajar en equipo

3. Raquel / abrir el libro de texto

4. tú / aprender los modismos de memoria

5. los estudiantes / compartir sus ideas

6. Ud. / practicar los sonidos del español

7. Felipe y tú (Uds.) / leer el diálogo

8. vosotros / aprender mucho

¿En esta clase? ¡Qué va! *Describa las cosas que nunca pasan en la clase de la profesora Reyes. Escriba oraciones usando el presente. Siga el modelo.*

> MODELO   los estudiantes / gritar
> → Los estudiantes nunca gritan.

Lo que no se hace en la clase
faltar *to be absent*
mascar chicle *to chew gum*
prender *to turn on (an appliance)*
el (teléfono) celular *cell phone*
utilizar una chuleta *to use a cheat sheet* (Spain)

1. nosotros / hablar por celular

2. Juan Diego / prender su iPad

3. yo / mandar mensajes de texto

4. Uds. / utilizar una chuleta

5. tú / interrumpir a la profesora

6. Isabel y Laura / faltar a la clase

7. Ud. / mascar chicle

8. vosotros / beber refrescos

E **¿Qué hacen sus profesores?** *Diga lo que sus profesores hacen o no hacen en la sala de clase escogiendo frases de la columna B para completar las frases de la columna A. Siga el modelo.*

> MODELO   Mi profesor de inglés...   hablar en voz alta / fumar
> → Mi profesor de inglés habla en voz alta.
>   Mi profesor de inglés no fuma.

A

1. Mi profesor de historia...

2. Nuestra profesora de química...

3. Nuestros profesores de matemáticas...

4. Las profesoras de español...

5. El profesor de música...

6. La profesora de informática...

B

a. enseñar bien

b. navegar por las redes sociales (*social media*)

c. discutir sus ideas

d. tocar el piano

e. prender los aparatos multimedia

f. escribir los problemas en la pizarra electrónica

g. cargar y descargar archivos

h. pasar lista (*to take attendance*)

i. esperar mucho de sus estudiantes

j. crear una base de datos

k. explicar los conceptos con claridad

F *Una fiesta de cumpleaños.* *Cecilia celebra su cumpleaños con una fiesta en su casa. Para saber cómo es, escriba la forma correcta del presente de los verbos indicados.*

Los padres y los hermanos de Cecilia _____ (1. planear) la fiesta. La mamá

_____ (2. cocinar) los platos favoritos de Cecilia y _____ (3. comprar) una torta de

chocolate. El padre y los hermanos de Cecilia _____ (4. colocar) globos y una piñata

en la sala. Cecilia _____ (5. invitar) a todos sus amigos. _____ (6. Llegar) la hora de la fiesta.

Paula, la mejor amiga de Cecilia, _____ (7. vivir) al lado y _____ (8. llegar) primero.

Durante la fiesta, todos _____ (9. comer), _____ (10. beber) y _____ (11. bailar).

Juan Pedro _____ (12. tocar) el piano y los otros amigos _____ (13. cantar). Mientras

Cecilia _____ (14. abrir) los regalos que _____ (15. recibir), su padre _____ (16. sacar)

fotos. Los invitados _____ (17. felicitar) a la cumpleañera y _____ (18. brindar (*to toast*))

por ella.

The Present Tense of Irregular Verbs

The following verbs have an irregular first person singular (**yo**) form in the present tense. All other forms are regular.

- -G- verbs are verbs that have an unexpected -**g**- in the **yo** form.

INFINITIVE	**yo** FORM	OTHER FORMS OF THE PRESENT TENSE
caer *to fall*	caigo	caes, cae, caemos, caéis, caen
hacer *to do, make*	hago	haces, hace, hacemos, hacéis, hacen
poner *to put*	pongo	pones, pone, ponemos, ponéis, ponen
salir *to go out*	salgo	sales, sale, salimos, salís, salen
traer *to bring*	traigo	traes, trae, traemos, traéis, traen
valer *to be worth*	valgo	vales, vale, valemos, valéis, valen

NOTES

1 · Verbs conjugated like **poner**: **componer** (*to compose*), **disponer** (*to dispose*), **exponer** (*to expose*), **imponer** (*to impose*), **posponer** (*to postpone*), **proponer** (*to propose*), **reponerse** (*to get well*), **suponer** (*to suppose*), etc.

2 · Verbs conjugated like **traer**: **atraer** (*to attract*), **contraer** (*to contract*), **distraer** (*to distract*), **sustraer** (*to remove, extract, subtract*), etc.

The following -**g**- verbs are irregular in other persons also.

decir *to say, tell*		**oír** *to hear*	
digo	decimos	**oigo**	oímos
dices	decís	oyes	oís
dice	dicen	oye	oyen

tener *to have*		**venir** *to come*	
tengo	tenemos	**vengo**	venimos
tienes	tenéis	vienes	venís
tiene	tienen	viene	vienen

NOTE Verbs conjugated like **tener**: **contener** (*to contain*), **detener** (*to stop, detain*), **mantener** (*to maintain*), **obtener** (*to obtain*), **retener** (*to retain*), etc.

- **Ir** (*to go*) is conjugated like an -**ar** verb. The **yo** form ends in -**oy**: **voy**. The stem of the verb is the letter **v**. Note that the **vosotros** form has no accent mark because it has only one syllable: **vais**.

ir *to go*	
voy	vamos
vas	vais
va	van

Ir + **a** + infinitive is used to refer to future time as is *to be going to* in English.

—Aquí está el cine. **Voy a estacionar** el coche.   *Here's the movie theater. **I'm going to park** the car.*
—Y **yo voy a comprar** los billetes.   *And **I'm going to buy** the tickets.*

- **Dar** (*to give*), like **ir**, is conjugated like an -**ar** verb. The **yo** form ends in -**oy**: **doy**. **Ver** (*to see*) is a regular -**er** verb except for the **yo** form: **veo**. The **vosotros** forms of these two verbs have no accent marks because they have only one syllable: **dais**, **veis**.

- **Saber** (*to know*) and **caber** (*to fit*) are irregular in the first person only.

INFINITIVE	**yo** FORM	OTHER FORMS OF THE PRESENT TENSE
saber *to know*	**sé**	sabes, sabe, sabemos, sabéis, saben
caber *to fit*	**quepo**	cabes, cabe, cabemos, cabéis, caben

- The verb **haber**, literally *to have*, is used almost exclusively as an auxiliary verb to form the compound tenses (see chapters 9, 11, and 12).

haber *to have* (lit.)	
he	hemos
has	habéis
ha	han

- In most verbs that end in a vowel + -**cer** or -**cir**, **c** changes to **zc** before **o** and **a**. In the present tense, the change occurs only in the first person singular (**yo**) form.

conocer *to know*	
conozco	conocemos
conoces	conocéis
conoce	conocen

NOTE Verbs conjugated like **conocer**: **reconocer** (*to recognize*), **desconocer** (*to be ignorant of*).

- Most verbs with infinitives in -**ecer** have -**zco** in the **yo** form like **conozco**. The other persons of the present tense are regular.

INFINITIVE	yo FORM
agradecer *to thank*	agradezco
aparecer *to appear*	aparezco
crecer *to grow*	crezco
desaparecer *to disappear*	desaparezco
embellecer *to make beautiful*	embellezco
establecer *to establish*	establezco
fallecer *to die*	fallezco
merecer *to deserve*	merezco
obedecer *to obey*	obedezco
ofrecer *to offer*	ofrezco
parecer *to seem*	parezco
permanecer *to remain*	permanezco
pertenecer *to belong*	pertenezco

- Verbs in -**ucir** also have -**zco** in the **yo** form, but are regular in the other persons.

conducir *to drive*

conduzco	conducimos
conduces	conducís
conduce	conducen

INFINITIVE	yo FORM
lucir *to shine; to show off*	luzco
producir *to produce*	produzco
reducir *to reduce*	reduzco
traducir *to translate*	traduzco

G *Un viaje de negocios.* *Ud. es jefe de una gran empresa multinacional. Su secretario le hace unas preguntas sobre su viaje de negocios a Europa. Conteste sus preguntas. Siga los modelos.*

MODELOS ¿Hace Ud. un viaje a Europa? (sí)
→ Sí, hago un viaje a Europa.

¿Hace Ud. un viaje a Medio Oriente? (no)
→ No, no hago un viaje a Medio Oriente.

1. ¿Sale Ud. la semana próxima? (sí)

2. ¿Viene Ud. a la oficina el viernes? (no)

3. ¿Va Ud. a España y Francia? (sí)

4. ¿Conoce Ud. a los directores franceses? (sí)

5. ¿Ve Ud. al gerente de ventas mañana? (sí)

6. ¿Traduce Ud. los documentos al ruso? (no)

7. ¿Sabe Ud. cuándo regresa? (no)

H *¡Cuánto trabajo tenemos!* *Varias personas reciben una invitación a una fiesta, pero no saben si tienen tiempo para ir. Siga el modelo.*

> MODELO   Juan
> → Viene si tiene tiempo.

1. José y yo   5. Ud.

2. tú   6. Carlos

3. Sara y Juan Miguel   7. Uds.

4. yo   8. vosotros

I *¿Oyes lo que dicen?* *Aunque se habla en voz baja, todo se oye. Escriba que todos oyen lo que dicen otras personas. Siga el modelo.*

> MODELO   María / Mateo
> → María oye lo que Mateo dice.

1. Carmen / Ud.   5. yo / Uds.

2. Pedro y Paco / yo   6. Uds. / nosotros

3. nosotros / tú   7. vosotros / Pablo

4. tú / Miguel y Teresa   8. ellas / vosotras

J *Lo hago yo.* *Conteste que es Ud. quien hace las siguientes cosas. Siga el modelo.*

> MODELO   ¿Quién hace una pregunta?
> → Yo hago una pregunta.

1. ¿Quién pone la mesa?   5. ¿Quién hace las maletas?

2. ¿Quién ve televisión?   6. ¿Quién va de compras?

3. ¿Quién da un paseo?   7. ¿Quién sale al cine?

4. ¿Quién trae el vino?   8. ¿Quién cae en un error?

K *¿Hablan en serio?* *Sus amigos tienen ideas geniales. ¿O es que le toman el pelo (they're pulling your leg)? Escriba lo que dicen. Siga el modelo.*

> MODELO   Carlota, ¿qué propones? (un plan para resolver todos los problemas del mundo)
> → Propongo un plan para resolver todos los problemas del mundo.

1. Eugenia, ¿qué mereces? (el Premio Nobel de Economía)

2. Gustavo, ¿qué compones? (una obra maestra mozartiana)

3. Paloma, ¿qué traduces? (novelas del vasco al árabe)

4. Mario, ¿qué conduces? (la limusina presidencial)

5. Franco, ¿qué supones? (que yo voy a vivir para siempre)

6. Ana, ¿qué obtienes? (una beca de cincuenta millones de dólares)

7. Antonio, ¿qué produces? (las películas más exitosas del cine)

L *Nadie conoce a esta gente.* *Use el verbo* **conocer** *para decir que nadie conoce a estas personas. Recuerde que tiene que usar la* **a** *personal. Siga el modelo. (Si necesita repasar la* **a** *personal, vea "Personal* **a** *and Direct Objects" en el capítulo 19.)*

> MODELO   ¿Sabe Juan si Paula es argentina?
> → No, no conoce a Paula.

1. ¿Sabes si esos programadores son trabajadores?

2. ¿Saben Uds. si Agustín es de México?

3. ¿Sabe Ud. si Julio es de origen italiano?

4. ¿Saben tus padres si este asesor financiero es responsable?

5. ¿Sabe Elena si sus vecinos son simpáticos?

6. ¿Sabéis si Sara es israelí?

M *¿Cuánto tiempo hace?* *Ud. le pregunta a su amigo cuánto tiempo hace que él y sus amigos se dedican a sus aficiones. Escriba cada pregunta de dos maneras usando las construcciones del modelo.*

> MODELO   Rafael / nadar en el equipo
> → ¿Cuánto tiempo hace que Rafael nada en el equipo?
> ¿Desde cuándo nada Rafael en el equipo?

1. tú / diseñar sitios web

2. Mario / cocinar a la italiana

3. Rosa y Jaime / bailar salsa

4. Uds. / hacer ejercicio

5. tu hermana / vender sus pinturas

6. Gabriel / leer el chino

N *Hace un año que...* *Su amigo le contesta las preguntas del ejercicio M de dos maneras, como en el modelo.*

> MODELO   Rafael / nadar en el equipo / seis meses
> → Hace seis meses que Rafael nada en el equipo.
> Rafael nada en el equipo desde hace seis meses.

1. tú / diseñar sitios web / dos años

2. Mario / cocinar a la italiana / un año

3. Rosa y Jaime / bailar salsa / siete semanas

4. Uds. / hacer ejercicio / cinco años

5. tu hermana / vender sus pinturas / un par de meses

6. Gabriel / leer el chino / cuatro años

O *Todos ayudamos.* En mi casa todo el mundo ayuda. Use **ir a** + el infinitivo indicado para expresar lo que cada persona va a hacer hoy. Siga el modelo.

MODELO   tú / arreglar la casa
                → Tú vas a arreglar la casa.

Las tareas del hogar (*household chores*)
barrer el suelo *to sweep the floor*
cortar el césped *to mow the lawn*
hacer la cama *to make the bed*
hacer la compra *to do the shopping*
lavar la ropa *to do the laundry*
limpiar la alfombra *to clean the carpet/rug*
pasar la aspiradora *to vacuum*
reciclar los periódicos *to recycle the newspapers*
sacar la basura *to take out the garbage*
quitar el polvo de los muebles *to dust the furniture*

1. mi hermano y yo / cortar el césped

2. mi abuela / lavar la ropa

3. yo / barrer el suelo

4. mamá / hacer la compra

5. mis hermanas / pasar la aspiradora

6. Ud. / reciclar los periódicos

7. Uds. / hacer las camas

8. papá / sacar la basura

9. tú / limpiar la alfombra

10. vosotros / quitar el polvo de los muebles

P *Expresar en español. La vida diaria.* Exprese en español algunas de las cosas que Ud. y otras personas hacen todos los días.

1. *I read and send emails.*

2. *Laura surfs the web.*

3. *I make breakfast.*

4. *You (Uds.) take the train.*

5. *Alejandro goes to the office.*

6. *Beatriz parks the car.*

7. *You (tú) download documents.*

8. *We talk on our cell phones.*

9. *Ricardo I and go out for dinner.*

10. *You (Ud.) print the reports.*

11. *The children do their homework.*

12. *You (vosotros) go to the mall.*

13. *We attend a lecture.*

14. *I take online classes.*

Q *Ejercicio oral. Diálogos. Pregúntele a su amigo/amiga lo que hace los fines de semana y cuando está de vacaciones. Dígale lo que Ud. hace. Algunas posibilidades:*

asistir a un concierto
bailar salsa y tango
hacer camping
comer en un restaurante
dar un paseo
dibujar
escuchar música
hacer deportes—esquiar, montar en bicicleta, montar a caballo, nadar, patinar, trotar
hacer ejercicio, hacer yoga
hacer turismo
ir al cine/a un concierto/al teatro/a una discoteca/al centro comercial/al gimnasio/a la piscina
ir de vacaciones al campo/a la sierra/al mar
mandar emails
navegar en la red
pintar
salir con su esposo/esposa, su novio/novia, sus hijos, sus amigos
tocar el piano/la flauta/la guitarra/el violín/el saxofón/el clarinete
tomar café en un café/tragos en un bar
tomar fotos
ver un partido de béisbol/de fútbol americano/de baloncesto/de tenis/de fútbol
visitar un museo de arte/de historia natural/de ciencias

Ser and estar

Spanish has two verbs that mean *to be*: **ser** and **estar**. Both verbs are irregular in the present tense. Both have **-oy** in the **yo** form, like **ir** (**voy**) and **dar** (**doy**).

ser *to be*		**estar** *to be*	
soy	somos	estoy	estamos
eres	sois	estás	estáis
es	son	está	están

NOTES

1 · The **vosotros** form of **ser**, **sois**, has no accent mark because it is a one-syllable form. Other one-syllable **vosotros** forms are **vais** (**ir**), **dais** (**dar**), and **veis** (**ver**).

2 · The forms of **estar** are all stressed on the endings.

The Uses of ser

Ser is used before most phrases beginning with **de**; for example, in expressing origin.

Soy de los Estados Unidos.   *I'm from the United States.*

Ser also expresses possession.

La cartera **es de Felipe**.   *The wallet is Felipe's.*

Ser is used to express what material something is made of.

La blusa **es de seda**.   *The blouse is (made of) silk.*

Ser is used before adjectives to indicate that the condition expressed by the adjectives does not result from a change. Thus, these adjectives express inherent qualities and characteristics such as nationality, age, physical and moral attributes, personality, religion, and color.

Mis amigas **son** españolas.	*My friends are Spanish.*
El presidente **es** joven.	*The president is young.*
Carlos **es** alto y rubio.	*Carlos is tall and blond.*
Nora **es** inteligente.	*Nora is intelligent.*
Mis primos **son** graciosos.	*My cousins are witty.*

| Esos señores **son** protestantes/ judíos/católicos. | *Those men and women are Protestant/ Jewish/Catholic.* |
| Nuestro coche **es** azul. | *Our car is blue.* |

Ser is used to link two nouns or pronouns or to link a noun and a pronoun. Both nouns and pronouns may appear in the sentence or be merely understood. Unlike English, Spanish omits the indefinite article **un/una** with a profession.

El señor Lara **es arquitecto**.	*Mr. Lara **is an architect**.*
Pilar Suárez **es médica**.	*Pilar Suárez **is a doctor**.*
Somos ingenieros.	***We're engineers.***

Ser is used to express time, dates, days of the week, and where an event takes place.

—¿Qué hora **es**?	*What time is it?*
—**Son** las ocho.	*It's eight o'clock.*
—¿Cuál **es** la fecha de hoy?	*What's today's date?*
—**Es** el seis de octubre.	*It's October 6th.*
—¿Qué día **es** hoy?	*What day is today?*
—**Es** miércoles.	*It's Wednesday.*
—¿El baile **es** en la universidad?	*Is the dance at the university?*
—No, **es** en el Hotel Palacio.	*No, it's at the Palacio Hotel.*

¿Qué horas son? is commonly used in Spanish America.

The Uses of **estar**

Estar is used to express location or position, whether permanent or temporary.

Santiago **está** en Chile.	*Santiago is in Chile.*
El perro **está** al lado del gato.	*The dog is next to the cat.*
La papelería **está** enfrente de la pastelería.	*The stationery store is opposite the pastry shop.*

Note that Spanish uses **estar** for the location of people or physical objects (see above examples), but **ser** for the location of events.

La reunión **es** en aquella sala.	*The meeting is in that room.*
La fiesta **es** en casa de Joaquín.	*The party is at Joaquin's house.*
El congreso **va a ser** en este hotel.	*The convention will be in this hotel.*

Estar is used before adjectives to indicate that the condition expressed by the adjective results from a change. The condition may be a phase of health, happiness, etc.; a temporary state of being tired, seated, etc.; or the result of an action such as a window being closed. **Estar** also may indicate that the adjective is the subjective impression of the speaker. **Estar** is therefore more common with adjectives that describe mental or physical states.

| —¿Cómo **está** Inés? | *How is Inés?* |
| —La pobre **está** enferma. | *The poor girl is (has gotten) sick.* |

—¿**Están** levantados los niños?	*Are the children up?*
—No, **están** acostados todavía.	*No, they're still in bed.*
—¿**Están** abiertas las ventanas?	*Are the windows open?*
—No, **están** cerradas.	*No, they are closed.*
—¿No reconoces a Luis?	*Don't you recognize Luis?*
—Apenas. **Está** muy gordo.	*Hardly. He's so fat. (He's gotten very fat. / He looks so fat to me.)*

Estar is used in the formation of the progressive tenses: **estar** + gerund (the present participle). The gerund or -**ndo** form is equivalent to the -*ing* form in English.

Están esperando.	*They're waiting.*
Estaba viviendo en París.	*He was living in Paris.*

Ser and **estar** are used with the past participle of the verb. **Ser** + past participle is passive; it can have an agent phrase introduced by **por**. **Estar** + past participle expresses the result of an action. (See Chapter 8.)

La puerta **fue abierta por** la chica.	*The door was opened by the girl.*
La puerta **está abierta**.	*The door is open.*
El trabajo **fue hecho por** él.	*The work was done by him.*
El trabajo **estaba hecho**.	*The work was done.*

The choice of **ser** or **estar** in a sentence is crucial to its meaning. A change in the verb will change the meaning.

Lola **es** delgada.	*Lola is thin. (Lola is a thin person.)*
Lola **está** delgada.	*Lola is thin. (Lola has gotten thin. / Lola looks thin to me.)*
Mario **es** nervioso.	*Mario is nervous. (He is a nervous person.)*
Mario **está** nervioso.	*Mario is feeling nervous. (Mario has gotten nervous/seems nervous to me.)*
Esos profesores **son** aburridos.	*Those professors are boring.*
Esos profesores **están** aburridos.	*Those professors are bored.*
Fernando **es** listo.	*Fernando is clever.*
Fernando **está** listo.	*Fernando is ready.*
La actriz **es** vieja.	*The actress is old.*
La actriz **está** vieja.	*The actress looks old.*
Los hombres **son** vivos.	*The men are sharp/quick.*
Los hombres **están** vivos.	*The men are alive.*
Beatriz **es** pálida.	*Beatriz is pale-complexioned.*
Beatriz **está** pálida.	*Beatriz is pale. (Beatriz looks pale to me.)*
Es seguro.	*It's safe.*
Está seguro.	*He's sure.*
Paquito **es** bueno.	*Paquito is good. (Paquito is a good boy.)*
La torta **está** buena.	*The cake is/tastes good.*

Note the difference in meaning between **ser** and **estar** when referring to food.

La carne **es** rica/mala.	*Meat is delicious/awful.* (in general)
La carne **está** rica/mala.	*The meat is/tastes delicious/awful.* (specific dish)

NOTES

1 · Adjectives used with **ser** and **estar** must agree with the subject in number and gender.

2 · Both **ser** and **estar** may also be used with **casado** and **divorciado**: **Fernando es/está casado. Marta es/está divorciada.**

Commonly Used Expressions with **ser**

es importante/necesario/posible	*it's important/necessary/possible*
es que	*the fact is that*
¿Cómo es Ud.?	*What are you like? / What do you look like?*
¿Cuál es la fecha de hoy?	*What's today's date?*
¿Cuál es su nacionalidad?	*What is your nationality?*
¿De dónde es Ud.?	*Where are you from?*
¿De qué color es...?	*What color is…?*
¿De qué origen es Ud.?	*What is your background?*
¿Qué hora es?	*What time is it?*

Commonly Used Expressions with **estar**

estar a punto de + *infinitive*	*to be about to (do something)*
estar conforme	*to be in agreement*
estar de acuerdo (con)	*to agree (with)*
estar de vacaciones	*to be on vacation*
estar de vuelta	*to be back*
estar para + *infinitive*	*to be about to (do something)*
estar por	*to be in favor of*
estar por + *infinitive*	*to be inclined to (do something)*
¿Cómo está Ud.?	*How are you?*

Estar used by itself with a person as subject means *to be in, to be home, to be available.*

—Busco al señor Soto.	*I'm looking for Mr. Soto.*
—Lo siento, pero **no está** en este momento.	*I'm sorry, but he's not in right now.*

A **Soy yo.** *Escriba en español quién llama a la puerta. Escriba la forma correcta del verbo* **ser.** *Siga el modelo.*

MODELO   ¿Quién es? (ella)
→ Es ella.

1. ¿Quién es? (yo)	5. ¿Quién es? (tú)
2. ¿Quién es? (Uds.)	6. ¿Quién es? (ellas)
3. ¿Quién es? (nosotros)	7. ¿Quién es? (Ud.)
4. ¿Quién es? (él)	8. ¿Quién es? (vosotros)

B *¿De dónde son? ¿De qué origen son?* *Escriba de dónde son y de qué origen son los amigos del Club Internacional. Siga el modelo.*

MODELO   Tomás / Inglaterra / alemán
→ Tomás es de Inglaterra pero es de origen alemán.

1. Pablo / la Argentina / inglés

2. los gemelos / Francia / ruso

3. la licenciada / el Canadá / japonés

4. Ud. / los Estados Unidos / irlandés

5. Ramón y Virginia / Puerto Rico / polaco

6. tú / España / portugués

7. Ud. y Raquel / México / griego

8. yo / Venezuela / italiano

C *Expresar en español. Una encuesta* (**survey**). *Ud. prepara una encuesta y necesita hacerles unas preguntas a sus amigos hispanos. Exprese en español las preguntas que va a hacerles. Use el verbo* **ser** *en todas las oraciones.*

1. *Who are you* (tú)?

2. *Where are you from?*

3. *What is your nationality?*

4. *What is your background?*

5. *What are you like? / What do you look like?*

6. *What color are your eyes?*

7. *What is your profession?*

D *Están de vacaciones.* *Escriba dónde y cómo están las siguientes personas usando el verbo* **estar***. Siga el modelo.*

MODELO   Pablo / Los Ángeles / preocupado
→ Pablo está en Los Ángeles y está preocupado.

1. Mercedes / Barcelona / contenta

2. Uds. / Lima / cansados

3. yo / Roma / feliz

4. tú / Las Vegas / estresado

5. nosotros / Jerusalén / emocionados

6. Consuelo y su marido / Londres / entusiasmados

7. vosotras / Beijing / nerviosas

8. Ud. / Moscú / inquieto

E *¿Cuál fue la pregunta?* *Lea lo que escribió una persona al contestar las preguntas de un formulario* (form). *Después escriba las preguntas. Use el verbo* **ser** *para cada pregunta.*

1. Antonia Gutiérrez
2. argentina
3. programadora de computadoras
4. soltera (estado civil)
5. el veintidós de mayo de 1982
6. alta, morena, de ojos castaños

F *Retratos biográficos.* *Escriba la forma correcta del verbo* **ser** *o* **estar** *para completar los retratos biográficos de las siguientes personas.*

Emiliano Estévez (1) _____ director de cine. Él (2) _____ célebre por sus comedias. Sus películas (3) _____ realmente muy divertidas. Estévez (4) _____ talentoso y encantador. (5) _____ mexicano pero (6) _____ en India este año porque rueda una película allí. Todos sus aficionados (7) _____ entusiasmados con la nueva película.

Camila de la Fuente (8) _____ diseñadora de ropa para mujeres. Su ropa (9) _____ de alta costura (*haute couture*) y (10) _____ muy cara. Este año los vestidos y los trajes que diseña (11) _____ de seda y lana. (12) _____ blancos, negros y de otros colores claros. La empresa De la Fuente (13) _____ en Nueva York, que (14) _____ una de las grandes capitales de la moda.

G *El museo de arte.* *Ud. es guía en un museo de arte y lleva a unos turistas a conocer el museo. Complete la descripción de la visita con las formas correctas de* **ser** *o* **estar**.

Buenas tardes, señoras y señores. Aquí (nosotros) (1) _____ en la entrada principal. A la derecha (2) _____ la librería. (3) _____ nueva y moderna. Y enfrente de la librería (4) _____ la sala de conferencias y conciertos. Esta noche precisamente hay una conferencia. Va a hablar Francisco Velázquez que (5) _____ profesor de arte en la universidad. (6) _____ especialista en la pintura renacentista y (7) _____ muy inteligente. La conferencia (8) _____ a las ocho. Va a (9) _____ muy interesante. Ahora, vamos a subir la escalera. Aquí a la derecha (10) _____ la sala de pintura impresionista. Esta exposición (11) _____ muy importante. Muchos de los cuadros que (12) _____ colgados aquí (13) _____ de otros museos europeos. Uds. (14) _____ viendo unas obras maestras que nunca habían salido de su país hasta ahora. Bueno, ya (15) _____ las tres y me parece que (16) _____ hora de terminar nuestra visita. Yo (17) _____ muy contenta de haber podido enseñarles el museo. Uds. que (18) _____ aficionados al arte deben volver a menudo. El museo (19) _____ abierto de martes a domingo. (20) _____ cerrado los lunes.

NOTA CULTURAL

El Museo Nacional del Prado, que se encuentra en Madrid, es una de las pinacotecas (*art museums*) más importantes del mundo. Fundado en 1819, El Prado tiene la colección más completa de pintura española. Llaman la atención los cuadros de Velázquez, Goya, El Greco, Ribera, Zurbarán y Murillo. El museo tiene naturalmente obras de otros pintores célebres como Rembrandt, Bosco (*Bosch*), Brueghel, Rubens, Tiziano (*Titian*), Caravaggio y Gainsborough. El edificio de estilo neoclásico fue construido por Juan de Villanueva por orden del rey español Carlos III (1716–1788) que reinó a partir del año 1759. Cerca del Museo del Prado se encuentran otros museos muy importantes: el Museo Arqueológico Nacional, el Museo Thyssen-Bornemisza y el Museo Reina Sofía. *https://www.museodelprado.es/en*

H *Un semestre en el extranjero. Ud. está pasando un semestre en Madrid para perfeccionar su español. Toma clases en la universidad y vive en casa de una familia española. Ud. les escribe un email a sus padres en el cual describe cómo es su vida en Madrid. Complete cada oración con la forma correcta de* **ser** *o* **estar**.

Queridos padres:

Ya hace dos meses que (1) _____ en Madrid y (2) _____ muy contento. (3) _____ una ciudad vieja y también moderna. Voy al Museo del Prado, al Parque del Retiro, a la Plaza Mayor y a muchos lugares turísticos. Hay cafés, restaurantes, teatros y cines, y la vida nocturna (4) _____ impresionante. ¡Claro que asisto a mis clases también! La clase de literatura española (5) _____ un poco difícil a veces porque el profesor habla muy rápido. Mi clase de historia (6) _____ muy buena. Los dos profesores (7) _____ inteligentes y simpáticos. Por desgracia, la profesora de lengua (8) _____ aburrida. La casa donde vivo (9) _____ en la calle Serrano. Enfrente de la casa (10) _____ el Museo Arqueológico Nacional. Algunas tiendas (11) _____ al lado de la casa también. Y la parada de autobuses (12) _____ delante de la casa. Así (13) _____ muy fácil recorrer la ciudad. La casa de la familia Ruiz (14) _____ grande y bonita y mi cuarto (15) _____ muy cómodo. Los señores Ruiz tienen cuatro hijos. (16) _____ siete personas en total porque la abuela vive con ellos también. Esteban, el hijo mayor, (17) _____ un buen amigo mío. (18) _____ pequeño y moreno. (19) _____ listo y simpático. Estela, la hija mayor, (20) _____ encantadora y muy guapa. Tiene novio. ¡(21) _____ una pena porque creo que (22) _____ enamorado de ella! (23) (¡_____ una broma!)

¿Cómo (24) _____ Uds.? Papá, (25) ¿_____ muy ocupado en la empresa? Mamá, ¿cómo (26) _____ los vecinos nuevos? ¿Simpáticos? ¿Y mis hermanos? Todos (27) _____ muy bien, espero. Claudia (28) _____ contenta en el nuevo colegio, ¿verdad? Espero recibir muchas noticias de Uds. Bueno, ya (29) _____ las cinco y media. Dos amigos que toman

clases conmigo van a pasar por mí a las seis. Jaime (30) _____ de Nueva York y Carlos

(31) _____ de Nuevo México. Vamos a ir al cine. Faltan dos meses y voy a (32) _____

de vuelta en casa con Uds. Hasta pronto.

Un abrazo muy fuerte de

Miguel

NOTA CULTURAL

Madrid, capital de España, se encuentra en una extensa llanura (*plain*) aproximadamente en el centro de la Península. La ciudad, a orillas del río Manzanares, fue llamada Magerit por los musulmanes, que se apoderaron de la Península en 711 y se quedaron hasta 1492 cuando fueron derrotados definitivamente en Granada por los Reyes Católicos. Los reyes borbones (*Bourbons*), especialmente Carlos III (1716–1788; rey 1759–1788), hicieron construir muchos monumentos y edificios y convirtieron la ciudad en el centro intelectual y artístico de España. Madrid no es solamente la capital de España, sino también uno de los centros culturales más importantes de la Unión Europea.

I ¿*Qué preguntó?* *A continuación hay unas respuestas que dio su amigo. Ud. no oyó las preguntas que le hizo otro amigo. ¿Puede imaginarse cuáles son las preguntas? Escoja entre* **ser** *y* **estar** *al formular cada pregunta. Siga el modelo.*

MODELO   ¿Hoy? El siete de marzo.
    → ¿Cuál es la fecha de hoy?

1. ¿La papelería? Enfrente del correo.

2. ¿Gloria? Rubia, alta y delgada.

3. ¿Los hermanos García? Brasileños.

4. ¿Juanito y Raúl? Preocupados y nerviosos.

5. ¿La familia Méndez? De origen español.

6. ¿Las primas de Paco? Encantadoras.

7. ¿El profesor Mora? En Costa Rica.

8. ¿El vestido? De algodón.

9. ¿La camisa y la corbata? Azules.

10. ¿Yo? Muy ocupado y cansado.

11. ¿Aquella casa? De los abuelos de Sara.

12. ¿Micaela? De Inglaterra.

J *Expresar en español. Unos nuevos estudiantes extranjeros.* *Exprese en español una conversación entre dos amigas sobre los nuevos estudiantes extranjeros en su universidad.*

1. Who are the new foreign students? Do you know where they're from?

2. I know María del Mar. She's in my economics class. She's from Argentina.

3. Yes, and her background is Italian. She's very nice and smart.

4. But she's sad because she wants to go back to Buenos Aires.

5. Lorenzo Tomé is French, but his grandparents are of Indian origin.

6. The family has been living in France for many years.

7. Lorenzo is studying biology and chemistry this year.

8. He says he wants to be a doctor.

K *Ejercicio oral. La familia.* *Pregúntele a su amigo/amiga cómo son y cómo están los miembros de su familia. Pregúntele también dónde están sus familiares ahora.*

Stem-Changing Verbs and Verbs with Spelling Changes

Stem-Changing Verbs Ending in -ar and -er

Many Spanish verbs change the vowel of the stem in the present tense in those forms where the vowel of the stem is stressed (the three forms of the singular and the third person plural). For -ar and -er verbs, the changes that occur are **e > ie** and **o > ue**.

You cannot predict from the infinitive which verbs will have a stem change and which will not. For instance, **volver** has a stem change (**vuelvo**, etc.), but **comer** does not (**como**, etc.). It is therefore necessary to memorize which verbs have a stem change.

Study the present tense forms of **pensar** (*to think*), **querer** (*to want*), **contar** (*to count, tell*), and **volver** (*to return*).

pensar (e > ie) *to think*		querer (e > ie) *to want*	
pienso	pensamos	quiero	queremos
piensas	pensáis	quieres	queréis
piensa	piensan	quiere	quieren

contar (o > ue) *to count, tell*		volver (o > ue) *to return*	
cuento	contamos	vuelvo	volvemos
cuentas	contáis	vuelves	volvéis
cuenta	cuentan	vuelve	vuelven

Verbs That Pattern like querer and pensar (e > ie)

acertar *to be on target, guess right*	**encender** *to light*
apretar *to be tight, squeeze*	**encerrar** *to lock in, contain*
ascender *to go up, promote*	**entender** *to understand*
atravesar *to cross*	**gobernar** *to govern*
cerrar *to close*	*helar *to freeze*
comenzar *to begin*	**merendar** *to have an afternoon snack*
confesar *to confess*	*nevar *to snow*
defender *to defend*	**perder** *to lose*
descender *to go down*	**quebrar** *to break*
despertar(se) *to wake; to wake up*	**recomendar** *to recommend*
empezar *to begin*	**sentar(se)** *to seat; to sit down*

*Impersonal verbs; conjugated only in the third person singular.

Verbs That Pattern like volver and contar (o > ue)

acordarse *to remember*
acostar(se) *to put to bed; to go to bed*
almorzar *to eat lunch*
conmover *to move (emotionally)*
costar *to cost*
demostrar *to show*
devolver *to return (something), give back (something)*
doler *to hurt, ache*
encontrar *to find*
envolver *to wrap up*
jugar (u > ue) *to play (a sport or game); to gamble, bet*

*llover *to rain*
mostrar *to show*
oler (o > hue) *to smell*
poder *to be able, can*
probar(se) *to try, taste; to try on*
recordar *to remember*
resolver *to solve*
rodar *to roll; to film*
rogar *to ask, request; to beg, plead*
soler *to be accustomed to (doing something)*
*tronar *to thunder*
volar *to fly*

NOTES

1 · **Pensar** + infinitive means *to intend to.*

2 · **Jugar** has the stem change **u > ue**. It is used with the preposition **a** and the definite article to indicate the sport or game played.

¿A qué juegan?   *What are they playing?*
Juegan al tenis.   *They're playing tennis.*

Some speakers omit the preposition **a** and the definite article: **jugar (al) tenis**, **jugar (al) béisbol**, **jugar (al) fútbol**.

3 · **Oler** has the stem change **o > hue**.

Huele bien.   *It smells good.*

A *Los deportes. Escriba el deporte al que juega cada persona. Siga el modelo.*

MODELO   Roberto / el fútbol
           → Roberto juega al fútbol.

1. yo / el tenis

2. Alejandro y Patricio / el béisbol

3. Carlota / el vólibol

4. tú / el baloncesto

5. Marcos y yo / el fútbol americano

6. Uds. / el golf

7. Ud. / el hockey sobre hielo

8. vosotros / el jai alai

---

*Impersonal verbs; conjugated only in the third person singular.

NOTA CULTURAL

- **El béisbol** es muy popular en México, Venezuela, Cuba, Centroamérica y la República Dominicana debido a la influencia estadounidense. Muchos beisbolistas de estos países y Puerto Rico han jugado en los equipos estadounidenses de Las Grandes Ligas de Béisbol (MLB). Entre los destacados peloteros dominicanos figuran Pedro Martínez, David Ortiz ("Big Papi"), Vladimir Guerrero (Sr.), Juan Marichal y Albert Pujols, todos miembros del Salón de la Fama del Béisbol salvo Pujols. Muchas palabras relacionadas con el béisbol han pasado del inglés al español, por ejemplo: el béisbol, el jonrón, el cácher, el fildeo, fildear, batear, cachear/cachar, jitear, pitchear (pichear), la base, embasar(se) (*to get on base*).

- **El jai alai** es un juego de pelota de origen vasco (*Basque*). Los jugadores lanzan la pelota con una pala (*bat or paddle*), una cesta (*basket*) o las manos contra un frontón (*wall*). El País Vasco (Euskadi) queda al norte de España. En las Vascongadas (*Basque Provinces*) se habla el euskera (el vascuence o el vasco en español) además del español. El euskera es un idioma aislado (*language isolate*), es decir, no está relacionado con ningún otro idioma del mundo.

B *El almuerzo.* *Escriba dónde y a qué hora almuerzan estas personas. Siga el modelo.*

> MODELO   yo / en casa / a las dos
>   → Yo almuerzo en casa a las dos.

1. Uds. / en un restaurante vegetariano / a la una
2. Regina / en casa de una amiga / a las doce y cuarto
3. Rafael y yo / en una cafetería / a las tres
4. Mauricio y Elena / en una pizzería / a las tres y veinte
5. tú / en el comedor de la compañía / a las once cincuenta
6. Uds. / en un café al aire libre / a las dos y media
7. vosotras / en un restaurante de comida rápida / a la una cuarenta y cinco

C *No puedo.* *Escriba que nadie puede hacer nada hoy. Siga el modelo.*

> MODELO   ¿Vas de compras hoy?
>   → No, no puedo ir de compras hoy.

1. ¿Uds. descargan las fotos de Internet hoy?
2. ¿Empieza Elena a escribir su informe hoy?
3. ¿Trabajan Josefa y Leonardo en la librería hoy?
4. ¿Rueda Ud. su película hoy?
5. ¿Ud. trae su cámara digital hoy?
6. ¿Visitamos el museo hoy?
7. ¿Contestas tu correo electrónico hoy?
8. ¿Merendáis en un café hoy?
9. ¿Devuelves los libros a la biblioteca hoy?

D **En un almacén.** *Margarita va a un almacén para comprar ropa. Termine la conversación que tiene con la dependienta. Complete el diálogo con la forma correcta de los verbos indicados. Siga el modelo.*

MODELO   Yo ___*pienso*___ (pensar) ir al almacén Macy's.

Dependienta   —Señorita, ¿en qué _____ (1. poder) servirle?

Margarita   —Es que yo no _____ (2. encontrar) los vestidos.

Dependienta   —Aquí están a la derecha. ¿Qué color _____ (3. querer) Ud.?

Margarita   —_____ (4. Pensar) que el café o el azul marino.

Dependienta   —Le _____ (5. mostrar) dos. Este azul es muy bonito, ¿verdad?

Margarita   —Ah sí. ¿_____ (6. Poder) mostrarme el otro?

Dependienta   —Cómo no. Aquí tiene el café. Yo _____ (7. encontrar) el estilo muy elegante.

Margarita   —Los dos son hermosos. ¿Cuánto _____ (8. costar)?

Dependienta   —El azul _____ (9. costar) ciento noventa dólares y el café _____ (10. costar) doscientos cinco dólares.

Margarita   —De veras no sé. Creo que me _____ (11. probar) los dos.

Quince minutos después.

—Me llevo los dos vestidos. ¿Ud. me los _____ (12. envolver), por favor?

Dependienta   —Con gusto. ¿Ud. _____ (13. querer) pagar con tarjeta de crédito?

Margarita   —Ah sí. Yo _____ (14. soler) pagar con mi tarjeta.

Dependienta   —Bien. Yo _____ (15. volver) en unos minutos.

E **Sinónimos.** *Consulte las listas de verbos que tienen cambios radicales en* "Verbs That Pattern like **querer** and **pensar** (e > ie)" *y* "Verbs That Pattern like **volver** and **contar** (o > ue)" *en este capítulo, y escoja sinónimos para los verbos que aparecen en letra cursiva (italics) en las siguientes oraciones. Escriba cada oración con la forma correcta del nuevo verbo. Siga el modelo.*

MODELO   El diccionario *vale* cien dólares.
          → El diccionario cuesta cien dólares.

1. Uds. *solucionan* los problemas de álgebra.
2. Los niños *cruzan* la calle con cuidado.
3. El concierto *empieza* a las ocho.
4. *Bajamos* al primer piso en ascensor.
5. Yo no *comprendo* su idea.
6. ¿*Regresas* el sábado o el domingo?
7. Pedro nos *enseña* el apartamento.
8. Los Salcedo *desean* salir a cenar esta noche.
9. Yo *prendo* la luz.
10. ¿Dónde *filman* la película?

F **Un día típico.** *Escriba lo que hacen estos estudiantes en un día típico. Siga el modelo.*

MODELO   Juana / encender las luces
          → Juana enciende las luces.

1. mi compañero de cuarto / despertar a todos nosotros

2. tú / empezar a mandar tu correo electrónico

3. Uds. / almorzar en un café

4. Ud. / devolver los libros a la biblioteca

5. mis amigos / volver a la residencia universitaria a las tres

6. nosotros / comenzar a estudiar a las cuatro

7. yo / soler hacer investigaciones en la red

8. los estudiantes / encontrar a sus profesores por el campus

G   **Hoy sí, mañana no.** *Escriba oraciones conjugando el segundo verbo de la construcción verbo conjugado + infinitivo para indicar que la acción ocurre hoy. Siga el modelo.*

> MODELO   Mis tíos van a volver mañana.
> → Mis tíos vuelven hoy.

1. Vas a recordar la fecha mañana.

2. Pablo y Lorenzo van a jugar al fútbol mañana.

3. Vamos a probar el nuevo plato mañana.

4. Alicia va a encontrar su secador mañana.

5. Yo voy a envolver los paquetes mañana.

6. Ud. va a resolver su problema mañana.

H   **Expresar en español. ¿Qué tiempo hace?** *Exprese en español el tiempo que hace hoy en varias ciudades.*

¿Qué tiempo hace?

Está nublado/despejado. *It's cloudy/clear.*	**la helada** *freeze, frost*
Hace buen/mal tiempo. *The weather's good/bad.*	**el hielo** *ice*
Hace calor/frío. *It's warm/cold.*	*****llover (o > ue)** *to rain*
Hace sol/viento. *It's sunny/windy.*	*****nevar (e > ie)** *to snow*
*****despejar** *to clear up*	**el relámpago** *lightning*
el granizo *hail*	**los truenos** *thunder*

1. *It's raining in San Francisco.*

2. *It's snowing in Geneva, Switzerland* (Ginebra, Suiza).

3. *It's cloudy in Santa Fe.*

4. *It's windy in Chicago.*

5. *It's beginning to snow in Punta Arenas, Chile.*

6. *It's clearing up in London* (Londres).

7. *It's clear in Sevilla.*

8. *It's cold in Barcelona.*

---

*Impersonal verbs; conjugated only in the third person singular.

NOTA CULTURAL

- **Sevilla**, a orillas del río Guadalquivir, es la capital de la Comunidad Autónoma de Andalucía. Es una típica ciudad andaluza con su barrio judío antiguo (Santa Cruz) de hermosos patios y calles estrechas. Sus muchos monumentos llaman la atención: la Catedral, de arquitectura gótica, el Alcázar, el Archivo de Indias, la Biblioteca Colombina (de Cristóbal Colón), el museo de pintura. Hay muchísimo turismo durante la Semana Santa y las ferias de abril.
- **Santa Fe**, capital del estado de Nuevo México, fue nombrada por la ciudad española que se encuentra en la provincia de Granada. Fue en esa ciudad española donde Cristóbal Colón y los Reyes Católicos firmaron los convenios (*agreements*) en 1492.
- **Barcelona**, segunda ciudad de España, es la capital de la Comunidad Autónoma de Cataluña (*Catalunya* en catalán). Va desde las orillas del Mediterráneo hasta el monte Tibidabo. Es un puerto muy importante y tiene la industria más importante del país. La ciudad está dividida en dos partes por las Ramblas, una hermosa avenida que baja hasta el puerto. Allí hay un monumento de Cristóbal Colón que conmemora su regreso triunfal de América en 1493. Fue recibido en Barcelona por los Reyes Católicos (Fernando II de Aragón e Isabel I de Castilla). Barcelona se destaca por su ambiente cosmopolita, su vida nocturna, sus impresionantes vistas y su animada vida cultural que consiste en extraordinarios museos, música y arquitectura como la icónica Basílica de la Sagrada Familia diseñada por el arquitecto catalán Antoni Gaudí, el Museo (*Museu* en catalán) Picasso, la Catedral de Barcelona, el Palacio (*Palau* en catalán) de la Música Catalana y la Fundación (*Fundació* en catalán) Joan Miró.
- **Punta Arenas**, Chile queda en Patagonia, una región de América del Sur, en la parte sur de Argentina y Chile. Se extiende hasta el Estrecho de Magallanes.

Stem-Changing Verbs Ending in -ir

Stem-changing verbs that end in **-ir** have three types of possible changes in the vowel of the stem: **e > ie, o > ue, e > i**. These **-ir** verbs have the changes in the vowel of the stem in all persons of the present tense except **nosotros** and **vosotros**. Note that **morir** (*to die*) is conjugated like **dormir**.

sentir *to regret*		**dormir** *to sleep*	
siento	sentimos	duermo	dormimos
sientes	sentís	duermes	dormís
siente	sienten	duerme	duermen

pedir *to ask for, request*	
pido	pedimos
pides	pedís
pide	piden

Verbs That Pattern like **sentir** (e > ie)

advertir *to notify, warn, inform, point out*	**hervir** *to boil*
convertir *to convert*	**mentir** *to lie*
convertirse en *to become*	**preferir** *to prefer*
divertirse *to have a good time*	**referirse (a)** *to refer (to)*

Verbs That Pattern like **pedir** (e > i)

conseguir *to get, obtain*	**reír(se)** *to laugh*
despedir *to fire*	**reñir** *to quarrel, scold*
despedirse (de) *to say good-bye (to)*	**repetir** *to repeat; to have a second helping*
gemir *to groan, moan*	**seguir** *to follow, continue*
impedir *to prevent*	**servir** *to serve*
medir *to measure*	**sonreír(se)** *to smile*
perseguir *to chase, pursue*	**vestir(se)** *to dress*

Note that **reír** and **sonreír** have **í** as the stem vowel in the singular and third person plural: **(son)río, (son)ríes, (son)ríe, (son)reímos, (son)reís, (son)ríen.**

I **En el restaurante.** *Escriba lo que piden estas personas que salen a comer. Siga el modelo.*

> MODELO   Francisco / carne
> → Francisco pide carne.

1. Ud. y José María / piña
2. la familia Herrera / paella
3. Pili y yo / ensalada
4. tú / flan

5. los chicos / helado
6. yo / arroz con pollo
7. vosotros / tapas
8. Ud. / un sándwich

J **¿Quién sirve?** *Escriba quién sirve cada bebida. Siga el modelo.*

> MODELO   Uds. / vino
> → Uds. sirven vino.

1. yo / limonada
2. Susana / refrescos
3. nosotros / cerveza
4. Eduardo y Dolores / jugo

5. tú / agua mineral
6. Ud. y Pepe / té
7. Ud. / café
8. vosotros / jerez

NOTA CULTURAL

- **La paella** es un plato tradicional de España de arroz con carne, pollo, mariscos (*shellfish*), pescado y guisantes. Es de origen valenciano, región conocida por su producción de arroz. Se usa el azafrán (*saffron*) para condimentar la paella y para darle al arroz su color amarillo.
- **Las tapas**, de origen español, son pequeñas porciones de comida que suelen acompañar un vino o una cerveza. Son aperitivos o entremeses que pueden ser de la tortilla española, queso manchego (de la Mancha), aceitunas (*olives*), chorizo (*pork sausage*), croquetas de bacalao (*cod croquettes*), ensaladilla

rusa (*potato salad*), calamares en su tinta (*squid in its ink*) o una ración de paella. En España sigue la divertida tradición de ir de tapas (tapear), o sea, salir de bar en bar degustando (*sampling, enjoying*) diversas tapas.

- **España, país vinícola** (*wine-producing*). El vino español más conocido en todo el mundo es el jerez (*sherry*) que se produce en la región de Jerez de la Frontera. Esta ciudad queda en la provincia de Cádiz, al suroeste de Sevilla.

K **¿Qué prefiere Ud. hacer?** *Escriba lo que prefiere hacer cada persona. Siga el modelo.*

MODELO   Isabel / ir de compras
→ Isabel prefiere ir de compras.

1. los primos / salir al campo
2. Julia / leer novelas históricas
3. nosotros / asistir a un concierto
4. Uds. / pedir tacos

5. yo / jugar al tenis
6. tú / bailar el tango
7. Ud. / ver películas policíacas
8. vosotros / ver videos en YouTube

L **A dormir.** *Escriba cuánto y cómo duermen estas personas. Siga el modelo.*

MODELO   Roberto / entre seis y siete horas
→ Roberto duerme entre seis y siete horas.

1. tú / profundamente
2. yo / mucho los fines de semana
3. Uds. / bien en este dormitorio
4. vosotros / muy poco
5. nosotros / mal en este colchón (*mattress*)
6. Ud. / diez horas los días feriados (*holidays*)

M **En otras palabras.** *Escriba lo que ocurre en las siguientes situaciones. Use la forma correcta de uno de los verbos que aparecen a continuación. Siga el modelo.*

MODELO   Todos tienen hambre. Tú ___*sirves*___ la comida.

divertir	vestir	reír
repetir	despedir	reñir
sonreír	mentir	referir
sentir	dormir	gemir
advertir	hervir	

1. La abuela baña y _____ a sus nietos antes de llevarlos al parque.

2. Va a llegar una tempestad del norte. El locutor de radio _____ al público.

3. Las chicas dejan caer los vasos. Dicen que lo _____.

4. Ya _____ el agua. Ahora podemos hacer el café.

5. Ud. juega al tenis toda la mañana y siente un cansancio tremendo. Ud. _____ toda la tarde.

6. Ramona exagera mucho. En realidad, ella _____.

7. Diana _____ a sus amigos con sus cuentos graciosos. Sin embargo, hay algunos

   de ellos que no _____, ¡ni siquiera _____!

8. Hace dos años que la empresa pierde dinero. Los jefes _____ a mil empleados.

9. ¿Te gustó la torta? ¿Por qué no _____?

10. Miguelito se porta mal. Por eso sus papás lo _____.

11. No comprendo lo que dice la profesora. ¿A qué se _____?

12. ¿Por qué tú _____? ¿Te duele algo?

Verbs Ending in **-uir**

Verbs ending in -**uir** (not including those ending in -**guir**) add **y** after the **u** in all forms except **nosotros** and **vosotros**.

construir *to build*	
construyo	construimos
construyes	construís
construye	construyen

Verbs That Pattern like **construir**

atribuir *to attribute*	**huir** *to flee*
concluir *to conclude*	**incluir** *to include*
contribuir *to contribute*	**influir** *to influence*
destruir *to destroy*	**intuir** *to have a sense of, feel*
distribuir *to distribute*	**sustituir** *to substitute*

N *Vamos a contribuir.* *Hubo un terremoto* (earthquake) *que destruyó muchas casas en la Ciudad de México. Ud. y sus amigos deciden recaudar* (to collect) *dinero para mandarles medicinas a los mexicanos afectados. Escriba la cantidad de dinero que contribuyen estas personas. Siga el modelo.*

MODELO   Vera / diez dólares
          → Vera contribuye diez dólares.

1. los padres de Vera / cien dólares

2. mi hermano y yo / ciento cincuenta dólares

3. tú / setenta dólares

4. Ud. / setenta y cinco dólares

5. Adriana / veinticinco dólares

6. los habitantes del barrio / mil quinientos dólares

7. yo / ochenta dólares

O *¡Qué desastre!* Hay un huracán en la Florida. Hay mucha gente sin casa. Escriba adónde *huye la gente para escapar del peligro. Siga el modelo.*

MODELO   la familia Rivas / al norte
→ La familia Rivas huye al norte.

1. tú / a la estación de tren

5. los señores Ortega / a un hotel

2. Uds. / al oeste

6. yo / al interior del estado

3. Fernando / a casa de sus abuelos

7. Ud. / al centro

4. nosotros / a la capital

8. vosotros / a un hospital

P *Un proyecto.* Unos amigos colaboran para realizar un proyecto para la clase de biología. *Escriba lo que propone incluir cada persona del grupo. Siga el modelo.*

MODELO   yo / una bibliografía
→ Yo incluyo una bibliografía.

1. Roberto / sus investigaciones científicas

2. Uds. / algunas fotos

3. Laura y yo / las estadísticas

4. Ud. / una presentación de PowerPoint

5. tú / un resumen

6. David y Gabriela / una introducción

7. yo / un sitio web

8. vosotros / una base de datos (*database*)

Verbs Ending in -iar and -uar

Some verbs that end in -**iar** or -**uar** stress the **i** (**í**) or the **u** (**ú**) in all forms except **nosotros** and **vosotros** in the present tense.

enviar *to send*		**continuar** *to continue*	
envío	enviamos	continúo	continuamos
envías	enviáis	continúas	continuáis
envía	envían	continúa	continúan

Verbs That Pattern like **enviar**

confiar (en) *to rely (on), confide (in)*
criar *to raise, bring up*
desafiar *to challenge, dare, defy*
espiar *to spy*
esquiar *to ski*
fiarse (de) *to trust*

guiar *to guide, lead, drive*
resfriarse *to catch cold*
rociar *to sprinkle, spray, water*
vaciar *to empty*
variar *to vary*

Verbs That Pattern like **continuar**

acentuar *to accent, stress, emphasize*	**evaluar** *to evaluate, assess*
actuar *to act*	**graduarse** *to graduate*
efectuar *to effect, carry out, do, execute*	**insinuar** *to hint*

Q *¿Cuándo se resfrían Uds.?* *Las personas tienen ideas diferentes sobre cómo y cuándo se resfrían. Escriba lo que creen las siguientes personas. Siga el modelo.*

MODELO   Ud. / en diciembre
→ Ud. se resfría en diciembre.

1. Tomás / todos los inviernos

2. Uds. / cuando duermen poco

3. Lidia y Miguel / tres veces al año

4. vosotros / cuando coméis mal

5. yo / cuando bebo en los vasos ajenos (*other people's*)

6. nosotros / cuando salimos bajo la lluvia

7. tú / cuando no tomas vitaminas

R *¿Cuándo es su graduación?* *Escriba cuándo se gradúan Ud. y sus amigos en la universidad. Siga el modelo.*

MODELO   Daniela / en junio
→ Daniela se gradúa en junio.

1. Micaela y Jorge / el año próximo

2. Ud. / dentro de dos años

3. Timoteo / en enero

4. Uds. / a fines del semestre

5. tú / el 14 de mayo

6. nosotros / a principios de junio

7. yo / el mes que viene

8. vosotros / el jueves

S *Los espías.* *Complete esta narración breve sobre el espionaje (espionage, spying). Escriba la forma correcta de los verbos indicados. Siga el modelo.*

MODELO   El espía ___*guía*___ (guiar) a sus colegas por el laberinto.

1. Los espías no _____ (fiarse) de nadie.

2. Todos los espías _____ (enviar) mensajes secretos.

3. El espía X _____ (confiar) solamente en el espía Y.

4. El espía Z _____ (continuar) su trabajo con los códigos (*codes*).

5. El espía 003 _____ (evaluar) las estrategias para evitar el ciberataque.

6. Nosotros _____ (espiar) en todos los países del mundo.

T   *¿Qué dice Ud.?* *Conteste las preguntas personales.*

1. ¿A Ud. le gustan las películas de espionaje y misterio? ¿Qué hacen los espías?

2. ¿Quiénes le envían a Ud. mensajes por correo electrónico?

3. ¿Se fía Ud. de los anuncios de televisión? ¿Por qué sí o por qué no?

4. ¿Qué hace y toma Ud. cuando se resfría?

5. ¿En quiénes confía Ud.?

6. ¿Cuándo se gradúa Ud.?

7. ¿Ud. esquía? ¿Dónde?

8. ¿Ud. actúa en obras de teatro? ¿En qué obras?

9. ¿Se fía Ud. de los desconocidos? ¿Por qué sí o por qué no?

Verbs with Spelling Changes in the Present Tense

For verbs that end in **-ger** and **-gir**, **g** changes to **j** before **o** and **a**. In the present tense, the change occurs only in the first person singular (**yo**) form.

escoger *to choose*	
escojo	escogemos
escoges	escogéis
escoge	escogen

Verbs That Pattern like **escoger**

acoger *to welcome, receive (someone)*	**encoger** *to shrink*
afligir *to afflict*	**exigir** *to demand*
coger* *to get, take*	**fingir** *to pretend*
corregir (**e** > **i**) *to correct*	**proteger** *to protect*
dirigir *to direct, conduct*	**recoger** *to gather, pick up, collect*
elegir (**e** > **i**) *to choose, elect*	**surgir** *to arise*

For verbs that end in **-guir**, **gu** changes to **g** before **o** and **a**. In the present tense, the change occurs only in the first person singular (**yo**) form.

distinguir *to distinguish*	
distingo	distinguimos
distingues	distinguís
distingue	distinguen

Extinguir (*to extinguish*) is conjugated like **distinguir**.

Seguir (*to follow, continue*) patterns like **distinguir** and also has the stem change **e** > **i**. This applies to related verbs ending in **-seguir**: **conseguir** (*to get, acquire*), **perseguir** (*to pursue, persecute*), **proseguir** (*to proceed*).

---

*This verb is taboo in much of South America; **tomar** and **agarrar** are used instead.

seguir *to follow*	
sigo	seguimos
sigues	seguís
sigue	siguen

For most verbs that end in -**cer** or -**cir**, **c** changes to **z** before **o** and **a**. In the present tense, the change occurs only in the first person singular (**yo**) form.

convencer *to convince*	
convenzo	convencemos
convences	convencéis
convence	convencen

Mecer (*to rock (a child); to swing (in a swing)*), **ejercer** (*to exercise, practice*), and **vencer** (*to conquer, overcome*) pattern like **convencer**. **Cocer** (*to cook*) and **torcer** (*to twist*) also follow this pattern and in addition have the stem change **o** > **ue**.

torcer *to twist*		**cocer** *to cook*	
tuerzo	torcemos	cuezo	cocemos
tuerces	torcéis	cueces	cocéis
tuerce	tuercen	cuece	cuecen

Most verbs are marked with their spelling changes in bilingual dictionaries. A typical presentation is **coger** (**g** > **j/o, a**). When the verb has both a stem change and a spelling change, it is usually marked as in this example: **torcer** (**o** > **ue, c** > **z/o, a**).

U *¿Qué elige Ud.? Nuestros amigos van a celebrar su aniversario de diez años el sábado. Por eso vamos a comprarles unos regalos. Escriba qué regalos elegimos. Siga el modelo.*

MODELO Ud. / un florero de cristal (*crystal vase*)
→ Ud. elige un florero de cristal.

1. yo / una caja de bombones

2. mis padres / una bandeja (*tray*) de plata

3. nosotros / un certificado de regalo

4. tú / dos tabletas

5. Uds. / un televisor

6. Raquel / una cámara digital

7. vosotros / un juego de vajilla (*dinnerware set*)

8. nuestros primos / un mueble

9. Ud. / unos billetes de concierto

V **¿Cuál es su trabajo?** *Escriba lo que hace cada persona escogiendo el verbo correcto de la lista abajo.*

dirigir   recoger   perseguir   mecer
extinguir   corregir   cocer

1. Soy campesino. Yo _____ manzanas y tomates.

2. Soy policía. Yo _____ a los ladrones.

3. Soy bombero. Yo _____ incendios.

4. Soy cocinera. Yo _____ platos muy sabrosos.

5. Soy director de orquesta. Yo _____ una orquesta sinfónica.

6. Soy profesora. Yo _____ exámenes y composiciones.

7. Soy papá. Yo _____ a mi hijito en el columpio (*swing*).

W **Un misterio.** *Escriba la forma correcta de los verbos indicados para describir el terror que experimenta el narrador.*

Es la una de la mañana. Yo _____ (1. seguir) por las calles vacías y desoladas

de la ciudad. Yo me _____ (2. dirigir) al hotel. De repente oigo pasos. Tengo miedo.

Me _____ (3. encoger) de hombros (*shrug*). Vuelvo la cabeza para ver quién camina detrás

de mí, quizás en pos de mí (*after me*). Yo _____ (4. distinguir) una sombra de persona.

No la _____ (5. reconocer). La persona deja de caminar y _____ (6. fingir) no verme.

Yo _____ (7. conseguir) ver que la persona _____ (8. lucir) un vestido blanco que brilla

a la luz de la luna. Yo _____ (9. proseguir) mi camino al hotel pero ahora camino más rápido.

La situación me _____ (10. producir) mucha angustia pero yo _____ (11. fingir) no estar

nervioso. Yo _____ (12. distinguir) un paquete que está a mis pies. Lo _____ (13. recoger).

Me da un escalofrío ver que yo soy el destinatario (*addressee*). Trato de persuadirme

que esto es una pesadilla. Por desgracia, no me _____ (14. convencer). ¡Aunque yo

_____ (15. desconocer) el camino voy corriendo por las calles como un loco!

X **Consiguen hacer algunas cosas.** *Escriba lo que consiguen hacer Ud. y sus amigos el sábado (**conseguir** + infinitivo (to manage to do something, succeed in doing something)). Siga el modelo.*

MODELO   Rosa y Margarita / terminar su informe
         → Rosa y Margarita consiguen terminar su informe.

1. Víctor / salir al centro comercial   4. yo / hacer unos platos riquísimos

2. Pablo y yo / reparar el coche   5. Uds. / arreglar los armarios

3. Ud. / ver la nueva exposición   6. tú / colgar los cuadros

Sinónimos. *Escoja de la siguiente lista el sinónimo del verbo en letra cursiva* (italics) *de cada oración. Escriba la nueva oración con la forma correcta del verbo.*

cocer   desconocer   conseguir
coger   seguir   distinguir
exigir   elegir
producir   fingir

1. *Continúa* con sus clases de pintura.

2. *Agarro* las monedas una por una.

3. *Ignoro* el motivo de los directores.

4. *Disimulo* tener interés en el proyecto.

5. *Cocinan* arroz para servirlo con el pollo.

6. No *diferencio* entre el mar y el cielo en el cuadro.

7. *Pido* más esfuerzos de parte de los miembros del equipo.

8. ¿*Seleccionas* tus clases para el próximo semestre?

9. No *logro* hablar con mis cuñados hoy.

10. *Cultivo* maíz y trigo en la finca.

Z **Expresar en español. Las noticias.** *Exprese en español los titulares* (headlines) *del periódico que Ud. lee. Trate de usar los verbos presentados en esta sección.*

1. *Leopoldo Soto is conducting the Philadelphia Orchestra* (la Orquesta de Filadelfia) *this week.*

2. *The firefighters put out thirty fires each day.*

3. *The parents are demanding better schools.*

4. *Senator Alonso is following the advice of his colleagues in the Senate* (el Senado).

5. *The Americans elect a new president this year.*

6. *Young couple succeeds in winning the lottery.*

7. *A new recipe: chef cooks soup with ice cream.*

8. *The campaign against illiteracy* (el analfabetismo) *proceeds.*

AA **Ejercicio oral. ¿Qué piensan Uds. hacer?** *Pregúnteles a sus amigos lo que piensan hacer y adónde quieren ir este fin de semana. Que digan también cómo se modificarán sus planes si llueve o nieva. Use verbos con cambios radicales donde sea posible, tales como* **pensar, querer, preferir, volver, poder,** *etc.*

The Preterit Tense

Regular Verbs

The preterit tense is used to express events that were completed in the past. Preterit tense endings are added to the stem of regular -**ar**, -**er**, and -**ir** verbs.

tomar *to take; to drink*		**comer** *to eat*	
tom**é**	tom**amos**	com**í**	com**imos**
tom**aste**	tom**asteis**	com**iste**	com**isteis**
tom**ó**	tom**aron**	com**ió**	com**ieron**

vivir *to live*	
viv**í**	viv**imos**
viv**iste**	viv**isteis**
viv**ió**	viv**ieron**

NOTES

1 · All preterit forms are stressed on the endings rather than on the stem.

2 · For -**ar** verbs:

- The first person singular (**yo**) form in the present tense and the third person singular (**él**, **ella**, **Ud.**) form in the preterit tense are distinguished only by the stress: tomo/tom**ó**.

- The first person plural (**nosotros**) form is the same in the present tense and the preterit tense: **tomamos**. The meaning is clarified by context.

3 · The preterit endings are the same for both -**er** and -**ir** verbs.

4 · For -**ir** verbs:

- The first person plural (**nosotros**) form is the same in the present tense and the preterit tense: **vivimos**. The meaning is clarified by context.

5 · For -**er** verbs:

- The present and preterit of the **nosotros** forms are different: com**emos**/com**imos**.

6 · -**Ar** and -**er** verbs that have changes in the vowel of the stem (**e** > **ie** or **o** > **ue**) in the present tense do not have these changes in any of the preterit forms. For example: p**ie**nso/pensé, v**ue**lven/volvieron.

7 · -**Ir** verbs that have a change in the vowel of the stem in the present tense also have a stem change in the preterit tense. In the preterit, the vowel changes from **e** > **i** or from **o** > **u** in the third person singular and plural.

pedir *to ask for*		**dormir** *to sleep*	
pedí	pedimos	dormí	dormimos
pediste	pedisteis	dormiste	dormisteis
pidió	pidieron	durmió	durmieron

8 · Some verbs that pattern like **pedir** in the preterit: **servir** (*to serve*), **divertirse** (*to have a good time*), **repetir** (*to repeat*), **medir** (*to measure*), **advertir** (*to point out, warn*), **mentir** (*to lie*), **convertir** (*to convert*), **vestirse** (*to dress*), **preferir** (*to prefer*), and **seguir** (*to follow*). Like **dormir**: **morir** (*to die*).

9 · The verbs **reír** and **sonreír** have a written accent mark on the **i** of the endings of the **yo**, **tú**, **nosotros**, and **vosotros** forms in the preterit: (**son**)re**í**, (**son**)re**í**ste, (**son**)ri**ó**, (**son**)re**í**mos, (**son**)re**í**steis, (**son**)rieron.

10 · -**Ir** verbs that have **ñ** directly before the ending drop the **i** of the ending in the third person singular and plural: **gruñir** (*to grunt*): **gruñó/gruñeron**; **reñir** (*to scold*): **riñó/riñeron**.

Verbs with Spelling Changes in the Preterit

Most verbs with spelling changes are regular in speech. The rules of Spanish, however, cause changes in their written forms.

-**Ar** verbs whose stems end in -**c**, -**g**, -**z** have the following spelling changes in the **yo** form of the preterit.

   c > **qu**
   g > **gu**
   z > **c**

Compare the spelling of some of these spelling change verbs in the **yo** form of the present and the preterit.

INFINITIVE	PRESENT TENSE	PRETERIT
buscar	busco	busqué
sacar	saco	saqué
llegar	llego	llegué
pagar	pago	pagué
alcanzar	alcanzo	alcancé
comenzar	comienzo	comencé

The reason for this change is that Spanish spells the sounds /k/, /g/, /s/ (spelled **z**) differently before **e** and **i**. Study the spelling of these sounds before the five vowels.

/k/	ca, **que**, **qui**, co, cu
/g/	ga, **gue**, **gui**, go, gu
/s/ (spelled **z**)	za, **ce**, **ci**, zo, zu

Verbs That Pattern like **buscar**

acercarse *to approach*

aparcar *to park*

arrancar *to pull/root out; to start up* (of a vehicle)

atacar *to attack*

chocar *to crash, collide with*

colocar *to put, place*

criticar *to criticize*

dedicarse *to devote oneself*

educar *to educate*

embarcar(se) *to embark, go on board*

equivocarse *to be mistaken*

explicar *to explain*

fabricar *to make, manufacture*

identificar *to identify*

indicar *to indicate*

justificar *to justify*

marcar *to dial; to mark*

mascar *to chew*

masticar *to chew*

pescar *to fish*

practicar *to practice*

publicar *to publish*

sacar *to take out*

secar *to dry*

tocar *to touch; to play a musical instrument*

volcar (o > ue) *to tip, knock over, upset*

Verbs That Pattern like **llegar**

agregar *to add*

ahogarse *to drown*

apagar *to put out, extinguish*

cargar *to load*

castigar *to punish*

colgar (o > ue) *to hang*

despegar *to take off* (of an airplane)

encargar *to put in charge, entrust; to order*

entregar *to hand in/over*

jugar (u > ue) *to play*

juzgar *to judge*

madrugar *to get up early*

navegar *to navigate; to surf (the web)*

negar (e > ie) *to deny*

pagar *to pay*

pegar *to stick, beat*

rogar (o > ue) *to beg, ask*

tragar *to swallow*

vengar *to avenge*

Verbs That Pattern like **comenzar**

abrazar *to hug, embrace*

actualizar *to bring up to date*

adelgazar *to get thin*

alcanzar *to reach, overtake*

almorzar (o > ue) *to have lunch*

amenazar *to threaten*

analizar *to analyze*

bostezar *to yawn*

cruzar *to cross*

deslizarse *to slip*

destrozar *to destroy, ruin*

empezar (e > ie) *to begin*

gozar *to enjoy*

lanzar *to throw*

organizar *to organize*

realizar *to fulfill*

rechazar *to reject*

rezar *to pray*

tranquilizarse *to calm down*

tropezar (e > ie) *to trip, stumble*

-Er and -ir Verbs with Stems Ending in a Vowel

-Er and -ir verbs that have a vowel immediately preceding the preterit ending change -ió to -yó in the third person singular and -ieron to -yeron in the third person plural in the preterit. These verbs also add a written accent to the i of the tú, nosotros, and vosotros endings.

leer *to read*		oír *to hear*	
leí	leímos	oí	oímos
leíste	leísteis	oíste	oísteis
leyó	leyeron	oyó	oyeron

Verbs that end in -uir also pattern this way; however, there is no written accent on the tú, nosotros, and vosotros forms of the verbs.

construir *to build*	
construí	construimos
construiste	construisteis
construyó	construyeron

Traer, which has an irregular preterit, as well as verbs with prefixes added to traer and verbs that end in -guir, are exceptions to the above pattern.

Verbs That Pattern like leer and oír

caer *to fall*
creer *to think, believe*
poseer *to have, possess*

Verbs That Pattern like construir

atribuir *to attribute*
concluir *to conclude*
contribuir *to contribute*
destruir *to destroy*
distribuir *to distribute*

huir *to flee*
incluir *to include*
influir *to influence*
intuir *to have a sense of, feel*
sustituir *to substitute*

A *¡Tanta tarea! Escriba las cosas que Ud. y sus compañeros de clase hicieron ayer. Siga el modelo.*

MODELO   Bárbara / practicar el ruso
→ Bárbara practicó el ruso.

1. vosotros / mandar textos
2. Rosa y Elena / solucionar los problemas de cálculo
3. tú / escribir un informe
4. nosotros / trabajar en la librería
5. yo / visitar unos sitios web
6. Uds. / contestar las preguntas de filosofía
7. Miguel / discutir unos temas
8. Ud. / aprender las fechas de historia de memoria

B *¡Vaya un día de examen!* Escriba las formas correctas del pretérito de los verbos indicados. Describa lo que le pasó a Pedro el día del examen. Siga el modelo.

MODELO   Rafael me ___despertó___ (despertar) a las siete.

En seguida yo me _____ (1. levantar) y me _____ (2. arreglar). _____ (3. Bajar) a la cocina donde _____ (4. saludar) a mis padres y a mi hermano. Mamá me _____ (5. preparar) cereal y pan tostado. Yo _____ (6. tomar) jugo y _____ (7. empezar) a repasar mi libro de química. Mi amigo Carlos _____ (8. pasar) por mí y _____ (9. desayunar) con nosotros. Él y yo _____ (10. terminar) el desayuno y yo _____ (11. coger) mi mochila. Carlos y yo _____ (12. salir) corriendo para la parada de autobuses. El número once _____ (13. llegar) casi inmediatamente. Nosotros _____ (14. subir) y _____ (15. viajar) quince minutos hasta llegar al colegio. Nosotros _____ (16. bajar) casi en la puerta principal. Tan pronto como el autobús _____ (17. arrancar) yo _____ (18. buscar) mi mochila. No la _____ (19. encontrar). ¡Ay, mis apuntes! ¡Qué susto! "Yo _____ (20. colocar) la mochila en el asiento, yo _____ (21. pensar). Carlos me _____ (22. mirar) con mi cara de angustia y _____ (23. hablar). "Chico, no te preocupes. Aquí la tienes," me _____ (24. explicar). Mi mejor amigo me _____ (25. entregar) la mochila y así me _____ (26. salvar) la vida.

C *Salimos a cenar.* Escriba qué tal Ud. lo pasó cuando salió a cenar con sus amigos. Siga el modelo.

MODELO   mis amigos y yo / salir a cenar / anoche
→ Mis amigos y yo salimos a cenar anoche.

1. yo / escoger / el Café Valencia
2. nosotros / llegar / al restaurante a las siete
3. Uds. / leer / la carta
4. el mesero / recomendar / el pescado al mango
5. Lorenzo / pedir / ternera y sopa
6. Eva y Diana / pedir / el bistec y ensalada
7. Ud. / preferir / el arroz con pollo
8. tú / comer / torta de postre
9. todos nosotros / tomar / vino
10. todo el mundo / beber / café
11. yo / pagar / la cuenta
12. Jaime / dejar / la propina
13. vosotros / cenar / muy bien
14. yo / gozar / de una cena riquísima
15. todos nosotros / divertirse mucho

NOTA CULTURAL

El arroz con pollo es un plato que se sirve en casi todos los países del mundo hispanohablante. Varía de un país a otro o de una región a otra en cuanto a los ingredientes, los condimentos y la preparación. Sigue una receta para este plato tradicional de Goya Foods, la empresa alimentaria hispana más grande de los Estados Unidos cuyos dueños son de la familia fundadora Unanue, de origen español y emigrantes a Puerto Rico. Goya Foods fue fundada en 1936. *https://www.goyapr.com/recetas/arroz-con-pollo*

D **Todo hecho ya.** *Su amigo le pregunta a Ud. si va a hacer ciertas cosas. Dígale que ya las hizo. Siga el modelo.*

MODELO   ¿Vas a apagar las luces?
→ Ya apagué las luces.

1. ¿Vas a sacar billetes para el concierto?

2. ¿Vas a jugar al tenis?

3. ¿Vas a tocar la flauta?

4. ¿Vas a colocar los documentos en el archivo?

5. ¿Vas a arrancar la mala hierba (*weeds*) del jardín?

6. ¿Vas a navegar en la red?

7. ¿Vas a descargar el documento?

8. ¿Vas a almorzar con Victoria?

9. ¿Vas a entregar el informe?

10. ¿Vas a empezar la novela inglesa?

E **Pasaron los años.** *Hace ocho años que Ud. no ve a estas personas. Ahora tiene noticias de ellas. Escriba lo que les pasó a lo largo de los años. Siga el modelo.*

MODELO   Jacinta / caer / enferma
→ Jacinta cayó enferma.

1. los hermanos Serrat / construir / muchas casas

2. el profesor Burgos / influir / mucho en la vida política

3. Francisca / leer / libros para una casa editora (*publishing house*)

4. Marco e Isabel / huir / a otro pueblo por un terremoto

5. Elvira / contribuir / mucho dinero a las caridades

6. Leonardo / concluir / los trámites de la empresa

F **¡Qué mala suerte!** *Ayer a Ud. todo le salió mal. Escriba lo que le pasó. Siga el modelo.*

MODELO   Yo me ___caí___ (caer) en la escalera.

1. Yo me _____ (equivocar) de número de teléfono

2. y _____ (marcar) mal cuatro veces.

3. Luego _____ (tropezar) con la pared

4. y me _____ (pegar) en el hueso de la alegría (*funny bone*).

5. Luego me _____ (deslizar) en una cáscara de plátano (*banana peel*).

6. En la cena _____ (mascar) la carne demasiado rápido

7. y _____ (tragar) mal.

8. Para tranquilizarme, me _____ (bañar).

9. Casi me _____ (ahogar) en la bañera.

10. ¡Claro que no me _____ (tranquilizar)!

G *Yo no hice eso.* *Escriba las formas correctas de los verbos indicados para describir lo que hicieron unas personas y lo que hizo Ud. Siga el modelo.*

MODELO   Alicia ___encargó___ unos vestidos. (encargar)

Yo ___encargué___ unas camisetas.

1. Jorge _____ la pelota en el partido. (lanzar)

   Yo _____ el bate.

2. Álvaro _____ unos cuentos. (publicar)

   Yo _____ una novela.

3. Tú te _____ a la pintura. (dedicar)

   Yo me _____ a la música.

4. Uds. _____ los datos. (descargar)

   Yo _____ los documentos.

5. Los Sierra _____ un viaje a Bruselas. (realizar)

   Yo _____ un viaje a Barcelona.

6. Ud. _____ para Tenerife. (embarcar)

   Yo _____ para Mallorca.

H *Una entrevista.* *Ud. acaba de volver de Puerto Rico donde pasó tres semanas con sus amigos. Ahora un periodista del periódico universitario le hace unas preguntas sobre el viaje. Contéstelas. Siga los modelos.*

MODELOS   ¿Qué día llegó a Puerto Rico? (el veinte de diciembre)
→ Llegué el 20 de diciembre.

¿Ud. sacó fotos? (muchas)
→ Sí, saqué muchas.

Turismo

el aeropuerto *airport*	**el mar** *sea, ocean*
almorzar (o > ue) *to have lunch*	**el museo** *museum*
aterrizar *to land*	**pescar** *to fish*
la estancia *stay*	**la playa** *beach*
la fortaleza *fortress*	**rezar** *to pray*
gozar (de) *to enjoy*	**la sinagoga** *synagogue*
la iglesia *church*	**visitar** *to visit*
el lugar turístico *tourist attraction*	

1. ¿Dónde aterrizó Ud.? (el aeropuerto de San Juan)

2. ¿Qué lugares turísticos visitó? (fortalezas, museos e iglesias)

3. ¿Rezó en una iglesia? (yo en la iglesia de San Juan y Sara en una sinagoga)

4. ¿Dónde almorzó? (en varias playas de la isla)

5. ¿Jugó al tenis? (y al fútbol también)

6. ¿Pescó en el mar? (y en los ríos también)

7. ¿Avanzó Ud. en su dominio del español? (mucho)

8. ¿Qué tal el viaje que realizó? (maravilloso)

9. ¿Gozó de su estancia en Puerto Rico? (muchísimo)

NOTA CULTURAL

El Estado Libre Asociado de Puerto Rico (*Commonwealth of Puerto Rico*) es un país que tiene el océano Atlántico al norte y el mar Caribe al sur. Es la isla más oriental de las Antillas Mayores cuyas otras islas más grandes son La Española (la República Dominicana y Haití), Jamaica y Cuba. La isla fue llamada Borinquen por los indígenas. Cristóbal Colón desembarcó en la isla en su segundo viaje en 1493. A los turistas les llaman la atención el Viejo San Juan, el Museo de Arte de Ponce, el Yunque (bosque), la Casa Blanca de Ponce de León, explorador de Puerto Rico y fundador de San Juan (1508). Hay también muchos festivales por toda la isla como el Festival Casals de música clásica que lleva el nombre del célebre violonchelista Pablo Casals que lo fundó en 1956. Casals nació en España en 1876 y murió en Puerto Rico en 1973 donde vivió por muchos años.

I ***Expresar en español. ¿Cómo reaccionó la gente?*** *Exprese en español cómo reaccionaron estas personas a una situación o a una noticia. Siga el modelo.*

MODELO   *Laura denied it.*
           → Laura lo negó.

1. *You (tú) smiled.*

2. *The boys had a second helping* (repetir).

3. *Patricio grunted.*

4. *We laughed.*

5. *You (Uds.) fell asleep* (dormirse).

6. *Mrs. Gil served the soup.*

7. *Chelo scolded the children.*

8. *The thieves lied.*

9. *Our friends warned us.*

10. *Paquita had a good time.*

11. *They were sorry.*

Irregular Verbs in the Preterit

Many Spanish verbs have an irregular stem plus a special set of endings in the preterit. The endings for these verbs are: **-e, -iste, -o, -imos, -isteis, -ieron**. Note that the **yo** and **él** forms are stressed on the stem, not on the ending.

decir *to say, tell*		**estar** *to be*	
dije	dijimos	estuve	estuvimos
dijiste	dijisteis	estuviste	estuvisteis
dijo	dijeron	estuvo	estuvieron

hacer *to do, make*		**poder** *to be able, can*	
hice	hicimos	pude	pudimos
hiciste	hicisteis	pudiste	pudisteis
hizo	hicieron	pudo	pudieron

poner *to put*		**querer** *to want, love*	
puse	pusimos	quise	quisimos
pusiste	pusisteis	quisiste	quisisteis
puso	pusieron	quiso	quisieron

saber *to know*		**tener** *to have*	
supe	supimos	tuve	tuvimos
supiste	supisteis	tuviste	tuvisteis
supo	supieron	tuvo	tuvieron

traer *to bring*		**venir** *to come*	
traje	trajimos	vine	vinimos
trajiste	trajisteis	viniste	vinisteis
trajo	trajeron	vino	vinieron

andar *to walk*		**caber** *to fit*	
anduve	anduvimos	cupe	cupimos
anduviste	anduvisteis	cupiste	cupisteis
anduvo	anduvieron	cupo	cupieron

producir *to produce*	
produje	produjimos
produjiste	produjisteis
produjo	produjeron

NOTES

1 · For the third person singular of **hacer** in the preterit, the stem is spelled **hiz-** (**hizo**). The spelling change **c** > **z** before **o** retains the /s/.

2 · Irregular preterits whose stems end in **-j**, such as **dij-** (**decir**) and **traj-** (**traer**), have **-eron** and not **-ieron** in the third person plural form: **dijeron, trajeron, produjeron**. Other verbs, ending in **-ducir**, are conjugated like **producir** in the preterit: **tradujeron** (**traducir** (*to translate*)), **condujeron** (**conducir** (*to drive*)), etc.

3 · Compound forms of the verbs **hacer** (**rehacer, satisfacer,** etc.), **poner** (**proponer, reponerse,** etc.), **tener** (**mantener, sostener,** etc.), **traer** (**atraer, distraer,** etc.), **venir** (**convenir, prevenir,** etc.) are conjugated the same way as the main verb.

4 · The preterit form of **hay** (*there is, there are*) is **hubo.**

5 · **Dar** takes the endings of regular **-er** and **-ir** verbs in the preterit. Note that the first and third person singular forms are written without an accent mark. **Ver,** regular in the preterit, has no written accent marks, like **dar.**

dar *to give*		**ver** *to see*	
di	dimos	vi	vimos
diste	disteis	viste	visteis
dio	dieron	vio	vieron

Ser (*to be*) and **ir** (*to go*) have the same conjugation in the preterit tense. Although isolated sentences may be ambiguous (for example, **fue** means both *he was* and *he went*), context usually clarifies which verb is meant.

ser/ir	
fui	fuimos
fuiste	fuisteis
fue	fueron

Some verbs take on a different meaning when they are used in the preterit. The distinction in meaning will be especially important when you study the difference between the preterit tense and the imperfect tense, which are two aspects or ways of looking at past time. In the case of these verbs used in the preterit, they focus on the beginning or completion of an action. For example, **conocí** means *I began to know,* that is, *I met.*

VERB	SPANISH	ENGLISH
saber *to know*	Supe la fecha hoy.	*I found out the date today.*
conocer *to know*	Conocimos a Carmen ayer.	*We met Carmen yesterday.*
tener *to have*	Tuvo una idea.	*He got an idea.*
poder *to be able to*	No pudieron salir.	*They didn't manage to go out.*
querer *to want*	No quisiste trotar.	*You refused to jog.*

J   *El pronóstico meteorológico. Su amiga comenta sobre el tiempo que hace en varias ciudades. Escriba qué tiempo hizo ayer. Siga el modelo.*

MODELO   Hace buen tiempo en Quito.
→ Hizo buen tiempo ayer también.

1. Está nublado en San Francisco.

2. Hace frío en París.

3. Llueve en Montevideo.

4. Hace sol en Guadalajara.

5. Está despejado en Jerusalén.

6. Nieva en Quebec.

7. Hace ochenta grados en Miami.

8. Hace fresco en Roma.

9. Truena en Londres.

10. Hay mucho viento en Chicago.

NOTA CULTURAL

- **Quito**, capital de Ecuador, queda a algunos 25 kilómetros de la línea ecuatorial, pero tiene los días calurosos y las noches frescas porque tiene una altitud de 2.850 metros. El metro equivale a 3.281 pies.
- **Montevideo** es la capital de Uruguay, el país hispanohablante más pequeño de América del Sur. Montevideo queda en la costa meridional (*southern*) del país, en el Río de la Plata. Es un resort veraniego (*summer* [adj.]) y el punto de partida para llegar a los balnearios (*beach resorts*) de la costa uruguaya, como Punta del Este.
- **Guadalajara** es la segunda ciudad de México en población y la capital del estado de Jalisco. Guadalajara es la cuna (*home, cradle*) del mariachi (*strolling Mexican musician or band*) y el tequila. El clima es templado (*mild*), seco y despejado todo el año aunque las noches pueden ser tormentosas.

K *Escenas breves. Escriba las formas correctas del pretérito de los verbos indicados para saber lo que se dice en los diálogos breves.*

1. —¿Qué _____ Ud. entonces? (decir)

   —Pues, no _____ nada.

2. —¿A qué hora _____ Uds. al cine? (ir)

   —_____ a las nueve.

3. —¿Dónde (tú) _____ el sábado? (estar)

   —_____ en el centro comercial.

4. —¿Las meseras les _____ el plato principal? (traer)

   —No, una mesera nos _____ el pan y nada más.

5. —¿Uds. _____ en coche? (venir)

   —Yo _____ en coche pero Teri _____ en tren.

6. —Yo _____ con Catalina anteayer. (dar con (*to run into*))

   —¿Ah sí? ¿Dónde la (Ud.) _____? (ver)

7. —¿Clara _____ lo que pasó? (oír)

   —Sí, lo _____ la semana pasada. (saber)

8. —Tú _____ la comida, ¿verdad? (hacer)

   —Claro. Y _____ la mesa también. (poner)

9. —¿José _____ el correo electrónico? (leer)

   —No, no _____. (querer)

10. —¿Quién _____ el postre? (hacer)

   —_____ yo. (ser)

L *¿Y qué pasó después?* *Para cada una de las siguientes situaciones hay una reacción. Para saber cuál es, complete las oraciones con la expresión correcta de la lista y conjugue el verbo en el pretérito. Siga el modelo.*

> MODELO   Yo invité a Marta a mi casa. (venir a verme)
> → Marta vino a verme.

hacerse daño	poner la mesa
tener frío	estar feliz
decir que sí	poder distinguir
ir tras ella	hacerse médico

1. Matilde ganó la lotería. Ella _____.

2. Juan Carlos se graduó en la facultad de medicina. Él _____.

3. Bajó mucho la temperatura entre las cinco y las seis de la tarde. Los niños _____.

4. Preparamos una cena para veinte invitados. Nosotros _____.

5. El pintor se cayó de la escalera. Él _____.

6. Fue un día de mucha niebla. Yo ni _____ la carretera.

7. Uds. le pidieron prestado el coche a Rodrigo. Rodrigo _____.

8. Tu novia salió de la conferencia. Y tú _____.

M *Ayer, al contrario...* *Generalmente Ud. hace cosas de cierta manera. Ayer, sin embargo, no fue así. Escriba cómo salieron sus actividades usando la información indicada. Siga el modelo.*

> MODELO   Generalmente me acuesto a las diez. (las once)
> → Pero ayer me acosté a las once.

1. Generalmente me despierto a las ocho. (las siete)

2. Generalmente almuerzo en el Café Bélgica. (el Café Atenas)

3. Generalmente voy de compras por la tarde. (por la mañana)

4. Generalmente hago un plato de pollo. (un plato de pescado)

5. Generalmente juego al ajedrez (*chess*) con Roberto. (con Ricardo)

6. Generalmente sigo por la calle Serrano. (la calle Atocha)

7. Generalmente empiezo a trabajar después del desayuno. (antes del desayuno)

8. Generalmente vengo en tren. (en taxi)

N *Una merienda en el campo.* *Unos amigos recuerdan lo bien que lo pasaron ese domingo en julio cuando fueron a merendar en el campo. Complete las oraciones con los verbos de la lista. Escriba los verbos usando el pretérito.*

tener	conducir	ir
hacer	traer	comenzar
recoger	ver	dar
oír	poder	estar

1. Todos nosotros _____ en carro.

2. Antonio y Francisco _____ los carros.

3. Por desgracia Pedro no _____ acompañarnos.

4. _____ muy buen tiempo.

5. Diego _____ un paseo con los niños.

6. Lila y Berta _____ flores.

7. Leticia y Manuel _____ sándwiches, ensaladas y jugo.

8. Los chicos _____ vacas y caballos

9. y _____ cantar los pájaros.

10. A las cinco de la tarde _____ a llover y

11. nosotros _____ que volver a la ciudad.

12. ¡Nosotros _____ muy contentos ese día!

O *Expresar en español. ¡Qué suspenso!* *Ud. es escritor/escritora de cuentos de misterio. Escriba un cuento de misterio expresando las siguientes oraciones en español.*

1. *The monster* (el monstruo) *came to the city.*

2. *It smashed* (hacer pedazos) *cars and destroyed buildings.*

3. *When the people saw the monster they shouted* (dar gritos).

4. *I got* (ponerse) *pale.*

5. *Felipe got a headache* (darle un dolor de cabeza a uno).

6. *Marisol got a stomachache* (darle un dolor de estómago a uno).

7. *We all started* (echarse a) *to run.*

8. *Some people didn't manage* (poder) *to escape* (escaparse).

9. *The suspense became* (hacerse) *unbearable* (insoportable, inaguantable)!

P *¿Qué dice Ud.?* *Conteste las siguientes preguntas personales.*

1. ¿Adónde fuiste el fin de semana?

2. ¿Qué hiciste el sábado (el domingo)?

3. ¿Adónde fuiste cuando saliste a comer?

4. ¿Con quiénes fuiste?

5. ¿Qué pidieron Uds.?

6. ¿Qué tal estuvo la comida?

7. ¿Qué tal sirvieron los meseros?

8. ¿Quién pagó la cuenta?

9. ¿Quién dejó la propina?

10. ¿Dónde pasaste las vacaciones de verano (invierno)?

11. ¿Con quiénes fuiste?

12. ¿Qué hicieron Uds. allí?

O *Los viajes.* Escriba las formas correctas del pretérito de los verbos indicados para saber lo que dicen estas personas de su viaje.

1. **Un vuelo directo**

   —¿Tú _____ (poder) reservar los billetes en línea?

   —Sí, yo _____ (hacer) todos los trámites (*arrangements*) a través de Internet.

   Yo _____ (encontrar) un vuelo directo a Madrid.

   —Estupendo. La última vez que nosotros _____ (viajar) a España (nosotros)

   _____ (tener) que hacer escala (*to make a stopover*).

   —No nos _____ (gustar) para nada. ¡_____ (Ser) un viaje interminable!

2. **En el aeropuerto**

   —¿Cómo te _____ (ir) en el aeropuerto?

   —Pan comido. (*A piece of cake.*) Yo _____ (llegar) temprano, _____ (facturar (*to check*))

   mi equipaje y _____ (sacar) mi tarjeta de embarque.

   —¿Luego tú _____ (seguir) a la puerta de embarque?

   —Primero yo _____ (comer) algo y _____ (comprar) unas revistas.

3. **A bordo del avión**

   —Yo _____ (subir) al avión y _____ (colocar) mi equipaje de mano arriba. Yo me

   _____ (acomodar) en mi asiento y me _____ (abrochar) el cinturón de seguridad.

   —Yo sé que el avión _____ (despegar) con un poco de retraso. ¿Qué (tú) _____ (hacer)?

   —Una vez en el aire, yo me _____ (dormir). Cuando me _____ (despertar),

   _____ (pedir) un vino y me _____ (poner) los auriculares (*headphones*) para oír

   música.

4. **El viaje de vuelta**

—¿Te acuerdas del aterrizaje (*landing*)? Nosotros _____ (aterrizar (*to land*))

en el aeropuerto pero (ellos) no nos _____ (dejar) bajar del avión por una hora.

—Ah sí, _____ (ser) horrendo. Por fin nosotros _____ (prender) el celular, _____ (bajar)

del avión y _____ (ir) a recoger nuestro equipaje.

—Luego nosotros _____ (pasar) por la aduana (*customs*) donde _____ (mostrar)

el pasaporte.

—¡Qué jet lag (nosotros) _____ (tener) al día siguiente!

5. **Un viaje en furgoneta** (*van*)

—Daniel me _____ (decir) que Uds. _____ (hacer) un viaje. ¿Adónde _____ (ir) (Uds.)?

—Nosotros _____ (alquilar) una furgoneta y _____ (recorrer) el sur del país.

—¿Uds. lo _____ (pasar) bien?

—Ah sí, nosotros nos _____ (divertir) mucho. _____ (Ver) unos paisajes

impresionantes.

6. **Una excursión a Toledo**

—Yo _____ (hacer) una excursión de Madrid a Toledo. _____ (Tomar) el tren

de alta velocidad y _____ (llegar) en media hora.

—¿Ud. _____ (ver) la pintura de El Greco?

—Claro. Para eso yo _____ (ir). Además, _____ (conocer) las iglesias, las sinagogas

y El Alcázar. Me _____ (encantar) caminar por las maravillosas calles medievales.

R *Ejercicio oral. Diálogos: El horario.* *Compare su rutina diaria con la de su amigo/amiga. Hable de las cosas que hizo ayer y diga a qué hora las hizo. Mencione a qué hora se despertó, se acostó, almorzó, fue a su lugar de trabajo y qué hizo allí. Describa lo que hizo el fin de semana. Después, dígale a su amigo/amiga que le hable de la rutina suya.*

5

The Imperfect Tense

Formation of the Imperfect

The markers for the imperfect tense are **-aba** for **-ar** verbs and **-ía** for **-er** and **-ir** verbs. These markers are attached to the stem of the verbs and the person endings are added to them.

hablar *to speak*

hablaba	hablábamos
hablabas	hablabais
hablaba	hablaban

vender *to sell*

vendía	vendíamos
vendías	vendíais
vendía	vendían

abrir *to open*

abría	abríamos
abrías	abríais
abría	abrían

NOTES

1 · The first and third person singular forms are identical for all verbs in the imperfect: **yo/él/ella/Ud. viajaba, corría, salía.**

2 · Since the forms of the imperfect tense are all stressed on the endings and not on the stem, the stem vowel does not change in any of the forms of the imperfect.

3 · For **-ar** verbs, the **nosotros** form is the only one with a written accent.

4 · For **-er** and **-ir** verbs, all forms have a written accent over the **i.**

5 · The imperfect of **hay** is **había** (*there was, there were*).

The verbs **ser, ir,** and **ver** are irregular in the imperfect.

ser *to be*

era	éramos
eras	erais
era	eran

ir *to go*

iba	íbamos
ibas	ibais
iba	iban

ver *to see*

veía	veíamos
veías	veíais
veía	veían

Basic Uses of the Imperfect

The imperfect tense is used to express an event or action going on in the past without any reference to its beginning or end. Because the imperfect is not concerned with the beginning or completion of an action, it is the tense used for expressing repeated actions in past time. Adverbs and adverbial phrases such as **todos los días, siempre,** and **muchas veces** are often clues for the selection of the imperfect rather than the preterit. The imperfect is therefore also the tense used for description and expressing background in the past. Common English equivalents for the Spanish imperfect are *used to do, was doing*.

—¿**Eras** estudiante entonces?	*Were you a student then?*
—No, yo **era** ingeniero ya.	*No, I was already an engineer.*
—**Querían** tocar en la orquesta.	*They wanted to play in the orchestra.*
—¿No **querían** cantar en el coro?	*Didn't they want to sing in the chorus?*
—¿Dónde **estaban** anoche?	*Where were you last night?*
—**Estábamos** en el teatro.	*We were at the theater.*
—**Leía** el periódico todos los días, ¿no?	*You used to read the newspaper every day, didn't you?*
—Sólo cuando **tenía** tiempo.	*Only when I had time.*
—¿Qué tiempo **hacía**?	*What was the weather like?*
—**Hacía** frío y **llovía**.	*It was cold and it rained.*

The imperfect tense is used to tell what time it was in the past. The preterit is never used for this purpose.

—¿Qué hora **era**?	*What time was it?*
—**Era** la una en punto.	*It was exactly one o'clock.*

The imperfect tense is used in indirect discourse (in other words, to report what someone said) after the preterit form of verbs such as **decir, escribir, avisar, anunciar,** and **informar**.

—¿Qué te dijo Loli?	*What did Loli tell you?*
—Me **dijo** que **venía**.	*She told me she was coming.*
—¿Les escribiste?	*Did you write to them?*
—Sí, les **escribí** que **viajaba**.	*Yes, I wrote them that I was traveling.*
—Paco nos **anunció** que **se casaba**.	*Paco announced to us he was getting married.*
—¡Y a mí me **informó** que **pensaba** romper con su novia!	*And he informed me that he intended to break up with his fiancée!*

A *Cuando yo era niño/niña...* *Ud. tiene nostalgia por esos años tan inolvidables de su niñez. Escriba sus recuerdos en su diario. Complete las oraciones usando el imperfecto de los verbos indicados. Siga el modelo.*

MODELO   Yo ___*visitaba*___ (visitar) a mis amigos.

El campo

al atardecer *at the end of the day, at dusk*	**fresco** *fresh*
el bosque *woods*	**el lago** *lake*
el campo *field*	**merendar** (**e > ie**) *to picnic*
la casa de campo *country house*	**el monte** *mountain*
cultivar *to grow, raise*	**nadar** *to swim*
la flor *flower*	**la sierra** *mountains, mountain range*

Yo _____ (1. vivir) en Madrid con mis padres y mis hermanos Jaime y Marisol. Jaime

_____ (2. ser) el mayor de los tres. Yo _____ (3. ir) al colegio y _____ (4. hacer) todas las

cosas que _____ (5. soler (*to usually do*)) hacer los niños. Mis hermanos, mis amigos y yo

_____ (6. ir) al cine, a los partidos de fútbol y a las fiestas. Lo que más me _____ (7. gustar)

de aquellos años _____ (8. ser) la estancia (*stay*) en la casa de campo. Allí en la sierra de

Guadarrama mis padres, mis hermanos y yo _____ (9. pasar) el mes de agosto. El aire

_____ (10. ser) tan fresco y puro y no _____ (11. hacer) tanto calor como en Madrid.

_____ (12. Haber) un campo detrás de la casa donde mis hermanos y yo _____ (13. jugar)

al fútbol. Mi mamá _____ (14. cultivar) rosas y buganvillas en el jardín. ¡Qué hermosas

_____ (15. ser)! Toda la casa _____ (16. oler) divinamente a flores. Nosotros _____ (17. salir)

a merendar en el bosque todas las tardes. (Nosotros) _____ (18. Subir) el monte hasta llegar

a un lugar desde donde se _____ (19. ver) todo el valle. Mamá nos _____ (20. servir)

los bocadillos (*sandwiches*) más sabrosos del mundo. A veces papá nos _____ (21. leer)

un cuento. Nosotros siempre _____ (22. ir) a nadar en uno de los lagos cristalinos (*crystal*

clear) de la sierra. Al atardecer (nosotros) _____ (23. estar) muy cansados. Mis hermanos

_____ (24. volver) caminando a la casa pero papá me _____ (25. llevar) a mí en brazos

porque yo _____ (26. ser) el bebé de la familia. ¡Qué felices recuerdos!

NOTA CULTURAL

La sierra de Guadarrama es una cadena de montañas que queda en el centro de España, entre Madrid y Segovia. El pico más alto de la sierra es el de Peñalara, a 2.428 metros de alto. Muchos madrileños pasan sus vacaciones de verano o de invierno en la sierra. Casi todos los españoles, como casi todos los europeos, salen de vacaciones durante el mes de agosto.

El metro equivale a 3.281 pies.

B   *Reunión de la clase del año X.* *Ud. y sus compañeros de la universidad se reúnen después de no verse por muchos años. Se hacen preguntas para ponerse al día* (catch up on the news). *Escriba lo que contestan sus amigos usando el imperfecto. Siga el modelo.*

> MODELO   Oye, Clara, ¿todavía estudias arte?
>   → Antes estudiaba arte, pero ya no.

1. Oye, Manolo, ¿todavía escribes para *El Tiempo*?

2. Oye, Dora, ¿todavía vas de vacaciones a México?

3. Oye, Pepe, ¿todavía sales con Lola?

4. Oye, Jorge, ¿todavía te gusta la cocina tailandesa?

5. Oye, Ana María, ¿todavía trabajas como programadora?

6. Oye, Paco, ¿todavía juegas en un equipo de fútbol?

7. Oye, Carmen, ¿todavía vienen tú y tu marido al pueblo en invierno?

8. Oye, Paula, ¿todavía almuerzas con tus padres los sábados?

9. Oye, Mario, ¿todavía eres socio del Club Atlántico?

10. Oye, Sofía, ¿todavía vive tu hijo en Chile?

11. Oye, Juan, ¿todavía tienes una cadena de restaurantes?

12. Oye, Laura, ¿todavía prefieres vivir en el centro?

13. Oye, Ramón, ¿todavía ves a nuestros profesores?

14. Oye, Maribel, ¿todavía ruedas películas?

C   *Un vuelo.* *Ud. acaba de aterrizar* (land) *en el aeropuerto donde lo/la espera su familia. Mientras van a buscar su equipaje, Ud. les habla de los viajeros que conoció en el vuelo. Escriba qué eran y adónde iban usando el imperfecto de los verbos irregulares* **ser** *e* **ir.** *Siga el modelo.*

> MODELO   Conocí al señor Torres. (abogado / Chicago)
>   → El señor Torres era abogado. Iba a Chicago.

1. Conocí a la señorita Fajardo. (gerente de fábrica / Miami)

2. Conocí a los señores Guzmán. (dueños de una pastelería / Buenos Aires)

3. Conocí al señor García. (profesor de economía / Irlanda)

4. Conocí a la señora Montoya. (banquera / Suiza)

5. Conocí a don Pedro Domínguez. (candidato a senador / Monterrey)

6. Conocí a Lorena Iglesias. (ama de casa / Costa Rica)

7. Conocí a los hermanos Machado. (músicos / Nueva York)

8. Conocí al señor Rubio. (cirujano / la India)

NOTA CULTURAL

- **Monterrey** queda al este de México, cerca de la frontera con Tejas. Es la capital del estado de Nuevo León y la tercera ciudad de México. Es un gran centro industrial y comercial.
- **Costa Rica**, país centroamericano, queda entre Nicaragua y Panamá con una costa en el Pacífico y otra en el Caribe. El país se destaca por su tradición democrática; en 1989 celebró el centenario de la democracia costarricense. Costa Rica ha tenido más adelantos económicos y sociales que ningún otro país centroamericano y goza del nivel de vida más alto de toda esa región.
- En el pueblo costarricense de **Turrialba**, que queda a 70 kilómetros de San José, capital de Costa Rica, se encuentra la fábrica Rawlings donde se producen las pelotas usadas por las Grandes Ligas de Béisbol (*Major League Baseball*) de los Estados Unidos.

D *¿Qué tal se veía?* *Las siguientes personas no podían ver ciertas cosas muy bien desde el lugar donde estaban. Describa lo que no podían ver usando la forma correcta del imperfecto del verbo* **ver**. *Siga el modelo.*

MODELO Pepe / el edificio suyo / la calle Mercado
→ Pepe no veía el edificio suyo desde la calle Mercado.

1. Carolina y Ramón / el mar Caribe / el avión

2. nosotros / la cara de los actores / el anfiteatro

3. Federica / el embotellamiento (*traffic jam*) / la ventana del dormitorio

4. Uds. / toda la cancha de fútbol / la tribuna (*stand*) del estadio

5. yo / la cumbre (*top*) de la montaña / el valle

6. vosotros / la discoteca / la esquina

7. tú / al público / la parte derecha del escenario

The Imperfect and the Preterit: Two Aspects of Past Time

The imperfect and preterit tenses express different ways of looking at past actions and events. The imperfect tense designates an action as going on in the past without any reference to its beginning or end. The preterit tense designates an action as completed in the past. Spanish speakers must select one of these two aspects—imperfect or preterit—for every past action they refer to. English sometimes expresses the differences between these past tenses, but not always.

Cuando estaba en la universidad, **estudiaba** chino.	*When I was at the university, **I studied** Chinese.* (OR ***I used to study** Chinese.*)
Ayer **estudié** chino.	*Yesterday **I studied** Chinese.*

Sometimes English uses entirely different verbs to express the difference between the imperfect and the preterit of some Spanish verbs. For example, **tenía** means *I was in the process of having* or *I had*; **tuve** means *I began to have* or *I got, I received*.

Sabía el precio.	*I knew the price.*
Supe el precio.	*I found out the price.*
Conocían a Sergio.	*They knew Sergio.*
Conocieron a Sergio.	*They met Sergio.*
No podíamos llegar para las cuatro.	*We couldn't arrive by four o'clock.* *(Doesn't say whether we arrived by four or not.)*
No pudimos llegar para las cuatro.	*We couldn't arrive by four o'clock.* *(We didn't arrive by four.)*
Laura **no quería** ir en metro.	*Laura didn't want to take the subway.*
Laura **no quiso** ir en metro.	*Laura refused to (didn't want to and didn't) take the subway.*

The imperfect and the preterit can be used in two different clauses in the same sentence. The imperfect expresses the background, a continuing action, or an ongoing state, against which a completed action or event takes place.

Mientras **trabajábamos**, Julia **durmió** la siesta.	*While we were working, Julia took a nap.*

It is possible to have sentences with all verbs in the imperfect if the speaker sees the past actions or events as ongoing processes.

Pilar **leía** mientras Marta **jugaba** al tenis.	*Pilar was reading while Marta was playing tennis.*

It is possible to have sentences with all verbs in the preterit if the speaker views the actions mentioned as a series of completed events.

Cené, me arreglé y **fui** al teatro.	*I ate dinner, got ready, and went to the theater.*

E **¿Qué tiempo hacía cuando...?** *Sus amigos quieren saber qué tiempo hacía cuando sucedieron ciertas cosas. Escriba oraciones usando el imperfecto para hablar del tiempo y el pretérito para hablar de los sucesos. Siga el modelo.*

MODELO   hacer buen tiempo / Ud. / salir
             → Hacía buen tiempo cuando Ud. salió.

1. llover / Beatriz y tú / volver

2. hacer frío / los Sorolla / levantarse

3. estar despejado / tú / ir al aeropuerto

4. hacer viento / José Antonio / venir a la casa

5. nevar / nosotros / terminar el trabajo

6. tronar / Ud. / entrar en el cine

7. hacer sol / yo / llegar a la playa

8. lloviznar (*drizzle*) / Uds. / irse

9. hacer calor / yo / ponerse en marcha

F **¿Qué hora era cuando…?** *Su amigo quiere saber a qué hora pasaron ciertas actividades. Escriba oraciones usando el imperfecto para hablar de la hora y el pretérito para hablar de las actividades. Siga el modelo.*

> MODELO las ocho / Carmen y Víctor / llamar
> → Eran las ocho cuando Carmen y Víctor llamaron.

1. las nueve y media / Consuelo y Berta / despedirse

2. la una / el programa / comenzar

3. mediodía / Sara / servir el almuerzo

4. las diez en punto / el empleado / abrir la taquilla (*box office*)

5. medianoche / nosotros / regresar de la fiesta

6. muy tarde / Uds. / dormirse

7. temprano / el cartero / traer el correo

8. las cinco y cuarto / yo / unirse a la reunión virtual (*to join the online meeting*)

9. las tres cuarenta / tú / reunirse con tus amigos

10. las once de la noche / el avión / aterrizar

G **Mientras estábamos de vacaciones…** *Durante las vacaciones de invierno pasaron muchas cosas. Escriba oraciones usando el imperfecto para dar información de fondo (background) y el pretérito para hablar de las cosas que sucedieron. Siga el modelo.*

> MODELO nosotros / estar de vacaciones : yo / leer cinco libros
> → Mientras estábamos de vacaciones, yo leí cinco libros.

1. tú / viajar : acabar / la telenovela

2. Marta y Miguel / quedarse en un hotel : un ladrón / forzar la entrada (*to break in*)

3. Estefanía / vivir / en el extranjero : sus padres / vender su casa de campo

4. Uds. / hacer un viaje : sus vecinos / montar una nueva empresa

5. yo / ver / las siete maravillas del mundo : añadirse a la lista / otras siete

6. Benito / trabajar en San Antonio : su novia / romper con él

7. el avión de Diego / aterrizar en Los Ángeles : el de su esposa / despegar en Atlanta

8. los turistas / conocer los Estados Unidos : la guerra / estallar en su país

9. nosotros / estar en el puerto : haber / un incendio en el barco

10. vosotros / caminar a la plaza mayor : yo / alcanzaros

11. Laura y yo / platicar : mi teléfono celular / sonar

12. tú / leer : nosotros / enviar el correo electrónico

NOTA CULTURAL

Los españoles pusieron nombres españoles, y especialmente nombres de los santos, a muchos lugares de América. Por ejemplo:

San Antonio, ciudad de Tejas, es donde ocurrió la batalla del Álamo en 1836. Cuando Tejas proclamó su derecho de separarse de México en 1835, Sam Houston asumió el mando del ejército tejano. En 1836 el general Santa Anna atacó el Álamo y mató a todos los soldados tejanos (23 de febrero–6 de marzo). El 21 de abril, Houston venció a Santa Anna en la batalla de **San Jacinto** después de la cual Tejas declaró su independencia.

Donde hubo colonización española hay nombres españoles: *California, Tejas, (la) Florida, Nevada, Los Ángeles, Las Vegas, Santa Fe, San Francisco, San Diego, Santa Ana, San Antonio, El Paso, Alamogordo, Las Cruces.*

H   *Y al mismo tiempo...*   *Escriba las cosas que hacían unas personas al mismo tiempo usando el imperfecto. Use las actividades de la siguiente lista o invente otras. Siga el modelo.*

MODELO   Sara escribía cartas mientras Teresa dibujaba.

arreglarse	divertirse	ir de compras	salir
caminar	ensayar	jugar al tenis	tocar
cocinar	escribir	leer	tomar
comer	esperar el tren	navegar en la red	trabajar
dibujar	estudiar	practicar	ver una película

I   *Perspectivas.*   *Gabriela Godoy recuerda la primera vez que sus padres la llevaron a ver una ópera. Seleccione el imperfecto o el pretérito de los verbos para completar su historia.*

El teatro

el/la acomodador(a) *usher*	**hacer el papel de** *to play the role of*
el aficionado/la aficionada a la ópera *opera fan*	**la obra** *work, piece*
	la ópera *opera*
apagar las luces *to turn off the lights*	**el programa** *playbill, program*
el/la cantante *singer*	**subir el telón** *to raise the curtain*
el decorado *scenery*	

Cuando yo (1. tenía / tuve) once años, mis padres me (2. llevaban / llevaron) por primera vez a ver una ópera. La acomodadora nos (3. sentaba / sentó) y nos (4. dio / daba) el programa. Mientras (5. leíamos / leímos) las notas sobre la obra, las luces (6. se apagaban / se apagaron). Luego (7. subían / subieron) el telón y (8. veíamos / vimos) la escena. (9. Había / Hubo) un decorado de palacio. Una cantante que (10. hizo / hacía) el papel de la reina (11. estaba / estuvo) sentada en el trono. Ella (12. llevó / llevaba) una corona (*crown*) de oro y (13. vestía / vistió) una capa de terciopelo (*velvet*) verde con armiño (*ermine*). El cantante que (14. hacía / hizo) el papel del rey (15. salió / salía) a la escena y (16. se ponía / se puso) a cantar. Yo (17. quedaba / quedé) tan impresionada con lo que vi y oí que (18. me hice / me hacía) aficionada a la ópera para siempre.

NOTA CULTURAL

El Teatro Colón, lugar conocido de Buenos Aires, es uno de los teatros de ópera más grandes del mundo. En este teatro todo dorado y de terciopelo rojo, ponen ópera, conciertos de la Orquesta Filarmónica de Buenos Aires, recitales y obras de ballet. La temporada es de abril a diciembre; está cerrado en enero y febrero. Recuerde que las estaciones están al revés en el hemisferio austral (sur). *http://www.teatrocolon.org.ar*

J *La vida de un periodista.* *Carlos Vega habla de su carrera y de su vida. Seleccione el imperfecto o el pretérito de los verbos para completar su historia.*

Hace ocho años (1. me graduaba / me gradué) en la Facultad de comunicaciones.

(2. Sacaba / Saqué) mi título en periodismo. (3. Esperaba / Esperé) encontrar trabajo en uno

de los periódicos grandes de la ciudad donde (4. nacía / nací). (5. Quería / Quise) quedarme

en Tejas porque mis padres y mis hermanos vivían allí. Por desgracia, no (6. había / hubo)

empleo en ningún periódico del estado. Por lo tanto, yo (7. mandaba / mandé) mi

currículum (*résumé*) a varios periódicos por todo el país. (8. Tenía / Tuve) suerte.

(9. Encontraba / Encontré) trabajo de reportero en un periódico que

(10. se publicaba / se publicó) en Maine. Al principio la vida en Maine me (11. era / fue)

muy difícil. Yo no (12. conocía / conocí) a nadie donde (13. vivía / viví) y no (14. estaba / estuve)

acostumbrado al clima (*weather*). ¡(15. Hacía / Hizo) un frío horrible en invierno! Pero un

día yo (16. conocía / conocí) a Juana quien (17. trabajaba / trabajó) en el periódico también.

Ella (18. era / fue) editora. ¡Y (19. era / fue) un flechazo (*love at first sight*)! En fin, Juana y yo

(20. nos casábamos / nos casamos). Yo (21. llegaba / llegué) a ser jefe de redacción

(*editor-in-chief*) del periódico. Juana y yo (22. teníamos / tuvimos) dos hijos. ¡Y todos

(23. vivíamos / vivimos) muy felices! (*And we all lived happily ever after!*)

K *Expresar en español. Contrastes.* *Exprese las siguientes ideas en español. Los contrastes surgen de la diferencia entre el imperfecto y el pretérito.*

1. *Bárbara thought Tomás knew her sister Luz.*
   Actually, he met Luz last night at dinner.

2. *The businessmen wanted to discuss the report.*
   Their lawyers refused to.

3. *The bride* (la novia) *didn't have any gifts.*
   Then she got twenty gifts this morning.

4. *We didn't know who had the documents.*
   We found out yesterday.

5. *I wasn't able to assemble* (armar) *the toy.*
   Javier (tried but) couldn't assemble it either.

L *¡Castillos de España!* *Describa una visita a un castillo español completando las oraciones con la forma correcta del verbo indicado. Escoja entre el imperfecto y el pretérito.*

El turismo

el alcázar *fortress, palace*	**el lugar histórico** *historic site*
el billete de avión *plane ticket*	**el palacio real** *royal palace*
el castillo *castle*	**el parador** *government-owned hotel in a historic building* (Spain)
la gira *tour, excursion*	**patrocinado por** *funded by, sponsored by*
hacer la reservación *to book*	**realizar mi sueño** *to realize my dream, make my dream*
hacer un viaje *to take a trip*	*come true*

Yo siempre _____ (1. querer) visitar un castillo en España. Por eso cuando mi esposo

y yo _____ (2. ir) a hacer un viaje en mayo, yo le _____ (3. decir) a Rolando que me

_____ (4. interesar) visitar un castillo español. A Rolando le _____ (5. gustar) la idea porque

no _____ (6. conocer) España. Rolando _____ (7. comprar) los billetes de avión y también

_____ (8. hacer) la reservación para el hotel. Nosotros _____ (9. pensar) hacer una gira

de tres semanas con visitas a Madrid, Toledo, Sevilla, Segovia y Santiago de Compostela.

Nosotros _____ (10. tomar) el avión y _____ (11. llegar) a Madrid el tres de mayo. Durante

las tres semanas nosotros _____ (12. visitar) varios lugares históricos y naturalmente

_____ (13. conocer) el Palacio Real en Madrid, el Alcázar de Sevilla, los de Segovia y Toledo

y otros castillos y palacios. Al llegar a Santiago de Compostela yo _____ (14. tener) una gran

sorpresa. En vez de simplemente visitar un castillo, nosotros _____ (15. poder) quedarnos

en uno por tres días. Es que el famoso castillo _____ (16. ser) un parador. Los paradores,

es decir, hoteles patrocinados por el gobierno español, _____ (17. estar) por todas partes

del país. ¡Por fin yo _____ (18. realizar) mi sueño de visitar un castillo en España!

NOTA CULTURAL

- **El Alcázar**, palabra de origen árabe, significa fortaleza (*fortress*), castillo o palacio (*palace*) real.
- La construcción del **Alcázar de Sevilla** comenzó bajo los almohades, una dinastía musulmana, en el siglo XII. Se siguió construyendo en época cristiana durante los reinos de Pedro I el Cruel, rey de Castilla y León (1334–1369), Juan II, rey de Castilla (1405–1454), los Reyes Católicos (Fernando II de Aragón (1452–1516) e Isabel I de Castilla (1451–1504)), Carlos V, rey de España y emperador de Alemania (1500–1558) y Felipe II, rey de España (1527–1598).
- **Santiago de Compostela**, capital de la Comunidad Autónoma de Galicia, queda al noroeste de España. En la Edad Media fue un importante lugar de peregrinación (*pilgrimage*), especialmente a partir del siglo XI. El supuesto sepulcro del Apóstol Santiago (*Saint James*), que fue descubierto a principios del siglo IX, se encuentra en la Catedral de Santiago de Compostela.

Del diario de un detective. *Aquí tiene Ud. una página de la libreta de apuntes (notebook) del famoso detective privado Samuel Espada. Para poder leer los apuntes e intentar desenredar (unravel) el misterio, complete las oraciones usando el imperfecto o el pretérito de los verbos indicados.*

El crimen

el/la chantajista *blackmailer*	**la pandilla** *gang*
la cita *appointment*	**la policía** *police*
el detective privado *private detective*	**el rescate** *ransom*
el dramón *melodrama, sob story*	**seguir la pista** *to follow the trail*
el ladrón *thief*	**sobresaltado** *startled*
maltés *Maltese*	**sollozar** *to sob*

Este ejercicio está basado libremente en El halcón maltés *(1941), película de cine negro (film noir) estadounidense.*

_____ (1. Ser) las diez de la mañana cuando _____ (2. sonar) el teléfono en mi oficina.

Yo _____ (3. estar) despierto desde la noche anterior. (Yo) _____ (4. descolgar) y

_____ (5. oír) la voz sobresaltada de una mujer. La mujer me _____ (6. decir) que una

pandilla de ladrones le _____ (7. robar) su estatuilla (*figurine*) del halcón (*falcon*) maltés

y que ahora ellos le _____ (8. pedir) un rescate por el halcón. Además, la señorita me

_____ (9. explicar) que _____ (10. tener) miedo de ir a la policía. Ella y yo

_____ (11. quedar) en vernos en el vestíbulo (*lobby*) del Hotel Casablanca. Ya _____ (12. ser)

las siete de la tarde cuando yo _____ (13. llegar) al hotel. Toda la tarde yo _____ (14. seguir)

la pista de los chantajistas hasta que _____ (15. llegar) la hora de la cita. En el vestíbulo yo

_____ (16. ver) a una señorita guapísima que _____ (17. estar) sentada en un sofá. Ella

_____ (18. tener) el pelo castaño y largo, los ojos verdes como dos esmeraldas (*emeralds*)

y _____ (19. llevar) una gardenia en la chaqueta. Ella _____ (20. fumar) un cigarrillo

igual que yo (¡porque todos los personajes de los años cuarenta fuman cigarrillos!).

Yo me _____ (21. acercar) y me _____ (22. sentar) a su lado. Ella _____ (23. oler) a un

perfume exótico. Yo le _____ (24. hablar) primero. "¿Es Ud. la señorita María Astor?"

le _____ (25. preguntar). Ella se _____ (26. poner) a llorar y me _____ (27. decir) sollozando:

"Samuel, es que tú no comprendes...". Pero sí, yo _____ (28. comprender) muy bien.

¡Esto _____ (29. ir) a ser otro dramón!

Remember that the Spanish construction **hace** + expression of time + **que** + verb in the present tense is used to label an action that began in the past and is continuing in the present. Similarly, the construction **hacía** + expression of time + **que** + verb in the imperfect tense is used to label an action that was continuing in the past when something else happened. The corresponding question is **¿Cuánto tiempo hacía...?** The word **tiempo** may be omitted.

—¿**Cuánto (tiempo) hacía que esperabas** cuando llegó el tren?	*How long had you been waiting when the train arrived?*
—**Hacía más de una hora** que esperaba.	*I had been waiting more than an hour.*

A verb in the imperfect tense + **desde hacía** + expression of time is also used to label an action that was continuing in the past when something else happened.

—¿**Desde cuándo rodaban** la película cuando **ocurrió** un terremoto?	*How long had they been shooting the film when there was an earthquake?*
—**Rodaban** la película **desde hacía siete semanas** cuando **ocurrió** un terremoto.	*They had been shooting the film for seven weeks when there was an earthquake.*

N *¿Cuánto tiempo hacía...?* Haga preguntas usando *¿Cuánto tiempo hacía que...?* y contéstelas usando la construcción **hacía** + expresión de tiempo + **que** + verbo en el imperfecto. Siga el modelo.

MODELO Leonor / estudiar inglés / salir para Inglaterra (dos años)
→ —¿Cuánto tiempo hacía que Leonor estudiaba inglés cuando salió para Inglaterra?
—Hacía dos años que estudiaba inglés.

1. Montserrat Pujol / cantar ópera / firmar un contrato con la Metropolitana (ocho años)
2. los señores Salazar / estar casados / su hija / nacer (cuatro años)
3. tú / vivir en París / tus padres / mudarse a Londres (once meses)
4. Susana y Lía / ser amigas / Susana / quitarle el novio a Lía (doce años)
5. Ud. / comprar billetes de lotería / ganar el premio gordo (*jackpot*) (quince años)
6. Patricio y Ud. / tocar el violonchelo / el conservatorio / darles una beca (nueve años)

O *Cambios políticos y económicos.* Hubo algunos cambios en la vida política y económica de un país latinoamericano. Escriba oraciones con la construcción verbo en imperfecto + **desde hacía** + expresión de tiempo para describir los cambios. Junte las dos frases con **hasta que**. Siga el modelo.

MODELO el gobierno / prometer muchas cosas / dos años : los ciudadanos / empezar a reclamar
→ El gobierno prometía muchas cosas desde hacía dos años hasta que los ciudadanos empezaron a reclamar.

Política y economía

los bienes *goods*	**la libertad** *liberty*
controlar la inflación *to control inflation*	**el libre mercado** *free market*
la década *decade*	**el obrero** *worker*
el dictador *dictator*	**la prensa** *press*
el/la economista *economist*	**el presidente/la presidenta** *president*
establecer la democracia *to establish democracy*	**privatizar la industria** *to privatize industry*
explotar el petróleo *to drill for oil*	**el pueblo** *the people*
el gobierno *government*	**reclamar** *to demand, protest*
el golpe de estado *coup d'état*	**el sindicato** *union*
intentar *to try, attempt*	**el sueldo** *salary*

1. el gobierno / explotar el petróleo / treinta años : el presidente / privatizar la industria

2. la gente / sufrir por la inflación / cinco años : los economistas / intentar controlarla

3. la prensa / no ser libre / cincuenta años : haber / un golpe de estado

4. los obreros / no recibir un sueldo decente / cinco décadas : formarse / los sindicatos

5. el país / no producir los bienes necesarios / varios años : el país / establecer el mercado libre

6. el pueblo / no tener ninguna libertad / cuarenta y cinco años : morir / el dictador / y / establecerse / la democracia

P *¿Qué dice Ud.?* *Conteste las siguientes preguntas personales.*

1. ¿Cuántos años tenía cuando se vestía solo/sola?

2. ¿Cuántos años tenía cuando empezó a estudiar en el colegio? ¿En la universidad?

3. Cuando era niño/niña, ¿adónde iba de vacaciones?

4. ¿Qué le gustaba hacer cuando era niño/niña?

5. ¿Cómo era de niño/niña?

6. Hable de las cosas que solía hacer todos los días cuando asistía a la universidad.

7. ¿Qué sueños quería realizar en la vida?

8. ¿Pudo realizar algunos ya?

Q *Expresar en español. Un viaje a México.* *Exprese esta historia en español. Escoja entre el pretérito y el imperfecto para hablar del pasado.*

1. *The first day Beatriz and I spent in Mexico City, we went to Chapultepec Park.*

2. *The weather was beautiful. It was sunny and warm.*

3. *There were many people in the park.*

4. *Little children were playing on the slides* (los resbalines) *and riding their bicycles.*

5. *As we walked through the park we saw Moctezuma's Tree and the Chapultepec Castle.*

6. *We arrived at the National Museum of Anthropology and went in.*

7. *We walked from room to room and saw the exhibit* (la exhibición) *of pre-Columbian* (precolombino) *art.*

8. *We spent two hours in the museum.*

9. *Then we went to the bookstore where I bought a book about the Aztecs and the Mayans.*

10. *We had lunch in the museum cafeteria.*

11. *It was five o'clock when we left the museum.*

NOTA CULTURAL

- **El Bosque de Chapultepec** queda al final del Paseo de la Reforma en plena Ciudad de México. El hermoso parque tiene miles de ahuehuetes (*Mexican cypress trees*), laberintos de caminos, lagos, un jardín botánico, un zoológico y varios museos.
- **El Castillo de Chapultepec**, situado en una colina, da hermosas vistas del valle de México desde sus balcones. La gran atracción del parque es el **Museo Nacional de Antropología** que presenta una espléndida exposición de las culturas mexicanas precolombinas, es decir, de los aztecas, los mayas y otros grupos indígenas que vivían allí antes de la llegada de Cristóbal Colón a América. *http://www.mna.inah.gob.mx*
- Moctezuma II era el emperador azteca (1466–1520) cuando llegó Hernán Cortés a México en 1519. Fue hecho prisionero por los conquistadores españoles poco después de su llegada. **El Árbol de Moctezuma**, un poco más abajo del Castillo, era inmenso—de algunos 60 metros (~196 pies) de alto. "El Sargento," como se le llama, se ha cortado hasta medir diez metros (~32.8 pies).

R *Ejercicio oral. Una encuesta. Prepare una lista de algunas actividades que Ud. hacía cuando era niño/niña. Después pregúnteles a unos amigos si también hacían esas actividades. Algunas posibilidades:*

jugar al béisbol/al tenis/al fútbol/al baloncesto
pintar cuadros al aire libre
pasar los veranos en un campamento
cocinar con mi mamá o papá
tocar un instrumento musical
montar en bicicleta
bucear (*dive*) en el mar
ir al centro comercial
navegar en la red

The Future and Conditional Tenses

Formation of the Future Tense

The future tense is formed in Spanish by adding a special set of endings to the infinitive. The endings are the same for -**ar**, -**er**, and -**ir** verbs.

firmar el documento *to sign the paper*

Firmar**é** el documento.	*I'll sign the paper.*
Firmar**ás** el documento.	*You'll sign the paper.*
Firmar**á** el documento.	*He'll/She'll/You'll sign the paper.*
Firmar**emos** el documento.	*We'll sign the paper.*
Firmar**éis** el documento.	*You'll sign the paper.*
Firmar**án** el documento.	*They'll/You'll sign the paper.*

correr el maratón *to run the marathon*

Correr**é** el maratón.	*I'll run the marathon.*
Correr**ás** el maratón.	*You'll run the marathon.*
Correr**á** el maratón.	*He'll/She'll/You'll run the marathon.*
Correr**emos** el maratón.	*We'll run the marathon.*
Correr**éis** el maratón.	*You'll run the marathon.*
Correr**án** el maratón.	*They'll/You'll run the marathon.*

asistir al concierto *to attend the concert*

Asistir**é** al concierto.	*I'll attend the concert.*
Asistir**ás** al concierto.	*You'll attend the concert.*
Asistir**á** al concierto.	*He'll/She'll/You'll attend the concert.*
Asistir**emos** al concierto.	*We'll attend the concert.*
Asistir**éis** al concierto.	*You'll attend the concert.*
Asistir**án** al concierto.	*They'll/You'll attend the concert.*

For some Spanish verbs, the future tense endings are added to modified versions of the infinitive. Some verbs have -**d**- in place of the infinitive vowel -**e**- or -**i**-.

poner	→ **pondré**	valer	→ **valdré**
salir	→ **saldré**	venir	→ **vendré**
tener	→ **tendré**		

Some verbs lose the infinitive vowel -**e**-.

caber   →   **cabré**
poder   →   **podré**
querer   →   **querré**
saber   →   **sabré**

Some verbs shorten the infinitive.

decir   →   **diré**
hacer   →   **haré**

-**Ir** verbs that have an accent mark in the infinitive—**oír, reír, sonreír**—lose the accent mark in the future: **oiré, reiré, sonreiré**.

The future of **hay** is **habrá** (*there will be*).

Compounds of the irregular verbs have the same irregularities: **componer** (**compondré**), **retener** (**retendré**), **prevenir** (**prevendré**), **contradecir** (**contradiré**), **satisfacer** (**satisfaré**), etc.

Uses of the Future Tense

The future tense is one of the ways in which Spanish expresses future time.

¿A qué hora **llegarán** Uds.?	*At what time **will you arrive**?*
Estaremos para las tres.	***We'll be** there by three o'clock.*

The future tense in Spanish is often replaced by the **ir a** + infinitive construction. This commonly used construction refers to the immediate future, whereas the future tense refers to both the immediate and the remote future.

Esquiaré en los Pirineos.	***I'll ski** in the Pyrenees.*
Voy a esquiar en los Pirineos.	***I'm going to ski** in the Pyrenees.*

The future tense is often replaced by the simple present tense when there is another element of the sentence that indicates future time.

Llamo **el jueves**.	*I'll call **on Thursday**.*

The future tense can be replaced by the present tense when asking for instructions (English: *shall* or *should*).

¿**Doblo** aquí?	***Shall** (**Should**) **I turn** here?*
¿**Imprimimos** el informe?	***Shall** (**Should**) **we print** the report?*

The future tense is commonly used in the main clause of a conditional sentence when the **si**-clause (*if*-clause) has the verb in the present tense.

Si Juana **va**, yo **iré** también.	*If Juana **goes, I'll go** too.*

The order of the clauses can be reversed with the **si**-clause following the main clause: Yo **iré** si **va** Juana.

A **Mis planes para el futuro.** *Cambie los verbos del presente al futuro en las oraciones para saber lo que hará Daniel después de graduarse. Siga el modelo.*

> MODELO   Trabajo en una oficina.
> → Trabajaré en una oficina.

1. Me gradúo en junio.

2. Mis amigos y yo celebramos con una fiesta.

3. Nuestros padres están muy contentos.

4. Yo hago un viaje a Europa en el verano.

5. Miguel me acompaña.

6. Nos encanta viajar.

7. Vamos a los países de la Europa oriental.

8. Andrés y Manuel quieren ir también.

9. Salimos para Polonia a mediados de junio.

10. Pasamos dos meses viajando.

11. Andrés vuelve antes porque

12. tiene que comenzar sus estudios graduados.

13. Al regresar yo empiezo a trabajar en una compañía multinacional.

14. Miguel puede trabajar en la empresa de sus padres.

15. Manuel sigue con sus clases en la facultad de ingeniería.

16. ¡Tenemos tiempo de vernos, espero!

B **¡Qué reacciones!** *¿Cómo reaccionarán estas personas al oír las noticias que Ud. tiene? Escriba sus reacciones usando el futuro de los verbos. Siga el modelo.*

> MODELO   Luisa / sonreír
> → Luisa sonreirá.

1. Mari Carmen / llorar

2. las tías / decir "¡ay de mí!"

3. Ramón / tener vergüenza

4. tú / volverse loco

5. Juan y Alicia / poner el grito en el cielo (*scream bloody murder*)

6. Uds. / enfadarse

7. nosotros / reírse a carcajadas

8. Ud. / ponerse de buen humor

9. vosotros / estar contento

C *¡Qué día!* *Mañana será un día sumamante ajetreado* (hectic), *con muchas ocupaciones para Ud. Diga lo que pasará, escribiendo los verbos en el futuro. Siga el modelo.*

MODELO Estudio todo el día.
→ Estudiaré todo el día.

1. ¡Mañana es un ajetreo continuo (*hustle and bustle*)!

2. Tengo mucho que hacer.

3. Hay clases todo el día

4. y tomo exámenes también.

5. Además, yo voy a una tienda por departamentos.

6. Le compro un regalo a mi hermana.

7. Sarita cumple diecisiete años pasado mañana.

8. Mamá hace una comida y una torta.

9. Papá y yo salimos para comprar vino.

10. También quiero terminar mi informe.

11. No puedo salir con mis amigos.

12. Me acuesto muy tarde.

D *Actividad y descanso.* *Ud. y sus amigos se dedicarán a ciertas cosas durante las vacaciones de invierno. Diga lo que piensan hacer, escribiendo los verbos en el futuro. Siga el modelo.*

MODELO Felipe / escuchar música
→ Felipe escuchará música.

1. Yolanda y Ana / patinar sobre hielo

2. tú / cocinar yacu-chupe y un sancochado

3. Julio / mandar textos

4. Consuelo / acostarse tarde

5. yo / pasear al perro

6. Uds. / jugar al baloncesto

7. Ud. / escribir correos electrónicos

8. nosotros / hacer una fiesta de disfraces (*costume party*)

9. vosotros / poder viajar al Canadá

10. Ud. / tomar una clase en línea

NOTA CULTURAL

La cocina peruana tiene muchos platos indígenas que les son exóticos a los extranjeros. **Yacu-chupe** es una sopa verde hecha a base de papas con queso, ajo (*garlic*), hojas de cilantro (*coriander*), perejil (*parsley*), pimentones, huevos, cebollas y menta. **El sancochado** es un guiso (*stew*) de carne y toda clase de legumbres y condimentado con ajo molido (*ground*).

E   *Todo depende. Ciertas cosas pasarán si pasan otras cosas. Para expresar esta idea, escriba oraciones que tienen la cláusula con* **si** *con el verbo en el presente y la cláusula principal con el verbo en el futuro. Siga el modelo.*

MODELO   tú / estudiar en la biblioteca : yo / trabajar allí también
             → Si tú estudias en la biblioteca, yo trabajaré allí también.

1. María / querer salir : nosotros / salir con ella

2. ellos / ir : Ud. / poder verlos

3. yo / hacer tu plato favorito : tú / venir a almorzar

4. Uds. / trabajar mucho : Uds. / tener éxito

5. tú / no saber qué pasó : yo / decirte

6. nosotros / no comprar harina : no haber tortillas esta noche

7. hacer calor : Carlos y Pedro / ir a la playa

8. llover : Celeste / querer ir al cine

The Future Tense Used to Express Probability or Conjecture

The future tense in Spanish is also used to express probability or conjecture in present time. The English equivalents of the future of probability (*I wonder, it's probably, it might,* etc.) are usually very unlike the Spanish structures.

The verbs most commonly used to express probability with the future are **estar**, **haber**, **ser**, and **tener**.

—¿Qué hora es?	*What time is it?*
—**Serán** las ocho.	***It's probably** eight o'clock.*
—**¿Quién tendrá** las llaves?	***I wonder who has** the keys.*
—Las **tendrá** Mario.	*Mario **probably has** them.*

Context will determine whether a verb in the future tense refers to the future or to probability in present time. For example, **¿Quién llamará?** means *Who will call?* as well as *I wonder who's calling.*

Deber de + infinitive is also used to express probability in the present: **Deben de ser las diez.** = **Serán las diez.**

F *¿Qué será?* *Ud. no está seguro de varias cosas. Por cada cosa exprese probabilidad o conjetura. Escriba los verbos en el futuro quitando la palabra o las palabras que indican probabilidad. Siga el modelo.*

MODELO   *Probablemente los Hidalgo están en casa.*
           → Los Hidalgo estarán en casa.

1. *Probablemente* son las seis.

2. *Me imagino que* Teodoro tiene veinte años.

3. *Supongo que* el reloj vale mucho.

4. *Probablemente* hay problemas entre los socios (*partners*) de la empresa.

5. *Supongo que* Teresa sabe la hora de la conferencia.

6. *Me imagino que* Esteban quiere ir a la reunión.

7. *Supongo que* los programadores vuelven pronto.

G *¿Qué habrá en esa caja?* *Ud. y sus amigos vieron a Juan Pedro llevando una caja enorme. Todos se mueren por saber lo que hay adentro. Uds. hacen conjeturas sobre el contenido usando el futuro de probabilidad. Siga los modelos.*

MODELOS   *It's probably big.*
          → Será grande.
          I wonder if it's beautiful.
          → ¿Será hermoso?

1. *I wonder if it's green.*

2. *It probably has batteries* (las pilas).

3. *I wonder if there are many parts.*

4. *Do you think it's made of wood?*

5. *Could it cost a lot?*

6. *It probably makes a noise.*

7. *It must be bigger than a breadbox* (una caja para el pan).

8. *Could everybody have one?*

9. *I wonder if it's alive.*

10. *It probably fits in your hand.*

Formation of the Conditional Tense

The conditional tense (English: *would*) is formed in Spanish by adding the endings of the imperfect tense of -**er** and -**ir** verbs to the infinitive. These endings are the same for the conditional of -**ar**, -**er**, and -**ir** verbs.

cobrar el cheque *to cash the check*

Cobraría el cheque.	*I'd cash the check.*
Cobrarías el cheque.	*You'd cash the check.*
Cobraría el cheque.	*He'd/She'd/You'd cash the check.*
Cobraríamos el cheque.	*We'd cash the check.*
Cobraríais el cheque.	*You'd cash the check.*
Cobrarían el cheque.	*They'd/You'd cash the check.*

entender el asunto *to understand the issue*

Entendería el asunto.	*I'd understand the issue.*
Entenderías el asunto.	*You'd understand the issue.*
Entendería el asunto.	*He'd/She'd/You'd understand the issue.*
Entenderíamos el asunto.	*We'd understand the issue.*
Entenderíais el asunto.	*You'd understand the issue.*
Entenderían el asunto.	*They'd/You'd understand the issue.*

recibir un email *to receive/get an email*

Recibiría un email.	*I'd receive an email.*
Recibirías un email.	*You'd receive an email.*
Recibiría un email.	*He'd/She'd/You'd receive an email.*
Recibiríamos un email.	*We'd receive an email.*
Recibiríais un email.	*You'd receive an email.*
Recibirían un email.	*They'd/You'd receive an email.*

Note that when *would* means *used to,* the imperfect tense rather than the conditional is used.

Cuando yo era niño, mi familia y yo **íbamos** al campo todos los veranos.	*When I was a child, my family and I* ***would go*** *to the country every summer.*

The verbs that have modified infinitives in the future tense have the same changes in the conditional tense.

caber	→ **cabría**		saber	→ **sabría**
decir	→ **diría**		salir	→ **saldría**
hacer	→ **haría**		tener	→ **tendría**
poder	→ **podría**		valer	→ **valdría**
poner	→ **pondría**		venir	→ **vendría**
querer	→ **querría**			

-Ir verbs that have an accent mark in the infinitive—**oír, reír, sonreír**—lose the accent mark in the conditional: **oiría, reiría, sonreiría**.

The conditional of **hay** is **habría** (*there would be*).

Compounds of the irregular verbs have the same irregularities: **componer** (**compondría**), **retener** (**retendría**), **prevenir** (**prevendría**), **contradecir** (**contradiría**), **satisfacer** (**satisfaría**), etc.

Uses of the Conditional Tense

The conditional is used commonly in subordinate (dependent) clauses after main verbs of communication (for example, **decir**) and knowledge or belief (**saber**, **creer**) when the main verb is in one of the past tenses. Observe a similar correspondence of tenses in Spanish and English: present/future and past/conditional.

Juan **dice** que **irá**.	*Juan says he'll go.*
Juan **dijo** que **iría**.	*Juan said he'd go.*
Sé que **llamarán**.	*I know they'll call.*
Sabía que **llamarían**.	*I knew they'd call.*

The conditional is commonly used in the main clause of a sentence that has the imperfect subjunctive in the **si**-clause (*if*-clause), that is, the subordinate or dependent clause. The condition expressed here is called contrary-to-fact. This pattern is practiced in greater depth in Chapter 12.

Si Elena **saliera**, yo **saldría** también.	*If Elena **were to leave**, I'd **leave** too.*

The conditional tense in Spanish is also used to express probability or conjecture in past time. The verbs most commonly used to express probability with the conditional are **estar**, **haber**, **ser**, and **tener**.

Sería la una.	*It **was probably** one o'clock.*
Habría algunas dificultades.	*There **were probably** some difficulties.*
El niño **tendría** nueve años.	*The boy **was probably** nine years old.*
El coche **costaría** un dineral.	*The car **probably cost** a fortune.*

Context will determine whether a verb in the conditional tense refers to the conditional or to probability in past time. For example, **Serían las tres** could mean either *It would be three o'clock (by the time we got there)* or *It was probably three o'clock.*

Deber de in the imperfect + infinitive may be used to express probability in past time. **Debían de ser las diez. = Serían las diez.**

H *Y Ud., ¿qué haría?* *¿Qué harían las personas en cada una de las siguientes situaciones? Escriba los verbos usando el condicional. Siga los modelos.*

> MODELOS   Estás en la clase de historia. El profesor hace preguntas. ¿Qué harías?
> contestar
> → Yo contestaría.
> cambiar el tema
> → Yo cambiaría el tema.

1. Ud. está en un almacén. Busca los abrigos pero no puede encontrarlos. ¿Qué haría?

   a. hablar con la dependienta

   b. ir a otro almacén

2. Carolina cena en casa de los Cela. Le encanta el arroz con pollo. ¿Qué haría?

   a. repetir (*to have a second helping*)

   b. pedir la receta

3. Estamos en el metro. Un pasajero grita "¡fuego!" ¿Qué haríamos?

   a. salir corriendo

   b. llamar a los bomberos

4. Osvaldo está en el teatro. Mientras busca su asiento le pisa el pie a una señora. ¿Qué haría?

   a. disculparse con la señora

   b. quitarle el zapato a la señora

5. La madre quiere bañar a sus hijos pero no hay agua caliente. ¿Qué haría?

   a. acostarlos sin bañarlos

   b. llamar al plomero

6. Pepe y Paco ven que hay diez pulgadas (*inches*) de nieve en la calle. ¿Qué harían?

   a. hacer un muñeco de nieve

   b. lanzar bolas de nieve

7. Hay un choque de coches no muy serio. Ud. es testigo del accidente. ¿Qué haría?

   a. decirle al policía lo que pasó

   b. ponerles vendas (*bandages*) a los heridos

I   *¡Qué bonanza! Ud. y sus amigos acaban de comprar un billete para la lotería que esta semana llegó a veinte millones de dólares. ¿Qué harían Uds. con veinte millones de dólares? Escriba algunas ideas empleando el condicional. Siga el modelo.*

    MODELO   yo / comprar tres casas
                  → Yo compraría tres casas.

1. Elena / pagar la matrícula en la universidad

2. mi primo Federico / venir a visitarnos

3. Uds. / hacer un viaje al Japón

4. Juan Pablo y Ana María / depositar la plata en el banco

5. tú / ya no tener deudas (*debts*)

6. mi hermano y yo / querer darles dinero a los huérfanos (*orphans*)

7. Rodrigo y yo / invertir en la Bolsa (*stock market*)

NOTA CULTURAL

La lotería es un juego público en el que se premian billetes que llevan ciertos números. A diferencia de los Estados Unidos donde las loterías son estatales, es decir, las dirigen los estados, España y los países latinoamericanos tienen loterías nacionales.

J **¿Qué dijeron?** *Dígale a un amigo lo que cada persona prometió hacer para ayudar con los preparativos para una fiesta. Complete las oraciones usando el condicional de los verbos indicados en las cláusulas subordinadas. Siga el modelo.*

MODELO   Pedro me dijo que ___*llamaría*___ (llamar) a los invitados.

1. Victoria nos dijo que le _____ (gustar) tener la fiesta en su casa.

2. Pablo le preguntó a Victoria si ella _____ (querer) planearla para el sábado.

3. Victoria nos aseguró que no _____ (haber) problema con ese día.

4. Isabel quería saber lo que nosotros _____ (poder) traer.

5. Victoria nos dejó saber que su esposo y ella se _____ (ocupar) de la comida.

6. José y yo le dijimos que _____ (hacer) una torta para la fiesta.

7. Marta y Carlos dijeron que _____ (poner) la mesa antes de la fiesta.

8. Todos le prometimos a Victoria que _____ (venir) muy temprano para ayudarla con los preparativos.

K **Probabilidad en el pasado.** *Exprese probabilidad o conjetura en el pasado al contestar las preguntas de su amiga. Use el condicional. Siga el modelo.*

MODELO   ¿Cuántos años tenía el primo de Fernando? (quince años)
           → Tendría quince años.

1. ¿Qué hora era cuando Uds. volvieron a casa? (las once)

2. ¿Cuántos invitados había en la fiesta? (sesenta)

3. ¿Cómo estaban tus padres después del viaje? (cansados)

4. ¿Cuánto costó el carro de Felipe? (treinta mil dólares)

5. ¿Cómo eran los nuevos consultores? (inteligentes)

L **Si yo fuera a la fiesta... (If I were going to the party . . .).** *Si ciertas personas fueran a la fiesta, algunas cosas pasarían. Para saber qué pasaría, escriba los verbos indicados de la cláusula principal en el condicional. Siga el modelo.*

MODELO   Si Matilde fuera a la fiesta, Guillermo ___*iría*___ (ir) también.

1. Si yo fuera, Uds. _____ (estar) contentos.

2. Si Uds. fueran, yo _____ (poder) llevarlos.

3. Si Catalina fuera, Tomás _____ (querer) bailar con ella.

4. Si todos nosotros fuéramos, los Herrera no _____ (caber) en el coche.

5. Si Ud. fuera, _____ (venir) conmigo.

6. Si tú fueras, te _____ (poner) un esmoquin (*tuxedo*).

7. Si todos los invitados fueran, no _____ (haber) lugar en la pista de baile (*dance floor*).

8. Si vosotros fuerais, nosotros _____ (tener) que servir champaña.

M *Expresar en español. Gustos e intereses.* Use el condicional para expresar lo que a Ud. le gustaría hacer y lo que a otros les gustaría hacer. Use estos verbos: **gustar**, **encantar**, **interesar**, **preferir** y **querer**.

1. *I'd like to . . .*

2. *My parents would prefer to . . .*

3. *My wife would want to . . .*

4. *My husband would love to . . .*

5. *My friend _____ would be interested in . . .*

6. *My brother and sister would like to . . .*

7. *I'd love to . . .*

8. *Our children would prefer to . . .*

9. *My colleagues* (colegas) *would be interested in . . .*

10. *My family would want to . . .*

N *Ejercicio oral.* Haga un diálogo con una amiga que tiene lugar en la empresa mexicana donde trabajan. Ud. es el director de mercadeo y ella es la gerenta de marca (brand manager). Ud. le hace preguntas a la gerenta sobre el viaje de negocios que harán a unas ciudades centroamericanas. La gerenta le contesta y le hace preguntas a Ud. sobre la campaña (campaign) de marketing que lanzarán (lanzar (to launch)). Use el futuro y el condicional lo más posible. Después cambien Uds. de papel. Por ejemplo:

Director   ¿A qué ciudades iremos? Me gustaría hacer los trámites para el viaje hoy.

Gerenta   Bueno, así será el itinerario—Guatemala, Ciudad de Guatemala, Costa Rica, San José y finalmente Panamá, Ciudad de Panamá.

Reflexive Verbs

Reflexive Verbs—Introduction and Conjugation

Spanish has a large class of verbs called reflexive verbs. These verbs always have an object pronoun called a reflexive pronoun that refers to the same person or thing as the subject. Most Spanish reflexive verbs correspond to English verbs that don't have a direct object (intransitive verbs) or English verb phrases consisting of *to be* or *to get* followed by an adjective or a past participle. Reflexive verbs appear in vocabulary lists with the reflexive pronoun **se** attached to the infinitive: **acostarse** (*to go to bed*), **lavarse** (*to wash up*), **sentarse** (*to sit down*), **vestirse** (*to get dressed*).

The reflexive pronoun **se** changes to agree with the subject of the verb. The reflexive pronoun precedes the conjugated verb in the simple tenses; it precedes the auxiliary verb **haber** in the compound tenses; it precedes the verb **estar** or is placed after the present participle (gerund) in the progressive tenses (and is attached to it in writing).

acostarse (o > ue) *to go to bed* (present tense)

me acuesto	nos acostamos
te acuestas	os acostáis
se acuesta	se acuestan

vestirse (e > i) *to dress, get dressed* (preterit tense)

me vestí	nos vestimos
te vestiste	os vestisteis
se vistió	se vistieron

lavarse *to wash up* (imperfect tense)

me lavaba	nos lavábamos
te lavabas	os lavabais
se lavaba	se lavaban

entusiasmarse *to get excited* (present perfect)

me he entusiasmado	nos hemos entusiasmado
te has entusiasmado	os habéis entusiasmado
se ha entusiasmado	se han entusiasmado

divertirse (e > ie, e > i) *to have a good time* (present progressive)	
me estoy divirtiendo	nos estamos divirtiendo
te estás divirtiendo	os estáis divirtiendo
se está divirtiendo	se están divirtiendo
estoy divirtiéndome	estamos divirtiéndonos
estás divirtiéndote	estáis divirtiéndoos
está divirtiéndose	están divirtiéndose

Most reflexive verbs can also be used nonreflexively. When they are used without the reflexive pronouns, they are transitive verbs—verbs that are used with a direct object. In transitive verbs, the subject and direct object refer to different things or people.

Yo **lavo** *el carro*.	*I wash the car.*
	(*I* = subject; *car* = direct object)
Yo **me lavo**.	*I wash up.*
	(subject and direct object refer to **yo**)
Ana **vistió** *a sus hijitas*.	*Ana dressed her little daughters.*
	(*Ana* = subject; *little daughters* = direct object)
Ana **se vistió**.	*Ana got dressed.*
	(subject and direct object refer to **Ana**)

The **se** of the infinitive must change to agree with the subject of the verb + infinitive construction. The reflexive pronoun may be placed either before the conjugated verb or after the infinitive. When placed after the infinitive, it is attached to it in writing.

quedarse *to stay, remain*		
Me quiero **quedar**.	Quiero **quedarme**.	*I want to stay.*
Te quieres **quedar**.	Quieres **quedarte**.	*You want to stay.*
Se quiere **quedar**.	Quiere **quedarse**.	*He/She wants to stay. / You want to stay.*
Nos queremos **quedar**.	Queremos **quedarnos**.	*We want to stay.*
Os queréis **quedar**.	Queréis **quedaros**.	*You want to stay.*
Se quieren **quedar**.	Quieren **quedarse**.	*They/You want to stay.*

The Reflexive Pronoun as Indirect Object

Certain reflexive verbs can appear with direct objects. In these cases, the reflexive pronoun is an indirect object, not a direct object. The equivalent of the indirect object reflexive pronoun in English is usually a possessive adjective. Most of these verbs express actions that have an effect on articles of clothing or parts of the body.

Los niños se ponen **el abrigo**.	*The children put on **their coats**.*
Y se ponen **las botas** también.	*And they put on **their boots** also.*
Marta se lavó **las manos**.	*Marta washed **her hands**.*
Nos lavamos **la cara**.	*We washed **our faces**.*

The reflexive pronoun in the preceding examples is closely related in function to the indirect object. If the indirect object reflexive pronoun is replaced by an indirect object referring to someone other than the subject, the relationship among the elements of the sentence changes.

| Le pongo el abrigo. | *I help him on with his coat.* |
| A los niños les ponemos los zapatos. | *We put the children's shoes on.* |

Spanish uses a singular noun for articles of clothing and parts of the body, even with plural subjects. It is assumed that each person has one item, unless the item comes in pairs. If each person has more than one item, Spanish uses a plural noun.

Here are some common reflexive verbs and expressions that are used in this pattern.

ponerse + *article of clothing*	*to put on*
probarse (**o** > **ue**) + *article of clothing*	*to try on*
quitarse + *article of clothing*	*to take off*
romperse + *article of clothing*	*to tear*
lavarse + *part of the body*	*to wash*
quebrarse (**e** > **ie**) + *part of the body*	*to break*
quemarse + *part of the body*	*to burn*
romperse + *part of the body*	*to break*

Here are some typical expressions using this pattern.

abrocharse (la chaqueta; el cinturón de seguridad)	*to button, zip (one's jacket); to buckle up, fasten (one's seat belt)*
afeitarse las piernas	*to shave one's legs*
amarrarse (los zapatos)	*to tie (one's shoes)*
atarse (los zapatos)	*to tie (one's shoes)*
cepillarse (los dientes, el pelo)	*to brush (one's teeth, one's hair)*
cortarse el pelo	*to get a haircut*
desabrocharse (la chaqueta; el cinturón de seguridad)	*to unbutton, unzip (one's jacket); to unbuckle, unfasten (one's seat belt)*
desamarrarse (los zapatos)	*to untie (one's shoes)*
desatarse (los zapatos)	*to untie (one's shoes)*
lastimarse el dedo	*to hurt one's finger*
lavarse la cabeza/el pelo	*to wash one's hair*
limarse las uñas	*to file one's nails*
limpiarse los dientes	*to brush one's teeth*
maquillarse la cara	*to put makeup on*
pintarse los labios	*to put lipstick on*
secarse el pelo	*to dry one's hair*
torcerse (**o** > **ue**) el tobillo	*to twist one's ankle*

A *¿Reflexivo o transitivo?* *Complete las oraciones escogiendo la forma reflexiva o transitiva del verbo indicado. Use el tiempo verbal indicado. Siga el modelo.*

MODELO   Rosita ___*bañó*___ a los niños y después ella ___*se bañó*___. (bañar—*preterit*)

1. Mañana yo _____ a las siete y _____ a mi hermana a las siete y cuarto. (despertar—*present*)

2. Aunque el profesor Vélez _____ a sus estudiantes, Miguel y Carlota no _____. (aburrir—*imperfect*)

3. Los novios _____ en la catedral de Burgos. El cura de la novia los _____. (casar—*preterit*)

4. Al jugar al escondite (*hide-and-seek*), nosotros _____ a los niñitos y luego nosotros

   _____. (esconder—*future*)

5. ¿Tú _____ ahora mismo o _____ primero a Luisita? (vestir—*present*)

6. Nosotros ya _____ y _____ al perro también. (pasear—*preterit*)

7. El correo electrónico que Carmen recibió ayer no la _____. Sin embargo al leerla Martín

   _____. (tranquilizar—*preterit*)

8. Yo _____ durante el primer acto de la obra pero los otros dos actos no me _____. (divertir—*preterit*)

9. Pepe me hacía tantas preguntas que francamente yo _____. ¡Ese chico _____ a todo el mundo! (marear—*imperfect*)

10. Daniel no tiene ganas de hacer nada. A ver si nosotros lo _____. Vamos a invitarlo

    a jugar al tenis. A ver si él _____. (animar—*present*)

11. Cuando Pablo y Laura eran niños _____ al ver las películas de terror. Las películas

    con fantasmas (*ghosts*) los _____ más que nada. (asustar—*imperfect*)

12. Uds. _____ por cualquier cosa. Menos mal que no _____ a otras personas. (ofender—*present*)

B *Todavía no, abuelita.* *La abuela llama desde Buenos Aires para hablar con sus nietos gemelos en Filadelfia. Ella les pregunta si pueden hacer ciertas cosas solos. Los niños le explican a su abuela que no pueden hacerlas solos todavía, que se las hace su mamá. Escriba oraciones—la pregunta de la abuelita y la respuesta de sus nietos—practicando los verbos como verbos transitivos y reflexivos. Siga el modelo.*

MODELO   bañarse
   → ¿Ustedes ya **se bañan** solos?
      No, abuelita. **Nos baña** mamá.

1. despertarse   4. atarse los zapatos

2. lavarse el pelo   5. cepillarse los dientes

3. peinarse   6. acostarse

C *Una excursión al campo.* *Escriba lo que Ud. y sus amigos se pusieron para ir al campo. Practique el uso del verbo reflexivo* **ponerse** *en el pretérito. Siga el modelo.*

MODELO   tú / los zapatos de tenis
          → Tú te pusiste los zapatos de tenis.

La ropa

el abrigo *overcoat*	**los jeans** *jeans*
la blusa *blouse*	**las medias** *socks* (Spanish America); *stockings* (Spain)
las botas *boots*	**los pantalones** *pants* (ALSO **el pantalón**)
la bufanda *scarf*	**el saco** *jacket*
los calcetines *socks* (Spain)	**las sandalias** *sandals*
la camisa *shirt*	**el smoking** *tuxedo* (ALSO **el esmoquin**)
la camiseta *T-shirt*	**el sombrero** *hat*
la chaqueta *jacket*	**el suéter** *sweater*
el cinturón *belt*	**el traje** *suit*
la corbata *tie*	**el traje de baño** *bathing suit*
la falda *skirt*	**el vestido** *dress*
el gorro *cap*	**los zapatos** *shoes*
los guantes *gloves*	**los zapatos de tacón alto** *high-heeled shoes*
el impermeable *raincoat*	**los zapatos de tenis** *sneakers*

¿De qué es?: Las telas

el algodón *cotton*	**la mezclilla** *denim*
el cuero *leather*	**la pana** *corduroy*
la franela *flannel*	**el poliéster** *polyester*
la lana *wool*	**la seda** *silk*
el lino *linen*	**el terciopelo** *velvet*

1. Marina y yo / los jeans

2. Arturo / un traje de baño

3. Uds. / un impermeable

4. yo / un suéter de lana

5. Víctor y Paco / un gorro

6. todos nosotros / una camiseta

7. Ud. / las sandalias

8. vosotros / una bufanda

D *¿Qué se pondrán para ir al trabajo?* *Escriba lo que se pondrán estas personas para ir al trabajo. Practique el uso del verbo reflexivo* **ponerse** *en el futuro. Siga el modelo.*

MODELO   Alberto / un saco de franela
          → Alberto se pondrá un saco de franela.

1. yo / un vestido de lino

2. Alicia / una blusa de poliéster

3. nosotros / zapatos de cuero

4. Uds. / una camisa de algodón

5. los jefes / un traje de lana

6. tú / una corbata de seda

7. Ud. / una falda de pana

8. vosotros / una chaqueta de mezclilla

E *¡Ya llega la fiesta de gala!* *Ud. y sus amigos están emocionados porque la fiesta de gala es el sábado. Todos Uds. necesitan probarse la ropa que van a llevar. Practique el uso del verbo reflexivo* **probarse** *en el presente. Siga el modelo.*

MODELO   nosotros / los zapatos de charol
→ Nosotros nos probamos los zapatos de charol.

1. Pilar y Luz / el vestido largo

2. yo / el abrigo de terciopelo

3. Lorenzo / el smoking

4. Uds. / los zapatos de tacón alto

5. tú / la blusa de seda

6. Antonio y Esteban / la corbata

7. vosotros / el sombrero

8. Ud. / los guantes

F *¡Qué malas noticias!* *Una amiga que acaba de volver de Panamá pregunta por sus amigos. Le toca a Ud. darle las malas noticias. Escriba los verbos reflexivos en el pretérito. Siga el modelo.*

MODELO   Alfonso / caerse / cruzando la calle
→ Alfonso se cayó cruzando la calle.

1. Miguel / romperse la pierna / montando a caballo

2. Ana / quemarse la mano / cocinando

3. el perro de Bernardo / perderse / en las afueras

4. Eunice / torcerse el tobillo / patinando sobre hielo

5. todos nosotros / enfermarse / comiendo hamburguesas poco hechas

6. yo / lastimarse / cortando el césped

7. el hermano de Pedro / quebrarse el dedo / jugando al baloncesto

G *Estimados televidentes.* *Ud. es locutor/locutora de televisión. Por desgracia las noticias de hoy son todas malas. Exprésalas en oraciones completas usando los verbos reflexivos en el pretérito. Siga el modelo.*

MODELO   dos panaderos / quemarse las manos / cuando hubo una explosión
en el horno
→ Dos panaderos se quemaron las manos cuando hubo una explosión
en el horno.

1. la actriz Ramona Arias / lastimarse / en el rodaje (*filming*) de su nueva película

2. el futbolista Diego Suárez / romperse el pie / en el partido de hoy

3. unos turistas norteamericanos / caerse / en la escalera mecánica del metro

4. un carpintero / cortarse la mano / serrando (*sawing*) madera

5. diez arqueólogos / hacerse daño / en una excavación en las pirámides

6. un bombero / quemarse / apagando un incendio

H *El aseo personal* (**Personal hygiene**). *Escriba oraciones explicando cuándo y cómo algunas personas hacen su aseo personal. Practique el uso de los verbos reflexivos en el presente. Siga el modelo.*

MODELO   Guillermo / lavarse los dientes / dos veces al día
→ Guillermo se lava los dientes dos veces al día.

1. Felisa / lavarse la cabeza / todos los días

2. yo / vestirse / rápidamente por la mañana

3. vosotros / ducharse / por la noche

4. Carlos / afeitarse / con una maquinilla de afeitar

5. Laura y Teresa / limarse las uñas / antes de ponerse el esmalte de uñas (*nail polish*)

6. tú / peinarse / con peine y cepillo

7. Benjamín y yo / arreglarse / después de desayunar

8. Ud. / cepillarse los dientes / antes de maquillarse

I *Hay que hacerlo.* *Escriba oraciones en las cuales se expresa que las personas* **quieren, van a, acaban de** *(u otra expresión) hacer ciertas cosas. Practique la construcción del verbo conjugado con el verbo reflexivo en el infinitivo. Escriba las oraciones de dos maneras. Siga el modelo.*

MODELO   Guillermo se afeita todos los días. (necesitar)
→ Guillermo necesita afeitarse todos los días.
Guillermo se necesita afeitar todos los días.

1. Samuel se coloca en una sucursal (*branch*) de la empresa. (querer)

2. Nosotros nos despertamos antes de las ocho. (deber)

3. Vosotros os reunís en casa de Felipe esta noche. (pensar)

4. Teresa se pesa (*weighs herself*) todas las semanas. (necesitar)

5. Yo me voy de vacaciones en julio. (ir a)

6. Las señoras se aprovechan de las liquidaciones (*sales*). (acabar de)

7. ¿Te sientas en esta fila? (querer)

8. Uds. se secan el pelo. (tener que)

The Imperative of Reflexive Verbs

Reflexive pronouns precede the verb in negative commands. In affirmative commands, reflexive pronouns are attached to the command form of the verb and an accent mark is added over the stressed syllable, except in **vosotros** commands and in some two-syllable forms.

No se acueste todavía.	***Don't go to bed*** *yet.*
Acuéstese más tarde.	***Go to bed*** *later.*
No te vayas.	***Don't go away.***
Vete.	***Go away.***

No se preocupen por nada.	*Don't worry about anything.*
Diviértanse.	*Have a good time.*
No os enojéis.	*Don't get angry.*
Tranquilizaos.	*Calm down.*

When the reflexive pronoun **nos** is added to a **nosotros** command form, the final -s of the verb form drops.

Quedémonos.	*Let's stay.*
Relajémonos.	*Let's relax.*
Divirtámonos.	*Let's have a good time.*
Reunámonos.	*Let's get together.*

As with other affirmative **nosotros** commands, **vamos a** + infinitive often replaces the command form derived from the subjunctive.

Vamos a quedarnos.	*Let's stay.*
Vamos a relajarnos.	*Let's relax.*
Vamos a divertirnos.	*Let's have a good time.*
Vamos a reunirnos.	*Let's get together.*

Following are some common reflexive verbs that refer to the daily routine. Their non-reflexive forms (usually transitive verbs) and meanings are also given.

REFLEXIVE VERBS	CORRESPONDING NONREFLEXIVE VERBS
acostarse (o > ue) *to go to bed*	**acostar (o > ue)** *to put (someone) to bed*
afeitarse *to shave*	**afeitar** *to shave (someone)*
arreglarse *to get ready (fix hair, clothing, etc.)*	**arreglar** *to arrange, fix*
bañarse *to bathe, take a bath*	**bañar** *to bathe (someone)*
cansarse *to get tired*	**cansar** *to tire (someone)*
colocarse *to place or position oneself, get a job*	**colocar** *to place, put*
cortarse *to cut oneself*	**cortar** *to cut*
despedirse (e > i) de *to say good-bye to*	**despedir (e > i)** *to fire, dismiss*
despertarse (e > ie) *to wake up*	**despertar (e > ie)** *to wake (someone) up*
dormirse (o > ue) *to fall asleep*	**dormir (o > ue)** *to sleep, put to sleep*
enfermarse *to get sick*	**enfermar** *to make ill*
lastimarse *to hurt oneself*	**lastimar** *to hurt*
lavarse *to wash up*	**lavar** *to wash (someone/something)*
levantarse *to get up*	**levantar** *to raise, pick up*
maquillarse *to put on makeup*	**maquillar** *to put makeup on (someone)*
peinarse *to comb one's hair*	**peinar** *to comb (someone's) hair*
reunirse (me reúno) (con) *to get together (with)*	**reunir (reúno)** *to join, gather*
vestirse (e > i) *to dress, get dressed*	**vestir (e > i)** *to dress (someone)*

Following are some common reflexive verbs expressing feelings and emotions. Corresponding nonreflexive verbs are usually transitive.

REFLEXIVE VERBS	CORRESPONDING NONREFLEXIVE VERBS
aburrirse *to get/be bored*	**aburrir** *to bore (someone)*
alegrarse *to be glad/happy*	**alegrar** *to make (someone) happy*
alterarse *to get upset*	**alterar** *to upset (someone)*
animarse *to cheer up, take heart, feel like doing something*	**animar** *to cheer (someone) up, encourage (someone)*
asustarse *to get scared*	**asustar** *to frighten (someone)*
calmarse *to calm down*	**calmar** *to calm (someone) down*
decidirse a *to make up one's mind*	**decidir** *to decide*
divertirse (e > ie, e > i) *to have a good time*	**divertir** (e > ie, e > i) *to amuse*
enfadarse *to get angry*	**enfadar** *to make (someone) angry*
enojarse *to get angry*	**enojar** *to make (someone) angry*
entusiasmarse *to get excited, feel thrilled*	**entusiasmar** *to excite, thrill, stir*
exasperarse *to get exasperated, lose one's patience*	**exasperar** *to exasperate, make (someone) lose his/her patience*
interesarse en *to be interested in*	**interesar** *to interest*
marearse *to get/feel dizzy*	**marear** *to make (someone) dizzy*
molestarse *to get annoyed*	**molestar** *to annoy, bother*
ofenderse *to get offended/insulted; to feel hurt*	**ofender** *to offend, insult, hurt (someone)*
preocuparse *to worry*	**preocupar** *to worry (someone)*
probarse (o > ue) *to try on*	**probar** (o > ue) *to try, taste*
sorprenderse *to be surprised*	**sorprender** *to surprise (someone)*
tranquilizarse *to calm down, stop worrying*	**tranquilizar** *to calm (someone) down, reassure*

J   *Mandatos* **(Commands).** *Dando consejos.* *Lea las siguientes situaciones y luego dé algunos consejos. Escriba los verbos indicados con la forma formal e informal singular del mandato. Siga el modelo.*

MODELO   Tengo calor. (quitarse el suéter)
           → Quítese el suéter.
             Quítate el suéter.

1. Me gustan los dos trajes. (probarse los dos)
2. Tengo muchísimo sueño. (acostarse temprano)
3. Tengo cita a las tres y ya son las tres menos cuarto. (darse prisa)
4. Empieza a llover. (ponerse el impermeable)
5. Voy a ver la nueva película española esta noche. (divertirse mucho)
6. Me encanta París. (quedarse otra semana entonces)
7. Tengo que recoger a mis padres en el aeropuerto. (irse ahora mismo)
8. Me siento nervioso. (tranquilizarse)

K   *¡No lo haga!* *Déle a la persona un mandato negativo empleando el verbo indicado.*
Escriba la forma formal e informal singular del mandato. Siga el modelo.

> MODELO   Me gusta el pelo largo. (no cortarse el pelo entonces)
> → No se corte el pelo entonces.
> No te cortes el pelo entonces.

1. Tengo fiebre. (no levantarse todavía)

2. Tengo los pies mojados por la lluvia. (no enfermarse)

3. A Roberta se le rompió mi reloj. (no enfadarse con ella)

4. Voy a coger el tren de las ocho. (no despertarse tarde)

5. Necesito estudiar para un examen de biología. (no dormirse)

6. Yo no tengo la menor idea de lo que pasó. (no hacerse el desentendido (*pretend not to understand, play dumb*))

7. Me como muchos dulces todos los días. (no ponerse gorda)

L   *¡Niños, hagan esto!* *Déles mandatos a los niños escribiendo la forma del mandato de los verbos indicados. Dígales las cosas que deben hacer. Siga el modelo.*

> MODELO   bañarse ahora
> → Niños, báñense ahora.

1. vestirse para salir

2. cepillarse los dientes

3. atarse los zapatos

4. ponerse serios

5. lavarse las manos

6. sentarse

7. tranquilizarse

8. acostarse

M   *¡Niños, pórtense bien!* *Déles mandatos a los niños escribiendo la forma del mandato de los verbos indicados. Esta vez, dígales las cosas que **no** deben hacer. Siga el modelo.*

> MODELO   no quitarse los guantes
> → Niños, no se quiten los guantes.

1. no ensuciarse (*get dirty*) la cara

2. no hacerse los sordos (*pretend not to hear*)

3. no caerse patinando

4. no olvidarse de guardar sus juguetes

5. no irse del jardín

6. no hacerse daño

7. no quejarse tanto

The Position of Reflexive Pronouns
with the Present Participle

In the progressive tenses, the reflexive pronouns may either precede the forms of **estar** or follow the present participle (gerund). When they follow, they are attached in writing and a written accent is added to the vowel before the **-ndo** of the gerund.

Me estoy vistiendo.	*I'm getting dressed.*
Ana **está arreglándose.**	*Ana is getting ready.*

Following are some commonly used reflexive verbs that refer to motion or to a change in position. In most cases, the corresponding nonreflexive verb is transitive.

REFLEXIVE VERBS	CORRESPONDING NONREFLEXIVE VERBS
acercarse (a) *to come closer, approach*	**acercar** *to bring (something) closer/over*
alejarse (de) *to move away from*	**alejar** *to move (something) away*
caerse *to fall down*	**caer** *to fall* (usually figurative)
correrse *to move over, make room for*	**correr** *to move (something)*
detenerse (e > ie) *to stop, come to a halt*	**detener (e > ie)** *to stop, bring to a halt*
instalarse *to move in*	**instalar** *to install*
levantarse *to get up, rise*	**levantar** *to lift*
moverse (o > ue) *to move, stir, budge*	**mover (o > ue)** *to move, put in motion*
pararse *to stand up* (especially Spanish America)	**parar** *to stop*
pasearse *to stroll*	**pasear** *to walk, take for a walk*
perderse (e > ie) *to get lost*	**perder (e > ie)** *to lose*
quedarse *to stay, remain*	**quedar** *to remain, be left*
sentarse (e > ie) *to sit down*	**sentar (e > ie)** *to seat*
tirarse *to jump, throw oneself; to lie down*	**tirar** *to throw*
volcarse (o > ue) *to get knocked over*	**volcar (o > ue)** *to knock over*

The following verbs of motion or change of position are used primarily as reflexives.

echarse *to lie down*
escaparse *to escape*
inclinarse *to bend over*
mudarse *to move* (*change residence*)
ponerse de pie *to stand up* (especially Spain)
recostarse (o > ue) *to lie down*

Following are some verbs that are used primarily or exclusively as reflexives in Spanish, at least with the meanings given. Verbs marked with an asterisk exist only as reflexives.

acatarrarse *to catch a cold*
acordarse (o > ue) (de) *to remember*
apoderarse (de) *to take possession (of)*
apresurarse (de) *to hurry*
aprovecharse (de) *to take advantage (of)*
apuntarse (a/para) *to register (for), sign up (for)*
***arrepentirse (e > ie) (de)** *to regret, repent*
***atreverse (a)** *to dare to (do something)*
ausentarse *to be out/away*

burlarse de *to laugh at, make fun of*
casarse (con) *to get married (to)*
comprometerse *to get engaged*
*desmayarse *to faint*
*divorciarse *to get divorced*
empeñarse (en) *to insist (on), persist (in)*
enamorarse (de) *to fall in love (with)*
encararse (con) *to face, confront*
enterarse (de) *to find out (about)*
*equivocarse *to make a mistake*
fiarse (me fío) (de) *to trust*
figurarse *to imagine*
fijarse (en) *to notice*
graduarse (me gradúo) *to graduate*
*jactarse (de) *to boast about*
matricularse *to register, enroll*
negarse (e > ie) (a) *to refuse to*
ocuparse (de) *to take care of*
olvidarse (de) *to forget*
oponerse (a) *to oppose, be against*
parecerse (a) *to resemble*
portarse bien/mal *to behave well/badly*
*quejarse (de) *to complain about*
reírse (e > i) (de) *to laugh at*
resfriarse (me resfrío) *to catch a cold*
sentirse (e > ie) *to feel*
*suicidarse *to commit suicide*

NOTE **Olvidar** is followed by a direct object, **olvidarse** by the preposition **de: Olvidaron el número. = Se olvidaron del número.** Both sentences mean *They forgot the number.* **Olvidarse** is also used with the indirect object pronoun to express unplanned occurrences, as in **Se les olvidó el número** (*They forgot the number*) (see "Other Uses of the Indirect Object" in Chapter 19).

Some verbs change considerably in meaning when they become reflexive.

NONREFLEXIVE VERBS	CORRESPONDING REFLEXIVE VERBS
despedir (e > i) *to fire, dismiss*	**despedirse de (e > i)** *to say good-bye to*
dormir (o > ue) *to sleep*	**dormirse (o > ue)** *to fall asleep*
empeñar *to pawn*	**empeñarse (en)** *to insist (on), persist (in)*
ir *to go*	**irse** *to go away*
llevar *to carry, take*	**llevarse** *to take away*
	llevarse bien/mal con *to get along/ not get along with*
meter *to put in, insert*	**meterse (en)** *to meddle, butt in*
negar (e > ie) *to deny*	**negarse (e > ie) (a)** *to refuse to*
parar *to stop*	**pararse** *to stand up* (Spanish America)
parecer (yo parezco) *to seem*	**parecerse (yo me parezco) (a)** *to resemble*
quedar *to remain, be left*	**quedarse** *to stay, remain*
volver (o > ue) *to return, go/come back*	**volverse (o > ue)** *to turn around*

N *¡Haciendo diabluras!* **(Making mischief!)** *En una reunión familiar, los niños están haciendo sus diabluras como de costumbre. Y los adultos están reaccionando como de costumbre. Escriba oraciones usando el presente progresivo para describir la escena. Escriba cada oración de dos maneras. Siga los modelos.*

MODELOS Sarita / mojarse con la sopa
→ Sarita está mojándose con la sopa.
Sarita se está mojando con la sopa.

la hermana de Sarita / quejarse
→ La hermana de Sarita está quejándose.
La hermana de Sarita se está quejando.

1. Luisito / portarse mal

2. los abuelos de Luisito / ponerse rojos (*get embarrassed*)

3. Adrianita / reírse como una loca

4. la tía de Adrianita / desmayarse

5. Fernandito / esconderse en un armario

6. el tío de Fernandito / asustarse

7. los gemelos (*twins*) / escaparse de su padre

8. el padre de los gemelos / enojarse

9. Pedrito / burlarse de sus primos

10. los primos de Pedrito / exasperarse

11. Mari Carmen / ensuciarse con el guacamole

12. la madre de Mari Carmen / avergonzarse (*to be ashamed/embarrassed*)

NOTA CULTURAL

El guacamole es una salsa o mole que se come en México, los países centro-americanos y Cuba. Se come mucho en los Estados Unidos también gracias a la popularidad de la cocina mexicana. La palabra guacamole es del náhuatl, lengua indígena de los aztecas, un pueblo precolombino del Valle de México. El guacamole se prepara machacando aguacates (o paltas) (*avocados*) en un mortero. A los aguacates machacados se le añaden tomates, sal, cilantro (*cori-ander*), cebolla, jugo de limón y otros condimentos.

O *Están en movimiento. Hay mucha actividad en el barrio hoy. Use el presente progresivo para decir lo que está haciendo cada persona. Escriba cada oración de dos maneras. Siga el modelo.*

MODELO ¿Qué hace Juan Pedro? (arreglarse)
→ Se está arreglando.
Está arreglándose.

1. ¿Qué hace tu mamá? (apresurarse para salir)

2. ¿Qué hacen los Pereira? (mudarse a otro barrio)

3. ¿Qué hacen los niños? (acercarse a la escuela)

4. ¿Qué hacen tus abuelos? (pasearse por el centro)

5. ¿Qué haces tú? (instalarse en un nuevo apartamento)

6. ¿Qué hacen Uds.? (reunirse en el comedor de la empresa)

7. ¿Qué hace Elena? (vestirse para salir)

8. ¿Qué hacéis? (divertirse con nuestros amigos)

Reflexive Verbs with Reciprocal Meaning

The plural forms of reflexive verbs are used to express reciprocal action corresponding to the English phrase *each other*. Because **se ven** means either *they see each other* or *they see themselves* (for example, in the mirror), the meaning must be clarified by the context.

—Jacinto y Laura **se quieren** mucho.	*Jacinto and Laura **love each other** very much.*
—**Se ven** todos los días.	***They see each other** every day.*
—¿Dónde **se conocieron** Uds.?	*Where **did you meet each other**?*
—**Nos conocimos** en una conferencia.	***We met** at a lecture.*

Spanish uses the phrase **el uno al otro** (or **uno a otro**) to focus on or to clarify the meaning *each other*. This phrase agrees with the gender and number of the people referred to: **el uno al otro/la una a la otra/los unos a los otros/las unas a las otras**.

Mis hermanos se ayudan **el uno al otro**.	*My brothers help **each other**.*
Las chicas se miran **la una a la otra**.	*The girls look at **each other**.*

The reflexive pronoun is not used to express *each other* with any preposition other than **a**.

Diana y Felisa no pueden ir de compras **la una sin la otra**.	*Diana and Felisa can't shop without **each other**.*

P *Mi mejor amigo/amiga y yo.* *Escriba oraciones en las cuales describe cómo es la relación entre Ud. y su mejor amigo/amiga. Practique el uso del reflexivo con el significado* each other. *Use el presente del verbo. Siga el modelo.*

MODELO   Pablo y yo / conocer muy bien
→ Pablo y yo nos conocemos muy bien.

1. Marisol y yo / hablar por teléfono cuatro veces al día

2. Jorge y yo / entender perfectamente

3. José María y yo / ver todos los días

4. Consuelo y yo / escribir correos electrónicos

5. Felipe y yo / ayudar con el trabajo

6. Victoria y yo / prestar ropa

7. David y yo / tutear (*address each other as* tú (*informally*))

Q *Un gran amor.* *¿Cómo llegaron Alejandra y Claudio a comprometerse? Para saberlo, escriba oraciones usando el pretérito con la forma recíproca del reflexivo. Siga el modelo.*

MODELO   ver por primera vez hace un año
               → Se vieron por primera vez hace un año.

1. conocer en una fiesta   5. comprar regalos

2. dar un beso   6. decir muchas cosas importantes

3. ver todos los días   7. hacer promesas

4. hablar constantemente   8. comprender muy bien

R *Travesuras en el parque* **(Mischief in the park).** *Dos niños estaban en el parque ayer. Complete el relato usando el pretérito de los verbos indicados para saber lo que les pasó. Ud. practicará el uso del verbo reflexivo con el significado de* each other.

Luisito y Juanito _____ (1. conocerse) en el parque ayer. _____ (2. Ponerse) a jugar.

Pronto, Luisito le quitó el camión a Juanito. Los niñitos _____ (3. enojarse) tanto que

_____ (4. pegarse). Las dos mamás _____ (5. acercarse) y trataron de calmar a sus hijos.

Por fin los niños _____ (6. tranquilizarse), _____ (7. abrazarse) y _____ (8. darse) un beso.

How to Say "Become" in Spanish

The English verb *to become* has several different translations in Spanish. When *to become* is followed by an adjective, the most common Spanish expression is **ponerse** + adjective. It is used for physical or emotional changes, where no effort is implied.

Esteban **se puso bravo** al leer la carta.	*Esteban **got angry** when he read the letter.*
Lidia y María **se pusieron pálidas** del susto.	*Lidia and María **turned pale** from fright.*
Juanita **se pone roja** porque es tímida.	*Juanita **blushes** (**gets red**) because she's shy.*

Volverse + adjective is used to express a sudden, involuntary change, most commonly in the expression **volverse loco** (*to go crazy/mad*). Changes indicated by **ponerse** may be superficial, while those indicated by **volverse** are more profound.

El psicólogo **se volvió loco**.	*The psychologist **went mad**.*
Los políticos **se volvieron muy arrogantes**.	*The politicians **got very arrogant**.*
¡Ese niño **se ha vuelto imposible**!	*That kid **has become impossible**!*

Hacerse and **llegar a ser** also mean *to become* and are used with nouns expressing profession or adjectives expressing social status. They imply effort on the part of the subject. **Pasar a ser**, stressing the process of change, is also used.

Sarita **se hizo abogada**.	*Sarita became a lawyer.*
Lola **llegó a ser abogada** también.	*Lola became a lawyer also.*
Pedro y yo **nos hicimos amigos**.	*Pedro and I became friends.*
Pedro y Tomás nunca **llegaron a ser amigos**.	*Pedro and Tomás never got to be friends.*
Laura **pasó a ser directora ejecutiva** de la compañía.	*Laura got to be executive director of the company.*
Y **se hizo rica** también.	*And she got rich too.*

The idioms **convertirse (e > ie) en** and **transformarse en** also express ideas related to the verb *to become*.

Atlanta **se convirtió en** una ciudad importante.	*Atlanta became an important city.*
El vino **se transformó en** vinagre.	*The wine turned to vinegar.*

Very often the idea of *to become* or *to get* is expressed by a reflexive verb in Spanish. Here are some examples.

alegrarse	*to become happy*
cansarse	*to get tired*
enojarse	*to get angry*
emocionarse	*to get excited*
*entristecerse (yo me entristezco)	*to become sad*

Some ideas can be expressed both with a verb meaning *to become* followed by an adjective and with a reflexive verb; the latter is more literary. Here are some examples.

hacerse rico ~ enriquecerse	*to become rich*
ponerse furioso ~ enfurecerse	*to become furious*
volverse orgulloso ~ enorgullecerse	*to become haughty*

There are some verbs in Spanish that express a change of state similar to **alegrarse** and **enojarse** that are not reflexive. These verbs have alternate constructions consisting of one of the verbs for *to become* followed by an adjective.

adelgazar ~ quedarse delgado	*to get thin*
*enflaquecer ~ ponerse flaco	*to get thin*
engordar ~ ponerse gordo	*to get fat*
*enloquecer ~ volverse loco	*to go mad*
*enmudecer ~ volverse mudo	*to become mute*
*ensordecer ~ volverse sordo	*to go deaf*
*envejecer ~ ponerse viejo	*to grow old*
*palidecer ~ ponerse pálido	*to turn pale*

---

*Most verbs with infinitives ending in -**ecer** have -**zco** in the **yo** form in present tense.

S *¿Cómo se dice* **to become** *en español?* *Indique cuál de las expresiones que significan* to become *corresponde en cada oración.*

1. Los chicos _____ contentísimos al ver su nueva bicicleta.
   a. se pusieron
   b. se hicieron

2. Después de unas campañas políticas muy duras, Jorge Cuevas _____ presidente.
   a. se volvió
   b. llegó a ser

3. ¡_____ locos por la cantidad de trabajo!
   a. Nos volvemos
   b. Nos hacemos

4. Rita _____ brava cuando el taxi chocó con su coche.
   a. se hizo
   b. se puso

5. Este pueblo está _____ en un centro turístico.
   a. poniéndose
   b. convirtiéndose

T *Expresar en español.* **To become y to get.** *Exprese las oraciones en español usando la expresión correcta para* to become *o* to get *en cada caso.*

1. *Ricardo became a millionaire.*

2. *The archaeologists got excited when they saw the ruins (las ruinas).*

3. *Magdalena often blushes (gets red) because she's very shy.*

4. *Daniel is marrying Tere because he wants to become an American citizen.*

5. *Carlitos has become impossible!*

6. *Felisa is getting very fat because of the cake and ice cream she eats every day.*

7. *The region became an important technological center.*

8. *Isabel became a programmer.*

Other Reflexive Verbs

There are cases of reflexive verbs that do not fit exactly into the categories given above and that require special attention.

Equivocarse has a basic meaning of *to be mistaken* or *to be wrong*.

Si crees que Paula te va a devolver el dinero, **te equivocas**.	*If you think Paula is going to return the money to you, **you're mistaken**.*

Note that **equivocarse** means *to be wrong* only when the subject is a person. **Estar equivocado** means *to be wrong* both for persons and things.

El físico **se equivocó**.	*The physicist **was wrong***.
El físico **estuvo equivocado**.	*The physicist **was wrong***.
La respuesta **está equivocada**.	*The answer **is wrong***.

The expression **equivocarse de** can translate other uses of English *wrong*.

Ud. **se ha equivocado** de casa.	*You've come to the **wrong** house*.
Nos equivocamos de carretera.	*We took the **wrong** highway*.

Quedarse has a basic meaning of *to remain, stay*.

Quédate en casa si no te sientes bien.	***Stay at home** if you don't feel well*.
Pensamos quedarnos en un parador en Segovia.	***We intend to stay** at an inn in Segovia*.

Quedarse can express *to become* to indicate a new state, either physical or emotional.

Todos **se quedaron atónitos**.	*Everyone **was astonished***.
Dos víctimas del terremoto **se quedaron ciegas y sordas**.	*Two victims of the earthquake **went blind and deaf***.

Nonreflexive **quedar** is used to mean different things.

El cuarto **queda bien/mal** con las nuevas cortinas.	*The room **looks good/bad** with the new curtains*.
Tu corbata roja **queda bien** con tu camisa azul.	*Your red tie **goes well** with your blue shirt*.
Paco **quedó bien** regalándole flores a su suegra.	*Paco **made a good impression** giving flowers to his mother-in-law*.
El director de la orquesta **quedó mal** con los músicos.	*The conductor **made a bad impression** on the musicians*.

Hacerse, when followed by the definite article and an adjective, means *to pretend to be* or *to act like*.

El ladrón **se hizo el desentendido** al ser encontrado por la policía.	*The thief **played dumb** (**pretended not to understand**) when he was found by the police*.
Lola **se hizo la sorda** cuando su hermana le pidió prestado el coche.	*Lola **pretended to be deaf** (**turned a deaf ear**) when her sister asked to borrow the car*.
Berta **se hizo la dormida** para no tener que hacer las labores domésticas.	*Berta **pretended to be asleep** so that she wouldn't have to do the household chores*.
Nicolás **se hacía el tonto** en la fiesta.	*Nicolás **was acting silly** (**playing the fool**) at the party*.

Both **acordarse de** and **recordar** mean *to remember*.

Si no **me acuerdo** mal. ⎫ Si no **recuerdo** mal. ⎭	*If **I remember** correctly*.

Recordar also means *to remind.*

Les recuerdo que mañana tenemos ensayo.	*I'm reminding them that we have a rehearsal tomorrow.*
Me recuerdas a tu mamá.	*You remind me of your mother.*

Some Expressions with Reflexive Verbs

darse cuenta (de)	*to realize*
darse prisa	*to hurry*
echarse a + *infinitive*	*to begin to*
hacerse daño	*to hurt oneself*
hacerse tarde	*to get late*
ponerse a + *infinitive*	*to begin to*
ponerse de acuerdo	*to come to an agreement*
quedarse con	*to keep, hold onto*
referirse (**e** > **ie**) (a)	*to refer to*
servirse (**e** > **i**) (de)	*to use*
tratarse (de)	*to be about, be a question of*
valerse (de)	*to use*

Certain verbs are made reflexive to stress participation by the subject or to convey an intensification of the action.

Compré un coche.	*I bought a car.*
Me compré un coche.	*I bought (myself) a car.*
Leo **comió** los pasteles.	*Leo ate the pastries.*
Leo **se comió** los pasteles.	*Leo gobbled up the pastries.*

U   *Preposiciones con verbos reflexivos. Complete las oraciones con las preposiciones correctas. Vea "The Position of Reflexive Pronouns with the Present Participle" en este capítulo.*

1. Este niño malcriado (*spoiled*) no se lleva bien _____ nadie.

2. Los turistas se fijaron _____ la arquitectura de los castillos.

3. No debemos aprovecharnos _____ las demás personas.

4. Jorge se arrepiente _____ haberles mentido a sus padres.

5. Yo me intereso mucho _____ la historia europea.

6. Los Cela se negaron _____ hacer cola en la taquilla.

7. ¿No te fías _____ tu abogado?

8. ¿Por qué se opuso Ud. _____ nuestra idea?

9. Los abuelos siempre se jactan (*brag*) _____ sus nietos.

10. Os olvidasteis _____ desenchufar (*unplug*) los aparatos eléctricos.

11. Daniel se casará _____ Luz en mayo.

12. Te pareces mucho _____ tu mamá.

En otras palabras. *Vuelva a escribir las oraciones usando un sinónimo de los verbos o expresiones que aparecen en letra cursiva. Todos los sinónimos se encuentran en este capítulo.*

1. *Si no recuerdo mal,* los Aranda se mudaron a Los Ángeles.

2. Ud. *no tiene razón.* Lima es la capital del Perú, no de Ecuador.

3. Dos personas *perdieron la vista* a causa del accidente.

4. *Parece que* la niña *está dormida* (pero no está).

5. Juan Carlos *ha bajado mucho de peso.*

6. Creíamos que íbamos a *volvernos locos* por el desorden de la casa.

7. Todos los habitantes *están enfureciéndose* por el número de robos en el barrio.

8. Diego *se ponía pálido* corriendo la última milla de la carrera.

 Ejercicio oral. Un día típico. *Descríbale a un amigo/una amiga cómo es un día típico para Ud. Hable de sus actividades diarias y a qué hora las hace. Use los verbos reflexivos que se presentan en este capítulo, por ejemplo,* **despertarse, vestirse, peinarse, arreglarse, lavarse la cabeza, acostarse.**

8

Passive Constructions

The Passive Voice—Formation and Use

The passive voice in Spanish consists of a form of **ser** + past participle. This is often followed by the agent phrase introduced by the preposition **por**. The past participle agrees in number and gender with the subject of the sentence.

La cena fue servida **por Margarita**.	*Dinner was served by Margarita.*
Los paquetes serán entregados **por el cartero**.	*The packages will be delivered by the mailman.*
El coche ha sido reparado **por los mecánicos**.	*The car has been repaired by the mechanics.*

The passive voice is used in Spanish to move the focus of the sentence from the performer of the action to the direct object of the verb.

ACTIVE VOICE   Los obreros construirán el rascacielos.
The workers will build the skyscraper.

PASSIVE VOICE   El rascacielos será construido por los obreros.
The skyscraper will be built by the workers.

Note that the direct object of the active sentence, **el rascacielos**, becomes the subject of the passive sentence. The subject of the active sentence (the performer of the action), **los obreros**, appears in the "agent phrase" introduced by **por**. In the rephrasing of the active sentence into a passive sentence, the speaker focuses on **el rascacielos** and on its building rather than on the performer of the action, **los obreros**.

 En la oficina. *Vuelva a escribir las oraciones cambiando la construcción activa a la construcción pasiva para describir las actividades que ocurren en la oficina. Mantenga el tiempo verbal de la oración en voz activa. Siga el modelo.*

MODELO   El secretario arregló los papeles.
           → Los papeles fueron arreglados por el secretario.

La oficina

actualizar *to update*	**el formulario** *form*
el administrador/la administradora de web *webmaster*	**el/la gerente, la gerenta** *manager*
la base de datos *database*	**la impresora** *printer*
el diseñador gráfico *graphic designer*	**la pantalla** *screen*
el folleto *brochure, pamphlet*	**el programador/la programadora** *programmer*

1. La recepcionista leyó el email.

2. Los empleados llenarán los formularios.

3. El diseñador gráfico ha preparado el folleto.

4. La programadora hizo la base de datos.

5. El administrador de web actualizará el sitio web.

6. Los agentes de viajes compraron los billetes electrónicos.

7. El técnico reparó la pantalla.

8. Los gerentes han resuelto los problemas.

B *Día de mudanza.* *Escriba oraciones usando la voz pasiva y en pretérito para describir lo que pasó en casa de los Pidal el día de su mudanza de San Salvador a Nueva York. Siga el modelo.*

MODELO   los muebles / llevar / cargadores (*movers*)
         → Los muebles fueron llevados por los cargadores.

1. las camas / subir a los dormitorios / tres hombres

2. la alfombra de la sala / correr / la señora Pidal

3. los cuadros / colgar en las paredes / Benito y Ramona

4. la secadora / bajar al sótano / un cargador

5. el sillón azul / colocar al lado de la ventana / el señor Pidal

6. las lámparas / poner en las mesas / Regina

NOTA CULTURAL

- Hay mucha **emigración** de México y ciertos países centroamericanos a los Estados Unidos por razones económicas, políticas y personales. Los inmigrantes más numerosos son de México. Muchos centroamericanos emigran de Guatemala, Honduras y El Salvador. De los inmigrantes sudamericanos, muchos son de Colombia, Perú y Ecuador. Después del 2020, ha aumentado mucho el número de inmigrantes cubanos y venezolanos a los Estados Unidos.

Se Constructions with Passive Meaning

Spanish uses the construction **se** + verb in third person singular or plural to deemphasize the performer of the action. The agent phrase with **por** is not used in this construction. Note that in English this **se** construction (**se** + verb) can be translated in many different ways. The verb in this construction is either third person singular or third person plural, depending on whether the grammatical subject is singular or plural.

El locutor **dio** los premios.	*The announcer **gave out** (**awarded**) the prizes.*
Los premios **fueron dados** por el locutor.	*The prizes **were given out** (**awarded**) by the announcer.*
Se dieron los premios.	*The prizes **were given out** (**awarded**).*
Se sabe el motivo.	*The reason **is known**. / **You/They/People know** the reason. / **One knows** the reason.*
Se entregó el informe.	*The report **was handed in**.*
Se entregaron los informes.	*The reports **were handed in**.*

For intransitive verbs, that is, those that do not take a direct object, the verb is always in third person singular.

Se sale por aquí.	***You go out** this way. / This **is the way out**.*
Se vive bien en este país.	***People live** well in this country.*
Se trabaja con entusiasmo.	***We/You/They work** enthusiastically.*

Note that reflexive verbs such as **divertirse** and **despertarse** can only show an unidentified or deemphasized subject with the addition of **uno** (or **una** if the reference is feminine) to a third person singular verb.

Uno se divierte mucho en esta ciudad.	***You** have a lot of fun in this city.*
Uno se despierta más tarde los domingos.	***People** wake up later on Sundays.*

Spanish also uses **la gente** with a third person singular verb to label an indefinite subject. Compare this usage to English *people*. This Spanish construction is less common than its English equivalent.

Para divertirse, **la gente** va a un concierto.	*To have a good time, **people** go to a concert.*

Spanish also uses the third person plural of the verb to label an indefinite subject. In this case, the subject pronouns **ellos/ellas** cannot be used.

Dicen que va a llover.	***They say** it's going to rain.*
Me **van** a invitar a la boda.	***They're going** to invite me to the wedding. (I'm going to be invited to the wedding.)*
Lo **entrevistaron** la semana pasada.	***They interviewed** him last week. (He was interviewed last week.)*

C ***¡Se están instalando todavía!*** *A los Pidal les quedan muchas cosas que hacer en instalarse. Diga cuáles son estas cosas, escribiendo oraciones con la construcción con* **se** *y el verbo en el futuro. Fíjese que esta vez no hay agente en las oraciones. Siga el modelo.*

MODELO   correr / las cortinas
   → Se correrán las cortinas.

1. enchufar / la nevera

2. encender / las lámparas

3. guardar / las cajas

4. poner / el sofá / en la sala

5. colocar / el lavaplatos / en la cocina

6. meter / las sábanas / en el armario

7. poner / las sillas / con la mesa del comedor

8. subir / las cómodas / a los dormitorios

D ***Titulares y anuncios del periódico.*** *Escriba oraciones usando la construcción con el sujeto indefinido* **se** *+ la tercera persona singular o plural del verbo. Mantenga el tiempo verbal de la oración original. Siga el modelo.*

MODELO   Los políticos estudian los problemas económicos.
   → Se estudian los problemas económicos.

1. La empresa busca programadores de computadoras.

2. La ley prohíbe el fumar en los restaurantes.

3. Los contadores (*accountants*) calculaban los impuestos.

4. Los inquilinos (*tenants*) alquilaron el condominio en la playa.

5. El Café Vietnám entrega comida a la casa hasta la una de la mañana.

6. Los clientes pagan con cheque o tarjeta de crédito.

7. Esta sucursal del Banco de Barcelona solicitará gerentes.

8. La compañía necesita asesores bilingües.

E ***Una excursión al zoológico.*** *Cambie las oraciones sobre una excursión al zoológico de la voz pasiva a la voz activa usando los sujetos indicados. Siga el modelo.*

MODELO   Se visita el zoológico. (nosotros)
   → Visitamos el zoológico.

1. Se va de excursión al zoológico. (mis amigos y yo)

2. Para llegar al zoológico, se toma el autobús en la calle Azorín. (nosotros)

3. Se ven leones, tigres, leopardos y panteras. (yo)

4. Se da de comer a los animales. (los guardianes)

5. Se entra en las jaulas para limpiarlas. (un trabajador)

6. Se comen las hojas de los árboles. (las jirafas)

7. Se tiran cacahuates a los elefantes. (tú)

8. Se juega tirando plátanos. (un mono)

9. Se grita en voz alta. (los loros)

10. Uno se baña en la piscina de la jaula. (los hipopótamos)

11. Se bebe una limonada. (Ud.)

12. Se compran palomitas y refrescos. (vosotros)

Ser and estar with the Past Participle

Both **ser** and **estar** are used with the past participle of the verb. Passive sentences have **ser** + past participle and usually have the agent phrase introduced by **por**. Sentences that have **estar** + past participle express the result of an action. They do not have an agent phrase introduced by **por**.

La torta **fue hecha** por el pastelero.	*The cake **was made** by the pastry chef.*
La torta **estaba hecha**.	*The cake **was made** (done, completed, finished).*

F ***Todo estaba hecho.*** *Cuando Ud. llegó, todo estaba hecho ya. Dígaselo a su amigo. Siga el modelo.*

> MODELO   ¿Quién abrió las ventanas?
> → No sé. Cuando yo llegué, las ventanas ya estaban abiertas.

1. ¿Quién arregló el cuarto?

2. ¿Quién preparó el almuerzo?

3. ¿Quién cerró la puerta?

4. ¿Quién apagó el microondas?

5. ¿Quién puso la mesa?

6. ¿Quién rompió los vasos?

7. ¿Quién mandó el documento escaneado (*scanned*)?

8. ¿Quién prendió las luces?

G ***Expresar en español. ¿Qué significa?*** *Su amigo español está pasando las vacaciones de verano en su casa. Mientras Uds. se pasean por la ciudad, su amigo le pregunta qué quieren decir los letreros que ve. Explíquele lo que dicen en español usando la construcción con* **se**.

1. *Newspapers and magazines are sold here.*

2. *You park here.*

3. *You eat well in this city.*

4. *One turns right.*

5. *You enter this way.*

6. *Spanish is spoken here.*

7. *Houses being built.*

8. *You leave by this door.*

H **¿Qué dice Ud.?** *Un nuevo estudiante extranjero en la universidad le hace unas preguntas sobre la vida universitaria. Conteste sus preguntas usando la construcción con* **se.**

1. ¿Qué materias toman?

2. ¿A qué hora almuerzan Uds.?

3. ¿Cómo llegan a la universidad?

4. ¿Dónde compran sus libros de texto?

5. ¿Cómo pueden sacar buenas notas?

6. ¿Qué hacen para divertirse los fines de semana?

7. ¿En qué restaurantes comen?

I **Ejercicio oral. Juego de adivinanza (Guessing game).** *En este juego Ud. y su amigo/su amiga tienen que decir el nombre del autor de una obra literaria bien conocida (novela, cuento, poesía, obra de teatro). Uno de Uds. dice el título de la obra y el otro tiene que decir lo más rápido posible el nombre del autor/de la autora de la obra. Hay que contestar usando la voz pasiva. ¡Un punto por cada respuesta correcta! Por ejemplo:*

—*1984.*
—La novela fue escrita por George Orwell.

—*Harry Potter y la piedra filosofal* (Harry Potter and the Sorcerer's Stone).
—La novela fue escrita por J. K. Rowling.

—*Mujercitas* (Little Women).
—La novela fue escrita por Louisa May Alcott.

—*La caída de la Casa Usher* (The Fall of the House of Usher).
—El cuento corto fue escrito por Edgar Allan Poe.

—*Oigo cantando a América* (I Hear America Singing).
—El poema fue escrito por Walt Whitman.

—*La muerte de un viajante* (Death of a Salesman).
—La obra teatral fue escrita por Arthur Miller.

The Compound Tenses

Formation of the Present Perfect

The perfect tenses in Spanish are similar to their English equivalents. They consist of a conjugated form of the auxiliary verb **haber** (*to have*) + past participle, which is the form of the verb ending in **-do**. The past participle of regular verbs is formed by dropping the infinitive ending and adding **-ado** to **-ar** verbs and **-ido** to **-er** and **-ir** verbs.

mandar	**mandado**	*sent*
comprender	**comprendido**	*understood*
servir	**servido**	*served*

These verbs have irregular past participles.

abrir	**abierto**	imprimir	**impreso**
cubrir	**cubierto**	morir	**muerto**
decir	**dicho**	poner	**puesto**
escribir	**escrito**	romper	**roto**
freír	**frito**	ver	**visto**
hacer	**hecho**	volver	**vuelto**

When a prefix is added to any of the above verbs, the past participle shows the same irregularities.

descomponer	**descompuesto**	posponer	**pospuesto**
describir	**descrito**	predecir	**predicho**
descubrir	**descubierto**	prever	**previsto**
deshacer	**deshecho**	rehacer	**rehecho**
devolver	**devuelto**	revolver	**revuelto**
imponer	**impuesto**	satisfacer	**satisfecho**

-Er and **-ir** verbs that have stems ending in a vowel have an accent mark over the **i** in the past participle.

caer	**caído**
creer	**creído**
leer	**leído**
oír	**oído**
traer	**traído**

The past participle forms of **ser** and **ir** are **sido** and **ido**, respectively.

The present perfect of **hay** is **ha habido** (*there has been, there have been*).

In the perfect tenses, object pronouns precede the forms of **haber** and are not attached to the past participle. In questions, subject pronouns follow the past participle. They are not placed between the auxiliary verb and the past participle as they are in English.

Se **lo** hemos hecho.	*We've done **it** for them.*
¿**Lo** has leído?	*Have you read **it**?*
¿Qué han visto **Uds.**?	*What have **you** seen?*
¿Todavía no se ha levantado **Ud.**?	*Haven't **you** gotten up yet?*

The present perfect consists of a conjugated form of the auxiliary verb **haber** + past participle. The past participle does not change to show gender or number in compound tenses where the auxiliary verb is **haber**. The present perfect is used in Spanish, as in English, to mark or describe past events that have an influence on the present or that continue into the present.

Han estado aquí todo el día.	*They have been here all day.*
He comenzado a escribir el informe.	*I've begun to write the report.*

ganar, comprender, salir

(yo) **he** ganado, comprendido, salido	(nosotros) **hemos** ganado, comprendido, salido
(tú) **has** ganado, comprendido, salido	(vosotros) **habéis** ganado, comprendido, salido
(él/ella/Ud.) **ha** ganado, comprendido, salido	(ellos/ellas/Uds.) **han** ganado, comprendido, salido

 Preparándose para un viaje. *Ud. y su familia se van de vacaciones. Antes de irse tienen que hacer ciertas cosas. Describa quién hizo cada cosa usando el pretérito perfecto (present perfect). Siga el modelo.*

> MODELO   papá / comprar / el mapa
> → Papá ha comprado el mapa.

Preparándose para un viaje

el baúl *trunk* (of a car)
el cristal *car window*
desenchufar los aparatos eléctricos
   to unplug the appliances
el equipaje *luggage*
hacer las maletas *to pack*

la linterna *flashlight*
llenar el tanque del coche *to fill the tank*
el mapa *map*
la pila *battery* (for a flashlight)
prepararse *to get ready*

1. Pedro / apagar / las luces

2. Cecilia y Pilar / hacer / las maletas

3. papá / llenar / el tanque del coche

4. Ud. / desenchufar / los aparatos eléctricos

5. David y Juan Carlos / meter / el equipaje en el baúl

6. yo / decirles / a los vecinos / que nos vamos

7. vosotros / poner / las pilas en la linterna

8. tú / limpiar / los cristales del coche

B *Una receta de cocina* (recipe). *Ud. y unos amigos han preparado un plato especial para servir en la cena. Describa paso a paso lo que han hecho, usando el pretérito perfecto. Siga el modelo.*

MODELO   Vera / comprar / los mariscos
→ Vera ha comprado los mariscos.

Una receta de cocina

el aguacate *avocado*
añadir *to add*
la cacerola *saucepan*
el camarón *shrimp*
la cebolla *onion*
cortar *to cut*
cubrir *to cover*
encender el fuego *to turn on the flame*
la ensalada *salad*
los espárragos *asparagus*
freír *to fry*
frito past participle of **freír**
   (**freído**—less commonly used)

los mariscos *shellfish*
picar *to chop*
la pimienta picante *hot pepper*
el pollo *chicken*
poner al horno *to put in the oven*
quemar *to burn*
la sal *salt*
la salchicha *sausage*
la salsa *salsa*
la sartén *frying pan*

1. nosotros / leer / la receta

2. Jorge / encender / el fuego

3. yo / hacer / la salsa

4. Alicia y Juan Diego / picar / las pimientas picantes

5. Ud. / freír / las cebollas

6. Estrella y yo / cortar / la salchicha

7. tú / lavar / los espárragos y los aguacates

8. Marianela / añadir / la sal

9. Uds. / poner / el pollo al horno

10. yo / mezclar / la ensalada de camarones

11. Martín / cubrir / la cacerola

12. vosotros / quemar / las sartenes

C *Vuelva a escribir las oraciones del ejercicio B cambiando el sustantivo por el pronombre de complemento directo correcto. Siga el modelo.*

MODELO   Vera ha comprado los mariscos.
→ Vera los ha comprado.

D ***¡Nos aburrimos como ostras* (oysters)! (We're dying of boredom!)** *Ud. y sus amigos quieren escaparse de una fiesta muy aburrida. Describa lo que han hecho, cambiando los verbos del tiempo presente al pretérito perfecto. Siga el modelo.*

MODELO   Pablo trata de huir.
          → Pablo ha tratado de huir.

1. María Dolores se duerme.

2. Ud. bosteza (*yawn*).

3. Yo me pongo el abrigo.

4. Carlos y Beatriz se despiden de la anfitriona (*hostess*).

5. ¡Nos matan de aburrimiento!

6. Tú te quejas que la comida te cayó mal.

7. Ud. y Clara dan excusas.

8. Nosotros decimos que nos enfermamos.

E ***Preguntas personales.*** *Conteste las preguntas usando el pretérito perfecto.*

1. ¿Se ha hecho Ud. socio/socia de (*Have you joined*) un club? ¿Qué club?

2. ¿A qué países han viajado Ud. y sus padres/su esposo/su esposa?

3. ¿Qué planes han hecho Ud. y su familia para el verano?

4. ¿Qué películas ha visto este año? ¿Cuál le ha gustado más?

5. ¿Cómo ha celebrado su cumpleaños?

6. ¿Qué regalo ha recibido? ¿Quiénes le han dado los regalos?

7. ¿Qué cosas han hecho Ud. y sus amigos hoy?

8. ¿Qué libros ha leído Ud. recientemente?

9. ¿Cuál le ha interesado más?

F ***¡Cosa hecha!*** *Conteste las preguntas usando el pretérito perfecto del verbo reflexivo en la oración original para explicar que las cosas ya están hechas. Siga el modelo.*

MODELO   ¿Cuándo van Uds. a mudarse?
          → Nos hemos mudado ya.

1. ¿Cuándo va Cristóbal a matricularse?

2. ¿Cuándo van Uds. a colocarse?

3. ¿Cuándo vas a instalarte en la nueva casa?

4. ¿Cuándo van Irene y Jaime a comprometerse (*to get engaged*)?

5. ¿Cuándo va Nora a enterarse de los líos de la familia?

6. ¿Cuándo vas a apuntarte en la lista de voluntarios?

7. ¿Cuándo vais a reuniros?

The Past Perfect

The past perfect consists of the imperfect of the auxiliary verb **haber** + past participle. The English equivalent of the past perfect is *had done something*.

---

llegar, comer, subir

(yo) **había** llegado, comido, subido	(nosotros) **habíamos** llegado, comido, subido
(tú) **habías** llegado, comido, subido	(vosotros) **habíais** llegado, comido, subido
(él/ella/Ud.) **había** llegado, comido, subido	(ellos/ellas/Uds.) **habían** llegado, comido, subido

---

The past perfect (or pluperfect) tense designates an event that happened prior to another past event that is further removed in the past.

Yo ya me había despertado cuando sonó el despertador.	*I had already awakened when the alarm clock went off.*
María ya había ido al teatro cuando Pedro la llamó.	*María had already gone to the theater when Pedro called her.*
Nosotros ya habíamos vuelto a casa cuando empezó a nevar.	*We had already gotten back home when it began to snow.*

G **Sí, había pasado antes.** *Explique cuándo había pasado cada una de las cosas mencionadas usando el pluscuamperfecto* (past perfect). *Siga el modelo.*

MODELO   Lorenzo / llegar / la semana pasada
          → Había llegado la semana pasada.

1. Uds. / ver la exposición / hace unos meses

2. Amelia / cortarse el pelo / el sábado

3. Ricardo y Leonor / casarse / en abril

4. nosotros / hacer una barbacoa / el cuatro de julio

5. tú / celebrar tu cumpleaños / hace un mes

6. Ud. / cambiar de idea / hace varios días

7. yo / ponerme en contacto con Felipe / hace tres semanas

8. Javier / devolverme los disquetes / la semana pasada

9. vosotros / escribir los informes / en noviembre

10. Marcos / romperse el codo / hace casi un año

H   **Tomás, el holgazán (loafer).** *Es que los amigos de Tomás no pueden contar con él porque no le gusta trabajar y siempre llega tarde. Cuando Tomás llega, todo ya está hecho. Escriba oraciones en las cuales explica lo que ya habían hecho los amigos cuando llegó Tomás por fin. Siga el modelo.*

> MODELO   Cuando Tomás llegó por fin... los amigos / lavar el carro
> → Cuando Tomás llegó por fin, los amigos ya habían lavado el carro.

1. Cuando Tomás llegó por fin... Raúl / hacer la pizza
2. Cuando Tomás llegó por fin... Uds. / poner la mesa
3. Cuando Tomás llegó por fin... Diana y Judit / ver el sitio web
4. Cuando Tomás llegó por fin... Ud. / sacar la basura
5. Cuando Tomás llegó por fin... yo / subir las cajas a la buhardilla (*attic*)
6. Cuando Tomás llegó por fin... tú / ir de compras
7. Cuando Tomás llegó por fin... Plácido y yo / volver de la tienda de cómputo

I   **Ya habíamos hecho muchas cosas.** *Escriba oraciones que explican lo que Ud. y otras personas habían hecho ya cuando pasaron ciertas cosas. Use el pretérito para la primera frase y el pluscuamperfecto para la segunda. Siga el modelo.*

> MODELO   sonar el teléfono : ellos / cenar
> → Cuando sonó el teléfono, ellos ya habían cenado.

1. Julia / venir a buscarnos : nosotros / hacer ejercicio
2. yo / ir a su casa : Virginia / dar una vuelta
3. Ud. / levantarse : sus padres / desayunar
4. nosotros / volver a casa : Juanita / escribir su email
5. los bomberos / llegar : Uds. / apagar el incendio en la cocina
6. los bisnietos / lograr ver a su bisabuelo : el bisabuelo / enfermarse

J   **Nunca habíamos visto...** *Ud. y su familia vuelven mañana a los Estados Unidos después de pasar seis semanas en España. Ahora que se van, se ponen a pensar en las cosas que no habían visto ni hecho en los viajes anteriores. Escriba oraciones usando el pluscuamperfecto en las cuales Ud. describe las cosas que no habían visto ni hecho antes. Siga el modelo.*

> MODELO   mamá / visitar la Catedral de Burgos
> → Mamá no había visitado la Catedral de Burgos.

1. Laura / ver una corrida de toros en Madrid
2. Rodolfo y Eva / dar una vuelta por las carreteras gallegas (de Galicia)
3. yo / hacer una excursión a El Escorial
4. tú y Susana / pasearse por el barrio de Santa Cruz
5. nosotros / subir al monte Tibidabo
6. Jaime / conocer la Alhambra
7. tú / pasar la Semana Santa en Sevilla
8. vosotros / conocer tantos restaurantes

NOTA CULTURAL

- **La Catedral de Burgos**—la ciudad de Burgos, capital de la provincia de Burgos, queda en Castilla la Vieja, al centro norte de España. Queda a las orillas del río Arlanzón. Su catedral, por sus dimensiones la tercera catedral española después de las de Sevilla y Toledo, se destaca por su estilo gótico. La construcción de la catedral empezó en el siglo XIII.
- **Las carreteras gallegas** se encuentran en la región de Galicia al noroeste de España. Comprende las provincias de La Coruña, Lugo, Orense y Pontevedra.
- **El Escorial** (El Real Monasterio de San Lorenzo de El Escorial) es el complejo de palacio, monasterio, basílica y biblioteca construido por el rey español Felipe II (1527–1598; rey 1556–1598) entre 1563 y 1584. Felipe II creó un gran monumento para honrar la memoria de su padre, Carlos V (Carlos I de España), emperador del Sacro Imperio Romano Germánico, que yacía (yacer (*to lie*)) en el panteón donde estaban enterrados los reyes españoles. Este majestuoso complejo, uno de los principales monumentos renacentistas españoles, queda en la sierra de Guadarrama al noroeste de Madrid.
- **El barrio de Santa Cruz**, que era el barrio judío en la Edad Media, es hoy el barrio más típico y pintoresco (*picturesque*) de Sevilla.
- **El monte Tibidabo** queda al noroeste de Barcelona. Desde la cima (*top, summit*) hay un hermoso panorama de Barcelona y el Mediterráneo. Hay un funicular (*cable car*) que lleva a la gente a lo alto del monte.
- **La Alhambra** es una obra maestra del arte islámico que se remonta al (*dates back to*) siglo IX cuando llegaron musulmanes de la dinastía nazarí del norte de África. Establecieron el reino nazarí y el rey fundador conocido por Alhamar hizo construir una sencilla fortaleza (*fortress*). Llegó a ser residencia real (*royal*) y de la corte de Granada. A lo largo de los siglos XIII–XV la fortaleza se convirtió en un monumental complejo de murallas (*walls*) y torres (*towers*) con una zona militar (Alcazaba) y una ciudad (la medina) donde se encuentran los palacios nazaríes.
- **La Semana Santa** (*Holy Week*) empieza con la celebración del Domingo de Ramos (*Palm Sunday*) y termina con la celebración del Domingo de Pascua (*Easter Sunday*), también conocido como Domingo de Resurrección. Las procesiones religiosas sevillanas son imponentes (*breathtaking*).

The Future Perfect

The future perfect consists of the future tense of the auxiliary verb **haber** + past participle.

llegar, comer, subir

(yo) **habré** llegado, comido, subido	(nosotros) **habremos** llegado, comido, subido
(tú) **habrás** llegado, comido, subido	(vosotros) **habréis** llegado, comido, subido
(él/ella/Ud.) **habrá** llegado, comido, subido	(ellos/ellas/Uds.) **habrán** llegado, comido, subido

In Spanish, as in English, the future perfect tense designates an event that will be completed in the future before another event occurs or before some point in time in the future.

Habrán vuelto para finales del mes.   ***They'll have returned*** *by the end of the month.*

Lo habré terminado todo antes de irme.   ***I'll have finished everything*** *before I leave.*

The future perfect is also used to express probability in past time. The future perfect of probability corresponds to the preterit or the present perfect.

Habrá pasado algo.
Probablemente pasó algo.
Probablemente ha pasado algo.   *Something probably happened.*

Deber de + perfect infinitive, which is the infinitive **haber** + past participle, can be used instead of the future perfect to express probability in past time.

Marta debe de haber llamado.   *Marta must have (probably) called.*

K   **¿Qué habrá ocurrido?** *Escriba oraciones usando el futuro perfecto para explicar para cuándo habrán ocurrido ciertas cosas. Siga el modelo.*

> MODELO   nosotros / almorzar / para las dos
> → Habremos almorzado para las dos.

1. Elena / graduarse / para el año próximo

2. Alfredo y Armando / mejorarse / antes de regresar a la oficina

3. nosotros / ahorrar dinero / antes de las vacaciones de invierno

4. yo / darte tu regalo / antes de tu fiesta de cumpleaños

5. Ud. y Laura / mudarse / para mediados del mes

6. tú / sacar un pasaporte / para julio

7. Ud. / volver del centro comercial / para las ocho

L   **Conjeturas (Conjectures).** *Exprese sus conjeturas sobre lo que pasó usando el futuro perfecto para expresar probabilidad en el pasado. Siga el modelo.*

> MODELO   *Probablemente* llegó el cartero.
> → Habrá llegado el cartero.

1. Su coche *probablemente* le costó un ojo de la cara (*an arm and a leg*).

2. Clara *probablemente* escribió el texto.

3. Felipe y Eduardo *probablemente* solicitaron una beca.

4. Uds. *probablemente* tomaron la merienda.

5. Martín y yo *probablemente* no entendimos el motivo.

6. Ud. *probablemente* hizo cola por mucho tiempo.

The Conditional Perfect

The conditional perfect consists of the conditional tense of the auxiliary verb **haber** + past participle. It corresponds to English *would have done something*.

---
llegar, comer, subir

(yo) **habría** llegado, comido, subido	(nosotros) **habríamos** llegado, comido, subido
(tú) **habrías** llegado, comido, subido	(vosotros) **habríais** llegado, comido, subido
(él/ella/Ud.) **habría** llegado, comido, subido	(ellos/ellas/Uds.) **habrían** llegado, comido, subido
---

The conditional perfect is used to designate an action or event that would have been completed in the past or when there is a real or implied condition.

Yo no lo **habría dicho**.	I *wouldn't have said* it.
Nosotros **nos habríamos quedado** más tiempo.	We *would have stayed* longer.

The conditional perfect is also used to express probability in past time. It corresponds to the past perfect + *probably*.

Ya **se habría ido**, me imagino.	*He had probably left*, I imagine.

The perfect infinitive consists of the infinitive **haber** + past participle. It is used after prepositions and as the complement of some verbs.

Lorenzo ha sacado excelentes notas **por haber estudiado** tanto.	Lorenzo has gotten excellent grades *for having studied* so much (because he studied so much).
No recuerdo **haberlo visto**.	I don't remember *having seen him*.

M *No lo habríamos hecho. Escriba oraciones que expresan que Ud. y otras personas no habrían hecho las cosas que hicieron algunas personas. Siga el modelo.*

MODELO   Gregorio pidió el plato de langosta (*lobster*) con salsa de chocolate. (yo)
→ Yo no lo habría pedido.

1. Diego y Jaime salieron a la calle durante la tormenta. (Patricia y yo)

2. Tere rompió su compromiso con su novio. (Sofía)

3. Uds. hicieron el viaje a California en autobús. (los turistas venezolanos)

4. Ariana se cortó el pelo en la peluquería Melenas. (tú)

5. Nosotros creímos lo que nos dijo Baltasar. (Ud.)

6. Te reíste cuando se te cayeron los vasos. (yo)

N *¡Felicidades!* *Ud. es el maestro de ceremonias del programa del premio Óscar. Les presenta la estatuilla del Óscar a los ganadores de las diferentes categorías artísticas de las películas del año. Practique el uso del infinitivo compuesto* (perfect infinitive) *tras* (after) **por**. *Siga el modelo.*

MODELO   Maribel Sánchez / trabajar en *Alma y corazón*
          → A Maribel Sánchez por haber trabajado en *Alma y corazón*.

1. Lope Cernuda / dirigir *Plátanos y cerezas*

2. Ernesto del Olmo / componer la música de *Mosquitos mágicos*

3. Ela Pantoja y Roberto Campillo / escribir el guión de *Agua hervida*

4. Agustín Domingo / cantar en *Después de haber bailado*

5. Beatriz Perales / ser primera actriz (*leading lady*) en *Salchichas al sol*

6. Mateo de León y Diana Duque / producir *Grapadora en la mesa*

7. Silvia Siles / hacer la escenografía de *Narices al aire*

8. Memo Morado / actuar en *Langostas en el cielo*

9. Edit Revueltas / diseñar el vestuario de *Tijeras de poliéster*

10. Pepe del Oeste / maquillar a los actores de *Tamales quemados*

O *Expresar en español. Nuestra hacienda.* *Exprese en español sus conjeturas sobre la hacienda que tenía su familia. Escriba oraciones de probabilidad usando el potencial compuesto* (conditional perfect).

1. *The ranch* (La hacienda) *had probably been very big.*

2. *The farmers* (Los agricultores) *probably had had chickens in a chicken coop* (el gallinero).

3. *The farm workers had probably picked cherries and strawberries.*

4. *The landscape of the countryside had probably been beautiful.*

5. *My great-grandfather* (bisabuelo) *had probably gone fishing in the lake that was nearby.*

6. *My great-grandmother* (bisabuela) *had probably cooked fresh fruits and vegetables from the harvest.*

7. *There had probably been horses and cows on the ranch.*

8. *The farmers had probably sowed* (sembrar) *seeds in the vegetable garden.*

9. *We probably would have loved life on the ranch.*

P *Ejercicio oral. Diálogos.* *Hable con un amigo/una amiga de las cosas que Ud. ha hecho este año. Su amigo/amiga le dice lo que él/ella habría hecho este año. Por ejemplo: —Yo he estudiado marketing este año. —**Yo habría estudiado informática.** Se puede hablar de la familia y las celebraciones familiares, del trabajo, de los deportes, los pasatiempos, las vacaciones, etcétera.*

10

The Gerund and
the Progressive Tenses

Formation of the Gerund (Present Participle)

The gerund or **-ndo** form in Spanish corresponds to the *-ing* form in English. For **-ar** verbs, the ending of the gerund is **-ando**; for **-er** and **-ir** verbs, the ending is **-iendo**.

tomar	tom**ando**
hablar	habl**ando**
aprender	aprend**iendo**
comer	com**iendo**
escribir	escrib**iendo**
abrir	abr**iendo**

-Er and **-ir** verbs whose stems end in a vowel use **-yendo** and not **-iendo** to form the gerund.

caer	ca**yendo**
creer	cre**yendo**
leer	le**yendo**
oír	o**yendo**
traer	tra**yendo**

-Ir verbs that have a change in the vowel of the stem in the third person singular of the preterit have the same change in the gerund.

INFINITIVE	PRETERIT	GERUND
decir	dijo	**diciendo**
dormir	durmió	**durmiendo**
morir	murió	**muriendo**
pedir	pidió	**pidiendo**
repetir	repitió	**repitiendo**
sentir	sintió	**sintiendo**
servir	sirvió	**sirviendo**
venir	vino	**viniendo**

Poder and **ir** have irregular gerunds.

poder	**pudiendo**
ir	**yendo**

Object and reflexive pronouns are attached to the present participle in writing, and an accent mark is written over the **a** or **e** of the gerund ending.

esperándolo
dándomelos
viéndolas
levantándose

The gerund in Spanish is usually equivalent to an English clause or gerund phrase beginning with *by, while, if, when,* or *because.*

Se aprende mucho **estudiando** con el profesor Padilla.	*You learn a lot **studying** (**when you study**) with Professor Padilla.*
Viajando en marzo, Nicolás ahorró mucho dinero.	***By traveling** in March, Nicolás saved a lot of money.*

With verbs of perception, such as **ver**, **mirar**, **oír**, and **escuchar**, either the infinitive or the gerund can be used, as in English.

Los oímos cantar.
Los oímos cantando. ⎫ ⎬ ⎭   *We heard them sing. / We heard them singing.*

A *La vecina entrometida* **(busybody).** *Su vecina se mete en todo. Ahora quiere saber lo que Ud. y otras personas hicieron hoy porque no los vio en todo el día. Contéstele usando* **pasar** + *gerundio. Siga el modelo.*

MODELO   ¿Trabajó Ud. en la oficina hoy?
→ Sí, pasé el día trabajando en la oficina.

1. ¿Habló Ud. por teléfono hoy?

2. ¿Carlos y Celeste navegaron en la red hoy?

3. ¿Paquito durmió la siesta hoy?

4. ¿Uds. leyeron su correo electrónico hoy?

5. ¿Oíste las noticias hoy?

6. ¿Imprimisteis los documentos hoy?

B *¡Cómo va volando el tiempo!* **(How time flies!)** *Ud. piensa en las cosas que hizo ayer y en cuánto tiempo le llevó cada cosa. ¡Qué rápido se le fue el día! Escriba oraciones usando* **pasar** + *gerundio para describir su horario de ayer. Siga el modelo.*

MODELO   yo / desayunar (media hora)
→ Yo pasé media hora desayunando.

1. yo / arreglarse (cuarenta y cinco minutos)

2. Estrella y yo / montar en bicicleta (una hora y media)

3. yo / escribir un informe (dos horas)

4. Fernando, Chelo y yo / comprar cosas en el centro comercial (un par de horas)

5. mis amigos y yo / vestirse (treinta minutos)

6. yo / ver un documental (una hora)

The Progressive Tenses

The progressive tenses consist of the present, past, future, or conditional forms of the verb **estar** followed by the gerund.

PRESENT PROGRESSIVE	Estoy escuchando música.	*I'm listening to music.*
IMPERFECT PROGRESSIVE	Estaba escuchando música.	*I was listening to music.*
PRETERIT PROGRESSIVE	Estuve escuchando música hasta que salimos.	*I was listening to music until we went out.*
FUTURE PROGRESSIVE	Estaré escuchando música toda la tarde.	*I'll be listening to music all afternoon.*
CONDITIONAL PROGRESSIVE	Estaría escuchando música.	*I'd be listening to music.*

The gerunds of **estar**, **ir**, and **venir** are not commonly used in progressive constructions.

The present, imperfect, and future progressive are different from the corresponding simple tenses in that they emphasize that the action is or was in progress. They may also suggest that the action is temporary, not habitual, or represents a change from the usual pattern.

Miguel juega al fútbol.	*Miguel plays soccer.* (habitual action)
Miguel está jugando al fútbol.	*Miguel's playing soccer.* (He's playing soccer right now OR He's begun to play soccer.)

The preterit progressive is used to show an action that was in progress in the past but is now completed.

Estuvimos estudiando latín hasta que Óscar vino a buscarnos.	*We were studying Latin until Oscar came to pick us up.*

The present progressive in Spanish can never refer to the future as the present progressive in English does. To express future time, Spanish uses the simple present, the **ir a** + infinitive construction, or the future tense.

Sacamos los boletos mañana.
Vamos a sacar los boletos mañana. } ***We're buying*** *the tickets tomorrow.*
Sacaremos los boletos mañana.

In the progressive tenses, object and reflexive pronouns may either precede the form of **estar** or be attached to the gerund in writing, in which case a written accent is added.

Isabel y Juan están paseándo**se**. } *Isabel and Juan are strolling.*
Isabel y Juan **se** están paseando.

The verb **seguir** is used with the gerund to mean *to be still doing something, to keep on doing something.*

Marta **sigue despertándose** antes de las seis.	*Marta **is still waking up** before six o'clock.*
Sigan buscando la llave.	***Keep on looking for*** *the key.*

Ir is commonly used with the gerund as well. It is used to convey the idea of *gradually* or *little by little*.

La empresa **va prosperando**.

The company **is gradually prospering**.

Las flores **se fueron secando** poco a poco.

The flowers **withered away** little by little.

C *En el campamento* (camp) *de verano.* *Use el presente progresivo para describir lo que están haciendo los niños en un día típico en el campamento. Siga el modelo.*

MODELO   Eva y Ángela trabajan en un campamento.
→ Eva y Ángela están trabajando en un campamento.

En el campamento

acampar *to camp*	**la linterna** *flashlight*
apagar el fuego *to put out the fire*	**la mochila** *backpack, knapsack*
la araña *spider*	**el mosquito** *mosquito*
asar *to roast*	**nadar** *to swim*
atrapar *to catch*	**el perro caliente** *hot dog*
desenvolver (o > ue) *to unroll*	**la picadura** *bite*
encender (e > ie) el fuego *to light the fire*	**la pila** *battery*
la hormiga *ant*	**el saco de dormir** *sleeping bag*
el hormiguero *anthill*	**la serpiente** *snake*
ir de camping *to go camping*	**la sierra** *mountains*
el lago *lake*	**la tienda de campaña** *tent*

1. Los niños acampan en la sierra.

2. Ricardo nada en el lago.

3. Lupe y yo llenamos la mochila.

4. Ester desenvuelve el saco de dormir.

5. Ud. y Andrés juegan al fútbol.

6. Pablo se acuesta en el saco de dormir.

7. Yo observo las hormigas en el hormiguero.

8. Tú enciendes el fuego para asar los perros calientes.

9. Vosotros metéis las pilas en la linterna.

10. Todos nosotros nos quejamos de las picaduras de los mosquitos.

11. Ud. se asusta al ver las arañas en la tienda de campaña.

12. Consuelo grita al ver una serpiente.

D **Acciones en progreso.** *Escriba oraciones usando el presente, el imperfecto o el futuro progresivo. Cambie los sustantivos a pronombres de complemento directo. Escriba cada oración de dos maneras. Siga el modelo.*

MODELO Carlos practica el ruso.
→ Está practicándolo.
Lo está practicando.

1. Leíamos los periódicos.

2. Uds. harán las maletas.

3. Me pongo el traje.

4. Ud. se lavaba la cabeza.

5. Nos dirás los planes.

6. Rita se abrocha el cinturón de seguridad.

7. Les servíamos los tacos.

E **Cuando estalló (broke out) el fuego,...** *Cuando estalló el fuego en la cocina del Hotel Dos Reyes en Cartagena, los huéspedes y los empleados del hotel estaban haciendo varias cosas. Describa lo que estaban haciendo usando el imperfecto progresivo. Escriba cada oración de dos maneras cuando sea posible. Siga el modelo.*

MODELO el señor Escudero / bañarse
→ El señor Escudero estaba bañándose.
El señor Escudero se estaba bañando.

En el hotel

el aire acondicionado *air conditioning*
el ascensor *elevator*
el botones *bellhop*
la camarera *hotel housekeeper, hotel cleaner*
el equipaje *luggage*
el gerente *manager*
el huésped *guest* (in a hotel)
el juego de toallas *set of towels*

el lavado *wash*
la lavandera *laundry woman*
el mesero *waiter*
el noveno piso *ninth floor*
la recepción *check-in desk*
registrarse *to check in*
tocar el timbre *to ring the bell*

1. los señores Sotomayor / registrarse

2. la señorita Serrano / pedir un juego de toallas

3. el botones / subirles el equipaje a unos huéspedes

4. las camareras / arreglar los cuartos

5. los meseros / servirles la cena a los clientes

6. el gerente / prender el aire acondicionado

7. el doctor López / afeitarse

8. la lavandera / devolverle el lavado a la señora Casona

9. los huéspedes del noveno piso / bajar en el ascensor

10. los turistas ingleses / tocar el timbre en la recepción

11. los cocineros / jactarse de los plátanos flameados que habían preparado

---

NOTA CULTURAL

La ciudad colombiana de **Cartagena** queda al noroeste del país en el mar Caribe. Fue fundada por Pedro de Heredia en 1533. Es un puerto importante que fue una de las bases principales en la colonización. Cartagena servía de almacén para las mercancías y riquezas que España recogía en sus colonias americanas destinadas a España y para mercancías enviadas a las colonias de España. Se construyeron murallas y fortalezas alrededor de la ciudad para protegerla de ataques por piratas.

F *¡Qué va! Siguen haciéndolo.* *Su amiga acaba de volver de Bogotá donde pasó un semestre estudiando español. Ella supone que ha habido muchos cambios mientras estaba en el extranjero. Ud. le dice que todo sigue siendo igual. Escriba oraciones usando* **seguir** *+ gerundio. Cambie los sustantivos que son complementos directos a pronombres. Siga el modelo.*

MODELO   Ya no estudias química, ¿verdad?
      → ¡Qué va! Sigo estudiándola.

1. Elena ya no dice chismes (*gossip*), ¿verdad?

2. Ya no construyen la autopista, ¿verdad?

3. Ya no lees ciencia-ficción, ¿verdad?

4. Tus hermanos ya no elaboran el presupuesto, ¿verdad?

5. Ud. ya no asiste a los conciertos de jazz, ¿verdad?

6. Nosotros, los Gatos Azules, ya no jugamos al fútbol en el estadio, ¿verdad?

NOTA CULTURAL

Bogotá, capital de Colombia, se encuentra en un altiplano a 2.650 metros de alto. Santa Fe de Bogotá, su nombre original, fue fundada por Gonzalo Jiménez de Quesada en 1538. La ciudad siempre ha sido el centro principal del país desde la Conquista. Lo más interesante de la ciudad es el centro histórico llamado La Candelaria. En este barrio se encuentra la Plaza Bolívar donde hay una estatua del Libertador, Simón Bolívar (1783–1830), el general y estadista venezolano que fue responsable por la independencia de Colombia, Venezuela y otros países hispanoamericanos de España, la madre patria.

G *Nosotros, los trasnochadores* (night owls). *A Ud. y a sus amigos les gusta trasnochar* (stay up all night). *Escriba oraciones usando el futuro progresivo para describir lo que Uds. estarán haciendo a esas horas. Siga el modelo.*

> MODELO   yo / hablar por celular / a la una de la mañana
> → Yo estaré hablando por celular a la una de la mañana.

1. Luisa / ver televisión / a las dos y media

2. Ud. / ducharse / a medianoche

3. mis amigos y yo / morirnos de sueño / a las cuatro

4. Pablo y Ramón / jugar videojuegos / a las doce y media

5. yo / escuchar música / a la una y media

6. tú / comer una pizza / a las tres

7. Uds. / enviarme un email / a las cinco

The Progressive Tenses with **llevar** to Express "Have Been Doing"

In addition to **hace** + expression of time + **que** + verb in the present tense, Spanish expresses actions that begin in the past and continue into the present with the present tense of **llevar** + gerund.

> **Llevo** tres años **estudiando** español. ⎫
> Hace tres años que estudio español. ⎬   *I've been studying Spanish for three years.*
> Estudio español desde hace tres años. ⎭

The gerund of **estar** is never used in a **llevar** + gerund construction. **Llevar** is used by itself to express *to have been*.

> **Llevo** dos horas aquí.   *I've been here for two hours.*

H *Una entrevista.* *Un periodista le entrevista al famoso pintor-escultor peruano Pablo de Lima. Conteste las preguntas usando la construcción* **llevar** + *gerundio. Siga el modelo.*

> MODELO   ¿Cuánto tiempo hace que Ud. hace esculturas? (quince años)
> → Llevo quince años haciendo esculturas.

La pintura

abstracto *abstract*	**el/la modelo** *model*
la cerámica *ceramics*	**el mural** *mural*
el cuadro *painting*	**el paisaje** *landscape*
dibujar *to draw*	**el pincel** *paintbrush*
el dibujo *drawing*	**pintar** *to paint*
el escultor/la escultora *sculptor*	**el pintor/la pintora** *painter*
la escultura *sculpture*	**la pintura** *painting; paint*
la galería *gallery*	**el retrato** *portrait*

1. ¿Cuánto tiempo hace que Ud. pinta retratos? (doce años)

2. ¿Cuánto tiempo hace que Ud. usa estos pinceles? (unos meses)

3. ¿Cuánto tiempo hace que Ud. dibuja con modelos? (varios años)

4. ¿Cuánto tiempo hace que Ud. se dedica a la pintura? (treinta años)

5. ¿Cuánto tiempo hace que Ud. vende sus cuadros de paisajes por Internet? (un año)

6. ¿Cuánto tiempo hace que Ud. se interesa en los murales? (poco tiempo)

7. ¿Cuánto tiempo hace que Ud. trabaja en cerámica? (nueve años)

8. ¿Cuánto tiempo hace que Ud. vive en Nueva York? (cinco años)

NOTA CULTURAL

Lima, capital del Perú, queda a orillas del río Rímac, no muy lejos del océano Pacífico. La ciudad fue fundada como "La ciudad de los Reyes" por Francisco Pizarro, conquistador español, en 1535. Lima tuvo una enorme importancia durante la época de la colonia hasta que Perú se independizó de España en 1821. Hay mucho que ver en Lima incluso la Universidad Nacional Mayor de San Marcos (fundada en 1551); la Catedral e iglesias; edificios públicos y casas históricas. Hay varios museos de las culturas precolombinas e historia peruana desde la Conquista—el Museo Nacional de Antropología y Arqueología, el Museo Oro del Perú y Armas del Mundo, el Museo Nacional de Historia y el Museo del Tribunal de la Santa Inquisición.

I   *Un partido de fútbol.* *Un locutor de televisión describe un partido de fútbol. Complete las oraciones usando el presente progresivo de los verbos indicados. Siga el modelo.*

    MODELO   Los aficionados ___*están*___ ___*llegando*___ al estadio. (llegar)

1. Los aficionados _____ _____ a sus equipos. (animar (*to cheer*))

2. Redondo _____ _____ el balón (*ball*). (robar)

3. Nosotros _____ _____ un partido emocionante. (ver)

4. Manrique _____ _____ un gol. (marcar (*to score*))

5. Los entrenadores (*trainers*) _____ _____ al campo de fútbol. (salir)

6. Cuéllar _____ _____ el balón. (regatear (*to dribble*))

7. Los técnicos (*coaches*) _____ _____ un gran esfuerzo a los jugadores. (pedirles)

8. Los aficionados _____ _____. (entusiasmarse)

9. Uds., los televidentes, _____ _____ los gritos de los aficionados. (oír)

10. Este partido de campeonato _____ _____ mucha atención. (atraer)

J **Expresar en español.** *Exprese las oraciones en español usando los tiempos progresivos.*

1. *We're having a wonderful time.*

2. *You (Ud.) were jogging until it began to rain.* [*use preterit progressive*]

3. *They're still serving dinner at the Hotel Palacio.*

4. *I'm getting to know Madrid little by little.*

5. *Mateo and Victoria will be playing tennis all afternoon.*

6. *Pedro and I kept on reading.*

K **Ejercicio oral. ¿Qué están haciendo?** *Use el presente progresivo para describir lo que Ud. y sus familiares y amigos están haciendo en este momento.*

The Subjunctive in Noun Clauses: Present and Present Perfect Subjunctive

Forms of the Present Subjunctive: Regular Verbs

The present subjunctive is formed by changing the vowel -a- of the present indicative to -e- in -ar verbs and the vowels -e- and -i- of the present indicative to -a- in -er and -ir verbs. Regular -er and -ir verbs have identical endings in all persons of the subjunctive.

estudiar

Quiere que estudie idiomas.	*He wants me to study languages.*
estudies	*He wants you to study languages.*
estudie	*He wants her to study languages.*
estudiemos	*He wants us to study languages.*
estudiéis	*He wants you to study languages.*
estudien	*He wants them to study languages.*

comprender

Espera que comprenda.	*She hopes I'll understand.*
comprendas	*She hopes you'll understand.*
comprenda	*She hopes he'll understand.*
comprendamos	*She hopes we'll understand.*
comprendáis	*She hopes you'll understand.*
comprendan	*She hopes they'll understand.*

vivir

Prefieren que viva aquí.	*They prefer that I live here.*
vivas	*They prefer that you live here.*
viva	*They prefer that she live here.*
vivamos	*They prefer that we live here.*
viváis	*They prefer that you live here.*
vivan	*They prefer that they live here.*

In the present subjunctive, the first person singular (**yo**) form and the third person singular (**él/ella/usted**) forms are identical.

-**Ar** and -**er** verbs that have changes in the vowel of the stem in the present indicative have these same changes in the present subjunctive.

Le aconsejan que pi**e**nse más.	*They advise her to think more.*
Nos aconsejan que pensemos más.	*They advise us to think more.*
Espera que yo enc**ue**ntre las llaves.	*He hopes that I find the keys.*
Espera que encontremos las llaves.	*He hopes that we find the keys.*

-Ir verbs that have the change **e > ie** or **e > i** in the present indicative have the same changes in the present subjunctive. However, unlike the present indicative, these verbs also have the **e > i** stem change in the **nosotros/nosotras** and **vosotros/vosotras** forms in the present subjunctive. **Dormir** and **morir** have the **o > ue** change in the present subjunctive, but they also have the **o > u** stem change in the **nosotros/nosotras** and **vosotros/vosotras** forms.

sentir		seguir		dormir	
si**e**nta	sintamos	si**g**a	sigamos	d**ue**rma	d**u**rmamos
si**e**ntas	sintáis	si**g**as	sigáis	d**ue**rmas	d**u**rmáis
si**e**nta	si**e**ntan	si**g**a	sigan	d**ue**rma	d**ue**rman

Verbs ending in **-iar** or **-uar** that have an accent mark on the **-i-** or **-u-** in the present indicative in all forms except **nosotros/nosotras** and **vosotros/vosotras** have an accent mark in the same persons of the present subjunctive. See Chapter 3 for more information on stem-changing verbs.

enviar		continuar	
env**í**e	enviemos	contin**ú**e	continuemos
env**í**es	enviéis	contin**ú**es	continuéis
env**í**e	env**í**en	contin**ú**e	contin**ú**en

A ***¡Pero yo sí quiero!*** *Un amigo suyo le menciona varias cosas que no suceden. Ud. le dice que quiere que pasen. Escriba oraciones usando el presente del modo* (mood) *subjuntivo. Siga el modelo.*

MODELO   Alicia no estudia química.
          → Pero yo quiero que estudie química.

1. Marcos no trabaja en el informe.

2. Yo no consigo empleo.

3. Federico y Paula no nos escriben.

4. Juanita no sigue nuestros consejos.

5. Nosotros no comemos fuera hoy.

6. Yo no vuelvo temprano.

7. Los niños no duermen la siesta.

8. Tú y yo no pedimos taxi.

9. No abren la tienda hoy.

10. Juan no entiende.

11. Amalia no piensa en nosotros.

12. La oficina no envía el paquete.

13. Yo no cierro las ventanas.

14. Tú y yo no nos divertimos.

15. No se gradúan este año.

Forms of the Present Subjunctive: Irregular Verbs

Verbs that have an irregularity such as -**g**- or -**zc**- in the **yo** form of the present indicative have that irregularity in all persons of the present subjunctive. These irregularities occur only in -**er** and -**ir** verbs, and therefore the present subjunctive endings of these irregular verbs all have the vowel -**a**-.

Here is a table of -**g**- verbs.

INFINITIVE	PRESENT INDICATIVE (**yo** FORM)	PRESENT SUBJUNCTIVE
caer	**caig**o	caiga, caigas, caiga, caigamos, caigáis, caigan
decir	**dig**o	diga, digas, diga, digamos, digáis, digan
hacer	**hag**o	haga, hagas, haga, hagamos, hagáis, hagan
oír	**oig**o	oiga, oigas, oiga, oigamos, oigáis, oigan
poner	**pong**o	ponga, pongas, ponga, pongamos, pongáis, pongan
salir	**salg**o	salga, salgas, salga, salgamos, salgáis, salgan
tener	**teng**o	tenga, tengas, tenga, tengamos, tengáis, tengan
traer	**traig**o	traiga, traigas, traiga, traigamos, traigáis, traigan
venir	**veng**o	venga, vengas, venga, vengamos, vengáis, vengan

Here is a table of the present subjunctive of other verbs that are irregular in the **yo** form.

INFINITIVE	PRESENT INDICATIVE (**yo** FORM)	PRESENT SUBJUNCTIVE
caber	**quep**o	quepa, quepas, quepa, quepamos, quepáis, quepan
conocer	**conozc**o	conozca, conozcas, conozca, conozcamos, conozcáis, conozcan
nacer	**nazc**o	nazca, nazcas, nazca, nazcamos, nazcáis, nazcan
parecer	**parezc**o	parezca, parezcas, parezca, parezcamos, parezcáis, parezcan
construir	**construy**o	construya, construyas, construya, construyamos, construyáis, construyan
destruir	**destruy**o	destruya, destruyas, destruya, destruyamos, destruyáis, destruyan
ver	**ve**o	vea, veas, vea, veamos, veáis, vean

Dar and **estar** are regular in the present subjunctive except for the accent marks. The first and third person singular forms of **dar** have the written accent (**dé**) and all of the present subjunctive forms of **estar** have the written accent, except the first person plural form **estemos**.

dar		estar	
dé	demos	**esté**	estemos
des	deis	**estés**	**estéis**
dé	den	**esté**	**estén**

Haber, **ir**, **saber**, and **ser** have irregular stems in the present subjunctive. However, their endings are regular.

INFINITIVE	SUBJUNCTIVE STEM	PRESENT SUBJUNCTIVE
haber	**hay-**	haya, hayas, haya, hayamos, hayáis, hayan
ir	**vay-**	vaya, vayas, vaya, vayamos, vayáis, vayan
saber	**sep-**	sepa, sepas, sepa, sepamos, sepáis, sepan
ser	**se-**	sea, seas, sea, seamos, seáis, sean

B   *Le parece muy bien.* *María se alegra de muchas cosas. Diga lo que son usando el presente de subjuntivo. Siga el modelo.*

MODELO   ¿Sabe María que viene Juan Carlos?
    → Sí. Se alegra de que venga.

1. ¿Sabe María que conoces a Pedro?
2. ¿Sabe María que tenemos un día libre?
3. ¿Sabe María que Alfredo le trae flores?
4. ¿Sabe María que te mudas al centro?
5. ¿Sabe María que los Ibáñez construyen una casa?
6. ¿Sabe María que Marcos y Julia salen juntos?
7. ¿Sabe María que tú y yo oímos música clásica?
8. ¿Sabe María que Uds. hacen un viaje?
9. ¿Sabe María que Raquel compone música?
10. ¿Sabe María que la fiesta es mañana?
11. ¿Sabe María que hay reunión la semana que viene?
12. ¿Sabe María que sus primos van a España?

Spelling Changes in the Present Subjunctive

1 · -**Ar** verbs whose stems end in -**c**, -**g**, or -**z** change those letters as follows in the present subjunctive.

c > qu
g > gu
z > c

Bus**c**amos casa.	→ Es necesario que bus**que**mos casa.
Lle**g**an el lunes.	→ Espero que lle**gue**n el lunes.
Almor**z**amos aquí.	→ Prefiero que almor**ce**mos aquí.

2 · -**Er** and -**ir** verbs whose stems end in -**g**, -**gu**, or -**c** change those letters as follows in the present subjunctive.

g > j
gu > g
c > z

Esco**g**es otro plato.	→ Queremos que esco**j**as otro plato.
Si**gu**en andando.	→ Es posible que si**g**an andando.
Te conven**c**e su idea.	→ Espero que te conven**z**a su idea.

3 · -**Ar** verbs whose stems end in -**j** do not change **j** to **g** before **e**.

Traba**j**o los domingos. → Quieren que traba**j**e los domingos.

4 · Irregular verbs such as **hacer** and **conocer** don't follow the spelling change in the second rule above, but instead have the irregularities of the **yo** form of the present indicative. See "Forms of the Present Subjunctive: Irregular Verbs" in this chapter.

Ha**c**es la cena.	→ Quiero que ha**g**as la cena.
Cono**c**en a Marta.	→ No creo que cono**zc**an a Marta.

C *Ortografía* (Spelling). *Complete las oraciones usando el presente de subjuntivo de los verbos indicados. Recuerde los cambios ortográficos.*

1. Espero que tú _____ (realizar) tus planes.

2. Es necesario que Uds. _____ (acercarse) más.

3. ¡Qué lástima que _____ (comenzar) a llover!

4. Se alegran de que yo _____ (dirigir) la orquesta.

5. Es probable que los chicos _____ (sacar) muy buenas notas.

6. Nos piden que _____ (recoger) las manzanas.

7. Es importante que Ud. _____ (dedicarse) a los negocios.

8. Me extraña que Vera no _____ (explicar) lo que pasó.

9. Te aconsejamos que _____ (entregar) el informe mañana.

10. Ojalá que Daniel _____ (conseguir) el puesto.

11. Tal vez Uds. _____ (organizar) la reunión.

12. No creo que Bárbara _____ (almorzar) antes de las dos.

13. Es difícil que yo los _____ (convencer).

14. Quieren que nosotros _____ (apagar) las luces.

15. Tenemos miedo de que los soldados no _____ (vencer) a sus enemigos.

Use of the Present Subjunctive in Noun Clauses

A noun clause is a clause that functions as a noun, that is, it can serve as either the subject or the object of a verb. Noun clauses that are incorporated into a longer sentence are called dependent or subordinate clauses and are introduced in Spanish by the conjunction **que**.

The Spanish tenses studied in previous chapters belong to the indicative mood. Verbs in the indicative mood express events or states that are considered factual, definite, or part of the speaker's experienced reality. The following examples have dependent noun clauses in the indicative. They show events perceived as part of reality because they are the objects of verbs such as **saber**, **parecer**, **oír**, and **ver**.

Sabes **que lo hizo Sandra**.	*You know **that Sandra did it**.*
Nos parece **que está lloviendo**.	*We think **it's raining**.*
He oído **que hay una buena noticia**.	*I've heard **there's good news**.*
Verán **que Juan no entiende**.	*You'll see **that Juan doesn't understand**.*

The present subjunctive in Spanish is used in dependent noun clauses that mark events or states that the speaker considers not part of reality or of his or her experience. These dependent noun clauses follow main clauses that express, as in the examples below, (1) expectation, skepticism, doubt, uncertainty; (2) demands, wants, needs, insistence, advice, impositions of will; (3) negated facts. The verbs in the main clauses are in the present, present perfect, future, or imperative.

(1) **Dudo** que Uds. **lleguen** para las tres.	*I **doubt** you'll **arrive** by three o'clock.*
(2) Paula **quiere** que la **visites**.	*Paula **wants** you **to visit** her.*
Le **hemos aconsejado** que **vuelva**.	*We've **advised** him **to come back**.*
Le **pediré** que me **acompañe**.	*I'll **ask** her **to go with** me.*
Insiste en que **paguen** la cuenta.	***Insist** that they **pay** the bill.*
(3) **No es cierto** que **nos quedemos**.	***It's not certain** that **we'll stay**.*

Verbs such as **desear** (*to want*), **esperar** (*to hope*), **insistir en** (*to insist on*), **necesitar** (*to need*), **preferir** (*to prefer*), and **querer** (*to want*) are followed by a dependent noun clause in the subjunctive unless the subjects of both clauses are the same. In that case, the verb in the dependent clause should be in the infinitive.

Verb in Main Clause + Dependent Noun Clause in Subjunctive (Two Clauses: Two Different Subjects)

Espero que Roberto **vaya.**	*I hope Roberto goes.*
Quieren que **salgamos.**	*They want us to go out.*
Insistimos en que Uds. **se queden.**	*We insist that you stay.*

Verb in Main Clause + Infinitive (the Same Subject in Both Parts of the Sentence)

Espero ir.	*I hope to go.*
Quieren salir.	*They want to go out.*
Insistimos en quedarnos.	*We insist on staying.*

The verbs **decir** (*to tell someone to do something*) and **pedir** (*to ask someone to do something*) are followed by a subjunctive clause. They may occur with an indirect object.

Le dicen a Felipe que **tenga** cuidado.	*They tell Felipe to be careful.*
Susana **nos pide** que **traigamos** el periódico.	*Susana asks us to bring the newspaper.*

Decir is followed by a dependent clause in the indicative when the dependent clause reports what someone said. For example, **José les dice: Leo mucho. Decir** is followed by a dependent clause in the subjunctive when it introduces a command, such as **José les dice: Lean mucho.** Contrast the use of the indicative and subjunctive after **decir.**

José les dice que **lee** mucho.	*José tells them he reads a lot.*
José les dice que **lean** mucho.	*José tells them to read a lot.*

Some verbs can be followed either by a noun clause in the subjunctive or by an infinitive without a change in meaning. These verbs include **aconsejar** (*to advise*), **exigir** (*to demand*), **impedir** (*to prevent*), **mandar** (*to order*), **permitir** (*to permit*), **prohibir** (*to forbid*), **recomendar** (*to recommend*), **rogar** (*to request, beg*), and **sugerir** (*to suggest*).

(Les) aconsejo que **tomen** el tren. **Les aconsejo tomar** el tren.	*I advise you to take the train.*
(Le) exigimos a Beatriz que **regrese.** **Le exigimos** a Beatriz **regresar.**	*We demand that Beatriz return.*

The verb **dejar** (*to let, allow*) can also be followed either by a noun clause in the subjunctive or by an infinitive without a change in meaning. **Dejar** takes a direct object pronoun before a subjunctive clause.

(Los) **dejan** que **entren.** Los **dejan entrar.**	*They let them come in.*

Some verbs that express an emotional state, an attitude, or a bias are followed by dependent noun clauses in the subjunctive. These verbs include **alegrarse (de)** (*to be glad/happy*), **extrañar** (*to surprise*), **gustar** (*to like*), **sentir** (*to regret*), **sorprender** (*to surprise*), **temer** (*to fear*), and **tener miedo (de)** (*to be afraid (of)*).

Me alegro (de) que Uds. **visiten** Lima.	*I'm glad that you're visiting Lima.*
¿No **te extraña** que Claudia no **llame**?	*Aren't you surprised that Claudia doesn't call?*
Los Ayala **temen** que sus hijos no **saquen** buenas notas.	*Mr. and Mrs. Ayala are afraid their children aren't getting good grades.*

Gustar, **extrañar**, and **sorprender** are usually used with an indirect object pronoun. (See Chapter 19 on the indirect object.)

In addition to the subordinate clauses introduced in this section by the subordinating conjunction **que**, Spanish also has coordinating conjunctions that connect clauses. The most common of these are **y** (*and*) and two Spanish equivalents of *but*, **pero** and **sino**.

The usual Spanish equivalent of English *but* is **pero**.

Yo voy, **pero** él, no.	*I'm going, but he's not.*
Dicen que la película es interesante, **pero** a mí no me gustó.	*They say that the film is interesting, but I didn't like it.*

After a negative, however, *but* is rendered **sino** when a contradiction is introduced. The meaning is *but rather, but instead.*

No lo hicimos nosotros, **sino** ellos.	*We didn't do it, but rather they did.*
No pedí helado, **sino** pastel.	*I didn't order ice cream, but rather pastry.*
El regalo no es para ti, **sino** para ella.	*The gift is not for you, but for her.*
Él no es inteligente, **sino** astuto.	*He is not intelligent, but sly.*
No me interesa ése, **sino** éste.	*I'm not interested in that one, but rather this one.*

Before a clause, **sino que** is used.

Ella no es estudiante, **sino que** ya trabaja.	*She's not a student, but rather is already working.*
Ellos no nos molestan, **sino que** nos ayudan.	*They aren't bothering us, but instead they are helping us.*
Los héroes no nacen, **sino que** se hacen.	*Heroes are not born, but rather made.*

Pero is used after a negative when the information that follows it doesn't negate what precedes, but instead adds something to it.

Yo no comprendí, **pero** ella, sí.	*I didn't understand, but she did.*
Él no es francés, **pero** conoce bien Francia.	*He's not French, but he knows France well.*

Sino (que) appears in the phrase **no sólo/solamente/solo... sino también** (*not only . . . but also*).

Vino no sólo él, **sino** también su esposa.	*Not only did he come, but his wife (did) too.*
No sólo robó, **sino que** también mató.	*He not only robbed, but he also killed.*

Note that a comma is written before **pero** and **sino**.

D *¿Indicativo o subjuntivo?* *Complete las oraciones usando el presente de indicativo o el presente de subjuntivo de los verbos indicados. Siga los modelos.*

MODELOS   Creo que Fernando __*llega*__ (llegar) el miércoles.

Prefiero que Fernando __*llegue*__ (llegar) el miércoles.

1. Daniel quiere que nosotros le _____ (decir) lo que pasó.

2. Vemos que estos chicos _____ (aprender) muchas fechas de memoria.

3. Siento que Javier no _____ (graduarse) este año.

4. Nos extraña que Uds. no _____ (comenzar) el trabajo.

5. Piensan que tú _____ (quejarse) de todo.

6. Mis padres insisten en que yo _____ (matricularse) lo antes posible.

7. Me alegro de que vosotros _____ (ir) a casaros.

8. Parece que Ud. no _____ (salir) hasta más tarde.

9. ¿Sabes que Raquel _____ (tener) mucho éxito?

10. Isabel comprende que nosotros no _____ (poder) ayudarla.

11. Le aconsejamos a Diego que _____ (ser) más responsable.

12. Les gusta que ya no _____ (haber) problemas con la casa.

13. Todo el mundo entiende que Uds. _____ (estar) ocupadísimos.

14. Yo exijo que tú me _____ (hacer) caso.

15. Pedro cree que yo lo _____ (saber) todo.

16. Debes darte cuenta de que ya no se _____ (conseguir) ese libro.

E *¡Viva México!* *Ud. y sus amigos están emocionados pensando en el viaje que van a hacer a México durante el verano. Escriba oraciones que expresen lo que quieren hacer en México. El sujeto de la cláusula principal y el de la subordinada (dependiente) deben ser el mismo. Use la construcción de verbo conjugado + infinitivo. Siga el modelo.*

MODELO   yo / querer / ver las pirámides de San Juan de Teotihuacán
→ Yo quiero ver las pirámides de San Juan de Teotihuacán.

1. Laura / esperar / perfeccionar su español

2. Ricardo y Beti / preferir / visitar la Catedral Metropolitana de la Ciudad de México

3. Ud. / deber / conocer Taxco

4. Pablo y yo / desear / ir a Puebla

5. tú / preferir / hacer una excursión a la Ciudad Universitaria

6. yo / sentir / no poder quedarme más tiempo en el Bosque de Chapultepec

7. Uds. / insistir en / escaparse un par de días a Mérida

8. todos nosotros / alegrarse de / estar en Oaxaca

NOTA CULTURAL

- **La Catedral Metropolitana de la Ciudad de México**, la más vieja y más grande de Latinoamérica, queda a un costado (*side*) del Zócalo, la Plaza Mayor de la zona más antigua de la ciudad. Fue el sitio del gran templo mayor de los aztecas, una civilización prehispánica o precolombina, es decir, que habitaba la región antes de la llegada de Cristóbal Colón. Los aztecas fundaron su capital de Tenochtitlán en 1325 que fue conquistada y destruida por los españoles en 1521. En ese mismo lugar los españoles empezaron la construcción de la catedral en 1573.
- **Mérida.** Capital del estado mexicano de Yucatán en la península de Yucatán, Mérida fue fundada en 1542 en el sitio de la ciudad maya de Tihoo. Esta península de la América Central, que queda entre el golfo de México y el mar Caribe, es un centro de turismo conocido por su arqueología maya y sus playas.
- **Oaxaca.** Esta pintoresca (*picturesque*) ciudad de arquitectura del siglo XVII y mercados indígenas queda a 531 kilómetros al sureste de la Ciudad de México.
- **Puebla (de los Ángeles).** "La ciudad de los Ángeles," una de las ciudades más antiguas y más famosas de México, queda al sur de la Ciudad de México. Es una ciudad colonial conocida por su catedral, iglesias y vistas de los volcanes.
- **San Juan de Teotihuacán** es un gran sitio arqueológico que queda en el Valle de México a unos 45 kilómetros al nordeste de la Ciudad de México. Fue un importante centro comercial, religioso y cultural de la civilización teotihuacana, una de las más importantes de Mesoamérica (*Middle America* (México y unos países de Centroamérica)). Lo que queda de la civilización teotihuacana, de orígenes desconocidos, son las increíbles pirámides: la Pirámide del Sol que se construyó a fines del siglo primero y la Pirámide de la Luna que se terminó alrededor del siglo dos.
- **Taxco.** Esta ciudad colonial muy pintoresca queda al sur de la Ciudad de México. El primer envío (*shipment*) de plata enviado a España desde el Nuevo Mundo fue de las minas de Taxco. Muchos turistas van a Taxco por los monumentos, las vistas y las platerías (*silversmiths*).

F **Con los amigos en México.** *Escriba oraciones que expresen lo que Ud. quiere que hagan los otros amigos en México. El sujeto de la cláusula principal es diferente del sujeto de la subordinada. Use el presente de subjuntivo. Siga el modelo.*

MODELO   yo / querer : Paco y Mari / ver las pirámides de San Juan de Teotihuacán
→ Yo quiero que Paco y Mari vean las pirámides de San Juan de Teotihuacán.

1. Laura / esperar : nosotros / perfeccionar nuestro español

2. Ricardo y Beti / preferir : Ud. / visitar la Catedral Metropolitana de la Ciudad de México

3. Ud. / necesitar : Leo / conocer Taxco

4. Pablo y yo / desear : Uds. / ir a Puebla

5. a ti / gustar : yo / hacer una excursión a la Ciudad Universitaria

6. yo / sentir : nosotros / no poder quedarse más tiempo en el Bosque de Chapultepec

7. Uds. / insistir en : los cuates (*pals (Mexico)*) / escaparse un par de días a Mérida

8. todos nosotros / alegrarse de : tú / estar en Oaxaca

G *Una familia unida* (**close**). *Los miembros de la familia Ayala son muy unidos. Todos se quieren mucho y comparten sus pensamientos y sentimientos. Escriba oraciones que expresen lo que quieren para los demás miembros de la familia. Use el presente de subjuntivo. Siga el modelo.*

MODELO   el abuelo / desear : su familia / vivir bien
　　　　　→ El abuelo desea que su familia viva bien.

Lazos familiares (*Family ties*)

la ahijada *goddaughter*	**el nieto** *grandson*
el ahijado *godson*	**los nietos** *grandchildren*
los ahijados *godchildren*	**la novia** *bride, fiancée*
la bisabuela *great-grandmother*	**el novio** *groom, fiancé*
el bisabuelo *great-grandfather*	**los recién casados** *newlyweds*
los bisabuelos *great-grandparents*	**la madrina** *godmother*
la cuñada *sister-in-law*	**el padrino** *godfather*
el cuñado *brother-in-law*	**los padrinos** *godparents*
los familiares *relatives*	**la suegra** *mother-in-law*
la nieta *granddaughter*	**el suegro** *father-in-law*

1. Elena / esperar : sus cuñados / tener éxito

2. el señor Ayala / pedirles : sus suegros / venir a verlos los domingos

3. la madrina / alegrarse : su ahijado / sacar buenas notas en el colegio

4. los padres / querer : sus hijos / ganarse la vida (*to earn a living*)

5. a la señora Ayala / gustarle : los bisabuelos / ser felices en la tercera edad (*old age*)

6. yo / aconsejarle : la nieta / hacerse arquitecta

7. Terencio / prohibirles : las ahijadas / ir solas al extranjero

8. tú / sentir : tu cuñado / no estar contento con el nuevo empleo

9. la suegra / preferir : los recién casados / mudarse con ella

10. Uds. / rogarles : los padrinos / aceptar su regalo

11. Ricardo y yo / necesitar : los nietos / darnos muchos besos y abrazos

12. los hijos / no dejar : sus padres / trabajar demasiado manteniéndolos

H *Un correo electrónico.* *Ana María Vázquez vive en Bogotá, Colombia. Le escribe un email a su amiga Isabel García que vive en Los Ángeles. Para enterarse de lo que Ana María escribe, complete las oraciones usando el presente de subjuntivo o el presente de indicativo de los verbos indicados.*

Querida Isabel:

Espero que tú _____ (1. encontrarse) bien. Mis papás, hermanos y yo _____ (2. estar) perfectamente. Recibí tu email ayer. Me alegro de que tú _____ (3. poder) venir a verme durante las vacaciones. Creo que yo _____ (4. ir) a ir a la playa con mi familia todo el mes de julio. Por eso es mejor que tú _____ (5. llegar) a principios de agosto. Mis padres quieren que tus papás y hermanos _____ (6. pasar) el mes con nosotros también. Les recomiendo que _____ (7. comprar) los boletos de avión lo antes posible. Les aconsejo también que _____ (8. traer) ropa un poco gruesa (*heavy*), un impermeable y un paraguas porque _____ (9. hacer) fresco, _____ (10. estar) nublado y _____ (11. llover). Tú _____ (12. deber) recordar que Bogotá queda en las montañas. Yo _____ (13. saber) que tú no _____ (14. ir) a aburrirte en Bogotá. Tú _____ (15. ir) a ver que _____ (16. haber) muchas cosas que ver y hacer aquí. Voy a insistir en que Uds. _____ (17. despertarse) muy temprano todos los días aunque vamos a trasnochar (*stay up late*) oyendo música y bailando en las discotecas. Así yo _____ (18. poder) enseñarles las muchas cosas que hay en la ciudad y las afueras. Bueno, querida amiga, yo _____ (19. tener) muchas ganas de volver a verte. ¡Espero que tú me _____ (20. escribir) con la buena noticia de que _____ (21. venir) tu familia también!

Cariños de Ana María

I *Pero, sino, o sino que.* *Escoja entre* **pero**, **sino** *o* **sino que** *para completar las oraciones.*

1. Ellos se quedaron en la playa, _____ nosotros, no.

2. No sirvieron cerveza, _____ vino.

3. A ella le gustan los medios sociales, _____ a Uds., no.

4. No va a ponerse los zapatos negros, _____ los marrones.

5. No puso la mesa, _____ hizo la comida.

6. No sólo bailaron, _____ cantaron también.

7. Yo no soy español, _____ conozco bien España.

8. El correo electrónico no es de Isabel, _____ de Mateo.

9. Él no hace programación, _____ diseña sitios web.

10. Nosotros fuimos al teatro, _____ tú, no.

NOTA CULTURAL

- **Bogotá**, capital de Colombia, está ubicada en el centro del país, en la cordillera (*mountain range*) oriental. Las vistas de los Cerros Orientales (*Eastern Hills*) son impresionantes. Además de sus excelentes museos, edificios históricos y paisajes, Bogotá tiene barrios pintorescos y animados (*lively*) como la Zona T que es conocida por su paseo peatonal (*pedestrian mall*) rebosante de (*bustling/brimming with*) tiendas, restaurantes de alta cocina (*haute cuisine, fine dining*) y una dinámica vida nocturna.

- **Música folklórica de Colombia.** Colombia se conoce por su variedad de música folklórica debido a sus cuatro regiones musicales que van de los Andes al Caribe: montañas, costa del Pacífico, costa del Caribe y los llanos (*plains*) orientales. El instrumento nacional es **el tiple**, una pequeña guitarra de 12 cuerdas. Hay varios ritmos y bailes colombianos tradicionales, entre ellos la cumbia, el bambuco, el joropó, el torbellino, el bullerengue y el mapalé, géneros musicales que demuestran sus raíces indígenas, africanas y españolas. Entre los bailes modernos son muy populares la champeta, que se originó en la costa caribeña y la salsa choke que se originó en la costa del Pacífico.

The Present Subjunctive in Noun Clauses After Impersonal Expressions

Impersonal expressions (expressions with no specific subject) require the subjunctive in dependent noun clauses if they suggest that the event or state mentioned in the dependent clause is not part of perceived reality. For example: **es necesario que** (*it's necessary that*), **es importante que** (*it's important that*), **es imposible que** (*it's impossible that*), **es improbable que** (*it's improbable that*), **es posible que** (*it's possible that*), **es preciso que** (*it's necessary that*), **es probable que** (*it's probable that*), and **Ojalá (que)** (*I hope (that)*).

—**Es necesario que discutamos** el asunto.	*It's necessary that we discuss the matter.*
—**Es posible que yo no tenga** tiempo hoy.	*It's possible I won't have time today.*
—Pero **es importante que resolvamos** algo.	*But it's important that we resolve something.*
—De acuerdo. **Es probable que podamos** discutirlo mañana.	*Agreed. It's probable we can discuss it tomorrow.*
—**Ojalá que tengas** razón.	*I hope you're right.*

Impersonal expressions that show the speaker's emotional attitude or bias toward the event or state of the dependent clause also require the subjunctive. **Es bueno que** (*it's good that*), **es inútil que** (*it's useless that*), **es malo que** (*it's bad that*), **es mejor que** (*it's better that*), **es peor que** (*it's worse that*), **es triste que** (*it's sad that*), **es útil que** (*it's useful that*), **más vale que** (*it's better that*). **Es una lástima que** (*It's a pity that*) and **¡qué lástima que...!** (*what a pity that . . . !*) are impersonal expressions that may be followed by the subjunctive or the indicative in the dependent clause.

—**Es triste** que José Luis **tenga** tantos problemas.	*It's sad that José Luis **has** so many problems.*
—**Es inútil** que **tratemos** de ayudarlo, ¿verdad?	*It's useless for **us to try** to help him, isn't it?*
—**Es una lástima** que no **haya** solución.	*It's a pity there's no solution.*

When the speaker does not identify a specific subject in the dependent clause, the impersonal expression is followed by an infinitive. Study the following pairs of sentences.

Es preciso saber la fecha.	*It's necessary to know the date.*
Es preciso que sepamos la fecha.	*It's necessary that we know the date.*
Es útil hacer investigaciones.	*It's useful to do research.*
Es útil que hagas investigaciones.	*It's useful for you to do research.*

There are certain verbs and expressions in Spanish that require the subjunctive in the dependent clause only when they are negative, that is, when they suggest that the event or state in the dependent clause is a negated fact. For example: **no es cierto que, no es evidente que, no es obvio que, no es que, no es/está seguro que, no es verdad que, no creer que,** and **no pensar que.** When they are not negative, they are followed by the indicative.

NOTE The negative constructions of **creer** and **pensar** (**no creer que** and **no pensar que**), as well as **tal vez** (*perhaps*), may be followed by the indicative as well as the subjunctive. The choice of the indicative by the speaker suggests that he or she thinks the event in the dependent clause is closer to reality while the use of the subjunctive suggests that the speaker is less certain about the event.

Creo que Lola y Paco **van** al cine.	*I think Lola and Paco are going to the movies.*
No creo que Lola y Paco **vayan** al cine.	*I don't think Lola and Paco are going to the movies.* (Speaker isn't sure whether Lola and Paco are going to the movies— it's quite possible they're going.)
No creo que Lola y Paco **van** al cine.	*I don't think Lola and Paco are going to the movies.* (Speaker thinks Lola and Paco are probably not going to the movies.)
Es verdad que Jaime **está** preocupado.	*It's true Jaime is worried.*
No es verdad que Jaime **esté** preocupado.	*It's not true Jaime is worried.*
Tal vez se enfadan.	*Perhaps they'll get angry.*
Tal vez se enfaden.	*Perhaps they might get angry.* (Speaker is less certain.)

When they are used in the affirmative, **dudar** (*to doubt*) and **es dudoso** (*it's doubtful*) require the use of the subjunctive in the dependent clause. Conversely, when **dudar** and **es dudoso** appear in the negative (indicating certainty), the verb in the dependent clause is in the indicative.

Dudamos que Andrés **vuelva** hoy.	*We doubt Andrés is coming back today.*
Es dudoso que Andrés **vuelva** hoy.	*It's doubtful Andrés is coming back today.*
No dudamos que Andrés **vuelve** hoy.	*We don't doubt Andrés is coming back today.*
No es dudoso que Andrés **vuelve** hoy.	*It's not doubtful Andrés is coming back today.*

J *¡Qué desorden! Y vienen los padres.* *Ud. comparte un apartamento con tres compañeras de cuarto. Este fin de semana vienen los padres a visitarlas. Uds. están contentas de ver a sus padres, pero están un poco preocupadas porque ellos van a ver que el apartamento es una pocilga* (pigsty). *Escriba oraciones usando el subjuntivo para describir la situación. Siga el modelo.*

MODELO   Vienen mis papás. (es bueno)
     → Es bueno que vengan mis papás.

Haciendo la limpieza

el desorden *mess*	**ordenar** *to clean up*
fregar (e > ie) las cacerolas *to scour the pans*	**el producto para la limpieza** *cleaning product*
guardar *to put away*	**la telaraña** *cobweb, spiderweb*
limpiar el polvo *to dust*	**el trapo** *cleaning rag*
meterse en *to get involved in*	

1. Ellos ven el desorden. (es malo)

2. Hacemos la limpieza del apartamento. (es necesario)

3. Lupe friega las cacerolas. (es importante)

4. Uds. recogen las cajas de pizza. (es probable)

5. Sus padres traen trapos y productos para la limpieza. (más vale)

6. Yo limpio el polvo. (es preciso)

7. Los papás se meten en todo esto. (es dudoso)

8. María y Diana guardan su ropa sucia en la cómoda. (es posible)

9. Tú quitas las telarañas del techo. (es mejor)

10. No nos relajamos en todo el día. (¡qué lástima que!)

K *Reacciones.* *Ud. reacciona a unas afirmaciones. Al reaccionar, escoja entre el presente de subjuntivo y el presente de indicativo. Siga los modelos.*

MODELOS   Manuela trabaja de mesera. (es verdad)
     → Es verdad que Manuela trabaja de mesera.

            Manuela trabaja de mesera. (no es verdad)
     → No es verdad que Manuela trabaje de mesera.

1. Lorenzo sigue enfermo. (no estoy seguro)

2. Teresa y Jesús se quieren mucho. (es obvio)

3. Uds. tienen problemas con el coche. (no es cierto)

4. Julia llega el sábado. (es que)

5. Alejandro es de origen ruso. (no es seguro)

6. Los niños están aburridos. (no es evidente)

7. Carmen lo sabe todo. (no es que)

8. Martín renuncia a su puesto. (es cierto)

L *Pereza del fin de año.* *Ahora que termina el año escolar y hace tan buen tiempo, sus amigos prefieren jugar al béisbol en vez de estudiar. Le toca a Ud. decirles que deben trabajar más. Escriba oraciones usando el presente de subjuntivo. Siga el modelo.*

MODELO   Pedro: No quiero asistir a la clase de química hoy. (es necesario)
→ Oye, Pedro, es necesario que asistas a la clase de química hoy.

1. Anita: No voy a estudiar para los exámenes finales. (insisto en)

2. Miguel: No deseo trabajar en la librería. (me sorprende)

3. Rebeca: No pienso escribir el informe para el proyecto. (más vale)

4. Tomás: No me gusta practicar el ruso. (es útil)

5. Graciela: No me interesa tomar apuntes en historia. (es importante)

6. Alfredo: Prefiero no hacer la tarea. (te ruego)

7. Carolina: No me importa sacar buenas notas. (espero)

8. Joaquín: Voy a jugar al béisbol todo el día. (te prohíbo)

M *Expresar en español. En un coloquio* (discussion). *Exprese en español las ideas de los participantes de un coloquio sobre el mundo en el siglo veintiuno. Use el presente de subjuntivo cuando sea necesario.*

1. *It's good there are so many technological advances* (adelantos).

2. *We prefer to use nuclear energy even more.*

3. *Everyone's happy to have the computer.*

4. *It's a pity that wars continue to break out* (estallar).

5. *We regret that the cities have so much crime.*

6. *We don't want to pay so many taxes* (los impuestos).

7. *It's probable that environmental pollution* (la contaminación ambiental) *is doing a lot of harm.*

8. *It's obvious that the free market* (mercado libre) *economy is the best.*

9. *It's necessary to control inflation and unemployment* (el desempleo).

10. *We advise the political leaders to spend money more accountably* (con más responsabilidad).

11. *I hope* (Ojalá) *there will be free elections in every country.*

12. *Nobody doubts that the 21st century is going to bring many changes.*

The Present Perfect Subjunctive: Forms and Uses

The present perfect subjunctive consists of the present subjunctive of **haber** + past participle.

Esperan que lo	**haya visto**.	*They hope I saw him.*
	hayas visto.	*They hope you saw him.*
	haya visto.	*They hope he saw him.*
	hayamos visto.	*They hope we saw him.*
	hayáis visto.	*They hope you saw him.*
	hayan visto.	*They hope they saw him.*

The present perfect subjunctive is used in the same kinds of dependent clauses as the present subjunctive. It is used to indicate that the action of the dependent clause happens before the action of the main clause.

Me alegro de que Uds. **salgan**.   *I'm glad you **are going out**.*
(two actions in the present)

Me alegro de que Uds. **hayan salido**.   *I'm glad you **went out**.*
(dependent clause action happens prior to action of main clause)

N   *¿Qué les parece?* *Escriba oraciones empleando la frase indicada en la cláusula principal. Cambie el verbo del pretérito al perfecto de subjuntivo. Siga el modelo.*

MODELO   Los Fernández llegaron. (es bueno)
→ Es bueno que los Fernández hayan llegado.

1. Uds. no vieron la exposición de arte. (Clara siente)

2. Vosotros escribisteis el contrato. (dudamos)

3. Carlos se hizo ciudadano. (me alegro)

4. Viste la nueva película policíaca. (esperan)

5. Murió el bisabuelo de Paco. (es una lástima)

6. Las chicas no dijeron nada. (es mejor)

7. Hubo un incendio en el metro. (nos sorprende)

8. Luz se puso brava. (no piensan)

9. Le gustó el concierto. (no creen)

O   *Expresar en español.* *Exprese las oraciones en español.*

1. *I'm glad Julia and Paco got married.*

2. *It's good that we saw those websites.*

3. *They doubt that the Tigers won the soccer championship.*

4. *We hope Fernando got rich.*

5. *Are you (Ud.) surprised that the Núñez family moved?*

6. *Ana doesn't think the boys broke the window.*

P ***Ejercicio oral. ¡Feliz año nuevo!*** *Escríbales tarjetas a sus amigos expresando sus deseos para el año nuevo. Use el indicativo de los verbos* **querer, esperar, desear,** *etcétera en la cláusula principal y el presente de subjuntivo en la subordinada.*

The Imperfect Subjunctive and Past Perfect Subjunctive; Conditional Sentences

Forms of the Imperfect Subjunctive

The forms of the imperfect subjunctive are derived from the third person plural form of the preterit. Any irregularity or vowel change in the stem of the third person plural of the preterit occurs in all persons of the imperfect subjunctive.

hablaron	→	que yo **hablara**
comieron	→	que yo **comiera**
escribieron	→	que yo **escribiera**
pidieron	→	que yo **pidiera**
hicieron	→	que yo **hiciera**
fueron	→	que yo **fuera**
durmieron	→	que yo **durmiera**
trajeron	→	que yo **trajera**

The preterit ending **-ron** is replaced by the following endings in all verbs.

		hablar	comer	escribir
-ra	Querían que	hablara	comiera	escribiera
-ras		hablaras	comieras	escribieras
-ra		hablara	comiera	escribiera
-ramos		habláramos	comiéramos	escribiéramos
-rais		hablarais	comierais	escribierais
-ran		hablaran	comieran	escribieran

The examples above express *They wanted me/you/him/her/us/you/them to speak/eat/ write.*

In the imperfect subjunctive, the first person singular (**yo**) form and the third person singular (**él/ella/Ud.**) forms are identical. The **nosotros** form has a written accent mark on the vowel before the **-r: habláramos, comiéramos, escribiéramos**.

There is an alternate form of the imperfect subjunctive that has endings in -**se**. The -**ra** and -**se** forms are largely interchangeable, but the -**se** forms are less common in colloquial speech.

		hablar	comer	escribir
-se	Querían que	hablase	comiese	escribiese
-ses		hablases	comieses	escribieses
-se		hablase	comiese	escribiese
-semos		hablásemos	comiésemos	escribiésemos
-seis		hablaseis	comieseis	escribieseis
-sen		hablasen	comiesen	escribiesen

A   **Imperfecto de subjuntivo.** *Complete las oraciones usando el imperfecto de subjuntivo de los verbos indicados. Escriba cada verbo con las dos desinencias* (endings) **-ra** y **-se**.

1. Yo esperaba que Manolo _____ / _____ cuenta. (darse)

2. Nos alegramos de que Lorna _____ / _____ su collar de perlas. (encontrar)

3. Rita insistió en que los niños _____ / _____ las botas. (ponerse)

4. No era cierto que nosotros lo _____ / _____. (saber)

5. Ojalá que _____ / _____ pescado en la carta. (haber)

6. Te aconsejaron que _____ / _____ derecho. (seguir)

7. Dudaban que Ud. _____ / _____ la siesta. (dormir)

8. No fue posible que yo los _____ / _____ hasta el jueves. (ver)

9. Habíamos querido que Uds. _____ / _____ con nosotros. (reunirse)

10. Le gustaría que nosotros _____ / _____ esta sinfonía. (oír)

11. Preferiríamos que vosotros nos lo _____ / _____. (decir)

12. No creían que los turistas _____ / _____ de Inglaterra. (ser)

13. Era preciso que se _____ / _____ nuevas casas en las afueras. (construir)

14. Yo querría que tú _____ / _____ los documentos. (traer)

15. Le dijeron a Mateo que no _____ / _____. (irse)

The Imperfect Subjunctive in Noun Clauses; the Sequence of Tenses

The imperfect subjunctive is used in dependent noun clauses requiring the subjunctive when the verb in the main clause is in the imperfect, preterit, past perfect, or conditional.

Queríamos que lo **hicieras**.	*We wanted you to do it.* (imperfect)
Quisimos que lo **hicieras**.	*We wanted you to do it.* (preterit)
Habíamos querido que lo **hicieras**.	*We had wanted you to do it.* (past perfect)
Querríamos que lo **hicieras**.	*We would want you to do it.* (conditional)

The present subjunctive is used when the verb in the main clause is in the present, present perfect, future, or imperative.

Queremos que lo **hagas.**	*We want you to do it.* (present)
Hemos querido que lo **hagas.**	*We've wanted you to do it.* (present perfect)
Querremos que lo **hagas.**	*We'll want you to do it.* (future)
Dígale que lo **haga.**	*Tell him to do it.* (imperative)

The English equivalents of many noun clauses in Spanish are in the infinitive, so the English sentences do not show the tense distinctions seen in the Spanish subjunctive clauses.

Queremos que lo **hagas.**	*We want you **to do** it.*
Queríamos que lo **hicieras.**	*We wanted you **to do** it.*

Remember that in Spanish, if the subjects of the main clause and the dependent clause are the same, the infinitive is used rather than the subjunctive.

Queremos **hacerlo.**	*We want **to do** it.*
Queríamos **hacerlo.**	*We wanted **to do** it.*

Ojalá used with the present subjunctive means *I hope.* **Ojalá** used with the imperfect subjunctive means *I wish.*

Ojalá que **saquen** boletos.	*I hope they'll get tickets.*
Ojalá que **sacaran** boletos.	*I wish they'd get tickets.*

Spanish uses the imperfect subjunctive, as well as the conditional, to soften a request or suggestion. The imperfect subjunctive of **querer**, **poder**, and **deber** is more courteous than the conditional, which is used with any verb.

Quisiera hablar con Ud.	***I'd like** to speak with you.*
¿Pudiera prestármelo?	***Could you** lend it to me?*
Uds. debieran volver a casa.	***You ought** to return home.*

In English, *would* is also used to soften a request.

¿Me lo **explicaría?**	***Would you explain** it to me?*

B *Un caso de celos.* *Narre la historia de dos chicos que quieren a Angélica. Cambie el verbo de la cláusula independiente según los verbos indicados, y el verbo de la cláusula dependiente al imperfecto de subjuntivo. Siga el modelo.*

MODELO   Felipe les dice a sus amigos que salgan. (dijo)
→ Felipe les dijo a sus amigos que salieran.

1. Felipe les sugiere que vayan a una discoteca. (sugirió)

2. Felipe espera que Angélica baile con él y nadie más. (esperaba)

3. Teodoro también desea que Angélica salga con él. (deseaba)

4. Angélica teme que los chicos tengan celos. (temía)

5. Es posible que Felipe y Teodoro se peleen por Angélica. (Era)

6. Felipe no cree que sea una buena idea ir a la discoteca. (no creía)

7. Felipe le propone a Angélica que vean una película. (propuso)

8. A Angélica le agrada que Felipe y Teodoro la quieran (agradaba), ¡pero ella estaba enamorada de Julio!

C *Expectativas. Cuando Timoteo fue a pasar un semestre en la Ciudad de Guatemala para estudiar español, tenía ciertas expectativas y preocupaciones sobre cómo iba a ser su experiencia. Para saber lo que pensaba, complete las oraciones usando el imperfecto de subjuntivo de los verbos indicados. Siga el modelo.*

MODELO   Timoteo deseaba que la casa donde iba a vivir ___quedara___ (quedar) cerca de la universidad.

1. Timoteo esperaba que _____ (haber) un chico de su edad en la familia.

2. Sentía que su mejor amigo no _____ (ir) a la Ciudad de Guatemala también.

3. Temía que nadie _____ (poder) comprender su español.

4. Era posible que Timoteo no _____ (llevarse) bien con sus compañeros de clase.

5. Tenía miedo de que la comida le _____ (caer) mal.

6. Dudaba que sus profesores le _____ (aprobar (o > ue) (*to pass*)) en todas las materias.

7. Era probable que Timoteo _____ (querer) mudarse a un hotel.

NOTA CULTURAL

Ciudad de Guatemala, capital de Guatemala, queda a 1.500 metros (~4.900 pies) sobre el nivel del mar en una meseta de la Sierra Madre. La capital fue fundada por decreto (*decree*) de Carlos III de España en 1776 después que un terremoto acabó con la capital anterior, Antigua Guatemala, en 1773. **Antigua**, fundada en 1543, fue una de las ciudades más atractivas de Centroamérica con una población de 60.000, varias iglesias grandes, una universidad (1680), una imprenta (1660) y famosos pintores, escultores, escritores y artesanos.

D *¿Qué tal le fue a Timoteo? Para saber cómo le fue, complete las oraciones usando el imperfecto de subjuntivo. Siga el modelo.*

MODELO   Los señores de la casa insistían en que Timoteo ___se quedara___ (quedarse) con ellos un mes más.

1. Era bueno que sus clases _____ (ser) tan interesantes.

2. Timoteo se alegró de que su profesora le _____ (dar) una buena nota en química.

3. Los señores permitían que Timoteo _____ (salir) con su hija Aurora.

4. La madre le pidió a Timoteo que los _____ (acompañar) a la sierra.

5. Los hijos de la familia le rogaron a Timoteo que _____ (jugar) al fútbol con ellos.

6. A Timoteo le sorprendió que todos lo _____ (tratar) tan bien.

7. El señor dejó que Timoteo _____ (conducir) el coche.

E *Vida de familia.* *Describa lo que los padres esperaban que sus hijos hicieran. Complete las oraciones usando el imperfecto de subjuntivo de los verbos indicados. Siga el modelo.*

MODELO   Mis papás querían que nosotros ___*estudiáramos*___ (estudiar) mucho.

1. Papá esperaba que yo _____ (hacerse) ingeniero.

2. Mamá insistía en que nosotros _____ (seguir) sus tradiciones.

3. Nuestros papás nos aconsejaban que _____ (tener) valores tradicionales.

4. Papá prefería que Pepe _____ (trabajar) con él en la empresa.

5. Nuestros padres deseaban que mis hermanos y yo _____ (casarse).

6. A nuestros papás les era importante que nosotros _____ (ser) responsables, honrados y trabajadores.

7. Mamá nos pedía que _____ (dedicarse) a nuestra familia.

8. Papá nos decía que _____ (ayudarse) los unos a los otros.

9. A nuestros padres les era necesario que mis hermanas _____ (vivir) cerca.

F *Me sobra tiempo.* **(I have plenty of time.)** *Sus padres le pidieron que hiciera unas cosas para ayudarlos. Ud. creía que le sobraba tiempo para hacerlas y fue a jugar al béisbol con sus amigos. Al regresar a casa, sus padres ven que todo ha quedado sin hacer. Complete las oraciones empleando el imperfecto de subjuntivo de los verbos indicados. Siga el modelo.*

MODELO   Hijo/Hija, yo quería que ___*buscaras*___ (buscar) el correo.

1. Hijo/Hija, te pedí que _____ (cortar) el césped.

2. Hijo/Hija, ¿no te dijimos que _____ (descongelar) la carne?

3. Hijo/Hija, te exigí que _____ (regar (*to water*)) los arbustos (*bushes*).

4. Hijo/Hija, esperábamos que _____ (hacer) la compra.

5. Hijo/Hija, yo quería que _____ (bañar) al perro.

6. Hijo/Hija, te rogamos que _____ (poner) el garaje en orden.

7. Hijo/Hija, yo deseaba que _____ (guardar) las herramientas (*tools*).

8. Hijo/Hija, insistíamos en que _____ (sacar) la basura.

9. Hijo/Hija, tu hermanito necesitaba que le _____ (reparar) su bicicleta.

G ¡Qué pesada! A Josefina no le queda ni un solo amigo porque se porta mal con todo el mundo. Para saber lo que pasó, complete las oraciones usando el imperfecto de subjuntivo de los verbos indicados. Siga el modelo.

MODELO   Josefina le pidió al novio de Lola que la ___llevara___ (llevar) al baile.

1. Josefina le dijo a Daniel que la _____ (sacar).

2. A los amigos no les gustaba que Josefina les _____ (mentir).

3. Josefina le aconsejó a Paquita que _____ (romper) con su novio.

4. Sus amigos sentían que Josefina _____ (tener) mala lengua (*vicious tongue*).

5. Josefina exigió que Pedro _____ (hacer) la tarea de cálculo por ella.

6. Josefina insistió en que los chicos la _____ (invitar) a todas sus reuniones.

7. Los amigos no querían que Josefina les _____ (tomar) el pelo.

8. Josefina les impidió a los amigos que _____ (ir) al cine sin ella.

9. A nadie le gustaba que Josefina _____ (ser) entrometida (*meddlesome, a busybody*).

H ¡Ojalá! A Ud. le gustaría que ciertas cosas sucedieran. Exprese sus deseos empleando el imperfecto de subjuntivo. Siga el modelo.

MODELO   mis primos / venir a visitarme
          → Ojalá que mis primos vinieran a visitarme.

1. yo / ir de vacaciones / en julio

2. Uds. / recibir / una beca

3. Diana / no quejarse / de todo

4. nuestro equipo / ganar / el campeonato

5. Bernardo y Marta / no discutir / tanto

6. tú / no preocuparse / por nada

7. tú y yo / poder asistir / al congreso (*conference*) en San Diego

8. vosotros / invitarnos / a vuestra hacienda

The Past Perfect (or Pluperfect) Subjunctive

The past perfect subjunctive consists of the imperfect subjunctive of **haber** + past participle. The most important use of the past perfect subjunctive is in conditional sentences. The past perfect subjunctive is also used to express a contrary-to-fact wish in the past after **ojalá (que)**.

saber

Ojalá (que)	hubiera sabido.	*I wish I had known.*
	hubieras sabido.	*I wish you had known.*
	hubiera sabido.	*I wish she had known.*
	hubiéramos sabido.	*I wish we had known.*
	hubierais sabido.	*I wish you had known.*
	hubieran sabido.	*I wish they had known.*

The past perfect subjunctive is used instead of the present perfect subjunctive to indicate that the action of the dependent clause happened before the action of the main clause when the main clause is in the preterit, imperfect, or conditional.

I ***¿Qué les parecía?*** *Escriba oraciones empleando las frases indicadas en la cláusula principal y el verbo de la cláusula dependiente en el pluscuamperfecto de subjuntivo. Siga el modelo.*

MODELO   Néstor había ganado la lotería. (esperábamos)
→ Esperábamos que Néstor hubiera ganado la lotería.

1. Rebeca había llegado a ser arquitecta. (era bueno)

2. Las hermanas Cela habían hecho un viaje a Santo Domingo. (nos gustó)

3. Uds. se habían quedado tanto tiempo. (me extrañó)

4. Tú habías comprado una computadora nueva. (era necesario)

5. Yo había conocido Roma. (era importante)

6. Juan y yo nos habíamos comprometido. (todos se alegraron)

NOTA CULTURAL

Santo Domingo, capital de la República Dominicana, es la más antigua de las ciudades americanas fundadas por los conquistadores. Fue fundada en 1496 por Bartolomé Colón, un hermano de Cristóbal Colón. La ciudad fue modernizada después que el huracán San Zenón la dejó totalmente destruida en 1930. Conserva cierto carácter colonial con sus muchos edificios y monumentos de interés histórico.

J ***Expresar en español.*** *Exprese las oraciones en español.*

1. You (tú) were hoping that they had been successful.

2. They were afraid that someone had told me (about it).

3. We were sorry that you (Ud.) hadn't heard what happened.

4. Sarita doubted that we had come back from the country.

5. I was glad that it had been warm and sunny.

6. I wish you (Uds.) had told us (about it) as soon as possible.

Conditional Sentences

In Spanish and English, conditional sentences consist of two clauses: a **si**-clause (*if*-clause) and a main clause. Both languages use similar tenses for the two clauses. The **si**-clause may come before or after the main clause.

Possible conditions are expressed in both languages by using the present in the **si**-clause and the future in the main clause.

si-CLAUSE	MAIN CLAUSE	
PRESENT	FUTURE	
Si vas,	**yo iré** también.	*If you go, I'll go too.*

To express a condition that is contrary to a fact or situation in present time, Spanish uses the imperfect subjunctive in the **si**-clause and the conditional in the main clause.

si-CLAUSE	MAIN CLAUSE	
IMPERFECT SUBJUNCTIVE	CONDITIONAL	
Si fueras,	**yo iría** también.	*If you were going, I'd go too.*

The sentence **Si fueras, yo iría también.** expresses a condition that is contrary-to-fact. The fact is that **tú no vas** and the result is that **yo no voy.** The meaning is *Si fueras* (*If you were going, which you're not*), *yo iría* también (*I'd go too*).

Spanish expresses a condition that is contrary to a fact or situation in past time by using the past perfect subjunctive in the **si**-clause and the conditional perfect or the past perfect subjunctive in the main clause.

si-CLAUSE	MAIN CLAUSE	
PAST PERFECT SUBJUNCTIVE	CONDITIONAL PERFECT OR PAST PERFECT SUBJUNCTIVE	
Si hubieras ido,	**yo habría ido** también.	*If you had gone, I would have*
Si hubieras ido,	**yo hubiera ido** también.	*gone too.*

The main clause may precede the **si**-clause, but the use of the tenses remains the same.

Yo habría ido también si tú hubieras ido. }
Yo hubiera ido también si tú hubieras ido. } *I would have gone too, if you had gone.*

Como si...

The imperfect subjunctive is used after **como si** (*as if*) to express an action contemporaneous with the action of the main clause.

Él habla **como si fuera** profesor.   *He speaks **as if he were** a teacher.*

Se abrazarán **como si no estuvieran**
enfadados.   *They'll hug each other **as if they weren't**
angry.*

Actúa **como si quisieras** estar con ellos.   *Act **as if you wanted** to be with them.*

Entraron **como si tuvieran** miedo.   *They came in **as if they were** afraid.*

The pluperfect subjunctive is used after **como si** to express an action that occurred prior to the action of the main clause.

Trabajaban **como si no hubieran entendido** las instrucciones.   *They were working **as if they hadn't understood** the instructions.*

Contestó **como si no hubiera leído** el libro.   *He answered **as if he hadn't read** the book.*

Él nos aconseja **como si hubiera estudiado** derecho.   *He advises us **as if he had studied** law.*

K *Todo está pendiente* (up in the air). *Complete las oraciones con la forma correcta de los verbos indicados. Use el presente de indicativo en las cláusulas que empiezan con* **si**. *Siga el modelo.*

MODELO Si Uds. ___*van*___ (ir), yo los ___*veré*___ (ver).

1. Si yo _____ (poder), los _____ (visitar).

2. Si ellos le _____ (ofrecer) el puesto a Daniel, lo _____ (aceptar).

3. Pepita y yo _____ (salir) si _____ (tener) tiempo.

4. Si Mario me _____ (llamar), yo se lo _____ (decir).

5. Si tú _____ (poner) la mesa , Isabel y Leo _____ (hacer) la cena.

6. _____ (Haber) mucha gente en la playa si _____ (hacer) un gran calor.

7. Tú _____ (tener) hambre si no _____ (comer) algo ahora.

8. Si Uds. no se lo _____ (preguntar) a Carlos, no _____ (saber) qué pasó.

9. Todos nosotros _____ (venir) en taxi si no _____ (haber) lugar en el coche de Manuel.

L *Si fuera posible...* *Complete las oraciones con la forma correcta de los verbos indicados. Use el imperfecto de subjuntivo en las cláusulas que empiezan con* **si**. *Siga el modelo.*

MODELO Si ___*fuera*___ (ser) posible, nosotros ___*iríamos*___ (ir).

1. Si yo _____ (tener) tiempo, _____ (hacer) un viaje a todos los países del mundo.

2. Los Madariaga _____ (venir) a visitarnos si nosotros los _____ (invitar).

3. Laura _____ (ver) esa obra de teatro si _____ (haber) entradas.

4. Si Diego _____ (ganar) más dinero, _____ (comprarse) un coche deportivo.

5. Si _____ (hacer) mucho viento, nosotros _____ (salir) con la cometa (*kite*).

6. Daniel _____ (dormir) la siesta si _____ (sentirse) cansado.

7. Si tú _____ (poder), _____ (resolver) el problema.

8. Vosotros _____ (salir) más temprano si _____ (ser) posible, ¿no?

9. Si Ana María y Esteban _____ (saber) los motivos, se los _____ (decir) a Uds.

M *Cuentos de hadas.* *Recuerde lo que pasa en estos cuentos de hadas* (fairy tales).
*Complete las oraciones con las formas correctas de los verbos indicados. Use el imperfecto
de subjuntivo en las cláusulas que empiezan con* **si**. *Siga el modelo.*

MODELO   «Si yo no ___tuviera___ (tener) sueño, no me ___acostaría___ (acostarse)
en la cama del osito», pensó Ricitos de Oro.

1. «Si yo _____ (encontrar) a la señorita que perdió la zapatilla de cristal,

   _____ (casarse) con ella», pensó el príncipe.

2. «Si una princesa me _____ (besar), yo _____ (dejar) de ser sapo (*toad*)

   y _____ (convertirse) en príncipe».

3. «Si _____ (haber) un guisante debajo de mi colchón, yo lo _____ (notar)»,
   dijo la princesa.

4. «Si Hansel y Gretel _____ (venir) a mi casa, yo me los _____ (comer)»,
   pensó la bruja.

5. «Si yo no _____ (mentir), no se me _____ (crecer) la nariz», dijo Pinocho.

6. «Si yo le _____ (dar) un beso a la bella durmiente, ella _____ (despertarse)»,
   dijo el príncipe.

7. «Si la reina no _____ (tener) celos de mí, no _____ (tener) que vivir con los siete
   enanos», pensó Blancanieves.

8. «Si yo _____ (soplar) fuerte, _____ (derrumbar) la casa de los tres cerditos»,
   pensó el lobo.

N *¡Viajes soñados!* *Complete las oraciones con la forma correcta de los verbos indicados.
Use el imperfecto de subjuntivo en la cláusula que empieza con* **si** *y el condicional en
la cláusula principal.*

1. Si yo _____ (ir) a Costa Rica, me _____ (gustar) hacer ecoturismo en los bosques
   nacionales.

2. Si Graciela y Miguel _____ (hacer) un viaje a Brasil, _____ (ir) a Río de Janeiro para
   ver el Carnaval.

3. Si Uds. _____ (poder) visitar Uruguay, _____ (quedarse) en Montevideo.

4. Si nosotros _____ (pasar) las vacaciones en Puerto Rico, _____ (tomar) el sol
   en la playa de el Dorado.

5. Si tú _____ (visitar) Chile, _____ (probar) vinos del Valle Central.

6. Si Felipe _____ (querer) viajar al Ecuador, _____ (conocer) Quito.

NOTA CULTURAL

- Hay mucho ecoturismo en **Costa Rica** gracias a su red de bosques naciona-les. En el de Monteverde, por ejemplo, hay más de 400 especies de aves (incluso el quetzal), monos, jaguares, pumas, reptiles y otros animales, 2.500 especies de plantas y más de 6.000 especies de insectos.
- **El Carnaval** es el período de diversiones que empieza el día de los Reyes (el 6 de enero), o sea la Epifanía, y termina el martes anterior al miércoles de Ceniza (*Ash Wednesday*). Se celebra por toda Latinoamérica. El Carnaval de Río de Janeiro es el más célebre.
- **Montevideo**, capital del Uruguay, es la única ciudad grande del país. Fue fundada por los españoles en 1726 como fortaleza contra los portugueses. Montevideo queda a orillas del río de la Plata que separa la ciudad de Bue-nos Aires, capital de la Argentina.
- **El Dorado** es una hermosa playa de Puerto Rico. Queda en el océano Atlán-tico cerca de San Juan.
- **Quito**, capital de Ecuador, queda a 25 kilómetros de la línea ecuatorial (*the equator*). Sin embargo, esta cuidad colonial, la segunda capital más alta de Latinoamérica, goza de días calurosos y noches frescas por su altitud. Quito era una ciudad del Imperio Inca cuando fue tomada por los soldados de Francisco Pizarro en 1534.

O   *Si hubiera sido posible…*   *Complete las oraciones con la forma correcta de los verbos indicados. Use el pluscuamperfecto de subjuntivo en la cláusula que empieza con* **si** *y el condicional compuesto* (conditional perfect) *o el pluscuamperfecto de subjuntivo en la cláusula principal. Siga el modelo.*

MODELO   Si __*hubiera sido*__ (ser) posible,

nosotros __*habríamos*__ / __*hubiéramos ido*__ (ir).

1. Si Uds. nos _____ (preguntar), se lo _____ / _____ (decir).

2. Yo te _____ / _____ (devolver) la cartera si te _____ (ver).

3. Si Jaime _____ (hacerse) médico, _____ / _____ (estar) más contento.

4. Eva y yo _____ / _____ (llamar) en seguida si lo _____ (saber).

5. Si yo _____ (jugar) al béisbol en el parque, no _____ / _____ (romper) la ventana de la casa.

6. Si tú _____ (leer) tu correo electrónico, _____ / _____ (entender) el problema.

P ***¿Campo o ciudad?*** *Pablo se crió en el campo y su prima Amelia se crió en la ciudad. Hablan de las maneras en las cuales hubiera sido diferente su vida si Pablo se hubiera criado en la ciudad y Amelia en el campo. Use el pluscuamperfecto de subjuntivo en la cláusula que empieza con* **si** *y el condicional compuesto o el pluscuamperfecto de subjuntivo en la cláusula principal. Siga el modelo.*

MODELO   Pablo / estudiar en un colegio grande / criarse en la ciudad
→ Pablo habría/hubiera estudiado en un colegio grande si se hubiera criado en la ciudad.

1. Pablo / asistir al teatro / vivir en la ciudad

2. Amelia / ordeñar (*to milk*) las vacas / nacer en una finca

3. Pablo / ponerse más nervioso / oír tanto ruido todos los días

4. Amelia / respirar aire no contaminado / vivir en el campo

5. Pablo / tomar el metro y los taxis / trabajar en la ciudad

6. Amelia / aprender a montar a caballo / pasar su vida en el campo

7. Pablo / comprar toda la comida en el supermercado / hacer la compra en la ciudad

8. Amelia / comer frutas y legumbres muy frescas / criarse en el campo

9. Pablo / llevar un traje, camisa y corbata / ganarse la vida trabajando en una empresa

10. Amelia / usar un sombrero de paja (*straw*) / cultivar la tierra

Q ***¡Julio el tardón* (slowpoke)!*** *A Julio le lleva tanto tiempo hacer cosas que siempre llega tarde a sus citas. Acaba de llegar a la fiesta de sus amigos, pero no ve a nadie. Despierta a su amigo Memo que le explica que la fiesta terminó a las dos de la mañana. Julio piensa en cómo le habría salido si hubiera llegado antes. Use el pluscuamperfecto de subjuntivo en la cláusula que empieza con* **si** *y el condicional compuesto o el pluscuamperfecto de subjuntivo en la cláusula principal. Siga el modelo.*

MODELO   Si yo ___*hubiera llegado*___ (llegar) antes, ___*habría/hubiera visto*___ (ver) a mis amigos.

1. Si yo _____ (terminar) mi trabajo para las diez, _____ (poder) llegar a tiempo.

2. Si yo _____ (planear) mejor mi horario, no me _____ (perder) la fiesta.

3. Si yo _____ (hacer) mi trabajo más eficazmente, _____ (bailar) con Julieta, la mujer de mis sueños.

4. Si yo no _____ (gastar) tanto tiempo echándome agua de colonia, _____ (disfrutar) de una comida rica.

5. Si yo _____ (manejar) más rápido, no _____ (atrasarse).

6. Si mis amigos _____ (divertirse) más, ellos _____ (quedarse) hasta las tres de la mañana.

7. Si Memo no _____ (acostarse) de inmediato, yo no _____ (tener) que tocar el timbre cien veces.

R   **Expresar en español.** *Exprese las oraciones en español.*

1. *If Victoria had had the key, she would have opened the suitcase.*

2. *If you (Uds.) were to take a trip this summer, where would you go?*

3. *If Pedro had been more careful, he wouldn't have lost his cell phone.*

4. *If you (Ud.) turn right at the corner, you'll see the museum.*

5. *If they gave good advice, I would pay attention to them.*

6. *If you (tú) had surfed the web more, you would have found the website.*

S   **Como si lo dijera.** *Complete las oraciones con la forma correcta del imperfecto de subjuntivo de los verbos indicados. Siga el modelo.*

    MODELO   Aurelia nos habla de Mallorca como si ___*conociera*___ (conocer) la isla.

1. Uds. se despiden como si _____ (ser) por última vez.

2. Los Madariaga me describían la casa como si _____ (vivir) en ella.

3. Laura se ríe como si no _____ (tener) ninguna preocupación.

4. Felipe te pedirá tu dirección electrónica como si _____ (pensar) escribirte.

5. Dígale a Ester la razón como si ella no la _____ (saber) ya.

6. Hablas como si no _____ (oír) nada de la conversación.

7. Ud. anda como si le _____ (doler) los pies.

8. Vosotros contestáis como si no _____ (comprender) la pregunta.

T   **Como si lo hubiera dicho.** *Complete las oraciones con la forma correcta del pluscuamperfecto de subjuntivo de los verbos indicados. Siga el modelo.*

    MODELO   Raimundo los saludó como si ___*hubiera estado*___ (estar) muy preocupado.

1. Los niños comían como si no _____ (comer) en todo el día.

2. Raquela está temblando como si _____ (ver) un fantasma.

3. Uds. reprendieron a Sara como si ella _____ (ser) la culpable.

4. Te quejabas de la fiesta como si no _____ (divertirse).

5. Gregorio gritó como si _____ (hacerse) daño.

6. Me hicieron unas preguntas como si yo _____ (poder) contestarlas.

U   **Ejercicio oral.** *Converse con sus colegas sobre lo que harían en cada caso. Pregúnteles, por ejemplo:* **¿Qué harías si tuvieras cincuenta millones de dólares?** *o* **Si tuvieras un año de vacaciones, ¿adónde irías?**

13

The Subjunctive: Adverb and Adjective Clauses

Adverb Clauses That Require the Subjunctive

A clause that modifies a verb the way an adverb does is called an adverb clause. Compare the use of adverbs and adverb clauses in the following pairs of sentences.

Salimos **temprano**.	*We went out **early**.*
Salimos **cuando terminamos**.	*We went out **when we finished**.*
Cantaron **bien**.	*They sang **well**.*
Cantaron **como les habían enseñado**.	*They sang **as they had been taught**.*

Adverb clauses are introduced by conjunctions, such as **cuando** and **como** in the examples above. The following conjunctions introduce adverb clauses in which the verb must be in the subjunctive: **a condición de que** (*on the condition that*), **a fin de que** (*in order that, so that*), **a menos que** (*unless*), **antes (de) que** (*before*), **con tal (de) que** (*provided that*), **en caso de que** (*in case*), **para que** (*so that*), and **sin que** (*without*). The same sequence-of-tense rules apply in adverb clauses as in noun clauses.

Saldré **antes de que** vuelvan.	*I'll leave before they get back.*
Salí **antes de que** volvieran.	*I left before they got back.*
Tito va a comprar huevos **para que** hagamos la torta.	*Tito's going to buy eggs so we can make the cake.*
Tito compró los huevos **para que** hiciéramos la torta.	*Tito bought eggs so that we might make the cake.*
Escondemos el regalo **sin que** Olga sepa dónde.	*We're hiding the gift without Olga knowing where.*
Escondimos el regalo **sin que** Olga supiera dónde.	*We hid the gift without Olga knowing where.*

A menos que and **con tal (de) que** are followed by the present subjunctive if the action of the dependent (subordinate) clause occurs at the same time as the action of the main clause. They are followed by the present perfect subjunctive if the action of the dependent clause occurs before the action of the main clause.

Hará su tarea de matemáticas con tal que le **devuelvas** su libro.	*He'll do his math homework provided that **you return** his book to him.*
Hará su tarea de matemáticas con tal que le **hayas devuelto** su libro.	*He'll do his math homework provided that **you've returned** his book to him.*

158

Adverb Clauses with Indicative or Subjunctive

Certain conjunctions are followed by the indicative when the action of the dependent (subordinate) clause is considered a known or established fact. They are followed by the subjunctive when the action of the dependent clause is considered uncertain or indefinite. The English equivalents of these subjunctive clauses often begin with conjunctions ending in -ever: *however, whenever, wherever.* These conjunctions include **aunque** (*although, even though*), **como** (*how*), **de manera que** (*so that*), **de modo que** (*so that*), **donde** (*where*), **mientras** (*while*), and **según** (*according to*).

Aunque va Elena, yo no voy.	***Even though** Elena **is going**, I'm not going.* (*I know Elena is going.*)
Aunque vaya Elena, yo no voy.	***Even though** Elena **may go**, I'm not going.*
Hágalo **como** ellos **dicen**.	*Do it **how** (**the way**) they say.* (*I know the way they say.*)
Hágalo **como** ellos **digan**.	*Do it **however** they say.* (*I don't know the way they say.*)
Iremos **donde** tú **quieres**.	*We'll go **where** you want.* (*We know where you want to go.*)
Iremos **donde** tú **quieras**.	*We'll go **wherever** you want to go.* (*We don't know yet where you want to go.*)

Adverb clauses introduced by conjunctions of time such as **así que** (*therefore, consequently, so*), **cuando** (*when*), **después (de) que** (*after*), **en cuanto** (*as soon as*), **hasta que** (*until*), **luego que** (*as soon as*), and **tan pronto (como)** (*as soon as*) are followed by the subjunctive when the main clause refers to the future or is a command.

Díselo **cuando lleguen**.	*Tell (it to) them **when they arrive**.*
Hablaremos **después de que se vayan** los invitados.	*We'll talk **after the guests leave**.*
Me quedaré **hasta que terminemos**.	*I'll stay **until we finish**.*
Avísame **tan pronto como te llamen**.	*Let me know **as soon as they call you**.*

If the action of the dependent clause is considered to be a habitual occurrence, the indicative, not the subjunctive, is used.

Se lo das **cuando llegan**.	*You (usually) give it to them **when they arrive**.*
Los niños se levantan de la mesa **en cuanto terminan de comer**.	*The children (usually) leave the table **as soon as they finish eating**.*
Me quedo **hasta que terminamos**.	*I (usually) stay **until we finish**.*

When the sentence relates a past action, the indicative is used after the conjunction of time since the event in the adverbial clause is considered to be part of reality.

Se lo di **cuando llegaron**.	*I gave it to them **when they arrived**.*
Los niños se levantaron de la mesa **en cuanto terminaron de comer**.	*The children (usually) left the table **as soon as they finished eating**.*
Me quedé **hasta que terminamos**.	*I stayed **until we finished**.*

The conjunction of time **antes (de) que** is an exception because it is always followed by the subjunctive even when the verb of the main clause is in a past tense.

Nora **salió** para el teatro **antes que**   *Nora **left** for the theater **before** Pablo*
    Pablo la **llamara.**   ***called** her.*

If the subject of the main clause and the dependent clause is the same, the dependent clause is replaced by an infinitive.

Estudien **hasta que Beti lo entienda.**   *Study until Beti understands it.*
Estudien **hasta entenderlo.**   *Study until you understand it.*

Voy a leer **antes que juguemos tenis.**   *I'm going to read before we play tennis.*
Voy a leer **antes de jugar tenis.**   *I'm going to read before I play (playing)*
                                              tennis.

Salimos **sin que Uds. almorzaran.**   *We went out without your having lunch.*
Salimos **sin almorzar.**   *We went out without having lunch.*

A *No se sabe todavía. Ud. no sabe cómo son las cosas mencionadas. Complete las cláusulas adverbiales con el presente de subjuntivo de los verbos indicados.*

1. Lo haré según Uds. _____ (mandar).

2. Viviremos donde Pepita _____ (aconsejar).

3. Aunque _____ (llover), habrá un partido de fútbol.

4. Guillermo quiere pintar los cuadros donde _____ (haber) mucha luz.

5. Realizarán el proyecto como tú _____ (querer).

6. Voy a leer el informe aunque no _____ (ser) muy interesante.

7. Vicente comerá donde Ud. _____ (preferir).

8. Prepara el plato según nosotros _____ (decir).

9. Van al cine aunque yo no _____(ir).

B *Haciendo las diligencias* (**Running errands**). *Explique que algunas personas hicieron ciertas cosas antes de que otras personas hicieran otras. Use el pretérito para el verbo de la cláusula principal y el imperfecto de subjuntivo para la cláusula adverbial. Siga el modelo.*

MODELO   Marta / ir a la pastelería : yo / ir a la carnicería
           → Marta fue a la pastelería antes de que yo fuera a la carnicería.

Las tiendas

el banco *bank*	**la librería** *bookstore*
la carnicería *butcher shop*	**la pastelería** *pastry shop*
el centro comercial *mall*	**la peluquería** *beauty salon, barber shop*
el cine *movie theater*	**el sello** *stamp*
la cita *appointment, date*	**el supermercado** *supermarket*
el correo *post office*	**la tienda de cómputo** *computer store*
la discoteca *discotheque*	**la tienda de mascotas** *pet store*
la farmacia *drugstore*	**la tienda de móviles** *cell phone store*
la gasolinera *gas station*	**la tintorería** *dry cleaner's*
la joyería *jewelry store*	**la zapatería** *shoe store*

1. Elena y Mario / salir del banco : nosotros / entrar en la zapatería

2. Ud. / encontrar la tienda de mascotas (*pets*) : yo / volver de la farmacia

3. Uds. / comprar los sellos en el supermercado : Miguel / poder ir al correo

4. Fernando y yo / estacionar en el centro comercial : tú / llegar al cine

5. yo / sacar la ropa de la tintorería : Juana / tener su cita en la peluquería

6. tú / ir a la joyería : Arturo y Bárbara / buscar una librería

7. vosotros / llegar a la gasolinera : Pedro y yo / regresar de la tienda de cómputo

C *¿Indicativo o subjuntivo?* *Complete las oraciones con la forma correcta de los verbos indicados. Escoja entre el indicativo y el subjuntivo (en presente o imperfecto). Siga el modelo.*

MODELO   No queremos ir al museo sin que tú ___*vayas*___ (ir).

1. Llamaré a Julio para que él _____ (saber) lo que está pasando.

2. Se quedaron hasta que Federico _____ (venir).

3. Iremos al centro comercial a menos que Uds. nos _____ (necesitar) aquí.

4. Le presté el dinero a Marisol para que _____ (poder) comprarse el vestido.

5. Tú puedes venir a la casa sin que nosotros te _____ (invitar).

6. Los vimos tan pronto como nosotros _____ (entrar) en la tienda de móviles (el móvil (*cell phone*) (Spain)).

7. No pensaban salir sin que su mamá les _____ (dar) de comer.

8. Carmen se puso de pie en cuanto _____ (terminar) la conferencia.

9. Nos reuniremos contigo cuando (tú) _____ (volver).

10. Los muchachos iban al cine a menos que Clarita no _____ (tener) ganas de ver la película.

D *Expresar en español.* *Exprese las oraciones en español.*

1. *I'll call them when I get to the airport.*

2. *We'll watch the soccer match until it begins to rain.*

3. *Consuelo set the table an hour before her friends arrived.*

4. *They stood in line at the box office after they had lunch.*

5. *You (Ud.) didn't want to go shopping without our going too.*

6. *Do it (Uds.) whichever way they want.*

7. *Even though it's cold out, we should take a walk.*

8. *I'll lend you (tú) the book so that you won't have to take it out of the library.*

9. *Carlos is going to study for his exam before playing tennis.*

Adjective Clauses That Require the Subjunctive

An adjective clause modifies a noun the way an adjective does. All relative clauses are adjective clauses. In the example, **una obra que se titula** *Don Quijote,* the clause **que se titula** *Don Quijote* modifies **obra** the way that the adjective **maravillosa** does in **una obra maravillosa.** The noun modified by an adjective clause is called the antecedent. Thus, **obra** is the antecedent of the **que** clause.

In Spanish, there are two types of antecedents—those considered part of reality, definite or existent, and those that are not part of reality, indefinite or nonexistent. When the antecedent is something or someone that exists and that the speaker can identify, the verb of the adjective clause appears in the indicative. For example, in the sentence **Tenemos un profesor que habla chino**, the antecedent, **un profesor**, is a definite person who can be identified by name. Therefore, the indicative **habla** is used. However, in adjective clauses that modify antecedents that are not part of reality or the speaker's experience, the subjunctive is used. These include clauses that refer to indefinite, undetermined, and negative antecedents.

Buscamos un profesor que **hable** chino.	*We're looking for* ***a*** *professor who speaks Chinese.*
Queremos un profesor que **hable** chino.	*We want* ***a*** *professor who speaks Chinese.*
Necesitamos un profesor que **hable** chino.	*We need* ***a*** *professor who speaks Chinese.*
No conozco a nadie que **hable** vasco.	*I* ***don't*** *know anyone who speaks Basque.*
No hay revista que le **guste**.	*There's* ***no*** *magazine he likes.*

Note that **buscar, necesitar, querer,** and other such verbs may also have direct objects that are definite and identifiable. In this case, adjective clauses that modify these objects are in the indicative. In the examples below, the professor being sought is known to the speakers.

Buscamos a la profesora que **habla** chino.	*We're looking for* ***the*** *professor who speaks Chinese.*
Necesitamos a la profesora que **habla** chino.	*We need* ***the*** *professor who speaks Chinese.*

The sequence-of-tense rules also apply in adjective clauses.

Quiero una novela que **tenga** un buen argumento.	*I* ***want*** *a novel that* ***has*** *a good plot.*
Quería una novela que **tuviera** un buen argumento.	*I* ***wanted*** *a novel that* ***had*** *a good plot.*
No hay casa que les **guste**.	*There's* ***no*** *house they* ***like***.
No había casa que les **gustara**.	*There was* ***no*** *house they* ***liked***.

In addition to **que,** other relative adverbs and pronouns such as **donde** and **quien** can introduce adjective clauses.

Buscan una florería **donde vendan** tulipanes.	*They're looking for a flower shop* ***where they sell*** *tulips.*

Tere quería una amiga **con quien pudiera** compartir sus ideas.

*Tere wanted a friend **with whom she could** share her ideas.*

E **Se busca apartamento.** *Describa el apartamento que Ud. y sus amigos esperan encontrar. Escriba oraciones usando el presente de subjuntivo en la cláusula adjetival y el presente de indicativo en la cláusula principal. Siga el modelo.*

MODELO nosotros / buscar un apartamento / tener cuatro dormitorios
→ Nosotros buscamos un apartamento que tenga cuatro dormitorios.

1. tú / querer un apartamento / tener dos baños

2. Mateo / necesitar un apartamento / donde / haber aire acondicionado

3. Javier y yo / buscar un apartamento / estar cerca de la universidad

4. Uds. / necesitar un apartamento / no costar un ojo de la cara (*not cost an arm and a leg*)

5. yo / querer un apartamento / no necesitar renovación

6. Pepe y Leo / desear un apartamento / ser moderno y fácil de limpiar

7. Octavio / buscar un apartamento / dar a una calle poco transitada (*a street with little traffic*)

8. Ud. / necesitar un apartamento / donde / caber todos los fiesteros (*partygoers*)

F **Mi novia ideal.** *Esteban le cuenta a su amigo Felipe cómo es la mujer ideal. Para saber lo que busca en una mujer, complete las cláusulas adjetivales usando el presente de subjuntivo de los verbos indicados.*

1. Busco una novia que _____ (saber) ser una buena amiga.

2. Quiero una chica con quien _____ (poder) hablar fácilmente.

3. Me hace falta una mujer que me _____ (comprender).

4. Quiero tener una novia con quien yo _____ (divertirse).

5. Necesito una chica que _____ (ser) inteligente.

6. Estoy buscando una novia que _____ (tener) un buen sentido del humor.

G **No hay candidatas para el puesto. (There are no candidates for the job.)** *Por desgracia, Felipe no puede ayudar a Esteban porque no tiene amigas que tengan todas las cualidades que su amigo exige. Complete las cláusulas adjetivales de las oraciones usando el presente de subjuntivo de los verbos indicados.*

1. No conozco a ninguna chica que _____ (reunir) todas estas características.

2. No hay nadie que _____ (ser) tan perfecta.

3. No conozco a ninguna mujer con quien tú _____ (querer) salir.

4. No hay ninguna que te _____ (ir) a interesar mucho.

5. No conozco a ninguna muchacha que _____ (tener) un cociente intelectual (*I.Q.*) tan alto como el tuyo.

6. ¡No hay ninguna chica que _____ (enamorarse) de ti tan fácilmente!

***En la cumbre* (At the top).** *Isabel Soriano es presidenta de su propia empresa multinacional y conoce el éxito y la prosperidad. Pero a veces Isabel se pone a pensar en el pasado. Complete las cláusulas adjetivales usando el imperfecto de subjuntivo de los verbos indicados para saber cómo era su vida antes de que llegara a la cumbre.*

Los negocios

compartir *to share*	**la fama** *name, reputation*
confiar en *to trust*	**el horario de trabajo** *work schedule*
la cumbre *the top*	**invertir** (e > ie) *to invest*
el dineral *fortune, a lot of money*	**los peldaños del éxito** *ladder of success*
la empresa *firm, company*	**la prosperidad** *prosperity*
esforzarse (o > ue) **por** *to strive to,*	**realizar** *to achieve*
try hard to	**trepar** *to climb*
el éxito *success*	**el valor** *value*

1. Yo buscaba una profesión que me _____ (dar) un dineral, fama y felicidad.

2. No había nadie que _____ (esforzarse) más que yo por conseguir el éxito.

3. Yo quería tener un horario de trabajo que me _____ (permitir) pasar mucho tiempo con mi familia.

4. Yo necesitaba un esposo que _____ (compartir) mis ideas y valores sobre la vida.

5. No conocía a nadie que _____ (invertir) más plata en su compañía que yo.

6. No había ninguna persona que _____ (ir) de vacaciones menos que yo.

7. Me hacían falta unos empleados en quienes yo _____ (poder) confiar.

8. Mi esposo y yo buscábamos una casa donde _____ (haber) mucho lugar para mi oficina y para los niños.

9. Yo quería tener una empresa que me _____ (dejar) realizar mis ambiciones.

NOTA CULTURAL

En muchos países hispánicos las letras **S.A.** aparecen tras el nombre de una empresa. **S.A.** es la abreviatura de Sociedad Anónima, el equivalente en español de *Inc.*

Adjective Clauses with Indicative or Subjunctive

In Spanish, a noun may be followed by a relative clause beginning with **que** that has a verb either in the indicative or the subjunctive. If the indicative is used, it suggests that the antecedent has already been identified. If the relative clause is in the subjunctive, it suggests that the antecedent has not yet been identified.

Traigo la torta que **quieres.**	*I'll bring the cake you want.*
(Yo sé cuál de las tortas te gustó.)	*(I know which of the cakes you liked.)*
Escoge la torta que **quieras.**	*Choose the cake you want.*
(Yo no conozco tus gustos.)	*(I don't know your tastes.)*

The meaning of the subjunctive in these adjective clauses can be conveyed in English by words ending in *-ever*.

Iremos al restaurante que tú **digas**.	*We'll go to **whichever** restaurant you say.*
Cenaré en el restaurante que ellos **quieran**.	*I'll have dinner in **whichever** restaurant they want.*

I **Expresar en español.** *Exprese las oraciones en español.*

1. *Mario and Carmen are looking for a house that has nine rooms.*

2. *There's no food that he likes.*

3. *I wanted a friend who would go to museums with me.*

4. *Don't you (Ud.) know anyone who's arriving before three o'clock?*

5. *Rosa will prepare whatever dish we choose.*

6. *They needed a secretary who worked on Saturdays.*

7. *We'll take the class with whichever professor teaches best.*

8. *I'll take the train at whatever time it arrives.*

9. *Roberto was looking for a website that had all the necessary information.*

10. *We'll stay at whatever hotel you (Uds.) like.*

11. *There was no Italian restaurant that was open at 1:00 in the morning.*

12. *They're looking for the programmers who work on weekends.*

J **Ejercicio oral.** *Hable con su amigo/amiga de las cualidades que Uds. buscan en las personas y las cosas. Complete las oraciones con cláusulas adjetivales. Por ejemplo:* **Busco unos profesores/unas profesoras que..., Quiero un novio/una novia que..., Necesito unos amigos que..., Deseo un empleo que..., Busco una casa que..., Deseo una computadora que..., Quiero un esposo/una esposa que...**

Commands

Command Forms for **Ud.** and **Uds.**

The command forms of a verb (the imperative) are used to tell someone to do or not to do something. The formal command forms for **Ud.** and **Uds.** are the same as the corresponding present subjunctive forms.

Escuche el ruido.	*Listen to the noise.*
Lea el libro.	*Read the book.*
Escriban el informe.	*Write the report.*
Traigan el periódico.	*Bring the newspaper.*

Negative formal commands are formed by the addition of **no** before the affirmative command.

No escuche los chismes.	*Don't listen to gossip.*
No escriban el informe.	*Don't write the report.*

A polite tone can be given to the command to soften it by the addition of **Ud.** or **Uds.** This is similar to the addition of *please* in English commands.

Espere.	*Wait.*
Espere Ud.	*Please wait.*
No griten.	*Don't shout.*
No griten Uds.	*Please don't shout.*

A *Una receta: La tortilla española.* *Póngase el gorro de cocinero y aprenda a preparar este plato español típico, cambiando el infinitivo de los verbos al imperativo formal. Trabajando paso a paso, Ud. llegará a ser un cocinero/una cocinera de primera categoría (a first-rate/top chef). Siga el modelo.*

MODELO   calentar el aceite de oliva en una sartén
   → Caliente el aceite de oliva en una sartén.

La cocina

a fuego lento *low heat, slowly*	**la fuente** *platter, serving dish*
el aceite de oliva *olive oil*	**el gorro de cocinero** *chef's hat*
añadir *to add*	**la patata** (Spain) *potato*
batir *to beat*	**pegar** *to stick*
calentar (e > ie) *to heat*	**pelar** *to peel*
la cebolla *onion*	**picar** *to chop*
cocinar *to cook*	**la pimienta** *pepper*
darle la vuelta *to turn over*	**la sal** *salt*
dorar *to brown*	**salpimentar** *to season*
espolvorear *to sprinkle*	**la** (OR **el**) **sartén** *frying pan*

1. añadir las patatas y cebollas peladas y picadas

2. cocinar a fuego lento

3. espolvorear con sal

4. batir los huevos

5. poner los huevos en la sartén

6. hacer dorar los huevos

7. darle la vuelta a la tortilla

8. no dejar que se pegue la tortilla

9. servir en una fuente

B *Una formación profesional.* *Unos jóvenes asesores comienzan un programa de formación profesional con la empresa de alta tecnología que acaba de contratarlos. Como jefe/jefa del programa, Ud. les dice lo que tienen que hacer. Escriba oraciones usando el imperativo. Siga el modelo.*

MODELO   llegar a las ocho menos cuarto todos los días
          → Lleguen a las ocho menos cuarto todos los días.

1. asistir a la reunión semanal en la oficina del director

2. traer la computadora

3. crear una base de datos

4. enviar el correo electrónico

5. seguir los consejos del gerente

6. actualizar (*update*) el sitio web

7. leer el manual sobre el programa de gráficas

8. hacer copias de seguridad (*backup*)

Trámites de banco **(Bank transactions).** *Ud. está de vacaciones en Santiago de Chile. Mientras Ud. está en el banco, oye algunas conversaciones. Escriba los verbos que aparecen en las preguntas usando el imperativo. Cambie los sustantivos a pronombres de complemento directo.* Siga el modelo.*

MODELO   ¿Debo abrir la cuenta?
          → Sí, ábrala.
            No, no la abra.

En el banco

la banca electrónica *online banking*
el cajero automático *ATM*
calcular *to compute*
el cheque *check*
la clave personal *PIN (personal identification number)*
la cuenta de ahorros *savings account*
la cuenta corriente *checking account*

firmar *to sign*
el formulario *(paper) form*
el interés *interest*
llenar *to fill out*
el peso *monetary unit of Chile and other Spanish American countries*
la planilla de retiro *withdrawal form/slip*
la plata *money*

1. ¿Debo buscar el cajero automático?

2. ¿Tengo que firmar la planilla de retiro?

3. ¿Debo llenar el formulario?

4. ¿Le doy el dinero en pesos?

5. ¿Puedo usar mi clave personal?

6. ¿Le calculo los intereses?

7. ¿Cierro la cuenta corriente?

8. ¿Le cobro los cheques?

9. ¿Debo probar la banca electrónica?

NOTA CULTURAL

- **Santiago**, capital de Chile, queda a orillas del río Mapocho. Tiene hermosos jardines públicos y se pueden ver los picos de los Andes desde la ciudad. Fundada por Pedro de Valdivia en 1541, Santiago tiene varias universidades y numerosas instituciones culturales, científicas y artísticas además de una pintoresca zona antigua.
- **El peso** es la moneda de Chile. Los otros países latinoamericanos que usan el peso como moneda son Argentina, México, Colombia, Uruguay, la República Dominicana y Cuba.

---

*To review the position of object pronouns with command forms, see "The Position of Object Pronouns with Command Forms" later in this chapter.

Command Forms for **nosotros** (let's, let's not)

The present subjunctive forms for **nosotros** are used as commands.

Tomemos el tren.	*Let's take the train.*
No hagamos nada.	*Let's not do anything.*

The affirmative **nosotros** command is often replaced by **vamos a** + infinitive. **Vamos a estudiar** may mean either *We're going to study* or *Let's study*. Because this does not apply to negative **nosotros** commands, **No vamos a estudiar** can only mean *We're not going to study*.

Vamos a salir esta noche. ⎫	
Salgamos esta noche. ⎬	*Let's go out tonight.*

Vamos is used instead of **vayamos** for *let's go*. The regular present subjunctive form is used for the negative: **no vayamos**.

Vamos al centro.	*Let's go downtown.*
No vayamos al cine.	*Let's not go to the movies.*

In affirmative **nosotros** commands, the final **-s** of the verb ending is dropped when the reflexive pronoun **nos** or the indirect object pronoun **se** is added and attached to the end. An accent mark is written over the stressed syllable.

Enseñémosela.	(**Enseñemos** + **se** + **la**)	*Let's show it to them.*
Hagámoselos.	(**Hagamos** + **se** + **los**)	*Let's make them for him.*
Lavémonos.	(**Lavemos** + **nos**)	*Let's wash up.*
Prestémoselo.	(**Prestemos** + **se** + **lo**)	*Let's lend it to her.*
Quedémonos.	(**Quedemos** + **nos**)	*Let's stay.*
Sentémonos.	(**Sentemos** + **nos**)	*Let's sit down.*
Vámonos.	(**Vamos** + **nos**)	*Let's go.*

D   ***Veámoslo todo en Perú.*** *Ud. y sus amigos están pasando las vacaciones en Perú. Recién llegados a Lima, Uds. hablan de sus planes. Escriba oraciones de dos maneras, usando la primera persona del plural del imperativo. Siga el modelo.*

MODELO   viajar a Nazca
      → Viajemos a Nazca.
        Vamos a viajar a Nazca.

1. dar un paseo por la zona de la Plaza de Armas

2. ir de compras en el Jirón de la Unión

3. conocer la Universidad de San Marcos

4. hacer una excursión a Machu Picchu

5. visitar la catedral y unas iglesias de Cuzco

6. quedarse en Miraflores

7. sentarse en el Malecón

NOTA CULTURAL

- **Lima**, capital del Perú, fue fundada por los españoles en 1535. Fue una ciudad rica e importante hasta que fue destruida por un terremoto en 1746. El casco antiguo (*old city*) de la ciudad conserva la arquitectura de la época colonial. Aquí se puede ver la Plaza de Armas alrededor de la cual se encuentran el Palacio de Gobierno, la catedral y otros lugares históricos.
- **La Universidad de San Marcos** (La Universidad Nacional Mayor de San Marcos) fue fundada en 1551.
- **Machu Picchu**, una ciudad inca, queda en el departamento de Cuzco al sudeste de Lima. Las ruinas de la ciudad sagrada, que consiste en una fortaleza, terrazas, escaleras, templos, palacios, torres, fuentes y un reloj de sol, fueron descubiertas en 1911.
- La ciudad de **Cusco** (Cuzco según la ortografía inglesa) fue fundada en el siglo XI por Manco Cápac y era capital del imperio inca hasta que Francisco Pizarro y los conquistadores españoles se apoderaron de la ciudad en 1533, nombrándola ciudad española en 1534. El quechua era el idioma de los incas. Se habla todavía en varios países de Sudamérica incluso Perú, Ecuador, Bolivia, Chile, Colombia y Argentina.
- **Miraflores** es el suburbio más grande y más importante de la capital peruana. Con sus muchos comercios, excelentes restaurantes y hoteles, Miraflores, con San Isidro, constituyen ahora el centro social de Lima. Desde la Avenida Diagonal hay una magnífica vista del litoral (*coastline*) de Lima. El malecón (*jetty*) pasa por todas estas estaciones balnearias (*seaside resorts*).
- **Nazca** es una ciudad que queda al sudeste de Lima. A unos 22 kilómetros al norte de Nazca se pueden ver las famosas líneas nazcas que son líneas paralelas, formas geométricas y las figuras de un perro, un mono, aves, una araña, un árbol y otras cosas. Se cree que fueron grabadas en las arenas de la Pampa Colorada por tres pueblos indígenas diferentes a partir de 900 antes de Jesucristo.

E   *Cómo no. Sus amigos le dicen que quieren hacer ciertas cosas hoy. Ud. les dice que está dispuesto/dispuesta a acompañarlos. Escriba oraciones usando el imperativo de **nosotros** de las dos maneras. Siga el modelo.*

MODELO   Quiero comprarle un regalo a Elisa.
       → Cómo no. Comprémoselo.
        Cómo no. Vamos a comprárselo.

1. Ana: Quiero darle a Maximiliano los CDs.

2. Raúl: Me encantaría sacar boletos para el concierto de la Sinfónica.

3. Felipe: Me gustaría ir al museo por la tarde.

4. Inés: Sería agradable caminar por el parque.

5. Laura: Quiero inscribirme en la clase de computación.

6. Pablo: Me gustaría jugar al tenis.

7. Paula: Me interesa conocer el nuevo centro comercial.

8. José: Me encantaría enseñarles el nuevo estadio a nuestros amigos.

9. Eva: Sería lindo tumbarse (*lie down*) en la playa.

Command Forms for **tú** and **vosotros**

Like formal commands, negative informal commands for **tú** and **vosotros** are derived from the present subjunctive.

tú		
	No compres más.	*Don't buy more.*
	No comas tanto.	*Don't eat so much.*
	No pidas cerveza.	*Don't order beer.*
	No digas eso.	*Don't say that.*
vosotros	**No compréis** más.	*Don't buy more.*
	No comáis tanto.	*Don't eat so much.*
	No pidáis cerveza.	*Don't order beer.*
	No digáis eso.	*Don't say that.*

Affirmative informal commands for **tú** and **vosotros** have their own endings. The affirmative **tú** commands are derived from the present indicative **tú** form minus the second person ending -**s**.

PRESENT INDICATIVE	COMMAND	
Contestas el teléfono.	→ **Contesta** el teléfono.	*Answer the telephone.*
Vendes el coche.	→ **Vende** el coche.	*Sell the car.*
Abres la ventana.	→ **Abre** la ventana.	*Open the window.*
Sirves la cena.	→ **Sirve** la cena.	*Serve dinner.*

The following verbs have irregular affirmative **tú** commands. Note that the negative **tú** commands of these verbs are regular. They are derived from the present subjunctive forms.

INFINITIVE	AFFIRMATIVE	NEGATIVE
decir	di	no digas
hacer	haz	no hagas
ir	ve*	no vayas
poner	pon	no pongas
salir	sal	no salgas
ser	sé	no seas
tener	ten	no tengas
venir	ven	no vengas

---

*The affirmative **tú** commands for **ir** and **ver** are the same: **ve**.

Affirmative **vosotros** commands are formed by replacing the **-r** of the infinitive with **-d**. They lose their final **-d** when the reflexive pronoun **os** is attached: **Acordaos** (*Remember*). The one exception to this rule is **idos** (*go away*).

contestar	→	Contesta**d** el teléfono.	*Answer the telephone.*
vende**r**	→	Vende**d** el coche.	*Sell the car.*
abri**r**	→	Abri**d** la ventana.	*Open the window.*
servi**r**	→	Servi**d** la cena.	*Serve dinner.*
arregla**rse**	→	Arregla**os**.	*Get ready.*

F **¡Venid a la fiesta!** *Vosotros estáis en España donde estáis organizando una fiesta para esta noche. Decid lo que los demás tienen que hacer y no hacer usando la segunda persona plural (**vosotros**) del imperativo. Seguid el modelo.*

MODELO   preparar las ensaladas / no cocinar la carne
→ Preparad las ensaladas, pero no cocinéis la carne.

1. hacer la torta / no ponerle el glaseado (*icing*)

2. abrir las botellas de vino / no cortar las rebanadas (*slices*) de naranja

3. sacar los platitos para las tapas / no preparar el chorizo (*pork sausage*)

4. poner la mesa / no colocar los claveles (*carnations*)

5. salir a comprar aceitunas / no ir al supermercado

6. remover la sangría / no servirla en este jarro

7. invitar a Pilar / no decirle nada a Consuelo

8. traer discos compactos / no traer vídeos

NOTA CULTURAL

- **La sangría** es una bebida española hecha con vino tinto, agua y azúcar a la cual se le puede añadir rebanadas de naranja, durazno y otras frutas.
- **El clavel** (*carnation*) es una flor muy apreciada por los españoles. Hay una canción española tradicional titulada "Clavelitos."

G *Expresar en español.* *Exprese los mandatos usando la segunda persona plural del imperativo (**vosotros**).*

1. *Be patient.*

2. *Go away.*

3. *Tell the truth.*

4. *Don't be unpleasant.*

5. *Don't get angry.*

6. *Don't leave yet.*

7. *Attend the lecture.*

8. *Play the piano.*

9. *Go to bed early.*

10. *Look for her on Facebook.*

H ***¡Tengo los nervios de punta!* (I'm on edge!)** *Manuela está nerviosísima estos días por los exámenes y el trabajo, y además se peleó con su novio. Dígale lo que debe hacer y no hacer para calmarse usando el imperativo. Siga el modelo.*

MODELO   comer bien
          → Come bien.

1. dar un paseo todos los días

2. hacer ejercicio

3. tomar una infusión de manzanilla (*chamomile tea*)

4. tranquilizarse escuchando música

5. no ponerse pesimista

6. salir a divertirte

7. reunirse con tus amigos

8. no preocuparse por tonterías

9. buscarse otro novio más compasivo

NOTA CULTURAL

La infusión de manzanilla (*chamomile tea*) se toma mucho en España para curar toda clase de problemas digestivos. Se conoce como calmante natural.

I ***Paquito, ¡no seas así!*** *Ud. está cuidando a un niño malcriado* (spoiled) *que hace diabluras* (is up to mischief). *Escriba oraciones usando el imperativo para decirle lo que debe hacer o no hacer. Siga el modelo.*

MODELO   limpiar la mancha del jugo
          → Limpia la mancha del jugo.

1. portarse bien

2. no hacer payasadas (*to clown around* (el payaso (*clown*)))

3. no ser terco

4. dejar al perro en paz (*to leave alone*)

5. recoger las migas (*crumbs*) de las galletas

6. no derramar (*to spill*) el perfume de tu mamá

7. hacerme caso

8. no encerrarse en el baño

9. venir acá inmediatamente

10. no tocar la computadora

J *Tito el desgraciado* (**unlucky guy**). *Todo le pasa a Tito porque tiene mala suerte. Déle consejos para ayudarlo. Escriba oraciones usando el imperativo de los verbos indicados. Siga los modelos.*

> MODELOS   Tito / mirar
> → Tito, mira.
>
> Tito / no correr
> → Tito, no corras.

1. Tito / darse prisa

2. Tito / no lastimarse

3. Tito / no cortarse el dedo

4. Tito / tener cuidado

5. Tito / no romperse el pie

6. Tito / no encender los fósforos (*matches*)

7. Tito / conducir más lentamente

8. Tito / ponerse una armadura (*suit of armor*)

K *La médica...* *Carlitos se quebró el tobillo jugando al fútbol. Su mamá lo lleva al consultorio donde la médica les da consejos a Carlitos y a su mamá. Complete las oraciones usando el imperativo de los verbos indicados para saber lo que les aconseja la médica. Siga los modelos.*

> MODELOS   Señora, ___póngale___ (ponerle) esta crema.
> Carlitos, ___anda___ (andar) con cuidado.

Las fracturas

escayolado *in a plaster cast*
la muleta *crutch*
la quebradura *fracture, break*

quebrarse (e > ie) *to break*
el tobillo *ankle*
el vendaje *dressing*

1. Señora, _____ (dejarlo) ir al colegio.

2. Carlitos, no _____ (mojarse) la pierna escayolada.

3. Señora, _____ (darle) estas pastillas si le duele el tobillo.

4. Carlitos, no _____ (jugar) deportes por ahora.

5. Señora, _____ (hacerle) una sopa de pollo.

6. Carlitos, no _____ (quitarse) el vendaje.

7. Señora, _____ (traerlo) al consultorio la semana próxima.

8. Carlitos, _____ (venir) a verme el miércoles o el jueves.

9. Carlitos, _____ (salir) a la calle con muletas.

The Position of Object Pronouns with Command Forms

In negative commands, object pronouns (direct, indirect, reflexive) are placed in their usual position before the verb.

No **lo** hagas.   *Don't do it.*

No **se lo** digas.   *Don't tell it to him.*

No **me la** traiga.   *Don't bring it to me.*

No **se** preocupen Uds.   *Please don't worry.*

No **nos** sentemos.	*Let's not sit down.*
No **te los** pongas. (los = guantes)	*Don't put them on.*

Object pronouns follow affirmative commands and are attached to them in writing. When pronouns are attached, an accent mark is placed over the stressed syllable, except when a single object pronoun is added to a one-syllable command form: **dime** (*tell me*); **dímelo** (*tell me it*). However, **dé**, **esté**, and **está** may keep their accent marks when a single object pronoun is added: **deme** or **déme**.

Hazlo.	*Do it.*
Díselo.	*Tell it to him.*
Tráigamela.	*Bring it to me.*
Quédense Uds.	*Please stay.*
Sentémonos.	*Let's sit down.*
Póntelos. (los = guantes)	*Put them on.*
Vete.	*Go away.*

L   *Sí, hágalo.*   *Conteste las preguntas con la forma correcta del imperativo—***Ud.***, ***tú***, ***Uds.** *Cambie los sustantivos a pronombres de complemento directo y haga todos los cambios necesarios. Siga el modelo.*

> MODELO   ¿Quieres que yo te traiga las revistas?
> → Sí, tráemelas.

1. ¿Quieres que yo les dé los informes a los jefes?

2. ¿Uds. quieren que yo les mande los correos electrónicos (a Uds.)?

3. ¿Ud. necesita que le entreguemos el contrato (a Ud.)?

4. ¿Quieres que yo te ponga el abrigo?

5. ¿Uds. necesitan que yo les prepare los tamales (a ellos)?

6. ¿Uds. quieren que les sirvamos el postre (a ellas)?

7. ¿Prefieres que yo te explique la idea?

8. ¿Te interesa que yo le diga los motivos (a ella)?

9. ¿Debemos enseñarle las fotos a Pedro?

M   *No, no lo haga.*   *Ahora, conteste las preguntas del ejercicio L con imperativos negativos. Siga el modelo.*

> MODELO   ¿Quieres que yo te traiga las revistas?
> → No, no me las traigas.

1. ¿Quieres que yo les dé los informes a los jefes?

2. ¿Uds. quieren que yo les mande los correos electrónicos (a Uds.)?

3. ¿Ud. necesita que le entreguemos el contrato (a Ud.)?

4. ¿Quieres que yo te ponga el abrigo?

5. ¿Uds. necesitan que yo les prepare los tamales (a ellos)?

6. ¿Uds. quieren que les sirvamos el postre (a ellas)?

7. ¿Prefieres que yo te explique la idea?

8. ¿Te interesa que yo le diga los motivos (a ella)?

9. ¿Debemos enseñarle las fotos a Pedro?

Indirect Commands

Indirect commands in Spanish consist of **que** + present subjunctive. Object and reflexive pronouns are placed before the verb. English equivalents are *Let/Have him/her/it/them do something.* Sometimes *I hope* is suggested in these sentences.

Que pase.	*Have him come in.*
Que espere.	*Let her wait.*
Que me llamen.	*Have them call me.*
Que lo busque en Google.	*Have her look for it with Google.*
Que se matriculen.	*Let them register.*
Que no se lo dé.	*Don't let him give it to them.*

Subject pronouns are added to indirect commands for emphasis: **Que lo haga *él.*** (*Let **him** do it.*)

Indirect commands of **se** constructions with indirect object pronouns (see "Other Uses of the Indirect Object" in Chapter 19) are usually the equivalents of regular commands in English.

Que no se te olvide tu licencia de manejar.	*Don't forget your driver's license.*
Que no se les acaben los cheques.	*I hope you don't run out of checks.*

N ***Que lo hagan los otros.*** *Rosario se niega a colaborar con sus compañeros de clase en el proyecto de ciencias. Incluso manda que sus amigos se ocupen de todo. Escriba lo que Rosario propone que los otros hagan usando el imperativo indirecto. Cambie el sustantivo a un pronombre de complemento directo. Siga el modelo.*

MODELO   No quiero aprender de memoria todos los elementos de la tabla periódica (*periodic table*). (los demás)
→ Que los aprendan de memoria los demás.

1. No voy a leer los libros de consulta (*reference books*). (Manolo)

2. No me interesa dibujar las tablas (*charts*). (Terencio y Elena)

3. No quiero observar los experimentos en el laboratorio. (Paulina)

4. Me niego a hacer los gráficos (*plot graphs*). (los otros)

5. No tengo ganas de investigar estas teorías. (Samuel)

6. No quiero limpiar las diapositivas de microscopio (*microscope slides*). (mis compañeros)

7. No pienso escribir el informe. (Federico)

O *Expresar en español.* *Exprese los mandatos indirectos en español.*

1. *Have her give it* (el cheque) *to you* (Ud.).

2. *Let them go away.*

3. *Have him send them* (las flores) *to her.*

4. *I hope you* (tú) *don't lose your wallet.* [*use* **se** *construction with indirect object pronoun*]

5. *Let them see our photos on Facebook.*

6. *I hope you* (Uds.) *don't run out of tacos.* [*use* **se** *construction with indirect object pronoun*]

Other Ways of Giving Commands

Often in newspaper ads for employment, recipes, notices, and instructions, the infinitive of the verb is used as an imperative rather than the command form. This type of command is only used in formal written language.

Interesados **mandar** currículum vitae.	*Interested persons,* **send** *your curriculum vitae.*
Enviar historial con fotografía a...	**Send** *résumé with photograph to . . .*
Interesados **llamar** al teléfono...	*Interested persons,* **call** *. . .*
Secar las berenjenas, **pasarlas** por harina y **freírlas** en aceite hirviendo.	**Dry** *the slices of eggplant,* **dip them** *in flour, and* **fry them** *in boiling oil.*

The infinitive rather than the command form is used with the following expressions that convey formality and politeness. They are the English equivalent of asking something with *please,* and may be used in written or spoken language.

Favor de llamarme mañana.	**Please call me** *tomorrow.*
Favor de esperar.	**Please wait.**
Tenga la bondad de sentarse.	**Please sit down.**
Haga el favor de firmar el documento.	**Please sign** *the paper.*
Hágame el favor de enviar el cheque.	**Please send** *the check.*

P *Libro de cocina.* *Escriba los verbos usando el infinitivo como imperativo. Siga el modelo.*

MODELO   Limpie el pollo.
        → Limpiar el pollo.

1. Córtelos a tiritas (*in strips*).

2. Añada el vino.

3. Déjelo evaporar.

4. Pártalos en trozos.

5. Tape las papas.

6. Seque los tomates.

7. Añádalas a la salsa.

8. Remuévalo (*stir*).

9. Póngala en una fuente (*serving dish*).

10. Cuézalo a fuego lento.

Q **El primer día de clase.** *El profesor de español les dice a sus estudiantes que hagan algunas cosas. Cambie el imperativo al infinitivo usando las expresiones indicadas. Siga el modelo.*

> MODELO   Estudien el primer capítulo. (favor de)
> → Favor de estudiar el primer capítulo.

1. Vayan a la biblioteca. (hagan el favor de)

2. Aprendan los diálogos de memoria. (tengan la bondad de)

3. Traigan el diccionario. (favor de)

4. Matricúlense si no lo han hecho todavía. (tengan la bondad de)

5. Compren el libro de texto y el cuaderno de trabajo. (háganme el favor de)

6. Apúntense en esta lista. (favor de)

7. Busquen sitios web en español. (hagan el favor de)

8. Vean películas en español. (tengan la bondad de)

R **Busque empleo en línea.** *Los anuncios para varios empleos aparecen en los periódicos que están en línea. Complételos usando el infinitivo de los verbos indicados como el imperativo. Elija entre* **enviar, dirigirse, llamar, mandar, concertar, escribir, ponerse en contacto, adjuntar, presentarse.** *Siga el modelo.*

> MODELO   Interesados ___*enviar*___ (*send*) curriculum vitae.

1. Interesados _____ (*call*) lunes día 3 al teléfono 91-742-42-63.

2. _____ (*Send*) historial y fotografía al Apto. (apartado = *box*) 36492, 28080 Madrid.

3. Interesados _____ (*write*) a: ARA Publicidad, 08008 Barcelona.

4. Interesados _____ (*apply*), lunes 3 de 9,30 a 14 horas y de 15,30 a 17,30 horas, en C/Alcalá, 54, Srta. Núñez.

5. Interesados _____ (*go to*) a: PAR-7. Avda. del Mediterráneo, 22, 28007 Madrid.

6. Interesados _____ (*attach*) fotografía reciente al apartado de Correos número 2.059 de Madrid.

7. Los interesados deben _____ (*get in touch*) con Ignacio Doncel llamando de 9 a 14 horas y de 16 a 18 horas al teléfono (91) 585-83-64.

8. Las personas interesadas, _____ (*arrange*) entrevista en el teléfono (91) 653-95-00.

S **Ejercicio oral. Situaciones.** *Usted y sus amigos crean escenas en las cuales los personajes emplean el imperativo. Por ejemplo, en el consultorio, la médica les aconseja a sus pacientes sobre sus problemas de salud; en la oficina, un programador le enseña a un compañero cómo hacer funcionar la computadora; en casa, los padres les dicen a sus hijos que arreglen su cuarto; en la clase de cocina, el chef les enseña a los cocineros en entrenamiento a preparar unos platos.*

The Infinitive

Verb + Infinitive Construction

In Spanish, an important function of the infinitive of the verb is to serve as a complement or completion form in verb + infinitive constructions. Many verbs can be followed directly by an infinitive.

—**Espero verlos** en la reunión.	*I hope to see you at the meeting.*
—Yo **pienso ir**, pero Miguel no **podrá asistir**.	*I intend to go, but Miguel won't be able to attend.*
—Laura **necesita tomar** dos cursos.	*Laura has to take two courses.*
—**Debe cursarlos** a distancia.	*She should take them online.*
—Uds. **necesitan tomar** una decisión lo antes posible.	*You need to make a decision as soon as possible.*
—**Procuramos tomarla** para mañana.	*We're trying to do it by tomorrow.*
—**Creo poder** sacar billetes para el concierto.	*I think I can get tickets for the concert.*
—Pero yo **prefiero ver** una película.	*But I prefer to see a film.*

The following verbs can be followed directly by an infinitive.

conseguir (e > i) *to succeed in, manage to*
creer *to think, believe*
deber *should, ought to*
decidir *to decide*
dejar *to let, allow*
desear *to want*
esperar *to hope, expect, wait*
hacer *to make*
impedir (e > i) *to prevent from*
intentar *to try to*
lograr *to succeed in*
mandar *to order to*
merecer *to deserve to*
necesitar *to need, have to*
ofrecer *to offer*
oír *to hear*
olvidar *to forget*
ordenar *to order*

parecer *to seem to*
pensar (e > ie) *to intend to*
permitir *to allow*
poder (o > ue) *can, to be able to*
preferir (e > ie) *to prefer*
pretender *to try to*
procurar *to try*
prohibir *to prohibit*
prometer *to promise to*
querer (e > ie) *to want*
recordar (o > ue) *to remember to*
resolver (o > ue) *to resolve to*
saber *to know how to*
sentir (e > ie) *to regret, be sorry*
soler (o > ue) *to be used to, be accustomed to*
temer *to be afraid to*
ver *to see*

Fiestas y celebraciones. *Practique la construcción del verbo conjugado + infinitivo. Vuelva a escribir las oraciones añadiendo los verbos indicados a las oraciones originales. Mantenga el tiempo verbal de la oración original. Siga el modelo.*

MODELO   Los Arriaga pasan la Nochebuena en casa. (preferir)
→ Los Arriaga prefieren pasar la Nochebuena en casa.

1. Los españoles celebraron el santo del rey. (querer)

2. Uds. siempre iban de vacaciones en la Semana Santa. (procurar)

3. Paco no salió con su novia el Día de los Enamorados. (poder)

4. Haces una barbacoa el Día de la Independencia. (soler)

5. Raúl y Pepita no asistieron a la Misa de Gallo este año. (conseguir)

6. Los niñitos recibían muchos regalos lindos el Día de Reyes. (esperar)

7. No gastas bromas el Día de los Inocentes. (resolver)

8. Hay unos desfiles el Día de la Raza. (deber)

9. Les trajimos flores y bombones a los tíos por el Año Nuevo. (decidir)

NOTA CULTURAL

- **La Nochebuena**, es decir, el 24 de diciembre, se celebra en todos los países hispanohablantes. Las familias suelen festejarla con una cena tradicional. Muchas personas van a la **Misa de Gallo** (*Rooster's Mass*) a medianoche.

- El 6 de enero es la Epifanía o **el Día de los Reyes**. Este día, cuando los Reyes Magos (*Magi*) les traen regalos a los niños, señala el fin de las fiestas de Navidad.

- **La Semana Santa** es el período de la Pascua Florida (*Easter*) cuando mucha gente toma sus vacaciones.

- **El Día de la Raza** (el Día de la Hispanidad, el Día del Encuentro de Dos Mundos) se celebra en la mayoría de los países hispanohablantes. Coincide con el Día de Colón en los Estados Unidos que conmemora la llegada del navegante italiano Cristóbal Colón al nuevo continente (el Nuevo Mundo para los europeos) el 12 de octubre de 1492. Los Reyes Católicos (Isabel I de Castilla y Fernando II de Aragón) financiaron el viaje del explorador en nombre de la Corona (*Crown*). Colón hizo tres viajes posteriores al continente americano.

- En muchos países hispanohablantes, **el día del santo** (*saint's day*) es más importante que el cumpleaños. En el catolicismo, la onomástica (o el onomástico (*name day*)), es el día en que según el santoral (*calendar of saints' days*), se celebra el santo en honor del cual se le puso el nombre a una persona.

- **El Día de los Enamorados** se celebra en el mundo hispánico el 14 de febrero tanto como el Día de San Valentín en los Estados Unidos.

- **El Día de los Inocentes**, parecido a *April Fools' Day*, se festeja en los países hispanohablantes el 28 de diciembre. En España es conocido como el Día de los Santos Inocentes.

B *Expansión de oraciones.* Practique la construcción del verbo conjugado + infinitivo. Vuelva a escribir las oraciones añadiendo los verbos indicados a las oraciones. Mantenga el tiempo verbal de la oración original. Siga el modelo.

MODELO   Sirvió la comida. (mandar)
          → Mandó servir la comida.

1. Nadaban muy bien. (saber)
2. Ud. ganó más plata. (merecer)
3. Terminé el proyecto. (lograr)
4. Felipe está solo en la casa. (temer)
5. Se sale por esa puerta. (prohibir)
6. Han tocado un vals. (preferir)
7. Limpiábamos la casa. (hacer)
8. ¿No escuchasteis estos discos? (querer)
9. Buscan los datos en ese sitio web. (impedir)
10. Encuentra a sus amigos en Facebook. (desear)

Conjugated Verb + Preposition + Infinitive

Some verbs require a preposition before an infinitive. The most common prepositions are **a** and **de**, but some verbs require **en** or **por**.

Van a pedir quesadillas.	*They're going to order quesadillas.*
Comenzó a llover hace media hora.	*It began to rain half an hour ago.*
Yo me encargué de hacer las investigaciones.	*I took charge of doing the research.*
No insistas en sentarte en la primera fila.	*Don't insist on sitting in the first row.*
¿Uds. no se interesaban por coleccionar sellos?	*Weren't you interested in collecting stamps?*

The following verbs take **a** before an infinitive.

acercarse a *to approach*	**enseñar a** *to show how to, teach to*
acostumbrarse a *to be accustomed to*	**invitar a** *to invite to*
animar a *to encourage to*	**ir a** *to be going to*
aprender a *to learn to*	**llegar a** *to get to, succeed in*
atreverse a *to dare to*	**llevar a** *to lead to*
ayudar a *to help*	**meterse a** *to start to*
comenzar (e > ie) a *to begin to*	**negarse (e > ie) a** *to refuse to*
cuidar a/de *to take care of*	**obligar a** *to force to, compel to*
decidirse a *to decide to*	**persuadir a** *to persuade*
dedicarse a *to devote oneself to*	**ponerse a** *to begin to*
disponerse a *to get ready to*	**prepararse a** *to get ready to*
echar(se) a *to begin to*	**renunciar a** *to renounce*
empezar (e > ie) a *to begin to*	**volver (o > ue) a** *to do (something) again*

—¿**Te decidiste a seguir** trabajando en esta oficina?	*Did you make up your mind to continue working in this office?*
—Sí. Ya **me he acostumbrado a trabajar** aquí.	*Yes. I've already gotten used to working here.*

—Mañana **empiezo a estudiar** en serio. *Tomorrow I'll start studying seriously.*
—Yo también **debo ponerme a trabajar**. *I ought to begin working too.*

—¿**Volvieron a pedirte** dinero? *Did they ask you for money again?*
—No. No **se atrevieron a pedirme** nada. *No. They didn't dare ask me for anything.*

After verbs of motion, **a** indicates the purpose of the action.

Bajo **a** ayudarte. *I'm coming downstairs (in order) to help you.*
Subo **a** ayudarte. *I'm coming upstairs (in order) to help you.*

Pasaron **a** verlo. *They stopped by to see him.*

The following verbs take **de** before an infinitive.

acabar de *to have just (done something)*
acordarse (o > ue) de *to remember*
arrepentirse (e > ie) de *to regret*
avergonzarse (o > üe) de *to be ashamed of*
cuidar de/a *to take care of*
dejar de *to stop*

encargarse de *to take charge of*
jactarse de *to boast of*
olvidarse de *to forget*
presumir de *to boast about*
terminar de *to stop*
tratar de *to try to*

—**No te olvides de venir** a cenar el jueves. *Don't forget to come have dinner on Thursday.*
—No te preocupes. **Acabo de anotar** el día y la hora. *Don't worry. I've just written down the day and the hour.*

The following verbs take **en** before an infinitive.

consentir (e > ie) en *to consent to, agree to*
consistir en *to consist of*
dudar en *to hesitate over*
empeñarse en *to insist on, be determined to*
esforzarse (o > ue) en/por *to strive to*

insistir en *to insist on*
interesarse en/por *to be interested in*
quedar en *to agree to*
tardar en *to delay in, be long in*
vacilar en *to hesitate to*

—Carlos **se interesa** mucho **en hablarme**. *Carlos is very interested in talking to me.*
—¿**Consentiste en verlo**? *Did you agree to see him?*
—Sí. **Quedamos en vernos** mañana. *Yes. We agreed to see each other tomorrow.*

The following verbs take **con** before an infinitive.

amenazar con *to threaten to*
contar (o > ue) con *to count on, rely on*
soñar (o > ue) con *to dream of/about*

—En vez de trabajar, Juanita **sueña** todo el día **con hacerse** actriz. *Instead of working, Juanita dreams all day of becoming an actress.*
—Por eso el jefe **amenazó con despedirla**. *That's why the boss threatened to fire her.*

The following verbs take **por** before an infinitive.

empezar (e > ie) por *to begin by*
esforzarse (o > ue) por/en *to strive to*
interesarse por/en *to be interested in*

optar por *to opt to, choose to*
votar por *to vote to*

—¿Los directores **votaron por renovar**   *Did the directors vote to renew the contract?*
el contrato?
—No, **optaron por terminarlo.**   *No, they opted to terminate it.*

There are two verbs that use **que** as the connector to the following infinitive.

Tener que hacer algo means *to have to do something.*

  —¿**Tienes que hacer** algo hoy?   *Do you have to do anything today?*
  —Sí, **tengo que llevar** mi carro al taller.   *Yes, I have to take my car to the mechanic's.*

Hay que hacer algo means *one must do something.* **Hay que** is not conjugated. It expresses a general obligation, not a personal one. Sometimes an English passive construction is the best equivalent for Spanish **hay que hacer algo.**

  —**Hay que trabajar** mucho hoy.   *We have to work hard today. / One has to*
                                         work hard today.
  —Sí, **hay que terminarlo** todo.   *Yes, everything has to be finished.*

C   *¿Qué hacen los estudiantes?* Practique el uso de las preposiciones. Complete las oraciones con las preposiciones correctas. Siga el modelo.

      MODELO   Empiezan ___*a*___ estudiar francés.

1. Ricardo se prepara _____ tomar los exámenes.

2. Carolina y Miguel quedaron _____ verse en la clase de física.

3. Jorge se empeña _____ sacar buenas notas este semestre.

4. Isabel se ha dedicado _____ hacer investigaciones.

5. Marco se jacta _____ saberlo todo.

6. Fernanda volverá _____ cursar biología.

7. Uds. se interesan _____ leer la literatura inglesa.

8. Tú y yo nos encargaremos _____ organizar los archivos.

9. Pablo sueña _____ graduarse el año que viene.

10. Teresa se decidió _____ matricularse en la escuela de verano.

11. Yo trato _____ ir a la biblioteca todas las tardes.

12. Pancho cuenta _____ terminar la carrera (*course of study*) este año.

13. Julia y Lorenzo acaban _____ completar sus requisitos (*requirements*).

14. Nosotros tendríamos _____ buscar otras optativas (*electives*).

D   *Expresar en español.* Exprese las oraciones en español usando la construcción verbo + preposición + infinitivo.

1. *We were accustomed to having dinner at 9:00 P.M.*

2. *Why did they take so long in calling us?*

3. *Esteban refused to lend Diego money.*

4. *Try to pay with a credit card.* (Ud.)

5. *Sing that song again.* (Uds.)

6. *I'm going to attend the lecture.*

7. *Silvia threatened to leave immediately.*

8. *They dream about becoming* (hacerse) *millionaires.*

E **Sinónimos.** *Escoja un sinónimo de las listas de verbos con y sin preposiciones para cada expresión escrita en letra cursiva. Siga el modelo.*

> MODELO   Los miembros del comité *acuerdan* reunirse el martes.
> → Los miembros del comité quedan en reunirse el martes.

1. Pedro *logró* hacerse presidente de la empresa.

2. Consuelo *tiene que* escribir su tesis.

3. *Procuramos* escribir un blog.

4. El profesor *mandó* cerrar los libros.

5. Uds. *sintieron* perderse la boda.

6. Yo no *recordé* recoger los pasteles.

7. ¿Cómo es que *te pusiste a* hacer el presupuesto (*budget*) a las dos de la mañana?

8. No se *dejaba* entrar en las salas de escultura.

9. Están *dudando en* invertir dinero en la compañía.

Infinitive After Prepositions

English uses the present participle (the verb form ending in -*ing*) after most prepositions. Spanish, however, does not allow the use of the present participle (the verb form ending in -**ndo**) after a preposition and requires the infinitive. The infinitive is used after many prepositions, such as **a**, **al**, **a pesar de**, **antes de**, **con el objeto de**, **con tal de**, **después de**, **en caso de**, **en lugar de**, **en vez de**, **hasta**, **para**, **por**, and **sin**. Study the contrasting usage in English and Spanish in the last two examples below.

Almorcemos **después de montar** en bicicleta.	*Let's have lunch **after we go for a** bicycle **ride**.*
Estudie más **para aprender** más.	*Study more **(in order) to learn** more.*
Me alegré **al oír** la buena noticia.	*I became happy **when I heard** the good news.*
Mario irá **con tal de ver** a Susana.	*Mario will go **provided that he sees** Susana.*
Llenen el formulario **antes de firmarlo**.	*Fill out the form **before signing it**.*
¿Entraste **sin vernos**?	*Did you come in **without seeing us**?*

F *Expresar en español.* *Exprese las oraciones en español. Practique usando el infinitivo después de las preposiciones.*

1. *We'll call you (tú) before we go out.*

2. *They traveled to Ponce by car without stopping.*

3. *Children, go (Uds.) to bed after you brush your teeth.*

4. *Bernardo should read a book instead of watching television.*

5. *I'll be in my office until I come home.*

6. *Elena will skate provided that Daniel skates too.*

7. *Invite (Ud.) them in case you see them.*

8. *When we got to the party, we started to dance.*

NOTA CULTURAL

Ponce, ciudad de Puerto Rico, queda en la costa sur de la isla. Se conoce como "La Ciudad Museo" debido a sus muchos museos, entre ellos el Museo de Arte, el Museo de la Historia de Ponce y el Museo de la Música Puertorriqueña. El Museo Castillo Serrallés, conocido como Museo de la Caña (*sugarcane*) y el Ron (*rum*) muestra la importancia de las industrias de la caña y el ron en la historia económica de Puerto Rico.

Al + Infinitive

The construction **al** + infinitive can replace an adverbial clause beginning with **cuando** when the subject of both clauses is the same.

Lo vieron cuando entraron.
→ Lo vieron **al entrar**.   *They saw him when they came in.*

Lo perdí cuando me fui.
→ Lo perdí **al irme**.   *I lost it when I left.*

The construction **al** + infinitive can also replace a clause beginning with **cuando** that refers to future time and is in the subjunctive.

Te lo diremos cuando lleguemos.
→ Te lo diremos **al llegar**.   *We'll tell you when we get there.*

Muéstrame el informe cuando lo termines.
→ Muéstrame el informe **al terminarlo**.   *Show me the report when you finish it.*

The **al** + infinitive phrase may also occur at the beginning of a sentence.

Al entrar, lo vieron.   *When they came in, they saw him.*

Al llegar, te lo diremos.   *When we get there, we'll tell you.*

The English equivalent of the **al** + infinitive construction is *upon doing something*, but this construction is literary and formal whereas **al** + infinitive is part of everyday speech in Spanish. Thus, **Lo vieron al entrar** may be translated as *They saw him upon entering*, but this English translation is much less common, especially in speech.

In everyday language, including in much modern writing, the **al** + infinitive construction may be used even when the subjects of the two verbs are different. The subject of the infinitive is merely placed after it.

Lo vieron cuando él entró en el café.
→ Lo vieron **al entrar él** en el café.   *They saw him when he came into the café.*

Me devolvió el libro cuando tú se lo
   recordaste.
→ Me devolvió el libro **al recordárselo tú**.   *She returned the book to me when you*
   reminded her about it.

Decidimos mudarnos cuando papá
   consiguió un ascenso.
→ Decidimos mudarnos **al conseguir**   *We decided to move when Dad got*
   papá un ascenso.   *a promotion.*

G   *La salud ante todo. Explique lo que hacen estas personas para mantenerse en forma. Reemplace las cláusulas que empiecen con* **cuando** *con la construcción* **al** + *infinitivo. Siga el modelo.*

MODELO   Hago ejercicio cuando me levanto.
         → Hago ejercicio al levantarme.

Para estar en forma

la comida sana *healthy food*	**mantenerse en forma** *to stay fit*
el gimnasio *gym(nasium)*	**trotar** *to jog*
levantar pesas *to lift weights*	

1. Mis padres toman sus vitaminas cuando desayunan.

2. Pablo y yo trotamos cuando salimos de la escuela.

3. Cuando salen del trabajo, Teresa y Laura van al gimnasio.

4. Tú levantas pesas cuando te despiertas.

5. Vosotros camináis cuando termináis de almorzar.

6. Cuando salgo a comer, pido comida sana.

7. Elena me llama cuando llega a la piscina.

8. Cuando termino un maratón, me tomo una botella de agua con electrolitos.

H   *¡Qué oficina! Cuente lo que pasa en la oficina del señor Montalbán. Reemplace las cláusulas que empiecen con* **cuando** *con la construcción* **al** + *infinitivo. Fíjese que en algunas de las oraciones los sujetos son diferentes en las dos cláusulas. Siga el modelo.*

MODELO   El señor Montalbán se enoja cuando sus empleados no cumplen con su deber.
         → El señor Montalbán se enoja al no cumplir sus empleados con su deber.

El mundo del trabajo

chismear *to gossip*	**dirigirse (a alguien)** *to address (someone)*
convocar una reunión *to call a meeting*	**gruñón/gruñona** *grumpy, grouchy*
cumplir con su deber *to do one's duty,*	**molestarse** *to get annoyed*
do what one is supposed to do	**ponerse** + adjetivo *to become*

1. Los empleados se quejan cuando el señor Montalbán exige demasiado.

2. Cuando ve un problema grande, el señor Montalbán convoca una reunión.

3. Los empleados se ponen gruñones cuando reciben el aviso de la reunión.

4. En la reunión, todo el mundo se calló cuando entró el señor Montalbán.

5. El señor Montalbán se puso muy serio cuando se dirigió a sus empleados.

6. Cuando se fue el señor Montalbán, todos empezaron a chismear.

Infinitive After Verbs of Perception

The infinitive is used after verbs of perception such as **ver** and **oír** to signal a completed action. The gerund, rather than the infinitive, is used to show an incomplete or in-progress action, but the gerund of verbs of motion is not common.

Los **oí cantar**.	*I heard them sing.*
Los **oí cantando**.	*I heard them singing.*
¿Uds. no nos **vieron entrar**?	*Didn't you see us come in?*
¿Uds. no nos **vieron haciendo las maletas**?	*Didn't you see us packing?*

The gerund is often replaced by **que** + imperfect in everyday spoken Spanish.

Los oí **que cantaban**.	*I heard them singing.*
Los vimos **que leían**.	*We saw them reading.*

The construction consisting of **que** + imperfect is preferred for verbs of motion.

Te vi **que salías**.	*I saw you going out.*
Los oímos **que caminaban** arriba.	*We heard them walking upstairs.*

I ***¿Qué oyó?*** *Lorenzo tiene problema del oído y va con una audioprotesista (hearing aid specialist) porque necesita un aparato. La especialista le pregunta lo que oyó. Siga el modelo.*

MODELO ¿Oyó Ud. el ruido de los coches? (frenar)
 → Sí, los oí frenar.

Los ruidos

el aterrizaje *landing*	**maullar** *to meow*
aterrizar *to land*	**el maullido** *meow*
despegar *to take off*	**roncar** *to snore*
el despegue *takeoff*	**los ronquidos** *snoring*
frenar *to brake*	**susurrar** *to whisper*
ladrar *to bark*	**el susurro** *whisper*
el ladrido *(dog) barking*	

1. ¿Oyó Ud. el ladrido de los perros? (ladrar)

2. ¿Oyó Ud. el maullido del gato? (maullar)

3. ¿Oyó Ud. el despegue y el aterrizaje de los aviones? (despegar, aterrizar)

4. ¿Oyó Ud. el susurro de las hojas? (susurrar)

5. ¿Oyó Ud. los gritos de sus hijos? (gritar)

6. ¿Oyó Ud. los ronquidos de su mujer? (roncar)

J ¿Qué vieron Uds.? *Escriba oraciones usando el verbo de percepción* **ver**. *Siga el modelo.*

    MODELO   María / bailar
               → La vimos bailar.

1. José y Pablo / trotar

2. vosotros / hacer ejercicio

3. Roberto / entrar en la discoteca

4. la señorita Barba / dictar una conferencia

5. Uds. [*masc.*] / hablar por celular

6. tú / escanear los documentos

7. Ud. [*fem.*] / salir de la tienda por departamentos

The Infinitive Preceded by que

The infinitive is often preceded by **que**. However, the **que** + infinitive construction cannot be used with verbs of searching, needing, and requesting. In these cases, **para** is used.

Nos han dado tantas cosas **que/para hacer**.	*They've given us so many things to do.*
Compra algo **que/para leer**.	*Buy something to read.*
Pidió algo **para aplacar** su sed.	*He ordered something to slake his thirst.*
Queríamos algo **para comer**.	*We wanted something to eat.*

K ¿Qué o para? *Complete las oraciones usando* **que** *o* **para** *antes del infinitivo.*

1. Teníamos mucho _____ hacer.

2. Están buscando algo _____ beber.

3. Quiero algo _____ leer.

4. Hay muchas cosas _____ tomar.

Adjective + *de* + Infinitive

The construction adjective + **de** + infinitive is used when the infinitive of a transitive verb is not followed by an object or a clause. The **de** is omitted when an object or a clause appears.

El vasco es muy difícil **de** aprender.	*Basque is very difficult to learn.*
Es muy difícil aprender vasco.	*It's very difficult to learn Basque.*
Su teoría es imposible **de** comprobar.	*His theory is impossible to prove.*
Es imposible comprobar su teoría.	*It's impossible to prove his theory.*

L *¿De o nada?* *Complete las oraciones con* de *antes del infinitivo cuando sea necesario. Si no es necesario escribir la preposición, escriba una X.*

1. No es posible _____ comprenderlo.

2. Eso es fácil _____ ver.

3. Es triste _____ pensar que ya no vuelven.

4. El japonés no es difícil _____ entender.

M *Ejercicio oral. Juego de expansión de oraciones.* *Se juega entre dos equipos. Uno de los equipos presenta una oración y un infinitivo. El otro equipo tiene que expandir la oración. Cada respuesta correcta vale un punto. Se juega hasta que uno de los equipos consiga diez puntos. Por ejemplo:*

Visitan nuestro sitio web. (necesitar)
→ Necesitan visitar nuestro sitio web.

Nieva. (comenzar)
→ Comienza a nevar.

Yo creé la base de datos. (encargarse)
→ Yo me encargué de crear la base de datos.

Nouns and Their Modifiers; Pronouns

Nouns and Articles

Gender of Nouns

In Spanish, all nouns are either masculine or feminine. There are ways to determine the gender of most nouns.

Most nouns that end in -**o** or that refer to males are masculine.

el banco	el libro
el doctor	el padre
el duque	el piano
el hijo	el profesor
el hombre	el señor
el laboratorio	el toro

Most nouns that end in -**a** or that refer to females are feminine.

la cartera	la madre
la computadora	la mujer
la duquesa	la oficina
la flauta	la profesora
la hija	la señora
la librería	la vaca

There are many nouns that end in -**a** and -**ma** that are masculine, and some nouns that end in -**o** that are feminine. The gender of these words must be memorized.

Masculine

el clima	el planeta
el día	el poema
el idioma	el problema
el mapa	el programa
el mediodía	el sistema
el panda	el tranvía

Feminine

la foto (*abbreviation of* la fotografía)
la mano
la moto (*abbreviation of* la motocicleta)
la radio

The gender of most nouns that end in **-e** or a consonant cannot be predicted and must therefore be memorized.

Masculine

el aceite	el disfraz *disguise*
el alfiler *pin*	el disquete
el arroz	el examen
el billete	el informe
el buzón *mailbox*	el jarabe *syrup*
el cine	el lápiz
el cobre *copper*	el papel
el desván *attic*	el plan

Feminine

la base	la luz
la clase	la piel
la gente	la red
la llave	la torre *tower*

Nouns that have endings in **-dad**, **-tad**, **-tud**, **-umbre**, **-ión**, **-ie**, **-cia**, **-ez**, **-eza**, **-nza**, **-sis**, and **-itis** are usually feminine.

la artritis	la multitud
la certidumbre *certainty*	la nación
la ciudad	la pereza *laziness*
la crisis	la presencia
la cumbre *(mountain) top*	la reunión
la diferencia	la sencillez *simplicity*
la esperanza *hope*	la serie *series*
la felicidad *happiness*	la sinusitis
la fraternidad	la superficie *surface*
la juventud *youth*	la tesis *thesis*
la libertad	la verdad

Nouns that refer to people (and some animals) that end in **-or**, **-és**, **-ón**, and **-ín** are usually masculine and add **-a** to make the feminine form. The accent mark of the masculine form is dropped in the feminine.

Masculine	Feminine
el anfitrión *host*	la anfitriona *hostess*
el asesor *consultant*	la asesora
el bailarín *dancer*	la bailarina
el campeón *champion*	la campeona
el director	la directora
el doctor	la doctora
el francés	la francesa
el león *lion*	la leona *lioness*
el profesor	la profesora

Nouns that end in **-aje**, **-ambre**, **-or**, **-án**, or a stressed vowel are usually masculine.

el alacrán *scorpion*	el equipaje
el amor	el paisaje
el calambre *cramp*	el refrán *proverb*
el champú	el rubí
el enjambre *swarm (of bees, etc.)*	el valor

In forming the feminine, some nouns that refer to people (or some animals) change only their article but not their form. Many of these nouns end in **-e**, **-a**, **-ista**, **-nte**, or a consonant.

el/la agente	el/la intérprete *interpreter*
el/la artista	el/la joven *young man/woman*
el/la atleta *athlete*	el/la líder *leader*
el/la cantante	el/la mártir *martyr*
el/la dentista	el/la pianista
el/la dependiente	el/la tigre *tiger* (ALSO *tigresa*)
el/la estudiante	el/la turista

A feminine form ending in **-nta** is common: **la dependienta, la estudianta**.

Sometimes the feminine form of a noun is not predictable from the masculine.

Masculine	Feminine
el actor *actor*	la actriz *actress*
el emperador *emperor*	la emperatriz *empress*
el príncipe *prince*	la princesa *princess*
el rey *king*	la reina *queen*

The days of the week are masculine.

Iremos a la sierra **el jueves** y volveremos **el lunes**.	*We'll go to the mountains on Thursday and we'll come back on Monday.*

The months of the year are masculine.

el enero más frío	*the coldest January*
el agosto más caluroso	*the hottest August*

The names of languages are masculine.

El español se habla en más de veinte países.	*Spanish is spoken in more than twenty countries.*
El inglés es el idioma internacional de la medicina.	*English is the international language of medicine.*

Compound nouns that consist of a verb and a noun are masculine.

el abrelatas *can opener*	el paraguas *umbrella*
el cumpleaños *birthday*	el portaaviones *aircraft carrier*
el lavaplatos *dishwasher*	el sacacorchos *corkscrew*
el limpiaparabrisas *windshield wiper*	el saltamontes *grasshopper*
el parachoques *bumper*	el salvavidas *lifeguard, life preserver*

Numbers (**el número**) are masculine.

El veintisiete de enero es el cumpleaños de Mozart.	*January 27 is Mozart's birthday.*
Mi número de suerte es **el 15**.	*My lucky number is 15.*

Colors are masculine when used as nouns.

Me gusta **el azul** más que **el marrón**.	*I like blue more than brown.*

Many names of trees are masculine, while their fruit is usually feminine.

El árbol	**La fruta**
el almendro *almond tree*	la almendra
el castaño *chestnut tree*	la castaña
el cerezo *cherry tree*	la cereza
el limonero *lemon tree*	el limón
el manzano *apple tree*	la manzana
el melocotonero *peach tree*	el melocotón
el naranjo *orange tree*	la naranja
el peral *pear tree*	la pera

All infinitives used as nouns are masculine.

El navegar en la red es divertido.	**Surfing** *the web is fun.*
El fumar hace daño.	**Smoking** *is harmful.*

Feminine nouns that begin with stressed **a** (spelled either **a** or **ha**) take the definite article **el** in the singular. However, in the plural, they take the usual feminine plural definite article **las**. Adjectives modifying these feminine singular nouns with **el** as the definite article appear in the feminine form. These nouns also take **un**, not **una**, as their indefinite article.

el agua *water*	el habla *speech, language*
el águila *eagle*	el hacha *hatchet*
el ala *wing*	el hada *fairy*
el alma *soul*	el hambre *hunger*
el área *area*	
el ave *bird*	

el agua fría del lago	*the cold water of the lake*
el hambre crónica	*chronic hunger*
las aguas tibias del Caribe	*the warm waters of the Caribbean*
un águila blanca	*a white eagle*
un alma generosa	*a generous soul*
un hada hermosa	*a beautiful fairy*
unas almas amorosas	*some loving souls*

The names of rivers, seas, and oceans are masculine.

Los Estados Unidos tiene costa en **el (océano) Atlántico** y **el Pacífico**.	*The United States has coasts on the Atlantic Ocean and on the Pacific.*
El (río) Amazonas atraviesa el Brasil.	*The Amazon River passes through Brazil.*

Some Spanish nouns have both a masculine and feminine gender, but with a difference in meaning.

Masculine	Feminine
el busca *beeper, pager*	la busca *search*
el capital *money*	la capital *capital city*
el coma *coma*	la coma *comma*
el cometa *comet*	la cometa *kite*

Masculine	Feminine
el frente *front* (*weather, military*)	la frente *forehead*
el mañana *tomorrow*	la mañana *morning*
el orden *order* (*tidiness*)	la orden *order* (*command*)
el policía *policeman*	la policía *policewoman, police force*

The word **arte** is masculine in the singular but feminine in the plural.

el arte español	*Spanish art*
las bellas artes	*fine arts*

Some nouns do not vary in gender and are applied to males and females, in some cases with a change in article.

el ángel	el personaje *character* (*in a book, play*)
el/la bebé	el/la testigo *witness*
el/la modelo	la víctima
la persona	

Thus you say **Juan fue *la* víctima más joven del accidente** but **Marta es *la* testigo más importante**.

Sometimes an inanimate feminine noun can be applied to a male person with a change in meaning. In this case, the new noun is masculine.

la cámara *camera*	**el** cámara *cameraman*
las medias *socks*	**los** Medias Rojas *the Red Sox*
la trompeta *trumpet*	**el** trompeta *trumpet player*

Spanish has borrowed many words from English in various technical and cultural fields. These borrowings are almost always masculine.

la app (el app)	el fax	el post
el blog	el film	el software
el campus	el jazz	el spa
el chat	el laptop	la suite
el déficit	el login/logon/logoff	el ticket
el email	el marketing	el/la web
el (e)spray *aerosol*	la pizza	

A few nouns can appear in either gender with no change in meaning.

el/la lente *lens*
el/la sartén *frying pan*

Many speakers change **la radio** to **el radio** under the influence of the ending **-o**. For other speakers, **el radio** refers to the appliance, while **la radio** refers to the medium of communication.

Se me descompuso **el radio**.	*My radio broke.*
Siempre escucho **la radio** mexicana.	*I always listen to Mexican radio.*

La mar de + adjective is used in colloquial speech to mean *very, extremely.*

Él es **la mar de** simpático.	*He is extremely nice.*

A **¿Masculino o femenino?** *Escriba la forma masculina o femenina del artículo definido para cada sustantivo de la lista.*

1. _____ concierto
2. _____ sistema
3. _____ escritor
4. _____ tierra
5. _____ drama
6. _____ mano
7. _____ natación
8. _____ día
9. _____ natalidad (*birthrate*)
10. _____ parque
11. _____ legumbre
12. _____ guión (*script*)
13. _____ capital (*capital city*)
14. _____ pararrayos (*lightning rod*)
15. _____ computadora
16. _____ seguridad (*security*)
17. _____ rompecabezas (*puzzle, riddle*)
18. _____ idioma
19. _____ dirección (*address*)
20. _____ escocés
21. _____ crisis
22. _____ verde
23. _____ frente (*forehead*)
24. _____ ascensor
25. _____ parabrisas (*windshield*)
26. _____ agua

B **Por parejas.** *Escriba quién es la pareja femenina (counterpart) de cada hombre. Practique usando la forma femenina de los sustantivos. Escriba el artículo también.*

1. el profesor / _____
2. el rey / _____
3. el artista / _____
4. el abogado / _____
5. el príncipe / _____
6. el gobernador (*governor*) / _____
7. el representante / _____
8. el policía / _____
9. el emperador / _____
10. el actor / _____
11. el estadista (*statesman*) / _____
12. el holandés (*Dutchman*) / _____
13. el cliente / _____
14. el atleta / _____
15. el programador / _____
16. el bailarín / _____

C **Expresar en español.** *Exprese las oraciones en español. Escriba los números con letras.*

1. Mr. Galíndez is leaving on a business trip on Tuesday and will return on Thursday.

2. Don't put (Ud.) the frying pan in the dishwasher.

3. English and French are the official languages of Canada.

4. Mozart was born on January 27, 1756.

5. My favorite colors are green and blue.

6. Let's pick apples from that (apple) tree.

7. The national bird (el ave) of the United States is the bald (calvo) eagle.

8. Did they like the cruise (crucero) in the Mediterranean or the Caribbean better?

9. Reading is so pleasant.

10. A tropical front will arrive tomorrow.

11. We'll invest our capital in a multinational company.

12. What are the names of the characters in the novel?

13. The cameraman lost his camera.

14. In the film we saw, the angels saved the baby [masc.].

15. The witnesses talked to the victim of the accident.

Number of Nouns

In Spanish, nouns that end in a vowel form the plural by adding -**s**.

Singular	Plural
la carretera *highway*	las carreteras
el cine	los cines
el clarinete	los clarinetes
la empresa	las empresas
el espejo *mirror*	los espejos
el hermano	los hermanos
el jefe	los jefes
la placa *license plate*	las placas

Nouns that end in a consonant, including **y**, form the plural by adding -**es**.

Singular	Plural
el celular	los celulares
el consultor *consultant*	los consultores
el examen	los exámenes
el huracán *hurricane*	los huracanes
el inglés	los ingleses
el lápiz	los lápices
la ley *law*	las leyes

Singular	Plural
el limón	los limones
el mes	los meses
la opinión	las opiniones
el origen	los orígenes
el país	los países
el peatón *pedestrian*	los peatones
el pez *fish*	los peces
el titular *headline*	los titulares
la voz *voice*	las voces

Notes on the Formation of the Plural

1 · Nouns stressed on the last syllable (with a written accent mark) in the singular lose their accent mark in the plural: **limón** → **limones, opinión** → **opiniones, inglés** → **ingleses, autobús** → **autobuses**. Exception: **país** → **países**.

2 · **Lápices** and all nouns that have a written accent on the next to the last syllable in the singular retain that accent in the plural: **azúcar** → **azúcares**.

3 · **Examen, joven**, and **origen** have an accent mark in the plural: **exámenes, jóvenes, orígenes**.

4 · A few common nouns shift their stress in the plural: **el carácter** → **los caracteres, el régimen** → **los regímenes, el espécimen** → **los especímenes**.

5 · When -**es** is added to final -**z**, the **z** is changed to **c**: **pez** → **peces, voz** → **voces, lápiz** → **lápices**.

6 · Nouns that end in a stressed -**í** or -**ú** add -**es** to form the plural: **el rubí** → **los rubíes, el tabú** → **los tabúes**.

7 · Nouns of more than one syllable ending in an unstressed vowel plus **s** do not add a plural ending.

el abrelatas *can opener* →	los abrelatas
el atlas →	los atlas
la crisis →	las crisis
el miércoles →	los miércoles
el paraguas →	los paraguas
el viernes →	los viernes

8 · The masculine plural of nouns referring to people can refer to a group of males or a group of males and females.

los abuelos *grandfathers, grandparents, grandmother and grandfather*
los hermanos *brothers, brothers and sisters*
los hijos *sons, children, sons and daughters*
los Reyes de España *the King and Queen of Spain*
los tíos *uncles, aunt and uncle, aunts and uncles*

9 · If a proper name refers to a family, it has no plural form. If a group of individuals happen to have the same name, a plural form is used. Names that end in -**z** are usually invariable.

Los Prado viven en esta calle.	*The Prado family lives on this street.*
La guía telefónica tiene tantos **Morelos** y **Blancos**.	*The telephone book has so many Morelos and Blancos (people named Morelo and Blanco).*
¿No conoces a **los Fernández**?	*Don't you know the Fernándezes?*

10 · Some nouns are always plural in Spanish, as they are in English.

los anteojos *eyeglasses*
los auriculares *earphones*
las gafas *eyeglasses*
los gemelos *twins, binoculars, cuff links*
las tijeras *scissors*

11 · Some nouns are usually plural in Spanish. Many of them appear in set expressions, for example: **hacerle cosquillas a alguien** (*to tickle someone*).

las afueras *outskirts*
los alrededores *surroundings*
los bienes *goods*
los celos *jealousy*
las cosquillas *tickling*
las ganas *urge, desire*
las vacaciones *vacation*

Note that **las ganas** (**tener ganas de (hacer algo)** (*to feel like (doing something)*)) appears in the singular in **No me da la gana** (*I don't feel like it*).

12 · The Spanish equivalent of *They washed their hair* is **Se lavaron la cabeza**. Notice that Spanish uses the singular noun **la cabeza** implying there is one for each person.

Se cortaron **la rodilla**.	*They cut their knees.*
Se pusieron **la chaqueta**.	*They put on their jackets.*
¿Tienen Uds. **novia**?	*Do you have girlfriends?*

D *En plural.* Escriba la forma plural de los sustantivos y sus artículos definidos.

1. el guante
2. el lavaplatos
3. la religión
4. el origen
5. la reunión
6. el color
7. la amistad
8. el rey
9. la voz
10. el martes
11. el irlandés
12. el paréntesis
13. el señor Sánchez
14. la luz
15. el té
16. el israelí

E ***El arca de Noé.*** *No se olvide de que hay dos animales de cada especie que suben al arca de Noé. Practique usando el plural de los sustantivos y sus artículos definidos. Siga el modelo.*

MODELO   caballo
         → los caballos

1. vaca
2. orangután
3. elefante
4. avestruz (*ostrich*)
5. león
6. castor (*beaver*)
7. loro (*parrot*)
8. cóndor

9. delfín (*dolphin*)
10. gorrión (*sparrow*)
11. faisán (*pheasant*)
12. pantera (*panther*)
13. tigre
14. oveja
15. mono (*monkey*)
16. camello

F ***Sobre gustos no hay nada escrito.* (Everyone to his or her own taste.)**
Escriba oraciones en las cuales Ud. explica lo que a cada persona le gusta comer. Cambie el sustantivo (la comida) al plural. Siga el modelo.

MODELO   Carlos / comer / haba
         → Carlos come habas.

Los alimentos

el aguacate *avocado*
el camarón *shrimp*
el chile *chile (chili) pepper*
el espárrago *asparagus*
el frijol *kidney bean*

el guisante *pea*
el haba *bean*
la palomita de maíz *popcorn (one piece)*
la papa *potato*

1. Lucía / pedir / guisante
2. yo / preferir / espárrago
3. tú / ordenar / papa
4. Claudia y Jesús / querer / chile
5. nosotros / tener ganas de comer / aguacate
6. Ud. y Luis / pedir / frijol
7. Ud. / querer / palomita de maíz
8. vosotros / comer / camarón

NOTA CULTURAL

Alimentos de la dieta mexicana

El aguacate, los frijoles, el maíz y el chile, alimentos básicos de la dieta mexicana, son los mismos hoy día que comían los indígenas precolombinos de México. A veces tienen otro nombre u otros nombres, por ejemplo, el aguacate se llama «palta» en Perú, Chile, Argentina, Uruguay y Bolivia; los frijoles son conocidos como «porotos» en Argentina, Uruguay, Chile, Bolivia y Paraguay; el maíz se llama «choclo» en México, Perú, Chile, Colombia y Ecuador; el chile se conoce como «chile» en México y América Central, «ají» en Puerto Rico, Cuba, Panamá y unos países de Sudamérica o «pimiento» en otros países sudamericanos. En España el aguacate es conocido como «aguacate», los frijoles se llaman «alubias» o «judías», el maíz se llama «maíz» y el chile es conocido como «pimiento» o «guindilla».

G ***¡Que toque la orquesta!*** *Escriba la forma plural de los sustantivos y sus artículos definidos.*

1. piano
2. flauta
3. viola
4. clarinete
5. violonchelo
6. violín

7. trompeta
8. trombón
9. arpa
10. oboe
11. tambor
12. tuba

The Definite Article: Forms and Uses

In Spanish, the definite article (English: *the*) changes its form to agree with the noun in gender (masculine/feminine) and number (singular/plural).

	MASCULINE	FEMININE
SINGULAR	el	la
PLURAL	los	las

el cuerpo   la cabeza
los cuerpos   las cabezas

In Spanish, unlike English, the definite article is used before a noun to refer to something in a general way (mass or uncountable nouns) or to refer to all the members of its class. Colors, like abstract nouns, also require the article.

La democracia es el mejor sistema de gobierno.	*Democracy is the best system of government.*
El agua mineral es buena para la digestión.	*Mineral water is good for digestion.*
El verde es el color que más me gusta.	*Green is the color I like best.*
No le gustan **las espinacas**.	*She doesn't like spinach.*

Note that the sentence in the preceding example, **No le gustan las espinacas**, is ambiguous out of context. It can mean she doesn't like all spinach, that is, spinach in general, or she doesn't like a particular spinach already mentioned in the conversation.

The definite article **el** is used before the names of languages except directly after **hablar** and after the prepositions **de** and **en**. It is also commonly omitted directly after the verbs **aprender**, **enseñar**, **estudiar**, **leer**, **practicar**, and **saber**.

Hablamos bien **el** español.	*We speak Spanish well.*
Hablamos español.	*We speak Spanish.*
Te presto el diccionario **de** chino.	*I'll lend you the Chinese dictionary.*
Escribió la carta **en** francés.	*He wrote the letter in French.*
Saben hebreo y **estudian** japonés.	*They know Hebrew and they're studying Japanese.*

The definite article is used before titles except when the person is being addressed directly. It is not used before **don/doña** and **Santo/San/Santa**.

El señor Lerma está bien.	*Mr. Lerma is well.*
Señor Lerma, ¿cómo está Ud.?	*Mr. Lerma, how are you?*
José nació el día de **San** José.	*José was born on San José's day.*

The definite article is used to express the time of day.

Son **las cuatro** y media.	*It's four thirty.*
Se acostaron a **la una** de la mañana.	*They went to bed at 1 A.M.*
Hoy me desperté a **las siete cincuenta**.	*I woke up at seven fifty today.*

The definite article is used with the days of the week.

Nos vemos **el jueves**, entonces.	*We'll see each other **on Thursday**, then.*
Los lunes el museo está cerrado.	***On Mondays** the museum is closed.*
¿Quién enseña la clase **del martes**?	*Who's teaching **Tuesday's** class?*

The definite article is omitted after forms of **ser**.

Hoy es **miércoles**.	*Today is **Wednesday**.*

However, the definite article is used after forms of **ser** when **ser** means *to happen, to take place*.

Eso fue **el domingo**.	*That was (happened) **on Sunday**.*
El concierto fue **el sábado**.	*The concert was **on Saturday**.*

The definite article is omitted before the names of the days of the week when a date follows.

viernes, cinco de agosto	***Friday**, August fifth*

The definite article is used with the names of the seasons. It can be omitted after the preposition **en** when it is suggested that the event mentioned occurs in that season every year.

Me encanta **el verano**.	*I love summer.*
Alano va a Madrid **en el otoño**.	*Alano is going to Madrid in the fall.*
Gonzalo viaja a Barcelona **en invierno**.	*Gonzalo travels to Barcelona in winter.*

Spanish uses the definite article rather than the possessive adjective commonly used in English with parts of the body and articles of clothing, especially with reflexive verbs.

Mauricio está cepillándose **los dientes**.	*Mauricio is brushing his teeth.*
Sofi se puso **los jeans**.	*Sofi put on her jeans.*

The definite article is used before infinitives that function as nouns. The article is often omitted when the infinitive is the subject of the sentence.

(El) Robar es malo.	*Stealing is bad.*
El estafar es también un vicio.	*Cheating is also a vice.*

The definite article is used with the names of rivers, oceans, and mountains.

El Sena pasa por París y **el Támesis** por Londres.	*The Seine flows through Paris and the Thames through London.*
Los Pirineos quedan entre España y Francia.	*The Pyrenees are between Spain and France.*

The definite article is traditionally used before the names of some countries, although it tends to be omitted more and more in contemporary Spanish. However, the definite article must be used before the name of a country, city, or continent that is modified.

en **(los)** Estados Unidos	*in the United States*
a través de **(del)** Canadá	*through Canada*
por **(la)** Argentina	*through Argentina*
hacia **(el)** Perú	*toward Peru*
sobre **(el)** Japón	*about Japan*
la Europa central	*Central Europe*
la España medieval	*Medieval Spain*

When the definite article is part of the name of a country or city, it is not omitted.

El Cairo	*Cairo*
El Salvador	*El Salvador*
La Coruña	*La Coruña (city in northwestern Spain)*
La Paz	*La Paz (capital of Bolivia)*
La República Dominicana	*The Dominican Republic*
Las Vegas	*Las Vegas*
Los Álamos	*Los Alamos*
Los Ángeles	*Los Angeles*

Some place names always take the definite article.

la India	*India*
los Países Bajos	*the Netherlands*
el Reino Unido	*the United Kingdom*

The definite article is used before nouns of measurement.

un dólar **la libra**	*a dollar a pound*
cincuenta centavos **el kilo**	*fifty centavos a kilo*

In Spanish, many set phrases that require the definite article do not have it in their English equivalents.

a/en/de **la** iglesia	*to/in/from church*
en **la** televisión	*on television*
en **el** mar	*at sea, on/in the sea*

H **El artículo definido.** *Para cada sustantivo, escriba el artículo definido singular, el artículo definido plural y el plural del sustantivo.*

1. aceituna (*olive*)	11. salvavidas	21. tenedor (*fork*)
2. ensayo	12. origen	22. pirámide
3. agua	13. foto	23. raíz
4. árbol	14. mes	24. sacapuntas (*pencil sharpener*)
5. dulce	15. serpiente	25. nación
6. demora (*delay*)	16. sillón	26. pintor
7. sal	17. miel	27. jardín
8. pasaporte	18. lápiz	28. jugador
9. volcán	19. francés	29. esquí
10. actividad	20. vez	30. pan

I **Retrato (portrait) de la heroína romántica.** *Armando, un pintor romántico, pinta el retrato de la mujer ideal. ¿Cómo es? Para saberlo, complete las frases con la forma correcta del artículo definido y el sustantivo. Siga el modelo.*

MODELO   La mujer ideal tiene...
               (*feet*) ___*los pies*___ pequeños

1. (*eyes*) _____ azules	6. (*teeth*) _____ como perlas
2. (*cheeks*) _____ rosadas	7. (*hair*) _____ como el oro
3. (*hands*) _____ suaves	8. (*neck*) _____ como cisne (*swan*)
4. (*fingers*) _____ largos	9. (*ears*) _____ bien formadas
5. (*lips*) _____ como cerezas	

J **¿Artículo definido o no?** *Complete las oraciones con la forma correcta del artículo definido cuando sea necesario. Si no es necesario escriba una X.*

1. Bogotá, _____ capital de Colombia, se encuentra en las montañas.

2. Nos interesa _____ cine.

3. Laura y Encarnación saben perfectamente _____ ruso.

4. Hay multa por _____ ensuciar las calles.

5. ¿Adónde va Ud., _____ señor Maldonado?

6. Volvimos a casa a _____ diez y cuarto.

7. Estas revistas están escritas en _____ árabe.

8. La comida fue _____ miércoles.

9. _____ legumbres son buenas para _____ salud.

10. _____ verano es la estación más agradable del año.

11. Hoy es _____ viernes.

12. Hicimos investigaciones sobre _____ España contemporánea.

13. _____ duraznos se venden a dos dólares _____ libra en verano.

14. ¿Habrá algo interesante en _____ televisión?

15. _____ señorita Suárez llega de _____ iglesia.

16. La boda será _____ domingo.

NOTA CULTURAL

El catalán se habla en Cataluña (*Catalunya* en catalán), la región al nordeste de España. El español y el catalán son oficiales en Cataluña. El catalán también se habla en Valencia (el dialecto se llama valenciano) y en las islas Baleares (el dialecto es el mallorquín).

K **Expresar en español.** *Exprese las oraciones en español.*

1. *The Sánchez family is going to Florida in the spring.*

2. *Florencia put on her socks.*

3. *Give (Ud.) us the Latin books.*

4. *Juli and Nicolás love swimming.*

5. *What did the tourists do at sea?*

6. *The twins washed their faces.*

7. *Elías knows Portuguese, speaks Italian, reads Russian, and is learning German.*

8. *The dance was on Saturday. It began at 9:30 P.M.*

9. *The novel was written in Polish and translated into Greek.*

The Definite Article: Omissions

The definite article is omitted before mass or count nouns that do not refer to the whole of their class but only to some of it or a part of it (an unspecified quantity).

Guadalupe tiene paciencia.	*Guadalupe is patient.*
Toman aspirinas.	*They're taking aspirin.*
Amparo compró carne.	*Amparo bought meat.*

Spanish usually omits the definite article after **haber**.

Hay gente en el comedor.	*There are people in the dining room.*
No hay interés en el proyecto.	*There's no interest in the project.*

When two nouns are joined by **de** to form a compound noun, the definite article is omitted before the second noun. Note that in these compound nouns, the order of the nouns is the reverse of their English equivalents.

la chuleta de ternera	*veal chop*
el cinturón de seguridad	*seat belt*
el dolor de cabeza	*headache*
el libro de historia	*history book*
la sala de espera	*waiting room*

To pluralize a compound noun joined by **de**, only the first noun is made plural.

las chuletas de ternera	*veal chops*
los cinturones de seguridad	*seat belts*
los dolores de cabeza	*headaches*
los libros de historia	*history books*
las salas de espera	*waiting rooms*

In some compound nouns joined by **de**, the second element is always plural.

la base de datos	*database*
la bolsa de valores	*stock exchange*
la silla de ruedas	*wheelchair*

The definite article is usually omitted in apposition.

Caracas, capital de Venezuela	*Caracas, the capital of Venezuela*
Santa Fe, capital de Nuevo México	*Santa Fe, the capital of New Mexico*
Mario Vargas Llosa, novelista	*Mario Vargas Llosa, the novelist*

The definite article is omitted before ordinal numbers with kings and other rulers.

Alfonso X (décimo)	*Alfonso the Tenth*
Carlos V (quinto)	*Charles the Fifth*

In Spanish, there are many set adverbial phrases that do not take the definite article, whereas their English equivalents usually do.

en nombre de	*in the name of*
a corto/largo plazo	*in the short/long run*
en camino	*on the way*

L ***¿Falta el artículo definido?*** *Escriba el artículo definido donde sea necesario.*
Si no es necesario escriba una X.

1. Plácido Domingo, _____ tenor, y Montserrat Caballé, _____ soprano, son españoles.

2. Juan Carlos _____ I (primero) subió al trono español en 1975.

3. Alfonsito tiene dolor de _____ estómago y Luisito tiene dolor de _____ muelas
por los bombones que comieron.

4. Los chicos compraron _____ refrescos más naturales para la fiesta.

5. Aurelia no está en casa porque ya está en _____ camino.

6. No hay _____ sillones en la sala todavía.

7. Tomamos _____ vitaminas para tener _____ energía.

8. ¿Por qué no pruebas la sopa de _____ legumbres?

NOTA CULTURAL

La música clásica
Hay varios artistas hispanos que han conseguido la fama internacional en la
música clásica. Entre los españoles figuran los tenores Plácido Domingo,
Alfredo Kraus y José Carreras, las sopranos Montserrat Caballé y Victoria de los
Ángeles, la pianista Alicia de Larrocha, el violonchelista Pablo Casals, el guita-
rrista Andrés Segovia y el director de orquesta Rafael Frühbeck de Burgos.
España ha tenido compositores de renombre como Manuel de Falla, Isaac
Albéniz, Enrique Granados, Joaquín Rodrigo y Rodolfo, Ernesto y Cristóbal
Halffter. También muy conocidos son los compositores mexicanos Carlos Chá-
vez, Manuel María Ponce y Silvestre Revueltas, y los compositores argentinos
Astor Piazzolla y Alberto Ginastera. Entre los artistas de países hispanoamericanos se destacan el pianista chileno Claudio Arrau y el pianista cubano Hora-
cio Gutiérrez. El tenor peruano Juan Diego Flórez ha triunfado en los teatros
de ópera más importantes del mundo y el director de orquesta venezolano
Gustavo Dudamel ha tenido un éxito destacado en el mundo musical.

The Neuter Article **lo**

Spanish has a neuter article **lo** that is placed before an adjective used as a noun to express
an abstract idea or a certain quality. The form **lo** is invariable; the adjective following **lo**
can be masculine or feminine, singular or plural. **Lo** + adjective + **que** expresses *how*.
Lo is also used with adverbs and adverbial phrases.

lo bueno	*the good part, what's good*
lo fácil	*the easy part, what's easy*
Lo importante es que nosotros pensamos **lo mismo**.	*The important thing is that we think the same.*
Vi **lo listo/lista** que es.	*I saw how clever he/she is.*
Oí **lo graciosos/graciosas** que son.	*I heard how witty they are.*
Pensaban en **lo bien** que lo iban a pasar.	*They were thinking about the good time they were going to have.*

Lo is used before a **de** phrase that means *the matter concerning.*

lo del ingeniero	*the matter concerning the engineer*
lo de tus documentos	*the business about your papers*

Lo is used in the phrases **lo más/menos posible** (*as much as possible/as little as possible*) and **lo antes posible** (*as soon as possible*).

M *Artículos en el museo. Cuando Ud. fue al museo con su amiga, vieron muchas cosas interesantes. Complete las oraciones con la forma correcta del artículo que falte. Escoja entre el artículo neutro **lo**, el artículo definido y el indefinido. Si no es necesario ningún artículo, escriba una X. (No se olvide de escribir las contracciones **al** y **del** cuando sean necesarias.)*

_____ (1) viernes yo fui con Emilia a _____ (2) museo de _____ (3) arte.

Todo _____ (4) de _____ (5) arte nos interesa mucho. _____ (6) bello de _____ (7)

museo son _____ (8) salas de _____ (9) escultura. Hay tantos artículos y piezas de

_____ (10) gran valor. No pudimos ver _____ (11) esculturas porque _____ (12) mes

pasado hubo _____ (13) robo en _____ (14) museo. Parece que _____ (15) ladrones

entraron a _____ (16) museo a _____ (17) tres de _____ (18) mañana. Se llevaron

_____ (19) estatuas preciosas. _____ (20) guardia muy simpático nos dijo que

_____ (21) de _____ (22) seguridad en _____ (23) museo es _____ (24) problema.

The Indefinite Article: Forms, Uses, and Omissions

The Spanish indefinite article (English: *a, an*) appears as **un** before a masculine noun and as **una** before a feminine noun. Like the definite article, the indefinite article changes to agree with the noun in gender (masculine/feminine) and number (singular/plural).

	MASCULINE	FEMININE
SINGULAR	**un**	**una**
PLURAL	**unos**	**unas**

The plural indefinite articles **unos/unas** are the equivalent of English *some, a few, a couple of.*

El and **un** are always used before feminine nouns that begin with a stressed **a** or **ha**. The plural of these nouns always uses **las** and **unas**. This rule does not apply where the first vowel is not stressed (**la alfombra, la ambición**) or when referring to the name of the letter **a** (**la a**) and the letter **h** (**la hache**).

el/un agua	**las/unas** aguas
el/un águila *eagle*	**las/unas** águilas
el/un alma *soul*	**las/unas** almas
el/un arca *ark*	**las/unas** arcas
el/un área	**las/unas** áreas

el/un arma *arm, weapon*	**las/unas** armas
el/un arpa *harp*	**las/unas** arpas
el/un haba *bean*	**las/unas** habas
el/un habla *language*	**las/unas** hablas
el/un hambre *hunger*	**las/unas** hambres

Since the change of **la** and **una** to **el** and **un** before these nouns is conditioned by the stressed /a/ sound, if another word comes between the article and the noun, **el** and **un** revert to **la** and **una**, respectively. Note that adjectives have their expected feminine forms before these feminine nouns.

la joven águila
una buena alma
una nueva arma

Other determiners, such as demonstratives, possessives, and quantifying adjectives, use the expected feminine forms before these nouns.

aquella agua
esta área
mucha hambre
tanta hambre

The indefinite article is omitted before predicate nouns that denote profession, occupation, nationality, religion, social status, and gender. If, however, the noun is modified by a phrase or an adjective, the indefinite article is expressed.

Amparo es violinista.	*Amparo is a violinist.*
Es una violinista brillante.	*She's a brilliant violinist.*
Francisco es carpintero.	*Francisco is a carpenter.*
Esos chicos son argentinos.	*Those kids are Argentine.*
Ester es judía/católica/protestante.	*Ester is Jewish/Catholic/Protestant.*

The indefinite article is usually omitted after the verbs **tener**, **llevar** (*to wear*), **usar** (*to wear habitually*), **comprar**, **buscar**, and **sacar**.

Asunción tiene jardín.	*Asunción has a garden.*
Nieves y Julián usan anteojos.	*Nieves and Julián wear glasses.*
Compra pasteles.	*Buy some pastries.*

The indefinite article is omitted in phrases with **¡qué...!** (*what a . . . !*) and before **otro** (*another*), **cierto** (*a certain*), **tal** (*such a*), **medio** (*half a*), **ciento** (*a hundred*), and **mil** (*a thousand*). The English equivalents of these words have the indefinite article.

¡Qué día!	*What a day!*
otro color y otro estilo	*another color and another style*
cierta persona	*a certain person*
tal problema	*such a problem*
medio kilo	*half a kilo*
cien dólares	*a hundred dollars*
mil dólares	*a thousand dollars*

N *El artículo indefinido.* *Para cada sustantivo, escriba el artículo indefinido singular, el artículo indefinido plural y el plural del sustantivo.*

1. mar	11. papel	21. voz
2. ángel	12. ley	22. desfile
3. hacha	13. menú	23. nación
4. comedor	14. cereal	24. lavaplatos
5. olor	15. buzón	25. lema
6. oboe	16. irlandés	26. sucursal (*branch, branch office*)
7. área	17. alma	27. ascensor
8. mochila	18. paraguas	28. habla
9. joven	19. camarón (*shrimp*)	29. postal (*postcard*)
10. nadador	20. garaje	30. agua

O *En el taller.* *El pintor Dionisio está pintando en su taller donde se encuentran las siguientes cosas. Escriba la forma correcta del artículo indefinido al lado del sustantivo.*

1. _____ cuadro

2. _____ pinturas

3. _____ pinceles (*brushes*)

4. _____ mural

5. _____ modelos [*fem.*]

6. _____ colección

7. _____ paisajes (*landscapes*)

8. _____ escultura

9. _____ retratos (*portraits*)

10. _____ paleta

11. _____ marco (*frame*)

12. _____ naturaleza muerta (*still life*)

P *¿Artículo indefinido o no?* *Complete cada oración con la forma correcta del artículo indefinido cuando sea necesario. Si no es necesario escriba una X.*

1. Sergio es _____ ingeniero.

2. Es _____ día muy caluroso.

3. Gabriel es _____ judío y Carmen es _____ católica.

4. Verónica gastó entre _____ cien y _____ mil dólares.

5. ¿Puede Ud. enseñarme _____ otro estilo de abrigo, por favor?

6. Simón Colón es _____ pianista muy talentoso.

7. La nueva vecina es _____ mexicana.

8. Todos los niños de esa familia usan _____ gafas.

9. No se puede encontrar _____ paraguas grande.

10. No le dijimos tal _____ cosa.

11. El cocinero preparó _____ cierto postre.

12. ¡Qué _____ idea!

Contractions **del** and **al**

There are two contractions in Spanish. The masculine article **el** combines with the preposition **de** to form **del** (*of the*) and with **a** to form **al** (*to the*). These prepositions do not contract with the other forms of the definite article: **la, los, las.** The contractions are not used if the definite article is part of a proper name.

Mateo es el gerente **del** hotel.	*Mateo is the manager of the hotel.*
Álvaro fue **al museo.**	*Álvaro went to the museum.*
Sol fue **a El Prado.**	*Sol went to El Prado.*
Ramón regresó **a El Salvador.**	*Ramón went back to El Salvador.*
Cervantes es el autor **de *El Quijote.***	*Cervantes is the author of* El Quijote.

Q ***¿Dónde están todos?*** *Exprese que las personas no están porque fueron a distintos lugares. Use la contracción* **al** *cuando sea necesario. Siga el modelo.*

MODELO   Nieves / teatro
→ Nieves fue al teatro.

1. Concepción y Simón / puesto de periódicos

2. yo / ayuntamiento (*town hall*)

3. Domingo y Brígida / supermercado

4. Ud. / heladería

5. Lourdes / iglesia

6. vosotros / farmacia

7. nosotros / estación de tren

8. tú / centro comercial

R ***¿De dónde salieron?*** *Diga de qué lugares salieron o volvieron estas personas. Use la contracción* **del** *cuando sea necesario. Siga el modelo.*

MODELO   Usted / salir / restaurante mexicano
→ Usted salió del restaurante mexicano.

1. tú y yo / volver / banco

2. Mercedes y Julio / salir / cine

3. yo / regresar / librería

4. Uds. / volver / tienda de zapatos

5. Pedro / salir / apartamento

6. tú / regresar / galería de arte

7. vosotros / salir / museo de ciencias naturales

8. Ud. / volver / aeropuerto

Possession

In Spanish, possession is expressed by the use of a prepositional phrase with **de**. Spanish titles such as **señor** and **profesora** must be preceded by the definite article when referring to the specific person.

Leí el informe **de Jacobo**.	*I read Jacobo's report.*
Leí todos los capítulos **del libro**.	*I read all the chapters of the book.*
Hoy es el día **del** examen final.	*Today is the day of the final exam.*
Cenaron en el restaurante **del** hotel.	*They had dinner in the hotel restaurant.*
¿Conoces el comercio **del** señor Bermúdez?	*Are you familiar with Mr. Bermúdez' store?*

In Spanish, **¿De quién?** followed by **ser** is equivalent to English *Whose?*

¿De quién es el cinturón?	*Whose belt is it?*
¿De quién son estos pendientes?	*Whose earrings are these?*
¿De quién son estas postales?	*Whose postcards are these?*
¿De quién es el barco? **¿De quiénes es** el barco?	*Whose boat is it?*

The form **¿De quiénes?** exists to refer to a plural possessor, but it is not common in the spoken language.

S **¿De quién es?** *Escriba preguntas y respuestas que demuestran la posesión. Siga el modelo.*

> MODELO   los libros de texto / el profesor
> → ¿De quién son los libros de texto?
>   Son del profesor.

1. el almacén / el señor Acosta

2. los peines / Adela y Matilde

3. el equipaje / los turistas

4. los discos compactos / el pianista

5. este llavero / la empleada

6. las sartenes / el cocinero

7. las raquetas / estas tenistas

8. el reloj / el doctor Villanueva

T **Expresar en español. ¿De quiénes son?** *Exprese las frases en español.*

1. *Mr. Valle's florist shop*

2. *the president's* [masc.] *office*

3. *the programmer's* [fem.] *disks*

4. *the dentist's* [fem.] *schedule*

5. *Dr.* [masc.] *Arriaga's employees* [masc.]

6. *the designer's* [masc.] *websites*

7. *Professor* [fem.] *Salas' lectures*

8. *the engineer's* [masc.] *project*

9. *Mr. and Mrs. Manrique's children*

10. *the boss's* [fem.] *report*

U **Ejercicio oral. Un programa de concursos (Quiz show).** *El presentador del programa lee unos sustantivos en voz alta. Los miembros de los dos equipos tienen que añadir el artículo definido o indefinido correcto. Se puede variar con frases de posesión, las contracciones* **al** *y* **del**, *etcétera. Al final se calculan los puntos ganados por cada equipo para saber quiénes sacaron el premio gordo* (grand prize, jackpot).

Adjectives

Agreement of Adjectives

Spanish adjectives agree in gender and number with the nouns they modify. Adjectives that have a masculine singular form ending in -o have four forms.

	bonito		**maravilloso**	
	MASCULINE	FEMININE	MASCULINE	FEMININE
SINGULAR	bonito	bonita	maravilloso	maravillosa
PLURAL	bonitos	bonitas	maravillosos	maravillosas

Adjectives that have a masculine singular ending in a consonant or in -e have only two forms, a singular and a plural. They do not change for gender.

	difícil	**triste**
	MASCULINE AND FEMININE	
SINGULAR	difícil	triste
PLURAL	difíciles	tristes

A small number of adjectives of nationality end in -a or in stressed -í or -ú. These also have only two forms.

	belga *Belgian*	**israelí** *Israeli*	**hindú** *Hindu, Indian*
	MASCULINE AND FEMININE		
SINGULAR	belga	israelí	hindú
PLURAL	belgas	israelíes	hindúes

Other similar adjectives are **azteca** (*Aztec*), **marroquí** (*Moroccan*), **iraní** (*Iranian*), **iraquí** (*Iraqi*), **paquistaní/pakistaní** (*Pakistani*), and **bantú** (*Bantu*). There are also adjectives ending in -ista, -sta, and -ita that follow this same pattern: **realista, entusiasta, nacionalista, cosmopolita**.

Adjectives ending in the suffixes **-dor**, **-ón**, and **-án** add **-a** to form the feminine and therefore have four forms like adjectives ending in **-o**. These adjectives form their masculine plural by adding **-es** and their feminine plural by adding **-as**. Those suffixes that are accented lose their accent mark when an ending is added.

hablador *talkative*	
	MASCULINE	FEMININE
SINGULAR	hablador	hablador**a**
PLURAL	hablador**es**	hablador**as**

preguntón *inquisitive*	
	MASCULINE	FEMININE
SINGULAR	preguntón	pregunton**a**
PLURAL	pregunton**es**	pregunton**as**

holgazán *lazy*	
	MASCULINE	FEMININE
SINGULAR	holgazán	holgazan**a**
PLURAL	holgazan**es**	holgazan**as**

Spanish adjectives usually follow the nouns they modify.

—En esa tienda de ropa venden cosas **maravillosas**.

In that clothing store, they sell wonderful things.

—Sí. Veo que te has comprado unos vestidos muy **bonitos**.

Yes. I see that you've bought yourself some very pretty dresses.

 ¿Cómo están? *Su amigo le pregunta cómo están varias personas. Contéstele usando los adjetivos indicados. Haga las concordancias (agreements) necesarias. Siga el modelo.*

MODELO   ¿Cómo está tu hermana? (ocupado)
→ Está ocupada.

1. ¿Cómo están tus padres? (feliz)

2. ¿Cómo estás [*masc.*]? (contento)

3. ¿Cómo se encuentra Raquel? (nervioso)

4. ¿Cómo se siente Claudio? (deprimido)

5. ¿Cómo se encuentran las hermanas de Augusto? (triste)

6. ¿Cómo están Uds. [*fem.*]? (cansado)

7. ¿Cómo se sienten los primos de Paco? (enfermo)

8. ¿Cómo estáis [*masc.*]? (preocupado)

9. ¿Cómo está tu tía? (aburrido)

B ¡*Don de gentes!* *Jacobo y su hermana Luisa son estudiantes de intercambio que llegaron de Tegucigalpa, capital de Honduras, el año pasado. Viven con una familia norteamericana y se llevan muy bien con todo el mundo. ¿Qué piensa la gente de los hermanos hondureños? Para saberlo, escriba oraciones usando los adjetivos indicados. Haga las concordancias necesarias. Siga el modelo.*

MODELO   Elena / creer / Luisa / honesto
          → Elena cree que Luisa es honesta.

Carácter y personalidad

buena gente *nice (person/people)*	**inteligente** *intelligent*
cortés *courteous*	**listo** *clever*
el don de gentes *charm, ability to get on well with people*	**responsable** *reliable*
	serio *serious*
encantador(a) *charming*	**simpático** *nice, pleasant*
generoso *generous*	**sincero** *sincere*
gracioso *witty*	**tener personalidad** *to have personality or character*
honesto *honest*	
independiente *independent*	**trabajador(a)** *hardworking*

1. Paco / creer / Jacobo / listo

2. la señora Alvarado / pensar / Luisa / encantador

3. el profesor de cálculo / encontrar / a los hermanos / inteligente y trabajador

4. Nieves / creer / Jacobo / sincero

5. el señor Alvarado / decir / Luisa / gracioso y generoso

6. las profesoras de computación / encontrar a Jacobo / serio y responsable

7. los hijos de los Alvarado / creer / Luisa / independiente y simpático

8. todo el mundo / decir / Jacobo y Luisa / buena gente y cortés

NOTA CULTURAL

Tegucigalpa, capital de Honduras, fue fundada como campamento de minas por los españoles en 1578. Los indígenas ya llamaban a la ciudad Tisingal. Tegucigalpa quiere decir "montaña de plata" en el idioma indígena original. La ciudad se convirtió en capital en 1880. A diferencia de la capital de Guatemala que fue casi totalmente destruida por terremotos, Tegucigalpa conserva mucha de su arquitectura original porque no queda en una falla (*fault*) geológica.

C ***¿Qué se piensa de ellos?*** *Juan y Teresa no le caen bien a nadie. ¿Qué piensa la gente de ellos? Complete las oraciones usando los adjetivos indicados. Haga las concordancias necesarias. Siga el modelo.*

MODELO   Laura dice: No soporto a Juan porque es ___*antipático*___.

Más carácter y personalidad

aguantar *to stand*	**molesto** *annoying*
antipático *unpleasant*	**No los puedo ver.** *I can't stand them.*
desleal *disloyal*	**odiar** *to hate*
engañoso *deceitful*	**soportar** *to stand*
Me cae mal. *I don't like him/her.*	**tacaño** *mean*
mentiroso *lying*	**tonto** *silly, stupid*

1. Ramón dice: Creo que Teresa es muy _____ (arrogante).

2. Patricio dice: No aguanto a Juan porque es _____ (molesto).

3. Matilde dice: Los encuentro _____ (tacaño).

4. Ana dice: No los puedo ver porque son _____ (tonto).

5. Luisa dice: Teresa me cae mal porque es _____ (mentiroso).

6. Joaquín dice: Yo odio a los dos porque son _____ (desleal).

7. Adela dice: Yo encuentro a los dos _____ (engañoso).

D ***¡El Príncipe Azul!* (Prince Charming!)** *El Príncipe Azul mira su ropa. Describa lo que tiene en su armario empleando los adjetivos de color. Fíjese bien si tiene ropa apropiada para pescar una princesa* (to catch a princess).

Para montar a caballo

1. una chaqueta _____ (rojo)

2. unos pantalones _____ (amarillo)

3. unas botas _____ (marrón)

4. unos guantes _____ (negro)

5. un sombrero con plumas _____ (azul), _____ (anaranjado) y _____ (verde)

Para ir a un baile de etiqueta (*dress ball*)

6. un esmoquin (*tuxedo*) _____ (blanco)

7. un sombrero de copa (*top hat*) _____ (negro)

8. una faja (*cummerbund*) _____ (rosado)

9. unos calcetines _____ (morado) y _____ (gris)

Position of Adjectives; Shortened Forms of Adjectives

Although descriptive adjectives in Spanish usually follow the noun they modify, descriptive and other adjectives can also appear before nouns in certain cases.

1 · Adjectives can precede nouns when they express an inherent characteristic of the noun that is known to all and do not add any new information about the noun.

la **blanca** nieve	*white snow*
el **tímido** cordero	*the timid lamb*
una **olorosa** rosa	*a fragrant rose*

2 · Adjectives can precede nouns when they express a subjective judgment of the speaker. **Bueno**, **malo**, and their comparatives **mejor** and **peor** fall into this category.

Vivimos en una **pequeña** ciudad.	*We live in a small city.*
Tenemos que leer una **larga** novela.	*We have to read a long novel.*
Sobrevolaron la **enorme** selva.	*They flew over the huge jungle.*
Es el **peor** libro que leímos.	*It's the worst book that we read.*
Prepararon una **buena** comida.	*They prepared a good meal.*

3 · Adjectives that express quantity precede the noun: **mucho**, **poco**, **bastante**, **suficiente**, **cuánto**, **alguno**, **ninguno**, **ambos** (*both*), and **varios** (*several*).

Alberto siempre tiene **muchas** ideas.	*Alberto always has a lot of ideas.*
No ganan **suficiente** dinero.	*They don't earn enough money.*
¿Hay **alguna** farmacia por aquí?	*Is there a (any) drugstore around here?*

4 · Adjectives can appear before the noun in exclamations with **¡Qué!**

¡Qué **mala** suerte!	*What bad luck!*
¡Qué **hermosa** plaza!	*What a beautiful square!*

When an adverb such as **más**, **tan**, or **muy** modifies the adjective, the adjective usually follows the noun.

¡Qué plaza **más hermosa**!	*What a beautiful square!*
Fue un proyecto **tan interesante**.	*It was such an interesting project.*
Prepararon una comida **muy buena**.	*They prepared a very good meal.*

The adjectives **bueno**, **malo**, **primero**, **tercero**, **uno**, **alguno**, and **ninguno** lose their final -o before a masculine singular noun. **Alguno** and **ninguno** add an accent mark when shortened (**algún**, **ningún**). The cutting off of the last sound or syllable(s) of a word is called *apocope* (**el apócope**).

—¿No conoces a **ningún** estudiante?	*Don't you know any students?*
—No conozco a nadie todavía. Es mi **primer** día aquí.	*I don't know anyone yet. It's my first day here.*

—¿Hay **algún** consejo que te pueda dar?	*Is there any advice that I can give you?*
—No, he tenido **un mal** día, nada más.	*No, I've had a bad day, that's all.*

The adjectives **cualquiera** (*any*) and **grande** shorten to **cualquier** and **gran** before any singular noun.

Cualquier restaurante por aquí es un **gran** restaurante.	*Any restaurant around here is a great restaurant.*

Cualquiera has its full form in the phrase **cualquiera de los/las dos** (*either one of the two*).

The adjective **Santo** shortens to **San** before all masculine saints' names except those that begin with **To-** and **Do-**, as in **Santo Tomás** and **Santo Domingo**. For example, **San Francisco** and **San Antonio**. The feminine form **Santa** has no shortened form, as in **Santa Bárbara** and **Santa María**.

Some adjectives have different English equivalents, depending on whether they precede or follow the nouns they modify.

nuestro **antiguo** jefe	una ciudad **antigua**
our former boss	*an old (ancient) city*
cierto país	una cosa **cierta**
a certain country	*a sure thing, a true thing*
una **nueva** casa	una casa **nueva**
another house	*a new house*
el **mismo** profesor	el profesor **mismo**
the same teacher	*the teacher himself*
un **pobre** hombre	un hombre **pobre**
a poor (unfortunate) man	*a poor (penniless) man*
un **gran** presidente	un hombre **grande**
a great president	*a big man*
diferentes libros	libros **diferentes**
various books	*different books*
Paco es **medio** español.	el español **medio**
Paco is half Spanish.	*the average Spaniard*
Este café es **pura** agua.	Prefiero beber agua **pura**.
This coffee is nothing but water.	*I prefer to drink pure water.*
Juan es un **simple** mesero.	Juan es un muchacho **simple**.
Juan is just a waiter.	*Juan is a simple boy.*
Me interesa **cualquier** película española.	Vamos a ver una película **cualquiera**.
I'm interested in any Spanish film.	*Let's see any old film.*
María es la **única** chica aquí.	María es una chica **única**.
María is the only girl here.	*María is a unique girl.*

E *Adjetivos pre- y pospuestos.* Complete las oraciones con los adjetivos indicados poniéndolos o antes o después de los sustantivos. Haga los cambios necesarios.

1. ¡Éste es el _____ día _____ de mi vida! (mejor)

2. Hay _____ discos compactos _____ en el escritorio. (alguno)

3. Ha habido _____ días _____ de lluvia este año. (mucho)

4. Los estudiantes leyeron unos _____ poemas _____. (renacentista)

5. Los franceses usan mucho la _____ energía _____. (nuclear)

6. El profesor dará el examen a _____ clases _____ el miércoles. (ambos)

7. Pili tiene los _____ ojos _____. (castaño)

8. No retiraron _____ plata _____ de su cuenta de ahorros. (suficiente)

9. Nos encanta el _____ vino _____. (tinto)

10. No se sabe _____ horas _____ de trabajo quedan. (cuánto)

11. Pedro tomó la _____ decisión _____ posible. (peor)

12. Miguel y Víctor se dedican al análisis de _____ teorías _____. (político)

F *¡Qué exclamación!* Amplíe cada exclamación con la forma correcta del adjetivo indicado. Haga los cambios necesarios. Siga los modelos.

MODELOS   ¡Qué casa! (lindo)
  → ¡Qué linda casa!

  ¡Qué casa! (más lindo)
  → ¡Qué casa más linda!

1. ¡Qué situación! (absurdo)

2. ¡Qué clima! (tan perfecto)

3. ¡Qué partido! (más emocionante)

4. ¡Qué paella! (tan rico)

5. ¡Qué zapatos! (hermoso)

6. ¡Qué ideas! (más estupendo)

7. ¡Qué problemas! (más complicado)

8. ¡Qué legumbres! (fresco)

9. ¡Qué niños! (cariñoso)

10. ¡Qué reunión! (tan animado)

G *Adjetivos: ¿apócope o no?* Complete las oraciones con la forma correcta del adjetivo indicado.

1. El cinco de septiembre es el _____ día del semestre. (primero)

2. No es _____ idea llevar el paraguas hoy. (malo)

3. Estos estadistas (*statesmen*) son _____ hombres. (grande)

4. Unas canicas (*marbles*) son un _____ juguete para Paquito. (bueno)

5. Ya es la _____ vez que me han invitado a salir. (tercero)

6. Esperamos que vengan a vernos _____ día. (alguno)

7. No hemos hecho _____ plan hasta ahora. (ninguno)

8. Yo nací el día de _____ Juan. (santo)

9. Sánchez dictó una serie de _____ conferencias. (bueno)

10. Albéniz fue un _____ compositor español. (grande)

11. No les gustó _____ bicicleta. (ninguno)

12. Pruebe _____ recetas de este libro de cocina italiana. (alguno)

13. _____ librería tendrá el libro que buscas. (Cualquiera)

14. ¿No celebras tu santo el día de _____ Rosa? (santo)

15. Jesús y Pepe fueron los _____ jugadores en llegar al estadio. (primero)

16. Carlos es el _____ rey de la dinastía. (tercero)

17. ¡No des _____ ejemplo para los niños! (malo)

H   *Adjetivos: antes o después del sustantivo.* *Complete las oraciones usando los adjetivos indicados. Póngalos antes o después de los sustantivos.*

1. Beti y yo vamos al _____ dentista _____. (*same*)

2. Atenas es una _____ ciudad _____. (*ancient*)

3. La fecha de su boda es una _____ cosa _____. (*sure*)

4. Tino es _____ portugués _____ y _____ mexicano _____. (*half, half*)

5. Bolívar fue un _____ soldado _____. (*great*)

6. Habla con un _____ funcionario _____. (*any old*)

7. ¡El _____ dramaturgo _____ no aguanta su obra! (*himself*)

8. La sopa que pedí es _____ agua _____. (*nothing but*)

9. Ricardo es una _____ persona _____. (*unique*)

10. _____ empresa _____ sigue perdiendo dinero. (*a certain*)

11. Los hermanos Ayala son _____ hombres _____ desde que su compañía quebró (*went bankrupt*). (*poor*)

12. La _____ casa _____ de Daniela y Pablo quedaba en las afueras de la ciudad. (*former*)

13. Mi biblioteca tiene _____ libros _____ sobre el _____ tema _____. (*several, same*)

14. A Leonor le va a encantar _____ regalo _____ que le demos. (*any*)

15. Agustín y Patricia son los _____ pianistas _____ que tocan con la orquesta. (*only*)

16. Le dimos el pésame (*we offered our sympathy*) a la _____ viuda (*widow*) _____. (*poor (sad, in mourning)*)

Adjectives of Nationality

Adjectives of nationality that end in -**o** in the masculine singular have the expected four forms of all adjectives whose masculine singular ends in -**o**.

	chileno *Chilean*		**mexicano** *Mexican*	
	MASCULINE	FEMININE	MASCULINE	FEMININE
SINGULAR	chileno	chilena	mexicano	mexicana
PLURAL	chilenos	chilenas	mexicanos	mexicanas

Adjectives of nationality or of origin that end in a consonant also have four forms. An -**a** is added to form the feminine. The masculine plural ends in -**es**, not -**os**. Adjectives of nationality that have an accent mark on the last syllable of the masculine singular lose that accent mark when an ending is added.

	español *Spanish*		**inglés** *English*	
	MASCULINE	FEMININE	MASCULINE	FEMININE
SINGULAR	español	española	inglés	inglesa
PLURAL	españoles	españolas	ingleses	inglesas

	alemán *German*		**andaluz** *Andalusian*	
	MASCULINE	FEMININE	MASCULINE	FEMININE
SINGULAR	alemán	alemana	andaluz	andaluza
PLURAL	alemanes	alemanas	andaluces	andaluzas

Adjectives of nationality or of origin that end in a vowel other than -**o** have only two forms. Many of these have the suffix -**ense** such as **canadiense** (*Canadian*) and **bonaerense** (*from Buenos Aires*).

Adjetivos de nacionalidad (gentilicios)*

Continente		Islas	
África	africano/a	las Antillas	antillano/a
la Antártida	antártico/a	las Bahamas	bahamiano/a
Asia	asiático/a	las Baleares	balear, baleárico/a
Australia	australiano/a	Mallorca	mallorquín/mallorquina
(Oceanía)		las Canarias	canario/a
Europa	europeo/a	las Filipinas	filipino/a
Norteamérica	norteamericano/a, estadounidense	las Galápagos	galapagueño/a
		las Malvinas	malvinense, malvinero/a
Sudamérica	sudamericano/a		

***El gentilicio** is the name given to a people of a particular country, city, or region that identifies them as coming from that place.

País	Gentilicio
Afganistán	afgano/a
Alemania	alemán/alemana
Andorra	andorrano/a
Arabia Saudita	saudí/saudita
Argelia (*Algeria*)	argelino/a
(la) Argentina	argentino/a
Australia	australiano/a
Austria	austríaco/a
Bélgica	belga
Bolivia	boliviano/a
Bosnia	bosnio/a
(el) Brasil	brasileño/a
Cachemira (*Kashmir*)	cachemir(a)
Camboya	camboyano/a
(el) Canadá	canadiense
Catar	catarí
Chile	chileno/a
China	chino/a
Colombia	colombiano/a
Corea (del Norte/Sur)	coreano/a (norte-coreano/a; surcoreano/a, sudcoreano/a)
Costa Rica	costarricense
Cuba	cubano/a
Dinamarca	danés/danesa
(el) Ecuador	ecuatoriano/a
Egipto	egipcio/a
El Salvador	salvadoreño/a
(los) Emiratos Árabes Unidos	emiratí
Escocia	escocés/escocesa
España	español(a)
(los) Estados Unidos	norteamericano/a, estadounidense
Etiopía	etíope
Filipinas	filipino/a
Finlandia	finlandés/finlandesa
Francia	francés/francesa
Gales (*Wales*)	galés/galesa
Gibraltar	gibraltareño/a
Gran Bretaña	británico/a
Grecia	griego/a
Guatemala	guatemalteco/a
Guinea Ecuatorial	guineoecuatoriano/a
Haití	haitiano/a
Holanda	holandés/holandesa
Honduras	hondureño/a
Hungría	húngaro/a
(la) India	indio/a
Indonesia	indonesio/a
Inglaterra	inglés/inglesa

País	Gentilicio
Irak/Iraq	iraquí
Irán	iraní
Irlanda	irlandés/irlandesa
Islandia	islandés/islandesa
Israel	israelí
Italia	italiano/a
Jamaica	jamaicano/a
(el) Japón	japonés/japonesa
Jordania	jordano/a
Kenia	keniano/a
Kuwait/Kuweit	kuwaití
Líbano	libanés/libanesa
Libia	libio/a
Luxemburgo	luxemburgués/luxemburgesa
Madagascar (República Malgache)	malgache
Malasia	malasio/a
Marruecos	marroquí
México	mexicano/a
Nicaragua	nicaragüense
Nigeria	nigeriano/a
Noruega	noruego/a
Nueva Zelanda	neocelandés/neocelandesa
los Países Bajos	holandés/holandesa
(el) Panamá	panameño/a
(el) Paraguay	paraguayo/a
Paquistán, Pakistán	paquistaní, pakistaní
(el) Perú	peruano/a
Polonia	polaco/a
Portugal	portugués/portuguesa
Puerto Rico	puertorriqueño/a
(la) República Dominicana	dominicano/a
Ruanda	ruandés/ruandesa
Rumania	rumano/a
Rusia	ruso/a
Siria	sirio/a
Somalia	somalí
Sudáfrica	sudafricano/a
Sudán	sudanés/sudanesa
Suecia	sueco/a
(la) Suiza	suizo/a
Tailandia	tailandés/tailandesa
Taiwán	taiwanés/taiwanesa
Túnez	tunecino/a
Turquía	turco/a
Ucrania	ucraniano/a, ucranio/a
Uganda	ugandés/ugandesa

País	Gentilicio
(el) Uruguay	uruguayo/a
Venezuela	venezolano/a
Vietnám	vietnamita
Yemen	yemení
Zimbabue	zimbabuense

Ciudad	Gentilicio	Ciudad	Gentilicio
Atenas	ateniense	Málaga	malagueño/a
Barcelona	barcelonés/barcelonesa	Moscú	moscovita
Berlín	berlinés/berlinesa	Nueva York	neoyorquino/a
Bilbao	bilbaíno/a	París	parisiense, parisino/a
Bogotá	bogotano/a	Quito	quiteño/a
Buenos Aires	bonaerense, porteño/a	Río de Janeiro	carioca
Caracas	caraqueño/a	Roma	romano/a
Florencia	florentino/a	Santiago	santiaguino/a
La Habana	habanero/a	Sevilla	sevillano/a
Lima	limeño/a	Toledo	toledano/a
Londres	londinense	Valencia	valenciano/a
Madrid	madrileño/a	Viena	vienés/vienesa

I ¿*De dónde son?* *Ud. y su amigo están preparando una lista de los estudiantes extranjeros de la facultad de ingeniería* (school of engineering). *Su amigo le pregunta si son de cierto país y Ud. lo confirma usando el adjetivo de nacionalidad. Siga el modelo.*

MODELO   Catalina es de Italia, ¿verdad?
→ Sí, es italiana.

1. Abrahán es de Rusia, ¿verdad?
2. Rosalinda y Arturo son del Canadá, ¿verdad?
3. David es de Israel, ¿verdad?
4. Mercedes es de Costa Rica, ¿verdad?
5. Hugo es de Guatemala, ¿verdad?
6. Javier y Paula son de Bélgica, ¿verdad?
7. Alano es del Japón, ¿verdad?
8. Perla es de la India, ¿verdad?
9. Isabel y Lucía son de Egipto, ¿verdad?
10. Margarita es de Inglaterra, ¿verdad?
11. Gerardo es de Corea del Sur, ¿verdad?
12. Cristina y Oliverio son de Francia, ¿verdad?

J *De muchos uno solo. Los Estados Unidos es un país de habitantes de miles de orígenes distintos. Sin embargo, son todos norteamericanos. Explique de qué origen son estos norteamericanos usando el adjetivo de nacionalidad. Siga el modelo.*

MODELO   Josefa e Ignacio / Panamá
→ Josefa e Ignacio son de origen panameño.

1. yo / Polonia
2. Teodoro e Irene / El Salvador
3. Uds. / Líbano
4. Gabriel / Vietnám
5. Adela y Rosa / Irán
6. Estanislao y Sofía / Grecia
7. tú / Nicaragua
8. Ud. y yo / Taiwán
9. Gualterio / Hungría
10. vosotros / Inglaterra

Panamá tiene al norte el océano Atlántico o mar Caribe, al este Colombia, al sur el océano Pacífico y al oeste Costa Rica. El Canal de Panamá es una gran encrucijada (*crossroad*) estratégica del mundo que hace comunicar los dos mares. El Canal, construido por los Estados Unidos, fue abierto en 1914. Los Estados Unidos controlaba la Zona del Canal hasta 1978 cuando los Estados Unidos y Panamá ratificaron un nuevo tratado (*treaty*) cambiando el nombre de la Zona al Área del Canal y dando soberanía (*sovereignty*) sobre el Canal a Panamá. Los Estados Unidos entregó el control del Canal a Panamá en el año 2000 y mantiene bases militares en el área.

More on the Agreement of Adjectives

Adjectives modifying two plural nouns of the same gender are in the plural of that gender.

libros y periódicos argentin**os**	*Argentine books and newspapers*
ciudades y provincias argentin**as**	*Argentine cities and provinces*

If two nouns of different genders, whether singular or plural, are modified by a single adjective, the adjective is masculine plural.

pantalones y chaquetas barat**os**	*inexpensive pants and jackets*
un colegio y una universidad antigu**os**	*an ancient school and university*

When a noun is used as an adjective, it usually does not agree in gender and number with the noun it modifies.

una visita **relámpago**	*a quick visit*
(relámpago (*lightning*))	
la luz **piloto** (piloto (*pilot*))	*pilot light (stove)*
apartamentos **piloto**	*model apartments*

Some of these nouns eventually become adjectives and show agreement. This is especially true of some nouns used as adjectives of color.

zapatos **marrón/marrones**	*brown shoes*
medias **café/cafés**	*light brown socks*

K **Sustantivos en plural.** *Complete las oraciones usando la forma plural de los adjetivos indicados.*

1. Hay _____ (bueno) almacenes y restaurantes en el centro comercial.

2. Conocimos varios pueblos y aldeas _____ (español).

3. Queremos manzanas y cerezas recién _____ (recogido).

4. Tengo mapas y guías _____ (inglés).

5. En la sala hay un sofá y dos sillones _____ (blanco).

6. Compre bollos y galletas _____ (fresco).

7. Laura necesita una blusa y unas medias _____ (gris).

8. Busquen un lavaplatos y una máquina de lavar _____ (rebajado).

9. No se vende ni agua ni sales _____ (mineral).

10. Después del choque tuvieron que poner un parachoques y una puerta _____ (nuevo).

11. Hay ofertas y liquidaciones _____ (magnífico) toda esta semana.

12. Clara tiene las pestañas y los ojos _____ (negro).

13. En Tecnolandia se venden computadoras y teléfonos celulares _____ (caro).

14. El administrador de web y la programadora eran muy _____ (creativo).

Two or More Adjectives Modifying a Noun

Typically, if two adjectives modify a noun, they both follow it and are joined by **y**.

una chica inteligente **y** simpática	*a nice, intelligent girl*
un día caluroso **y** agradable	*a warm, pleasant day*

If **y** is left out, the adjective that the speaker wishes to emphasize comes last.

artistas europeos **modernos**	**modern** *European artists* (*out of all European artists, the modern ones*)
artistas modernos **europeos**	*modern* **European** *artists* (*out of all modern artists, the European ones*)

However, if one of the two adjectives usually precedes the noun, it is placed there.

cierto país europeo	**a certain** *European country*
el único asesor español	**the only** *Spanish consultant*
diferentes libros científicos	**various** *scientific books*
otra ciudad moderna	**another** *modern city*
ese **pobre** hombre enfermo	*that* **poor** *sick man*

L *El rodaje de una película* (**The shooting of a film**). *Comente sobre el rodaje de una película del director de cine Federico Felino, poniendo los elementos de cada grupo en su orden correcto. Cada grupo consiste en un sustantivo, un adjetivo que aparece antes del sustantivo, y un adjetivo descriptivo. Escriba la oración completa haciendo los cambios necesarios.*

1. Federico Felino es el director de cine / mejor / joven

2. *El tango rojo* es su film / doblado (*dubbed*) / primero

3. Será una película / grande / extranjero

4. Tiene escenas / romántico / alguno

5. Se oye diálogo / bueno / uno

6. Hay efectos / diferente / fotográfico

7. Escribieron guión (*script*) / uno / inteligente

8. Trabajaron en el film intérpretes [*masc. and fem.*] / principal (*star, lead*) / alguno

9. Hay subtítulos / alguno / bien traducido

10. La película tiene argumento (*plot*) / interesante / uno

11. La película ganará un premio / importante / cinematográfico

The Past Participle as an Adjective

The past participle of most verbs can function as an adjective.

El ladrón entró por la ventana **abierta**.	*The thief got in through the open window.*
Quiero dominar la lengua **escrita** y **hablada**.	*I want to master the written and spoken language.*
Encontré los documentos **perdidos**.	*I found the lost documents.*
Trato **hecho**.	*It's a deal. / Done deal.*

The Spanish past participle is used to describe positions of people and objects where the present participle is used in English.

Todos están **sentados** en el comedor.	*Everyone is **sitting** in the dining room.*
A estas horas hay mucha gente **parada** en el metro.	*At this hour, there are a lot of people **standing** in the subway.*

M *Diálogos. Complete los diálogos usando la forma correcta del participio pasado como adjetivo. Todos los adjetivos son participios pasados. El adjetivo se encuentra en el modismo o se deriva del verbo del modismo. Siga el modelo.*

MODELO   meter(se) en sí mismo *to withdraw into oneself*

Felipe: —Últimamente me es difícil tener una conversación con Clara. ¿Qué tendrá?

Isabel: —No tengo idea. Parece que está muy ___*metida*___ en sí misma.

1. estar frito *to be all washed up*
   Diana: ¡Qué mala nota saqué en el examen! ¡Estoy _____!
   Mateo: Yo también. ¡Los dos estamos _____!

2. estar hecho una sopa *to be soaking wet*
   Raúl: Está lloviendo a cántaros. (*It's raining cats and dogs.*) Estoy _____ una sopa.
   Sara: ¡Yo estoy _____ una sopa también!

3. morir(se) de risa *to die laughing*
   Roberto: Mira a Clara e Inés. Están _____ de risa.
   Dorotea: Fíjate que Pepe y Esteban también están _____ de risa.

4. comer(se) de envidia *to be eaten up with envy*
   Julia: ¿Sabes que Aurelia está _____ de envidia porque yo salgo con Matías?
   Anita: ¡No sólo Aurelia sino todas las chicas están _____ de envidia!

5. meter(se) en lo que no le importa *to butt into someone else's business*
   Lola: Como siempre, Raúl está _____ en lo que no le importa.
   Paco: Así son sus hermanos también, siempre están _____ en lo que no les importa.

6. estar muy pagado de sí mismo *to have a high opinion of oneself*
   Alfredo: Chico, ya no salgo con Brígida porque está muy _____ de sí misma.
   Nicolás: Haces muy bien. ¡Yo rompí con Tere, Eva y Paloma porque están muy _____
   de sí mismas!

7. dormir(se) en los laureles *to rest on one's laurels*
   Tito: Veo que no te esfuerzas porque estás _____ en los laureles.
   José: Cuando logres algo como yo, ¡tú también estarás _____ en los laureles!

8. estar hecho una lástima *to be a sorry sight, be in a sad state*
   Leonor: ¿Qué les pasa a Paula y Dora? Están _____ una lástima.
   Alicia: A lo mejor tienen lo que tiene Mari que también está _____ una lástima.

N *¿Qué están haciendo?* *Use participios pasados como adjetivos para explicar la posición
de ciertas personas. Complete las oraciones usando la forma correcta del adjetivo y del
verbo* **estar**. *Siga el modelo.*

MODELO   Mario __*está levantado*__ (levantar) ya.

1. Rosa _____ (echar) en el sofá.

2. Clemente _____ (parar (*to stand*)) en la puerta de la casa esperando a su novia.

3. Los García _____ (sentar) a la mesa para charlar.

4. Pili _____ (asomar (*to lean out*)) a la ventana.

5. Los niños _____ (arrodillar) en el suelo jugando con sus cochecitos.

6. Adolfo y Javier _____ (tirar) en el suelo por los puñetazos que se dieron.

7. Paloma _____ (inclinar (*to bow*)) mientras el público le aplaude.

O *¡Preparados! ¡Listos! ¡Ya!* **(Ready! Set! Go!)** *Su amiga le pregunta cuándo Ud. y otras
personas van a hacer ciertas cosas porque tiene prisa por salir. Explíquele que Uds. están
listos porque esas cosas ya están hechas. Use el participio pasado como adjetivo.
Siga el modelo.*

MODELO   ¿Cuándo van Uds. a arreglarse?
          → Ya estamos arreglados/arregladas.

1. ¿Cuándo va Gerardo a bañarse?

2. ¿Cuándo van Elías e Isaac a afeitarse?

3. ¿Cuándo va Juliana a maquillarse?

4. ¿Cuándo van Uds. a vestirse?

5. ¿Cuándo va Ud. a peinarse?

6. ¿Cuándo vais a ducharos?

7. ¿Cuándo vas a arreglarte?

P *A comer pues.* *Ya es hora de comer. Su mamá quiere que Ud. y los otros miembros de su familia hagan ciertas cosas. Pero parece que todo está hecho ya. Siga el modelo.*

MODELO   Polo, prende el horno, por favor.
          → Ya está prendido.

1. Margarita, pon los cubiertos (*place settings*), por favor.

2. Benjamín, sirve el agua, por favor.

3. Abuela, prepara el dulce de leche, por favor.

4. Pancho, rompe los huevos, por favor.

5. Pepe y Nano, corten el pan, por favor.

6. Trini, haz la ensalada, por favor.

7. Hijita, fríe las papas, por favor.

8. Toni, pela unos dientes de ajo (*garlic cloves*), por favor.

Adjectives Used as Nouns (Nominalization of Adjectives)

Spanish adjectives can be used as nouns when the noun they modify is deleted.

—Las camisas verdes son más caras que **las rojas.**	*The green shirts are more expensive than **the red ones.***
—Pero yo prefiero **las verdes.**	*But I prefer **the green ones.***
—La casa vieja es más grande que **la moderna.**	*The old house is bigger than **the modern one.***
—Por eso vamos a comprar **la vieja.**	*That's why we're going to buy **the old one.***

When the noun is deleted, the masculine singular indefinite article changes from **un** to *uno*: **un libro nuevo** → *uno nuevo*, **un profesor comprensivo** → *uno comprensivo*.

—Él tiene dos carros, un carro grande y **uno** pequeño.	*He has two cars, a big car and a small one.*
—Ella se compró dos suéteres azules y **uno** negro.	*She bought herself two blue sweaters and one black one.*

Q *Opciones y preferencias.* *Sus amigos le preguntan qué cosas prefiere. Conteste las preguntas usando los adjetivos como sustantivos. Escriba la respuesta de dos maneras. Siga el modelo.*

MODELO   ¿Cuál prefieres, la novela histórica o la novela fantástica?
          → Prefiero la histórica.
            Prefiero la fantástica.

1. ¿Cúal te gusta más, la música instrumental o la música vocal?

2. ¿Cuáles prefieres, los programas serios o los programas cómicos?

3. ¿Dónde prefieres comer, en el restaurante chino o en el restaurante francés?

4. ¿Cuáles te gustan más, los trajes azules o los trajes marrones?

5. ¿Prefieres el apartamento moderno o el apartamento viejo?

6. ¿Cuál te gusta más, la universidad particular (*private*) o la universidad estatal (*state*)?

7. ¿Cuál prefieres, las películas norteamericanas o las películas extranjeras?

8. ¿Dónde quieres vivir, en la ciudad grande o en la ciudad pequeña?

9. ¿Cuáles te interesan más, las clases de ciencias políticas o las clases de ciencias naturales?

Comparative of Adjectives

One object or person may be seen as having more, less, or the same amount of a characteristic as another. To express this, Spanish and English use the comparative construction.

Comparison of Superiority (**más** + adjetivo + **que**)

La avenida es **más ancha que** nuestra calle.	*The avenue is **wider than** our street.*

Comparison of Inferiority (**menos** + adjetivo + **que**)

Pero la avenida es **menos ancha que** la autopista.	*But the avenue is **less wide than** (**not as wide as**) the superhighway.*

Note that in English the comparison of inferiority is usually expressed as *not as*: *The avenue is **not as wide as** the superhighway.*

Comparison of Equality (**tan** + adjetivo + **como**)

La avenida es **tan ancha como** el Paseo de Miraflores.	*The avenue is as wide as Miraflores Boulevard.*

The adjectives **bueno** and **malo** have irregular comparative forms.

bueno → **mejor**
malo → **peor**

Este restaurante es **mejor** que el otro.	*This restaurant is better than the other one.*
El ruido aquí es **peor** que en el barrio mío.	*The noise is worse here than in my neighborhood.*

Más bueno and **más malo** are used to refer to moral qualities.

Grande and **pequeño** have irregular comparative forms when they refer to age.

grande → **mayor** *older*
pequeño → **menor** *younger*

Mi hermana es **mayor** que mi hermano.	*My sister is older than my brother.*
Mi hermano es **menor** que mi hermana.	*My brother is younger than my sister.*

Adverbs are compared in the same way as adjectives.

Ella contesta **más cortésmente que** él.	*She answers **more politely than** he does.*
Ella contesta **menos cortésmente que** él.	*She answers **less politely than** he does.*
Ella contesta **tan cortésmente como** él.	*She answers **as politely as** he does.*

Some common adverbs have irregular comparative forms.

bien *well*	→	mejor *better*
mal *badly*	→	peor *worse*
mucho *much, a lot*	→	más *more*
poco *little, not much*	→	menos *less*

When **mejor** and **peor** are adverbs, they are invariable.

In comparing verbs and nouns, **tan** changes to **tanto**. **Tanto** is invariable with verbs, but agrees with nouns that follow it.

Comparing verbs:

Yo trabajo **más que** tú.	*I work **more than** you do.*
Yo trabajo **menos que** tú.	*I work **less than** you do.*
Yo trabajo **tanto como** tú.	*I work **as much as** you do.*

Comparing nouns:

—Creo que tú tienes **menos exámenes que** Amalia.	*I think you have **fewer exams than** Amalia.*
—Te equivocas. Tengo **tantos exámenes como** ella, y **más trabajos** escritos.	*You're mistaken. I have **as many exams as** she has, and **more papers**.*

Que (*than*) is followed by subject pronouns unless the pronoun is the direct or indirect object of the verb. In that case, **que** is followed by **a** + stressed pronoun.

Yo estudio más **que tú**.	*I study more **than you do**.*
A mí me gusta más **que a ti**.	*I like it more **than you do**.*

Que is followed by **nada**, **nadie**, and **nunca** where English uses *anything, anyone,* and *ever.*

El curso es difícil, más **que nada**.	*The course is hard, more **than anything**.*
Luis Alberto baila mejor **que nadie**.	*Luis Alberto dances better **than anyone**.*
Todo es más fácil **que nunca**.	*Everything is easier **than ever**.*

Que is replaced by **de** before a numeral.

Ganan más **de** quinientos mil dólares por año.	*They earn more than five hundred thousand dollars a year.*

Que is replaced by **de lo que** before a clause implying a standard for comparison.

—Este libro es más difícil **de lo que** cree el profesor.

This book is more difficult than the teacher thinks.

—Y menos interesante **de lo que** yo me imaginaba.

And less interesting than I imagined.

In the preceding example, the basis for comparison is how difficult the teacher thought the book was or how interesting I imagined the book was.

Que is replaced by **de** before **el que**, **la que**, **los que**, and **las que**. The article represents a deleted noun.

Necesito más plata **de la que** me prestaste. (**la que** = la plata que)

I need more money than (the money) you lent me.

Encontramos menos problemas **de los que** esperábamos. (**los que** = los problemas que)

We found fewer problems than (the problems) we expected.

R ***En comparación.*** *Combine las dos oraciones de cada grupo en una sola que exprese una comparación. Escriba las oraciones de dos maneras. Use la nominalización del adjectivo. Siga el modelo.*

MODELO   Lorenzo es listo. / Julio es más listo.
       → Julio es más listo que Lorenzo.
          Lorenzo es menos listo que Julio.

1. Ana es astuta. / Luisa es más astuta.

2. El museo de arte es bueno. / El museo de historia natural es mejor.

3. Mi novio es inteligente. / Yo soy más inteligente.

4. El cuarto de Elena es hermoso. / Tu cuarto es más hermoso.

5. La película inglesa es aburrida. / La película francesa es más aburrida.

6. Los bailarines son talentosos. / Los cantantes son más talentosos.

7. Las blusas de algodón son elegantes. / Las blusas de seda son más elegantes.

8. Tu hermano es grande. / Tu hermana es mayor.

S ***Comparación de adverbios.*** *Escriba oraciones comparativas usando adverbios de tres maneras:* **más**, **menos** *y* **tan**. *Use el pretérito. Siga el modelo.*

MODELO   Él / correr / rápidamente / ella
       → Él corrió más rápidamente que ella.
          Ella corrió menos rápidamente que él.
          Él corrió tan rápidamente como ella.

1. José / hablar / francamente / Consuelo

2. Los enfermeros / trabajar / cuidadosamente / los médicos

3. Virginia / resolver los problemas / fácilmente / Cristina

T *Adjetivos: igualdad.* *Escriba oraciones que demuestren la comparación de igualdad de los dos sustantivos. Siga el modelo.*

MODELO   Eduardo / diligente / Memo
→ Eduardo es tan diligente como Memo.

1. la obra de teatro / divertida / la película

2. las clases de física / fáciles / las clases de cálculo

3. los documentales / artísticos / los reportajes

4. los platos griegos / sabrosos / los platos húngaros

5. esta actriz / célebre / ese actor

6. el arroz / bueno / el maíz

7. el príncipe / valiente / el rey

8. Francisca / trabajadora / su hermana María

9. la inflación actual / baja / la inflación de hace tres años

U *Sustantivos: igualdad.* *Escriba oraciones que demuestren la comparación de igualdad.*

1. Alejandro / mandar / correo electrónico / Felipe

2. Miriam / tener / paciencia / Catalina

3. ellos / pasar / horas / en línea / nosotros

4. ella / comer / comida rápida / tú

5. sus amigos / ver / programas de realidad / Uds.

6. los asesores / demostrar / interés en el proyecto / vosotros

7. a él / quedarle / dinero / a ti

8. yo / conocer / clubes de jazz / Marcos

Superlative of Adjectives; Absolute Superlative

Spanish has no special superlative form. Instead, the definite article (or a possessive adjective) precedes a comparative construction with **más** or **menos** to express the idea of a superlative.

—Quiero ver una película **más emocionante**. (*comparative*) — *I want to see a **more exciting** film.*

—Ésta es **la película más emocionante** que he visto. (*superlative*) — *This is **the most exciting film** that I've seen.*

—Queremos **un** libro **mejor**. (*comparative*) — *We want **a better** book.*

—Pero éste es **el mejor libro** que hay. (*superlative*) — *But this is **the best book** there is.*

After a superlative, *in* is translated as **de**.

—Estamos en la ciudad más importante **del** país.	*We're in the most important city **in** the country.*
—Y ésta es la calle más elegante **de** la ciudad.	*And this is the most elegant street **in** the city.*

Spanish has a suffix **-ísimo**, called the absolute superlative, that is added to adjectives. This suffix adds the idea of *very* to the adjective. Note that **c** and **g** change to **qu** and **gu**, respectively, and **z** changes to **c** when **-ísimo** is added. Adjectives in **-ísimo** are four-form adjectives.

lindo → lindísimo
feo → feísimo
fácil → facilísimo
rico → riquísimo
largo → larguísimo
feliz → felicísimo

V ***¿Cómo son los estudiantes?*** *Use los signos aritméticos para escribir oraciones usando superlativos que describan a los estudiantes de la clase. Haga los cambios necesarios. Siga los modelos.*

MODELOS   Claudia / + erudito
→ Claudia es la estudiante más erudita.

Carlos / − atento
→ Carlos es el estudiante menos atento.

1. Juan Pablo / + aplicado
2. Daniel y Arturo / − obediente
3. Silvia / + simpático
4. Irene y María / − trabajador
5. Verónica / + inteligente
6. Diana y Esteban / + hablador
7. Sergio / + encantador
8. Rosa y Jacinto / − preparado

W ***¡Qué parque más precioso!*** *Confirme las observaciones de su amigo respecto al parque que están visitando. Escriba oraciones usando el superlativo absoluto del adjetivo. Siga el modelo.*

MODELO   El parque es lindo.
→ Sí. Es lindísimo.

1. La vegetación es interesante.
2. Ese árbol es viejo.
3. Esas flores son hermosas.
4. El zoológico del parque es grande.
5. Ese león parece feroz.
6. Los monos son simpáticos.
7. Las veredas (*paths*) son largas.
8. El lago es bello.

X *Visitando la ciudad.* *Raquel les enseña su ciudad a sus amigos. Escriba lo que les dice a sus amigos usando superlativos. Haga los cambios necesarios. Siga el modelo.*

MODELO   aquí está / biblioteca / importante / ciudad
→ Aquí está la biblioteca más importante de la ciudad.

1. allí se encuentra / plaza / imponente / ciudad

2. aquí ven / catedral / antiguo / estado

3. en frente hay / universidad / conocido / país

4. ésta es / calle / largo / ciudad

5. en esta calle hay / tiendas / hermoso / zona

6. allí está / tienda de comestibles / estimado / barrio

7. delante de nosotros hay / hotel / internacional / país

8. en este barrio se encuentran / restaurantes / concurrido (*busy, much frequented*) / ciudad

9. aquí ven / teatro / viejo / ciudad

10. pronto veremos / estadio / grande / región

Y *La clase de literatura.* *El profesor y los estudiantes describen las obras que estudian con superlativos. Escriba lo que dicen. Haga los cambios necesarios. Siga el modelo.*

MODELO   novela / interesante / siglo
→ Es la novela más interesante del siglo.

1. poema / conocido / literatura europea

2. obra de teatro / presentado / año

3. comedia / aplaudido / teatro nacional

4. novela / vendido / literatura moderna

5. tragedia / estimado / nuestro teatro

6. poeta / respetado / su siglo

7. novelista [*masc.*] / leído / mundo

8. dramaturgo / apreciado / nuestra época

Z *Expresar en español.* *Exprese las oraciones en español.*

1. *I read more than you (Ud.) do.*

2. *They know less than we do.*

3. *Ignacio complains as much as his wife does.*

4. *I have more compact discs than Federico.*

5. *Eva sees fewer films than Margarita.*

6. *We take as many trips as they do.*

7. *We have more than ten thousand books in our library.*

8. *The soccer game was more exciting than they expected.*

9. *Ruiz is the best programmer in the company.*

10. *This is the most beautiful beach in the country.*

11. *You (vosotros) live in the most elegant neighborhood in the city.*

12. *She liked the film more than we did.*

13. *Rolando surfs the web more than anyone.*

14. *You (Uds.) get together more than ever.*

 Ejercicio oral. Descripciones. *Converse con un amigo/una amiga con el fin de describir a sus parientes y a sus amigos. Describa cómo son (carácter, personalidad, lo físico), de dónde son, de qué origen son y cómo están. Compárelos con otros familiares y amigos.*

Demonstratives and Possessives

Demonstrative Adjectives

Spanish has three demonstrative adjectives: **este** (*this*) (near the speaker), **ese** (*that*) (near the person spoken to), and **aquel** (*that*) (removed from both the speaker and the person spoken to). The demonstrative adjectives agree in gender and number with the noun they modify.

	MASCULINE	FEMININE	MASCULINE	FEMININE	MASCULINE	FEMININE
SINGULAR	**este**	**esta**	**ese**	**esa**	**aquel**	**aquella**
PLURAL	**estos**	**estas**	**esos**	**esas**	**aquellos**	**aquellas**

Este apartamento tiene más habitaciones que **aquellas** casas.

This apartment has more rooms than those houses (over there).

Préstame **ese** bolígrafo que tienes en la mano. **Este** bolígrafo ya no escribe.

Lend me that ballpoint pen that you have in your hand. This ballpoint doesn't write anymore.

Note that the three demonstratives correspond to the three place words for *here* and *there*.

```
este   ~ aquí
ese    ~ ahí
aquel ~ allí
```

The demonstrative **ese** can also be placed after the noun to convey a note of contemptuousness.

No sé por qué una muchacha tan inteligente como Margarita saldría con el chico **ese**.

I don't know why a girl as intelligent as Margarita would go out with a guy like that.

A **Útiles de escuela.** *Cambie el artículo definido o indefinido a la forma correcta del adjetivo demostrativo para hablar de sus útiles de escuela. Escriba cada oración de tres maneras. Siga el modelo.*

MODELO Necesito un cuaderno.
→ Necesito este cuaderno.
    Necesito ese cuaderno.
    Necesito aquel cuaderno.

Útiles de escuela

el bolígrafo *ballpoint pen*	**el lápiz** *pencil*
el borrador *eraser*	**el laptop** *laptop*
la calculadora de bolsillo *pocket calculator*	**el libro de texto** *textbook*
el compás *compass*	**el mapa** *map*
el diccionario *dictionary*	**la regla** *ruler*
la enciclopedia *encyclopedia*	**la tarjeta de memoria** *memory stick*

1. Los libros de texto están bien escritos.

2. Compré un compás anteayer.

3. Consultaré el mapa.

4. Prefiero la tarjeta de memoria.

5. El lápiz no tiene borrador.

6. Me gusta el diccionario de español.

7. Los bolígrafos no sirven.

8. Encontré las reglas en el escritorio.

9. Las enciclopedias están en línea.

B *De compras en El Corte Inglés.* *Complete los siguientes diálogos entre unos amigos que van de compras. Use la forma correcta del adjetivo demostrativo.*

En la sección de ropa para mujeres

1. Irene: —Oye, Trini, ¿qué te parece _____ (*this*) traje?

2. Trini: —¿Cuál? ¿_____ (*That*) traje azul?

3. Irene: —Sí. ¿Verdad que _____ (*this*) color es muy bonito?

4. Trini: —Francamente me gusta más _____ (*that, over there*) traje verde.

5. Irene: —Pero me gustan _____ (*these*) blusas y no hacen juego con el traje verde.

6. Trini: —Bueno, chica, llévate _____ (*that*) traje azul y _____ (*those*) blusas entonces.

   Y si te queda dinero todavía, cómprate el traje verde con

   _____ (*that, over there*) blusa negra. ¡El conjunto (*outfit*) te quedará fenómeno!

En la sección de ropa para hombres

7. Lupe: —Bueno, Tito, ayúdame. ¿Qué le regalo a Mateo por su cumpleaños?

   ¿_____ (*This*) corbata roja o _____ (*that*) cinturón negro?

8. Tito: —Querida hermana, no me gustan ni _____ (*these*) corbatas ni _____ (*those*)

   cinturones. Mateo es un gran chico. _____ (*This*) novio tuyo se merece algo

   más interesante e importante. Mira _____ (*this*) sección de deportes...

   _____ (*that*) bate, o _____ (*that, over there*) guante para jugar al béisbol...

   o quizás _____ (*that*) raqueta de tenis, o...

9. Lupe: —Tito, yo comprendo lo que estás haciendo. Quieres que Mateo te preste

su nuevo bate o guante o raqueta. _____ (*This*) no puede ser. ¡Es mejor que

escoja el regalo yo!

Demonstrative Pronouns

Demonstrative pronouns in Spanish have the same form as demonstrative adjectives. The noun is deleted and an accent mark is added over the stressed vowel of the demonstrative.

—Estas tortas son más ricas que **aquéllas**.

*These cakes are more delicious than **those** (**over there**).*

—Pero aquellas galletas no son tan buenas como **éstas**.

*But those cookies (over there) aren't as good as **these**.*

—¿Qué camisa prefiere Ud.? ¿**Ésta** o **ésa**?

*Which shirt do you prefer? **This one** or **that one**?*

—Creo que me gusta más **aquélla** que está en el otro mostrador.

*I think that I like **that one** on the other counter better.*

—Aquellos anteojos son más bonitos que **ésos**.

*Those eyeglasses (over there) are prettier than **those**.*

—Puede ser, pero **éstos** tienen la montura que más me gusta.

*That may be, but **these** have the frame I like best.*

—¿Quiénes son los dos muchachos que figuran en la foto?

Who are the two boys in the photograph?

—**Éste** es mi primo Carlos y **ése** es su amigo.

***This one** is my cousin Carlos and **that one** is his friend.*

NOTE In modern usage, the written accent is usually omitted from demonstrative pronouns.

Spanish has three neuter demonstrative pronouns ending in -**o**: **esto**, **eso**, and **aquello**. These never have a written accent. They refer to situations or ideas, not to specific nouns.

—Dicen que Pedro toma y que después maneja.

They say that Pedro drinks and then drives.

—No hay nada más peligroso que **eso**.

*There's nothing more dangerous than **that**. (**eso** = drinking and driving)*

—El tío Marcos tenía antes una tienda de ropa en el centro.

Uncle Marcos used to have a clothing store downtown.

—**Aquello** fue hace muchos años, ¿verdad?

***That** was many years ago, wasn't it? (**aquello** = that he had a clothing store downtown)*

The neuter demonstratives can be followed by **de** to express *this/that situation regarding* or *this/that matter of/about* (see "The Neuter Article **lo**" in Chapter 16).

Esto de trabajar demasiado no te hace ningún bien.

***This situation of (your) working too much** is not doing you any good.*

| **Aquello de tu hermano Mateo** me puso triste. | *That business about your brother Mateo made me sad.* |

C *Un crítico de restaurantes.* Ud. es crítico de restaurantes. Alguien le hace una entrevista sobre ciertas comidas que probó. Contéstele usando los pronombres demostrativos en su respuesta. Siga el modelo.

MODELO   ¿Qué queso le gustó más? ¿Este queso o ese queso?
→ Me gustó éste más que ése.
o Me gustó ése más que éste.

1. ¿Qué salsa de champiñones (*mushrooms*) le gustó más? ¿Esa salsa o aquella salsa?

2. ¿Qué fideos le gustaron más? ¿Aquellos fideos o estos fideos?

3. ¿Qué bizcocho le gustó más? ¿Este bizcocho o ese bizcocho?

4. ¿Qué salchichas le gustaron más? ¿Esas salchichas o aquellas salchichas?

5. ¿Qué guisado (*stew*) le gustó más? ¿Este guisado o ese guisado?

6. ¿Qué panes le gustaron más? ¿Estos panes o aquellos panes?

7. ¿Qué sopa de legumbres le gustó más? ¿Esta sopa de legumbres o esa sopa de legumbres?

Possessive Adjectives

Possessive adjectives in Spanish agree with the noun they modify. Possessive adjectives referring to the singular pronouns and to the third person plural have only two forms: a singular and a plural. The possessives **nuestro/nuestra** and **vuestro/vuestra** are four-form adjectives because they agree in gender as well as in number.

(yo)	**mi/mis**	(nosotros)	**nuestro/nuestra/nuestros/nuestras**
(tú)	**tu/tus**	(vosotros)	**vuestro/vuestra/vuestros/vuestras**
(él/ella/Ud.)	**su/sus**	(ellos/ellas/Uds.)	**su/sus**

—¿Has visto **mis** libros?	*Have you seen **my** books?*
—Sí, aquí están **tus** libros.	*Yes, here are **your** books.*
—¿Venís a **nuestra** casa?	*Are you coming to **our** house?*
—Sí, vamos a **vuestra** casa.	*Yes, we're going to **your** house.*

The possessive adjective **su/sus** means *his, her, its, your,* and *their.* To clarify the person(s) to whom **su/sus** refers, a phrase consisting of **de** + pronoun may be added.

—¡Qué bueno! Allí están Sergio y Marisa. Necesito su libro.	*Great! There are Sergio and Marisa. I need (his/her/their) book.*
—¿El libro **de él** o el libro **de ella**?	*His book or her book?*
—¿Qué computadora te gustó más?	*Which computer did you like best?*
—La computadora **de Uds.** No me gustó tanto la computadora **de ellos**.	*Your computer. I didn't like their computer so much.*

Spanish has a set of long-form or stressed possessive adjectives that can be used to contrast one possessor with another (*It's **my** book, not **your** book*). These are all four-form adjectives and follow the noun they modify.

(yo)	**el** libro **mío**	**la** casa **mía**
	los libros **míos**	**las** casas **mías**
(tú)	**el** libro **tuyo**	**la** casa **tuya**
	los libros **tuyos**	**las** casas **tuyas**
(el/ella/Ud.)	**el** libro **suyo**	**la** casa **suya**
	los libros **suyos**	**las** casas **suyas**
(nosotros)	**el** libro **nuestro**	**la** casa **nuestra**
	los libros **nuestros**	**las** casas **nuestras**
(vosotros/vosotras)	**el** libro **vuestro**	**la** casa **vuestra**
	los libros **vuestros**	**las** casas **vuestras**
(ellos/ellas/Uds.)	**el** libro **suyo**	**la** casa **suya**
	los libros **suyos**	**las** casas **suyas**

The phrases consisting of **de** + pronoun clarify the person to whom **suyo** refers.

—Rogelio y Paula escribieron muchos artículos.	*Rogelio and Paula wrote a lot of articles.*
—**Los** artículos **de él** se publicaron en España y **los** artículos **de ella** en México.	***His** articles were published in Spain and **her** articles in Mexico.*
—**El** celular **mío** no funciona. ¿Me prestas el celular **tuyo**?	***My** cell phone doesn't work. Can you lend me **your** cell phone?*
—Lo siento. **El** celular **mío** no funciona tampoco.	*I'm sorry. **My** cell phone doesn't work either.*

The long-form possessive adjectives can also occur with the indefinite article.

unos amigos **míos**	*some friends of mine*
una idea **tuya**	*an idea of yours*

After **ser** the definite article is frequently omitted after long-form possessives.

Este coche es **mío**.	*This car is mine.*
Esas maletas son **nuestras**.	*Those suitcases are ours.*

When the definite article does appear with a long-form possessive after forms of **ser**, there is a difference in meaning that is difficult to express in English.

Esta casa es **mía**.	*This house is mine. (I own it. The focus is on ownership.)*
En esta calle hay varias casas. ¿Cuál es la **tuya**?	*There are several houses on this street. Which one is yours? (The focus is on which one of many belongs to someone.)*
Esta casa es **la mía**.	*This house is mine.*

D   ***En el depósito de artículos perdidos* (lost and found).** *A sus amigos siempre se les pierden sus cosas. Ud. y su amiga buscan esos artículos en el depósito donde suelen acabar. Dígale a su amiga de quiénes serán las cosas. Use un adjetivo posesivo en su respuesta. Siga el modelo.*

MODELO   Esta raqueta de tenis será de Paco, ¿no? (Jorge)
            → No, no es suya. Será de Jorge.

1. Este guante será de Rebeca, ¿no? (Martina)

2. Estas llaves serán de Carlos y Pepe, ¿no? (nosotros)

3. Este celular será de Amparo, ¿no? (Enrique)

4. Estos apuntes de historia serán del nuevo estudiante, ¿no? (Uds.)

5. Estas calculadoras serán de Fernando y Graciela, ¿no? (tú)

6. Esta bolsa será de Anita, ¿no? (la profesora Márquez)

7. Este paquete será de Uds., ¿no? (ellos)

E   ***Viajes.*** *¿Qué se lleva de viaje? Escriba frases usando un adjetivo posesivo de forma larga. Siga el modelo.*

MODELO   la guía / (yo)
            → la guía mía

Hacer un viaje

el billete electrónico *e-ticket*
la bolsa de viaje *travel bag*
la computadora portátil *laptop*
el equipaje de mano *hand luggage*
la guía *guidebook*
la maleta *suitcase*

el maletín *small suitcase*
la mochila *backpack*
el pasaporte *passport*
la tarjeta de crédito *credit card*
la visa *visa*

1. las maletas / (tú)

2. el equipaje de mano / (nosotros)

3. las tarjetas de crédito / (ellos)

4. la bolsa de viaje / (Ud.)

5. los maletines / (tú y yo)

6. la mochila / (Uds.)

7. el pasaporte / (yo)

8. las visas / (ellas)

9. los billetes electrónicos / (tú)

10. la computadora portátil / (vosotros)

Possessive Pronouns

Spanish possessive pronouns consist of the definite article plus the long-form possessive adjective. The noun is deleted.

—Javier se compró un coche espléndido.

—Sí, **el suyo** costó mucho más que **el nuestro**.

Javier bought himself a terrific car.

*Yes, **his** cost much more than **ours** did.*

—Los estudiantes míos son muy buenos este semestre. ¿Y **los suyos**?
*My students are very good this semester. What about **yours**?*

—**Los míos** también son excelentes.
Mine are excellent too.

—Mira mi computadora nueva.
Look at my new computer.

—Es fabulosa. Creo que **la tuya** tiene más memoria que **la mía**.
*It's fabulous. I think **yours** has more memory than **mine**.*

The masculine plural of the possessive pronoun can refer to family members or to teams.

—¿Cómo están **los tuyos**?
How's your family?

—¿**Los míos**? Perfectamente, gracias.
My family? Just fine, thanks.

—Espero que ganen **los nuestros**.
I hope our team wins.

—Por desgracia, los suyos son muy buenos también.
Unfortunately, theirs is very good too.

The neuter article **lo** + the masculine singular of the long-form possessive forms a neuter possessive pronoun meaning *whose part* or *whose task.*

—Denme **lo mío** y me voy.
*Give me **my share** and I'll leave.*

—**Lo tuyo** son veinte dólares.
***Your part** is twenty dollars.*

No encontramos **lo nuestro**, señor.
*We can't find **our things**, sir.*

Lo suyo es crear una base de datos.
***His task** is to create a database.*

F *Fernando el fanfarrón* (**braggart**). *Cada vez que alguien dice que tiene algo bueno, Fernando se jacta (brags) de tener algo mejor. Escriba lo que dice Fernando usando los pronombres posesivos. Siga el modelo.*

MODELO   Martín: Mi coche es muy lujoso.
Fernando: _¡Pero el mío es más lujoso que el tuyo!_

1. Lorenzo: Mi apartamento es muy moderno.

Fernando: _____

2. Patricia: Mi celular es nuevo.

Fernando: _____

3. Ricardo: Mi novia es muy simpática.

Fernando: _____

4. Dalia: Mi computadora es rápida.

Fernando: _____

5. Carlos: Mis revistas de deportes son muy interesantes.

Fernando: _____

6. Clara: Mis notas son muy buenas.

Fernando: _____

7. Leo: Mi perro es sumamente inteligente.

Fernando: _____

G *¿Dónde está?* *Explique dónde cree Ud. que están las siguientes cosas. Conteste las preguntas usando los pronombres posesivos. Siga el modelo.*

> MODELO   ¿Dónde está el anillo de Virginia? (en el dormitorio)
> → El suyo estará en el dormitorio.

1. ¿Dónde están los manuales de José? (en el estante (*shelf*))

2. ¿Dónde está tu permiso de manejar? (en mi cartera)

3. ¿Dónde están las pulseras de Lola y Nieves? (en la cómoda)

4. ¿Dónde están sus (de Uds.) sellos? (en la gaveta (*drawer*))

5. ¿Dónde está nuestra agenda electrónica? (en el escritorio)

6. ¿Dónde están vuestros frascos de agua de colonia? (en el baño)

7. ¿Dónde está su (de Ud.) guitarra? (encima del piano)

H *¡Qué niño más mimado!* **(What a spoiled brat!)** *Angelito siempre se sale con la suya* (gets his own way). *Y estas otras personas, ¿siempre se salen con la suya? Use el pronombre posesivo correcto en contestar que sí o que no. Siga el modelo.*

> MODELO   la hermanita de Angelito (sí)
> → Sí, se sale con la suya.

1. las hermanas mayores de Angelito (no)

2. Rafaelito (no)

3. Ud. (sí)

4. Bárbara (no)

5. Uds. (no)

6. tú [*fem.*] (sí)

7. vosotros (sí)

8. los amigos de Angelito (sí)

I *Expresar en español.* *Exprese las oraciones en español.*

1. *This business about the company is difficult to understand.*

2. *That situation regarding our trip has to be resolved.*

3. *We'll have to talk about that matter of buying a new car.*

4. *An old friend of mine is arriving on Saturday.*

5. *How's your (tú) family?*

6. *We hope our team wins.*

7. *Your (Ud.) part (task) is to bring the flowers.*

8. *My task is to make copies.*

J *Ejercicio oral. ¿Este? Es mío.* Practique el uso de los demostrativos y los posesivos. *Pregúnteles a sus amigos a quiénes les pertenecen ciertas cosas. Por ejemplo:* —¿De quién *es este cuaderno?* —**Es mío** o —**Es suyo** (**Es de él**) *(señalando a otro amigo).*

Personal Pronouns: Subject, Object, Prepositional

Subject Pronouns

Here are the subject pronouns in Spanish.

SINGULAR	PLURAL
yo *I*	**nosotros, nosotras** *we*
tú *you* (informal singular)	**vosotros, vosotras** *you* (informal plural, Spain only)
él *he*	**ellos** *they* [masc.]
ella *she*	**ellas** *they* [fem.]
Ud. (**usted**) *you* (formal singular)	**Uds.** (**ustedes**) *you* (formal and informal plural in Spanish America, formal plural in Spain)

There are several important differences between the personal pronouns in English and Spanish.

1 · Each of the four Spanish equivalents for English *you* specifies number (singular vs. plural) and formality (formal vs. informal). All Spanish-speaking countries use the singular forms **tú** (informal) and **Ud.** (formal), and the plural form **Uds.** (formal/informal), which can be used for any group of two or more people. In addition to these three forms, the plural **vosotros** (informal) replaces the informal use of **Uds.** in Spain.

2 · Since all Spanish nouns are either masculine or feminine, **él** and **ella** refer to things as well as to people. As subject pronouns, **él** and **ella** refer only to people, not to objects.

3 · **Ud.** and **Uds.** are often abbreviated **Vd.** and **Vds.** in Spain.

4 · Subject pronouns are less common in Spanish than in English because the verb endings show who is performing the action. They are used, however, to contrast or emphasize the subject of the verb.

—¿Qué haces mañana?	*What are you doing tomorrow?*
—Trabajo.	*I'm working.*
—¿Qué hacen (Uds.) mañana?	*What are you doing tomorrow?*
—**Ella** tiene el día libre, pero **yo** trabajo.	*She has the day off, but I'm working.*

In many parts of Spanish America, the pronoun **tú** is replaced by **vos**. **Vos** is the informal pronoun used in most of Central America, in parts of Venezuela and Ecuador, and in Paraguay, Bolivia, Uruguay, Argentina, and Chile. Verb forms used with **vos** have their own endings. Here are examples of the present tense forms used with **vos** from Argentina and Chile.

Standard Spanish	Argentina	Chile
tú cantas	vos cantás	vos cantái(s)
tú comes	vos comés	vos comí(s)
tú vives	vos vivís	vos viví(s)

In Chile, **vos** is characteristic of lower-class speech. Middle- and upper-class Chileans use **tú**. In Argentina, however, **vos** is the only familiar form used in spontaneous speech. It is considered standard and taught in the schools.

Note the following use of the subject pronouns with **ser** (colloquial English translations appear in parentheses).

Soy yo. *It is I.* (*It's me.*)	**Somos nosotros. Somos nosotras.** *It is we.* (*It's us.*)
Eres tú. *It is you.*	**Sois vosotros. Sois vosotras.** *It is you.*
Es él. *It is he.* (*It's him.*)	**Son ellos.** *It is they.* (*It's them.*) [masc.]
Es ella. *It is she.* (*It's her.*)	**Son ellas.** *It is they.* (*It's them.*) [fem.]
Es Ud. *It is you.*	**Son Uds.** *It is you.*

A *Identifique el sujeto de cada oración.* *Escriba el pronombre sujeto al lado de la oración. Si hay más de una posibilidad, escriba todos los pronombres posibles. Siga el modelo.*

> MODELO   ¡Lees una cantidad de libros!
> → tú

1. Estacionemos en esta calle.
2. Es español.
3. Sois simpáticas.
4. Buscaban casa.
5. Tengo razón.

6. Está contentísima.
7. Cenasteis a las nueve.
8. Lo verás.
9. Eran bellas.
10. Es inglesa.

B *Yo... pero tú...* *Practique usando el pronombre sujeto combinando las dos oraciones en una. Siga el modelo.*

> MODELO   Estudias español. Estudia (ella) francés.
> → Tú estudias español, pero ella estudia francés.

1. Trabajo de lunes a viernes. Trabajas los fines de semana.
2. Estudiamos en una universidad particular. Estudian (Uds.) en una universidad estatal.
3. Viven (ellas) en pleno centro. Vive (Ud.) en las afueras.
4. Vas de compras el sábado. Vamos de compras el jueves.
5. Es (él) abogado. Soy profesor.

6. Desayuna (Ud.) fuerte. Desayuna (ella) poco.

7. Escuchan (ellos) música clásica. Escucháis rock.

Pronouns After Prepositions (Prepositional Pronouns)

After a preposition, Spanish uses the subject pronouns, except for **yo** and **tú**.

para **mí**	para **nosotros/nosotras**
para **ti**	para **vosotros/vosotras**
para **él**	para **ellos**
para **ella**	para **ellas**
para **Ud.**	para **Uds.**

Note that **mí** has a written accent but **ti** does not.

Three irregular forms exist with the preposition **con**: **conmigo** (*with me*), **contigo** (*with you*) (informal singular), and **consigo** (*with himself, with herself, with yourself* (**Ud.**), *with yourselves* (**Uds.**), *with themselves*).

—¿Puedes ir **conmigo**?	*Can you go with me?*
—Hoy no. Mañana voy **contigo**.	*Not today. Tomorrow I'll go with you.*
—Alicia está enojada con nosotros.	*Alicia is angry with us.*
—Debería estar enojada **consigo** misma. Ella tiene la culpa de todo.	*She should be angry with herself. She's to blame for everything.*

When used after prepositions, **él** and **ella** can refer to things as well as people.

After the prepositions **como** (*like*), **según** (*according to*), **salvo** (*except*), **excepto** (*except*), **menos** (*except*), and **entre** (*between, among*), subject pronouns are used even in the first and second persons singular: **entre tú y yo** (*between you and me*), **todos menos tú** (*everyone except you*), and **según yo** (*according to me*). **Yo** and **tú** replace **mí** and **ti** after **y** with other prepositions.

No hay problemas entre tú y **yo**.	*There are no problems between you and me.*
Lo dijo delante de Ud. y **yo**.	*He said it in front of you and me.*

C ***Pronombres preposicionales.*** *Escriba cada preposición con la forma correcta del pronombre. Haga los cambios necesarios. Siga el modelo.*

MODELO de / yo
     → de mí

1. para / él
2. con / tú
3. según / tú
4. por / nosotros
5. salvo / yo
6. sobre / Ud.
7. con / yo

8. de / vosotros
9. para / ellas
10. por / tú
11. menos / tú
12. como / yo
13. en / ella
14. entre / tú y yo

D *Más pronombres preposicionales.* *Conteste las preguntas usando los pronombres preposicionales correctos. Siga el modelo.*

> MODELO   ¿Trajiste algo para Elenita?
> → Sí, traje algo para ella.

1. ¿Vive Ud. cerca de las tiendas?

2. ¿Trabajaba Timoteo en esa oficina?

3. ¿Lograron Uds. hablar sobre esos asuntos?

4. ¿Pagaste un dineral (*fortune*) por el nuevo televisor?

5. ¿Salió Ud. con Isabel y Alfonso?

6. ¿Hay mucho trabajo para la clase de filosofía?

7. ¿Se casó María Elena con el pintor?

8. ¿Felicitaste a los jugadores por la victoria?

E *Te equivocas.* *Conteste las preguntas de su amigo diciéndole que Ud. no hizo ciertas cosas ni con las personas ni para las personas que él menciona. Escriba oraciones usando los pronombres preposicionales. Siga el modelo.*

> MODELO   Saliste con Gabriela, ¿verdad?
> → No, con ella, no.

1. Almorzaste con Paquita y Laura, ¿verdad?

2. Fuiste al cine con Víctor, ¿verdad?

3. Hiciste el informe para la profesora Godoy, ¿verdad?

4. Trabajaste en la librería por tu hermana, ¿verdad?

5. Compraste un regalo para tus padres, ¿verdad?

6. Escribiste el trabajo por Daniel, ¿verdad?

7. Jugaste al tenis con los Vilas, ¿verdad?

8. Preparaste el almuerzo para mí, ¿verdad?

Personal a and Direct Objects

A direct object noun in Spanish is joined directly to its verb, without a preposition, if it refers to a thing. Direct object nouns that refer to specific people are preceded by **a**. This is called the personal **a**.

—¿Alquilaste **la película**?   *Did you rent **the film**?*
—Sí, y compré **palomitas de maíz**.   *Yes, and I bought **popcorn**.*

—No veo **a tu abuela**.   *I don't see **your grandmother**.*
—Está en la cocina ayudando **a mi   *She's in the kitchen helping **my mother**.*
   madre**.

In the preceding examples, the nouns **película**, **palomitas de maíz**, **abuela**, and **madre** are direct objects. Only the direct objects that refer to people use the personal **a**.

The personal **a** is not used before nouns referring to people unless they are specific.

Este restaurante busca **meseros**.	*This restaurant is looking for waiters.*
También necesitan **un cajero**.	*They also need a cashier.*
La empresa necesita **programadores**.	*The firm needs programmers.*
Admiten **cientos de estudiantes**.	*They admit hundreds of students.*

Nouns preceded by numbers are not considered specific and usually do not take the personal **a**.

Contrataron **(a) cien empleados nuevos**.	*They hired one hundred new employees.*
Vieron **(a) miles de aficionados**.	*They saw thousands of fans.*

However, the personal **a** is required before **alguien** and **nadie**, and before **alguno**, **ninguno**, and **cualquiera** when they modify a noun referring to people or are used as pronouns referring to people. The phrase **todo el mundo** is also preceded by the personal **a** when it is a direct object.

—¿**A quién** llamas?	***Whom*** *are you calling?*
—No puedo llamar **a nadie**. El teléfono está descompuesto.	*I can't call **anyone**. The telephone is out of order.*
—¿Despidieron **a alguien**?	*Did they fire **anyone**?*
—Creo que despidieron **a algunos empleados**.	*I think they fired **a few employees**.*
—¿Conoces **a algunos profesores** en Madrid?	*Do you know **any professors** in Madrid?*
—No, no conozco **a ningún profesor**.	*No, I don't know **any**.*
—¿Invitaste **a alguien**?	*Did you invite **anyone**?*
—No, no invité **a nadie**.	*No, I didn't invite **anyone**.*
—Nunca he visto **a nadie** que hable tanto como él.	*I've never seen **anyone** who talks as much as he does.*
—Sí, él es capaz de marear **a cualquiera**.	*Yes, he can make **anyone** dizzy.*
—Laura está dispuesta a ayudar **a cualquier amigo**.	*Laura is willing to help **any friend**.*
—Sí, ella siempre ayuda **a todo el mundo**.	*Yes, she always helps **everyone**.*

The personal **a** is also used before pronouns referring to people.

—Hoy llevo **a los míos** al centro.	*Today I'm taking **my family** downtown.*
—¿Puedo ir con Uds.? Me encantaría conocer **a los tuyos**.	*Can I go with you? I would love to meet **your family**.*

The personal **a** is generally used before **¿cuántos?** when it refers to people but is often omitted before the number that may appear in the answer to the question.

—¿**A cuántos** invitaron?	*How many of them* did they invite?
—Invitaron (**a**) **setecientos**.	*They invited seven hundred.*
—¿**A cuántos candidatos** eligieron?	*How many candidates did they elect?*
—Eligieron (**a**) **doce**.	*They elected twelve.*

The personal **a** is not usually used after **tener**.

—¿**Qué profesora** tienes para sicología?	*Which teacher do you have for psychology?*
—Tengo **la mejor profesora** que hay.	*I have the best teacher there is.*

When the personal **a** is used after **tener**, it implies having a person in a certain condition or in a certain role.

Tiene **a su mujer** como asistenta.	*He has his wife as his assistant.*
Tengo **a mi hija** en la universidad ahora.	*I've got my daughter in college now.*

The personal **a** is also used after **tener** when **tener** means *to hold*.

La mujer **tenía a su bebé** en brazos.	*The woman held her baby in her arms.*

When the personal **a** is used after **querer**, the verb means *to love* or *to like*. When the personal **a** is omitted after **querer**, the verb means *to want*.

Ricardo quiere **a** Sofía.	*Ricardo loves Sofía.*
No quieren **a su cocinero**.	*They don't like their cook.*
Quieren **otro cocinero**.	*They want another cook.*

Several verbs that take a direct object in Spanish have English equivalents that have prepositions.

aprovechar algo	*to take advantage of something*
buscar algo/a alguien	*to look for something/for someone*
escuchar algo/a alguien	*to listen to something/to someone*
esperar algo/a alguien	*to wait for something/for someone*
mirar algo/a alguien	*to look at something/at someone*
pagar algo	*to pay for something*
pedir algo	*to ask for something*

F *La a personal. Complete las oraciones con la a personal. Si no es necesario añadir la a personal, escriba una X. No se olvide de escribir la contracción al (a + el) cuando haga falta.*

1. Yo buscaba _____ los sobres.

2. Encontré _____ los niños en el patio.

3. Busquen _____ los documentos en el escritorio.

4. Encontraron _____ el arquitecto en su oficina.

5. Paco conoció _____ su novia hace seis meses.

6. ¿_____ quién viste en el teatro?

7. Llevamos _____ nuestros amigos a la sierra.

8. ¿No comprendes _____ el problema todavía?

9. Me gustaría conocer _____ la ciudad.

10. Llévate _____ el paquete.

11. Vamos a buscar _____ Mari Carmen.

12. No he encontrado _____ el número de teléfono.

13. Jesús y Tito llevan _____ la camiseta de su equipo.

14. ¿Quién llamó _____ el médico?

15. Ayuda _____ tu hermano.

16. ¿Conoce Ud. _____ ese centro comercial?

17. Voy a ver _____ mis tíos mañana.

18. Nadie comprende _____ el profesor Delgado.

19. ¿Es verdad que no pudiste encontrar _____ el hotel?

20. ¿_____ quiénes llamaste?

G *¡Un flechazo!* **(Love at first sight!)** *Simón le explica a su amigo cómo se enamoró en Palma de Mallorca. Complete las oraciones con la **a** personal. Si no es necesario añadir la **a** personal, escriba una X.*

1. Pedro: Entonces, ¿ya conocías _____ algunos estudiantes de la facultad de ciencias sociales?

2. Simón: Por desgracia, las primeras semanas no conocí _____ ninguno de los estudiantes.

3. Pedro: ¿Pero no viste _____ muchos chicos en la universidad?

4. Simón: Claro que los vi pero no me presenté _____ ellos porque no dominaba (dominar (*to master, be fluent in*)) el español.

   Pedro: ¿Cómo es que cambió la situación entonces?

5. Simón: Bueno, después de un mes más o menos conocí _____ alguien de la facultad de ingeniería que me llevó a una fiesta.

6. Pedro: Allí conociste _____ mucha gente, ¿verdad?

7. Simón: _____ muchas personas, no, pero _____ una muy especial sí. Es que vi _____ tantas chicas muy lindas.

8. Pedro: Y querías sacar a bailar _____ todas, ¿no?

   Simón: Sí, al principio. ¡Hasta que me fijé en una que me dejó boquiabierto (literally, *openmouthed; took my breath away*)!

9. Pedro: ¡Un flechazo! No invitaste _____ ninguna a salir...

10. Simón: ¡Excepto _____ Josefa!

NOTA CULTURAL

Palma de Mallorca es la capital de la provincia de Baleares, las islas españolas en el Mediterráneo. Es también capital de la isla de Mallorca, la mayor de las Baleares. Por su hermoso paisaje y clima perfecto, Mallorca es un gran centro de turismo internacional. Un lugar de visita es la Cartuja de Valldemosa (*Carthusian Monastery of Valldemosa*), donde el compositor polaco Frédéric Chopin (1810–1849) y la escritora francesa la baronesa Dudevant, cuyo seudónimo era George Sand, pasaron el invierno de 1838.

H *Expresar en español. Verbos.* *Exprese las oraciones en español. No se olvide de que varios verbos en español que tienen complemento directo y no tienen preposición corresponden a verbos con preposición en inglés.*

1. *Ask* (Ud.) *for another bottle of wine.*

2. *Let's take advantage of this sale.*

3. *Look* (tú) *at the beautiful ocean.*

4. *I'll wait for them until three o'clock.*

5. *He's looking for his brother and sister.*

6. *Did their parents pay for the furniture?*

7. *Let's listen to the orchestra.*

Direct Object Pronouns: Forms and Position

Direct object nouns can be replaced by direct object pronouns. Here are the direct object pronouns in Spanish.

me	nos
te	os
lo	los
la	las

NOTES

1 · **Lo, la, los, las** refer to both people and things.

2 · **Lo, la, los, las** are also the direct object pronouns for **Ud.** and **Uds.**, so they mean *you* as well as *him, her, it,* and *them.*

3 · In Spain, **lo** is usually replaced by **le** when referring to people.

Direct object pronouns precede the conjugated verb in Spanish, whereas in English they follow the conjugated verb.

—¿Dónde estarán los niños? Hace quince minutos que **los** busco y no **los** encuentro.
—**Los** vi en el parque.

*Where can the children be? I've been looking for **them** for fifteen minutes and I can't find **them**.*
*I saw **them** in the park.*

—¡Ay! No tengo mi libro de química.
  Lo dejé en el laboratorio.

Oh! I don't have my chemistry book. I left
  ***it** at the lab.*

—Aquí tengo el mío. ¿**Lo** quieres?

*I have mine here. Do you want **it**?*

—**Me** avisará si hay un cambio en
  el horario de mañana, ¿verdad?

*You'll inform **me** if there's a change in
  tomorrow's schedule, won't you?*

—Cómo no, señora. Cualquier cosa
  y **la** llamo en seguida.

*Of course, madam. If anything comes up,
  I'll call **you** immediately.*

—¿Vas al centro ahora? ¿**Nos** llevas?

*Are you going downtown now? Will you
  take **us**?*

—Con mucho gusto. **Los** dejo
  delante del correo. ¿Está bien?

*Gladly. I'll leave **you** in front of the post
  office. Is that all right?*

In compound tenses, the direct object pronouns are placed before the auxiliary verb
haber.

—Carlos, ¡qué milagro! No **te** hemos
  visto por tanto tiempo.

*Carlos, what a surprise! We haven't seen
  you for such a long time.*

—Es que **me** han contratado en una
  empresa de las afueras.

*That's because I was hired at a firm in the
  suburbs.*

In verb + infinitive constructions, the direct object pronoun may either precede the first
verb or be attached to the infinitive in writing.

—¿Has visto la nueva película
  española?

Have you seen the new Spanish film?

—No, pero **la** quiero ver. ⎫
—No, pero quiero ver**la**. ⎭

No, but I want to see it.

In the progressive tenses, the direct object pronoun can either be placed before the form
of **estar** or be attached to the present participle in writing. When the pronoun is attached
to the present participle, an accent mark is added to the vowel before the **-ndo**.

—¿Has leído la nueva novela de
  Atienza?

Have you read the new novel by Atienza?

—**La** estoy leyendo ahora. ⎫
—Estoy ley**é**ndo**la** ahora. ⎭

I'm reading it now.

The direct object pronoun is also attached to affirmative command forms. An accent
mark is added to the stressed vowel of the command form, except in the case of one-
syllable commands.

—Ah, tienes el periódico. **Ponlo** en
  la mesa.

*Ah, you have the newspaper. Put it on the
  table.*

—No, **cógelo** tú y **llévalo** arriba.

No, you get it and take it upstairs.

—Éstas son las palabras nuevas,
  chicos. **Apréndanlas** de memoria.

*These are the new words, kids. Learn them
  by heart.*

—Por favor, **repáselas** con nosotros,
  profesor.

Please, review them with us, sir.

To emphasize or contrast direct object pronouns referring to people, a phrase consisting of **a** + the corresponding prepositional pronoun is added to the sentence.

—¿Reconociste a Laura y a Marcos?	*Did you recognize Laura and Marcos?*
—**La** reconocí **a ella**, pero no **lo** vi **a él**.	*I recognized **her**, but I didn't see **him**.*
—Parece que las secretarias son más simpáticas que el jefe.	*It seems that the secretaries are nicer than the boss.*
—Sí, **a ellas las** encuentro encantadoras, pero **a él** no **lo** aguanto.	*Yes, I find **them** delightful, but I can't stand **him**.*

When a direct object noun *precedes* the verb, the direct object pronoun must be present. Compare **Veo *a Juan*** with ***A Juan lo* veo**. This is true even if the direct object is a thing. Compare **Dejé *los libros* en la mesa** with ***Los libros los* dejé en la mesa**.

I   **Mi coche.** *Conteste las preguntas sobre el cuidado de su coche cambiando el sustantivo a un pronombre de complemento directo. Siga el modelo.*

> MODELO   ¿Compraste la bomba de aire (*air pump*)?
> → No, no la compré.
>   Voy a comprarla.

El coche

la caja de herramientas *toolbox*	**las piezas de repuesto** *spare parts*
el faro *headlight*	**la placa de matrícula** *license plate*
el gato *jack*	**el silenciador** *muffler*
el parachoques *bumper*	**el volante** *steering wheel*

1. ¿Cambiaste el aceite?

2. ¿Reparaste el parachoques?

3. ¿Pediste las placas de matrícula?

4. ¿Llevaste la caja de herramientas y las piezas de repuesto?

5. ¿Usaste el gato?

6. ¿Pusiste otros faros?

7. ¿Arreglaste el volante?

8. ¿Instalaste el silenciador?

J   **Bernardo y los coches.** *Bernardo acaba de sacar su licencia de conducir y piensa mucho en su coche. Escriba oraciones sobre la afición de Bernardo cambiando el sustantivo a un pronombre de complemento directo. Escriba la respuesta de dos maneras. Siga el modelo.*

> MODELO   Bernardo quiere limpiar el baúl.
> → Quiere limpiarlo.
>   Lo quiere limpiar.

El coche

la avería *breakdown*	**el coche todo terreno** *jeep, SUV*
el baúl *trunk*	**el pinchazo** *blowout*
cargar la batería *to charge the battery*	**la señal de tráfico** *road sign*
el coche descapotable *convertible*	

1. Piensa comprar el coche todo terreno.

2. Tiene que llenar el tanque de gasolina.

3. Trata de leer todas las señales de tráfico.

4. Prefiere conducir el coche descapotable.

5. Debe cargar la batería.

6. Teme tener un pinchazo.

7. Procura evitar las averías.

8. Necesita cerrar el baúl.

K *Lo significa* **you.** *El complemento directo* **lo, la, los, las** *también reemplaza* **Ud.** *y* **Uds.** *Conteste las preguntas empleando el complemento directo en su respuesta. Siga el modelo.*

> MODELO   ¿Me conoce Ud.?
> → Sí, señor, lo conozco.

1. ¿Me conoce Ud.?

   Sí, señorita, _____.

2. ¿Nos comprende Ud.?

   Sí, señores, _____.

3. ¿Me llama Ud.?

   No, señora, no _____.

4. ¿Nos busca Ud.?

   No, señoras, no _____.

5. ¿Me lleva Ud.?

   Sí, señor, _____.

6. ¿Nos espera Ud.?

   No, señoritas, no _____.

7. ¿Me ayuda Ud.?

   Sí, profesor, _____.

8. ¿Nos ve Ud.?

   No, señores, no _____.

L *¡Míralo!* *Dé mandatos a varias personas diciéndoles lo que deben hacer y no hacer en ciertos deportes. Escriba mandatos afirmativos y negativos colocando el pronombre de complemento directo en su posición correcta. Siga el modelo.*

> MODELO   ver / Ud. / los Juegos Olímpicos
> → Véalos.
>   No los vea.

1. marcar / Ud. /goles

2. llamar / tú / al árbitro (*umpire*)

3. recoger / Uds. / los bates

4. saltar / Ud. / vallas (*hurdles*)

5. hacer / tú / gimnasia

6. mirar / Uds. / la cancha

7. lanzar / Ud. / la pelota

8. felicitar / tú / al plusmarquista [*masc.*] (*record holder*)

9. levantar / Uds. / las pesas

M *¿Lo ha visto Ud.?* *Unos amigos quieren saber si Ud. ha visto a ciertas personas y cosas hoy. Conteste usando el pronombre de complemento directo. Siga el modelo.*

MODELO   ¿Ha visto a Paulina hoy? (sí / no)
→ Sí, la he visto.
No, no la he visto.

1. ¿Has visto al señor Domínguez hoy? (sí)

2. ¿Ha visto Ud. a los decanos (el decano (*dean*)) de la universidad? (no)

3. ¿Han visto Uds. la cámara digital? (sí)

4. ¿Ha visto Ud. los alicates (*pliers*)? (no)

5. ¿Has visto a las hermanas Moya? (no)

6. ¿Han visto Uds. las tarjetas de crédito? (sí)

7. ¿Ha visto Ud. el recibo? (sí)

8. ¿Has visto a la ortodontista? (no)

N *La catedral de Sevilla.* *La catedral se remonta* (dates back) *al siglo XV cuando se empezó a construir. Ud. vive en la Edad Media y es testigo de la construcción. Describa las actividades que está viendo, cambiando el sustantivo al pronombre de complemento directo. Escriba las oraciones de dos maneras. Siga el modelo.*

MODELO   Yo estoy viendo la construcción.
→ Yo estoy viéndola.
Yo la estoy viendo.

La catedral de Sevilla: su construcción

el albañil *bricklayer, mason*	**el fraile** *monk*
los andamios *scaffolding*	**el maestro de obras** *master builder*
la argamasa *mortar* (mezcla de cemento, arena y agua)	**la mezquita** *mosque*
	la monja *nun*
el dibujante *draftsman*	**rezar las oraciones** *to say prayers*
echar los cimientos *to lay the foundation*	

1. Los arquitectos están empleando el estilo gótico.

2. Los constructores van cubriendo la mezquita.

3. Los dibujantes están dibujando las ventanas.

4. Los maestros de obras están echando los cimientos.

5. Los frailes y las monjas siguen rezando sus oraciones.

6. Los trabajadores siguen colocando los andamios.

7. Los albañiles van trayendo piedras.

8. Los obreros están poniendo la argamasa.

NOTA CULTURAL

La catedral de Sevilla es por sus dimensiones la primera de España y la tercera del mundo cristiano después de San Pedro del Vaticano y San Pablo de Londres. Es una de las últimas catedrales góticas españolas y tiene algunas influencias renacentistas. La construcción de la catedral fue comenzada en 1402 y terminada a principios del siglo XVI. La catedral fue construida sobre las ruinas de una mezquita (*mosque*) que se remonta al siglo XII.

Hubo influencia árabe en España a partir de la batalla de Guadalete en 711 en la cual los árabes derrotaron a Don Rodrigo, el último rey visigodo, y se apoderaron de la península Ibérica. Duró la influencia árabe en España ocho siglos hasta que perdieron la campaña (*campaign*) de Granada en 1492. Sin embargo, la influencia árabe en España perdura en la toponimia (nombres de lugares), léxico, arquitectura, arte y comida. Hay herencia de la mezquita en la catedral de Sevilla—la Giralda, campanario de la catedral, era un alminar (*minaret*) de la mezquita.

O *Pili lo arregla todo.* *David vuelve a casa después de un viaje de negocios. Le hace unas preguntas a su sobrina Pili para saber dónde están sus cosas y los otros miembros de su familia. ¿Qué le dice Pili a su tío David? Use el complemento directo en primer lugar. Siga el modelo.*

MODELO   ¿Dónde está tu tía? (ver salir hace una hora)
         → A mi tía la vi salir hace una hora.

1. ¿Dónde está mi celular? (poner en tu mesa de trabajo)

2. ¿Dónde están tus primos? (llevar al colegio)

3. ¿Dónde está mi tablet? (dejar en el jardín)

4. ¿Dónde están tus padres? (ver en la sala)

5. ¿Dónde están mis libros? (colocar en tu oficina)

6. ¿Dónde están las cartas que escribí? (echar al correo)

7. ¿Dónde está mi abrigo? (colgar en el armario)

8. ¿Dónde están las galletas que compré? (comer)

Indirect Object Pronouns: Forms and Position

Indirect objects are joined to the verb by the preposition **a**. Indirect objects most commonly refer to people.

Here are the indirect object pronouns in Spanish.

me	nos
te	os
le	les

Indirect object pronouns follow the same rules of position as direct object pronouns.

Te dije la verdad.
Le debo decir la verdad. OR Debo decir**le** la verdad.
Les estoy diciendo la verdad. OR Estoy diciéndo**les** la verdad.
Nos han dicho la verdad.
Díga**me** la verdad.

An indirect object noun in Spanish is usually accompanied by the corresponding indirect object pronoun (**le** or **les**, depending on whether the noun is singular or plural).

—¿**Les** escribiste **a tus padres?**   *Did you write to your parents?*
—Sí, y también **le** mandé un email   *Yes, and I also sent my sister an email.*
   a mi hermana.

Some verbs that take an indirect object in Spanish take a direct object in English.

contestarle a alguien	*to answer someone*
pedirle algo a alguien	*to ask someone for something*
preguntarle a alguien	*to ask someone*
recordarle a alguien	*to remind someone*

Many verbs take an indirect object of the person (**le… a alguien**) and an inanimate direct object (**algo**).

contarle algo a alguien	*to relate/recount something to someone*
darle algo a alguien	*to give something to someone*
decirle algo a alguien	*to tell/say something to someone*
devolverle algo a alguien	*to return something to someone*
enseñarle algo a alguien	*to show something to someone*
entregarle algo a alguien	*to hand over something to someone*
enviarle algo a alguien	*to send something to someone*
escribirle algo a alguien	*to write something to someone*
explicarle algo a alguien	*to explain something to someone*
mandarle algo a alguien	*to send something to someone*
mostrarle algo a alguien	*to show something to someone*
ofrecerle algo a alguien	*to offer something to someone*
pedirle algo a alguien	*to ask someone for something*
recordarle algo a alguien	*to remind someone of something*
regalarle algo a alguien	*to give something to someone as a gift*
traerle algo a alguien	*to bring something to someone*
venderle algo a alguien	*to sell something to someone*

The indirect object is often the equivalent of English *from* or *of* with verbs meaning *take away, steal, remove*, etc.

arrancarle algo a alguien	*to snatch/grab something from someone*
arrebatarle algo a alguien	*to snatch/grab something from someone*
comprarle algo a alguien	*to buy something from someone*
esconderle algo a alguien	*to hide something from someone*

exigirle algo a alguien	*to demand something of someone*
ganarle algo a alguien	*to win something from someone*
ocultarle algo a alguien	*to hide something from someone*
pedirle prestado algo a alguien	*to borrow something from someone*
quitarle algo a alguien	*to take something away from someone*
robarle algo a alguien	*to steal something from someone*
sacarle algo a alguien	*to get something out of someone*
solicitarle algo a alguien	*to ask/request something of someone*
suspenderle algo a alguien	*to revoke/cancel something of someone*

¿A quién le compraste el coche?	*Whom did you buy the car from?*
Me exigieron mis documentos de identidad.	*They demanded my identification papers (of/from me).*
Le solicité trabajo **al padre de Lucas.**	*I applied for work with/from Lucas's father.*
Al turista le quitaron el pasaporte.	*They took the tourist's passport from him.*

To emphasize or contrast indirect object pronouns, a phrase consisting of **a** + the corresponding prepositional pronoun is added to the sentence.

—¿Qué **les** pidieron los aduaneros **a ustedes**?	*What did the customs officers ask **you** for?*
—**A mí me** pidieron el pasaporte, pero **a él le** pidieron todos los documentos.	*They asked **me** for **my** passport, but they asked **him** for all of **his** documents.*
—¿**A ustedes les** regalaron algo?	*Did they give **you** anything as a gift?*
—**A nosotros nos** regalaron muchas cosas, pero **a ellos** no **les** dieron nada.	*They gave **us** many things, but they didn't give **them** anything.*

P   *El complemento indirecto.* *Vuelva a escribir las oraciones cambiando el pronombre de complemento indirecto. Siga el modelo.*

> MODELO   Le pedí unas revistas. (a ellos)
> → Les pedí unas revistas.

1. Les traje los refrescos. (a ti)

2. Me dieron flores. (a nosotros)

3. Le mandó una tarjeta postal. (a mí)

4. Nos dijeron los precios. (a Ud.)

5. Te ofrecimos el escritorio. (a él)

6. Les preguntó la hora. (a ella)

7. Le expliqué mis ideas. (a vosotros)

8. Me recordaron el cumpleaños de Leo. (a Uds.)

Q *Salir ganando o salir perdiendo.* *Añada a cada oración una frase que consiste en **a** + el pronombre enfático para hacer énfasis en o contraste de los pronombres de complemento indirecto. Siga el modelo.*

MODELO   _A mí_ me enviaron mucha plata, pero _a ella_ (Roberta) no le enviaron nada.

1. _____ nos mostraron el castillo, pero _____ (Ud. y Felipe) les mostraron solamente el establo de caballos.

2. Marta me contó _____ la pura verdad, pero _____ te contó puras mentiras.

3. Yo le escribí una carta de amor _____ (Daniel), pero le escribí una carta de odio _____ (su novia).

4. _____ te dimos la llave de la casa, pero _____ (Catarina y Jorge) les dimos una carta de despedida.

5. _____ os regalaron unos discos compactos fabulosos, pero _____ nos regalaron unos discos rayados (*scratched*).

6. _____ (Elena y Margarita) les trajo unos bombones, pero _____ (Ud.) le trajo una caja vacía.

R *Titulares de periódico.* *Componga estos titulares para el periódico de hoy. Debe haber un pronombre de complemento indirecto en cada titular. Escriba oraciones usando el presente de indicativo. Siga el modelo.*

MODELO   (ellos) / a una señora / robarle el carro / mientras compra leche en una tienda
→ A una señora le roban el carro mientras compra leche en una tienda.

1. (ellos) / a tres jóvenes / suspender el permiso de manejar

2. (los políticos) / a nosotros / ocultar los problemas económicos del país

3. (ellos) / al pueblo / exigir más sacrificios

4. (nuestro país) / a España / ir a comprar barcos

5. (el gobierno) / a tres extranjeros / quitar la visa

Verbs Usually Appearing with an Indirect Object Pronoun (e.g., **gustar**)

Certain verbs in Spanish are almost always used with an indirect object pronoun. This construction is different from the English equivalents of these verbs. The most common of these is **gustar**. These are known as reverse construction verbs.

Me gusta la torta. *I like the cake.*
Me gustan las galletas. *I like the cookies.*

Te gusta la torta. *You like the cake.*
Te gustan las galletas. *You like the cookies.*

Le gusta la torta. *He/She likes/You like the cake.*
Le gustan las galletas. *He/She likes/ You like the cookies.*

Nos gusta la torta. *We like the cake.*
Nos gustan las galletas. *We like the cookies.*

Os gusta la torta. *You like the cake.*
Os gustan las galletas. *You like the cookies.*

Les gusta la torta. *They/You like the cake.*

Les gustan las galletas. *They/You like the cookies.*

Note that the verb agrees with the subject of the Spanish sentence, **torta** or **galletas**.

When the grammatical subject of a verb like **gustar** is an infinitive, the verb is always third person singular.

—**Me encanta patinar** sobre hielo.	*I love to ice skate.*
—A mí **me gusta más esquiar.**	*I like skiing better.*

Here are some other verbs and verbal phrases that function like **gustar**.

agradarle a uno	*to like something, find something pleasing*
caerle bien/mal a uno	*to like/dislike (usually a person)*
convenirle a uno	*to suit someone, be good for someone*
desagradarle a uno	*to dislike something, find something unpleasant*
disgustarle a uno	*to dislike something, find something unpleasant*
encantarle a uno	*to love something*
entusiasmarle a uno	*to be excited about something*
faltarle a uno	*to be missing something, not to have something*
fascinarle a uno	*to be fascinated by something; to like something*
hacerle falta a uno	*to need something*
importarle a uno	*to care about something; to mind; to matter*
interesarle a uno	*to be interested in something*
quedarle a uno	*to have something left*
sobrarle a uno	*to have more than enough of something*
tocarle a uno	*to be someone's turn*
urgirle a uno	*to be urgent for someone to do something*

—¿**Te importa** acompañarme a la exposición de arte?	*Would you mind accompanying me to the art show?*
—**Me encantaría. Me interesa** mucho la pintura.	*I'd love to. I'm very interested in painting.*
—Creo que **te convendría** salir un poco.	*I think it would be good for you to go out a little.*
—Sé que **me hace falta**, pero **me sobra** trabajo.	*I know I need to, but I have too much work.*
—Parece que no **te entusiasman** mucho estos juegos.	*It seems that you're not very excited about these games.*
—Cada vez que **me toca a mí**, pierdo.	*Every time it's my turn, I lose.*
—**Nos hace falta** un carro nuevo.	*We need a new car.*
—Y **les hace falta** también el dinero para comprarlo, me imagino.	*And you also need the money to buy it, I imagine.*
—Cuando estás lejos no sabes **cuánta falta me haces.**	*When you're away you don't know how much I miss you.*
—Sí, lo sé, porque tú **a mí me haces mucha falta** cuando no estamos juntos.	*Yes, I do know, because I miss you a lot when we're not together.*

To emphasize or contrast the indirect object pronouns, a phrase consisting of **a** + the corresponding prepositional pronoun is added to the sentence. This prepositional phrase is also used for "short responses."

—¿Cuánto dinero nos queda?	*How much money do we have left?*
—A mí me quedan doscientos pesos. ¿Y a ti?	*I have two hundred pesos left. How about you?*
—Chicos, ¿a quién le gusta la torta de chocolate?	*Kids, who likes chocolate cake?*
—¡A mí! ¡A mí! ¡A mí!	*I do! I do! I do!*

The phrase **¿Y a ti?** is short for **Y a ti, ¿cuánto dinero te queda?** The phrase **¡A mí!** is short for **A mí me gusta la torta de chocolate.**

S **En plural.** *Cambie el sujeto de las oraciones al plural. Todos los verbos son del tipo* **gustar.** *No se olvide de hacer todos los cambios necesarios. Siga el modelo.*

MODELO   Me gusta ese suéter.
                → Me gustan esos suéteres.

1. Le encanta ese perfume.

2. Nos interesa esta novela.

3. Les queda un examen.

4. Te entusiasma la comedia.

5. Os importa la idea.

6. Me hace falta una guía.

7. Les fascina esta materia.

8. Le falta un cuaderno.

T **En el futuro.** *Añada la construcción* **ir a** + *infinitivo a las oraciones con verbos como* **gustar.** *Siga los modelos.*

MODELOS   Me gusta esa película.
                  → Me va a gustar esa película.

                  Me gustan esas películas.
                  → Me van a gustar esas películas.

1. Nos importan sus problemas.

2. No les queda mucho dinero.

3. Le encanta visitar a sus abuelos.

4. No les sobra comida.

5. Os conviene viajar en tren.

6. Te fascinan esos cuadros.

7. Me entusiasman sus obras.

8. No le interesan esos programas.

U **¿Quién y a quién?** *Conteste las preguntas escogiendo entre el pronombre sujeto y la frase con* **a.** *Siga el modelo.*

MODELO   ¿Quién estudia chino? (Yo. / A mí.)
                → Yo.

1. ¿A quién le gusta jugar al baloncesto? (Él. / A él.)

2. ¿Quiénes vieron a los niños? (Ellos. / A ellos.)

3. ¿A Juana le quedan cincuenta dólares? (Ella no. / A ella no.)

4. ¿Conociste a Diana? (Yo no. / A mí no.)

5. ¿Comprendieron al profesor? (Nosotros sí. / A nosotros sí.)

6. ¿A quién le interesan estos poemas? (Ud. / A Ud.)

7. ¿Te hace falta manejar? (Yo sí. / A mí sí.)

8. ¿Devolvieron los libros a la biblioteca? (Ellas sí. / A ellas sí.)

V   *Expresar en español. La familia Castellón planea un viaje. Exprese en español la conversación que tienen los señores Castellón y sus tres hijos sobre el viaje que piensan hacer en el verano. Escriba oraciones usando los verbos como **gustar**.*

1. Alicia: *I'd like to take a trip to Spain.*

2. Rafael: *I'd love to visit my relatives in Chile and Argentina.*

3. Lorenzo: *I'd be interested in going camping in New Mexico or Arizona.*

4. Nora: *And I'd like (be fascinated) to see the new Italian fashions.*

5. Carlos: *I'd be very excited to do water sports.*

6. Rafael: *It's good for us to make a decision as soon as possible.*

7. Lorenzo: *We have more than enough suggestions. Let's draw lots!* (echar suertes)

8. Nora: *It's my turn first!*

Other Uses of the Indirect Object

The indirect object in Spanish is often the equivalent of the English possessive with parts of the body and articles of clothing. This is also true of reflexive pronouns.

—¿**Te quito** el abrigo?	*Shall I help you off with your coat?*
—No, gracias. Siempre **me haces daño** en el brazo cuando me lo quitas.	*No, thank you. You always hurt my arm when you help me off with it.*
—Ven, Carlitos. **Te lavo** las manos.	*Come, Carlitos. I'll wash your hands.*
—No, no. Yo mismo **me las lavo**.	*No, no. I'll wash them myself.*

The indirect object tells for whose benefit or disadvantage something is done.

—¿**Me haces** el almuerzo, mamá?	*Can you make my lunch for me, Mom?*
—Sí, si **me llevas** las bolsas de comida a la cocina.	*Yes, if you carry the bags of food to the kitchen for me.*
—Espero que no **nos** caiga otra vez la vecina con sus dos hijos.	*I hope the neighbor doesn't drop in on us again with her two children.*
—Sí, la última vez esos dos diablitos casi **nos** destruyeron la casa.	*Yes, the last time those two little rascals almost destroyed our house.*
—¡Y **nos** comieron todas las galletas que teníamos!	*And they ate up all the cookies that we had!*

The indirect object pronouns can be added to certain impersonal expressions.

Es difícil caminar cuando nieva.	*It's hard to walk when it snows.*
Me es difícil caminar cuando nieva.	*It's hard for me to walk when it snows.*
Es necesario estudiar más.	*It's necessary to study more.*
Nos es necesario estudiar más.	*It's necessary for us to study more.*

The indirect object pronoun can be added to a **se** construction with certain verbs to express unplanned occurrences. These constructions focus on the object affected rather than on the person involved.

acabársele a uno	*to run out of*
averiársele a uno	*to get damaged, break down, fail*
caérsele a uno	*to drop*
descomponérsele a uno	*to have something break down*
ocurrírsele a uno	*to dawn on, get the idea of*
olvidársele a uno	*to forget*
perdérsele a uno	*to lose*
quebrársele a uno	*to break*
quedársele a uno	*to leave something behind*
rompérsele a uno	*to break*

—Veo que **se te rompieron** los anteojos. — *I see that you broke your glasses.*

—Sí, **se me cayeron** en la calle. — *Yes, I dropped them in the street.*

—¿Cómo **se les ocurrió** venir ayer? — *How did they get the idea to come yesterday?*

—**Se les había olvidado** que la reunión era mañana. — *They had forgotten that the meeting was tomorrow.*

—**Se nos está acabando** la gasolina. Tenemos que comprar. — *We're running out of gas. We have to buy some.*

—Ay, **se me quedó** la tarjeta de crédito en casa. — *Oh, I left my credit card at home.*

W **Sucesos inesperados.** *Escriba los elementos de la oración que faltan. Todas las oraciones expresan la idea de un suceso inesperado. Use el pretérito de los verbos indicados y el complemento indirecto + construcción con* **se**.

1. No pudimos hacer los sándwiches.

   _____ el pan. (acabársele)

2. Plácido no pudo entrar en su casa.

   _____ las llaves. (perdérsele)

3. No le mandé una tarjeta a Beatriz.

   _____ la fecha de su cumpleaños. (olvidársele)

4. ¡Pero estáis mojadísimos!

   ¿_____ el paraguas en casa? (quedársele)

5. ¡Cuidado de no cortarte la mano!

   ¿Cómo _____ los vasos? (rompérsele)

6. Pasando por Madrid, Uds. no visitaron a los tíos.

   ¿Ni _____ llamarlos? (ocurrírsele)

7. Los niños están recogiendo todos los papeles en el suelo.

   ¿Cómo _____? (caérsele)

Prevenir **(to warn)** *contra lo inesperado.* *Escriba oraciones previniendo a unas personas contra ciertas cosas. Fíjese que el imperativo de los verbos como* **acabársele** *es un mandato indirecto. Siga el modelo.*

> MODELO   tú / no caérsele / los platos
>   → Que no se te caigan los platos.

1. Uds. / no olvidársele / asistir a la conferencia

2. él / no perdérsele / los anteojos

3. Ud. / no acabársele / la paciencia

4. vosotros / no quedársele / los cheques

5. ella / no rompérsele / las estatuillas de porcelana (*china figurines*) .

6. tú / no ocurrírsele / tales cosas

7. ellos / no caérsele / la torta de chocolate

Y *Expresar en español.* *Exprese los diálogos en español usando la construcción del suceso inesperado.*

1. *Did you (Ud.) lose your wallet?*
   No, I had left it at home.

2. *They're running out of pastries at the bake shop.*
   Didn't it occur to you (tú) to buy them this morning?

3. *Be (Uds.) careful! You're going to drop the cups!*
   We already broke two!

4. *She forgot to pick Tere and Leo up.*
   Didn't it dawn on her that they were waiting all night?

Double Object Pronouns

In Spanish, a direct object pronoun and an indirect object pronoun can appear together with a verb. The indirect object pronoun precedes the direct object pronoun.

—Necesito mil euros. ¿**Me los** prestas?	*I need a thousand euros. Will you lend **them to me**?*
—**Te los** presto con tal de que **me los** devuelvas la semana que viene.	*I'll lend **them to you** as long as you return **them to me** next week.*
—Nos interesa tu colección de sellos. ¿**Nos la** enseñas?	*We're interested in your stamp collection. Will you show **it to us**?*
—Claro. Ahora **se la** traigo.	*Of course. I'll bring **it to you** right now.*

When a third person indirect object pronoun (**le** or **les**) precedes a third person direct object pronoun (**lo, la, los, las**), the indirect object pronoun changes to **se**.

le/les + lo	→	se lo
le/les + la	→	se la
le/les + los	→	se los
le/les + las	→	se las

Double object pronouns cannot be separated from each other. They follow the same rules of position as single object pronouns. When double object pronouns are added to an infinitive, present participle, or affirmative command in writing, an accent mark is always added, even to infinitives and command forms of one syllable: **Quiero dártelo**, **Dándomelo**, **Dámelo**.

—¿Cuándo le va a entregar Ud. el informe al jefe?	*When are you going to submit the report to the boss?*
—Ya **se lo** he entregado.	*I've already submitted it to him.*
—Hay un problema que no comprendo.	*There's a problem that I don't understand.*
—Mué**stramelo**. A ver si **te lo** puedo explicar.	*Show it to me. Let's see if I can explain it to you.*
—Mué**stramelo**. A ver si puedo **explicártelo**.	
—¿Dónde están nuestras maletas?	*Where are our suitcases?*
—El botones **nos las** está subiendo ahora.	*The bellhop is bringing them up for us now.*
—El botones está subiéndo**noslas** ahora.	

Sentences with **se** out of context can be ambiguous. Context or a phrase consisting of **a** + prepositional pronoun clarifies to whom **se** refers.

—¿La niñita se puso los zapatos?	*Did the little girl put on her shoes?*
—Sí, **se los** puso. (**se** = reflexive pronoun referring to **la niña**)	*Yes, she put them on.*
—¿La niñita se puso los zapatos?	*Did the little girl put on her shoes?*
—No, **yo se los puse**. (**se** = indirect object pronoun referring to **la niña**)	*No, I put them on (for her).*
—¿El gerente y la directora tienen copias del informe?	*Do the manager and the director have copies of the report?*
—Sí, a él **se lo** mandé por correo y a ella **se lo** di personalmente.	*Yes, I sent it to him by mail and I gave it to her personally.*

Z *Dos pronombres de complementos directo e indirecto.* Escriba oraciones cambiando el sustantivo complemento directo a un pronombre y haga todos los cambios necesarios. Algunas oraciones tienen dos respuestas posibles. Siga el modelo.

MODELO   Les entregaré las cartas el martes.
          → Se las entregaré el martes.

1. Me dijeron los motivos.

2. Le hemos puesto los zapatos.

3. Está explicándoles la idea.

4. Os muestro el paquete.

5. ¿Te darían la beca?

6. Les cuentas los chismes.

7. Nos ha hecho las chuletas de cordero.

8. Devuélvame el cortacésped (*lawnmower*).

9. Me estaban enseñando las fotos.

10. ¿A quién le vendiste tu velero (*sailboat*)?

11. Os había escrito una tarjeta postal.

12. ¿Nos prestarás unos disquetes?

13. Apréndanse la letra (*lyrics*) de memoria.

14. ¿Estáis preguntándole el por qué?

15. Le pusieron la multa.

16. Les preparó arroz y carne.

17. Estará bajándome el equipaje.

18. Vendámosles la casa.

19. Estuvimos trayéndole los periódicos ingleses.

20. Te apagaré la televisión.

AA *Algo pasará./Algo pasó.* *Añada la construcción* **ir a** + *infinitivo o* **acabar de** + *infinitivo a las oraciones. Haga los cambios necesarios respecto a los verbos y a los pronombres de complemento directo e indirecto. Escriba cada oración de dos maneras. Siga los modelos.*

MODELOS Se los doy. (ir a)
     → Voy a dárselos.
       Se los voy a dar.

     Se los doy. (acabar de)
     → Acabo de dárselos.
       Se los acabo de dar.

1. Me la traen. (ir a)

2. Te lo dice. (acabar de)

3. Se los hacemos. (ir a)

4. Os las pongo. (acabar de)

5. Se lo muestra. (ir a)

6. Nos la compráis. (acabar de)

7. Me los cuentas. (ir a)

8. Se las arreglo. (acabar de)

9. Te la suben. (ir a)

10. Os lo damos. (acabar de)

11. Se lo describimos. (ir a)

12. Se la ofrezco. (acabar de)

13. Te los limpia. (ir a)

14. Se las encuentro. (acabar de)

15. Me la piden. (ir a)

16. Nos lo buscas. (acabar de)

17. Os los llevamos. (ir a)

18. Se las sirve. (acabar de)

19. Se lo devolvéis. (ir a)

20. Te la canto. (acabar de)

BB **¡Mami, papi, cómprenmelo!** *Esta niña Rita vuelve loca a toda su familia. No deja de pedir cosas y por desgracia, sus familiares se lo conceden todo. Por eso es una niña mal criada (spoiled brat). Escriba diálogos entre Rita y sus familiares en los cuales Ud. emplea los pronombres de complemento directo e indirecto con mandatos y los verbos en tiempo presente. Siga el modelo.*

MODELO   Mami / comprarme / una bicicleta
→ Rita: *Mami, cómpramela.*
Mamá: *Sí, hijita, te la compro.*   (Sí, hijita)

1. Papi / darme / los bombones

   Rita: _____

   Papá: _____ (Sí, hijita)

2. Mami / comprarme / todos estos juguetes

   Rita: _____

   Mamá: _____ (Sí, hijita)

3. Juan / prestarme / tu patineta (*scooter*)

   Rita: _____

   Juan: _____ (Sí, hermanita)

4. Amparo / enseñarme / tu celular

   Rita: _____

   Amparo: _____ (Sí, hermanita)

5. Abuelo / regalarme / este juego de Lego

   Rita: _____

   Abuelo: _____ (Sí, hijita)

6. Elvira / servirme / todo el helado de chocolate

   Rita: _____

   Elvira: _____ (Sí, hermanita)

7. Tía / ponerme / tus joyas de oro

   Rita: _____

   Tía: _____ (Sí, hijita)

8. Abuela / traerme / mis muñecas

   Rita: _____

   Abuela: _____ (Sí, hijita)

¿Las cosas claras? *Exprese las oraciones en inglés aclarando a quién(es) se refiere el ambiguo* **se.** *Unas oraciones pueden tener más de una sola traducción.*

1. a. Se la dio Fernando.

   b. Se la dio a Fernando.

2. a. Se lo dijeron los asesores.

   b. Se lo dijeron a los asesores.

3. a. Se las prestó el analista.

   b. Se las prestó al analista.

4. a. Se los pidieron mis colegas.

   b. Se los pidieron a mis colegas.

5. a. Se la devolvió Laura.

   b. Se la devolvió a Laura.

Special Uses of the Object Pronouns

The object pronoun **lo** is invariable and has no equivalent in English. It is used to replace a clause or an adjective or predicate noun, which can be masculine or feminine, or singular or plural.

—Los Ochoa se mudaron a Ecuador.	*The Ochoas moved to Ecuador.*
—Sí, **lo sé.** (**lo** = que se mudaron a Ecuador)	*Yes, I know.*
—¿María Elena es simpática?	*Is María Elena nice?*
—Sí, **lo es.** (**lo** = simpática)	*Yes, she is.*
—¿Son profesoras Marta y Sara?	*Are Marta and Sara teachers?*
—**Lo** fueron. Ahora son abogadas. (**lo** = profesoras)	*They were. Now they're lawyers.*

Nouns that follow forms of **hay** are considered direct objects and can be replaced by direct object pronouns.

—¿**Hay papel**?	*Is there any paper?*
—Sí, **lo hay.**	*Yes, there is.*
—¿**Hay manzanas**?	*Are there any apples?*
—No, no **las hay.**	*No, there aren't any.*

The object pronouns **la** and **las** appear in many idioms without any antecedent. They must be memorized as part of the idiom.

apañárselas	*to manage, get by*
arreglárselas	*to manage, get by*
componérselas	*to manage, get by*
echárselas de + *adjective* OR *noun*	*to boast of being*
habérselas con	*to be up against, face, have to deal with*
tenérsela jurada a alguien	*to have it in for someone*
vérselas con	*to explain oneself to*

—Creo que el profesor Méndez **me la tiene jurada**.

I think Professor Méndez has it in for me.

—No te preocupes. **Te las arreglarás** bien en su clase.

Don't worry. You'll manage fine in his class.

—Oscar siempre **se las echa de rico**.

Oscar always boasts of being rich.

—Y no tiene dónde caerse muerto. No sé cómo **se las apaña**.

And he doesn't have a penny. I don't know how he manages.

—Este profesor tiene que **habérselas con una clase mediocre**.

This teacher has to face a class of mediocre students.

—Y si no hacen progresos, tiene que **vérselas con el director**.

And if they don't do well, he has to explain why to the principal.

DD *Expresar en español.* *Exprese las oraciones en español.*

1. *Do you* (tú) *know if the stores are open?*
   I couldn't (sabría) *tell you.*

2. *I don't know how Raúl manages. He thinks that everyone has it in for him.*

3. *Any student who behaves badly will have to explain himself to me.*

4. *Are Ramón and Sergio engineers?*
   No, they're not. They're programmers.
   I think they're very intelligent.
   Yes, they are.

5. *Pedrito couldn't put on his coat, so I helped him on with it.*

6. *Should I ask Alicia and Pablo for their history notes?*
   Ask (tú) *him for them. Don't ask her for them.*

7. *Javier, please send me the reports.*
   Consuelo, I sent them to you last week.
   I'm sorry. I lost them.

EE *Ejercicio oral.* *Hable con un amigo/una amiga de los libros que leyeron y las películas que vieron este año. Usen pronombres de complemento directo e indirecto.*

Relative Pronouns

The Relative Pronoun que

Relative pronouns are used to join two sentences into a single sentence. The clause introduced by the relative pronoun is the relative clause. A relative clause modifies a noun in the same way that an adjective does. That is why it is also called an adjective clause. The noun that the relative clause refers to is called the antecedent.

The relative pronoun **que** can refer to animate or inanimate antecedents (persons or things) and can be either the subject or direct object of the verb of the relative clause it introduces. **Que** can refer to both singular and plural nouns and is the most common relative pronoun in everyday conversation.

el hombre **que** trabaja aquí (*que refers to **hombre** and is the subject of its clause*)	*the man who works here*
los paquetes **que** están en la mesa (*que refers to **paquetes** and is the subject of its clause*)	*the packages that are on the table*
los abogados **que** conozco (*que refers to **abogados** and is the direct object of its clause*)	*the lawyers whom I know*
la casa **que** compré (*que refers to **casa** and is the direct object of its clause*)	*the house that I bought*

In English, the relative pronoun can be omitted when it is the object of the verb: *the lawyers I know, the house I bought*. In Spanish, **que** is never omitted.

When **nadie** or **alguien** is the antecedent of a relative clause, **que** is used as the subject or direct object of the clause. When **todo** is the antecedent, it is followed by **lo que** to express *all that*.

—Si hay **alguien que** comprende, es él.	*If there's someone who understands, it is he.*
—No, él no comprende tampoco. No hay **nadie que** comprenda.	*No, he doesn't understand either. There's no one who understands.*
Esto es **todo lo que** tengo.	*This is all (everything) I have.*

A *Seamos precisos.* *Conteste las preguntas de su amigo con una cláusula relativa para que él sepa de qué objeto o persona se trata. Siga los modelos.*

MODELOS ¿Qué libro quieres? (El libro está en la estantería.)
→ Quiero el libro que está en la estantería.

¿Qué suéter lleva Paula? (Su novio le compró el suéter en Ecuador.)
→ Lleva el suéter que su novio le compró en Ecuador.

1. ¿A qué médico ves? (Tiene su consulta en aquel edificio.)

2. ¿Qué película quieres ver? (La película se rodó en Perú.) (rodar (o > ue) (*to film, shoot*))

3. ¿Qué revistas te gustan más? (Las revistas se publican en Asunción.)

4. ¿Qué restaurante prefieres? (El restaurante sirve comida del Caribe.)

5. ¿A qué peluquería vas? (La peluquería está en la calle del Conde.)

6. ¿Qué libros queréis comprar? (El profesor nos recomendó los libros.)

7. ¿Qué computadora usas? (Mis padres me regalaron la computadora.)

8. ¿Con qué secretaria hablaban Uds.? (Contratamos a esa secretaria la semana pasada.)

9. ¿Qué mecánico repara tu coche? (Mi vecino conoce al mecánico.)

10. ¿Qué email estás leyendo? (Silvia me mandó este email ayer.)

NOTA CULTURAL

- **Asunción**, capital del Paraguay, fue fundada en 1537 por Juan de Salazar y Gonzalo de Mendoza. Fue una importante base de penetración de la Conquista española por la cuenca (*basin*) del río de la Plata. Es una ciudad colonial que tiene monumentos interesantes y jardines lindos. Muchas avenidas están bordeadas (*lined*) de árboles de caucho (*rubber*) y naranjos.

- Casi todos los paraguayos hablan no sólo el español sino también **el guaraní**, la lengua de los indígenas. El guaraní es el idioma cooficial con el español. Se enseña en los colegios particulares, se publican periódicos y revistas en guaraní y hay un teatro guaraní.

B *Más precisiones* (clarifications). *La persona que habla usa cláusulas relativas para indicar exactamente a qué objeto o persona se refiere. Escriba sus precisiones según el modelo.*

MODELO   ¿Qué computadora?
(Olivia la usa.) → La computadora que usa Olivia.
(Tiene mucha memoria.) → La computadora que tiene mucha memoria.

1. ¿Qué profesora?
(Todos los estudiantes la admiran.)
(Enseña francés y español.)
(Acaba de casarse.)
(Mis padres la conocen.)

2. ¿Qué casa?
(Juana y Rafael la compraron.)
(Tiene patio y piscina.)
(La construyeron en 2018.)
(Es de ladrillos.)

3. ¿Qué regalo?
(Mis hermanos y yo lo recibimos hace dos días.)
(Mis tíos nos lo mandaron.)
(Te lo enseñé ayer.)
(Nos gustó tanto.)

4. ¿Qué restaurante?
(Nuestros amigos lo abrieron el año pasado.)
(Sirve comida española.)
(Tiene manteles rojos.) (el mantel (*placemat*))
(Muchos artistas lo frecuentan.)

5. ¿Qué senador?
(Lo eligieron el año pasado.)
(Prometió reducir los impuestos.)
(Es casado con una arquitecta.)
(Era jefe de una empresa.)

The Relative Pronoun **quien**

When **que** is the direct object of the verb in the relative clause and it has an antecedent that is a person, it can be replaced by **a quien** or, if the antecedent is plural, **a quienes**. **A quien** and **a quienes** are somewhat more formal than **que**.

El empleado **a quien** conocíamos ya no trabaja aquí.	*The employee (whom) we knew doesn't work here any longer.*
Busqué a los estudiantes **a quienes** vi ayer, pero no los encontré.	*I looked for the students (whom) I saw yesterday, but I couldn't find them.*

Quien and **quienes** can also serve as the subject of a relative clause if that clause is set off by commas (nonrestrictive clause).

José Pedro fue a hablar con la profesora Umbral, **quien** siempre tiene tiempo para sus estudiantes.	*José Pedro went to speak with Professor Umbral, who always has time for her students.*

El profesor, quien... **Quien** y **quienes** *sirven también de sujeto de una cláusula relativa si esa cláusula está apartada con unas comas. Combine las oraciones con* **quien/quienes** *para describir a algunas personas que están en la universidad. Siga el modelo.*

MODELO   Cajal, Toledano y Puche aprobaron sus exámenes. /
            Ellos son compañeros de cuarto en una residencia universitaria.
      → Cajal, Toledano y Puche, quienes son compañeros de cuarto
          en una residencia universitaria, aprobaron sus exámenes.

La universidad

aprobar (o > ue) *to pass*   **jubilarse** *to retire*
los archivos *files*   **el rector** *president, head of a university*
el ayudante *assistant*   **el salón de actos** *assembly hall, auditorium*
el congreso *conference*   **el secretario general** *registrar*
el decano *dean*   **el tribunal de exámenes** *board of examiners*
dictar una conferencia *to deliver a lecture*

1. El señor Mora es secretario general de la universidad. / Él se encarga de los archivos.

2. El profesor Uriarte enseña química. / Él asistió a un congreso en la UNAM.

3. Los estudiantes tienen que entregar una tesis. / Ellos se gradúan en junio.

4. La doctora Arrieta tiene dos ayudantes de laboratorio. /
Ella figura en el tribunal de exámenes.

5. Estos decanos trabajan en la facultad de ingeniería. / Ellos planean el programa.

6. El rector de la universidad es abogado. / Él dicta conferencias de ciencias políticas.

7. Algunos estudiantes de medicina fueron a hablar con el profesor Quijano. /
Él estaba ya en el salón de actos.

8. La profesora Arenas se jubila el año que viene. / Ella hace investigaciones de biología.

NOTA CULTURAL

- La **UNAM**, la Universidad Nacional Autónoma de México, fue fundada en 1910. La universidad antecesora de la UNAM, llamada la Real y Pontífica Universidad de México, fue fundada en 1551, el mismo año en que se fundó la Universidad de San Marcos de Lima. Unas universidades hispanoamericanas fundadas después incluyen la de Córdoba (Argentina) (1621), la Javierana de Bogotá (1622), la de Caracas (1721), la de La Habana (1728) y la de Buenos Aires (1821).

- La **Ciudad Universitaria**, el campus principal de la UNAM, queda a 18 kilómetros al sur de la Ciudad de México. Tiene una fama mundial por su arquitectura, obra del arquitecto mexicano Juan O'Gorman (1905–1982). Se destaca la torre de la biblioteca cubierta por fuera de mosaicos que narran la historia del conocimiento científico desde la astronomía azteca hasta la teoría molecular. La Rectoría (edificio administrativo del presidente de la universidad) es notable por su mural de David Siqueiros y el estadio Olímpico por su pintura-escultura de Diego Rivera. *http://www.unam.mx*

D *... a quien/... a quienes.* **A quien** *y* **a quienes** *se usan como complemento directo de un verbo cuando el antecedente es una persona. Combine las oraciones en una con* **a quien** *o* **a quienes** *para describir a ciertas personas. Siga el modelo.*

MODELO   Las chicas vinieron a vernos. / Las conocimos en el teatro.
→ Las chicas a quienes conocimos en el teatro vinieron a vernos.

1. Mis primos están de vacaciones en los Estados Unidos. / Los vi en Caracas hace dos años.

2. La pintora sólo pinta acuarelas (la acuarela (*watercolor*)). / La vieron en la exposición.

3. La muchacha me dio las gracias hoy. / Yo le di un regalo ayer.

4. Los amigos no quisieron salir. / Los llamamos a la una de la mañana.

5. Los vecinos se habían mudado. / Los buscábamos.

6. La dependienta ya no trabaja en esta tienda. / Ud. la conoció el año pasado.

7. El señor es mi profesor de cálculo. / Lo encontraste en la calle.

NOTA CULTURAL

Caracas, capital de Venezuela, fue fundada en 1567 por el conquistador español Diego de Losada. Como otras ciudades de países hispanohablantes, Caracas ha nombrado sus grandes avenidas y plazas por sus héroes nacionales. La avenida Bolívar fue nombrada por Simón Bolívar (1783–1830), que nació en Caracas y se formó en las ideas de los escritores de la Ilustración europea (*the Enlightenment*). Bolívar, el Libertador, fue el gran líder del movimiento independentista de los países sudamericanos. La avenida Andrés Bello fue nombrada por el gran filósofo, filólogo, poeta y político (1781–1865). Caraqueño también, Bello fue uno de los maestros de Bolívar.

E *¿Sujeto u objeto?* *Complete las oraciones escogiendo* **quien(es)** *si se refiere al sujeto de una cláusula relativa o* **a quien(es)** *si se refiere al complemento directo del verbo.*

1. Te presento al señor (quien / a quien) conocimos ayer.

2. Llamemos a aquella señorita (quien / a quien) siempre está dispuesta a ayudarnos.

3. Voy a la casa de los señores (a quienes / quienes) compraron la casa de enfrente.

4. ¿Conoces a los chicos (a quienes / quienes) invité a la fiesta?

5. Esos arquitectos (a quienes / quienes) trabajan en el rascacielos nuevo, son mis cuñados.

6. ¿Comprendéis a la locutora (quien / a quien) yo no comprendo bien?

7. Jorge llama a su novia (a quien / quien) quiere muchísimo.

8. La novia de Jorge está enamorada de Alfredo (quien / a quien) es el mejor amigo de Jorge.

The Relative Pronouns el que, el cual

The relative pronouns **el que** and **el cual** have four forms each: **el que, la que, los que, las que; el cual, la cual, los cuales, las cuales**. They can replace **que** or **a quien/a quienes** when the antecedent is animate and the relative pronoun is the object of the verb. The personal **a** must precede these relative pronouns when they are the direct object of the verb of the relative clause, and this personal **a** contracts with the **el** of **el que** and **el cual** to form **al que** and **al cual**.

los españoles **a los que** he conocido	*the Spaniards (whom) I've met*
el electricista **al que** he llamado	*the electrician (whom) I called*
la vecina **a la que** no soportamos	*the neighbor (whom) we can't stand*

In nonrestrictive clauses (those set off by commas), **el que** and **el cual** can function as either subject or object and can refer to either people or things. Since **el que** and **el cual** show gender and number distinctions, they are used to avoid confusion when there is more than one possible antecedent for **que** or **quien**.

El amigo de mi prima, **el que/el cual** estudia física, llega mañana de Caracas.	*My (female) cousin's (male) friend, who (refers to the male friend) studies physics, is arriving from Caracas tomorrow.*
El amigo de mi prima, **la que/la cual** estudia física, llega mañana de Caracas.	*My (female) cousin's (male) friend, who (refers to the female cousin) studies physics, is arriving from Caracas tomorrow.*

The neuter relative pronouns **lo que** and **lo cual** refer to a preceding clause or idea. They only occur in clauses set off by commas (nonrestrictive clauses).

Su hija le dijo que no quería seguir estudiando, **lo que/lo cual** no le gustó para nada al señor Lara.	*His daughter told him that she didn't want to continue with her studies, which Mr. Lara didn't like at all.*

F ¿**El que o lo que?** *Escoja el pronombre* **el que, la que, los que, las que** *o* **lo que** *para completar las oraciones.*

1. Me cayeron muy bien los turistas a _____ conocimos en la excursión.

2. Los Merino nos invitaron a pasar el fin de semana en su barco, _____ nos agradó mucho.

3. La hermana de mi amigo, _____ vive en Bogotá, estudiará administración de empresas en los Estados Unidos.

4. Nadie vio llegar a Isabel, _____ nos sorprendió.

5. Por fin subimos en la montaña rusa, _____ nos dejó medio muertos.

6. El amigo de mi prima, _____ trabaja en Barcelona, se casará en mayo.

7. Esas chicas tan antipáticas con _____ saliste son mis primas.

G *¿El cual o lo cual?* *Ahora reemplace los pronombres relativos del ejercicio anterior con* **el cual, la cual, los cuales, las cuales** *o* **lo cual.**

1. Me cayeron muy bien los turistas a _____ conocimos en la excursión.

2. Los Merino nos invitaron a pasar el fin de semana en su barco, _____ nos agradó mucho.

3. La hermana de mi amigo, _____ vive en Bogotá, estudiará administración de empresas en los Estados Unidos.

4. Nadie vio llegar a Isabel, _____ nos sorprendió.

5. Por fin subimos en la montaña rusa, _____ nos dejó medio muertos.

6. El amigo de mi prima, _____ trabaja en Barcelona, se casará en mayo.

7. Esas chicas tan antipáticas con _____ saliste son mis primas.

Relative Pronouns After Prepositions

Que may be used after the prepositions **a, de,** and **con** when the antecedent is not a person.

Éste es el tema **a que** nos limitamos.	*This is the subject to which we will limit ourselves.*
¿Comprendes los problemas **de que** te hablé?	*Do you understand the problems that I spoke to you about?*
Mi abuelo me mostró el bastón **con que** camina.	*My grandfather showed me the cane he walks with.*

En que is common after expressions of time and to express imprecise location.

el mes **en que** se fueron	*the month they went away*
un siglo **en que** la vida era muy difícil	*a century in which life was very difficult*
el edificio **en que** trabajamos	*the building we work in*
la materia **en que** se interesa	*the subject she's interested in*

The **en** of **en que** can be omitted after expressions of time.

el día **(en) que** la vi	*the day I saw her*

When **en** expresses physical location inside an object, **en el que/en la que/en los que/en las que** are used.

Abrió la gaveta **en la que** había metido las llaves.	*He opened the drawer in which he had put the keys.*

Donde can replace **en** + relative pronoun to express location. See "The Relative Pronoun **cuyo; donde** as a Relative Pronoun" later in this chapter.

Abrió la gaveta **donde** había metido las llaves.	*He opened the drawer where he had put the keys.*

Quien/quienes or **el que** are used after prepositions for human antecedents. Some speakers also use **el cual**.

el tío **a quien/al que** Pablito se parece	*the uncle (whom) Pablito looks like*
la chica **con quien/con la que** se casó mi hermano	*the girl (whom) my brother married*
los amigos **de quienes/de los que** me fío	*the friends (whom) I trust*

After prepositions other than **a**, **de**, **con**, and **en**, the relative pronoun **que** is not used. **Quien/quienes** may be used for people, and **el que** and **el cual** for both people and things. **El cual** is especially common after prepositions of more than one syllable (**para**, **según**, **hacia**, **desde**, **contra**, **mediante**, **durante**, **sobre**) and with compound prepositions (**a causa de**, **delante de**, **detrás de**, **encima de**, **debajo de**, **por medio de**, **enfrente de**, **al frente de**, **antes de**, **después de**).

una guerra **durante la cual** cayeron muchos soldados	*a war during which many soldiers died*
el edificio **delante del cual** la vi	*the building in front of which I saw her*
los problemas **a causa de los que** dejé de jugar al tenis	*the problems because of which I stopped playing tennis*
los señores **para quienes** (**para los que/para los cuales**) trabajo	*the men for whom I work*
las ancianas al lado **de quienes** (**al lado de las que/al lado de las cuales**) vivimos	*the elderly women next door to whom we live*

H *Te enseño mi ciudad. Ud. le enseña su ciudad a un amigo extranjero. Exprese la información indicada con una cláusula relativa. Escriba la respuesta de por lo menos dos maneras. Siga el modelo.*

MODELO   Hay un festival de teatro durante el verano.

→ El verano es la estación _durante la cual hay un festival de teatro_.
durante la que hay un festival de teatro.

1. Hay varias líneas de metro debajo de estas calles.

   Éstas son las calles _____.

2. Vivimos cerca de la facultad.

   Allí ven la facultad _____.

3. Hay un restaurante enfrente de ese cine.

   Allí está el cine _____.

4. Solemos pasar los domingos aquí.

   Ven y te presento a los muchachos _____.

5. Hay una exposición de arte en medio de la plaza.

   Ésta es la plaza _____.

6. Hay un mercado al aire libre detrás de aquellos edificios.

   Aquéllos son los edificios _____.

7. Ahora caminamos hacia un barrio muy antiguo.

   El barrio _____.

8. Unas tiendas elegantes se encuentran al otro lado de este río.

   Éste es el río _____.

I ***En de varios significados.*** *Complete las frases con el pronombre relativo correcto. Recuerde que hay una diferencia entre el* **en** *concreto que significa* **dentro de** *y el* **en** *que expresa una relación abstracta.*

1. los libros _____ me intereso (en que / en los que)

2. el armario _____ cuelgo mi ropa (en que / en el que)

3. la exactitud _____ insiste el profesor (en que / en la que)

4. el arreglo _____ quedaron (en que / en el que)

5. el bolsillo _____ tengo mi celular (en que / en el que)

6. los cuadernos _____ escribo (en que / en los que)

7. los métodos _____ creemos (en que / en los que)

8. las bolsas _____ llevaban la comida (en que / en las que)

J ***Expresar en inglés.*** *Exprese las oraciones en inglés.*

1. El concierto benéfico fue un evento mediante el cual la universidad recibió mucho dinero.

2. Se ha construido un nuevo rascacielos desde el cual hay fabulosas vistas de la ciudad.

3. Éstos son los libros según los cuales el profesor Sorolla sacó sus conclusiones.

4. Siempre me acuerdo de las ruinas griegas entre las cuales caminamos.

5. Se abrió un hotel al lado del cual se abrirá un centro comercial.

6. Vamos a reunirnos en la facultad de ingeniería enfrente de la cual nos conocimos.

7. Allí está la fuente delante de la cual nos enamoramos.

8. ¿Cómo se llama la empresa para la cual Antonio trabaja?

9. ¿Sabéis cuáles son las ideas sobre las cuales los investigadores basaron sus teorías?

The Relative Pronoun **cuyo**; **donde** as a Relative Pronoun

Cuyo means *whose*. It agrees in gender and number with the noun that follows.

La doctora Paredes es la profesora **cuyas clases** cursé con mucho provecho.	*Dr. Paredes is the teacher whose classes I took and benefited greatly from.*
Ése es el autor **cuyos libros** leemos en la clase de literatura.	*That's the author whose books we read in literature class.*
Él es un hombre sobre **cuya vida** se comenta mucho.	*He's a man about whose life people comment a lot.*

Donde is used after prepositions to refer to a place. It can also replace **en el que** when the relative pronoun refers to a concrete place. As a relative pronoun, **donde** does not take a written accent.

la avenida **donde** hay muchos cafés	*the avenue on which (where) there are many cafés*
la puerta **por donde** salieron	*the door through which they went out*
la playa **hacia donde** caminábamos	*the beach toward which we were walking*

K **Cuyo.** *Complete las oraciones usando la forma correcta del pronombre relativo* **cuyo.**

1. Éste es el nuevo cantante _____ canciones han ganado muchos premios.

2. Éstos son los señores _____ hijos asisten a la universidad con los nuestros.

3. Tengo que buscar a la persona _____ coche está estacionado delante de mi garaje.

4. Quieren conocer al compositor _____ sinfonía será estrenada (*premiered*) el sábado.

5. Habla con tu vecino _____ perro ladra (*barks*) toda la noche.

6. Se habla mucho de la profesora de arqueología _____ clases son tan interesantes.

7. Es un país _____ historia no se estudia lo suficiente.

8. Ésos son los técnicos _____ equipos han llegado al campeonato.

L **Expresar en inglés.** *Exprese las oraciones en inglés.*

1. Ahora sabes la razón por la cual me enfadé.

2. Vivíamos en un barrio donde había muchas tiendas.

3. Allí a la derecha está la puerta por donde entran y salen los actores.

4. Yo no entiendo los motivos por los cuales el sindicato (*union*) declaró la huelga (*strike*).

5. Los muchachos no me dijeron para donde iban.

6. Son las horas durante las cuales Miguel navega en la red.

7. Aquí está el quiosco detrás del cual Sergio y Sol quedaron en verse.

8. Te presentaré al joven cuyo padre era mi profesor de mercadeo.

9. Jaime no nos invitó a su fiesta, lo cual nos sorprendió.

M *Ejercicio oral. **Juego de adivinanzas** (**Guessing game**). Cree un acertijo* (riddle) *para un amigo/una amiga. Las pistas* (hints) *se forman con cláusulas relativas:* **Es algo que...,** **Es alguien quien..., Es un lugar donde..., Es una persona con quien..., Es un hombre cuyo...** *Dé cinco pistas después de las cuales su amigo/amiga tratará de adivinar lo que es. Sí él/ella logra resolver el acertijo, le tocará a Ud. crear uno.*

Other Elements
of the Sentence

Adverbs

Formation of Adverbs

Most Spanish adverbs are formed by adding the suffix -**mente** to the feminine form of the adjective. Spanish -**mente** corresponds to the English adverbial suffix -*ly*.

MASCULINE	FEMININE		ADVERB
histórico *historic*	histórica	→	históricamente *historically*
intenso *intense*	intensa	→	intensamente *intensely*
lento *slow*	lenta	→	lentamente *slowly*
cariñoso *loving*	cariñosa	→	cariñosamente *lovingly*
profundo *deep*	profunda	→	profundamente *deeply*
serio *serious*	seria	→	seriamente *seriously*

Adjectives that do not have a distinct feminine form add -**mente** to the masculine/feminine singular.

amable *kind*	→	amablemente *kindly*
fácil *easy*	→	fácilmente *easily*
feliz *happy*	→	felizmente *happily*
inteligente *intelligent*	→	inteligentemente *intelligently*
triste *sad*	→	tristemente *sadly*

Several adverbs either have irregular forms or are identical to the corresponding adjectives.

bueno *good*	→	bien *well*
malo *bad*	→	mal *badly*
mejor *better*	→	mejor *better*
peor *worse*	→	peor *worse*

Many adverbs of quantity have no suffix but are identical to the masculine singular form of the adjective.

mucho

poco

demasiado

tanto

más

menos

Adverbs referring to loudness and softness have no ending but are identical to the masculine singular form of the adjective.

| hablar alto/bajo | to speak loudly/softly |
| hablar fuerte | to speak loudly |

Some adverbs have alternate forms that are the same as the masculine singular form of the adjective.

El tren corre rápidamente. }
El tren corre rápido.   }   *The train moves quickly.*

Masculine singular adjectives that function as adverbs are more commonly used in Spanish America than in Spain.

| La niña dibuja muy bonito. | *The girl draws very beautifully.* |
| ¡Qué lindo juegan los niños! | *How nicely the children play!* |

Solamente (*only*) has the alternate form **sólo** (also written **solo** with this meaning).

Sólo a ti te lo digo.   *I'm telling only you.*

A **Para describir acciones.** *Escriba los adverbios que corresponden a los adjetivos. Siga el modelo.*

> MODELO   maravilloso
>   → maravillosamente

1. alegre
2. descuidado
3. cruel
4. artístico
5. normal
6. abierto
7. franco
8. nervioso
9. evidente
10. responsable
11. débil
12. verdadero
13. torpe (*clumsy*)
14. violento
15. perspicaz (*perceptive*)
16. burlón (*mocking*)
17. comercial
18. sagaz (*wise*)
19. honrado
20. humilde
21. difícil
22. admirable
23. estupendo
24. afectuoso
25. vulgar

B *¿Cómo hablaron?* *Escriba oraciones que describan cómo algunas personas hablaron en ciertas situaciones. Siga el modelo.*

MODELO   Marisol habló. ¿Fue sincera?
→ Sí, habló sinceramente.

1. Hernán ganó un premio muy importante. ¿Estaba orgulloso?

2. Matías pidió disculpas (*apologized*). ¿Fue sincero?

3. Anita y Bárbara contaron sus problemas. ¿Estaban tristes?

4. Ud. se enojó con un amigo. ¿Estuvo furioso?

5. La señorita Cortés se quejó. ¿Estaba malhumorada (*peevish, grouchy*)?

6. A Uds. se les rompieron nueve vasos. ¿Estuvieron avergonzados (*embarrassed*)?

7. Hablaste por teléfono. ¿Estabas distraído?

8. Gladis chocó con un árbol montando en bicicleta. ¿Estuvo incoherente?

9. Vuestro equipo ganó el campeonato. ¿Fuisteis felices?

Adverbs of Manner

Adverbs of manner (adverbs that tell how something is done), such as the ones presented in the previous section, come right after the verbs they modify, or as close to the verb as possible.

—Hiciste **mal** el trabajo.	*You did the work poorly.*
—¿Qué dices? Lo hice **bien**. De todas formas, lo hice **mejor** que tú.	*What are you talking about? I did it well. Anyway, I did it better than you did.*
—Mentira. Yo trabajé **cuidadosamente**.	*Not true. I worked carefully.*
—A mí me parece que no hiciste nada **sistemáticamente**.	*I think you didn't do anything systematically.*

Adverbs cannot come between an auxiliary verb and the main verb, as they often do in English.

El huracán ha destruido el pueblo **totalmente**.	*The hurricane has **totally** destroyed the town.*
El enfermo está mejorando **rápidamente**.	*The patient is **rapidly** improving.*

Direct objects, including negative and indefinite words such as **algo**, **nada**, **nadie**, and neuter demonstratives, often come between the verb and the adverb.

Leyó **el artículo** atentamente.	*He read the article attentively.*
No explicó **nada** claramente.	*He didn't explain anything clearly.*
Dijo **eso** torpemente.	*He said that awkwardly.*

When two or more adverbs ending in **-mente** modify the same verb, the suffix **-mente** is dropped from all but the last adverb.

Nos habló **franca** y **abiertamente**.	*He spoke to us frankly and openly.*
Hay que explicar las cosas **clara** e **inteligentemente**.	*One has to explain things clearly and intelligently.*
Hicieron su trabajo **diligente** y **cuidadosamente**.	*They did their work diligently and carefully.*

Adverbs ending in **-mente** can be replaced by **con** + corresponding noun.

alegremente	→	con alegría
claramente	→	con claridad
cuidadosamente	→	con cuidado
elegantemente	→	con elegancia
inteligentemente	→	con inteligencia
torpemente	→	con torpeza

Adverbs as Intensifiers

Intensifiers, or adverbs that modify adjectives and other adverbs, such as **completamente**, **muy**, **tan**, etc., precede the adjective or adverb they modify. Intensifiers enhance or emphasize the meaning of the adjective or adverb.

completamente inútil	*completely useless*
elegantemente vestido	*elegantly dressed*
extremadamente inteligente	*extremely intelligent*
muy bonito	*very pretty*
muy rápidamente	*very quickly*
sumamente bien	*extremely well*
tan fácilmente	*so easily*
totalmente ridículo	*totally ridiculous*

In colloquial speech, the words **súper** and **medio** are used as adverbs that modify adjectives.

Es una carrera **súper** interesante.	*It's a really interesting course of study.*
Nos llevaron a un restaurante **súper** caro.	*They took us to a really expensive restaurant.*
Es un tipo **medio** cínico.	*He's a pretty cynical guy.*
Vivimos en una zona **medio** árida.	*We live in a pretty arid region.*

C *Cada adverbio en su lugar.* *Ordene los elementos para formar oraciones colocando los adverbios en su lugar correcto. Siga el modelo.*

MODELO   problema / claramente / el / explicó
                → Explicó el problema claramente.

1. las / mal / frases / pronunciaron

2. responsablemente / trabajaron / muy

3. bien / cosas / las / andaban

4. hijos / que / felizmente / mis / quiero / vivan

5. su / interesante / última / fue / película / muy

6. padres / inocentemente / a / niño / miraba / el / sus

7. esos / sumamente / Patricia / difíciles / encontró / problemas

8. salgan / la / rápidamente / de / muy / casa

9. totalmente / proyecto / encontramos / ridículo / el

10. súper / esta / estamos / semana / ocupados

11. estaba / medio / dormido / Carlos

D ***En otras palabras.*** *Vuelva a escribir las oraciones, cambiando el sustantivo a la forma verbal y el adjetivo al adverbio correspondiente. Siga el modelo.*

MODELO   Juan es un hablador apasionado.
         → Juan habla apasionadamente.

1. Martín y Fernando son unos trabajadores inteligentes.

2. Lola es una cantante maravillosa.

3. Carmen y Pilar son escritoras hábiles.

4. Rafa es un conductor prudente.

5. Lucas es un estudiante diligente.

6. Marcos es un pintor divino.

7. Carla y Pedro son viajeros frecuentes.

8. Alfonso es un jugador enérgico.

E ***Con + sustantivo = adverbio + -mente.*** *Cambie el adverbio que termina en* **-mente** *a una frase que consiste en la preposición* **con** *+ sustantivo.*

1. inteligentemente

2. armónicamente

3. elegantemente

4. diligentemente

5. delicadamente

6. cariñosamente

7. alegremente

8. ligeramente

9. lealmente

10. suavemente

11. fuertemente

12. felizmente

13. tristemente

14. calurosamente

15. claramente

16. violentamente

F **_Expresar en español._** _Exprese los diálogos en español. Tenga presente especialmente el uso de los adverbios._

1. _Did you (Ud.) go to the supermarket already?_
   Not yet. I haven't gotten dressed yet.

2. _I'll be back right away._
   Come (tú) here right now!

3. _Mariana can't find her cat anywhere._
   Look (Ud.) up there! The cat's in the tree.

4. _Are the boys around here?_
   They're probably in the house.
   Do you (tú) know if they're upstairs or downstairs?
   They're probably hiding behind some piece of furniture.

5. _Is the computer store far away?_
   No, it's nearby. And there's a wonderful ice cream store next to it.

Adverbs of Time and Place

Ya means _already, now, right now._ **Ya no** means _no longer, not anymore._

—Tocan a la puerta.	_Someone's at the door._
—**Ya** voy.	_I'll be right there._
—¿**Ya** has visto la nueva película?	_Have you already seen the new film?_
—No, **ya no** voy al cine.	_No, I don't go to the movies anymore._

The adverb **recién** appears before past participles with the meaning _newly, just, recently._ This is especially common in Spanish American Spanish.

un niño **recién** nacido	_a newborn child_
los **recién** casados	_the newlyweds_
una casa **recién** construida	_a newly built house_

Common Adverbs of Time

ahora	_now_	mucho antes	_much before, a long time before_
ahora mismo	_right now_	mucho después	_much later, a long time after_
anteriormente	_formerly_	posteriormente	_subsequently_
antes	_before_	siempre	_always_
apenas	_hardly, scarcely_	tarde	_late_
aún	_still, yet_	temprano	_early_
después	_after, afterward_	todavía	_still, yet_
en seguida	_right away_	todavía no	_not yet_
entonces	_then, afterward_	ya	_already, right now_
luego	_then, afterward_	ya no	_no longer_

—¿**Ya** han llegado los invitados?	_Have the guests arrived already?_
—No, **todavía no**.	_No, not yet._

—¿Carlos salió **en seguida**?	*Did Carlos leave right away?*
—No, salió **mucho después**.	*No, he left much later.*
—Tenías que llamar **temprano**, a las nueve.	*You were supposed to call early, at nine.*
—Sí, pero llamé **mucho antes**.	*Yes, but I called much before that.*

Spanish has several words meaning *even*. **Incluso** and **inclusive** are the most common, although **inclusive** is more widely used in the Americas than in Spain. The words **aun** and **hasta** are also used with the meaning of *even*. (Don't confuse **aún** (*still, yet*) and **aun** (*even*).) The phrase **ni siquiera** means *not even*.

Incluso en los países ricos hay pobreza.	***Even*** *in rich countries there is poverty.*
Inclusive me prestaron dinero.	*They* ***even*** *lent me money.*
Hasta mi hijo de dos años lo sabía.	***Even*** *my two-year-old son knew it.*
Aun si nos invitan, no iremos.	***Even*** *if they invite us, we won't go.*
Ni siquiera nos saludaron.	*They didn't* ***even*** *greet us.*

The basic adverbs of place in Spanish are **aquí** (*here*), **ahí** (*there*) (near the person spoken to), and **allí** (*there*) (not near the speaker or the person spoken to). The adverbs **acá** and **allá** are used in the phrases **para acá** (*this way, in this direction*) and **para allá** (*that way, in that direction*). **Allá** means *way over there, somewhere over there*. In Spanish America, **acá** often replaces **aquí** in speech.

—**Aquí** hay excelentes escuelas.	*There are excellent schools here.*
—**Allá** en mi país también.	*Back in my country also.*
—¿Qué veo **ahí** en tu impresora?	*What do I see there on your printer?*
—Es mi cartera.	*It's my wallet.*

Common Adverbs of Place

a la derecha/izquierda	*on the right/left*
a mano derecha/izquierda	*on the right/left*
abajo	*down, downstairs; underneath*
al fondo	*in back, at the bottom*
al lado	*next door, next to it*
arriba	*up, upstairs; above*
atrás	*behind*
cerca	*close, nearby*
delante	*in front*
en lo alto	*up, up there, up high*
encima	*on top*
fuera, afuera	*outside*
lejos	*far off, far away*
por algún sitio/lado	*somewhere*
por ningún sitio/lado	*nowhere*

Adverbs of place can combine with various prepositions and with each other.

por aquí	*around here*
por ahí	*around there*
por allí	*around there*
por allá	*around there (far away)*
desde aquí	*from here*
hasta allí	*up to there*
hacia allá	*toward that place far away*
allí arriba	*up there*
aquí abajo	*down here*
aquí cerca	*near here*
para atrás	*backward, to the back*

Adverbs of place can also express time in certain phrases.

de aquel momento para acá	*from that time until now*
por allá por el año 1920	*around the year 1920*
de ayer acá	*from yesterday until now*
allá en mi juventud	*back then in my youth*

NOTA CULTURAL

En algunos países hispanohablantes como España, Argentina y Uruguay, **la planta baja** se refiere al piso del edificio que está al nivel de la calle, es decir, *ground floor*, mientras en otros países de habla hispana como Chile, Perú y Colombia, el piso que está a nivel de la calle es el primer piso (*first floor*) como en los Estados Unidos.

G *Un adverbio más otro. Escriba frases con dos adverbios para describir cómo se hicieron ciertas cosas. Cambie los adjetivos a la forma correcta del adverbio.*

1. elegante y cuidadoso

2. lento y suave

3. cariñoso y caluroso

4. oportuno y apasionado

5. ligero y perezoso

6. fiel y leal

7. sabio y astuto

8. deprimido y triste

Comparison of Adverbs

Adverbs are compared much the way adjectives are (see Chapter 17).

Él habla **más claramente que** tú.	*He speaks more clearly than you do.*
Él habla **menos claramente que** tú.	*He speaks less clearly than you do.*
Él habla **tan claramente como** tú.	*He speaks as clearly as you do.*

The superlative of adverbs does not use the definite article and therefore has no special form. Its meaning is inferred from context.

El que **más claramente** habla soy yo.	*The one who speaks most clearly is I.*

Adverbs can also be formed from the feminine form of the absolute superlatives of adjectives (see Chapter 17).

MASCULINE	FEMININE	ADVERB	
clarísimo	clarísima	clarísimamente	*very clearly*
malísimo	malísima	malísimamente	*very badly*
tontísimo	tontísima	tontísimamente	*very foolishly*

H *Comparaciones. Escriba oraciones de comparación usando los elementos indicados. Siga los modelos.*

MODELOS Luisa / trabajar / + hábil / sus compañeras
→ Luisa trabaja más hábilmente que sus compañeras.

Luisa / trabajar / − hábil / sus compañeras
→ Luisa trabaja menos hábilmente que sus compañeras.

Luisa / trabajar / = hábil / sus compañeras
→ Luisa trabaja tan hábilmente como sus compañeras.

1. él / escribir / + sarcástico / tú

2. tú / analizar el artículo / − crítico / yo

3. ellos / hacerlo / = fácil / nosotros

4. Ana / hablar / + franco / Lucía

5. este niño / jugar / − alegre / aquél

6. ella / expresarse / = lógico / tú

7. nosotros / mandar los emails / + frecuente / ellos

8. vosotros / recibirnos / = afectuoso / Pablo y Lucero

I *Ejercicio oral. Diálogos con adverbios. Pregúntele a un amigo/una amiga cómo se hicieron ciertas cosas. Ud. pregunta por ejemplo: —¿Cómo te habló tu hermana? Su amigo/amiga contesta usando un adverbio:* **—Me habló abiertamente.** *Después cambien de papel para que los dos tengan la oportunidad de preguntar y contestar.*

Prepositions

A preposition is a word that links a noun to a verb, an adjective, or another noun. Prepositions can also link verbs to each other.

el libro **de** Paula
entra **en** la cocina
darle el dinero **a** Pablo
dejar **de** fumar

The Preposition a

A has many uses in Spanish. (Remember its contraction: **a** + **el** → **al**.) The preposition **a**

- indicates motion toward a place

regresar a casa	*to return home*
ir a la ciudad	*to go to the city*
llegar al teatro	*to arrive at the theater*

- labels the animate, specific direct object (This is also known as the personal **a** (see Chapter 19).)

ver a Consuelo	*to see Consuelo*
ayudar a los niños	*to help the children*

- labels the indirect object noun and is usually accompanied by the corresponding indirect object pronoun (especially in Spanish America)

Le di el paquete a Carla.	*I gave Carla the package.*
Les compré helado a los chicos.	*I bought the children ice cream.*

- connects verbs of motion to infinitives, conveying the idea of purpose

salir a comer	*to go out to eat*
venir a vernos	*to come to see us*

- labels the rate or price

¿A cuánto está el dólar hoy?	*What's the exchange rate of the dollar today?*
Condujimos a sesenta millas por hora.	*We drove at sixty miles an hour.*
Estos coches se venden a cuarenta mil dólares.	*These cars sell at/for forty thousand dollars.*

Voy al gimnasio dos veces al mes/ a la semana.	*I go to the gym twice a month/a week.*

- labels the manner in which something is done

a pie	*on foot*
a caballo	*on horseback*
andar a gatas	*to crawl on all fours*
a regañadientes	*reluctantly*
a doble espacio	*double-spaced*
escribir a lápiz	*to write in pencil*
hecho a mano	*made by hand*
a la española	*Spanish-style*
a la americana/lo americano	*American-style*

- expresses location (instead of **en**) in certain fixed expressions of place and time

estar sentado a la mesa	*to be seated at the table*
tocar a la puerta	*to knock at the door*
a la izquierda/derecha	*on the left/right*
a mano izquierda/derecha	*on the left/right*
a la salida del pueblo	*at the edge of town*
a la salida del trabajo	*upon leaving work*
al final de la calle	*at the end of the street*
a dos kilómetros de aquí	*two kilometers from here*
a la vuelta de la esquina	*around the corner*
a(l) mediodía	*at noon*
a medianoche	*at midnight*
a las dos de la tarde	*at two in the afternoon*
a nuestra llegada	*upon our arrival*
estar a dieta/a régimen	*to be on a diet*

- is found in idiomatic expressions

al mes de trabajar aquí	*after working here for one month*
paso a paso	*step by step*
uno a uno	*one by one*
a veces	*sometimes*
a escondidas	*stealthily, behind someone's back*
a espaldas de uno	*behind someone's back*
a mi juicio	*in my opinion*
a mi parecer	*in my opinion*

A **¿A o nada?** *Complete las oraciones con la preposición* **a** *cuando sea necesaria. Si no es necesario usarla, escriba una X. No se olvide de la contracción* **al**.

1. Les envié un email _____ mis amigos.

2. ¿Conociste _____ la Alhambra?

3. No pudimos ir _____ verlos.

4. Leonardo habló con nosotros _____ dos veces.

5. Llegué _____ pueblo _____ la una.

6. Viajaban _____ cien millas por hora.

7. ¿_____ cuánto está el dólar hoy?

8. Ya son _____ las ocho.

9. La parada queda _____ seis cuadras de mi casa.

B *Expresar en español.* *Exprese las oraciones en español.*

1. *I wrote the paper double-spaced.*

2. *Upon his arrival at midnight, he went to bed.*

3. *The baby crawls on all fours.*

4. *I love the clothing that's made by hand.*

5. *The children ate all the cookies behind our backs.*

6. *The mall is seven miles from my house.*

The Preposition **de**

The preposition **de**, like **a**, has many uses in Spanish. (Remember its contraction: **de** + **el → del**.) The preposition **de**

- indicates motion from a place

El avión llega de Colombia.	*The plane is arriving from Colombia.*
Vengo de la farmacia.	*I'm coming from the drugstore.*
Salgo de casa a las ocho menos diez.	*I leave home at ten to eight.*

- indicates origin and possession

el tren de Buenos Aires	*the train from Buenos Aires*
Son de Venezuela.	*They're from Venezuela.*
la mochila de Pedrito	*Pedrito's backpack*
la casa de mis tíos	*my aunt and uncle's house*

- indicates the material of which something is made or the contents of a container

una casa de ladrillos	*a brick house*
un reloj de oro	*a gold watch*
una camisa de algodón	*a cotton shirt*
una taza de café	*a cup of coffee*
un vaso de agua	*a glass of water*
una caja de juguetes	*a box of toys*

- is often the equivalent of English *with* or *in* in descriptive expressions

lleno de agua	*filled with water* (ALSO *full of water*)
cubierto de nieve	*covered with snow*
forrado de plumón	*down lined, lined with down*
vestido de negro	*dressed in black*
pintado de azul	*painted (in) blue*

- forms noun phrases that are the equivalent of either noun + noun or present participle + noun constructions in English

una lección de música	*a music lesson*
una exposición de arte	*an art exhibit*
la máquina de lavar	*the washing machine*
la facultad de medicina	*the medical school*
el cuarto de baño	*the bathroom*
la base de datos	*the database*

- indicates a characteristic of a noun

una persona de dinero	*a wealthy person*
la mujer del sombrero rojo	*the woman in the red hat*
una chica de talento	*a talented girl*
un hombre de porte medio	*a man of medium build*

- indicates a limitation or restriction on a verb or adjective

ciego del ojo izquierdo	*blind in one's left eye*
alto de estatura	*tall*
ancho de espaldas	*broad-shouldered*
un pie de largo/de ancho/de alto	*a foot long/wide/high*
Trabajo de programador.	*I work as a programmer.*

- indicates time in certain fixed expressions

muy de mañana	*very early in the morning*
trabajar de día/de noche	*to work days/nights*
Es de día/de noche.	*It's daytime/nighttime.*

- indicates the manner in which something is done

ponerse de pie	*to stand up*
ponerse de rodillas	*to get on one's knees*
estar de luto	*to be in mourning*
servir de intérprete	*to serve as interpreter*
hacer algo de buena fe	*to do something in good faith*
hacer algo de mala gana	*to do something unwillingly*
beber algo de un trago	*to drink something in one gulp*
Se viste de policía.	*He dresses up as a policeman.*
Se disfraza de policía.	*He disguises himself as a policeman.*

- connects nouns in often humorous or mocking descriptions of people

el loco de Pedro	*crazy Pedro*
la muy tonta de Marta	*silly Marta*
el pobre de mi cuñado	*my poor brother-in-law*
aquel burro de recepcionista	*that jerk of a receptionist*

- indicates the cause or reason

saltar de alegría	*to jump for joy*
gritar de dolor	*to scream in pain, scream because of the pain*
morir de hambre	*to starve to death*
estar loco de alegría	*to be mad with joy*
no poder moverse de miedo	*to be paralyzed with fear*

- indicates the topic (English: *about*)

hablar de filosofía   *to talk about philosophy*
saber poco de aquella familia   *to know little about that family*

C **¿De o nada?** *Complete las oraciones con la preposición* **de** *cuando sea necesaria. Si no es necesario usarla, escriba una X. No se olvide de la contracción* **del.**

1. ¡Qué hermosa es tu blusa _____ seda!

2. Esos turistas son _____ chilenos.

3. Diana lleva un vestido _____ azul.

4. Éstos son los documentos _____ el ingeniero.

5. La niñita saltó _____ alegremente.

6. Salieron _____ casa a las diez y cuarto.

7. Pedro tomará su lección _____ piano el jueves.

8. Sírvame una taza _____ té, por favor.

D **Expresar en español.** *Exprese las oraciones en español.*

1. *They gave me (as a gift) a gold bracelet and silver earrings.*

2. *Bernardo is tall and broad-shouldered.*

3. *Do you (tú) want to work days or nights?*

4. *Her poor aunt is in mourning.*

5. *They got down on their knees.*

The Preposition **en**

The basic meaning of the preposition **en** is to express location. It is the equivalent of English *in, on,* or *at*. The preposition **en**

- indicates location (English: *in, on, at*)

en el comedor   *in the dining room*
en la mesa   *on the table*
en el aeropuerto   *at the airport*

- indicates extent of time

Vuelvo en unos minutos.   *I'll be back in a few minutes.*
Roma no se construyó en un día.   *Rome wasn't built in a day.*

- is used in some expressions of manner

en serio   *seriously*
en broma   *not seriously, as a joke*
estar en contra   *to be against something*

- labels the amount by which measured quantities differ

más alto que yo en una cabeza	*a head taller than I*
Los precios han aumentado en un 20 por ciento.	*Prices have gone up (by) 20%.*

- labels the price

Te lo doy en diez dólares.	*I'll give it to you for ten dollars.*

- labels the means by which an action occurs

ir en avión/en barco/en tren/en coche	*to go by plane/by boat/by train/by car*
Te reconocí en la voz/en el andar.	*I recognized you by your voice/by your way of walking.*

E ***Expresar en inglés.*** *Exprese las oraciones en inglés.*

1. La reconocí en la voz.

2. Me lo vendieron en dos mil dólares.

3. El valor ha subido en un quince por ciento.

4. Los obreros están en contra de la huelga.

5. Se reunieron en el café Segovia.

F ***Expresar en español.*** *Exprese las oraciones en español.*

1. *We plan to go by plane.*

2. *I'll pick you (Uds.) up at the airport.*

3. *Miguel is taller than Juan by a head.*

4. *Are you (tú) saying this seriously or as a joke?*

5. *They will go out in an hour.*

The Preposition **con**

The preposition **con** expresses the idea of accompaniment or the means by which something is done. Its most common English equivalent is *with*. The preposition **con**

- expresses accompaniment

salir con los amigos	*to go out with friends*
llegar con un ramillete de flores	*to arrive with a bouquet of flowers*
té con limón	*tea with lemon*

- expresses attitude (sometimes **para con**)

generoso con uno	*generous to someone*
Es muy amable conmigo.	*He's very nice to me.*
insolente para con el maestro	*fresh to the teacher*

- labels the means by which something is done

abrir la puerta con una llave	*to open the door with a key*
atar el paquete con cuerda	*to tie the package with string*

- labels the action as a means, using the **con** + infinitive construction

Con pulsar esta tecla, se guarda el archivo.	*By pushing this key, you save the file.*

- labels the manner in which something is done

Nos recibió con una sonrisa.	*He received us with a smile.*
Lo hice con mucho esfuerzo.	*I did it with a great deal of effort.*

- expresses *in spite of* or *notwithstanding*

Con todos sus problemas, se hizo abogado.	*In spite of all his problems, he became a lawyer.*
Con tener tanto dinero de su tío, acabó sin un centavo.	*In spite of all the money he had from his uncle, he wound up penniless.*

- can label the content of a container and is less ambiguous than **de**

una cesta con ropa	*a basket of clothing*
una bolsa con cebollas	*a bag of onions*

G ¿Con qué? *Complete las oraciones con una de las expresiones con* **con**. *Escoja entre* **con caramelos, con un apretón, con cuerda, con llave, con esfuerzo** *y* **con leche.**

1. Tomó café _____.

2. Abrieron la puerta _____.

3. Se ató el paquete _____.

4. Nos saludó _____ de manos.

5. Búscame la caja _____.

6. Lo hacen todo _____.

H ¿Qué falta? *Complete las oraciones con la preposición correcta. Escoja entre* **a, de, en** *y* **con**. *No se olvide de escribir las contracciones* **al** *y* **del** *cuando sean necesarias.*

1. ¿Viste a la señora _____ el vestido blanco?

2. _____ todos sus defectos, José me parece una buena persona.

3. Vivo _____ dos cuadras de la oficina.

4. ¿Hablas _____ serio?

5. Tengo que terminar mi tesis _____ una semana.

6. El señor Salas es muy generoso _____ sus hijos.

7. Es una mujer _____ estatura media.

8. El dólar está _____ dos euros.

9. Las calles están cubiertas _____ nieve.

10. Limpio el suelo _____ un trapo.

11. ¿Me puedes dar agua _____ hielo?

12. Hay un buen restaurante _____ la estación de trenes.

13. Ahora me voy. Hablaremos _____ mi regreso.

14. Vengan a sentarse _____ la mesa.

15. La reconocí _____ la voz.

16. El inocente _____ mi hermano se compró un coche usado que no funciona.

17. Este jarro fue hecho _____ máquina.

18. Hace frío. Ponte el gorro _____ lana.

19. ¡Qué viaje más largo! Se mueren _____ sueño.

20. La sala es grande. Tiene cinco metros _____ largo.

21. _____ año de trabajar en la empresa, Víctor renunció a su puesto.

22. _____ principio, no nos gustaba la casa.

The Prepositions **para** and **por**

The prepositions **para** and **por** are often difficult for English speakers because both correspond to English *for* in many cases. It is most useful to consider the different relationships each expresses.

Para

The preposition **para**

- labels the destination, the time by which something will occur, or the figurative goal

Tomaron el tren para Córdoba.	*They took the train for Cordoba.* (destination)
Los chicos salieron para el colegio.	*The kids left for school.* (destination)
Terminaré para el martes.	*I'll finish by Tuesday.* (time by which)
El regalo es para ti.	*The gift is for you.* (figurative goal)
Estudio para médico.	*I'm studying to be a doctor.* (figurative goal)
Es un honor para nosotros.	*It's an honor for us.* (figurative goal)
Leo para perfeccionar mi español.	*I read to improve my Spanish.* (infinitive as figurative goal)
Busqué otro empleo para ganar más plata.	*I looked for another job in order to earn more money.* (infinitive as figurative goal)

- labels the standard for comparison

Para profesor, tiene poca paciencia.	*For a teacher, he's not very patient.*
Para doctora, sabe poco.	*For a doctor, she doesn't know much.*

- labels the information in the sentence as someone's opinion

Para mí, la obra fue excelente.	*In my opinion, the play was excellent.*
Para ella, el precio es bueno.	*In her opinion, the price is good.*

- appears in some common expressions and idioms

para entonces	*by that time*
para otra vez	*for another (later) occasion*
para siempre	*forever*
para variar	*just for a change*
ser tal para cual	*to be two of a kind*
estar para	*to be about to*

Por

The preposition **por**

- expresses motion through a place or location somewhere in a place (imprecise location)

Salga por esa puerta.	*Go out through that door.* (motion through)
Hay varios restaurantes por este barrio.	*There are several restaurants in (around) this neighborhood.* (imprecise location)
por todas partes, por todos lados	*everywhere* (imprecise location)
No lo he visto por aquí.	*I haven't seen him around here.* (imprecise location)

- expresses duration of time or imprecise point in time

Trabajó por muchos años.	*He worked for many years.* (duration)
Tuve que hacer cola por tres horas.	*I had to stand in line for three hours.* (duration)
Ayer por la tarde.	*Yesterday afternoon.* (imprecise point in time)
Nos veremos por Navidad.	*We'll see each other around Christmas.* (imprecise point in time)

- designates the cause or reason

Se ofenden por cualquier cosa.	*They get insulted at/over any little thing.*
Te felicito por tus buenas notas.	*I congratulate you on your good grades.*
Lo pasé mal en Panamá por el calor.	*I had a bad time of it in Panama because of the heat.*

- designates the means by which something is done

Mándeme un mensaje por correo electrónico.	*Send me a message by email.*

- designates motivation or incentive (It also designates the person for whose sake something is done.)

Brindaron por el equipo vencedor.	*They toasted the winning team.*
Todo lo hice por mi familia.	*Everything I did was for my family.*
Me callé por ti.	*I kept quiet for your sake.*

- expresses exchange or substitution

Pagamos mucho dinero por el coche.	*We paid a lot of money for the car.*
Enseñé la clase por el profesor.	*I taught the class for (instead of) the teacher.*

- adds the idea of motion to prepositions of location

El caballo saltó **por encima de** la valla.	*The horse jumped over the hurdle.*
El mesero pasó **por detrás de** las sillas.	*The waiter passed behind the chairs.*
El perro corrió **por debajo de** la mesa.	*The dog ran under the table.*

- labels the agent in passive constructions (see Chapter 8)

El libro fue escrito por un historiador inglés.	*The book was written by an English historian.*
El sitio web será creado por la administradora de web.	*The website will be created by the webmaster.*

- appears in idiomatic expressions

dar gato por liebre (*hare*)	*to put something over on someone*
(de) una vez por todas	*once and for all*
en un dos por tres	*in a jiffy*
escaparse por un pelo	*to have a narrow escape, escape by the skin of one's teeth*
estar por	*to be in the mood for something*
pasar un examen por los pelos	*to barely get through an exam*
poner por las nubes	*to praise to the skies*
por las buenas o por las malas	*whether one likes it or not*
por los cuatro costados	*on both sides (of the family)*
por motivo de	*on account of*
por si las moscas	*just in case*
siete por dos son catorce	*seven times two is fourteen* (mathematics)
traído por los pelos	*far-fetched*

Common Expressions with por

por acá/ahí/allá/aquí	*around here/there/there/here*
por ahora	*for now*
por añadidura	*in addition*
por aquel entonces	*at that time*
por casualidad	*by chance*
por cierto	*certainly*

por completo	*completely*
por consecuencia	*consequently*
por consiguiente	*consequently*
por culpa de	*the fault of*
por dentro y por fuera	*inside and outside*
por desgracia	*unfortunately*
por ejemplo	*for example*
por esa época	*around that time*
por escrito	*in writing*
por eso	*therefore, that's why*
por favor	*please*
por fin	*finally*
por lo común	*usually*
por lo demás	*furthermore*
por lo general	*generally*
por lo menos	*at least*
por lo mismo	*for that very reason*
por lo pronto	*for the time being*
por lo tanto	*therefore*
por lo visto	*apparently*
por medio de	*by means of*
por mi parte	*as far as I'm concerned*
por poco	*almost*
por primera vez	*for the first time*
por si acaso	*just in case*
por su cuenta	*on one's own*
por su parte	*as far as one is concerned*
por supuesto	*of course*
por todas partes	*everywhere*
por todos lados	*everywhere*
por último	*finally*
por un lado, por otro	*on the one hand, on the other*

Para and **por** contrast with each other in certain contexts.

para esa época	*by that time*
por esa época	*around that time*
Para algo lo hizo.	*He did it for some purpose.*
Por algo lo hizo.	*He did it for some reason or other.*
—¿Para quién trabaja Ud.?	*For whom are you working?*
—Trabajo para el señor Domínguez.	*I'm working for Mr. Domínguez.* *(he's my boss)*
—¿Por quién trabaja Ud.?	*For whom are you working?*
—Trabajo por el señor Domínguez.	*I'm working for Mr. Domínguez.* *(in his place)*

I *¿Para qué?* *Ud. es el hermano modelo para su hermanito. Por eso él tiene interés en saber todo lo que Ud. hace y por qué lo hace. Ud. le contesta dándole muy buenos consejos. Use la preposición* **para** + *infinitivo en su respuesta. Siga el modelo.*

MODELO   ¿Para qué estudias tanto? (sacar buenas notas)
→ Para sacar buenas notas.

1. ¿Para qué trabajas en la biblioteca? (ganar dinero)

2. ¿Para qué lees tantos libros? (aprender mucho)

3. ¿Para qué te quedas en casa los sábados hasta las tres? (ayudar a mis papás)

4. ¿Para qué le compras flores y bombones a tu novia? (demostrarle mi cariño)

5. ¿Para qué practicas español cuatro horas al día todos los días? (perfeccionarlo)

6. ¿Para qué votas en todas las elecciones? (ser buen ciudadano)

7. ¿Para qué hablas de los principios éticos? (llevar una vida moral y feliz)

J *¡Una semana muy ocupada!* *Hay tantas cosas que hacer y tan poco tiempo para hacerlas. Escriba para cuándo todas las cosas se tienen que hacer. Conteste las preguntas usando la preposición* **para**. *Siga el modelo.*

MODELO   ¿Para cuándo te cortas el pelo? (el jueves)
→ Para el jueves.

1. ¿Para cuándo tienes que entregar el informe? (pasado mañana)

2. ¿Para cuándo arreglaste cita con el dentista? (la semana entrante)

3. ¿Para cuándo vas a entrevistarte para el empleo? (el martes)

4. ¿Para cuándo necesitas devolver los libros a la biblioteca? (finales del semestre)

5. ¿Para cuándo necesitas el regalo para el aniversario de tus papás? (el mes próximo)

6. ¿Para cuándo debes recoger la ropa en la tintorería? (las cinco de la tarde)

7. ¿Para cuándo vas a alquilar un coche? (el fin de semana)

K *¡Pepita la preguntona* (busybody)*!* *Pepita pregunta muchas cosas por curiosa. Conteste sus preguntas usando la preposición* **por** *en sus respuestas. Siga el modelo.*

MODELO   ¿Por qué se durmió Ud. tan temprano? (un tremendo sueño)
→ Me dormí tan temprano por un tremendo sueño.

1. ¿Por qué fue Ud. al almacén? (un par de zapatos)

2. ¿Por qué felicitaron Uds. a Verónica? (su cumpleaños)

3. ¿Por qué te duele la espalda? (jugar al tenis / cuatro horas)

4. ¿Por qué no terminó Javier el informe? (pereza)

5. ¿Cuándo veremos a Carlos y Elena? (la tarde)

6. ¿Cómo salieron los Salcedo de la ciudad? (el puente más céntrico)

7. ¿Por qué cosas irán Uds. a la tienda de conveniencia? (salchicha y queso)

8. ¿Cómo tendrás que hacer la tarea? (escrito)

9. ¿Por dónde darán un paseo los muchachos? (el bulevar Alameda)

10. ¿Por quiénes vas a pasar por la casa de los Granados? (Micaela y Angustias)

L *¿Qué tal la película?* *A su amiga le gustó tanto la película* Mangos del Caribe *que la vio cinco veces. Ud. quiere saber por qué le gustó tanto porque Ud. la encontró francamente aburrida. Escriba sus respuestas usando la preposición* **por.** *Siga el modelo.*

MODELO   ¿Por qué te gustó la película tanto? (los actores principales)
           → Por los actores principales.

1. ¿Por qué la viste cinco veces? (la fotografía)

2. ¿Por qué te interesa tanto? (el argumento)

3. ¿Por qué quedaste tan impresionada? (la dirección)

4. ¿Por qué te llamó la atención? (el guión (*script*))

5. ¿Por qué estás loca por ella? (el escenario (*scenery*))

6. ¿Por qué la encontraste tan buena? (la música)

7. ¿Por qué le haces un relato entusiasta (*rave review*)? (los efectos especiales)

8. ¿Por qué estás tan entusiasmada por el film? (el diálogo)

NOTA CULTURAL

El centenario del **cine español** se celebró el 14 de mayo de 1996, fecha de la primera proyección en Madrid. Algunos directores españoles han logrado una fama internacional, entre ellos Luis Buñuel, Carlos Saura, Luis García Berlanga, Víctor Erice, Juan Antonio Bardem y Pedro Almodóvar. Almodóvar formó parte de «la movida», el movimiento innovador y experimental en las artes que surgió con la muerte de Francisco Franco en 1975 y el fin de la censura. Hay varios festivales de cine españoles como los de Valladolid, Huelva, Madrid, Alcalá de Henares, Barcelona, Valencia, Bilbao y Sitges, pero el más prestigioso de todos es el Festival Internacional de Cine de San Sebastián, una ciudad muy apreciada como centro cultural y balneario (*beach resort*).

M *¿Para o por?* *Complete los diálogos escogiendo* **para** *o* **por.**

1. —¿Cuándo sale el tren de Madrid _____ Barcelona?

   —Sale _____ la mañana pasando _____ Zaragoza _____ la tarde.

2. —¿Van tú y Mari Carmen al centro comercial _____ ver escaparates?

   —Ah, sí, una vez _____ semana.

3. —_____ peluquera, Teresa no sabe cortar el pelo.

   —_____ eso ya no voy a esa peluquería.

4. —Hagamos una excursión _____ la sierra _____ mediados de julio.

   —_____ variar, viajemos _____ las islas _____ principios de agosto.

5. —¿_____ quién es este hermoso traje hecho a la medida?

—Es _____ mi hermana Rosa. Fue hecho _____ Gabriela, la famosa modista.

6. —¿Le dijiste a Juan lo de Armando _____ teléfono?

—¡Qué va! _____ darle esta noticia tengo que hacerlo _____ escrito.

—Es decir, ¡será _____ el 30 de febrero del año que viene!

7. —¿Cuánto pagaste _____ los boletos?

—_____ mí, un precio especial—¡el doble del precio normal!

8. —Parece que el ladrón se escapó _____ los pelos.

—¿_____ dónde entró en la tienda?

—_____ lo que leí en el periódico, entró _____ una ventana del sótano.

9. —Rodrigo estuvo enfermo _____ la leche estropeada que tomó.

—Yo sé. Él me llamó para pedirme que fuera al trabajo _____ él.

NOTA CULTURAL

Zaragoza, capital de la Comunidad Autónoma de Aragón, queda a orillas del río Ebro en el noreste de España. Está bien situada entre Madrid y Barcelona y entre Bilbao y Valencia. El matrimonio de Fernando II de Aragón e Isabel I de Castilla, los Reyes Católicos, en 1469 unieron los reinos de Aragón y Castilla, base de la futura nación española. Zaragoza fue fundada por los romanos en el año 24 a.C. en el mismo sitio donde hubo un pueblo fortificado ibero. Nombrada Caesaraugusta por los romanos, fue una importante colonia del Imperio romano. Fue conquistada por los árabes en 714 y por el rey Alfonso I de Aragón en 1118. Su monumento más importante es la basílica de Nuestra Señora del Pilar.

N *Expresar en inglés.* *Exprese las oraciones en inglés. Fíjese especialmente en las preposiciones* **para** *y* **por**.

1. Soy norteamericano por los cuatro costados.

2. Iremos con Uds. más temprano por si las moscas.

3. Ponen al compositor por las nubes.

4. Ricardo habrá llamado para algo.

5. Tres por ocho son veinticuatro.

6. Mortadelo y Filemón son tal para cual.

7. «Te querré para siempre», le dijo don Quijote a Dulcinea.

NOTA CULTURAL

Don Quijote es el protagonista de la novela *El ingenioso hidalgo Don Quijote de la Mancha* que fue escrita por Miguel de Cervantes Saavedra (1547–1616), considerado el creador de la novela moderna. La primera parte del Quijote fue publicada en 1605 y la segunda en 1615. Cervantes escribió su obra maestra como una parodia de los libros de caballerías (*chivalry*) que eran muy populares. Cervantes cuenta la historia de un hidalgo (*nobleman*) manchego (de la Mancha) Alonso Quijano que pierde la razón (*who loses his mind*) leyendo libros de caballerías. Creyéndose un caballero andante (*knight errant*), toma el nombre de don Quijote, escoge a Sancho Panza como su escudero (*squire*) e inventa una dama enamorada, Dulcinea del Toboso. Imita las hazañas (*deeds, feats*) de los héroes de las novelas confundiendo lo real con lo imaginario. Don Quijote, como don Juan, son personajes literarios que llegaron a ser figuras universales, los dos creados por autores españoles.

Mortadelo y **Filemón** (*Mort & Phil* en inglés) son los graciosos espías de las historietas españolas. Su creador Francisco Ibáñez empezó a escribir estas historias en forma de tiras cómicas (*comic strips*) en los tebeos (*comic books*), que son publicaciones infantiles ilustradas, en 1958. Mortadelo y Filemón comenzaron siendo una parodia de Sherlock Holmes y el doctor Watson.

O *¡Vivan los fiesteros!* **(Hooray for the party lovers!)** *Les toca a los estudiantes hacer una fiesta del fin de curso. Cada persona salió a comprar algo y ahora cuenta lo que compró y cuánto costó. Escriba oraciones usando la preposición* **por***. Siga el modelo.*

MODELO   yo / ir / los manteles : pagar / doce dólares
→ Yo fui por los manteles. Pagué doce dólares por ellos.

1. Beatriz / ir / panecillos : pagar / treinta dólares

2. Carlos y Leo / ir / refrescos : pagar / cincuenta y cinco dólares

3. Paula y yo / ir / servilletas : pagar / siete dólares

4. tú / ir / fiambres (*cold cuts*) : pagar / cien dólares

5. yo / ir / torta : pagar / dieciocho dólares

6. Uds. / ir / vino : pagar / cuarenta y tres dólares

7. Ud. / ir / fruta : pagar / veintidós dólares

8. vosotros / ir / quesos : pagar / sesenta y un dólares

Other Common Simple Prepositions

desde	*from*
durante	*during*
entre	*between, among*
excepto	*except*
hacia	*toward*
hasta	*until*
menos	*except*
salvo	*except*
según	*according to*
sin	*without*
sobre	*above, about*

Desde is more specific than **de** in labeling the starting point.

Lo vi desde la ventana.	*I saw him from the window.*
Desde aquel día hemos sido buenos amigos.	*From that day on we have been good friends.*

Hacia can refer to attitudes and feelings as well as direction.

Siente mucho cariño hacia sus sobrinos.	*He feels deep affection for his nieces and nephews.*

Note the following combinations of **hacia** + adverb.

hacia adelante	*forward; toward the front*
hacia atrás	*backward; toward the rear*
hacia arriba	*upward*
hacia abajo	*downward*

Hasta can mean *even* as well as *until*.

Hasta mis abuelos vinieron a la fiesta.	*Even my grandparents came to the party.*

Sin + infinitive has a variety of English equivalents.

El trabajo quedó sin hacer.	*The work remained undone.*
Las calles están sin pavimentar.	*The streets are unpaved.*
Habla sin parar.	*He talks without stopping.*
Quedamos sin comer.	*We ended up not eating.*

Sobre means *about* as well as *above, on top of*. It can also mean *about* in the sense of *approximately*.

Leí un artículo sobre la industria mexicana.	*I read an article on (about) Mexican industry.*
Vamos a comer sobre las siete.	*We'll eat at about seven o'clock.*

P *Expresar en español.* *Exprese las oraciones en español.*

1. *My homework is unfinished.*

2. *I put one book on top of the other.*

3. *I saw him go out toward the rear.*

4. *She lived for (during) many years among the indigenous people* (los indígenas).

5. *It's hot even in the mountains.*

6. *The immigrants feel love for their new country.*

7. *They followed us from the door of the movie theater.*

8. *I'm reading a book about Puerto Rico.*

Sets of Prepositions and Compound Prepositions

Antes de (before), ante, delante de (in front of)

Antes de is used to mean *before* with time expressions, whereas **ante** is figurative. **Delante de** expresses physical location.

antes de su llegada	*before your arrival*
antes de Navidad	*before Christmas*
antes de las ocho	*before eight o'clock*
comparecer ante el juez	*to appear before the judge*
ante todo	*first of all, above all*
No sé qué hacer ante tantas posibilidades.	*I don't know what to do faced with so many possibilities.*
Hay un jardín delante de la casa.	*There's a garden in front of the house.*

Debajo de (under) and bajo

Debajo de usually means *under* in a literal sense, whereas **bajo** is generally figurative.

debajo del puente	*under the bridge*
bajo la administración de González	*under the González government*
bajo Carlos V	*under Charles the Fifth*
bajo ningún concepto	*in no way*
diez grados bajo cero	*ten degrees below zero*
bajo llave	*under lock and key*
bajo juramento	*under oath*

En contra de (against) and contra

En contra de usually expresses being *against* someone's ideas, policies, or political views. **Contra** means *against* in most other contexts.

escribir un artículo en contra de la guerra	*to write an article against (opposing) the war*
hablar en contra del proyecto	*to speak against the project*

Los hechos van en contra de sus ideas.	*The facts run counter to your ideas.*
apoyarse contra el árbol	*to lean against the tree*
pastillas contra la gripe	*pills for the flu*
luchar contra el enemigo	*to fight against the enemy*

Frente a and enfrente de (opposite, facing across from)

Frente a and **enfrente de** (*opposite, facing, across from*) are synonyms. Note that **delante de** should be used to mean *in front of.*

Hay una parada de autobuses frente a nuestra casa.
Hay una parada de autobuses enfrente de nuestra casa.

There's a bus stop across from our house.

Tras (behind, after), detrás de (behind), después de (after)

Tras means *behind, after* in certain set expressions. Generally, **detrás de** means *behind* and **después de** means *after.*

año tras año	*year after year*
un artículo tras otro	*one article after another*
detrás de la casa	*behind the house*
después de la clase	*after class*

Other Common Compound Prepositions

The prepositions **a** and **de** in compound prepositions contract with the definite article **el** when **el** follows directly.

a causa de	*because of*
acerca de	*about* (*concerning*)
al lado de	*next to*
a lo largo de	*throughout, along, over*
a pesar de	*in spite of*
a través de	*through*
cerca de	*near; about* (*approximately*)
dentro de	*inside of*
encima de	*on, upon, on top of* (similar to **sobre**, but cannot mean *approximately*)
fuera de	*outside of*
afuera de	*outside of*
junto a	*close to, right next to*
lejos de	*far from*
por medio de	*by means of* (a synonym of **mediante**)
respecto a	*about* (*concerning*)

Q   *Ejercicio de conjunto.*   *Escoja la preposición que complete correctamente las oraciones.*

1. No pudieron lanzar el nuevo cohete _____ mal tiempo que hacía.
   a. por medio del
   b. junto al
   c. a causa del

2. Todo lo que sé lo supe _____ sitio web.
   a. encima del
   b. sobre el
   c. a través del

3. No puedo salir de la oficina a las cinco. Por eso llegaré al restaurante _____ las seis.
   a. a pesar de
   b. respecto a
   c. después de

4. El señor Aranda tuvo un ataque de nervios _____ la perspectiva de perder su empleo.
   a. ante
   b. para
   c. al lado de

5. Ricardo mandó email _____ email y nunca recibió una respuesta.
   a. tras
   b. atrás
   c. detrás de

6. Si alquilas un apartamento tan _____ la oficina, tendrás que viajar por lo menos una hora para llegar al trabajo.
   a. junto a
   b. lejos de
   c. por medio de

7. En la radio están hablando constantemente _____ peligro de un ciclón.
   a. sobre el
   b. encima del
   c. cerca del

8. El coche resbaló, salió de la carretera y fue _____ por la cuesta.
   a. afuera
   b. hacia abajo
   c. cerca

9. Miré por la ventana mientras mi avión volaba _____ Nueva York.
   a. entre
   b. por encima de
   c. antes de

10. Alfredo tiene gripe. _____ lo tanto, no viene hoy.
   a. Por
   b. En
   c. De

11. El tren de alta velocidad viaja _____ 270 kilómetros _____ hora.
   a. por, de
   b. en, para
   c. a, por

12. Bueno, eso es todo _____ ahora.
   a. para
   b. hacia
   c. por

13. _____ culpa de él, el proyecto quedó _____ terminar.
   a. Para, en
   b. Con, hasta
   c. Por, sin

14. A mi sobrinito travieso lo quiero _____ todo.
   a. a pesar de
   b. a lo largo de
   c. frente a

15. Los ciclistas tienen que pasar _____ los coches cuando hay mucho tráfico.
   a. por entre
   b. ante
   c. después de

16. Varios senadores votaron _____ la propuesta de ley (*bill*).
   a. por medio de
   b. en contra de
   c. dentro de

17. Todos estos sarapes están hechos _____ mano.
   a. a
   b. con
   c. de

18. Pedro Camacho es el señor _____ traje gris.
   a. con el
   b. dentro del
   c. del

19. —¿No vino Zenaida?
   —No. Vinieron todos _____ ella.
   a. con
   b. después de
   c. menos

20. Este autor vivió _____ los Reyes Católicos.
   a. debajo de
   b. sin
   c. bajo

R *Ejercicio oral. Preposiciones: **para** y **por**. Hágale preguntas a su amigo/amiga que empiezan con ¿para qué? o ¿por qué? Su amigo/amiga le contesta usando la preposición* **para** *o* **por**. *Por ejemplo: —¿Para qué compraste bombones? —**Para regalar.** o —¿Por qué te interesó la novela tanto? —**Por el argumento.** Después su amigo/amiga le hace preguntas a Ud. y Ud. le contesta usando las mismas preposiciones.*

Interrogative Words and Question Formation

Interrogative Words in Information Questions

Questions that begin with an interrogative word such as **¿Cuándo?** or **¿Quién?** ask for a piece of information (*When is the meeting? Who is that man? Which one do you want?*). They are called information questions.

Interrogative words have a written accent. These are the most important interrogative words.

¿cuál? ¿cuáles?	*which one(s)?*
¿cuándo?	*when?*
¿cuánto? ¿cuánta?	*how much?*
¿cuántos? ¿cuántas?	*how many?*
¿cómo?	*how?*
¿dónde?	*where?* (*at what place?*)
¿adónde?	*where?* (*to what place?*)
¿de dónde?	*from where?*
¿qué?	*what?/which?*
¿para qué?	*for what purpose?*
¿por qué?	*why?*
¿quién? ¿quiénes?	*who?* (subject)
¿a quién? ¿a quiénes?	*whom?* (object)
¿de quién? ¿de quiénes?	*whose?*

Some of the interrogatives are not used exactly like their English equivalents.

¿Cómo?

¿Cómo? has different meanings depending on whether it is used with **ser** or **estar**.

¿Cómo está tu hermano?	*How is your brother?* (asks about health or mental state)
¿Cómo es tu hermano?	*What does your brother look like? / What is your brother like?* (asks about character, personality)

¿Cómo? is used to ask for repetition of something you didn't understand or to express surprise at something you have just heard (English uses *what* for this purpose).

—Hay examen de física hoy.	*There's a physics exam today.*
—¿Cómo?	*What?*

¿Cómo? cannot precede adjectives or adverbs directly. Unlike English *how* in questions such as *How heavy is the package? How wide is the river? How fast does he run?*, Spanish asks for measurements using different structures.

¿Cuánto pesa el paquete? ¿Cómo es de pesado el paquete? } ¿Cuánto es de pesado el paquete?	*How heavy is the package?*
¿Cómo es el río de ancho? ¿Cuánto es el río de ancho? ¿Cuánto tiene el río de ancho? } ¿Qué anchura tiene el río? ¿Cuánto mide el río de ancho?	*How wide is the river?*
¿Con qué rapidez corre?	*How fast does he run?*

In Spanish America, the colloquial form **¿Qué tan ancho es el río?** is also used.

¿Cuál?

¿Cuál? and **¿cuáles?** ask *which?* when a noun does not immediately follow.

¿Cuál prefieres?	*Which (one) do you prefer?*

¿Cuál? and **¿cuáles?** are replaced by **¿qué?** before a noun in standard Spanish.

¿Qué libros leíste?	*Which books did you read?*
¿Qué materias escogiste?	*Which subjects did you choose?*

However, in parts of Spanish America, such as Mexico and Cuba, sentences such as **¿Cuáles materias escogiste?** are acceptable.

¿Cuál? is used for English *what?* when an identification is asked for.

¿Cuál es la diferencia?	*What's the difference?*
¿Cuál es la capital de Nicaragua?	*What's the capital of Nicaragua?*
¿Cuál es la fecha de hoy?	*What's today's date?*
¿Cuál fue el resultado?	*What was the result?*
¿Cuál fue el año de la crisis económica?	*What was the year of the economic crisis?*

Note that **¿qué?** before **ser** asks for a definition.

¿Qué es la programación?	*What is programming?*
¿Qué es un nanosegundo?	*What is a nanosecond?*

¿Dónde? vs. ¿adónde?

¿Dónde? is used to ask about location. **¿Adónde?** asks direction and is used with verbs of motion.

¿Dónde trabaja Jimena?	*Where does Jimena work?*
¿Adónde va Jimena?	*Where is Jimena going?*

Many speakers use **¿dónde?** instead of **¿adónde?** with verbs of motion.

¿Para dónde? and **¿hacia dónde?** mean *toward where?*

¿De quién(es)?

Questions beginning with **¿de quién(es)?** have a different word order than their English equivalents.

¿De quién es el libro?   *Whose book is it?*

Prepositions always precede the interrogative word in Spanish.

¿Con cuántas personas llegó?   *How many people did he arrive with?*

¿Para quiénes es el regalo?   *Whom is the gift for?*

¿Sobre qué hablaron?   *What did they talk about?*

¿En qué casa vive Nélida?   *Which house does Nélida live in?*

A **Los detalles, por favor.** *Cuando su amigo le habla de lo que hacen unas personas, Ud. le pide más detalles usando las palabras interrogativas con las preposiciones apropiadas. Siga el modelo.*

MODELO   Francisca se lamenta de todo.
          → ¿De qué se lamenta?

1. Monserrat se quejaba de su trabajo.

2. Jorge y Maribel se interesan en el cine.

3. Eduardo se jacta de sus logros.

4. Carlota se casará con Pedro.

5. Cristóbal y Tere se metieron en un lío.

6. Luz se fija en el paisaje.

7. Hernán se ríe de todo.

8. Elvira se enamoró de Roberto.

9. Pablo soñó con su novia.

B **¿Quiénes son?** *Lea los datos sobre cada persona y derive preguntas con palabras interrogativas de ellos. Siga el modelo.*

MODELO   Es venezolano.
          → ¿De dónde es?
            o ¿De qué nacionalidad es?

A. Leonardo Gustavo Sáenz

1. Es argentino.

2. Es ingeniero.

3. Trabaja para su suegro.

4. Vive en Nueva York.

5. Es casado con una norteamericana.

6. Tiene tres hijos.

B. Delmira Danielo

7. Nació en Francia.

8. Sus abuelos son de España.

9. Se mudó al Canadá cuando tenía cuatro años.

10. Hace estudios posgraduados en química en una universidad canadiense.

11. Terminará sus estudios el año próximo.

12. Vive con sus padres y hermanos en las afueras de Montreal.

C. Claudio del Mundo

13. Ganó la gran carrera de bicicletas.

14. Es un héroe nacional en España.

15. Fue condecorado por el rey español.

16. Tiene cuarenta y dos bicicletas.

17. Le gusta más su italiana amarilla.

18. Quiere descansar.

19. Irá de vacaciones al Caribe.

20. Llevará a su mujer y a sus dos hijas.

C *¿Cómo? ¡Habla más fuerte!* *Su amiga llama para invitarlo/invitarla a ir de compras con ella. Por desgracia, hay interferencias en la línea y Ud. le pregunta lo que dijo usando las palabras interrogativas apropiadas. Escriba más de una pregunta cuando sea posible. Siga el modelo.*

MODELO   Voy al centro comercial.
→ ¿Adónde?

1. El centro comercial queda en la carretera de Salamanca.

2. Hay ochenta y siete tiendas en el centro comercial.

3. Hay unos veintiséis restaurantes y cafés en el centro comercial.

4. Voy a comprar dos pares de zapatos.

5. Necesito comprarle un regalo a mi cuñada.

6. Trataré de gastar menos de cincuenta dólares.

7. Quizás le compre una blusa de seda.

8. No sé si le gustará más la blusa azul o la verde.

9. Pagaré con tarjeta de crédito.

10. Voy a llegar al centro comercial en coche.

11. Saldré para el centro comercial a eso de las dos.

12. Volveré a casa antes de la cena.

D *Estudiantes.* *Complete las oraciones con las palabras interrogativas correctas.*

A

1. Nati: ¿_____ materias estás tomando este semestre?
   Sergio: Estoy tomando cuatro.

2. Nati: ¿_____ son?
   Sergio: Historia de los Estados Unidos, literatura inglesa, física y español.

3. Nati: ¿_____ enseña la clase de historia?
   Sergio: El profesor Durán.

4. Nati: ¿_____ es la clase?
   Sergio: ¡Excelente, y fuerte! El profe es estupendo. No hay cosa que no sepa.

5. Nati: ¿_____ estudiantes hay en la clase?

6. Sergio: Creo que somos veintidós. ¿_____ te interesa tanto?

7. Nati: Es que soy aficionada a la historia norteamericana. Es posible que tome

   la clase de oyente (*auditor*). ¿_____ se reúnen Uds.?
   Sergio: En el edificio de ciencias políticas, aula número 387.

8. Nati: ¿_____ días?
   Sergio: Lunes, miércoles y jueves.

9. Nati: ¿_____ hora?
   Sergio: De las diez y media hasta las doce.

B

10. Diego: Oye, Paco, ¿_____ es esta carpeta (*briefcase*)? ¿De Baltasar?

11. Paco: ¿_____ dice adentro? ¿No tiene nombre ni papeles?

12. Diego: ¿_____ (*Where?*) Yo no veo nada. Mira.

13. Paco: ¿_____ color es la de Jaime? ¿No tiene él una así?

14. Diego: No me acuerdo. Vamos a llamarlo. ¿_____ es su número de teléfono?
    Paco: No creo que lo encontremos en la casa porque lo vi hace poco por aquí.

15. Diego: ¿_____ iba?
    Paco: No tengo la menor idea.

16. Diego: ¿Con _____ estaba?
    Paco: Ni te puedo decir porque yo hablaba con Aurelia.

17. Diego: ¿_____? (*What?*) ¿_____ dices? ¿Tú y Aurelia otra vez?

18. Paco: Ay, chico, ¿_____ quieres que yo haga? La quiero mucho. ¿_____ me
    hablas de esto ahora?

19. Diego: Bueno, es tema por otro día. Por ahora, ¿_____ no llamamos a Jaime
    en su celular?

E **Un testigo.** *Ud. está paseándose por la calle cuando ve un choque de coches. Un policía acaba de llegar a la escena del accidente y quiere hacerle unas preguntas. Escriba las preguntas usando las palabras interrogativas correctas.*

1. ¿_____ estaba Ud. cuando vio ocurrir el accidente?

2. ¿_____ pasó? Déme todos los detalles.

3. ¿_____ pasó? Dígame la hora exacta.

4. ¿_____ de los dos coches fue responsable del accidente?

5. ¿_____ pasó la luz roja sin parar?

6. ¿_____ iba el conductor del coche blanco?

7. ¿_____ venía el conductor del coche rojo?

8. ¿_____ peatones (*passersby*) se acercaron a la escena?

9. ¿_____ tiempo transcurrió (*elapsed*) entre el choque y la llegada de la policía?

F **Una conversación telefónica.** *Ud. está escuchando lo que dice su amigo mientras él habla por teléfono. Porque no oye lo que dice la otra persona, Ud. tiene que imaginarse lo que ésta le pregunta a su amigo. Escriba las preguntas que se habrán hecho. Siga el modelo.*

MODELO — *¿Qué tiempo hace?*
—Hace calor.

1. —_____
—De parte de Jaime Vega.

2. —_____
—La casa queda en la calle Olmo.

3. —_____
—El coche es de Roberto.

4. —_____
—Es verde oscuro.

5. —_____
—Voy a llevar a Ofelia.

6. —_____
—Llegaremos a las nueve.

7. —_____
—Tengo veintinueve años.

8. —_____
—Pienso ver a Leo y a Matilde.

9. —_____
—Será el sábado.

10. —_____
—Llegan mis primos.

11. —_____
    —Gasté mucha plata.

12. —_____
    —Está lloviendo.

13. —_____
    — César y Josefa se encuentran muy bien.

14. —_____
    —Me quedo hasta el domingo.

15. —_____
    —No quiero ninguno de los dos.

16. —_____
    —De origen ruso.

G *Expresar en español. Vamos a comprar boletos.* *Exprese las siguientes oraciones en español. Preste mucha atención a las palabras interrogativas.*

1. *When are we going to buy the tickets for the play?*

2. *How about going tomorrow? Where's the box office?*

3. *On Pamplona Avenue. How many tickets do we need?*

4. *Six. How much do they cost?*

5. *Fifty dollars each. Who's paying for them?*

6. *Each one will pay for his/her ticket. What day are we going?*

7. *Thursday. What time does the show start?*

8. *At eight o'clock. Whom are you inviting?*

9. *Nobody! The ticket is very expensive! How are we getting there?*

10. *By car or by train.*

H *¡Maravillas naturales de las Américas!* *Escriba preguntas acerca de la magnitud de estos lugares tan conocidos. Siga el modelo.*

MODELO   el río Grande / ser 1900 millas / largo
          → ¿Cómo es el río Grande de largo?
          o ¿Cuánto es el río Grande de largo?

1. el río Iguazú / tener 1.320 kilómetros / largo

2. el río Amazonas / tener 6.500 kilómetros / longitud

3. el río Mississippi / medir 2350 millas / largo

4. el lago Titicaca / ser 3.815 metros / altura

5. el desierto de Atacama / tener 600 millas / largo

6. el monte McKinley / tener 20,320 pies / altura

7. la cumbre Aconcagua / medir 6.959 metros / alto

NOTA CULTURAL

- **Un kilómetro** (1.000 metros) equivale aproximadamente a 5/8 de una milla. Un metro equivale a 39.37 pulgadas (*inches*).
- **El río Iguazú** se encuentra al sur del Brasil y desemboca en (*flows into*) el Paraná donde se unen Argentina, Brasil y Paraguay.
- **El río Amazonas** nace en los Andes de Perú y atraviesa (*crosses*) Brasil.
- **El río Mississippi** (en español **Misisipí**) desemboca en el golfo de México por un ancho delta.
- **El lago Titicaca** se encuentra en la altiplanicie (*high plateau*) andina de Perú y Bolivia.
- **El desierto de Atacama**, que queda al norte de Chile, es una región rica en cobre (*copper*) y nitrato (*saltpeter*).
- **El monte McKinley** es la cumbre (*peak*) más alta de las montañas Rocosas (*Rocky*). La sierra se extiende desde Alaska, donde se encuentra el monte McKinley, hasta México.
- **Aconcagua**, la cumbre más alta de América del Sur, se encuentra en los Andes argentinos.

I *¿Cuál es?* Complete las oraciones con las palabras interrogativas correctas. Escoja **¿cuál?**, **¿cómo?** o **¿qué?**

1. ¿_____ es la capital de Costa Rica?
2. ¿_____ es la computación?
3. ¿_____ es la montaña de alto?
4. ¿_____ fue el problema?
5. ¿_____ están por tu casa?
6. ¿_____ es la fecha de hoy?
7. ¿_____ es la termodinámica?

J *Escriba preguntas derivadas de las oraciones. Tenga presente que la preposición precede la palabra interrogativa. Siga el modelo.*

MODELO   Van *para el mar.*
→ ¿Para dónde van?

1. Estas rosas son *para Susana.*
2. Los ingenieros hablaron *sobre el nuevo puente.*
3. Celeste trabaja *en aquella oficina.*
4. Alberto fue *con otras siete personas.*
5. Los celulares son *de Uds.*
6. Daniel caminaba *hacia el río.*
7. Jeremías entró *por aquí.*
8. Soñó *con su novia.*
9. Se metieron *en un lío.*
10. Vienen *del club de jazz.*

Yes/No Questions

Questions that do not begin with a question word require either *yes* or *no* as an answer. These yes/no questions are referred to in Spanish as **preguntas generales**.

To make a statement into a yes/no question in Spanish, the intonation changes from falling to rising at the end of the sentence without changing the word order.

¿Los chicos tienen juguetes?	*Do the children have toys?*
¿Laura trabaja mañana?	*Is Laura working tomorrow?*
¿Martín compró los boletos?	*Did Martín buy the tickets?*

Yes/no questions can also be formed from statements by inverting the subject and the verb.

¿Tienen los chicos juguetes?	*Do the children have toys?*
¿Trabaja Laura mañana?	*Is Laura working tomorrow?*
¿Sacó Martín las entradas?	*Did Martín buy the tickets?*

The subject can be placed at the end of the sentence to emphasize it.

¿Trabaja Laura mañana?	*Is Laura working **tomorrow**?* (focus on *tomorrow*)
¿Trabaja mañana Laura?	*Is **Laura** working tomorrow?* (focus on *Laura*)

In yes/no questions consisting of just a subject and verb, either the subject or the verb may come at the end of the sentence, depending on which element is the focus of the question. Thus, the questions **¿Carlos se va?** and **¿Se va Carlos?** require different answers, since their focus is different.

—¿Carlos se va?	*Is Carlos **leaving**? (focus on the verb)*
—No, se queda.	*No, he's **staying**.*
—¿Se va Carlos?	*Is **Carlos** leaving? (focus on who's leaving)*
—No, Carlos no. Se va Raúl.	*No, not Carlos. **Raúl** is leaving.*

Statements consisting of a subject, **ser** or **estar**, and an adjective are usually made into yes/no questions by placing the subject at the end of the sentence, not right after the verb as in English.

El coche es caro.	*The car is expensive.*
¿Es caro el coche?	*Is the car expensive?*
Las tiendas están cerradas.	*The stores are closed.*
¿Están cerradas las tiendas?	*Are the stores closed?*

Spanish can add phrases such as **¿verdad?**, **¿no es verdad?**, **¿no es cierto?**, and **¿no?** to statements to turn them into questions. The added phrases are called tags. These tag questions signal that the speaker expects the answer *yes*. Note that if the statement is negative, only **¿verdad?** can be used as a tag.

Vienes con nosotros, ¿no es cierto?	*You're coming with us, aren't you?*
Te gustó la película, ¿no?	*You liked the film, didn't you?*
No tienes hambre, ¿verdad?	*You're not hungry, are you?*

K *¿Cuál es la pregunta?* Escriba preguntas generales derivadas de las oraciones colocando el sujeto inmediatamente después del verbo. Siga el modelo.

MODELO   Raúl estudia arquitectura.
→ ¿Estudia Raúl arquitectura?

1. Gustavo y Juana aprenden francés.
2. Pepe trabaja en una tienda de deportes.
3. Ud. toca el piano.
4. Los niños se han vestido.
5. Cristóbal jugará al béisbol.
6. Elena se matriculó anteayer.
7. Uds. deben quedarse unos días más.
8. Ramona está a dieta.

L *¿Ser/estar + adjetivo + sujeto?* Escriba preguntas generales derivadas de las oraciones. Ponga el verbo **ser** o **estar** primero, seguido del adjetivo y al final el sujeto. Siga el modelo.

MODELO   El edificio es alto.
→ ¿Es alto el edificio?

1. Estos niños son traviesos.
2. Las margaritas (*daisies*) son bonitas.
3. El televisor estaba descompuesto.
4. El museo está abierto.
5. La revista es italiana.
6. Las joyas fueron robadas.
7. Los pantalones están rotos (*torn*).
8. Esta marca es buena.
9. El espectáculo fue impresionante.
10. Las chuletas de cordero están ricas.

M *Para hacer un picnic.* Unos amigos quieren hacer un picnic y necesitan hacer ciertas cosas para que resulte bien. ¿Quién se ocupa de cada cosa? Para saberlo, conteste las siguientes preguntas generales usando los nombres indicados. Siga el modelo.

MODELO   ¿Trae la carne Marianela? (Clarita)
→ No, Marianela no. La trae Clarita.

1. ¿Trae los panes Pedro? (Memo)
2. ¿Compran el vino Domingo y Toni? (Manolo y Juan)
3. ¿Va a preparar las ensaladas Dora? (Leonor)
4. ¿Traerá el bate y la pelota Jorge? (Miguel)
5. ¿Piensa llevar las servilletas Carmen? (Marcos)
6. ¿Harán los bocadillos Uds.? (Olivia y Nacho)
7. ¿Sirven las tortas ellos? (tú)
8. ¿Quiere comprar la fruta Mari? (yo)

Questions in Indirect Speech

When a question is not asked directly, but is incorporated into a larger sentence as a dependent clause, it is called an indirect question. Compare the following examples. The first one has a question quoted directly, the second one has the same question reported indirectly by being incorporated into a larger sentence.

> *She asked me, "Where is the post office?"*
> *She asked me where the post office was.*

Information questions are turned into indirect questions as subordinate clauses. The question word retains its accent mark.

Me preguntaron: —¿De dónde vienes?	*They asked me, "Where are you coming from?"*
Me preguntaron de dónde venía.	*They asked me where I was coming from.*
Te pregunté: —¿Cuándo regresarás?	*I asked you, "When will you return?"*
Te pregunté cuándo regresarías.	*I asked you when you would return.*
Siempre nos preguntan: —¿Qué quieren?	*They always ask us, "What do you want?"*
Siempre nos preguntan qué queremos.	*They always ask us what we want.*

Yes/no questions are turned into indirect questions by means of the word **si** (*whether, if*).

DIRECT QUESTION	INDIRECT QUESTION
¿Sales, Juan?	Le pregunté a Juan si salía.
Are you going out, Juan?	*I asked Juan if he was going out.*

If **preguntar** is in the present or future, then the tense of the original question is kept in the indirect question.

DIRECT QUESTION	INDIRECT QUESTION
Me pregunta —¿Para qué lo haces?	Me pregunta para qué lo hago.
He asks me, "Why do you do it?	*He asks me why I do it.*
Nos pregunta —¿Cuándo vendrá Marta?	Nos pregunta cuándo vendrá Marta.
He asks us, "When will Marta come?"	*He asks us when Marta will come.*
Me preguntará —¿Quiénes regresaron?	Me preguntará quiénes regresaron.
She will ask me, "Who returned?"	*She will ask me who returned.*

However, if the verb in the main clause of the indirect question (**preguntar**) is in the preterit, the tense of the original direct question changes in the indirect question.

DIRECT QUESTION		INDIRECT QUESTION
PRESENT ¿Para qué lo haces?	→ IMPERFECT	Me preguntó para qué lo hacía.
FUTURE ¿Cuándo vendrá Marta?	→ CONDITIONAL	Me preguntó cuándo vendría Marta.
PRETERIT ¿Quiénes regresaron?	→ PLUPERFECT	Me preguntó quiénes habían regresado.
	OR → PRETERIT	Me preguntó quiénes regresaron.

N ***¡Cuántas preguntas!*** *Unas personas le machacaron los oídos* (repeated over and over again) *con tantas preguntas hoy que Ud. se encuentra mareado/mareada* (dizzy). *Ahora Ud. le cuenta a un amigo lo que le preguntaron usando la pregunta indirecta. Siga el modelo.*

> MODELO Anita me preguntó: —¿Adónde vas?
> → Anita me preguntó adónde iba.

1. Felipe me preguntó: —¿Qué harás en la tarde?

2. Isabel me preguntó: —¿Con quiénes saliste?

3. Carlos me preguntó: —¿Por qué no quieres jugar al baloncesto?

4. Sol me preguntó: —¿A qué hora volviste a casa?

5. Claudio me preguntó: —¿Para cuándo necesitas escribir el informe?

6. Mi hermana me preguntó: —¿Cuándo me llevas a una discoteca?

7. Mis colegas me preguntaron: —¿Por qué no nos invitas a tomar una copa?

8. El director me preguntó: —¿Quién hizo el presupuesto (*budget*)?

9. Yo me pregunté a mí mismo: —¿Por qué te levantaste de la cama?

O ***Ejercicio oral: Una adivinanza*** (**Guessing game**). *Ud. piensa en una persona, una cosa o un acontecimiento histórico. Sus amigos tienen que hacerle preguntas hasta adivinar en qué piensa. Le toca a la persona que lo adivine pensar en otra persona, cosa o acontecimiento.*

Negative and Indefinite Words

Negative Words and Expressions

Study the following list of Spanish negative words and expressions and their affirmative counterparts.

nunca, jamás *never*	alguna vez *sometime*
	algunas veces *sometimes*
	a veces *sometimes*
	muchas veces *often*
	a menudo *often*
	siempre *always*
nunca más *never again*	otra vez *again*
nada *nothing*	algo *something*
nadie *no one, nobody*	alguien *someone, somebody*
tampoco *neither, not either*	también *also*
ni *not even*	o *or*
ni siquiera *not even*	o *or*
ni... ni *neither . . . nor*	o... o *either . . . or*
en/por ninguna parte *nowhere*	en/por alguna parte *somewhere*
en/por ningún lado/sitio/lugar *nowhere*	en/por algún lado/sitio/lugar *somewhere*
ya no *no longer*	todavía *still*
de ninguna manera *in no way*	de alguna manera *somehow, in some way*
de ningún modo *in no way*	de algún modo *somehow, in some way*

Spanish also has negative and affirmative adjectives: **ninguno** (*no, not a*) and **alguno** (*some*). **Ninguno** and **alguno** are shortened to **ningún** and **algún** before a masculine singular noun.

Laura trabaja en **algún** edificio del centro.	*Laura works in some building downtown.*
Mercedes trabaja en **alguna** oficina.	*Mercedes works in some office.*
Hay **algunos** anuncios en el periódico.	*There are some ads in the newspaper.*
Conozco **algunas** tiendas elegantes por aquí.	*I know some elegant stores around here.*

Ninguno is not used in the plural unless the noun it modifies is always used in the plural such as **anteojos, tijeras,** or **vacaciones**.

No hay **ningún** hospital aquí.	*There is no hospital here. (There are no hospitals here.)*
No recibí **ninguna** respuesta.	*I didn't receive any answer.*
Este año no tenemos **ningunas** vacaciones.	*This year we don't have any vacation.*

When negative words follow the verb, **no** precedes it.

—**No** hice **nada** hoy.	*I didn't do anything today.*
—Catalina **no** hizo **nada tampoco**.	*Catalina didn't do anything either.*
No vamos **nunca** a esquiar.	*We never go skiing.*

However, if a negative word precedes the verb, then **no** is not used.

—**Nunca** voy al cine.	*I never go to the movies.*
—Yo **tampoco** voy mucho.	*I don't go much either.*

Personal **a** is used before **alguien** and **nadie** when they are direct objects and also before forms of **alguno** and **ninguno** when they refer to people and are direct objects.

—¿Viste **a alguien** en la plaza?	*Did you see anyone in the square?*
—No, no vi **a nadie**.	*No, I didn't see anyone.*
—¿Invitaste **a alguno** de los vecinos?	*Did you invite any of the neighbors?*
—No, no llamé **a ninguno**.	*No, I didn't call any (of them).*

When words joined by **o… o** are the subject of a sentence, the verb is usually singular. The first **o** can be omitted. When words joined by **ni… ni** are the subject of a sentence, the verb generally appears in the plural. In usage, **ni… ni** used with a singular verb is also possible, especially when the verb precedes the subject.

Vio la película **o Esteban o Elena**.	*Either Esteban or Elena saw the film.*
Él o ella estacionó el coche.	*Either he or she parked the car.*
Ni él ni ella salieron.	*Neither he nor she went out.*
No me llamaron **ni Claudia ni Felipe**.	*Neither Claudia nor Felipe called me.*
No dijo nada **ni él ni ella**.	*Neither he nor she said anything.*

A single **ni** means *not even*. **Ni siquiera** is a more emphatic form.

—¿Cuántos asistieron a la reunión?	*How many attended the meeting?*
—**Ni siquiera** uno.	*Not even one.*
—¿Te ofrecieron algo?	*Did they offer you anything?*
—**Ni** un vaso de agua.	*Not even a glass of water.*

A **¡No!** *Conteste las preguntas negativamente usando* **no** *y las palabras negativas que corresponden a las afirmativas. Siga el modelo.*

MODELO   ¿Quieres tomar *algo*?
→ No, no quiero tomar nada.

1. ¿Fuiste *alguna vez* a la Isla de Pascua?

2. ¿Aprendieron Uds. chino *también*?

3. *¿Alguien* ha llamado esta tarde?

4. ¿Va Isabel a tomar álgebra *otra vez*?

5. ¿Leerás *o* la novela *o* el guión de la película?

6. *¿Algunos* jefes renunciaron al puesto?

7. ¿Conoció Osvaldo *a alguien* por fin?

8. ¿Quedan *algunos* duraznos?

9. *¿Siempre* limpias la casa los sábados?

10. ¿Has visto *a alguna* de las empleadas?

NOTA CULTURAL

La Isla de Pascua (*Easter Island*) queda en el océano Pacífico a unas 2.300 millas de Valparaíso. Este territorio chileno es uno de los lugares más remotos y de condiciones ambientales más severas del mundo. La isla es conocida por sus enormes estatuas de piedra volcánica que fueron construidas por gente de origen polinesio. La isla se llamaba Rapa Nui en la lengua de la isla que es un idioma de la familia polinesia. Se cree que estas casi mil estatuas religiosas datan de entre 1100 y 1650. Se encuentran en el Parque Nacional Rapa Nui que ocupa más del 40% de la isla. En octubre de 2022 estalló un incendio en la isla que causó daños irreparables a numerosas estatuas de este sitio arqueológico.

B *Angustias, la aguafiestas* **(the party pooper).** *Angustias lo ve todo negro, es decir, es muy pesimista. Lea sus comentarios sobre una fiesta, cambiando la posición de la palabra negativa. Siga el modelo.*

MODELO   Nadie se divierte.
→ No se divierte nadie.

1. Nada queda de la comida.

2. Tampoco hay refrescos.

3. Ni los chicos ni las chicas bailan.

4. Ninguno de los chicos se acerca para hablarme.

5. Ningún cantante canta bien.

6. Nadie tiene ganas de quedarse.

7. Nunca dan fiestas divertidas.

¡Qué iluso (dreamer)! *Humberto pasa la vida soñando... pero son mirlos blancos (impossible dreams) (mirlo = blackbird). Necesita un chequeo de la realidad. Escriba oraciones usando las palabras negativas apropiadas. Siga el modelo.*

MODELO   Siempre gano becas.
     → ¡Qué va! Nunca ganas becas.
     o ¡Qué va! Jamás ganas becas.

1. Alguien me regaló dos millones de dólares.

2. Algunas chicas dicen que soy un Adonis.

3. Muchas veces saco un diez en mis exámenes.

4. Los reyes de España me mandaron algo.

5. Yo también voy a la luna.

6. Conchita va a salir conmigo otra vez.

7. Mis padres me van a regalar un Rolls-Royce y un Lamborghini.

Other Uses of Negative Words

Spanish, unlike English, allows two or more negative words in a sentence.

Nadie trae **nada nunca.**	*Nobody ever brings anything.*

Alguno can have an emphatic negative meaning when placed after the noun.

No hay problema **alguno.**	*There is no problem at all.*
No recibimos carta **alguna.**	*We received no letter at all.*

In Spanish, negative words are used in certain constructions where English uses indefinite words.

Spanish uses negatives after **que** (*than*) in comparative sentences.

—La lluvia fue peor **que nada.**	*The rain was worse than anything.*
—Sí, y yo me mojé más **que nadie.**	*Yes, and I got wetter than anyone.*
—Lo que es la guerra lo sabe este país mejor **que ningún otro.**	*This country knows better than any other what war is.*
—El pueblo ha sufrido más aquí **que en ningún otro lugar.**	*The people have suffered more here than anywhere else.*
—Hoy habló el profesor mejor **que nunca.**	*Today the teacher spoke better than ever.*
—Y aprendimos más **que en ningún otro momento.**	*And we learned more than at any other time.*

Spanish uses negatives after **antes de**, **antes que**, and **sin**.

Antes de hacer **nada**, lee las instrucciones.	*Before doing anything, read the instructions.*
Has llegado **antes que nadie.**	*You've arrived before anyone else.*
Lo hizo **sin** pedir **nada a nadie nunca.**	*He did it without ever asking anything of anyone.*

Spanish uses negatives after **imposible**, **inútil**, **poco probable**, expressions of doubt, and other similar words that imply negation.

Es **imposible** hacer **nada** aquí.	*It's impossible to do anything here.*
Es **inútil** pedirle **nada**.	*It's useless to ask him for anything.*
Dudo que venga **nadie**.	*I doubt that anyone will come.*

The conjunction **pero** is replaced by **sino** after a negative clause.

| No viene ella, **sino** él. | *Not she, but he, is coming.* |

Note also **no solamente/sólo/solo... sino también** *not only . . . but also.*

| **No solamente** viene ella, **sino** también él. | ***Not only*** *is she coming,* ***but*** *he is too.* |

D *Hay que ser negativo.* *Complete las oraciones con las expresiones negativas o indefinidas apropiadas. Véase "Negative and Indefinite Words in Idiomatic Expressions" en este capítulo.*

1. Es imposible decirle _____ a este chiquillo porque no le hace caso a _____.

2. ¡_____ he oído tantas barbaridades!

3. El programa no fue _____ bueno, pero los locutores sí fueron _____ interesantes.

4. ¿No probaste la sopa? Y salió mejor que _____.

5. No sólo visitamos Córdoba, _____ nos quedamos ocho días en Granada.

6. Aunque Diego y yo nos conocimos hace un año es como si él no me conociera _____.

7. ¡Qué señora más distinguida! Será _____.

8. ¡Ay, sus cuentos tan largos y siempre con los mismos temas! Son los cuentos de _____.

9. Maribel es tan torpe; no sabe nada _____.

10. Mauricio es siempre el primero en llegar. Llega antes que _____.

11. —¿Vino Alicia Delgado?

    —Sí, y _____ ella, _____ su hermano Francisco.

12. Muchos dicen que Toledo es más interesante por su arte e historia que _____ otra ciudad española.

NOTA CULTURAL

- **Córdoba** es una pintoresca ciudad andaluza que queda a orillas del río Guadalquivir. Sus monumentos más importantes incluyen la catedral (que era mezquita (*mosque*)), el Alcázar (fortaleza y palacio real) y un puente romano sobre el Guadalquivir. Durante la Edad Media las artes y las ciencias florecieron en Córdoba. Allí nacieron tres grandes filósofos: el estoico romano Séneca, el judío Maimónides y el musulmán Averroes.

- **Granada**, otra hermosa ciudad andaluza, queda al pie de la Sierra Nevada. Algunos monumentos que destacan son la Alhambra (el palacio de los reyes moros), el palacio de Carlos V, la Catedral y el Generalife (el palacio y jardines de los reyes moros). Granada, la última defensa de los moros en España, fue conquistada por los Reyes Católicos en 1492.
- **Toledo**, una gran ciudad rica en historia y arte, queda al sur de Madrid a orillas del río Tajo. Entre los monumentos más impresionantes se destacan la catedral gótica, Santa María la Blanca (la sinagoga Ben Shoshan, contruida en 1180); la iglesia de Santo Tomé donde se ve la pintura más famosa de El Greco, *El entierro del Conde de Orgaz*; la sinagoga de El Tránsito (la sinagoga de Samuel Halevi, construida en 1357; hoy el Museo Sefardí) y la casa de El Greco. Este gran pintor que nació en Creta en 1541 (o 1542) vivió muchos años en Toledo y murió allí en 1614. Su obra fue profundamente inspirada por Toledo. Se puede ver su obra maestra *Vista de Toledo* expuesta en el Museo Metropolitano de Nueva York.

Negative Words in Conversation

Negative words frequently serve as one-word answers to questions.

—¿Vas a menudo al café estudiantil?	*Do you often go to the student café?*
—**Nunca.**	*Never.*
—¿Quién te ayudó con el trabajo?	*Who helped you with the work?*
—**Nadie.**	*Nobody.*

Negative words, including **no**, often appear with subject pronouns or with phrases consisting of **a** + prepositional pronoun as short answers to questions.

—¿Cursan tú y Carla español?	*Are you and Carla taking Spanish?*
—Yo, sí. **Ella, no.**	*I am. She's not.*
—No voy a la conferencia hoy. ¿Y tú?	*I'm not going to the lecture today. What about you?*
—**Yo tampoco.**	*Neither am I.*
—A mí no me gusta este plato.	*I don't like this dish.*
—**A nosotros tampoco.**	*We don't either.*
—A mí siempre me escriben.	*People are always writing to me.*
—**A nosotros nunca.**	*Never to us.*

Some non-negative expressions such as **en absoluto** and **en la vida** can function as negatives.

—**En la vida** he visto un espectáculo tan bueno.	*I have never in my life seen such a good show.*
—Yo tampoco.	*Neither have I.*
—¿Contrataría Ud. a ese analista?	*Would you hire that analyst?*
—**En absoluto.**	*Absolutely not.*

Algo and **nada** can function as adverbs and modify adjectives and verbs.

—El discurso fue **algo** confuso.	*The speech was somewhat confusing.*
—Y no fue **nada** interesante.	*And it wasn't at all interesting.*
—Tomás trabaja **algo**.	*Tomás works a little.*
—Pero no se concentra **nada**.	*But he doesn't concentrate at all.*

Para nada is an emphatic replacement for **nada**: **No se concentra para nada.**

Algo de and **nada de** are used before nouns.

—¿Quieres **algo de** chocolate?	*Do you want a little chocolate?*
—No, no debo comer **nada de** dulces.	*No, I'm not supposed to eat any sweets.*

Algo de is a synonym for **un poco de**.

Negative and Indefinite Words in Idiomatic Expressions

Nunca and jamás

casi nunca	*hardly ever*
el cuento de nunca acabar	*the never-ending story*
jamás de los jamases	*never ever*
nunca jamás	*never ever*
nunca más	*never again, no more*
¡Hasta nunca!	*Good-bye forever!*

Ni

ni hablar	*nothing doing*
ni modo	*nothing doing*
Ni lo pienses.	*Don't even think about it.*
No lo puedo ver ni en pintura.	*I can't stand him at all.*
No tengo ni idea.	*I haven't the slightest idea.*

Nada

antes de nada	*first of all*
casi nada	*hardly*
como si nada	*as if it were nothing at all*
dentro de nada	*in a moment*
más que nada	*more than anything*
nada de eso	*nothing of the sort*
nada de extraordinario	*nothing unusual*
nada de nada	*nothing at all*
nada más	*that's all*
no servir para nada	*to be useless*
no tener nada de + *noun*	*to not have (to have no) _____ at all*
no tener nada de particular	*to have nothing special about*
por nada del mundo	*for nothing in the world*
quedarse en nada	*to come to nothing*
tener en nada	*to think very little of; to take no notice of*
No por nada vendimos la casa.	*We had good reason to sell the house.*
No por nada lo llaman "tonto".	*They don't call him "foolish" for nothing.*

¡De eso nada, monada! (*slang*)	*None of that! / No way!*
De nada.	*You're welcome. / Don't mention it.*
Por nada.	*You're welcome. / Don't mention it.*
¡Nada de salir antes de terminar la tarea!	*Forget about going out before you finish your homework!*
No me conoce de nada.	*He doesn't know me from Adam.*

Nadie

nadie más	*nobody else*
Es un don nadie.	*He's a nobody.*
Tú no eres nadie para quejarte.	*You have no right to complain.*

Expressions with Indefinite Words

algo así	*something like that*
tener algo que ver con	*to have something to do with*
ser alguien	*to be somebody*
Algo es algo.	*Something is better than nothing.*
Más vale algo que nada.	*Something is better than nothing.*
Ya es algo.	*That's something at least. / It's a start.*
¡Por algo será!	*There must be a reason.*
De algo lo conozco.	*I know you from somewhere.*
Nos vemos a la hora de siempre.	*We'll see each other at the usual time.*
Es lo de siempre.	*It's the same old story.*
Para siempre.	*Forever.*

E   ***¿Cómo se dice eso en inglés?*** *Exprese las oraciones en inglés. Tenga en cuenta especialmente las expresiones con palabras negativas e indefinidas.*

1. No la puedo ver ni en pintura.

2. De algo la conozco.

3. Van a verse a la hora de siempre.

4. No por nada la llaman encantadora.

5. Si Isabel te dijo eso por algo será.

6. Todo el tiempo y todos los planes se quedaron en nada.

7. Al fin y al cabo todo el discutir no sirvió para nada.

8. Lo que dices no tiene nada que ver con la situación actual.

F   ***¿Algo? ¿Nada? ¿Nunca?*** *Indique cuál de las expresiones con* **nunca, jamás, algo, nada** *o una palabra indefinida corresponde a cada oración.*

1. Eso es inútil.
   a. No sirve para nada.
   b. Por nada del mundo.

2. ¿Ir al cine? ¡Ni hablar!
   a. Algo es algo.
   b. ¡Nada de salir!

3. Es lo de siempre.
   a. Nunca jamás.
   b. Nada de extraordinario.

4. X está relacionado con Y.
   a. X tiene algo que ver con Y.
   b. X se queda en nada.

5. No volveremos a vernos.
   a. Nos veremos más que nunca.
   b. Nunca más nos veremos.

6. Se le acabó la paciencia.
   a. No tiene nada de paciencia.
   b. Más vale algo que nada.

7. Camilo tendrá algún motivo.
   a. Por algo será.
   b. Por nada.

8. Van poco a ese café.
   a. Como si nada.
   b. Casi nunca.

9. Olga vuelve muy pronto.
   a. Dentro de nada.
   b. Antes de nada.

10. Nos queremos toda la vida.
    a. Jamás de los jamases.
    b. Para siempre.

Other Indefinite Words and Constructions

The pronoun **cualquiera** means *anyone* or *any one* and can refer to people or things.

—¿Cuál de los dos pasteles quieres?	*Which of the two pastries do you want?*
—**Cualquiera** de los dos.	*Any one (either one) of the two.*
—**No cualquiera** podría hacer esto.	*Not just anyone would be able to do this.*
—Al contrario. **Cualquiera** lo habría hecho mucho mejor.	*On the contrary. Anyone would have done it much better.*

Note also the idiomatic use of **cualquiera** as a noun: **Él es un cualquiera.** (*He's a nobody.*)

When used as an adjective, **cualquiera** becomes **cualquier.**

El tren puede llegar en **cualquier** momento.	*The train can arrive at any moment.*
La vida es más fácil en **cualquier** otro lugar.	*Life is easier anywhere else.*
Está contento con **cualquier** cosa.	*He's happy with anything.*

Spanish also indicates "indefiniteness" by the subjunctive. English often uses *whatever* or *wherever* in these cases. Compare the following pairs of sentences.

Lee el libro que recomiendan.	*Read the book that they recommend.* (INDICATIVE: speaker knows which book it is)
Lee el libro que **recomienden**.	*Read whatever book they recommend.* (SUBJUNCTIVE: speaker does not know which book it is)
Haga lo que quiere.	*Do what you want.* (INDICATIVE: we already know what you want to do)
Haga lo que **quiera**.	*Do whatever you want.* (SUBJUNCTIVE: we don't yet know what you want to do)

Todo is usually followed by the definite article and noun.

por **todo el** país	*throughout the whole country*
toda la casa	*the whole house*
todos los músicos	*all the musicians*
todas las calles	*every street*

Todo followed by the indefinite article means *quite the, a real,* or *just like a.*

Él es **todo un** cocinero.	*He's quite the cook.*
Ella es **toda una** reina.	*She's just like a queen.*

When **todo** is followed directly by a singular noun, it means *every* or *any.*

Todo estudiante tiene computadora.	*Every student has a computer.*
Nos sirvieron **toda clase** de pescado.	*They served us every kind of fish.*
Todo jugo de fruta es bueno.	*Any fruit juice is good.*

Note also the use of **todo** with place names.

Hay paradores por **toda España**.	*There are government inns all over Spain.*
En casi **todo Santiago** hay servicio de metro.	*The subway serves almost all of Santiago.*

Todo can also be used as a pronoun or in pronominal phrases.

Todo es interesante en los Estados Unidos.	*Everything is interesting in the U.S.* (**Todo** takes a singular verb.)
Todos son amables.	*Everyone is nice.* (**Todos** takes a plural verb.)
Todo el mundo trata de ayudar.	*Everyone/Everybody tries to help.* (**Todo el mundo** takes a singular verb.)

G *Expresar en español.* *Exprese las oraciones en español. Tenga en cuenta especialmente las expresiones con palabras negativas o indefinidas.*

1. He had good reason to quit his job.

2. They'll call at any moment.

3. We walked the whole day through the whole city.

4. Anyone could help us with the work.

5. Every avenue is blocked during rush hour.

6. There are Roman ruins all over Spain.

NOTA CULTURAL

Las ruinas romanas—Los romanos llegaron a la península ibérica en los primeros años del siglo II a.C. A lo largo de siete siglos, lograron unificar la península ibérica a través de su lengua (el latín) y su administración. Le pusieron el nombre Hispania a la península, nombre del cual deriva «España». Los romanos construyeron impresionantes obras públicas que han durado por siglos— acueductos, puentes, caminos, anfiteatros y arcos de triunfo, algunos de los cuales se han conservado en Sevilla, Córdoba, Tarragona y otros sitios. El imponente acueducto de Segovia, obra maestra de la ingeniería romana, fue construido sin argamasa (*mortar*) a principios del siglo II d.C.

H *Expresar en español.* **Finales dramáticos o Lo que el viento se llevó** (Gone with the Wind). *Le toca a Ud. como guionista (scriptwriter) escribir las últimas palabras de unas películas. Escríbalas en español. Tenga en cuenta las expresiones con palabras negativas e indefinidas.*

1. Although I'll love you forever, I must say, "good-bye forever!"

2. Something is better than nothing.

3. Forget (tú) about going to Mars before you graduate!

4. And here ends the never-ending story!

5. I know you (Ud.) from somewhere. You must be somebody.

6. Do (tú) whatever you want! Go wherever you want! I shall never ever forget you!

7. This ending? That ending? I'm happy with either one!

8. That's all. Tomorrow is another day!

I *Ejercicio oral.* *Usted afirma algo. Su amigo/amiga contesta haciendo negativa la afirmación. Después, se hace al inverso, es decir, uno de Uds. dice algo usando palabras o expresiones negativas y el otro contesta con una respuesta afirmativa.*

Numbers; Dates; Time

Cardinal Numbers

Cardinal numbers are used for counting. Here are the Spanish cardinal numbers from 1 to 99.

0 cero	10 diez	20 veinte
1 uno (una)	11 once	21 veintiuno (-una)
2 dos	12 doce	22 veintidós
3 tres	13 trece	23 veintitrés
4 cuatro	14 catorce	24 veinticuatro
5 cinco	15 quince	25 veinticinco
6 seis	16 dieciséis	26 veintiséis
7 siete	17 diecisiete	27 veintisiete
8 ocho	18 dieciocho	28 veintiocho
9 nueve	19 diecinueve	29 veintinueve
30 treinta	40 cuarenta	70 setenta
31 treinta y uno (una)	50 cincuenta	80 ochenta
32 treinta y dos	60 sesenta	90 noventa

Numbers ending in *one* agree in gender with the following noun. **Uno** shortens to **un** before a masculine noun. The number **veintiún** has a written accent in the masculine.

veintiún libros	*21 books*
veintiuna revistas	*21 magazines*
cincuenta y un estudiantes	*51 students*
cincuenta y una profesoras	*51 female teachers*

Una also shortens to **un** before a noun beginning with a stressed **a** sound.

un águila	*one eagle*
veintiún aulas	*21 lecture halls*
cuarenta y un hachas	*41 axes*

Numbers ending in **-uno** are used in counting and when no masculine noun follows directly.

—¿Cuánto es? ¿Treinta y dos dólares?	*How much is it? 32 dollars?*
—No, treinta y uno.	*No, 31.*

The numbers from 16 to 19 and from 21 to 29 can be written as three words: **diez y seis,
diez y siete, diez y ocho, diez y nueve, veinte y uno (una), veinte y dos, veinte y tres.**
No accent marks are used when these numbers are spelled as three words. Compare
veintiséis and **veinte y seis.**

Here are the Spanish numbers from 100 to 999.

100	cien	400	cuatrocientos/cuatrocientas
101	ciento uno (una)	500	quinientos/quinientas
110	ciento diez	600	seiscientos/seiscientas
167	ciento sesenta y siete	700	setecientos/setecientas
200	doscientos/doscientas	800	ochocientos/ochocientas
300	trescientos/trescientas	900	novecientos/novecientas

NOTES

1 · **Cien** becomes **ciento** before another number: **ciento sesenta** (*160*).

2 · Spanish does not use **y** to connect hundreds to the following number the way English
may use *and*: **doscientos cuarenta** (*two hundred **and** forty*).

3 · The hundreds from 200 to 900 agree in gender with the noun they modify. This
agreement takes place even when other numbers come between the hundreds and
the noun.

doscient**os** edificios	*two hundred buildings*
doscient**as** casas	*two hundred houses*
doscient**as** treinta y cuatro casas	*two hundred thirty-four houses*

Here are the numbers above 1,000.

1.000	mil	100.000	cien mil
2.000	dos mil	250.000	doscientos cincuenta mil
6.572	seis mil quinientos setenta y dos	1.000.000	un millón
10.000	diez mil	2.000.000	dos millones

NOTES

1 · Numerals ending in **-cientos** agree across the word **mil**: **seiscient*as* cincuenta mil
empresas.**

2 · Some Spanish-speaking countries use the period to separate thousands in writing
numbers and the comma as a decimal point: $7.560 = **siete mil quinientos sesenta
dólares**; $7,50 = **siete dólares cincuenta centavos.**

3 · Spanish does not count by hundreds above 1,000. Thus, *seventeen hundred* must be
rendered **mil setecientos**, *thirty-two hundred* as **tres mil doscientos.**

4 · **Millón** is a noun and is followed by **de** when it appears before another noun unless
another number comes between **millón** and the noun that follows it: **un millón de
euros; dos millones de euros; un millón doscientos mil euros.**

5 · *A billion* in Spanish is **mil millones**. **Un billón** means *a trillion*.

6 · Traditionally, the Spanish word **o** (*or*) was written **ó** between numerical figures to avoid confusion with zero: **5 ó 6**. This rule has recently been abolished.

A   ***Para hacer un inventario.*** *Ud. trabaja de empleado/empleada de tiempo parcial en una tienda de útiles de oficina* (office supplies store). *Hoy le toca hacer el inventario de las existencias* (stock). *Escriba los números con letras. Siga el modelo.*

MODELO   escritorios / 386
           → trescientos ochenta y seis escritorios

Los útiles de oficina
el bolígrafo *ballpoint pen*
la caja *box*
el calendario *calendar*
la cámara digital *digital camera*
el cartucho de tinta *ink cartridge*
el escritorio *desk*
la etiqueta *label*
las existencias *stock*
la goma *rubber band*
la grapa *staple*
la grapadora *stapler*
hacer un inventario *to take inventory*
la impresora *printer*
el lápiz *pencil*
la pluma *pen*
el rotulador *marker*
el sobre *envelope*
los sujetapapeles *paper clips*
el (teléfono) celular *cell phone*
tiempo completo *full-time*
tiempo parcial *part-time*

1. grapadoras / 100

2. teléfonos celulares / 1.821

3. rotuladores, plumas y bolígrafos / 1.549

4. cajas de gomas, grapas y sujetapapeles / 751

5. cartuchos de tinta / 467

6. calendarios y lápices / 909

7. sobres y etiquetas / 1.000

8. cámaras digitales / 1.381

B *La entrada de datos* (**Data entry**). *Ud. es analista que se encarga de entrar en una base de datos el número de habitantes y el de usuarios de Internet de algunos países hispanohablantes. Las cifras son de 2021. Convierta los números a letras. Véase* https://en.wikipedia.org/wiki/List_of_countries_by_number_of_Internet_users.

País	Habitantes		Usuarios de Internet	
1. España	47,486,935	_____	42,400,756	_____
2. México	128,972,439	_____	92,010,000	_____
3. Panamá	4,351,267	_____	2,371,852	_____
4. Costa Rica	5,153,957	_____	3,511,549	_____
5. Guatemala	17,608,483	_____	11,750,000	_____
6. Puerto Rico	3,256,028	_____	2,664,928	_____
7. La República Dominicana	11,117,873	_____	6,997,472	_____
8. Colombia	51,516,562	_____	30,548,252	_____
9. Argentina	45,276,780	_____	33,561,876	_____
10. Uruguay	3,426,260	_____	2,360,269	_____
11. Chile	19,493,184	_____	14,864,456	_____
12. Perú	33,715,471	_____	15,674,241	_____

Ordinal Numbers

Ordinal numbers are used for ranking (*first, second, third*). In conversation, usually only the ordinal numbers through *tenth* are used. Spanish ordinal numbers are adjectives that agree with the noun they modify in gender and number.

primero	*first*	sexto	*sixth*
segundo	*second*	séptimo	*seventh*
tercero	*third*	octavo	*eighth*
cuarto	*fourth*	noveno	*ninth*
quinto	*fifth*	décimo	*tenth*

Ordinal numbers usually precede the noun. **Primero** and **tercero** become **primer** and **tercer** before a masculine singular noun.

el **primer** día	*the first day*
la **segunda** hija	*the second daughter*
el **tercer** capítulo	*the third chapter*
la **séptima** sinfonía	*the seventh symphony*

Ordinals often follow nouns such as **siglo** and the names of kings and queens. The definite article is not used after names of royalty.

el siglo segundo	*the second century*
Carlos Quinto	*Charles the Fifth*

Above *tenth*, Spanish generally uses the cardinal numbers after the noun instead of the ordinals. Sometimes the cardinal numbers are used even below *tenth*.

Vive en el piso quince.	*He lives on the fifteenth floor.*
Vamos a leer el capítulo tres.	*We're going to read the third chapter.*

Ordinals are abbreviated in various ways in Spanish: **1ᵉʳ, 1ᵉʳᵃ, 1º, 2ª, 3ʳᵒ, 5ᵗᵒ, 7ᵐᵃ, 8º**.

C ***Todos juntos en los Estados Unidos.*** *Alberto y un grupo de amigos chilenos están en los Estados Unidos para estudiar inglés durante el verano. Todos viven en la misma residencia. Alberto les escribe a sus padres y les dice en qué piso vive cada uno de sus amigos. Escriba oraciones usando números ordinales y cardinales. Siga el modelo.*

MODELO   Ramón / 6
→ Ramón vive en el sexto piso.

1. Silvia y Adela / 12	5. Ana María / 10
2. Carlos / 5	6. Patricio / 4
3. yo / 1	7. Lucía / 3
4. José Miguel / 9	8. Daniela / 14

Days, Dates, and Years

The days of the week and the months of the year are not capitalized in Spanish. Note that the Hispanic week begins with Monday.

Days of the Week

lunes	*Monday*
martes	*Tuesday*
miércoles	*Wednesday*
jueves	*Thursday*
viernes	*Friday*
sábado	*Saturday*
domingo	*Sunday*

Months of the Year

enero	*January*	julio	*July*
febrero	*February*	agosto	*August*
marzo	*March*	septiembre	*September*
abril	*April*	octubre	*October*
mayo	*May*	noviembre	*November*
junio	*June*	diciembre	*December*

Seasons

la primavera	*spring*
el verano	*summer*
el otoño	*fall, autumn*
el invierno	*winter*

Expressions for Situating Events in Time

al cabo de un año	*a year later*
al día siguiente	*the next day*
de hoy en ocho días	*a week from now, a week from today*
ayer	*yesterday*
anteayer	*the day before yesterday*
mañana	*tomorrow*
pasado mañana	*the day after tomorrow*
pasando un día	*every other day*
un día de por medio	*every other day*
la semana pasada/próxima	*last/next week*
el mes pasado/próximo	*last/next month*
el año pasado/próximo	*last/next year*
la semana/el mes/el año que viene	*next week/month/year*
la próxima vez	*next time*
la vez pasada	*last time*
A los diez minutos se fue.	*After ten minutes she left.*
Nos vimos el martes pasado.	*We saw each other last Tuesday.*
Nos veremos el próximo martes.	*We'll see each other next Tuesday.*

In Spanish, there are several patterns for using the preceding words in expressions of time.

1 · The singular definite article **el** means *on* before the days of the week.

Nos vamos **el** lunes.	*We're leaving on Monday.*

2 · The plural definite article **los** indicates repeated action or regular occurrence.

Van a la iglesia **los** domingos.	*They go to church on Sundays.*

3 · The preposition **en** is used before months of the year and the names of the seasons: **en enero**, **en otoño**. The definite article is sometimes used after **en** with the names of the seasons: **en la primavera**.

To express dates, Spanish uses cardinal numbers, except for **el primero** (some speakers say **el uno**). The definite article **el** precedes the date. The order is day-month-year and the preposition **de** is placed before the month and also the year, if it is given. Note that as with days of the week, no preposition is used for *on*.

—Creía que tus primos llegaban el treinta de noviembre.	*I thought your cousins were arriving on November thirtieth.*
—No, vienen el primero de diciembre.	*No, they're coming December first.*

NOTES

1 · The definite article **el** in dates is usually left out after the day of the week: **martes, 5 de mayo**.

2 · When abbreviating dates, the Spanish order day-month-year is used. Roman numerals are often used for the month: **16-XI-28, el dieciséis de noviembre de dos mil veintiocho**.

3 · As in English, the last two numbers are often used in speech to express the years of the century. In this case, the definite article **el** precedes the year.

Llegamos a los Estados Unidos en el '23.   *We arrived in the United States in 2023.*

Here are some useful expressions for talking about the days and dates or that use the days and months in idiomatic ways.

¿Cuál es la fecha de hoy?	*What's today's date?*
¿Qué fecha es hoy?	*What's today's date?*
¿A cuántos estamos hoy?	*What's today's date?*
Es el primero de junio.	*It's June first.*
Estamos a diez de octubre.	*It's October tenth.*
¿Qué día es hoy?	*What day is today?*
Hoy es jueves.	*Today is Thursday.*
a principios de marzo	*at the beginning of March*
a mediados de julio	*in the middle of July*
a fines de/a finales de septiembre	*at the end of September*
No es cosa del otro jueves.	*It's nothing special.*
martes trece	*Tuesday the 13th* (equivalent of Friday the 13th)

D *El Premio Nobel. Once escritores hispanohablantes han recibido el Premio Nobel de literatura desde que el premio fue otorgado (awarded) por primera vez en 1901. Aquí tiene Ud. una lista de los once galardonados (prize winners) con el año del premio y las fechas de nacimiento y muerte. Escriba los números con letras.*

1. Mario Vargas Llosa (Perú, España)

    Premio Nobel: 2010 _____

    nacimiento: 1936 _____

2. Octavio Paz (México)

    Premio Nobel: 1990 _____

    nacimiento: 1914 _____

    muerte: 1998 _____

3. Camilo José Cela (España)

    Premio Nobel: 1989 _____

    nacimiento: 1916 _____

    muerte: 2002 _____

4. Gabriel García Márquez (Colombia)

    Premio Nobel: 1982 _____

    nacimiento: 1928 _____

    muerte: 2014 _____

5. Vicente Aleixandre (España)

    Premio Nobel: 1977   _____

    nacimiento: 1898   _____

    muerte: 1984   _____

6. Pablo Neruda (Chile)

    Premio Nobel: 1971   _____

    nacimiento: 1904   _____

    muerte: 1973   _____

7. Miguel Ángel Asturias (Guatemala)

    Premio Nobel: 1967   _____

    nacimiento: 1899   _____

    muerte: 1974   _____

8. Juan Ramón Jiménez (España)

    Premio Nobel: 1956   _____

    nacimiento: 1881   _____

    muerte: 1958   _____

9. Gabriela Mistral (Chile)

    Premio Nobel: 1945   _____

    nacimiento: 1889   _____

    muerte: 1957   _____

10. Jacinto Benavente (España)

    Premio Nobel: 1922   _____

    nacimiento: 1866   _____

    muerte: 1954   _____

11. José Echegaray (España)

    Premio Nobel: 1904   _____

    nacimiento: 1833   _____

    muerte: 1914   _____

E *Los huracanes.* *A lo largo de la historia ha habido huracanes originados en el Caribe que han ocasionado enormes pérdidas humanas y materiales. Lea la lista parcial de huracanes con su fecha y el número (estimado) de muertos que causaron. Escriba los números (incluso los romanos) con letras.*

1. El Gran Huracán de 1780
   País, región o estado: Martinica, Puerto Rico, la República Dominicana, Barbados

   Fecha: 10/X–16/X/1780 _____

   Número de muertos: 22,000 _____

2. Fifi
   País, región o estado: Honduras

   Fecha: 19–20/IX/1974 _____

   Número de muertos: 8,000 _____

3. Gordon
   País, región o estado: Costa Rica, Honduras, Nicaragua, la Florida

   Fecha: 8–21/XI/1994 _____

   Número de muertos: 1,145 _____

4. Mitch
   País, región o estado: Honduras, Nicaragua

   Fecha: 22/X–5/XI/1998 _____

   Número de muertos: 11,000 _____

5. Jeanne
   País, región o estado: Puerto Rico, la República Dominicana, Haití, la Florida

   Fecha: 13–28/IX/2004 _____

   Número de muertos: 3,025 _____

6. Katrina
   País, región o estado: Luisiana, Bahamas, Cuba, la Florida

   Fecha: 23–30/VIII/2005 _____

   Número de muertos: 1,836 _____

7. María
   País, región o estado: Puerto Rico e islas del Caribe

   Fecha: 20–21/IX/2017 _____

   Número de muertos: 2,975 _____

Telling Time

All times begin with **Son las**, except for **Es la una** (*It's one o'clock*). To ask the time say, **¿Qué hora es?** In Spanish America **¿Qué horas son?** is very common.

Es la una.	*It's one o'clock.*
Son las tres.	*It's three o'clock.*
Son las tres y diez.	*It's ten after three.*
Son las tres y cuarto/y quince.	*It's a quarter after three. / It's three fifteen.*
Son las tres y media/y treinta.	*It's three thirty.*
Son las cuatro menos veinte.	*It's twenty to four.*
Son las cuatro menos cuarto/menos quince.	*It's a quarter to four.*

An alternative system for expressing the times between the half hour and the following hour is very common in Spanish America. The verbs used are **faltar** and **ser**.

Faltan/Son quince (minutos) para las cuatro.	*It's a quarter to four.*
Falta/Es un cuarto para las cuatro.	*It's a quarter to four.*

Digital clock time is also used in Spanish.

Son las siete cincuenta.	*It's seven fifty.*
Son las diez cincuenta y cinco.	*It's ten fifty-five.*

The equivalents of English A.M. and P.M. in Spanish are the phrases **de la mañana, de la tarde, de la noche** added to the expression of time. Spanish Americans often use A.M. and P.M. as in English. For noon and midnight, people say **Son las doce del día, Son las doce de la noche** or **Es mediodía, Es medianoche.**

Son las diez de la mañana.	*It's 10 A.M.*
Son las seis de la tarde.	*It's 6 P.M.*
Son las once y media de la noche.	*It's 11:30 P.M.*

To express the time at which something occurs, Spanish uses the preposition **a**.

A las ocho de la mañana.	*At 8 A.M.*
A veinte para las siete.	*At twenty to seven.*

In Spanish-speaking countries, a 24-hour clock is used for official purposes such as train and plane schedules and show times. In the 24-hour clock, the minutes past the hour are counted from 1 to 59. **Cuarto** and **media** are replaced by **quince, treinta**, and **cuarenta y cinco**; and the phrases **de la mañana, de la tarde**, and **de la noche** are not used.

Mi avión sale a las **trece treinta**.	*My plane leaves at 1:30 P.M.*
La película es a las **veinte cuarenta**.	*The film is at 8:40 P.M.*

The word **horas** often appears when using the 24-hour clock.

El programa es a las dieciocho horas.	*The program is at 6 P.M.*

Some Useful Expressions for Talking About the Time of Day

Son las seis en punto.	*It's six o'clock sharp.*
Es tarde.	*It's late.*

Es temprano.	*It's early.*
Se levanta tarde/temprano.	*He gets up late/early.*
Siento llegar tarde.	*I'm sorry to be late.*
Llego con anticipación.	*I'm early.*
Llego puntualmente.	*I'm on time.*
Mi reloj está adelantado/retrasado.	*My watch is fast/slow.*
Son las tres pasadas.	*It's after three. / It's past three.*
ser madrugador/madrugadora	*to be an early riser*
pegársele a uno las sábanas	*to sleep late, sleep in*

F **En el tren turístico.** *La Renfe, la marca comercial de la empresa nacional de trenes españoles, se deriva del acrónimo RENFE (Red Nacional de los Ferrocarriles Españoles, 1941–2005). La Renfe ofrece al público viajes turísticos en tren desde Madrid a los lugares históricos más importantes de España. Lea el programa de esta excursión de dos días a las tierras del Cid en Castilla la Vieja y conteste las preguntas con los días y las horas oficiales indicados en el programa. Escriba los números con letras. Siga el modelo.*

MODELO   ¿Cuándo se reúnen los viajeros para empezar la excursión?
→ Los viajeros se reúnen para empezar la excursión el sábado
a las siete treinta.

Tren tierras del Cid

Burgos. Tierra del Campeador. Punto de encuentro de Románico y Gótico. Punto de encuentro con el arte Medieval. Con el tren Tierras del Cid conócela a fondo. Recorre Covarrubias, Silos y La Yecla. Sal a su encuentro.

PROGRAMA
Sábado

07:30 h.	Recepción de viajeros en el punto de información de la estación de Madrid-Chamartín.
08:00 h.	Salida hacia Burgos.
11:36 h.	Llegada a Burgos. Traslado en autocar a Covarrubias, visita a la Colegiata. Tiempo libre para almorzar.
16:00 h.	Salida en autocar para visitar Santo Domingo de Silos y la Yecla.
20:00 h.	Llegada a Burgos. Traslado al hotel. Tiempo libre.
21:30 h.	Saludo del Ayuntamiento en el antiguo Monasterio de San Juan. Vino, aperitivos y actuaciones folklóricas.

Domingo

09:30 h.	Desayuno en el hotel.
10:30 h.	Salida en autocar para visitar el Monasterio de las Huelgas.
14:00 h.	Tiempo libre para el almuerzo.
16:30 h.	Concentración en la puerta de la Catedral para visitarla. Traslado en autocar a la estación de ferrocarril.
18:39 h.	Salida de la estación de Burgos hacia Madrid.
21:55 h.	Llegada a Madrid-Chamartín. Fin de viaje.

1. ¿Cuándo salen los turistas para visitar Santo Domingo de Silos?

2. ¿Cuándo llegan los viajeros a Burgos donde se hospedan en un hotel?

3. ¿Cuándo salen los turistas en autocar para visitar el Monasterio de las Huelgas?

4. ¿Cuándo visitan los turistas la Catedral de Burgos?

5. ¿Cuándo salen los viajeros de la estación ferroviaria de Burgos para Madrid?

6. Terminado el recorrido (*tour*), ¿cuándo llegan los viajeros a la estación Madrid-Chamartín?

NOTA CULTURAL

Rodrigo (Ruy) Díaz, el Cid Campeador (*valiant warrior*), nació c. 1048 en Vivar, un pueblo que queda a siete kilómetros de Burgos. En la magnífica Catedral de Burgos, obra maestra de arquitectura gótica cuya construcción empezó en 1221, se encuentra el sepulcro (*sepulcher, final resting place*) de Rodrigo Díaz de Vivar y su esposa Jimena (*Ximena* en español medieval). Fue un gran caballero (*knight*) que entabló batalla (*engaged in battle*) durante la Reconquista y llegó a ser personaje legendario y héroe nacional por sus hazañas (*heroic feats*). Al morir el Cid, su fama aumentó mediante el monumental poema épico *El Cantar de Mío Cid*, poema anónimo que fue compuesto alrededor del año 1200, es decir, un siglo después de su muerte en 1099. Este cantar de gesta (*poem of heroic deeds; chanson de geste* en francés), recitado por un juglar (*troubadour*) anónimo, es una de las primeras grandes obras medievales y el único poema épico español conservado casi completo.

Arithmetic Operations, Fractions, and Percentages

Here is how the basic arithmetic operations are read in Spanish.

$15 + 12 = 27$	quince **más** doce **son/es igual a** veintisiete
$40 - 24 = 16$	cuarenta **menos** veinticuatro **son/es igual a** dieciséis
$10 \times 15 = 150$	diez **por** quince **son/es igual a** ciento cincuenta
$120 \div 12 = 10$	ciento veinte **dividido por** doce **son/es igual a** diez

For division, the preposition **entre** is also used to mean divided by: **ciento veinte entre doce son diez**. Some Spanish-speaking countries use **para: ciento veinte para doce son diez**.

Except for **un medio** (*one-half*) and **un tercio** (*one-third*), fractions have the same form as masculine ordinal numbers.

un cuarto	*one-fourth*
tres quintos	*three-fifths*

Above one-tenth, the suffix **-avo** is added to the cardinal number to form the corresponding fraction: **un onceavo** (*one-eleventh*), **tres veinteavos** (*three-twentieths*).

Note also the fractions **un centavo** or **un centésimo** (*one-hundredth*) and **un milésimo** (*one-thousandth*).

Percentages in Spanish usually have an article (either **un** or **el**) before the figure.

Dan un veinte por ciento de descuento.	*They give a twenty percent discount.*
El diez por ciento de la población habla español.	*Ten percent of the population speaks Spanish.*

Here are the words for mathematical operations.

sumar	*to add*	el quebrado	*fraction*
restar	*to subtract*	por ciento	*percent*
multiplicar	*to multiply*	el porcentaje	*percentage*
dividir	*to divide*		

G *Operaciones matemáticas.* *Ayude a un amigo hispano que no habla inglés a resolver estos problemas. Primero, escriba los problemas con números y luego resuélvalos. Después escriba la solución con letras.*

1. ciento setenta y cuatro más ochenta y nueve son _____

2. seiscientos tres menos doscientos ochenta y uno son _____

3. cuarenta y nueve por cinco son _____

4. mil doscientos ochenta y cuatro dividido por cuatro son _____

5. tres cuartos de ochenta son _____

6. Juan ganó ochenta mil dólares en la lotería. Tiene que pagar un veinticinco por ciento de impuestos. ¿Cuánto tiene que pagar de impuestos? _____

NOTA CULTURAL

La palabra **álgebra** proviene de la palabra árabe *al-gabr*, una de las más de 4.000 palabras que fueron introducidas al español del árabe a través de ocho siglos de influencia árabe en España. Otras palabras españolas de origen árabe en el campo de las matemáticas incluyen **el cero**, **la cifra** y **el cenit**. Muchas palabras de origen árabe han pasado a otras lenguas europeas por medio del español.

H *Ejercicio oral. ¿En qué año fue?* *Ud. hace referencia a un acontecimiento histórico y les pregunta a sus compañeros en qué año sucedió. Ellos le contestan. Después les toca a sus compañeros hacerle preguntas a Ud. Por ejemplo:*

Ud. *¿En qué año fue adoptada la Declaración de la Independencia de los Estados Unidos?*
Él   Fue adoptada en mil setecientos setenta y seis.

Él   *¿En qué año estalló (estallar (to break out)) la Primera Guerra Mundial?*
Ud. Estalló en mil novecientos catorce.

Ud. *¿En qué año terminó la Primera Guerra Mundial?*
Ella Terminó en mil novecientos dieciocho.

Ella *¿En qué año llegó Cristóbal Colón a América?*
Ud. Cristóbal Colón llegó a América en mil cuatrocientos noventa y dos.

Idiomatic Usage

Idioms, Expressions, and Proverbs

Idioms and Expressions with **tener**

tener ángel/mal ángel	*to be charming/lack charm*
tener buena/mala estrella	*to be lucky/unlucky*
tener calor/frío	*to be warm/cold*
tener corazón de piedra	*to be hard-hearted*
tener cuidado	*to be careful*
tener dolor de cabeza/estómago	*to have a headache/stomachache*
tener en la punta de la lengua	*to have on the tip of one's tongue*
tener éxito	*to be successful*
tener ganas de	*to feel like*
tener hambre/sed	*to be hungry/thirsty*
tener inconveniente	*to mind, object to*
tener la culpa de	*to be to blame for*
tener la palabra	*to have the floor*
tener la razón de su parte	*to be in the right*
tener líos	*to have difficulties*
tener los huesos molidos	*to be exhausted*
tener los nervios de punta	*to have one's nerves on edge*
tener lugar	*to take place*
tener madera para	*to be cut out for, made for*
tener mala cara	*to look bad*
tener malas pulgas	*to be short-tempered*
tener miedo de	*to be afraid of*
tener mundo	*to be sophisticated, know how to act in society*
tener ojos de lince	*to have (sharp) eyes like a hawk (literally, lynx)*
tener pájaros en la cabeza	*to have bats in the belfry*
tener palabra	*to keep one's word*
tener por	*to consider someone to be*
tener prisa	*to be in a hurry*
tener que ver con	*to have to do with*
tener razón	*to be right*
tener sueño	*to be sleepy*
tener suerte	*to be lucky*
tener un disgusto	*to have a falling out*

tener vergüenza de	to be ashamed of
no tener arreglo	not to be able to be helped
no tener donde caerse muerto	not to have a penny to one's name
no tener nombre	to be unspeakable
no tener pelo de tonto	to be nobody's fool
no tener pelos en la lengua	to be very outspoken
no tener pies ni cabeza	to not make any sense, have no rhyme or reason

A **Tener.** *Complete las oraciones con una expresión o un modismo con* **tener** *como reacción lógica a la oración escrita.*

1. A Manolo le dieron un ascenso y un aumento de sueldo también.

   Tuvo _____.

2. Yo no comprendo nada de este libro.

   Para mí, el libro no tiene _____.

3. El nombre del actor es...

   ¡Caramba! Lo tengo _____.

4. Este niño es muy listo.

   ¿Verdad que no tiene _____?

5. Pablo corrió tanto que ni puede levantarse por cansado.

   El chico tiene _____.

6. Carmen ganó el premio gordo de la lotería.

   Esta señorita tiene _____.

7. Rebeca siempre está molesta y se queja de todo.

   Ella tiene _____.

8. El detective Sierra lo ve todo. No se le pierde nada.

   En efecto. Él tiene _____.

9. Álvaro se ve mal y está nerviosísimo.

   El pobre chico tiene _____ y (tiene) _____.

10. Los padres de Gonzalito se sienten avergonzados porque su hijo siempre causa problemas en el colegio.

    Los señores tienen _____ porque Gonzalito tiene muchos _____ en el colegio.

Idioms and Expressions with tomar

tomar algo a bien/mal	to take something well/badly
tomar a broma/risa	to take as a joke
tomar a pecho	to take to heart
tomar aliento	to catch one's breath

tomar en serio	*to take seriously*
tomar la palabra	*to take the floor*
tomar partido por	*to side with*
tomar la delantera	*to get ahead of*
tomarle el pelo	*to pull someone's leg*
tomárselo con calma	*to take it easy*

B **Tomar.** *Escriba una paráfrasis de las oraciones usando una expresión con* **tomar.**

1. Amparo lo aceptó tranquilamente.

2. Los García se pusieron tristes por la muerte del vecino.

3. Pedro se rió viendo las diabluras de su hijo.

4. La profesora se enojó por lo que le dijo Marianela.

5. Paco apoyó a Juan Carlos en la discusión.

Idioms and Expressions with estar

está despejado/claro	*it's clear*
está nublado	*it's cloudy*
estar a sus anchas	*to be comfortable*
estar calado/mojado hasta los huesos	*to be soaked (to the skin), to be soaking wet*
estar como el pez en el agua	*to be right at home*
estar con el alma en un hilo/en vilo	*to be in suspense*
estar de más	*to be in excess*
estar de sobra	*to be in excess*
estar en condiciones	*to be in good shape, be able (to do something)*
estar en la luna	*to have one's head in the clouds*
estar en las nubes	*to be in the clouds, daydreaming*
estar fuera de sí	*to be beside oneself emotionally (positive and negative)*
estar hecho polvo	*to be worn out*
estar hecho una fiera	*to be furious*
estar hecho una sopa	*to be soaked*
estar loco de atar	*to be completely crazy*
estar loco de remate	*to be completely crazy*
estar sin blanca	*to be flat broke*

C **Estar.** *Escriba una expresión con* **estar** *que sea sinónimo de la palabra o la frase indicada.*

1. cansarse

2. mojarse

3. no tener dinero

4. ponerse furioso

5. sentirse cómodo

Idioms and Expressions with **echar**

echar a perder	*to ruin, spoil*
echar chispas	*to be furious, get angry*
echar de menos	*to miss*
echar flores	*to flatter, sweet-talk*
echar la bronca a uno	*to give someone a dressing down*
echar la culpa	*to blame*
echarse a	*to start to*
echárselas de	*to fancy oneself as, boast of being*

D **¿Qué le pasó a don Juan?** *Complete las oraciones usando las expresiones con* **echar.**

1. Lorenzo le dijo a Beti que la echaba _____ cuando ella estaba de vacaciones.

2. Al mismo tiempo, Lorenzo les echaba _____ a Marisol y a Gloria.

3. Lorenzo _____ de don Juan.

4. Al volver, Beti se enteró de la situación y echó _____.

5. Beti le echó _____ a Lorenzo y rompió con él.

Idioms and Expressions with **dar**

dar a	*to face*
dar a luz a un niño/un hijo	*to give birth to a child*
dar asco	*to disgust*
dar calabazas	*to jilt; to flunk*
dar carta blanca a uno	*to give someone a free hand/carte blanche*
dar cuerda a	*to wind*
dar con	*to find; to run into*
dar de comer	*to feed*
dar de beber	*to give a drink to*
dar el golpe de gracia	*to finish (someone) off, give the coup de grâce to*
dar gritos	*to shout*
dar guerra	*to cause/make trouble*
dar la hora	*to strike the hour*
dar (la) lata	*to make a nuisance of oneself*
dar las gracias	*to thank*
dar por sentado	*to take for granted; to regard as settled*
dar rienda suelta a	*to give free rein to*
dar un abrazo	*to hug, embrace*
dar un paseo	*to take a walk/ride*
dar una vuelta	*to take a walk/ride*
dar vueltas a algo	*to think something over, thoroughly examine*
darse cuenta de	*to realize*
darse la mano	*to shake hands*
darse por vencido	*to give up*
darse prisa	*to hurry*

E *¿Qué se dio en cada caso?* Complete las oraciones usando las expresiones con **dar**.

1. Paquita era tan molesta y mal criada. Ella daba _____.

2. Los soldados dejaron de luchar. Se dieron _____.

3. Los soldados ultimaron a sus enemigos. Les dieron _____.

4. No deje que los chicos hagan esas cosas. No les dé _____.

5. Ya tomamos la decisión y dimos el asunto _____.

Idioms and Expressions with **hacer**

hace + *time expression* + preterit	*ago*
hace buen/mal tiempo	*it's good/bad weather*
hace calor/frío	*it's warm/cold*
hace viento	*it's windy*
hacer caso	*to pay attention, heed*
hacer (buenas) migas (con alguien)	*to hit it off (with someone)*
hacer de las suyas	*to be up to one's old tricks*
hacer un papel	*to play a role*
hacer juego	*to match*
hacer la vista gorda	*to turn a blind eye, pretend not to notice*
hacer las paces	*to make peace*
hacer época	*to be sensational, attract public attention*
hacer pedazos/añicos	*to break to pieces*
hacer su agosto	*to make a killing*
hacer un viaje	*to take a trip*
hacerse + *profession, status, etc.*	*to become*
hacerse daño	*to hurt oneself*
hacerse tarde	*to become late*
hacérsele agua la boca	*to make someone's mouth water*

F *¿Qué quieren hacer?* Complete las oraciones usando las expresiones con **hacer**.

1. dos amigos dejan de pelear

   Quieren _____.

2. una persona que estudia la Bolsa e invierte mucho dinero

   Espera _____.

3. a una actriz le interesa la nueva película que van a rodar

   Quiere _____.

4. unos padres que tienen vergüenza de las diabluras de sus hijos

   Prefieren _____.

5. un niñito travieso que ya no trata de portarse bien

   Vuelve a _____.

Idioms and Expressions with **ir**, **llevar**, and **quedar**

Ir

ir al grano	*to go straight to the point*
ir de juerga	*to be out on a spree*
ir sobre ruedas	*to run smoothly*
ir tirando	*to get by*

Llevar

llevar a cabo	*to carry out*
llevar la contraria	*to take an opposite point of view, contradict*
llevar leña al monte	*to carry coals to Newcastle*
llevarse como el perro y el gato	*to be always fighting, fight like cats and dogs*
llevarse un chasco	*to be disappointed*

Quedar

quedar boquiabierto	*to be left openmouthed in astonishment*
quedarse con	*to keep*
quedarse con el día y la noche	*to be left penniless*
quedarse de una pieza	*to be dumbfounded*
quedar en	*to agree on*
quedarse sin blanca	*to be flat broke; to go broke*

G **Ir, llevar, quedar: Sinónimos.** *Escriba oraciones usando los modismos de esta sección.*

1. El proyecto progresa sin problemas.

   El proyecto _____.

2. Nos pusimos de acuerdo para vernos delante del cine.

   _____ vernos delante del cine.

3. No me gusta ir a su casa. Siempre discuten.

   No me gusta ir a su casa. _____.

4. Si viniste a ver a Micaela, vas a quedar sin satisfacción. Ella no está.

   Si viniste a ver a Micaela, vas a _____. Ella no está.

5. Es difícil hablar con Alfonso. Nunca está de acuerdo con nadie.

   Es difícil hablar con Alfonso. Siempre _____.

6. No sé si vamos a poder realizar este plan.

   No sé si vamos a poder _____ este plan.

7. Cuando me dijo eso, no pude hacer nada más que mirarlo en silencio.

   Cuando me dijo eso, _____.

8. El negocio del señor Ortega quebró y su familia quedó sin un centavo.

   El negocio del señor Ortega quebró y su familia _____.

Idioms and Expressions with **meter** and **poner**

Meter

meter la pata	*to put one's foot in one's mouth*
meter las narices	*to snoop around*
meterse en donde no le llaman	*to meddle, snoop around*
meterse en la boca del lobo	*to enter the lion's den*
meterse en un callejón sin salida	*to get into a jam*

Poner

poner en ridículo	*to make look ridiculous*
poner las cartas sobre la mesa	*to put one's cards on the table*
poner los puntos sobre las íes	*to dot the i's and cross the t's*
poner a alguien por las nubes	*to praise someone to the skies*
poner pleito	*to sue*
ponerse las pilas	*to pull oneself together, get to work*
ponérsele a uno la carne de gallina	*to get goose bumps*
ponérsele los cabellos/pelos de punta	*to have one's hair stand on end, be terrified*

H *Definiciones.* *Empareje la definición de la columna A con el modismo de la columna B que le corresponda.*

A	B
_____ 1. entrar en un lugar peligroso	a. meterse en un callejón sin salida
_____ 2. llevar ante el juez o al tribunal	b. meter la pata
_____ 3. decir o hacer algo inapropiado y ofensivo	c. poner en ridículo
_____ 4. sentir pánico	d. meterse en la boca del lobo
_____ 5. buscarse un problema que no tiene solución	e. poner pleito
_____ 6. revelar las cosas	f. poner por las nubes
_____ 7. alabar a alguien con entusiasmo	g. poner las cartas sobre la mesa
	h. ponérsele los pelos de punta
	i. poner los puntos sobre las íes
	j. meterse en donde no le llaman

Idioms and Expressions with **ser**

ser de buena pasta	*to be a good guy, have a nice disposition*
ser de película	*to be sensational*
ser de poca monta	*to be of little value*
ser el colmo	*to be the limit*
ser harina de otro costal	*to be a horse of a different color*
ser el ojo derecho	*to be someone's pet*
ser la flor y nata	*to be the best*

ser otro cantar	*to be a horse of a different color*
ser pan comido	*to be as easy as pie*
ser para chuparse los dedos	*to taste delicious*
ser todo oídos	*to be all ears*
ser un cero a la izquierda	*to be of no value, count for nothing (of a person)*
ser un mirlo (*blackbird*) blanco	*to be an impossible dream*
ser una lata	*to be annoying*
ser una perla	*to be a jewel/treasure*
ser uña y carne	*to be close as can be*
no ser cosa del otro jueves	*to be nothing out of the ordinary*

I **¿Cuál es?** *Indique cuál de los modismos con* **ser** *significa lo mismo que la oración principal.*

1. Ya has llegado al límite.
    a. Esto es pan comido.
    b. Esto es un mirlo blanco.
    c. Esto es el colmo.

2. Esta situación me fastidia mucho.
    a. Es una lata.
    b. Es de película.
    c. Es otro cantar.

3. Esas dos chicas son muy buenas amigas. Siempre están juntas.
    a. Son la flor y la nata.
    b. Son de buena pasta.
    c. Son uña y carne.

4. Lo que me dices ahora es algo totalmente distinto.
    a. Es una perla.
    b. Es harina de otro costal.
    c. Es de poca monta.

5. Este flan está riquísimo.
    a. Es todo oídos.
    b. Es para chuparse los dedos.
    c. Es un cero a la izquierda.

Other Verbal Expressions

andar de boca en boca	*to be generally known*
andarse por las ramas	*to beat around the bush*
armarse un escándalo	*to cause a row*
buscar tres pies al gato	*to split hairs*
no caber en sí	*to be beside oneself with joy, anger, etc.; to be presumptuous*
no caber en su piel	*to be beside oneself with joy, anger, etc.; to be presumptuous*

caerse el alma a los pies	*to be down in the dumps*
consultar con la almohada	*to sleep on it*
decirle cuatro verdades	*to tell someone a thing or two*
no decir ni pío	*to not say a word*
dejar caer	*to drop*
dejar de + *infinitive*	*to stop (doing something)*
dejar plantado	*to stand someone up*
no dejar piedra por/sin mover	*to leave no stone unturned*
dorar la píldora	*to sugarcoat something*
dormir a pierna suelta	*to sleep like a log*
dormir la mona	*to sleep off a hangover*
dormirse en/sobre los laureles	*to rest on one's laurels*
faltarle a uno un tornillo	*to have a screw loose*
hablar hasta por los codos	*to talk incessantly*
llamar al pan pan y al vino vino	*to call a spade a spade*
mandar a freír espárragos	*to tell someone to go jump in the lake/ go fly a kite*
matar la gallina de los huevos de oro	*to kill the goose that lays the golden eggs*
matar dos pájaros de un tiro	*to kill two birds with one stone*
no importar un bledo/comino/ pepino	*to not give a damn about*
pasar las de Caín	*to go through hell*
pedir peras al olmo	*to expect the impossible*
no pegar ojo en toda la noche	*to not sleep a wink all night*
quemarse las cejas	*to burn the midnight oil*
querer decir	*to mean*
no saber a qué carta quedarse	*to be unable to make up one's mind*
sacar a luz	*to publish*
sacar en limpio/claro	*to make clear*
salir a luz	*to publish*
salirse con la suya	*to get one's own way*
saltar a la vista	*to be obvious*
tocar en lo vivo	*to hurt deeply*
tragarse la píldora	*to be taken in, swallow a lie*
valer la pena	*to be worthwhile*
valer un mundo/ojo de la cara/ Potosí	*to be worth a fortune*
venir de perlas	*to be just the thing, be just right*
verlo todo color de rosa	*to see life through rose-tinted glasses*
verlo todo negro	*to be pessimistic*
no poder verlo ni en pintura	*to not be able to stand the sight of someone*
volver a las andadas	*to go back to one's old ways*
volver en sí	*to regain consciousness*

J *Sinónimos.* Empareje el modismo de la columna A con su sinónimo de la columna B.

A	B
_____ 1. llamar al pan pan y al vino vino	a. ser evidente
_____ 2. costar un ojo de la cara	b. buscar tres pies al gato
_____ 3. dormir a pierna suelta	c. dormir profundamente
_____ 4. faltarle un tornillo	d. no abrir la boca
_____ 5. no decir ni pío	e. exigir lo imposible
_____ 6. pedir peras al olmo	f. llamar las cosas por su nombre
_____ 7. saltar a la vista	g. no ir al grano
_____ 8. andarse por las ramas	h. valer un Potosí
	i. no estar completamente bien de la cabeza
	j. volver en sí

K *Antónimos.* Escoja de la columna B un antónimo para cada modismo de la columna A.

A	B
_____ 1. andar de boca en boca	a. comportarse mejor que antes
_____ 2. no importarle un bledo	b. no decir ni pío
_____ 3. no pegar ojo	c. tomar una decisión
_____ 4. volver a las andadas	d. caerse el alma a los pies
_____ 5. dejar plantado	e. preocuparse mucho
_____ 6. no saber a qué carta quedarse	f. ser muy amigo de uno
_____ 7. no poder verlo ni en pintura	g. ser una cosa ignorada de todos
_____ 8. hablar hasta por los codos	h. sacar en limpio
	i. dormir a pierna suelta
	j. acudir a la cita

Other Idioms

¡A otro perro con ese hueso!	*Nonsense! / Don't give me that!* (literally, *to another dog with that bone*)
a pedir de boca	*perfectly, smoothly*
como el que más	*as well or better than anyone else*
contra viento y marea	*against all odds* (literally, *against wind and tide*)
dar gato por liebre	*to sell a pig in a poke, take someone in*
de buenas a primeras	*right off the bat*

de carne y hueso	*flesh and blood*
de categoría	*of importance*
de mal en peor	*from bad to worse*
de segunda mano	*secondhand*
desde que el mundo es el mundo	*since the world began*
Dios mediante	*God willing*
el qué dirán	*what people say*
entre la espada y la pared	*between the devil and the deep blue sea*
	(la espada = *sword*)
en un abrir y cerrar de ojos	*in the twinkling of an eye*
está chupado/tirado	*it's a piece of cake*
peces gordos	*big shots, important people*
sin más ni más	*without further hesitation*
tocar madera	*to touch wood, knock on wood*
todo el santo día	*the whole darn day*
Hay gato encerrado.	*There's something fishy.*
Hay moros en la costa.	*The coast isn't clear, be careful.*
	(literally, *There are Moors on the coast.*)
Más vale cuatro ojos que dos.	*Two heads are better than one.*
¡Ojo!	*Be careful!*
Trato hecho.	*It's a deal.*

L **Sinónimos.** *Escoja de la columna B un sinónimo para cada modismo de la columna A.*

A	B
_____ 1. está chupado	a. engañar
_____ 2. el qué dirán	b. existe una cosa sospechosa que no vemos
_____ 3. dar gato por liebre	c. con mucha rapidez
_____ 4. hay gato encerrado	d. la opinión de los demás
_____ 5. de segunda mano	e. desde el principio
_____ 6. en un abrir y cerrar de ojos	f. con gran esfuerzo
_____ 7. de categoría	g. es pan comido
_____ 8. de buenas a primeras	h. entre dos peligros
	i. usado, no nuevo
	j. de importancia

Proverbs and Sayings

A caballo regalado no se le mira el colmillo.	*Don't look a gift horse in the mouth.* (colmillo = *canine tooth*)
A lo hecho, pecho.	*It's no use crying over spilled milk.* (literally, *Chest out to what has been done.*)

Al que madruga, Dios le ayuda.

Antes que te cases, mira lo que haces.
Aunque la mona se vista de seda,
   mona se queda.

Cuando a Roma fueres, haz como
   vieres. OR Allá donde fueres,
   haz como vieres.
Del dicho al hecho hay gran trecho.

De tal palo, tal astilla.

Desgraciado en el juego, afortunado
   en amores.
Dios los cría y ellos se juntan.
El infierno está lleno de buenos
   propósitos, y el cielo de buenas
   obras.
El sapo a la sapa tiénela por muy
   guapa.

En tierra de ciegos, el tuerto es rey.

En una hora no se ganó Zamora.
Eso es el cuento de la lechera.
   OR Hacer las cuentas de la lechera.
Las paredes oyen.
Los dineros del sacristán, cantando
   se vienen y cantando se van.
Más vale pájaro en mano que ciento
   volando.
No es oro todo lo que reluce (brilla).
Obras son amores, que no buenas
   razones.
Ojos que no ven, corazón que no
   siente.
Poderoso caballero es don Dinero.
Quien mala cama hace, en ella se yace.

Sobre gustos no hay nada escrito.
Ver y creer.

The early bird catches the worm.
   (madrugar = to get up early)
Look before you leap.
You can't make a silk purse out of a sow's ear.
   (literally, Although the monkey may dress
   in silk, she remains a monkey.)
When in Rome, do as the Romans do.
   (**Fueres** and **vieres** are old future
   subjunctive forms.)
There's many a slip 'twixt the cup and the lip.
   (el trecho = distance)
A chip off the old block. (el palo = stick;
   la astilla = splinter)
Unlucky in cards, lucky in love.

Birds of a feather flock together.
The road to hell is paved with good
   intentions.

Beauty is in the eye of the beholder.
   (el sapo = toad; la sapa = female toad;
   tiénela = la tiene)
In the land of the blind, the one-eyed is king.
   (tuerto = one-eyed)
Rome wasn't built in a day.
Don't count your chickens before they hatch.

The walls have ears.
Easy come, easy go. (el sacristán = church
   sexton)
A bird in the hand is worth two in the bush.

All that glitters is not gold.
Actions speak louder than words.
   (razones = speech, talk)
Out of sight, out of mind.

Money talks.
You made your bed, now lie in it!
   (yacer [old] = to lie down)
Everyone to his own taste.
Seeing is believing.

M *¿Qué se diría?* *Escoja el refrán apropiado para cada situación.*

1. Uno nota que un muchacho se comporta exactamente como su padre.
   a. No es oro todo lo que reluce.
   b. De tal palo, tal astilla.
   c. Obras son amores, que no buenas razones.

2. Uno le advierte a su compañero que deben ser discretos en caso de que alguien los escuche.
   a. Las paredes oyen.
   b. Ver y creer.
   c. Aunque la mona se vista de seda, mona se queda.

3. Uno le dice a un amigo que hay que olvidar los errores del pasado.
   a. A lo hecho, pecho.
   b. Sobre gustos no hay nada escrito.
   c. Cuando a Roma fueres, haz como vieres.

4. Uno le advierte a su amigo que debe actuar con prudencia en una situación complicada.
   a. Más vale pájaro en mano que ciento volando.
   b. El sapo a la sapa tiénela por muy guapa.
   c. Antes que te cases, mira lo que haces.

5. Un muchacho le reprocha a su novia por no haberle escrito cuando estaba en el extranjero.
   a. Los dineros del sacristán cantando se vienen y cantando se van.
   b. Del dicho al hecho hay gran trecho.
   c. Ojos que no ven, corazón que no siente.

N *El zoológico de expresiones.* *Los siguientes modismos, proverbios y expresiones nombran a ciertos animales. Consulte las listas anteriores para completar las oraciones con los nombres de los animales correctos. Después exprese la oración en inglés.*

1. Aunque _____ se vista de seda, _____ se queda.

2. Más vale _____ en mano que ciento volando.

3. A otro _____ con ese hueso.

4. Que no le dé _____ por _____.

5. _____ a _____ tiénela por muy guapa.

6. Son los _____ gordos de la industria.

7. A _____ regalado no se le mira el colmillo.

8. Creo que hay _____ encerrado.

9. Mató _____ de los huevos de oro.

10. Es bueno que hayamos matado dos _____ de un tiro.

11. Su plan fue un _____ blanco.

12. Sin darse cuenta, se metió en la boca del _____.

13. Se le puso la carne de _____.

14. ¡Qué dos! Se llevan como el _____ y el _____.

15. Ella lo ve todo. Tiene ojos de _____.

16. Lo que dice no tiene sentido. Tiene _____ en la cabeza.

Word Formation and Diminutives

Forming Nouns from Verbs

Some nouns related to verbs consist of the verb stem + **-o** or **-a**.

aumentar *to increase*	→ el aumento *increase*
ayudar *to help*	→ la ayuda *help*
contar *to count*	→ la cuenta *bill*
contar *to tell, recount*	→ el cuento *story*
charlar *to chat*	→ la charla *chat, talk*
dudar *to doubt*	→ la duda *doubt*
encontrar *to meet*	→ el encuentro *meeting, sports match*
espantar *to frighten*	→ el espanto *fright, scare*
esperar *to wait*	→ la espera *waiting*
fracasar *to fail*	→ el fracaso *failure*
gastar *to spend*	→ el gasto *expense*
practicar *to practice*	→ la práctica *practice*
regresar *to return*	→ el regreso *return*
volar *to fly*	→ el vuelo *flight*

Many nouns are formed from the past participle of verbs. They consist of the verb stem + the suffix **-ada** (for **-ar** verbs) or **-ida** (for **-er** and **-ir** verbs).

bajar *to go down(stairs)*	→ la bajada *way down; decline*
caer *to fall*	→ la caída *fall*
comer *to eat*	→ la comida *meal, food*
correr *to run*	→ la corrida (de toros) *bullfight* (literally, *running (of bulls)*)
entrar *to enter*	→ la entrada *entrance*
ir *to go*	→ la ida *trip to somewhere, first leg of journey*
llegar *to arrive*	→ la llegada *arrival*
mirar *to look (at)*	→ la mirada *look, glance*
salir *to go out*	→ la salida *exit*
subir *to go up*	→ la subida *way up, rise*
volver *to go/come back*	→ la vuelta *return, trip back*

Many nouns are formed from **-ar** verbs with the suffix **-ción**. Most of these have English cognates ending in *-tion*.

admirar	→ la admiración
invitar	→ la invitación
organizar	→ la organización
separar	→ la separación

Not all English words ending in *-tion, -sion* have Spanish equivalents ending in **-ción, -sión**.

transportation ~ el transporte (**la transportación** is rare)

A **¿Y el verbo original?** *Escriba al lado de cada sustantivo el verbo del que se deriva.*

1. la formación
2. la programación
3. la dominación
4. la preparación

5. la grabación
6. la presentación
7. la obligación
8. la complicación

The suffixes **-ancia** and **-encia** are used to form nouns from verbs. Most of the nouns have English cognates.

coincidir	→ la coincidencia
preferir	→ la preferencia
tolerar	→ la tolerancia
vigilar	→ la vigilancia

Note also **la estancia** (*stay*) from **estar**.

The suffix **-miento** is widely used to form nouns from verbs. **-Ar** verbs have the vowel **a** before this suffix; both **-er** and **-ir** verbs have the vowel **i**.

| agotar *to exhaust* | → el agotamiento *exhaustion* |
| entender *to understand* | → el entendimiento *understanding* |

B **El sustantivo que falta.** *Complete la tabla con los sustantivos correctos.*

1. comportarse *to behave* _____ *behavior*
2. encarcelar *to jail, imprison* _____ *jailing*
3. consentir *to consent* _____ *consent*
4. mover *to move* _____ *movement*
5. pensar *to think* _____ *thought*
6. plantear *to pose (a problem)* _____ *posing*
7. tratar *to treat* _____ *treatment*
8. nombrar *to nominate* _____ *nomination*
9. crecer *to grow, increase* _____ *growth*
10. sufrir *to suffer* _____ *suffering*

Forming Verbs from Nouns

-Ear is one of the most commonly used suffixes for converting nouns into verbs. It can convey the impression of repeated movement or action of the noun.

párpado *eyelid* → parpadear *to blink*
paso *step* → pasear *to walk*

Most of these verbs can then form a noun ending in **-eo**: **el parpadeo** (*blinking*), **el paseo** (*walk*).

C **Verbos nuevos.** *Adivine el significado de los verbos en letra cursiva* (italics) *partiendo de los sustantivos de los cuales se han formado. Escriba el infinitivo del verbo en español y el significado del verbo en inglés.*

1. el sabor *taste*
   Come lentamente y *saborea* estos platos.

2. la gota *drop (of liquid)*
   El agua *goteaba* del techo de la casa.

3. el golpe *blow, hit*
   El hombre *golpeaba* al perro cruelmente.

4. la tecla *key (on a keyboard)*
   La pianista *tecleaba* con gran velocidad.

5. la hoja *leaf, sheet of paper*
   La bibliotecaria *hojeaba* las páginas del libro.

6. el zapato *shoe*
   Todos *zapateaban* al compás (*rhythm*) de la música.

7. la pata *paw; foot* (slang)
   El jugador *pateó* el balón muy fuerte.

Some nouns can be transformed into verbs by the prefix **en-** + infinitive ending **-ar**.

la cadena *chain* → encadenar *to chain*
la máscara *mask* → enmascarar *to mask, masquerade, hide, disguise*
el veneno *poison* → envenenar *to poison*

The prefix **-en** is **-em** before **b** and **p**.

el brujo *sorcerer* → embrujar *to cast a spell over, bewitch*
el papel *paper* → empapelar *to wallpaper*

Some of these verbs allow a new noun to be formed by adding **-miento**.

el encadenamiento   *chaining*
el envenenamiento   *poisoning*
el enmascaramiento   *masking, masquerading, hiding*
el embrujamiento   *bewitching, spell, sorcery*
el empapelamiento   *papering*

D *Palabras relacionadas.* Complete la tabla de palabras relacionadas.

1. SPANISH   la casilla   _____   el encasillamiento
   ENGLISH   *mailbox, pigeonhole*   *to pigeonhole*   *pigeonholing*

2. SPANISH   la grasa   engrasar   _____
   ENGLISH   _____   _____   *lubrication*

3. SPANISH   la saña   _____   el ensañamiento
   ENGLISH   *rage, fury*   *to enrage, infuriate*   *raging, fury*

4. SPANISH   la botella   _____   _____
   ENGLISH   *bottle*   *to bottle (up)*   *traffic jam*

5. SPANISH   la pareja   emparejar   _____
   ENGLISH   *couple*   *to match, pair*   *pairing, mating*

6. SPANISH   la frente   enfrentar   _____
   ENGLISH   *forehead, brow, face*   *to face, confront*   *clash, confrontation*

Forming Verbs from Adjectives

Certain adjectives can be transformed into verbs by the prefix **a-** + infinitive ending **-ar**.

fino *fine*   → afinar *to refine, tune*
liso *smooth* → alisar *to smooth*
llano *flat*   → allanar *to flatten, level*
manso *tame*   → amansar *to tame, domesticate*

E *El diccionario.* Empareje los verbos de la columna A con su equivalente inglés de la columna B. Cada verbo deriva de un adjetivo que Ud. ya sabe.

A   **B**

_____ 1. acertar   a. *assure*

_____ 2. aclarar   b. *lengthen*

_____ 3. achicar   c. *enlarge*

_____ 4. aflojar   d. *drive mad (with joy or delight)*

_____ 5. agrandar   e. *guess right, hit the mark*

_____ 6. alargar   f. *clarify*

_____ 7. alocar   g. *loosen*

_____ 8. asegurar   h. *reduce in size*

The suffix **-ecer** is added to the stem of some adjectives and nouns to create a new verb.

oscuro → oscurecer *to get dark*
pálido → palidecer *to grow pale*

Like all **-ecer** verbs, the first person singular and the present subjunctive have **-zc-** before the endings: **Temo que *oscurezca* antes de que lleguemos.** (*I'm afraid it will get dark before we arrive.*)

F *Adivine qué significan estas palabras. Escriba el significado en inglés.*

1. florecer

2. fortalecer

3. robustecer

4. humedecer

5. *What household appliance is* la humedecedora?

Many adjectives can be made into verbs with the prefix **en-** (**em-** before **b** and **p**) and the suffix **-ecer**. Adjectives whose stems end in **-c** change the **c** to **qu** before **-ecer**.

triste   → entristecer *to sadden*
pobre   → empobrecer *to impoverish*
rico   → enriquecer *to enrich*
flaco   → enflaquecer *to get thin*
loco   → enloquecer *to go crazy*
bruto   → embrutecer *to brutalize*

G ***Formación de verbos.*** *¿Cuáles son los verbos que derivan de estos adjetivos? Todos tienen el sufijo* **-ecer.**

1. duro   6. negro

2. bello   7. rojo

3. flaco   8. ronco (*hoarse*)

4. noble   9. sordo

5. loco

Suffixes Added to Nouns to Form New Nouns

The suffix **-ada** can have three different meanings.

1 · The full measure of the noun or the amount that the noun holds (**-ado** is used with some nouns)

la cuchara *spoon* → la cucharada *spoonful*
la pala *shovel*   → la palada *shovelful*
el puño *fist*   → el puñado *fistful*
la boca *mouth*   → el bocado *mouthful* (ALSO la bocanada *mouthful, swallow*)

2 · A blow with the object designated by the noun

el cuchillo *knife*	→ la cuchillada *slash made with a knife*
el puñal *dagger*	→ la puñalada *stab*
la pata *foot, paw*	→ la patada *kick*

3 · An act typical of the object or person designated by the noun

el animal *animal*	→ la animalada *stupid or gross thing to do*
el payaso *clown*	→ la payasada *clown-like action, action worthy of a clown*
el muchacho *boy, kid*	→ la muchachada *kid's prank*

The suffix -**astro** is the equivalent of English *step-* with relatives.

el hermanastro *stepbrother*
la madrastra *stepmother*

The suffix -**azo**, like -**ada**, can signify a blow with the object designated by the noun. In Latin America, -**azo** can also be an augmentative suffix.

la bala *bullet*	→ el balazo *shot, bullet wound*
el codo *elbow*	→ el codazo *nudge, push with the elbow*
los ojos *eyes*	→ los ojazos *big eyes*

The suffix -**era** designates the container for the object expressed by the noun. Some nouns use -**ero** as the suffix for this meaning.

| la sopa *soup* | → la sopera *soup bowl* |
| la pimienta *pepper* | → el pimentero *pepper shaker* |

The suffix -**ero** has other important functions.

1 · The owner or person in charge

| la cárcel *jail* | → el carcelero *jailer* |
| el molino *mill* | → el molinero *miller* |

2 · The person who makes or sells the object denoted by the noun

| el libro *book* | → el librero *bookseller* |
| el reloj *watch* | → el relojero *watchmaker* |

3 · The person fond of whatever the noun designates

| el queso *cheese* | → el quesero *cheese lover, person who is fond of cheese* |
| el café *coffee* | → el cafetero *coffee drinker, coffee lover, person who is fond of coffee* |

The suffix -**ería**, derived from -**ero**, designates the corresponding store or place of business.

la librería *bookstore*
la relojería *watchmaker's store, watch store*

H *¿Qué significa?* *Escriba el significado de las palabras, analizando la raíz y el sufijo.*

1. el pastelero
2. la cucharada
3. la sombrerería
4. la cafetera
5. la ensaladera
6. el lapicero

7. la bobada
8. la barcada
9. el portazo
10. la hijastra
11. el salero
12. el fiestero

Diminutives and Augmentatives

Diminutives are widely used in Spanish to add a note of smallness or endearment to the noun. The most common diminutive suffix is **-ito/-ita**, added to nouns and personal names. The following spelling changes occur when **-ito/-ita** is added: **c > qu, g > gu, z > c.**

la silla *chair*	→ la sillita *small chair*
el hermano *brother*	→ el hermanito *little brother, younger brother*
la cuchara *spoon*	→ la cucharita *teaspoon*
el gato *cat*	→ el gatito *kitten*
abuela *grandmother*	→ abuelita *grandma*
Paco	→ Paquito
Diego	→ Dieguito
Lorenza	→ Lorencita

The diminutive suffix **-ito/-ita** changes to **-cito/-cita** if the noun ends in **-n** or **-r**, or if the noun ends in **-e** and has more than one syllable.

el pintor *painter*	→ el pintorcito *painter, third-rate painter* (often sarcastic)
la joven *young girl, teenage girl*	→ la jovencita *young girl* (endearing)
la madre *mother*	→ la madrecita *dear mother*
el puente *bridge*	→ el puentecito *little bridge*

Nouns of two syllables whose first syllable has **ie** or **ue** and that end in **-o** or **-a** drop the **-o** or **-a** and add **-ecito/-ecita** to form the diminutive. The same is true of one-syllable nouns ending in a consonant.

la piedra *stone*	→ la piedrecita *little stone*
la fiesta *party*	→ la fiestecita *little party*
el cuerpo *body*	→ el cuerpecito *little body* (could be sarcastic)
la puerta *door*	→ la puertecita *little door*
la flor *flower*	→ la florecita *little flower*

Other diminutive endings are **-ico** (a regional variant of **-ito**), **-illo** (which can convey contempt as well as endearment), and **-uelo** (a diminutive ending that often conveys a note of contempt). These endings add **c** or **ec** (**z** or **ez** in the case of **-uelo**) the way **-ito** does.

la cuesta *slope*	→	la cuestecilla *slight slope*
un abogado *lawyer*	→	un abogadillo *third-rate lawyer*
una república *republic*	→	una republiquilla *a miserable little country*
la cosa *thing*	→	la cosilla *insignificant thing*
un rey *a king*	→	un reyezuelo *a poor excuse for a king*
un escritor *a writer*	→	un escritorzuelo *a very bad writer*
un muchacho *boy*	→	un muchachuelo *small boy*

Words with a diminutive suffix may take on an independent meaning.

el zapato *shoe*	→	la zapatilla *slipper*
la mano *hand*	→	la manecilla *hand of a watch or clock*
la bolsa *bag*	→	el bolsillo *pocket*

NOTA CULTURAL

- El diminutivo **-ico/-ica** se usa tanto en la república centroamericana de Costa Rica que se les ha apodado (*nicknamed*) a los costarricenses «**los ticos**».
- **Costa Rica** es una nación democrática cuya estabilidad presenta un contraste con el trágico caos político y social de otros países centroamericanos. El ex-presidente de Costa Rica, Oscar Arias, que se esforzó incansablemente por resolver de una manera pacífica los conflictos de Nicaragua y El Salvador, recibió el Premio Nobel de la Paz en 1987.

The suffix **-ucho/-ucha** conveys the idea of ugliness.

la casa *house*	→	la casucha *hovel*
el cuarto *room*	→	el cuartucho *small, miserable, uncomfortable room*

The most common augmentative suffix in Spanish is **-ón/-ona**.

la mancha *stain*	→	el manchón *big, dirty stain*
la mujer *woman*	→	la mujerona *big, hefty woman*
la novela *novel*	→	el novelón *long, boring novel*

Note, however, that in **el ratón** (*mouse*) from **la rata** (*rat*) the suffix **-ón** functions as a diminutive.

The suffix **-ón/-ona** can also be added to some verb stems to form adjectives meaning *given to doing the action of the verb.*

contestar *to answer*	→	contestón *given to answering back*
llorar *to cry*	→	llorón *crybaby, always crying*
mirar *to look at*	→	mirón *given to staring*
preguntar *to ask*	→	preguntón *inquisitive, given to asking too many questions*
responder *to answer*	→	respondón *fresh, insolent, given to answering back*
burlarse *to make fun of*	→	burlón *mocking, derisive*
comer *to eat*	→	comilón *big eater, gluttonous*

dormir *to sleep*	→	dormilón *sleepyhead, given to sleeping*
gritar *to shout, scream*	→	gritón *loud-mouthed, always yelling*

The suffix **-azo/-aza** is also augmentative, especially in Spanish America.

el perro *dog*	→	el perrazo *big dog*
el éxito *success*	→	el exitazo *great success, hit*

The augmentative suffix **-ote/-ota** often adds a note of contempt to the idea of bigness.

la palabra *word*	→	la palabrota *bad word, dirty word*
el animal *animal*	→	el animalote *big animal; gross, ignorant person*

As with diminutives, the addition of an augmentative suffix sometimes creates an independent word.

soltero *unmarried*	→	el solterón *old bachelor,* la solterona *unmarried woman*
la silla *chair*	→	el sillón *armchair*
la caja *box*	→	el cajón *drawer; crate*

Diminutive and augmentative suffixes can be added to adjectives and some adverbs. The suffixes vary in form as with nouns.

pobre *poor*	→	pobrecito *an unfortunate person*
feo *ugly*	→	feíto *somewhat ugly, a little ugly*
viejo *old*	→	viejito *rather old, getting on in years*
flaco *thin*	→	flacucho *skinny*
inocente *innocent*	→	inocentón *naive, gullible*
guapo *good-looking*	→	guapote *really good-looking*
poco *little, not much*	→	poquito *very little, rather little*
ahora *now*	→	ahorita *right now*
tarde *late*	→	tardecito *rather late, a little late*
cerca *nearby*	→	cerquita *really close, not at all far away*
en seguida *right away*	→	en seguidita *in just a moment*

I **Diminutivos.** *Escriba el diminutivo terminando en* **-ito/-ita** *que corresponda a estas palabras.*

1. la voz

2. la carta

3. el traje

4. el pez

5. el cuento

6. la pierna

7. el caballo

8. el bosque

9. el dolor

10. la cabeza

11. el lago

12. suave

13. el viento

14. el jugo

15. el carro

16. fuerte

17. chico

18. nuevo

19. fresco

20. la luz

¡Ojo! Common Errors and Pitfalls

Dejar vs. salir

Dejar and **salir** both mean *to leave*, but they are not interchangeable. **Dejar** is a transitive verb that means *to leave something or someone behind.*

—¿Dónde **dejaste las llaves** del coche?	*Where did you leave the car keys?*
—Creo que **las dejé** en la mesa del comedor.	*I think I left them on the dining room table.*
—¿Dónde **los puedo dejar**?	*Where can I leave you (off)?*
—**Déjeme a mí** delante del cine y **deje a mi marido** en la estación.	*Leave me in front of the movie theater and drop (leave) my husband at the station.*

Salir is an intransitive verb that means *to go out* or *to leave*. The preposition **de** follows **salir** before the name of the place being left.

—Nuestro tren **sale** a las tres y media.	*Our train leaves at three thirty.*
—En ese caso debemos **salir de casa** a las tres para no llegar tarde.	*In that case, we should leave the house at three in order not to be late.*

Compare the following examples where **salir** and **dejar** contrast.

Salió de la casa a las cinco.	*He left the house at five o'clock.*
Dejó la casa hecha un desastre.	*He left the house in a mess.*

Note that **irse** and **marcharse** also mean *to leave* in the sense of *to go away*. They also require **de** before the name of the place. **Marcharse** may imply leaving forever or for a long period of time.

—**Me voy** de la oficina a las cinco.	*I'm leaving the office at five o'clock.*
—Ayer **te fuiste** a las cuatro, ¿verdad?	*Yesterday you left at four, didn't you?*
—**Se marchó** porque odiaba el trabajo aquí.	*He left because he hated the work here.*
—A ver si yo también **me marcho** pronto.	*Let's see if I (can) leave soon too.*

Dejar + infinitive means *to let*. **Dejar** + **de** + infinitive means *to stop doing something.*

—¿Cuándo me **dejarás** salir, mamá?	*When will you let me go out, Mom?*
—Cuando **deje de** llover.	*When it stops raining.*

Salir + adjective or adverb means *to turn out*. An indirect object is often added.

Ese coche **te saldrá** muy caro.	*That car will turn out to be very expensive for you.*
Nos salió bien el proyecto.	*The project turned out well for us.*
Los nuevos empleados **salieron** muy trabajadores.	*The new employees turned out to be very hardworking.*

A *¿Cómo se dice?* *Complete las oraciones con la forma correcta de* **salir, dejar** *o* **irse,** *según convenga.*

1. No debemos _____ nada en el cuarto de hotel.

2. Si llueve, no quiero _____ a la calle. Prefiero esperar a que _____ de llover.

3. No _____ (tú [*imperative*]), por favor. No me _____ solo aquí en el parque.

4. Ese sinvergüenza (*scoundrel*) _____ [*preterit*] del país y _____ a su mujer y a sus hijos sin un centavo.

5. Juan _____ del correo y se dirigió al banco.

6. Oye, Carlitos, _____ de molestarme. Te dije que no podías _____ a jugar.

7. La fiesta de Francisca _____ estupenda. Yo lo pasé muy bien.

8. Casi todos los estudiantes _____ mal en el examen de física porque fue muy difícil.

9. Mis padres no me _____ [*present*] manejar de noche.

Saber vs. conocer

Saber and **conocer** both mean *to know*. **Saber** is used for facts, information, or knowledge that can be stated.

—¿**Sabes** la dirección de Marta?	*Do you know Marta's address?*
—No, pero **sé** su número de teléfono.	*No, but I know her phone number.*

Conocer means *to know a person* or *to be familiar with a place*. With places, **conocer** is often translated as *to have been* in English.

—¿**Conoces** a Pedro Gómez?	*Do you know Pedro Gómez?*
—No, pero **conozco** a su hermana.	*No, but I know his sister.*
—¿**Conocen** Uds. la universidad?	*Are you familiar with the university?*
—No, no la **conocemos**.	*No, we've never been there.*

In modern usage, **conocer** frequently replaces **saber** for *to know a piece of information*.

—Eres muy amigo de Carlos Lozano, ¿no?	*You're very friendly with Carlos Lozano, aren't you?*
—Sí, pero no **conozco** su dirección.	*Yes, but I don't know his address.*

Saber + infinitive means *to know how to do something*.

—¿**Sabes** cocinar?	*Do you know how to cook?*
—**Sé** preparar algunos platos sencillos.	*I know how to prepare some simple dishes.*

B **¿Saber o conocer?** *Escoja el verbo correcto para completar las oraciones.*

1. Alfredo no _____ (sabe / conoce) a nadie en esta ciudad.

2. ¿Uds. no _____ (saben / conocen) Galicia? Entonces, tienen que ir.

3. ¿_____ (Sabe / Conoce) Ud. cuántos habitantes hay en Caracas?

4. No _____ (sé / conozco) esta computadora. ¿Cómo funciona?

5. Marisol no _____ (sabe / conoce) manejar todavía.

Oreja vs. oído

Oreja and **oído** both mean *ear*. **Oreja** refers to the outer ear; **oído** refers to the inner ear, and thus the sense of hearing or the ear canal.

El peluquero me cortó **la oreja**.	*The hairdresser cut my ear.*
El bebé tiene infección de **oído**.	*The baby has an ear infection.*

C **¿Oyes?** *Complete las oraciones con **oreja** u **oído**, escogiendo entre las posibilidades indicadas.*

1. —¿Por qué llora tu hijo?

   —Creo que tiene dolor de _____ (orejas / oídos).

2. Después de la corrida de toros, le ofrecen _____ (la oreja / el oído) del toro al torero.

3. Tiene _____ (buena oreja / buen oído) para la música.

4. Le dio un golpe en _____ (la oreja / el oído).

5. Mi abuelo no oye bien. Es duro de _____ (oreja / oído).

NOTA CULTURAL

En **la corrida de toros**, si el torero torea bien según los jueces, le conceden una de las orejas del toro. Si torea sumamente bien, existe la posibilidad de que los jueces le premien con las dos orejas y el rabo (*tail*) del toro.

Meanings of quedar

Quedar means *to remain*. One of its most frequent uses is to ask for the location of places.

—¿Dónde **queda** el estadio?	*Where's the stadium?*
—**Queda** lejos, cerca del aeropuerto.	*It's far away, near the airport.*

When referring to people, **quedar** means *to remain* or *to be in a certain emotional or physical state.*

quedar boquiabierto	*to be openmouthed with astonishment*
quedar ciego/sordo/cojo	*to go blind/deaf/lame*
quedar en ridículo	*to look foolish*
quedar bien	*to come off well, make a good impression*
quedar mal	*to come off badly, make a bad impression*
hacer algo por quedar bien	*to do something to make a good impression*

Quedar means *to have left*, and in this usage it is often accompanied by an indirect object pronoun. See "Verbs Usually Appearing with an Indirect Object Pronoun (e.g., **gustar**)" in Chapter 19.

—¿Cuánto dinero **te queda**?	*How much money do you have left?*
—**Me quedan** mil pesos.	*I have a thousand pesos left.*
Me quedan tres páginas por escribir.	*I have three pages left to write.*
Quedan cinco kilómetros.	*There are five kilometers left (to go).*
Quedan seis estudiantes en la clase.	*There are six students left in the class.*
Quedan pocos días para las vacaciones.	*There aren't many days left until vacation.*

Quedarse means *to stay, remain.*

quedarse en un hotel	*to stay at a hotel*
quedarse en casa de sus amigos	*to stay at one's friends' house*

Quedarse con means *to keep*; **quedarse sin** means *to run out of.*

Se quedó con mi libro de química.	*He kept my chemistry book.*
Me quedo con éste.	*I'll take this one.* (in a store)
Quédese Ud. con la vuelta.	*Keep the change.*
Me he quedado sin azúcar.	*I've run out of sugar.*
Lidia **se ha quedado sin** trabajo.	*Lidia has lost her job.*

In colloquial usage, the phrase beginning with **con** in the idiom **quedarse con** is often replaced by a direct object pronoun.

—Entonces, ¿le gusta esta computadora?	*So, you like this computer?*
—Sí, me la quedo. (FORMAL: Me quedo con ella.)	*Yes, I'll take it.*

Some Expressions with **quedar(se)**

No me queda más remedio.	*I have no choice/alternative.*
Queda a tres millas de aquí.	*It's three miles from here.*
Quedar con uno para ir al cine.	*To make a date with someone to go to the movies.*
Quedan en salir el domingo.	*They agree/arrange to go out on Sunday.*
¿En qué quedamos?	*What did we decide to do?*
No se queda con la cólera dentro.	*He can't hide his anger.*
No quise quedarme en menos.	*I refused to be outdone.*
Se quedó en nada.	*It came to nothing.*

D *Expresar en español. Quedar.* *Escriba oraciones en español usando el verbo* **quedar(se)**.

1. *We have two weeks left in Puerto Rico.*

2. *Keep* (tú) *the money. I don't need it.*

3. *I have run out of job opportunities.*

4. *They stayed with a Mexican family.*

5. *You* (Uds.) *have three sentences left to translate.*

6. *He went deaf because of the explosion.*

7. *Where's the post office, please?*

8. *Paula and I agreed to go to the movies.*

"To Break" and "To Tear"

The Spanish verb **romper** covers the meanings of English *to break* and *to tear*.

La ventana está rota.	*The window is broken.*
Mi camisa está rota. }	
Tengo la camisa rota. }	*My shirt is torn.*

Romperse + article of clothing is often used with the meaning *to tear something*.

Cuidado, o te vas a romper el pantalón.	*Careful, or you'll tear your pants.*

To be broken in the sense of *to be out of order* is usually **estar descompuesto**. The verb is **descomponerse** and it may also appear with an indirect object pronoun (the unplanned occurrences construction): **descomponérsele a uno**.

El ascensor está descompuesto.	*The elevator is broken (out of order).*
Se descompuso el aire acondicionado.	*The air conditioner went on the blink.*
Se me descompuso el coche.	*My car broke down.*

Expressions with **romper**

romper a llorar	*to burst out crying*
romper con alguien	*to break off with someone*
romper el fuego	*to open fire*
romper en llanto	*to burst out crying*
romper las hostilidades	*to start hostilities*
Quien rompe paga.	*Actions have consequences.*
No te preocupes. No te vas a romper.	*Don't worry. You're not so fragile.*

E *Expresar en español. Exprese las oraciones en español.*

1. *Who tore my newspaper?*

2. *My chair is broken.*

3. *The radio is broken.*

4. *My coat is torn.*

5. *I hope the car doesn't break down on us.*

6. *We don't understand why she burst out crying.*

7. *Don't (tú) tear your jacket.*

8. *Elena broke off with her boyfriend.*

9. *The enemy opened fire.*

10. *Actions have consequences.*

"Wrong"

There is no one Spanish word that covers all the meanings of English *wrong*. When *wrong* means *morally* or *ethically wrong*, Spanish often uses **malo**.

Hiciste algo muy **malo**.	*You did something very wrong.*
¿Qué tiene eso de **malo**?	*What's wrong with that?*

When *wrong* means *incorrect*, Spanish has several possibilities, not all interchangeable.

1 · When *wrong* is said of people, Spanish uses **no tener razón**, **equivocarse**, or **estar equivocado**.

—Mónica dijo que la lámpara costaba cincuenta dólares.	*Monica said that the lamp cost fifty dollars.*
—**No tiene razón.** Cuesta cuarenta.	*She's wrong. It costs forty.*
—Quisiera hablar con el señor Lares.	*I'd like to speak with Mr. Lares.*
—Aquí no vive ningún señor Lares. Ud. **se ha equivocado** al marcar el número.	*There's no Mr. Lares (living) here. You've dialed the wrong number.*
—¿Aquí no vive la familia Laínez?	*Doesn't the Laínez family live here?*
—No. Ud. **se ha equivocado de casa**.	*No. You've come to the wrong house.*
—Creo que la respuesta es cinco y tres octavos.	*I think the answer is five and three-eighths.*
—Ud. **está equivocado**. La respuesta es seis.	*You're wrong. The answer is six.*

2 · When *wrong* refers to information or answers, Spanish uses **incorrecto**, **inexacto**, **equivocado**, and **mal**.

La respuesta es **incorrecta**. ⎫	*The answer is wrong.*
La respuesta es **inexacta**. ⎭	
Estos datos están **equivocados**.	*This data is wrong.*
La receta está **mal**.	*The recipe is wrong.*
Mi reloj anda **mal**.	*My watch is wrong.*
Ud. escribió **mal** mi dirección.	*You wrote my address wrong.*
Uds. me comprendieron **mal**.	*You didn't understand me correctly.*
El estudiante contestó **mal**.	*The student answered incorrectly.*

3 · When *wrong* means *inopportune, unwanted,* it is often translated as **no... adecuado**, **no... apropiado**, **impropio**, or **inoportuno**.

No es el momento **adecuado**
    para hablar de esas cosas.   *It's the wrong time to speak about those*
No es el momento **apropiado**   *things.*
    para hablar de esas cosas.

Decir algo **inoportuno** en español   *To say the wrong thing in Spanish is*
    es «meter la pata».   *"meter la pata."*

4 · When *wrong* expresses a result or outcome not desired or sought, it can have a variety of translations.

Éste no es el libro que hacía falta.	*This is the wrong book.*
Éste no es el tren que debíamos tomar. Nos hemos equivocado de tren.	*This is the wrong train.*
Tienes los calcetines al revés.	*Your socks are wrong side out.*
Mi profesión no me conviene.	*I'm in the wrong profession.*
Tocó una nota falsa.	*He played a wrong note.*
La silla está mal colocada.	*The chair is in the wrong place.*
Ud. maneja por el lado prohibido.	*You're driving on the wrong side of the road.*

5 · When *wrong* means *amiss, to have something wrong,* the verb **pasar** is used.

—¿Qué te pasa, Luis?	*What's wrong with you, Luis?*
—No me pasa nada.	*Nothing is wrong with me.*
—¿Pasa algo aquí?	*Is something wrong here?*
—No, señora, no pasa nada.	*No, ma'am. Nothing is wrong.*
—Le pasa algo a la computadora.	*Something's wrong with the computer.*
—Hay que llamar al técnico.	*We have to call the technician.*

6 · Note also the following expressions.

Distinguir entre el bien y el mal.	*To tell right from wrong.*
Entiéndeme bien.	*Don't get me wrong.*
Todo salió mal.	*Everything went wrong.*
Hiciste mal en prestarle el dinero.	*You were wrong to lend him the money.*

F   *Expresar en español. Exprese las oraciones en español.*

1. *I dialed the wrong number.*

2. *He took the wrong train.*

3. *What's wrong with the cell phone?*

4. *This is not the right time.*

5. *I read the title wrong.*

6. *Your (tú) gloves are wrong side out.*

7. *He's got the wrong job.*

8. *The definition is wrong.*

9. *I was wrong not to believe him.*

10. *You (Ud.) added* (sumar) *wrong.*

"To Miss"

The verb *to miss* has several very different meanings in English, each of which is translated by a different Spanish verb. When *miss* means *to long for a person or thing*, Spanish uses **echar de menos** or, especially in Spanish America, **extrañar**.

—Echo de menos a mi familia.	*I miss my family.*
—Yo también extraño a mis padres.	*I also miss my parents.*

Spanish uses the verb **perder** for *to miss a plane or train*.

—Date prisa. Vamos a perder el tren.	*Hurry up. We're going to miss the train.*
—Ya lo hemos perdido. Tomaremos el siguiente.	*We've already missed it. We'll take the next one.*

Spanish uses the verb **perderse** for *to miss a show or event*.

—Me perdí la nueva película.	*I missed the new film.*
—Te has perdido algo muy bueno.	*You've missed something very good.*

Note that *to miss class* is usually **faltar a clase**.

Spanish uses **errar el tiro** or **fallar (el blanco)** for *to miss the target, miss the mark, not to hit.*

Apuntó, pero erró el tiro.	*He aimed, but missed.*
Es un método que nunca falla.	*It's a method that never misses (fails).*
El ladrón disparó, pero falló el blanco.	*The thief shot, but missed.*

To be missing can be expressed in two ways in Spanish, depending on the meaning.

Encontraron a los estudiantes desaparecidos.	*They found the missing students.*
Nos faltan tres documentos.	*We're missing three documents.*
Complete las oraciones con las palabras que faltan.	*Complete the sentences with the missing words.*

Here are other uses of *to miss.*

No puedes dejar de encontrarlo.	*You can't miss it.*
Llegué tarde y no lo encontré.	*I arrived late, so I missed him.*
No dejes de ir a los museos cuando estés en México.	*Don't miss the museums when you're in Mexico.*
No entendí lo que dijiste.	*I missed what you said.*

G *A completar.* Complete las oraciones con una expresión adecuada que exprese la idea de *to miss.*

1. Anoche mi hermana no pudo salir. Por eso _____ la obra de teatro.

2. Si Alfonso _____ tantas veces a clase, va a salir muy mal en el curso.

3. Vamos rápido. No quiero _____ el avión.

4. El pillo (*hoodlum*) trató de romper la ventana con una piedra, pero _____.

5. Otra vez, por favor. Hay tanto ruido aquí que yo _____ lo que dijiste.

6. Con este programa, tienes que aprender inglés. Dicen que es un sistema que nunca

    _____.

7. —¿Todos los socios del club ya han llegado?

    —No, todavía _____ dos o tres.

8. Ojalá pudiera ver a mi novia. No sabes cuánto la _____.

9. Hubo muchos soldados _____ al terminar la guerra.

Review

Review Exercises

1 The Present Tense

A **The present tense.** Write the present tense form of the regular -**ar**, -**er**, or -**ir** verb in parentheses that correctly completes each of the following sentences.

1. Yo _____ un informe. (escribir)

2. Ricardo _____ en una empresa multinacional. (trabajar)

3. ¿Dónde _____ Uds.? (vivir)

4. Tú no _____ mi idea, ¿verdad? (comprender)

5. Nosotros te _____ en el café. (esperar)

6. ¿Ud. _____ administración de empresas? (estudiar)

7. Ellos _____ sano. (comer)

8. Sofía _____ español y francés. (aprender)

B **The present tense.** Write the present tense **yo** form of the irregular verb in the question to correctly complete each of the following responses.

1. ¿Sales a las siete? No, _____ a las ocho.

2. ¿Conoces a Felipe? No, pero _____ a su esposa.

3. ¿Haces pescado esta noche? No, _____ pollo.

4. ¿Das un paseo por el centro? No, _____ un paseo por el parque.

5. ¿Vas de vacaciones en abril? No, _____ de vacaciones en julio.

6. ¿Sabes su dirección? No, pero _____ su número de celular.

7. ¿Tienes hambre? No, pero _____ mucha sed.

8. ¿Vienes en carro? No, _____ en tren.

2 Ser and estar

C **Ser and estar.** Write the present tense form of **ser** or **estar** that correctly completes each of the following sentences.

1. Nosotros _____ de los Estados Unidos.

2. Todos los museos _____ abiertos hoy.

3. Daniel _____ más alto que su hermano.

4. Yo _____ de acuerdo contigo.

5. Isabel y Miguel _____ ingenieros.

6. Este traje _____ de una lana muy fina.

7. Tus hijos _____ acatarrados, ¿no?

8. Yo _____ de origen inglés y ruso.

9. Me parece que Ud. _____ ocupadísimo.

10. ¿De dónde _____ (tú)?

11. Claudia y yo ya _____ de vuelta.

12. La tienda de cómputo _____ en la esquina.

13. La reunión _____ en la oficina del director.

14. ¿_____ italianos esos turistas?

3 Stem-Changing Verbs and Verbs with Spelling Changes

D **Stem-changing verbs.** Write complete sentences with stem-changing verbs in the present tense, using the elements given.

1. mis padres / volver / el viernes

2. Beatriz / pedir / postre con el café

3. Uds. / poder / comprar boletos en línea

4. yo / pensar / en el futuro

5. llover / toda la semana

6. ¿tú / querer / acompañarnos?

7. nosotros / empezar a / navegar en la red

8. Ud. / servir / unos platos riquísimos

4 The Preterit Tense

E **The preterit tense.** Write the preterit tense form of the regular -ar, -er, or -ir verb in parentheses that correctly completes each of the following sentences.

1. Yo _____ una computadora. (comprar)

2. Rafael _____ el maratón ayer. (correr)

3. ¿Tú no _____ el paquete? (recibir)

4. Uds. _____ su casa, ¿no? (vender)

5. ¡Nos _____ los regalos! (encantar)

6. Yo _____ a analizar los datos. (comenzar)

7. Pilar _____ una novela muy aburrida. (leer)

8. Yo _____ al tenis por la tarde. (jugar)

9. La abuela _____ a sus nietecitos. (vestir)

10. Las niñas _____ la siesta. (dormir)

11. Yo _____ al perro. (buscar)

12. ¿Qué les _____ Ud. a los invitados? (servir)

F **The preterit tense.** Write the preterit tense form of the irregular verb in parentheses that correctly completes each of the following sentences.

1. Yo no les _____ nada. (decir)

2. Ellos nos _____ un lindo regalo. (traer)

3. ¿Cuándo _____ (tú) el viaje a Inglaterra? (hacer)

4. Nosotros _____ lo del huracán ayer.   (saber)

5. Antonio _____ mucho éxito. (tener)

6. ¿Uds. _____ al centro comercial el sábado? (ir)

7. Raquel no _____ mandar el email. (poder)

8. Los chicos no _____ pasear al perro. (querer)

9. Nosotras _____ a ver a los abuelos. (venir)

10. ¡Yo _____ contentísimo! (estar)

5 The Imperfect Tense

G **The imperfect tense.** Write the imperfect tense form of the verb in parentheses that correctly completes each of the following sentences.

1. Nosotros _____ el español todos los días. (practicar)

2. _____ las diez cuando salimos del teatro. (ser)

3. Yo _____ ponerme en contacto con ellos. (querer)

4. Los gemelos _____ once años. (tener)

5. Tú _____ en este barrio, ¿no? (vivir)

6. Uds. no _____ nada desde allí. (ver)

7. Juan Carlos no _____ cuando llegamos. (estar)

8. _____ muchos pasajeros en el tren. (haber)

9. ¿Es cierto que Ud. _____ a estudiar medicina? (ir)

10. Paloma y yo _____ en la red. (navegar)

H   **The imperfect and the preterit.** Write the imperfect or preterit tense form of the verbs in parentheses to correctly complete each of the following sentences. Each sentence will have one verb in the imperfect and one verb in the preterit.

1. _____ fuerte cuando (nosotros) _____ a casa. (llover / volver)

2. Mientras Ud. _____, _____ su celular. (cenar / sonar)

3. Sara _____ la mesa cuando _____ sus invitados. (poner / llegar)

4. _____ la una y media cuando yo _____ a trabajar. (ser / empezar)

5. Pedro _____ un ruido extraño cuando _____ la siesta. (oír / dormir)

6. Yo les _____ que (yo) _____ a invitarlos a la fiesta. (decir / ir)

7. _____ mucha neblina cuando el avión _____. (haber / despegar)

8. ¿_____ algo mientras tú _____ un paseo? (pasar / dar)

9. Nos _____ cuando _____ estudiantes. (conocer / ser)

10. Mi prima me _____ que la empresa _____ trasladarla a Chile. (escribir / pensar)

11. Nosotros _____ el postre cuando José _____ más sopa. (tomar / pedir)

12. Mientras ellas _____ en el extranjero, se les _____ su perro. (estar / morir)

6 The Future and Conditional Tenses

I   **The future tense.** Rewrite each of the following sentences, changing the verb from the present to the future tense.

1. Imprimo estos documentos.

2. Brindamos por su salud.

3. ¿Prendes la tele?

4. La reunión comienza a las dos.

5. Me pongo la camisa blanca.

6. Los actores se divierten mucho.

7. Te pruebas los zapatos nuevos, ¿no?

8. Salimos para la oficina en media hora.

9. Diego se gradúa el año que viene.

10. Yo vuelvo el miércoles.

11. ¿Qué hay en la bolsa?

12. La boda es en el hotel Plaza.

J   **The future tense.** Rewrite each of the following sentences, using a verb in the future tense in place of the verb + infinitive construction. Use the infinitive from the original construction as the replacement verb.

1. Mateo prefiere venir la semana próxima.

2. Todos Uds. no pueden caber en el carro.

3. ¿Tus amigos no te van a decir la verdad?

4. Tenemos que hacer escala en Madrid.

5. Espero reunirme con todo el equipo.

6. El anillo debe valer una fortuna.

7. Quedamos en vernos el domingo.

8. ¿Piensas aprovecharte de las ofertas?

9. Mis colegas se empeñan en saberlo todo.

10. Yo me pongo a arreglarme.

K **The conditional tense.** Write the conditional tense form of the verb in parentheses that correctly completes each of the following sentences.

1. Uds. _____ los datos. (analizar)

2. José _____ los gastos del apartamento. (compartir)

3. Me _____ seguir con mis clases en línea. (gustar)

4. ¿Nosotros _____ instalarnos en la casa? (poder)

5. _____ mucha gente en el parque. (Hay)

6. Tú _____ muy emocionada. (estar)

7. _____ setenta y ocho grados. (Hacer)

8. A ellos les _____ estudiar en el extranjero. (interesar)

9. Ud. no _____ miedo, ¿verdad? (tener)

10. ¿Qué _____ nosotros en ese caso? (decir)

7 Reflexive Verbs

L **Reflexive verbs.** Write complete sentences with reflexive verbs in the present tense, using the elements given.

1. nosotros / quedarse en la ciudad

2. él / acostarse a las once

3. ellos / lavarse las manos

4. yo / probarse la chaqueta

Write complete sentences with reflexive verbs in the preterit, using the elements given.

5. nosotros / ponerse de pie

6. Uds. / divertirse en el baile

7. ella / cortarse el pelo

8. tú / despertarse temprano

Write complete sentences with reflexive verbs in the imperative, using the elements given. Write each item as both an affirmative and a negative command.

9. Ud. / despedirse de ellos

10. Uds. / acostarse

11. tú / irse

12. nosotros / vestirse

13. Ud. / reírse

14. Uds. / acercarse

15. tú / dormirse

16. nosotros / ponérnoslo

8 Passive Constructions

M **The passive voice.** Rewrite each of the following sentences, changing from the active to the passive voice. Follow the *modelo*.

> MODELO El estudiante leyó el libro.
> → El libro fue leído por el estudiante.

1. El asesor elaboró el presupuesto.

2. La cocinera preparó los platos principales.

3. Nora y Jaime pusieron la mesa.

4. Esos secretarios escribieron los emails.

5. Una programadora creó el software.

6. Andrés resolvió todos los problemas.

7. Un técnico reparó mi computadora.

8. La compañía envió a unos gerentes a Buenos Aires.

N **The se construction.** Rewrite each of the following sentences, using the **se** construction with the verb in present tense. Follow the *modelos*.

> MODELOS Guardo los documentos.
> → Se guardan los documentos.
>
> Entramos por aquí.
> → Se entra por aquí.

1. Firma los contratos.

2. Trabajamos de lunes a jueves.

3. Alquila apartamentos.

4. Hablas inglés.

5. Llegan en tren.

6. Venden flores.

7. Pagas los impuestos.

8. Servimos comida vegetariana.

9. Calcula los gastos.

10. Salgo por aquella puerta.

11. Visitan la ciudad vieja.

12. Hago copias.

9 The Compound Tenses

O **The present perfect.** Rewrite each of the following sentences, changing the verb from the present tense to the present perfect.

1. El viajero llega a la puerta de embarque.

2. ¿Bebes té o café?

3. ¿Qué ocurre?

4. Los profesores entienden la teoría.

5. Alfonso abre los ficheros.

6. Hay mucho tráfico últimamente.

7. Rebeca se maquilla la cara.

8. No vemos a nadie.

9. El niño se los pone.

10. No se lo digo a nadie.

11. Los gerentes no pueden entregarle el informe a su jefe.

12. Te la devolvemos.

P **The present perfect.** Write complete sentences with the verb in the present perfect, using the elements given. Then write another sentence that shows the resulting condition. Follow the *modelo*.

  MODELO el director / rodar / la película
       → El director ha rodado la película.
       → La película está rodada.

1. la cantante / grabar / la canción

2. yo / subir / los archivos

3. los contadores / pagar / las cuentas

4. el niño / tirar / sus juguetes

5. nosotros / desarrollar / el plan de negocios

6. el presidente / tomar una decisión

7. Alonso / vender / su carro

8. Uds. / prender / la tele

Q **The past perfect (pluperfect).** Rewrite each of the following sentences, changing the verb from the preterit to the past perfect.

1. Tú regresaste a la oficina.

2. Nosotros nos mudamos.

3. Yo busqué al nuevo diseñador.

4. El auxiliar de vuelo se puso el cinturón de seguridad.

5. Ellos no oyeron la noticia.

6. Uds. le pidieron más plata.

7. Yo apagué las luces.

8. ¿Los muchachos se lo leyeron?

10 The Gerund and the Progressive Tenses

R **The present progressive.** Rewrite each of the following sentences, changing the verb from the present tense to the present progressive. When there is more than one way to express the sentence in the present progressive, write both sentences.

1. Hablo con mis amigos.

2. Comemos al aire libre.

3. Nieva hoy.

4. ¿Imprimes el contrato?

5. El avión aterriza.

6. Te despiertas.

7. Nosotros se lo servimos.

8. Yo se las traigo.

11 The Subjunctive in Noun Clauses: Present and Present Perfect Subjunctive

S **The present subjunctive.** Write the present subjunctive form of the verb in parentheses that correctly completes each of the following sentences.

1. Quiero que Uds. _____ al concierto conmigo. (asistir)

2. No creemos que Felipe _____ el problema. (entender)

3. Te aconsejo que _____. (tranquilizarse)

4. Insisto en que Ud. _____ el español todos los días. (practicar)

5. Los Aguilar esperan que sus hijos _____ muy felices. (ser)

6. Me alegro de que nosotros _____ un vuelo directo. (tener)

7. No nos gusta que tú _____ así. (ponerse)

8. Les recomiendo que Uds. _____ ejercicio. (hacer)

9. Ojalá que nosotros _____ mucho. (divertirse)

10. Exigen que yo les _____ exactamente lo que pasó. (decir)

T **Present subjunctive or present indicative.** Write either the present subjunctive or the present indicative form of the verb in parentheses to correctly complete each of the following sentences.

1. Blanca prefiere que nosotros _____ este fin de semana. (venir)

2. Es una lástima que tú y Paco no _____ bien. (llevarse)

3. No pensamos que esa película _____ muy buena. (ser)

4. Es verdad que Raúl _____ fácilmente. (molestarse)

5. Deseamos que tú nos _____ con el proyecto. (apoyar)

6. Mis tíos saben que sus hijos no les _____ caso. (hacer)

7. Nos sorprende que Ud. no _____ de lo ocurrido. (saber)

8. Creo que Leonor _____ muy estresada. (estar)

U **The present subjunctive.** Rewrite each of the following sentences with a noun clause in the present subjunctive. Use the cue in parentheses.

1. Es importante disfrutar de la vida. (Ud.)

2. Es bueno leer las obras maestras de la literatura universal. (nosotros)

3. Es posible graduarse en enero. (ellos)

4. Es imprescindible comer sano. (Uds.)

5. Es útil traer la computadora. (ella)

6. Es triste estar lejos de la familia. (tú)

7. Es bueno llevar una vida tranquila. (tú y yo)

8. Es necesario aprovecharse de esta oportunidad. (yo)

V **The present perfect subjunctive.** Rewrite each of the following sentences, using the phrase in parentheses in the main clause. Change the tense of the verb from the preterit to the present perfect subjunctive.

1. Mario escribió otra novela. (nos alegramos)

2. No dijimos nada. (es mejor que)

3. No te devolvieron el dinero. (me sorprende)

4. ¿Hubo muchos problemas políticos? (dudas)

5. Tuviste mucha suerte. (espero)

6. Al futbolista se le rompió el pie. (sienten)

12 The Imperfect Subjunctive and Conditional Sentences

W **The imperfect subjunctive.** Write the imperfect subjunctive form of the verb in parentheses that correctly completes each of the following sentences. Use the **-ra** endings.

1. Tomás y Rita esperaban que su hijo _____ ingeniero. (hacerse)

2. Los Reyes nos pidieron que _____ a verlos. (pasar)

3. Queríamos que Uds. _____ esta exhibición de arte. (ver)

4. Si _____ posible, yo los acompañaría. (ser)

5. Era posible que Jorge _____ el puesto. (conseguir)

6. Ojalá que _____ reunirnos más a menudo. (poder)

7. Nosotros haríamos ecoturismo si _____ a Costa Rica. (ir)

8. Nos gustaría que tú _____ con nosotros. (salir)

14 Commands

X **Commands.** Write affirmative and negative commands for each item. Change direct object nouns to pronouns and make all necessary changes.

Ud.

1. trabajar los lunes

2. escribir el ensayo

3. leer los documentos

4. ir a la clase

5. probarse la camisa

Uds.

6. salir ahora mismo

7. darles las llaves

8. explicarme sus ideas

9. devolverles el coche

10. lavarse la cara

tú

11. ser amable

12. venir conmigo

13. salir a las cuatro

14. hacernos la cena

15. ponerte el traje

nosotros

16. ir de compras

17. relajarnos

18. servirles el postre

19. quitarnos las botas

20. cepillarnos los dientes

19 Personal Pronouns: Subject, Object, Prepositional

Y   **Reverse construction verbs.** Express the following sentences in Spanish, using reverse construction verbs.

1. *I like these museums.*

2. *We're very interested in archaeology.*

3. *They care about the environment.*

4. *Didn't you (Uds.) like that guy?*

5. *Were you (tú) excited about the shows?*

6. *We would love to take a trip.*

7. *It was his turn.*

8. *You (Ud.) need to make up your mind.*

Z   **Unplanned occurrences.** Write sentences in the preterit to express the idea of an unplanned occurrence, using the elements given.

1. (a él) perdérsele / la mochila

2. (a mí) quedársele / el paraguas / en la oficina

3. (a ellos) descomponérsele / el carro

4. (a Ud.) rompérsele / las gafas oscuras

5. (a Uds.) acabársele / la energía

6. (a ti) caérsele / los vasos

7. (a nosotros) ocurrírsele / algo

8. (a ella) olvidársele / el cumpleaños de su hermana

Appendices

Verb Charts

Regular Verbs

-ar verbs

cantar *to sing*

INDICATIVE MOOD

PRESENT	canto, cantas, canta · cantamos, cantáis, cantan
IMPERFECT	cantaba, cantabas, cantaba · cantábamos, cantabais, cantaban
PRETERIT	canté, cantaste, cantó · cantamos, cantasteis, cantaron
FUTURE	cantaré, cantarás, cantará · cantaremos, cantaréis, cantarán
CONDITIONAL	cantaría, cantarías, cantaría · cantaríamos, cantaríais, cantarían
PRESENT PERFECT	he cantado, has cantado, ha cantado · hemos cantado, habéis cantado, han cantado
PLUPERFECT	había cantado, habías cantado, había cantado · habíamos cantado, habíais cantado, habían cantado
PRETERIT PERFECT	hube cantado, hubiste cantado, hubo cantado · hubimos cantado, hubisteis cantado, hubieron cantado
FUTURE PERFECT	habré cantado, habrás cantado, habrá cantado · habremos cantado, habréis cantado, habrán cantado
CONDITIONAL PERFECT	habría cantado, habrías cantado, había cantado · habríamos cantado, habríais cantado, habrían cantado

SUBJUNCTIVE MOOD

PRESENT	cante, cantes, cante · cantemos, cantéis, canten
IMPERFECT	cantara, cantaras, cantara · cantáramos, cantarais, cantaran
	cantase, cantases, cantase · cantásemos, cantaseis, cantasen
PRESENT PERFECT	haya cantado, hayas cantado, haya cantado · hayamos cantado, hayáis cantado, hayan cantado
PLUPERFECT	hubiera/hubiese cantado, hubieras/hubieses cantado, hubiera/hubiese cantado · hubiéramos/hubiésemos cantado, hubierais/hubieseis cantado, hubieran/hubiesen cantado

IMPERATIVE MOOD

	canta / no cantes (tú), cante (Ud.) · cantemos (nosotros), cantad / no cantéis (vosotros), canten (Uds.)

-er verbs

comer *to eat*

INDICATIVE MOOD

PRESENT	como, comes, come · comemos, coméis, comen
IMPERFECT	comía, comías, comía · comíamos, comíais, comían
PRETERIT	comí, comiste, comió · comimos, comisteis, comieron
FUTURE	comeré, comerás, comerá · comeremos, comeréis, comerán
CONDITIONAL	comería, comerías, comería · comeríamos, comeríais, comerían
PRESENT PERFECT	he comido, has comido, ha comido · hemos comido, habéis comido, han comido
PLUPERFECT	había comido, habías comido, había comido · habíamos comido, habíais comido, habían comido
PRETERIT PERFECT	hube comido, hubiste comido, hubo comido · hubimos comido, hubisteis comido, hubieron comido
FUTURE PERFECT	habré comido, habrás comido, habrá comido · habremos comido, habréis comido, habrán comido
CONDITIONAL PERFECT	habría comido, habrías comido, habría comido · habríamos comido, habríais comido, habrían comido

SUBJUNCTIVE MOOD

PRESENT	coma, comas, coma · comamos, comáis, coman
IMPERFECT	comiera, comieras, comiera · comiéramos, comierais, comieran
	comiese, comieses, comiese · comiésemos, comieseis, comiesen
PRESENT PERFECT	haya comido, hayas comido, haya comido · hayamos comido, hayáis comido, hayan comido
PLUPERFECT	hubiera/hubiese comido, hubieras/hubieses comido, hubiera/hubiese comido · hubiéramos/hubiésemos comido, hubierais/hubieseis comido, hubieran/hubiesen comido

IMPERATIVE MOOD

come / no comas (tú), coma (Ud.) · comamos (nosotros),
comed / no comáis (vosotros), coman (Uds.)

-ir verbs

vivir *to live*

INDICATIVE MOOD

PRESENT	vivo, vives, vive · vivimos, vivís, viven
IMPERFECT	vivía, vivías, vivía · vivíamos, vivíais, vivían
PRETERIT	viví, viviste, vivió · vivimos, vivisteis, vivieron
FUTURE	viviré, vivirás, vivirá · viviremos, viviréis, vivirán
CONDITIONAL	viviría, vivirías, viviría · viviríamos, viviríais, vivirían
PRESENT PERFECT	he vivido, has vivido, ha vivido · hemos vivido, habéis vivido, han vivido
PLUPERFECT	había vivido, habías vivido, había vivido · habíamos vivido, habíais vivido, habían vivido
PRETERIT PERFECT	hube vivido, hubiste vivido, hubo vivido · hubimos vivido, hubisteis vivido, hubieron vivido
FUTURE PERFECT	habré vivido, habrás vivido, habrá vivido · habremos vivido, habréis vivido, habrán vivido
CONDITIONAL PERFECT	habría vivido, habrías vivido, habría vivido · habríamos vivido, habríais vivido, habrían vivido

SUBJUNCTIVE MOOD

PRESENT	viva, vivas, viva · vivamos, viváis, vivan
IMPERFECT	viviera, vivieras, viviera · viviéramos, vivierais, vivieran
	viviese, vivieses, viviese · viviésemos, vivieseis, viviesen
PRESENT PERFECT	haya vivido, hayas vivido, haya vivido · hayamos vivido, hayáis vivido, hayan vivido
PLUPERFECT	hubiera/hubiese vivido, hubieras/hubieses vivido, hubiera/hubiese vivido · hubiéramos/hubiésemos vivido, hubierais/hubieseis vivido, hubieran/hubiesen vivido

IMPERATIVE MOOD

vive / no vivas (tú), viva (Ud.) · vivamos (nosotros),
vivid / no viváis (vosotros), vivan (Uds.)

Verbs with Changes in the Vowel of the Stem

pensar (e > ie) *to think*

PRESENT INDICATIVE	pienso, piensas, piensa · pensamos, penséis, piensan
PRESENT SUBJUNCTIVE	piense, pienses, piense · pensemos, penséis, piensen
IMPERATIVE	piensa / no pienses, piense · pensemos, pensad / no penséis, piensen

Other tenses and forms have no changes in the vowel of the stem.

entender (e > ie) *to understand*

PRESENT INDICATIVE	entiendo, entiendes, entiende · entendemos, entendéis, entienden
PRESENT SUBJUNCTIVE	entienda, entiendas, entienda · entendamos, entendáis, entiendan
IMPERATIVE	entiende / no entiendas, entienda · entendamos, entended / no entendáis, entiendan

Other tenses and forms have no changes in the vowel of the stem.

recordar (o > ue) *to remember*

PRESENT INDICATIVE	recuerdo, recuerdas, recuerda · recordamos, recordáis, recuerdan
PRESENT SUBJUNCTIVE	recuerde, recuerdes, recuerde · recordemos, recordéis, recuerden
IMPERATIVE	recuerda / no recuerdes, recuerde · recordemos, recordad / no recordéis, recuerden

Other tenses and forms have no changes in the vowel of the stem.

volver (o > ue) *to return*

PRESENT INDICATIVE	vuelvo, vuelves, vuelve · volvemos, volvéis, vuelven
PRESENT SUBJUNCTIVE	vuelva, vuelvas, vuelva · volvamos, volváis, vuelvan
IMPERATIVE	vuelve / no vuelvas, vuelva · volvamos, volved / no volváis, vuelvan

Other tenses and forms have no changes in the vowel of the stem.

Stem-changing **-ir** verbs have three types of possible changes in the vowel of the stem: **e > ie, e > i, o > ue**. In addition to the expected changes in the present subjunctive and imperative, verbs having the change **e > ie** and **e > i** have **i** as the stem vowel and verbs having the change **o > ue** have **u** as the stem vowel in the following forms:

- The **nosotros** and **vosotros** forms of the present subjunctive
- The **nosotros** command and the negative **vosotros** commands
- The third person singular and third person plural forms of the preterit
- All persons of the imperfect subjunctive (both **-ra** and **-se** forms)
- The present participle

Sample Conjugations

sentir (e > ie) *to feel, regret*

PRESENT INDICATIVE	siento, sientes, siente · sentimos, sentís, sienten
PRESENT SUBJUNCTIVE	sienta, sientas, sienta · sintamos, sintáis, sientan
IMPERATIVE	siente / no sientas, sienta · sintamos, sentid / no sintáis, sientan
PRETERIT	sentí, sentiste, sintió · sentimos, sentisteis, sintieron
IMPERFECT SUBJUNCTIVE	sintiera, sintieras, sintiera · sintiéramos, sintierais, sintieran
	sintiese, sintieses, sintiese · sintiésemos, sintieseis, sintiesen
PRESENT PARTICIPLE	sintiendo

Other tenses and forms have no changes in the vowel of the stem.

pedir (e > i) *to ask for*

PRESENT INDICATIVE	pido, pides, pide · pedimos, pedís, piden
PRESENT SUBJUNCTIVE	pida, pidas, pida · pidamos, pidáis, pidan
IMPERATIVE	pide / no pidas, pida · pidamos, pedid / no pidáis, pidan
PRETERIT	pedí, pediste, pidió · pedimos, pedisteis, pidieron
IMPERFECT SUBJUNCTIVE	pidiera, pidieras, pidiera · pidiéramos, pidierais, pidieran
	pidiese, pidieses, pidiese · pidiésemos, pidieseis, pidiesen
PRESENT PARTICIPLE	pidiendo

Other tenses and forms have no changes in the vowel of the stem.

dormir (o > ue) *to sleep*

PRESENT INDICATIVE	duermo, duermes, duerme · dormimos, dormís, duermen
PRESENT SUBJUNCTIVE	duerma, duermas, duerma · durmamos, durmáis, duerman
IMPERATIVE	duerme / no duermas, duerma · durmamos, dormid / no durmáis, duerman
PRETERIT	dormí, dormiste, durmió · dormimos, dormisteis, durmieron
IMPERFECT SUBJUNCTIVE	durmiera, durmieras, durmiera · durmiéramos, durmierais, durmieran
	durmiese, durmieses, durmiese · durmiésemos, durmieseis, durmiesen
PRESENT PARTICIPLE	durmiendo

Other tenses and forms have no changes in the vowel of the stem.

Verbs with Spelling Changes

These changes occur in the first person singular of the preterit, in all persons of the present subjunctive, and in imperative forms derived from the present subjunctive.

Verbs Ending in -car (c > qu before -e)

tocar *to play an instrument; to touch*

PRETERIT	to**qu**é, tocaste, tocó · tocamos, tocasteis, tocaron
PRESENT SUBJUNCTIVE	to**qu**e, to**qu**es, to**qu**e · to**qu**emos, to**qu**éis, to**qu**en
IMPERATIVE	toca / no to**qu**es, to**qu**e · to**qu**emos, tocad / no to**qu**éis, to**qu**en

Verbs Ending in -gar (g > gu before -e)

llegar *to arrive*

PRETERIT	lle**gu**é, llegaste, llegó · llegamos, llegasteis, llegaron
PRESENT SUBJUNCTIVE	lle**gu**e, lle**gu**es, lle**gu**e · lle**gu**emos, lle**gu**éis, lle**gu**en
IMPERATIVE	llega / no lle**gu**es, lle**gu**e · lle**gu**emos, llegad / no lle**gu**éis, lle**gu**en

Verbs Ending in -zar (z > c before -e)

cruzar *to cross*

PRETERIT	cru**c**é, cruzaste, cruzó · cruzamos, cruzasteis, cruzaron
PRESENT SUBJUNCTIVE	cru**c**e, cru**c**es, cru**c**e · cru**c**emos, cru**c**éis, cru**c**en
IMPERATIVE	cruza / no cru**c**es, cru**c**e · cru**c**emos, cruzad / no cru**c**éis, cru**c**en

Verbs Ending in -ger and -gir (g > j before -a and -o)

recoger *to pick up*

PRESENT INDICATIVE	reco**j**o, recoges, recoge · recogemos, recogéis, recogen
PRESENT SUBJUNCTIVE	reco**j**a, reco**j**as, reco**j**a · reco**j**amos, reco**j**áis, reco**j**an
IMPERATIVE	recoge / no reco**j**as, reco**j**a · reco**j**amos, recoged / no reco**j**áis, reco**j**an

exigir *to demand*

PRESENT INDICATIVE	exi**j**o, exiges, exige · exigimos, exigís, exigen
PRESENT SUBJUNCTIVE	exi**j**a, exi**j**as, exi**j**a · exi**j**amos, exi**j**áis, exi**j**an
IMPERATIVE	exige / no exi**j**as, exi**j**a · exi**j**amos, exigid / no exi**j**áis, exi**j**an

Verbs Ending in -guir (gu > g before -a and -o)

seguir *to follow*

PRESENT INDICATIVE	sigo, sigues, sigue · seguimos, seguís, siguen
PRESENT SUBJUNCTIVE	siga, sigas, siga · sigamos, sigáis, sigan
IMPERATIVE	sigue / no sigas, siga · sigamos, seguid / no sigáis, sigan
PRESENT PARTICIPLE	siguiendo

Verbs Ending in a Consonant + -cer, -cir (c > z before -a and -o)

convencer *to convince*

PRESENT INDICATIVE	convenzo, convences, convence · convencemos, convencéis, convencen
PRESENT SUBJUNCTIVE	convenza, convenzas, convenza · convenzamos, convenzáis, convenzan
IMPERATIVE	convence / no convenzas, convenza · convenzamos, convenced / no convenzáis, convenzan

-Er Verbs Having Stems Ending in a Vowel

These verbs change the **i** of the preterit endings **-ió** and **-ieron** and the **i** of the present participle ending **-iendo** to **y**. The **y** appears in all persons of the imperfect subjunctive. These verbs also add written accents to the endings of the second person singular and the first and second person plural forms of the preterit and the past participle.

creer *to believe*

PRETERIT	creí, creíste, creyó · creímos, creísteis, creyeron
IMPERFECT SUBJUNCTIVE	creyera (creyese), creyeras, creyera · creyéramos, creyerais, creyeran
PRESENT PARTICIPLE	creyendo
PAST PARTICIPLE	creído

-Ar Verbs Having Stems Ending in Syllabic -i or -u (Not as Part of a Diphthong)

These verbs have an accent mark over the **i** or **u** in all persons of the singular and in the third person plural of the present indicative and present subjunctive, and in all imperative forms except **nosotros** and **vosotros**.

enviar *to send*

PRESENT	envío, envías, envía · enviamos, enviáis, envían
PRESENT SUBJUNCTIVE	envíe, envíes, envíe · enviemos, enviéis, envíen
IMPERATIVE	envía / no envíes, envíe · enviemos, enviad / no enviéis, envíen

continuar *to continue*

PRESENT	continúo, continúas, continúa · continuamos, continuáis, continúan
PRESENT SUBJUNCTIVE	continúe, continúes, continúe · continuemos, continuéis, continúen
IMPERATIVE	continúa / no continúes, continúe · continuemos, continuad / no continuéis, continúen

Irregular Verbs

Only tenses with irregular forms are shown.

Verbs Ending in a Vowel + -cer or -ucir

These verbs change the final -c of the stem to -zc before -a and -o. The -zc appears in the first person singular of the present indicative, in all persons of the present subjunctive, and in imperative forms derived from the present subjunctive.

The verb **mecer** (*to rock a child/cradle*) is conjugated like **convencer**, and not like **conocer**: present **mezo**, **meces**, etc.; present subjunctive **meza**, **mezas**, etc. The verb **cocer** is also conjugated like **convencer** and, in addition, has the stem change **o > ue**: present **cuezo**, **cueces**, etc.; present subjunctive **cueza**, **cuezas**, etc.

conocer *to know*

PRESENT INDICATIVE	conozco, conoces, conoce · conocemos, conocéis, conocen
PRESENT SUBJUNCTIVE	conozca, conozcas, conozca · conozcamos, conozcáis, conozcan
IMPERATIVE	conoce / no conozcas, conozca · conozcamos, conoced / no conozcáis, conozcan

conducir *to drive*

PRESENT INDICATIVE	conduzco, conduces, conduce · conducimos, conducís, conducen
PRESENT SUBJUNCTIVE	conduzca, conduzcas, conduzca · conduzcamos, conduzcáis, conduzcan
IMPERATIVE	conduce / no conduzcas, conduzca · conduzcamos, conducid / no conduzcáis, conduzcan

Verbs Ending in -uir (Not Including Those Ending in -guir)

These verbs add **y** before a vowel other than **i** and change the unaccented **i** between vowels to **y**. The **y** appears in all singular forms and in the third person plural of the present, in the third person singular and plural of the preterit, in all persons of the present and imperfect subjunctive, and in all imperative forms except the affirmative **vosotros** command.

construir *to build*

PRESENT INDICATIVE	construyo, construyes, construye · construimos, construís, construyen
PRETERIT	construí, construiste, construyó · construimos, construisteis, construyeron
IMPERATIVE	construye / no construyas, construya · construyamos, construid / no construyáis, construyan
PRESENT SUBJUNCTIVE	construya, construyas, construya · construyamos, construyáis, construyan
IMPERFECT SUBJUNCTIVE	construyera (construyese), construyeras, construyera · construyéramos, construyerais, construyeran
PRESENT PARTICIPLE	construyendo

Other Irregular Verbs

Only tenses with irregular forms are shown.

andar *to walk*

PRETERIT	anduve, anduviste, anduvo · anduvimos, anduvisteis, anduvieron
IMPERFECT SUBJUNCTIVE	anduviera (anduviese), anduvieras, anduviera · anduviéramos, anduvierais, anduvieran

caber *to fit*

PRESENT INDICATIVE	quepo, cabes, cabe · cabemos, cabéis, caben
PRETERIT	cupe, cupiste, cupo · cupimos, cupisteis, cupieron
FUTURE	cabré, cabrás, cabrá · cabremos, cabréis, cabrán
CONDITIONAL	cabría, cabrías, cabría · cabríamos, cabríais, cabrían
IMPERATIVE	cabe / no quepas, quepa · quepamos, cabed / no quepáis, quepan
PRESENT SUBJUNCTIVE	quepa, quepas, quepa · quepamos, quepáis, quepan
IMPERFECT SUBJUNCTIVE	cupiera (cupiese), cupieras, cupiera · cupiéramos, cupierais, cupieran

caer *to fall*

PRESENT INDICATIVE	caigo, caes, cae · caemos, caéis, caen
PRETERIT	caí, caíste, cayó · caímos, caísteis, cayeron
IMPERATIVE	cae / no caigas, caiga · caigamos, caed / no caigáis, caigan
PRESENT SUBJUNCTIVE	caiga, caigas, caiga · caigamos, caigáis, caigan
IMPERFECT SUBJUNCTIVE	cayera (cayese), cayeras, cayera · cayéramos, cayerais, cayeran
PRESENT PARTICIPLE	cayendo
PAST PARTICIPLE	caído

dar *to give*

PRESENT INDICATIVE	doy, das, da · damos, dais, dan
PRETERIT	di, diste, dio · dimos, disteis, dieron
IMPERATIVE	da / no des, dé · demos, dad / no deis, den
PRESENT SUBJUNCTIVE	dé, des, dé · demos, deis, den
IMPERFECT SUBJUNCTIVE	diera (diese), dieras, diera · diéramos, dierais, dieran

decir *to say, tell*

PRESENT INDICATIVE	digo, dices, dice · decimos, decís, dicen
PRETERIT	dije, dijiste, dijo · dijimos, dijisteis, dijeron
FUTURE	diré, dirás, dirá · diremos, diréis, dirán
CONDITIONAL	diría, dirías, diría · diríamos, diríais, dirían
IMPERATIVE	di / no digas, diga · digamos, decid / no digáis, digan
PRESENT SUBJUNCTIVE	diga, digas, diga · digamos, digáis, digan
IMPERFECT SUBJUNCTIVE	dijera (dijese), dijeras, dijera · dijéramos, dijerais, dijeran
PRESENT PARTICIPLE	diciendo
PAST PARTICIPLE	dicho

estar *to be*

PRESENT INDICATIVE	estoy, estás, está · estamos, estáis, están
PRETERIT	estuve, estuviste, estuvo · estuvimos, estuvisteis, estuvieron
IMPERATIVE	está / no estés, esté · estemos, estad / no estéis, estén
PRESENT SUBJUNCTIVE	esté, estés, esté · estemos, estéis, estén
IMPERFECT SUBJUNCTIVE	estuviera (estuviese), estuvieras, estuviera · estuviéramos, estuvierais, estuvieran

haber *to have* (auxiliary verb)

PRESENT INDICATIVE	he, has, ha · hemos, habéis, han
PRETERIT	hube, hubiste, hubo · hubimos, hubisteis, hubieron
FUTURE	habré, habrás, habrá · habremos, habréis, habrán
CONDITIONAL	habría, habrías, habría · habríamos, habríais, habrían
PRESENT SUBJUNCTIVE	haya, hayas, haya · hayamos, hayáis, hayan
IMPERFECT SUBJUNCTIVE	hubiera (hubiese), hubieras, hubiera · hubiéramos, hubierais, hubieran

hacer *to do, make*

PRESENT INDICATIVE	hago, haces, hace · hacemos, hacéis, hacen
PRETERIT	hice, hiciste, hizo · hicimos, hiciste, hicieron
FUTURE	haré, harás, hará · haremos, haréis, harán
CONDITIONAL	haría, harías, haría · haríamos, haríais, harían
IMPERATIVE	haz / no hagas, haga · hagamos, haced / no hagáis, hagan
PRESENT SUBJUNCTIVE	haga, hagas, haga · hagamos, hagáis, hagan
IMPERFECT SUBJUNCTIVE	hiciera (hiciese), hicieras, hiciera · hiciéramos, hicierais, hicieran
PAST PARTICIPLE	hecho

ir *to go*

PRESENT INDICATIVE	voy, vas, va · vamos, vais, van
IMPERFECT	iba, ibas, iba · íbamos, ibais, iban
PRETERIT	fui, fuiste, fue · fuimos, fuisteis, fueron
IMPERATIVE	ve / no vayas, vaya · vamos / no vayamos, id / no vayáis, vayan
PRESENT SUBJUNCTIVE	vaya, vayas, vaya · vayamos, vayáis, vayan
IMPERFECT SUBJUNCTIVE	fuera (fuese), fueras, fuera · fuéramos, fuerais, fueran
PRESENT PARTICIPLE	yendo

oír *to hear*

PRESENT INDICATIVE	oigo, oyes, oye · oímos, oís, oyen
PRETERIT	oí, oíste, oyó · oímos, oísteis, oyeron
IMPERATIVE	oye / no oigas, oiga · oigamos, oíd / no oigáis, oigan
PRESENT SUBJUNCTIVE	oiga, oigas, oiga · oigamos, oigáis, oigan
IMPERFECT SUBJUNCTIVE	oyera (oyese), oyeras, oyera · oyéramos, oyerais, oyeran
PRESENT PARTICIPLE	oyendo
PAST PARTICIPLE	oído

poder *to be able, can*

PRESENT INDICATIVE	puedo, puedes, puede · podemos, podéis, pueden
PRETERIT	pude, pudiste, pudo · pudimos, pudisteis, pudieron
FUTURE	podré, podrás, podrá · podremos, podréis, podrán
CONDITIONAL	podría, podrías, podría · podríamos, podríais, podrían
PRESENT SUBJUNCTIVE	pueda, puedas, pueda · podamos, podáis, puedan
IMPERFECT SUBJUNCTIVE	pudiera (pudiese), pudieras, pudiera · pudiéramos, pudierais, pudieran
PRESENT PARTICIPLE	pudiendo

poner *to put*

PRESENT INDICATIVE	pongo, pones, pone · ponemos, ponéis, ponen
PRETERIT	puse, pusiste, puso · pusimos, pusisteis, pusieron
FUTURE	pondré, pondrás, pondrá · pondremos, pondréis, pondrán
CONDITIONAL	pondría, pondrías, pondría · pondríamos, pondríais, pondrían
IMPERATIVE	pon / no pongas, ponga · pongamos, poned / no pongáis, pongan
PRESENT SUBJUNCTIVE	ponga, pongas, ponga · pongamos, pongáis, pongan
IMPERFECT SUBJUNCTIVE	pusiera (pusiese), pusieras, pusiera · pusiéramos, pusierais, pusieran
PAST PARTICIPLE	puesto

producir *to produce*

PRESENT INDICATIVE	produzco, produces, produce · producimos, producís, producen
PRETERIT	produje, produjiste, produjo · produjimos, produjisteis, produjeron
IMPERATIVE	produce / no produzcas, produzca · produzcamos, producid / no produzcáis, produzcan
PRESENT SUBJUNCTIVE	produzca, produzcas, produzca · produzcamos, produzcáis, produzcan
IMPERFECT SUBJUNCTIVE	produjera (produjese), produjeras, produjera · produjéramos, produjerais, produjeran

querer *to want*

PRESENT INDICATIVE	quiero, quieres, quiere · queremos, queréis, quieren
PRETERIT	quise, quisiste, quiso · quisimos, quisisteis, quisieron
FUTURE	querré, querrás, querrá · querremos, querréis, querrán
CONDITIONAL	querría, querrías, querría · querríamos, querríais, querrían
IMPERATIVE	quiere / no quieras, quiera · queramos, quered / no queráis, quieran
PRESENT SUBJUNCTIVE	quiera, quieras, quiera · queramos, queráis, quieran
IMPERFECT SUBJUNCTIVE	quisiera (quisiese), quisieras, quisiera · quisiéramos, quisierais, quisieran

saber *to know*

PRESENT INDICATIVE	sé, sabes, sabe · sabemos, sabéis, saben
PRETERIT	supe, supiste, supo · supimos, supisteis, supieron
FUTURE	sabré, sabrás, sabrá · sabremos, sabréis, sabrán
CONDITIONAL	sabría, sabrías, sabría · sabríamos, sabríais, sabrían
IMPERATIVE	sabe / no sepas, sepa · sepamos, sabed / no sepáis, sepan
PRESENT SUBJUNCTIVE	sepa, sepas, sepa · sepamos, sepáis, sepan
IMPERFECT SUBJUNCTIVE	supiera (supiese), supieras, supiera · supiéramos, supierais, supieran

salir *to go out*

PRESENT INDICATIVE	salgo, sales, sale · salimos, salís, salen
FUTURE	saldré, saldrás, saldrá · saldremos, saldréis, saldrán
CONDITIONAL	saldría, saldrías, saldría · saldríamos, saldríais, saldrían
IMPERATIVE	sal / no salgas, salga · salgamos, salid / no salgáis, salgan
PRESENT SUBJUNCTIVE	salga, salgas, salga · salgamos, salgáis, salgan

ser *to be*

PRESENT INDICATIVE	soy, eres, es · somos, sois, son
IMPERFECT	era, eras, era · éramos, erais, eran
PRETERIT	fui, fuiste, fue · fuimos, fuisteis, fueron
IMPERATIVE	sé / no seas, sea · seamos, sed / no seáis, sean
PRESENT SUBJUNCTIVE	sea, seas, sea · seamos, seáis, sean
IMPERFECT SUBJUNCTIVE	fuera (fuese), fueras, fuera · fuéramos, fuerais, fueran

tener *to have*

PRESENT INDICATIVE	tengo, tienes, tiene · tenemos, tenéis, tienen
PRETERIT	tuve, tuviste, tuvo · tuvimos, tuvisteis, tuvieron
FUTURE	tendré, tendrás, tendrá · tendremos, tendréis, tendrán
CONDITIONAL	tendría, tendrías, tendría · tendríamos, tendríais, tendrían
IMPERATIVE	ten / no tengas, tenga · tengamos, tened / no tengáis, tengan
PRESENT SUBJUNCTIVE	tenga, tengas, tenga · tengamos, tengáis, tengan
IMPERFECT SUBJUNCTIVE	tuviera (tuviese), tuvieras, tuviera · tuviéramos, tuvierais, tuvieran

traer *to bring*

PRESENT INDICATIVE	traigo, traes, trae · traemos, traéis, traen
PRETERIT	traje, trajiste, trajo · trajimos, trajisteis, trajeron
IMPERATIVE	trae / no traigas, traiga · traigamos, traed / no traigáis, traigan
PRESENT SUBJUNCTIVE	traiga, traigas, traiga · traigamos, traigáis, traigan
IMPERFECT SUBJUNCTIVE	trajera (trajese), trajeras, trajera · trajéramos, trajerais, trajeran
PRESENT PARTICIPLE	trayendo
PAST PARTICIPLE	traído

valer *to be worth*

PRESENT INDICATIVE	valgo, vales, vale · valemos, valéis, valen
FUTURE	valdré, valdrás, valdrá · valdremos, valdréis, valdrán
CONDITIONAL	valdría, valdrías, valdría · valdríamos, valdríais, valdrían
IMPERATIVE	vale / no valgas, valga · valgamos, valed / no valgáis, valgan
PRESENT SUBJUNCTIVE	valga, valgas, valga · valgamos, valgáis, valgan

venir *to come*

PRESENT INDICATIVE	vengo, vienes, viene · venimos, venís, vienen
PRETERIT	vine, viniste, vino · vinimos, vinisteis, vinieron
FUTURE	vendré, vendrás, vendrá · vendremos, vendréis, vendrán
CONDITIONAL	vendría, vendrías, vendría · vendríamos, vendríais, vendrían
IMPERATIVE	ven / no vengas, venga · vengamos, venid / no vengáis, vengan
PRESENT SUBJUNCTIVE	venga, vengas, venga · vengamos, vengáis, vengan
IMPERFECT SUBJUNCTIVE	viniera (viniese), vinieras, viniera · viniéramos, vinierais, vinieran
PRESENT PARTICIPLE	viniendo

ver *to see*

PRESENT INDICATIVE	veo, ves, ve · vemos, veis, ven
IMPERFECT	veía, veías, veía · veíamos, veíais, veían
PRETERIT	vi, viste, vio · vimos, visteis, vieron
IMPERATIVE	ve / no veas, vea · veamos, ved / no veáis, vean
PRESENT SUBJUNCTIVE	vea, veas, vea · veamos, veáis, vean
IMPERFECT SUBJUNCTIVE	viera (viese), vieras, viera · viéramos, vierais, vieran
PAST PARTICIPLE	visto

Written Conventions

Spanish has several written conventions that are different from those we observe in English.

Capitalization

Spanish capitalizes proper names (**México, Chile, Estados Unidos**) but does not capitalize adjectives derived from these names: **mexicano, chileno, estadounidense**. Spanish does not capitalize names of religions or the words referring to believers in those religions: **el catolicismo, católico/católica, el protestantismo, protestante, el judaísmo, judío/judía, el islam, musulmán/musulmana**. Spanish also does not capitalize titles of government officials: **el presidente de México, el rey/la reina de España**.

The names of the months and the days of the week are not capitalized in Spanish: **jueves**, 23 de **agosto**. In Spanish book and movie titles, all words except the first one are written with lowercase letters unless there are proper names in the title: ***Como agua para chocolate, La historia oficial, Lo que el viento se llevó*** (*Gone with the Wind*). But Spanish does capitalize the words in the titles of newspapers and magazines: ***El País, La Prensa, El Vocero, El Universal, El Economista***.

Punctuation

Questions in Spanish begin with an inverted question mark ¿ and end with a question mark identical to the one used in English. Exclamations in Spanish begin with an inverted exclamation point ¡ and end with an exclamation point identical to the one used in English. The Spanish treatment of questions and exclamations in writing parallels the English treatment of quotations, in which quotation marks are placed at both the beginning and end of the quote.

¿Quién es ese muchacho?

¡Qué artículo más interesante!

Within certain sentences, the inverted question mark or exclamation point is placed not at the beginning of the sentence but at the beginning of the actual question or exclamation.

Pero, ¡qué bueno!

Entonces, dime, ¿cuándo sales para Europa?

Accent Marks

Spanish uses diacritics, or accent marks, over certain letters (**acento** or **tilde** in Spanish).

The **tilde** over the letter **n** creates a different letter with its own sound: **ñ** (called **eñe**).

 año
peña
sueño

The accent mark (´) is placed over a vowel to show that the word it appears in violates one of the rules of Spanish stress.

The rules for stress in Spanish are simple. Words ending in a vowel or the consonant -**n** or -**s** are stressed on the next-to-the-last syllable, also called the penultimate syllable. These words are called **palabras llanas**.

administran
aprendizaje
desconectas
disquete
permitido
realizan

Words ending in a consonant other than -**n** or -**s** are stressed on the final syllable. These words are called **palabras agudas**.

capataz
celular
digital
gratitud
internacional
Internet
representar
usted

In order to calculate the position of stress you have to understand the Spanish classification of vowels. The vowels **a**, **e**, and **o** are considered strong vowels. The vowels **i** and **u** are considered weak vowels. When two strong vowels appear in succession, they constitute separate syllables.

co-rre-o
le-al
ma-es-tro
pa-se-ar
pe-o-res
po-e-ma
ro-er
to-a-lla

When a strong and a weak vowel appear together they constitute a diphthong. A diphthong is a combination of two vowels pronounced in the same syllable. In diphthongs, the weak vowels **i** and **u** have the sound values /y/ and /w/. These diphthongs count as single vowels for the purpose of determining stress.

aurora
b**ai**le
b**oi**na
c**au**sa
c**ie**ncia
d**eu**da
p**ei**ne
p**ue**s
r**ei**na
s**ie**nto
s**ua**ve
v**ue**lto

When a word violates one of the above rules of stress, a written accent mark is placed over the vowel of the stressed syllable.

Words ending in a vowel or the consonant **-n** or **-s** that are not stressed on the penultimate syllable but instead on the final syllable or on the third-from-the-last syllable, require a written accent mark to indicate this deviation from the rule. Words stressed on the third-from-the-last syllable are called **palabras esdrújulas**. The third-from-the-last syllable is called the antepenultimate syllable in English.

abrir**ás**
an**á**lisis
ánimo
coraz**ón**
eli**gió**
hablar**án**
lev**án**tate
matem**á**ticas
Panam**á**
ru**bí**
sic**ó**logo
química
Tom**ás**
vínculo

Words ending in a consonant other than **-n** or **-s** that are not stressed on the final syllable but instead on the penultimate syllable or on the antepenultimate syllable require a written accent mark to indicate this deviation from the rule.

Alb**é**niz
alc**á**zar
alf**é**rez
az**ú**car
Berm**ú**dez
car**á**cter
Rodr**í**guez

When a strong and a weak vowel in succession are pronounced not as a diphthong but as two separate syllables, a written accent is placed over the weak vowel.

actúa
ataúd
baúl
lío
país
reúne
ríe
tecnología

The accent mark in Spanish is also used to distinguish in writing words that are otherwise identical in speech. Usually one member of each of these pairs of words can carry stress in the phrase or sentence it occurs in, and that is the member of the pair that is written with an accent mark. For instance, the definite article **el** is not stressed but the subject pronoun **él** can carry stress.

UNSTRESSED WORD	STRESSED WORD
de *of, from*	**dé** *give!*
el *the*	**él** *he*
mas *but* (literary)	**más** *more*
mi *my*	**mí** *me* [object of a preposition]
que [relative pronoun]	**qué** [interrogative pronoun]
se [pronoun]	**sé** *I know; be!*
si *if*	**sí** *yes*
solo *alone*	**sólo** *only* (ALSO **solo** *only*)
te *you* [object pronoun]	**té** *tea*
tu *your*	**tú** *you* [subject pronoun]

Interrogative words in Spanish are written with an accent mark. They retain this accent mark even when incorporated into a larger sentence.

—¿**Cuándo** sale Juan?   *When is Juan leaving?*
—No sé **cuándo** sale.   *I don't know when he is leaving.*

When interrogative words are written without accents, they are conjunctions or relative pronouns.

Lo veré **cuando** llegue.   *I'll see him when he gets here.*

Es el colega con **quien** trabajo.   *It's the colleague whom I work with.*

Most publications distinguish demonstrative adjectives from demonstrative pronouns by placing an accent mark over the stressed vowel of the pronoun. In modern usage, the written accent is sometimes left off demonstrative pronouns.

A él le gusta **aquel** libro, pero a mí   *He likes **that** book, but I like **this one**.*
me gusta **éste** (**este**).

—¿Qué te parece **esta** cartera, señora?   *How do you like **this** handbag, ma'am?*
—**Ésa** (**Esa**) no tanto. **Aquéllas**   *I don't like **that one** so much. I like **those**
(**Aquellas**) me gustan más.   **over there** more.*

Answer Key

I Verbs—Forms and Uses

1 The Present Tense

A

1. navego
2. leen
3. administramos
4. repara
5. analizas
6. escribe
7. trabajan
8. imprimimos
9. diseñáis
10. manda
11. crean
12. usa
13. elaboran
14. comparto

B

1. escuchamos
2. toco
3. encarga
4. caminan
5. comes
6. leen
7. bebéis
8. mira

C

1. Yo repaso los tiempos verbales.
2. Nosotros trabajamos en equipo.
3. Raquel abre el libro de texto.
4. Tú aprendes los modismos de memoria.
5. Los estudiantes comparten sus ideas.
6. Ud. practica los sonidos del español.
7. Felipe y tú leen el diálogo.
8. Vosotros aprendéis mucho.

D

1. Nosotros nunca hablamos por celular.
2. Juan Diego nunca prende su iPad.
3. Yo nunca mando mensajes de texto.
4. Uds. nunca utilizan una chuleta.
5. Tú nunca interrumpes a la profesora.
6. Isabel y Laura nunca faltan a la clase.
7. Ud. nunca masca chicle.
8. Vosotros nunca bebéis refrescos.

E

Answers will vary.

F

1. planean
2. cocina
3. compra
4. colocan
5. invita
6. Llega
7. vive
8. llega
9. comen
10. beben
11. bailan
12. toca
13. cantan
14. abre
15. recibe
16. saca
17. felicitan
18. brindan

G

1. Sí, salgo la semana próxima.
2. No, no vengo a la oficina el viernes.
3. Sí, voy a España y Francia.
4. Sí, conozco a los directores franceses.
5. Sí, veo al gerente de ventas mañana.
6. No, no traduzco los documentos al ruso.
7. No, no sé cuándo regreso.

H

1. Venimos si tenemos tiempo.
2. Vienes si tienes tiempo.
3. Vienen si tienen tiempo.
4. Vengo si tengo tiempo.
5. Viene si tiene tiempo.
6. Viene si tiene tiempo.
7. Vienen si tienen tiempo.
8. Venís si tenéis tiempo.

I

1. Carmen oye lo que Ud. dice.
2. Pedro y Paco oyen lo que yo digo.
3. Nosotros oímos lo que tú dices.
4. Tú oyes lo que Miguel y Teresa dicen.
5. Yo oigo lo que Uds. dicen.
6. Uds. oyen lo que nosotros decimos.
7. Vosotros oís lo que Pablo dice.
8. Ellas oyen lo que vosotras decís.

J

1. Yo pongo la mesa.
2. Yo veo televisión.
3. Yo doy un paseo.
4. Yo traigo el vino.
5. Yo hago las maletas.
6. Yo voy de compras.
7. Yo salgo al cine.
8. Yo caigo en un error.

K

1. Merezco el Premio Nobel de Economía.
2. Compongo una obra maestra mozartiana.
3. Traduzco novelas del vasco al árabe.
4. Conduzco la limusina presidencial.
5. Supongo que voy a vivir para siempre.
6. Obtengo una beca de cincuenta millones de dólares.
7. Produzco las películas más exitosas del cine.

L

1. No, no conozco a esos programadores.
2. No, no conocemos a Agustín.
3. No, no conozco a Julio.
4. No, no conocen a este asesor financiero.
5. No, no conoce a sus vecinos.
6. No, no conocemos a Sara.

M

1. ¿Cuánto tiempo hace que diseñas sitios web? / ¿Desde cuándo diseñas sitios web?
2. ¿Cuánto tiempo hace que Mario cocina a la italiana? / ¿Desde cuándo cocina Mario a la italiana?
3. ¿Cuánto tiempo hace que Rosa y Jaime bailan salsa? / ¿Desde cuándo bailan salsa Rosa y Jaime?
4. ¿Cuánto tiempo hace que Uds. hacen ejercicio? / ¿Desde cuándo hacen Uds. ejercicio?
5. ¿Cuánto tiempo hace que tu hermana vende sus pinturas? / ¿Desde cuándo vende tu hermana sus pinturas?
6. ¿Cuánto tiempo hace que Gabriel lee el chino? / ¿Desde cuándo lee Gabriel el chino?

N

1. Hace dos años que diseño sitios web. / Diseño sitios web desde hace dos años.
2. Hace un año que Mario cocina a la italiana. / Mario cocina a la italiana desde hace un año.
3. Hace siete semanas que Rosa y Jaime bailan salsa. / Rosa y Jaime bailan salsa desde hace siete semanas.
4. Hace cinco años que hacemos ejercicio. / Hacemos ejercicio desde hace cinco años.
5. Hace un par de meses que mi hermana vende sus pinturas. / Mi hermana vende sus pinturas desde hace un par de meses.
6. Hace cuatro años que Gabriel lee el chino. / Gabriel lee el chino desde hace cuatro años.

O

1. Mi hermano y yo vamos a cortar el césped.
2. Mi abuela va a lavar la ropa.
3. Yo voy a barrer el suelo.
4. Mamá va a hacer la compra.
5. Mis hermanas van a pasar la aspiradora.
6. Ud. va a reciclar los periódicos.
7. Uds. van a hacer las camas.
8. Papá va a sacar la basura.
9. Tú vas a limpiar la alfombra.
10. Vosotros vais a quitar el polvo de los muebles.

P

1. Yo leo y mando correos electrónicos (emails).
2. Laura navega en la red.
3. Yo hago el desayuno.
4. Uds. toman el tren.
5. Alejandro va a la oficina.
6. Beatriz estaciona el coche.
7. Tú descargas (bajas) los documentos.
8. Hablamos por teléfono celular.
9. Ricardo y yo salimos a cenar.
10. Ud. imprime los informes.
11. Los niños hacen su tarea.
12. Vosotros vais al centro comercial.
13. Nosotros asistimos a una conferencia.
14. Yo tomo clases en linea (a distancia).

Q

Answers will vary.

2 Ser and estar

A

1. Soy yo.
2. Son Uds.
3. Somos nosotros.
4. Es él.
5. Eres tú.
6. Son ellas.
7. Es Ud.
8. Sois vosotros.

B

1. Pablo es de la Argentina pero es de origen inglés.
2. Los gemelos son de Francia pero son de origen ruso.
3. La licenciada es del Canadá pero es de origen japonés.
4. Ud. es de los Estados Unidos pero es de origen irlandés.
5. Ramón y Virginia son de Puerto Rico pero son de origen polaco.
6. Tú eres de España pero eres de origen portugués.

7. Ud. y Raquel son de México pero son de origen griego.
8. Yo soy de Venezuela pero soy de origen italiano.

C

1. ¿Quién eres?
2. ¿De dónde eres?
3. ¿De qué nacionalidad eres?
4. ¿De qué origen eres?
5. ¿Cómo eres?
6. ¿De qué color son tus ojos?
7. ¿Cuál es tu profesión?

D

1. Mercedes está en Barcelona y está contenta.
2. Uds. están en Lima y están cansados.
3. Yo estoy en Roma y estoy feliz.
4. Tú estás en Las Vegas y estás estresado.
5. Nosotros estamos en Jerusalén y estamos emocionados.
6. Consuelo y su marido están en Londres y están entusiasmados.
7. Vosotras estáis en Beijing y estáis nerviosas.
8. Ud. está en Moscú y está inquieto.

E

1. ¿Cuál es su nombre?
2. ¿Cuál es su nacionalidad?
3. ¿Cuál es su profesión?
4. ¿Cuál es su estado civil?
5. ¿Cuál es su fecha de nacimiento?
6. ¿Cómo es Ud.?

F

1. es	8. es
2. es	9. es
3. son	10. es
4. es	11. son
5. Es	12. Son
6. está	13. está
7. están	14. es

G

1. estamos	11. es
2. está	12. están
3. Es	13. son
4. está	14. están
5. es	15. son
6. Es	16. es
7. es	17. estoy
8. es	18. son
9. ser	19. está
10. está	20. Está

H

1. estoy	17. es
2. estoy	18. Es
3. Es	19. Es
4. es	20. es
5. es	21. Es
6. es	22. estoy
7. son	23. Es
8. es	24. están
9. está	25. estás
10. está	26. son
11. están	27. están
12. está	28. está
13. es	29. son
14. es	30. es
15. es	31. es
16. Son	32. estar

I

1. ¿Dónde está la papelería?
2. ¿Cómo es Gloria?
3. ¿De dónde son los hermanos García? (¿De qué nacionalidad son los hermanos García?)
4. ¿Cómo están Juanito y Raúl?
5. ¿De qué origen es la familia Méndez?
6. ¿Cómo son las primas de Paco?
7. ¿Dónde está el profesor Mora?
8. ¿De qué es el vestido?
9. ¿De qué color son la camisa y la corbata?
10. ¿Cómo está? (¿Cómo estás?)
11. ¿De quién es aquella casa? (¿De quiénes es aquella casa?)
12. ¿De dónde es Micaela?

J

1. ¿Quiénes son los nuevos estudiantes extranjeros? ¿Sabes de dónde son?
2. Yo conozco a María del Mar. Está en mi clase de economía. Es de la Argentina.
3. Sí, y es de origen italiano. Es muy simpática e inteligente.
4. Pero está triste porque quiere volver a Buenos Aires.
5. Lorenzo Tomé es francés pero sus abuelos son de origen indio.
6. Hace muchos años que la familia vive en Francia.
7. Lorenzo estudia biología y química este año.
8. Él dice que quiere ser médico.

K

Answers will vary.

3 Stem-Changing Verbs and Verbs with Spelling Changes

A

1. Yo juego al tenis.
2. Alejandro y Patricio juegan al béisbol.
3. Carlota juega al vólibol.
4. Tú juegas al baloncesto.
5. Marcos y yo jugamos al fútbol americano.
6. Uds. juegan al golf.
7. Ud. juega al hockey sobre hielo.
8. Vosotros jugáis al jai alai.

B

1. Uds. almuerzan en un restaurante vegetariano a la una.
2. Regina almuerza en casa de una amiga a las doce y cuarto.
3. Rafael y yo almorzamos en una cafetería a las tres.
4. Mauricio y Elena almuerzan en una pizzería a las tres y veinte.
5. Tú almuerzas en el comedor de la compañía a las once cincuenta.
6. Uds. almuerzan en un café al aire libre a las dos y media.
7. Vosotras almorzáis en un restaurante de comida rápida a la una cuarenta y cinco.

C

1. No, no podemos descargar las fotos de Internet hoy.
2. No, no puede empezar a escribir su informe hoy.
3. No, no pueden trabajar en la librería hoy.
4. No, no puedo rodar mi película hoy.
5. No, no puedo traer mi cámara digital hoy.
6. No, no podemos visitar el museo hoy.
7. No, no puedo contestar mi correo electrónico hoy.
8. No, no podemos merendar en un café hoy.
9. No, no puedo devolver los libros a la biblioteca hoy.

D

1. puedo	9. cuesta
2. encuentro	10. cuesta
3. quiere	11. pruebo
4. Pienso	12. envuelve
5. muestro	13. quiere
6. Puede	14. suelo
7. encuentro	15. vuelvo
8. cuestan	

E

1. Uds. resuelven los problemas de álgebra.
2. Los niños atraviesan la calle con cuidado.
3. El concierto comienza a las ocho.
4. Descendemos al primer piso en ascensor.
5. Yo no entiendo su idea.
6. ¿Vuelves el sábado o el domingo?
7. Pedro nos muestra el apartamento.
8. Los Salcedo quieren salir a cenar esta noche.
9. Yo enciendo la luz.
10. ¿Dónde ruedan la película?

F

1. Mi compañero de cuarto despierta a todos nosotros.
2. Tú empiezas a mandar tu correo electrónico.
3. Uds. almuerzan en un café.
4. Ud. devuelve los libros a la biblioteca.
5. Mis amigos vuelven a la residencia universitaria a las tres.
6. Nosotros comenzamos a estudiar a las cuatro.
7. Yo suelo hacer investigaciones en la red.
8. Los estudiantes encuentran a sus profesores por el campus.

G

1. Recuerdas la fecha hoy.
2. Pablo y Lorenzo juegan al fútbol hoy.
3. Probamos el nuevo plato hoy.
4. Alicia encuentra su secador hoy.
5. Yo envuelvo los paquetes hoy.
6. Ud. resuelve su problema hoy.

H

1. Llueve (Está lloviendo) en San Francisco.
2. Nieva (Está nevando) en Ginebra, Suiza.
3. Está nublado en Santa Fe.
4. Hace viento en Chicago.
5. Empieza a nevar en Punta Arenas, Chile.
6. Despeja en Londres.
7. Está despejado en Sevilla.
8. Hace frío en Barcelona.

I

1. Ud. y José María piden piña.
2. La familia Herrera pide paella.
3. Pili y yo pedimos ensalada.
4. Tú pides flan.
5. Los chicos piden helado.
6. Yo pido arroz con pollo.
7. Vosotros pedís tapas.
8. Ud. pide un sándwich.

J

1. Yo sirvo limonada.
2. Susana sirve refrescos.
3. Nosotros servimos cerveza.
4. Eduardo y Dolores sirven jugo.
5. Tú sirves agua mineral.
6. Ud. y Pepe sirven té.
7. Ud. sirve café.
8. Vosotros servís jerez.

K

1. Los primos prefieren salir al campo.
2. Julia prefiere leer novelas históricas.
3. Nosotros preferimos asistir a un concierto.
4. Uds. prefieren pedir tacos.
5. Yo prefiero jugar al tenis.
6. Tú prefieres bailar el tango.
7. Ud. prefiere ver películas policíacas.
8. Vosotros preferís ver videos en YouTube.

L

1. Tú duermes profundamente.
2. Yo duermo mucho los fines de semana.
3. Uds. duermen bien en este dormitorio.
4. Vosotros dormís muy poco.
5. Nosotros dormimos mal en este colchón.
6. Ud. duerme diez horas los días feriados.

M

1. viste
2. advierte
3. sienten
4. hierve
5. duerme
6. miente
7. divierte / ríen / sonríen
8. despiden
9. repites
10. riñen
11. refiere
12. gimes

N

1. Los padres de Vera contribuyen cien dólares.
2. Mi hermano y yo contribuimos ciento cincuenta dólares.
3. Tú contribuyes setenta dólares.
4. Ud. contribuye setenta y cinco dólares.
5. Adriana contribuye veinticinco dólares.
6. Los habitantes del barrio contribuyen mil quinientos dólares.
7. Yo contribuyo ochenta dólares.

O

1. Tú huyes a la estación de tren.
2. Uds. huyen al oeste.
3. Fernando huye a casa de sus abuelos.
4. Nosotros huimos a la capital.
5. Los señores Ortega huyen a un hotel.
6. Yo huyo al interior del estado.
7. Ud. huye al centro.
8. Vosotros huís a un hospital.

P

1. Roberto incluye sus investigaciones científicas.
2. Uds. incluyen algunas fotos.
3. Laura y yo incluimos las estadísticas.
4. Ud. incluye una presentación de PowerPoint.
5. Tú incluyes un resumen.
6. David y Gabriela incluyen una introducción.
7. Yo incluyo un sitio web.
8. Vosotros incluís una base de datos.

Q

1. Tomás se resfría todos los inviernos.
2. Uds. se resfrían cuando duermen poco.
3. Lidia y Miguel se resfrían tres veces al año.
4. Vosotros os resfriáis cuando coméis mal.
5. Yo me resfrío cuando bebo en los vasos ajenos.
6. Nosotros nos resfriamos cuando salimos bajo la lluvia.
7. Tú te resfrías cuando no tomas vitaminas.

R

1. Micaela y Jorge se gradúan el año próximo.
2. Ud. se gradúa dentro de dos años.
3. Timoteo se gradúa en enero.
4. Uds. se gradúan a fines del semestre.
5. Tú te gradúas el 14 de mayo.
6. Nosotros nos graduamos a principios de junio.
7. Yo me gradúo el mes que viene.
8. Vosotros os graduáis el jueves.

S

1. se fían
2. envían
3. confía
4. continúa
5. evalúa
6. espiamos

T

Answers will vary.

U
1. Yo elijo una caja de bombones.
2. Mis padres eligen una bandeja de plata.
3. Nosotros elegimos un certificado de regalo.
4. Tú eliges dos tabletas.
5. Uds. eligen un televisor.
6. Raquel elige una cámara digital.
7. Vosotros elegís un juego de vajilla.
8. Nuestros primos eligen un mueble.
9. Ud. elige unos billetes de concierto.

V
1. recojo	5. dirijo
2. persigo	6. corrijo
3. extingo	7. mezo
4. cuezo	

W
1. sigo	9. prosigo
2. dirijo	10. produce
3. encojo	11. finjo
4. distingo	12. distingo
5. reconozco	13. recojo
6. finge	14. convenzo
7. consigo	15. desconozco
8. luce	

X
1. Víctor consigue salir al centro comercial.
2. Pablo y yo conseguimos reparar el coche.
3. Ud. consigue ver la nueva exposición.
4. Yo consigo hacer unos platos riquísimos.
5. Uds. consiguen arreglar los armarios.
6. Tú consigues colgar los cuadros.

Y
1. Sigue	6. distingo
2. Cojo	7. Exijo
3. Desconozco	8. Eliges
4. Finjo	9. consigo
5. Cuecen	10. Produzco

Z
1. Leopoldo Soto dirige la Orquesta de Filadelfia esta semana.
2. Los bomberos extinguen treinta fuegos cada día.
3. Los padres exigen mejores escuelas.
4. El senador Alonso sigue los consejos de sus colegas en el Senado.
5. Los norteamericanos eligen un nuevo presidente este año.
6. Joven pareja consigue ganar la lotería.

7. Una nueva receta: cocinero cuece sopa con helado.
8. La campaña contra el analfabetismo prosigue.

AA
Answers will vary.

4   The Preterit Tense

A
1. Vosotros mandasteis textos.
2. Rosa y Elena solucionaron los problemas de cálculo.
3. Tú escribiste un informe.
4. Nosotros trabajamos en la librería.
5. Yo visité unos sitios web.
6. Uds. contestaron las preguntas de filosofía.
7. Miguel discutió unos temas.
8. Ud. aprendió las fechas de historia de memoria.

B
1. levanté	14. subimos
2. arreglé	15. viajamos
3. Bajé	16. bajamos
4. saludé	17. arrancó
5. preparó	18. busqué
6. tomé	19. encontré
7. empecé	20. coloqué
8. pasó	21. pensé
9. desayunó	22. miró
10. terminamos	23. habló
11. cogí	24. explicó
12. salimos	25. entregó
13. llegó	26. salvó

C
1. Yo escogí el Café Valencia.
2. Nosotros llegamos al restaurante a las siete.
3. Uds. leyeron la carta.
4. El mesero recomendó el pescado al mango.
5. Lorenzo pidió ternera y sopa.
6. Eva y Diana pidieron el bistec y ensalada.
7. Ud. prefirió el arroz con pollo.
8. Tú comiste torta de postre.
9. Todos nosotros tomamos vino.
10. Todo el mundo bebió café.
11. Yo pagué la cuenta.
12. Jaime dejó la propina.
13. Vosotros cenasteis muy bien.
14. Yo gocé de una cena riquísima.
15. Todos nosotros nos divertimos mucho.

D

1. Ya saqué los billetes para el concierto.
2. Ya jugué al tenis.
3. Ya toqué la flauta.
4. Ya coloqué los documentos en el archivo.
5. Ya arranqué la mala hierba del jardín.
6. Ya navegué en la red.
7. Ya descargué el documento.
8. Ya almorcé con Victoria.
9. Ya entregué el informe.
10. Ya empecé la novela inglesa.

E

1. Los hermanos Serrat construyeron muchas casas.
2. El profesor Burgos influyó mucho en la vida política.
3. Francisca leyó libros para una casa editora.
4. Marco e Isabel huyeron a otro pueblo por un terremoto.
5. Elvira contribuyó mucho dinero a las caridades.
6. Leonardo concluyó los trámites de la empresa.

F

1. equivoqué
2. marqué
3. tropecé
4. pegué
5. deslicé
6. masqué
7. tragué
8. bañé
9. ahogué
10. tranquilicé

G

1. lanzó / lancé
2. publicó / publiqué
3. dedicaste / dediqué
4. descargaron / descargué
5. realizaron / realicé
6. embarcó / embarqué

H

1. Aterricé en el aeropuerto de San Juan.
2. Visité fortalezas, museos e iglesias.
3. Sí, yo recé en la iglesia de San Juan y Sara rezó en una sinagoga.
4. Almorcé en varias playas de la Isla.
5. Sí, jugué al tenis y al fútbol también.
6. Sí, pesqué en el mar y en los ríos también.
7. Sí, avancé mucho en mi dominio del español.
8. Realicé un viaje maravilloso.
9. Sí, gocé muchísimo de mi estancia en Puerto Rico.

I

1. Tú sonreíste.
2. Los chicos repitieron.
3. Patricio gruñó.
4. Nosotros reímos.
5. Uds. se durmieron.
6. La señora Gil sirvió la sopa.
7. Chelo riñó a los niños.
8. Los ladrones mintieron.
9. Nuestros amigos nos advirtieron.
10. Paquita se divirtió.
11. Ellos lo sintieron.

J

1. Estuvo nublado ayer también.
2. Hizo frío ayer también.
3. Llovió ayer también.
4. Hizo sol ayer también.
5. Estuvo despejado ayer también.
6. Nevó ayer también.
7. Hizo ochenta grados ayer también.
8. Hizo fresco ayer también.
9. Tronó ayer también.
10. Hubo mucho viento ayer también.

K

1. dijo / dije
2. fueron / Fuimos
3. estuviste / Estuve
4. trajeron / trajo
5. vinieron / vine / vino
6. di / vio
7. oyó / supo
8. hiciste / puse
9. leyó / quiso
10. hizo / Fui

L

1. estuvo feliz
2. se hizo médico
3. tuvieron frío
4. pusimos la mesa
5. se hizo daño
6. pude distinguir
7. dijo que sí
8. fuiste tras ella

M

1. Pero ayer me desperté a las siete.
2. Pero ayer almorcé en el Café Atenas.
3. Pero ayer fui de compras por la mañana.
4. Pero ayer hice un plato de pescado.
5. Pero ayer jugué al ajedrez con Ricardo.
6. Pero ayer seguí por la calle Atocha.
7. Pero ayer empecé a trabajar antes del desayuno.
8. Pero ayer vine en taxi.

N

1. fuimos	7. trajeron
2. condujeron	8. vieron
3. pudo	9. oyeron
4. Hizo	10. comenzó
5. dio	11. tuvimos
6. recogieron	12. estuvimos

O

1. El monstruo llegó (vino) a la ciudad.
2. Hizo pedazos a los coches y destruyó edificios.
3. Al ver al monstruo la gente dio gritos. (Cuando la gente vio al monstruo dio gritos.)
4. Yo me puse pálido/a.
5. A Felipe le dio dolor de cabeza.
6. A Marisol le dio dolor de estómago.
7. Todos nos echamos a correr.
8. Algunas personas no pudieron escaparse.
9. ¡El suspenso se hizo insoportable (inaguantable)!

P

Answers will vary.

Q

1. pudiste / hice / encontré / viajamos / tuvimos / gustó / Fue
2. fue / llegué / facturé / saqué / seguiste / comí / compré
3. subí / coloqué / acomodé / abroché / despegó / hiciste / dormí / desperté / pedí / puse
4. aterrizamos / dejaron / fue / prendimos / bajamos / fuimos / pasamos / mostramos / tuvimos
5. dijo / hicieron / fueron / alquilamos / recorrimos / pasaron / divertimos / Vimos
6. hice / Tomé / llegué / vio / fui / conocí / encantó

R

Answers will vary.

5 The Imperfect Tense

A

1. vivía	7. gustaba
2. era	8. era
3. iba	9. pasábamos
4. hacía	10. era
5. solían	11. hacía
6. íbamos	12. Había

13. jugábamos	20. servía
14. cultivaba	21. leía
15. eran	22. íbamos
16. olía	23. estábamos
17. salíamos	24. volvían
18. Subíamos	25. llevaba
19. veía	26. era

B

1. Antes escribía para *El Tiempo,* pero ya no.
2. Antes iba de vacaciones a México, pero ya no.
3. Antes salía con Lola, pero ya no.
4. Antes me gustaba la cocina tailandesa, pero ya no.
5. Antes trabajaba como programadora, pero ya no.
6. Antes jugaba en un equipo de fútbol, pero ya no.
7. Antes mi marido y yo veníamos al pueblo en invierno, pero ya no.
8. Antes almorzaba con mis padres los sábados, pero ya no.
9. Antes era socio del Club Atlántico, pero ya no.
10. Antes mi hijo vivía en Chile, pero ya no.
11. Antes tenía una cadena de restaurantes, pero ya no.
12. Antes prefería vivir en el centro, pero ya no.
13. Antes veía a nuestros profesores, pero ya no.
14. Antes rodaba películas, pero ya no.

C

1. La señorita Fajardo era gerente de fábrica. Iba a Miami.
2. Los señores Guzmán eran dueños de una pastelería. Iban a Buenos Aires.
3. El señor García era profesor de economía. Iba a Irlanda.
4. La señora Montoya era banquera. Iba a Suiza.
5. Don Pedro Domínguez era candidato a senador. Iba a Monterrey.
6. Lorena Iglesias era ama de casa. Iba a Costa Rica.
7. Los hermanos Machado eran músicos. Iban a Nueva York.
8. El señor Rubio era cirujano. Iba a la India.

D

1. Carolina y Ramón no veían el mar Caribe desde el avión.
2. Nosotros no veíamos la cara de los actores desde el anfiteatro.
3. Federica no veía el embotellamiento desde la ventana del dormitorio.
4. Uds. no veían toda la cancha de fútbol desde la tribuna del estadio.
5. Yo no veía la cumbre de la montaña desde el valle.
6. Vosotros no veíais la discoteca desde la esquina.
7. Tú no veías al público desde la parte derecha del escenario.

E

1. Llovía cuando Beatriz y tú volvieron (volvisteis).
2. Hacía frío cuando los Sorolla se levantaron.
3. Estaba despejado cuando fuiste al aeropuerto.
4. Hacía viento cuando José Antonio vino a la casa.
5. Nevaba cuando nosotros terminamos el trabajo.
6. Tronaba cuando Ud. entró en el cine.
7. Hacía sol cuando yo llegué a la playa.
8. Lloviznaba cuando Uds. se fueron.
9. Hacía calor cuando yo me puse en marcha.

F

1. Eran las nueve y media cuando Consuelo y Berta se despidieron.
2. Era la una cuando el programa comenzó.
3. Era mediodía cuando Sara sirvió el almuerzo.
4. Eran las diez en punto cuando el empleado abrió la taquilla.
5. Era medianoche cuando regresamos de la fiesta.
6. Era muy tarde cuando Uds. se durmieron.
7. Era temprano cuando el cartero trajo el correo.
8. Eran las cinco y cuarto cuando me reuní a la reunión virtual.
9. Eran las tres cuarenta cuando te reuniste con tus amigos.
10. Eran las once de la noche cuando el avión aterrizó.

G

1. Mientras tú viajabas, acabó la telenovela.
2. Mientras Marta y Miguel se quedaban en un hotel, un ladrón forzó la entrada.
3. Mientras Estefanía vivía en el extranjero, sus padres vendieron su casa de campo.
4. Mientras Uds. hacían un viaje, sus vecinos montaron una nueva empresa.
5. Mientras yo veía las siete maravillas del mundo, se añadieron otras siete a la lista.
6. Mientras Benito trabajaba en San Antonio, su novia rompió con él.
7. Mientras el avión de Diego aterrizaba en Los Ángeles, el de su esposa despegó en Atlanta.
8. Mientras los turistas conocían los Estados Unidos, la guerra estalló en su país.
9. Mientras nosotros estábamos en el puerto, hubo un incendio en el barco.
10. Mientras vosotros caminabais a la plaza mayor, yo os alcancé.
11. Mientras Laura y yo platicábamos, mi teléfono celular sonó.
12. Mientras tú leías, nosotros enviamos el correo electrónico.

H

Answers will vary.

I

1. tenía
2. llevaron
3. sentó
4. dio
5. leíamos
6. se apagaron
7. subieron
8. vimos
9. Había
10. hacía
11. estaba
12. llevaba
13. vestía
14. hacía
15. salió
16. se puso
17. quedé
18. me hice

J

1. me gradué
2. Saqué
3. Esperaba
4. nací
5. Quería
6. había
7. mandé
8. Tuve
9. Encontré
10. se publicaba
11. fue
12. conocía
13. vivía
14. estaba
15. Hacía
16. conocí
17. trabajaba
18. era
19. fue
20. nos casamos
21. llegué
22. tuvimos
23. vivimos

K

1. Bárbara creía que Tomás conocía a su hermana Luz. En realidad, él conoció a Luz anoche en la cena.
2. Los hombres de negocios querían hablar del informe. Sus abogados no quisieron.
3. La novia no tenía regalos. Entonces tuvo veinte regalos esta mañana.
4. No sabíamos quién tenía los documentos. Lo supimos ayer.
5. Yo no podía armar el juguete. Javier no pudo armarlo tampoco.

L

1. quería
2. íbamos
3. dije
4. interesaba
5. gustó
6. conocía
7. compró
8. hizo
9. pensábamos
10. tomamos
11. llegamos
12. visitamos
13. conocimos
14. tuve
15. podíamos
16. era
17. estaban
18. realicé

M

1. Eran
2. sonó
3. estaba
4. descolgué
5. oí
6. dijo
7. robó
8. pidieron
9. explicó
10. tenía
11. quedamos
12. eran
13. llegué
14. seguía
15. llegó
16. vi
17. estaba
18. tenía
19. llevaba
20. fumaba
21. acerqué
22. senté
23. olía
24. hablé
25. pregunté
26. puso
27. dijo
28. comprendí
29. iba

N

1. ¿Cuánto tiempo hacía que Montserrat Pujol cantaba ópera cuando firmó un contrato con la Metropolitana? / Hacía ocho años que cantaba ópera.
2. ¿Cuánto tiempo hacía que los señores Salazar estaban casados cuando nació su hija? / Hacía cuatro años que estaban casados.
3. ¿Cuánto tiempo hacía que vivías en París cuando tus padres se mudaron a Londres? / Hacía once meses que yo vivía en París.
4. ¿Cuánto tiempo hacía que Susana y Lía eran amigas cuando Susana le quitó el novio a Lía? / Hacía doce años que eran amigas.
5. ¿Cuánto tiempo hacía que Ud. compraba billetes de lotería cuando ganó el premio gordo? / Hacía quince años que compraba billetes de lotería.
6. ¿Cuánto tiempo hacía que Patricio y Ud. tocaban el violonchelo cuando el conservatorio les dio una beca? / Hacía nueve años que tocábamos el violonchelo.

O

1. El gobierno explotaba el petróleo desde hacía treinta años hasta que el presidente privatizó la industria.
2. La gente sufría por la inflación desde hacía cinco años hasta que los economistas intentaron controlarla.
3. La prensa no era libre desde hacía cincuenta años hasta que hubo un golpe de estado.
4. Los obreros no recibían un sueldo decente desde hacía cinco décadas hasta que se formaron los sindicatos.
5. El país no producía los bienes necesarios desde hacía varios años hasta que el país estableció el mercado libre.
6. El pueblo no tenía ninguna libertad desde hacía cuarenta y cinco años hasta que murió el dictador y se estableció la democracia.

P

Answers will vary.

Q

1. El primer día que Beatriz y yo pasamos en la Ciudad de México fuimos al Bosque de Chapultepec.
2. Hacía muy buen tiempo. Hacía sol y calor.
3. Había mucha gente en el parque (el bosque).
4. Unos niñitos jugaban en los resbalines y montaban en bicicleta.
5. Mientras caminábamos por el parque (el bosque) vimos el Árbol de Moctezuma y el Castillo de Chapultepec.
6. Llegamos al Museo Nacional de Antropología y entramos.
7. Caminábamos de una sala a otra y vimos la exhibición de arte precolombino.
8. Pasamos dos horas en el museo.
9. Después fuimos a la librería donde yo compré un libro sobre los aztecas y los mayas.

10. Almorzamos (Tomamos el almuerzo) en la cafetería del museo.
11. Eran las cinco cuando salimos del museo.

R

Answers will vary.

6 The Future and Conditional Tenses

A

1. Me graduaré en junio.
2. Mis amigos y yo celebraremos con una fiesta.
3. Nuestros padres estarán muy contentos.
4. Yo haré un viaje a Europa en el verano.
5. Miguel me acompañará.
6. Nos encantará viajar.
7. Iremos a los países de la Europa oriental.
8. Andrés y Manuel querrán ir también.
9. Saldremos para Polonia a mediados de junio.
10. Pasaremos dos meses viajando.
11. Andrés volverá antes porque
12. tendrá que comenzar sus estudios graduados.
13. Al regresar yo empezaré a trabajar en una compañía multinacional.
14. Miguel podrá trabajar en la empresa de sus padres.
15. Manuel seguirá con sus clases en la facultad de ingeniería.
16. ¡Tendremos tiempo de vernos, espero!

B

1. Mari Carmen llorará.
2. Las tías dirán "¡ay de mí!"
3. Ramón tendrá vergüenza.
4. Tú te volverás loco.
5. Juan y Alicia pondrán el grito en el cielo.
6. Uds. se enfadarán.
7. Nosotros nos reiremos a carcajadas.
8. Ud. se pondrá de buen humor.
9. Vosotros estaréis contentos.

C

1. ¡Mañana será un ajetreo continuo!
2. Tendré mucho que hacer.
3. Habrá clases todo el día
4. y tomaré exámenes también.
5. Además, yo iré a una tienda por departamentos.
6. Le compraré un regalo a mi hermana.

7. Sarita cumplirá diecisiete años pasado mañana.
8. Mamá hará una comida y una torta.
9. Papá y yo saldremos para comprar vino.
10. También querré terminar mi informe.
11. No podré salir con mis amigos.
12. Me acostaré muy tarde.

D

1. Yolanda y Ana patinarán sobre hielo.
2. Tú cocinarás yacu-chupe y un sancochado.
3. Julio mandará textos.
4. Consuelo se acostará tarde.
5. Yo pasearé al perro.
6. Uds. jugarán al baloncesto.
7. Ud. escribirá correos electrónicos.
8. Nosotros haremos una fiesta de disfraces.
9. Vosotros podréis viajar al Canadá.
10. Ud. tomará una clase en línea.

E

1. Si María quiere salir, nosotros saldremos con ella.
2. Si ellos van, Ud. podrá verlos.
3. Si yo hago tu plato favorito, tú vendrás a almorzar.
4. Si Uds. trabajan mucho, tendrán éxito.
5. Si tú no sabes qué pasó, yo te diré.
6. Si nosotros no compramos harina, no habrá tortillas esta noche.
7. Si hace calor, Carlos y Pedro irán a la playa.
8. Si llueve, Celeste querrá ir al cine.

F

1. Serán las seis.
2. Teodoro tendrá veinte años.
3. El reloj valdrá mucho.
4. Habrá problemas entre los socios de la empresa.
5. Teresa sabrá la hora de la conferencia.
6. Esteban querrá ir a la reunión.
7. Los programadores volverán pronto.

G

1. ¿Será verde?
2. Tendrá pilas.
3. ¿Habrá muchas partes?
4. ¿Será de madera?
5. ¿Costará (Valdrá) mucho?
6. Hará un ruido.
7. Será más grande que una caja para el pan.
8. ¿Todo el mundo tendrá uno? (¿Todos tendrán uno?)
9. ¿Estará vivo?
10. Cabrá en la mano.

H

1. a. Buscaría a la dependienta.
   b. Iría a otro almacén.
2. a. Repetiría.
   b. Pediría la receta.
3. a. Saldríamos corriendo.
   b. Llamaríamos a los bomberos.
4. a. Se disculparía con la señora.
   b. Le quitaría el zapato a la señora.
5. a. Los acostaría sin bañarlos.
   b. Llamaría al plomero.
6. a. Harían un muñeco de nieve.
   b. Lanzarían bolas de nieve.
7. a. Yo le diría al policía lo que pasó.
   b. Yo les pondría vendas a los heridos.

I

1. Elena pagaría la matrícula en la universidad.
2. Mi primo Federico vendría a visitarnos.
3. Uds. harían un viaje al Japón.
4. Juan Pablo y Ana María depositarían la plata en el banco.
5. Tú ya no tendrías deudas.
6. Mi hermano y yo querríamos darles dinero a los huérfanos.
7. Rodrigo y yo invertiríamos en la Bolsa.

J

1. gustaría	5. ocuparían
2. querría	6. haríamos
3. habría	7. pondrían
4. podríamos	8. vendríamos

K

1. Serían las once.
2. Habría sesenta invitados.
3. Estarían cansados.
4. Costaría treinta mil dólares.
5. Serían inteligentes.

L

1. estarían	5. vendría
2. podría	6. pondrías
3. querría	7. habría
4. cabrían	8. tendríamos

M

Answers will vary.

N

Answers will vary.

7   Reflexive Verbs

A

1. me despierto / despierto
2. aburría / se aburrían
3. se casaron / casó
4. esconderemos / nos esconderemos
5. te vistes / vistes
6. nos paseamos / paseamos
7. tranquilizó / se tranquilizó
8. me divertí / divirtieron
9. me mareaba / mareaba
10. animamos / se anima
11. se asustaban / asustaban
12. se ofenden / ofenden

B

1. ¿Uds. ya se despiertan solos? / No, abuelita. Nos despierta mamá.
2. ¿Uds. ya se lavan el pelo solos? / No, abuelita. Nos lava el pelo mamá. (Nos lo lava mamá.)
3. ¿Uds. ya se peinan solos? / No, abuelita. Nos peina mamá.
4. ¿Uds. ya se atan los zapatos solos? / No, abuelita. Nos ata los zapatos mamá. (Nos los ata mamá.)
5. ¿Uds. ya se cepillan los dientes solos? / No, abuelita. Nos cepilla los dientes mamá. (Nos los cepilla mamá.)
6. ¿Uds. ya se acuestan solos? / No, abuelita. Nos acuesta mamá.

C

1. Marina y yo nos pusimos los jeans.
2. Arturo se puso un traje de baño.
3. Uds. se pusieron un impermeable.
4. Yo me puse un suéter de lana.
5. Víctor y Paco se pusieron un gorro.
6. Todos nosotros nos pusimos una camiseta.
7. Ud. se puso las sandalias.
8. Vosotros os pusisteis una bufanda.

D

1. Yo me pondré un vestido de lino.
2. Alicia se pondrá una blusa de poliéster.
3. Nosotros nos pondremos zapatos de cuero.
4. Uds. se pondrán una camisa de algodón.
5. Los jefes se pondrán un traje de lana.
6. Tú te pondrás una corbata de seda.
7. Ud. se pondrá una falda de pana.
8. Vosotros os pondréis una chaqueta de mezclilla.

E

1. Pilar y Luz se prueban el vestido largo.
2. Yo me pruebo el abrigo de terciopelo.
3. Lorenzo se prueba el smoking.
4. Uds. se prueban los zapatos de tacón alto.
5. Tú te pruebas la blusa de seda.
6. Antonio y Esteban se prueban la corbata.
7. Vosotros os probáis el sombrero.
8. Ud. se prueba los guantes.

F

1. Miguel se rompió la pierna montando a caballo.
2. Ana se quemó la mano cocinando.
3. El perro de Bernardo se perdió en las afueras.
4. Eunice se torció el tobillo patinando sobre hielo.
5. Todos nosotros nos enfermamos comiendo hamburguesas poco hechas.
6. Yo me lastimé cortando el césped.
7. El hermano de Pedro se quebró el dedo jugando al baloncesto.

G

1. La actriz Ramona Arias se lastimó en el rodaje de su nueva película.
2. El futbolista Diego Suárez se rompió el pie en el partido de hoy.
3. Unos turistas norteamericanos se cayeron en la escalera mecánica del metro.
4. Un carpintero se cortó la mano serrando madera.
5. Diez arqueólogos se hicieron daño en una excavación en las pirámides.
6. Un bombero se quemó apagando un incendio.

H

1. Felisa se lava la cabeza todos los días.
2. Yo me visto rápidamente por la mañana.
3. Vosotros os ducháis por la noche.
4. Carlos se afeita con una maquinilla de afeitar.
5. Laura y Teresa se liman las uñas antes de ponerse el esmalte de uñas.
6. Tú te peinas con peine y cepillo.
7. Benjamín y yo nos arreglamos después de desayunar.
8. Ud. se cepilla los dientes antes de maquillarse.

I

1. Samuel quiere colocarse en una sucursal de la empresa. / Samuel se quiere colocar en una sucursal de la empresa.
2. Nosotros debemos despertarnos antes de las ocho. / Nosotros nos debemos despertar antes de las ocho.
3. Vosotros pensáis reuniros en casa de Felipe esta noche. / Vosotros os pensáis reunir en casa de Felipe esta noche.
4. Teresa necesita pesarse todas las semanas. / Teresa se necesita pesar todas las semanas.
5. Yo voy a irme de vacaciones en julio. / Yo me voy a ir de vacaciones en julio.
6. Las señoras acaban de aprovecharse de las liquidaciones. / Las señoras se acaban de aprovechar de las liquidaciones.
7. ¿Quieres sentarte en esta fila? / ¿Te quieres sentar en esta fila?
8. Uds. tienen que secarse el pelo. / Uds. se tienen que secar el pelo.

J

1. Pruébese los dos. / Pruébate los dos.
2. Acuéstese temprano. / Acuéstate temprano.
3. Dése prisa. / Date prisa.
4. Póngase el impermeable. / Ponte el impermeable.
5. Diviértase mucho. / Diviértete mucho.
6. Quédese otra semana entonces. / Quédate otra semana entonces.
7. Váyase ahora mismo. / Vete ahora mismo.
8. Tranquilícese. / Tranquilízate.

K

1. No se levante todavía. / No te levantes todavía.
2. No se enferme. / No te enfermes.
3. No se enfade con ella. / No te enfades con ella.
4. No se despierte tarde. / No te despiertes tarde.
5. No se duerma. / No te duermas.
6. No se haga el desentendido. / No te hagas el desentendido.
7. No se ponga gorda. / No te pongas gorda.

L

1. Niños, vístanse para salir.
2. Niños, cepíllense los dientes.
3. Niños, átense los zapatos.
4. Niños, pónganse serios.
5. Niños, lávense las manos.

6. Niños, siéntense.
7. Niños, tranquilícense.
8. Niños, acuéstense.

M

1. Niños, no se ensucien la cara.
2. Niños, no se hagan los sordos.
3. Niños, no se caigan patinando.
4. Niños, no se olviden de guardar sus juguetes.
5. Niños, no se vayan del jardín.
6. Niños, no se hagan daño.
7. Niños, no se quejen tanto.

N

1. Luisito está portándose mal. / Luisito se está portando mal.
2. Los abuelos de Luisito están poniéndose rojos. / Los abuelos de Luisito se están poniendo rojos.
3. Adrianita está riéndose como una loca. / Adrianita se está riendo como una loca.
4. La tía de Adrianita está desmayándose. / La tía de Adrianita se está desmayando.
5. Fernandito está escondiéndose en un armario. / Fernandito se está escondiendo en un armario.
6. El tío de Fernandito está asustándose. / El tío de Fernandito se está asustando.
7. Los gemelos están escapándose de su padre. / Los gemelos se están escapando de su padre.
8. El padre de los gemelos está enojándose. / El padre de los gemelos se está enojando.
9. Pedrito está burlándose de sus primos. / Pedrito se está burlando de sus primos.
10. Los primos de Pedrito están exasperándose. / Los primos de Pedrito se están exasperando.
11. Mari Carmen está ensuciándose con el guacamole. / Mari Carmen se está ensuciando con el guacamole.
12. La madre de Mari Carmen está avergonzándose. / La madre de Mari Carmen se está avergonzando.

O

1. Se está apresurando para salir. / Está apresurándose para salir.
2. Se están mudando a otro barrio. / Están mudándose a otro barrio.
3. Se están acercando a la escuela. / Están acercándose a la escuela.
4. Se están paseando por el centro. / Están paseándose por el centro.

5. Me estoy instalando en un nuevo apartamento. / Estoy instalándome en un nuevo apartamento.
6. Nos estamos reuniendo en el comedor de la empresa. / Estamos reuniéndonos en el comedor de la empresa.
7. Se está vistiendo para salir. / Está vistiéndose para salir.
8. Nos estamos divirtiendo con nuestros amigos. / Estamos divirtiéndonos con nuestros amigos.

P

1. Marisol y yo nos hablamos por teléfono cuatro veces al día.
2. Jorge y yo nos entendemos perfectamente.
3. José María y yo nos vemos todos los días.
4. Consuelo y yo nos escribimos correos electrónicos.
5. Felipe y yo nos ayudamos con el trabajo.
6. Victoria y yo nos prestamos ropa.
7. David y yo nos tuteamos.

Q

1. Se conocieron en una fiesta.
2. Se dieron un beso.
3. Se vieron todos los días.
4. Se hablaron constantemente.
5. Se compraron regalos.
6. Se dijeron muchas cosas importantes.
7. Se hicieron promesas.
8. Se comprendieron muy bien.

R

1. se conocieron
2. Se pusieron
3. se enojaron
4. se pegaron
5. se acercaron
6. se tranquilizaron
7. se abrazaron
8. se dieron

S

1. a
2. b
3. a
4. b
5. b

T

1. Ricardo se hizo (llegó a ser) millonario.
2. Los arqueólogos se entusiasmaron al ver las ruinas.
3. Magdalena se pone roja a menudo porque es muy tímida.
4. Daniel se casa con Tere porque quiere llegar a ser (hacerse) ciudadano (norte)americano.
5. ¡Carlitos se ha vuelto imposible!
6. Felisa está poniéndose muy gorda por la torta y el helado que come todos los días.

7. La región se convirtió en un importante centro de tecnología.
8. Isabel se hizo (llegó a ser) programadora.

U

1. con	7. de
2. en	8. a
3. de	9. de
4. de	10. de
5. en	11. con
6. a	12. a

V

1. Si me acuerdo bien, los Aranda se mudaron a Los Ángeles.
2. Ud. se equivoca. Lima es la capital del Perú, no de Ecuador.
3. Dos personas se quedaron ciegas a causa del accidente.
4. La niña se hace la dormida.
5. Juan Carlos se ha enflaquecido.
6. Creíamos que íbamos a enloquecernos por el desorden de la casa.
7. Todos los habitantes están poniéndose furiosos por el número de robos en el barrio.
8. Diego se palidecía corriendo la última milla de la carrera.

W

Answers will vary.

8 Passive Constructions

A

1. El email fue leído por la recepcionista.
2. Los formularios serán llenados por los empleados.
3. El folleto ha sido preparado por el diseñador gráfico.
4. La base de datos fue hecha por la programadora.
5. El sitio web será actualizado por el administrador de web.
6. Los billetes electrónicos fueron comprados por los agentes de viajes.
7. La pantalla fue reparada por el técnico.
8. Los problemas han sido resueltos por los gerentes.

B

1. Las camas fueron subidas a los dormitorios por tres hombres.
2. La alfombra de la sala fue corrida por la señora Pidal.
3. Los cuadros fueron colgados en las paredes por Benito y Ramona.
4. La secadora fue bajada al sótano por un cargador.
5. El sillón azul fue colocado al lado de la ventana por el señor Pidal.
6. Las lámparas fueron puestas en las mesas por Regina.

C

1. Se enchufará la nevera.
2. Se encenderán las lámparas.
3. Se guardarán las cajas.
4. Se pondrá el sofá en la sala.
5. Se colocará el lavaplatos en la cocina.
6. Se meterán las sábanas en el armario.
7. Se pondrán las sillas con la mesa del comedor.
8. Se subirán las cómodas a los dormitorios.

D

1. Se buscan programadores de computadoras.
2. Se prohíbe el fumar en los restaurantes.
3. Se calculaban los impuestos.
4. Se alquiló el condominio en la playa.
5. Se entrega comida a la casa hasta la una de la mañana.
6. Se paga con cheque o tarjeta de crédito.
7. Se solicitarán gerentes.
8. Se necesitan asesores bilingües.

E

1. Mis amigos y yo vamos de excursión al zoológico.
2. Para llegar al zoológico, tomamos el autobús en la calle Azorín.
3. Yo veo leones, tigres, leopardos y panteras.
4. Los guardianes dan de comer a los animales.
5. Un trabajador entra en las jaulas para limpiarlas.
6. Las jirafas comen las hojas de los árboles.
7. Tú tiras cacahuates a los elefantes.
8. Un mono juega tirando plátanos.
9. Los loros gritan en voz alta.
10. Los hipopótamos se bañan en la piscina de la jaula.
11. Ud. bebe una limonada.
12. Vosotros compráis palomitas y refrescos.

F
1. No sé. Cuando yo llegué, el cuarto ya estaba arreglado.
2. No sé. Cuando yo llegué, el almuerzo ya estaba preparado.
3. No sé. Cuando yo llegué, la puerta ya estaba cerrada.
4. No sé. Cuando yo llegué, el microondas ya estaba apagado.
5. No sé. Cuando yo llegué, la mesa ya estaba puesta.
6. No sé. Cuando yo llegué, los vasos ya estaban rotos.
7. No sé. Cuando yo llegué, el documento escaneado ya estaba mandado.
8. No sé. Cuando yo llegué, las luces ya estaban prendidas.

G
1. Se venden periódicos y revistas aquí.
2. Se estaciona aquí.
3. Se come bien en esta ciudad.
4. Se dobla a la derecha.
5. Se entra por aquí.
6. Se habla español aquí.
7. Se construyen casas.
8. Se sale por esta puerta.

H
Answers will vary. Suggested responses:
1. Se toman física, historia y matemáticas.
2. Se almuerza a la una. (Se toma el almuerzo a la una.)
3. Se llega andando o en autobús.
4. Se compran los libros de texto en la librería Academia.
5. Se puede sacar buenas notas estudiando mucho.
6. Se va a un concierto o al cine.
7. Se come en el Café Miraflores o en el restaurante Cuatro Caminos.

I
Answers will vary.

9 The Compound Tenses

A
1. Pedro ha apagado las luces.
2. Cecilia y Pilar han hecho las maletas.
3. Papá ha llenado el tanque del coche.
4. Ud. ha desenchufado los aparatos eléctricos.

5. David y Juan Carlos han metido el equipaje en el baúl.
6. Yo les he dicho a los vecinos que nos vamos.
7. Vosotros habéis puesto las pilas en la linterna.
8. Tú has limpiado los cristales del coche.

B
1. Nosotros hemos leído la receta.
2. Jorge ha encendido el fuego.
3. Yo he hecho la salsa.
4. Alicia y Juan Diego han picado las pimientas picantes.
5. Ud. ha frito las cebollas.
6. Estrella y yo hemos cortado la salchicha.
7. Tú has lavado los espárragos y los aguacates.
8. Marianela ha añadido la sal.
9. Uds. han puesto el pollo al horno.
10. Yo he mezclado la ensalada de camarones.
11. Martín ha cubierto la cacerola.
12. Vosotros habéis quemado las sartenes.

C
1. Nosotros la hemos leído.
2. Jorge lo ha encendido.
3. Yo la he hecho.
4. Alicia y Juan Diego las han picado.
5. Ud. las ha frito.
6. Estrella y yo la hemos cortado.
7. Tú los has lavado.
8. Marianela la ha añadido.
9. Uds. lo han puesto al horno.
10. Yo la he mezclado.
11. Martín la ha cubierto.
12. Vosotros las habéis quemado.

D
1. María Dolores se ha dormido.
2. Ud. ha bostezado.
3. Yo me he puesto el abrigo.
4. Carlos y Beatriz se han despedido de la anfitriona.
5. ¡Nos han matado de aburrimiento!
6. Tú te has quejado que la comida te cayó mal.
7. Ud. y Clara han dado excusas.
8. Nosotros hemos dicho que nos enfermamos.

E
Answers will vary.

F
1. Cristóbal se ha matriculado ya.
2. Nos hemos colocado ya.
3. Yo me he instalado en la nueva casa ya.

4. Irene y Jaime se han comprometido ya.
5. Nora se ha enterado de los líos de la familia ya.
6. Yo me he apuntado en la lista de voluntarios ya.
7. Nos hemos reunido ya.

G

1. Uds. habían visto la exposición hace unos meses.
2. Amelia se había cortado el pelo el sábado.
3. Ricardo y Leonor se habían casado en abril.
4. Nosotros habíamos hecho una barbacoa el cuatro de julio.
5. Tú habías celebrado tu cumpleaños hace un mes.
6. Ud. había cambiado de idea hace varios días.
7. Yo me había puesto en contacto con Felipe hace tres semanas.
8. Javier me había devuelto los disquetes la semana pasada.
9. Vosotros habíais escrito los informes en noviembre.
10. Marcos se había roto el codo hace casi un año.

H

1. Cuando Tomás llegó por fin, Raúl ya había hecho la pizza.
2. ..., Uds. ya habían puesto la mesa.
3. ..., Diana y Judit ya habían visto el sitio web.
4. ..., Ud. ya había sacado la basura.
5. ..., yo ya había subido las cajas a la buhardilla.
6. ..., tú ya habías ido de compras.
7. ..., Plácido y yo ya habíamos vuelto de la tienda de cómputo.

I

1. Cuando Julia vino a buscarnos, nosotros ya habíamos hecho ejercicio.
2. Cuando yo fui a su casa, Virginia ya había dado una vuelta.
3. Cuando Ud. se levantó, sus padres ya habían desayunado.
4. Cuando nosotros volvimos a casa, Juanita ya había escrito su email.
5. Cuando los bomberos llegaron, Uds. ya habían apagado el incendio en la cocina.
6. Cuando los bisnietos lograron ver a su bisabuelo, el bisabuelo ya se había enfermado.

J

1. Laura no había visto una corrida de toros en Madrid.
2. Rodolfo y Eva no habían dado una vuelta por las carreteras gallegas.
3. Yo no había hecho una excursión a El Escorial.
4. Tú y Susana no se habían paseado por el barrio de Santa Cruz.
5. Nosotros no habíamos subido al monte Tibidabo.
6. Jaime no había conocido la Alhambra.
7. Tú no habías pasado la Semana Santa en Sevilla.
8. Vosotros no habíais conocido tantos restaurantes.

K

1. Elena se habrá graduado para el año próximo.
2. Alfredo y Armando se habrán mejorado antes de regresar a la oficina.
3. Nosotros habremos ahorrado dinero antes de las vacaciones de invierno.
4. Yo te habré dado tu regalo antes de tu fiesta de cumpleaños.
5. Ud. y Laura se habrán mudado para mediados del mes.
6. Tú habrás sacado un pasaporte para julio.
7. Ud. habrá vuelto del centro comercial para las ocho.

L

1. Su coche le habrá costado un ojo de la cara.
2. Clara habrá escrito el texto.
3. Felipe y Eduardo habrán solicitado una beca.
4. Uds. habrán tomado la merienda.
5. Martín y yo no habremos entendido el motivo.
6. Ud. habrá hecho cola por mucho tiempo.

M

1. Patricia y yo no habríamos salido.
2. Sofía no habría roto su compromiso con su novio.
3. Los turistas venezolanos no habrían hecho el viaje a California en autobús.
4. Tú no te habrías cortado el pelo en la peluquería Melenas.
5. Ud. no habría creído lo que dijo Baltasar.
6. Yo no me habría reído.

N

1. A Lope Cernuda por haber dirigido *Plátanos y cerezas.*
2. A Ernesto del Olmo por haber compuesto la música de *Mosquitos mágicos.*
3. A Ela Pantoja y Roberto Campillo por haber escrito el guión de *Agua hervida.*
4. A Agustín Domingo por haber cantado en *Después de haber bailado.*
5. A Beatriz Perales por haber sido primera actriz en *Salchichas al sol.*
6. A Mateo de León y Diana Duque por haber producido *Grapadora en la mesa.*
7. A Silvia Siles por haber hecho la escenografía de *Narices al aire.*
8. A Memo Morado por haber actuado en *Langostas en el cielo.*
9. A Edit Revueltas por haber diseñado el vestuario de *Tijeras de poliéster.*
10. A Pepe del Oeste por haberles maquillado a los actores de *Tamales quemados.*

O

1. La hacienda habría sido muy grande.
2. Los agricultores habrían tenido gallinas (pollos) en un gallinero.
3. Los campesinos habrían recogido cerezas y fresas.
4. El paisaje del campo habría sido hermoso.
5. Mi bisabuelo habría ido a pescar en el lago que quedaba cerca.
6. Mi bisabuela habría cocinado frutas y verduras frescas de la cosecha.
7. Habría habido caballos y vacas en la estancia.
8. Los granjeros habrían sembrado semillas en el huerto.
9. Nos habría encantado la vida de la estancia.

P

Answers will vary.

10 The Gerund and the Progressive Tenses

A

1. Sí, pasé el día hablando por teléfono.
2. Sí, pasaron el día navegando en la red.
3. Sí, pasó el día durmiendo la siesta.
4. Sí, pasamos el día leyendo nuestro correo electrónico.
5. Sí, pasé el día oyendo las noticias.
6. Sí, pasamos el día imprimiendo los documentos.

B

1. Yo pasé cuarenta y cinco minutos arreglándome.
2. Estrella y yo pasamos una hora y media montando en bicicleta.
3. Yo pasé dos horas escribiendo un informe.
4. Fernando, Chelo y yo pasamos un par de horas comprando cosas en el centro comercial.
5. Mis amigos y yo pasamos treinta minutos vistiéndonos.
6. Yo pasé una hora viendo un documental.

C

1. Los niños están acampando en la sierra.
2. Ricardo está nadando en el lago.
3. Lupe y yo estamos llenando la mochila.
4. Ester está desenvolviendo el saco de dormir.
5. Ud. y Andrés están jugando al fútbol.
6. Pablo está acostándose (se está acostando) en el saco de dormir.
7. Yo estoy observando las hormigas en el hormiguero.
8. Tú estás encendiendo el fuego para asar los perros calientes.
9. Vosotros estáis metiendo las pilas en la linterna.
10. Todos nosotros estamos quejándonos (nos estamos quejando) de las picaduras de los mosquitos.
11. Ud. está asustándose (se está asustando) al ver las arañas en la tienda de campaña.
12. Consuelo está gritando al ver una serpiente.

D

1. Estábamos leyéndolos. / Los estábamos leyendo.
2. Estarán haciéndolas. / Las estarán haciendo.
3. Estoy poniéndomelo. / Me lo estoy poniendo.
4. Estaba lavándosela. / Se la estaba lavando.
5. Estarás diciéndonoslos. / Nos los estarás diciendo.

6. Está abrochándoselo. / Se lo está abrochando.
7. Estábamos sirviéndoselos. / Se los estábamos sirviendo.

E

1. Los señores Sotomayor estaban registrándose. / Los señores Sotomayor se estaban registrando.
2. La señorita Serrano estaba pidiendo un juego de toallas.
3. El botones estaba subiéndoles el equipaje a unos huéspedes. / El botones les estaba subiendo el equipaje a unos huéspedes.
4. Las camareras estaban arreglando los cuartos.
5. Los meseros estaban sirviéndoles la cena a los clientes. / Los meseros les estaban sirviendo la cena a los clientes.
6. El gerente estaba prendiendo el aire acondicionado.
7. El doctor López estaba afeitándose. / El doctor López se estaba afeitando.
8. La lavandera estaba devolviéndole el lavado a la señora Casona. / La lavandera le estaba devolviendo el lavado a la señora Casona.
9. Los huéspedes del noveno piso estaban bajando en el ascensor.
10. Los turistas ingleses estaban tocando el timbre en la recepción.
11. Los cocineros estaban jactándose de los plátanos flameados que habían preparado. / Los cocineros se estaban jactando de los plátanos flameados que habían preparado.

F

1. ¡Qué va! Elena sigue diciéndolos.
2. ¡Qué va! Siguen construyéndola.
3. ¡Qué va! Yo sigo leyéndola.
4. ¡Qué va! Mis hermanos siguen elaborándolo.
5. ¡Qué va! Yo sigo asistiendo a los conciertos de jazz.
6. ¡Qué va! Seguimos jugando al fútbol en el estadio.

G

1. Luisa estará viendo televisión a las dos y media.
2. Ud. estará duchándose a medianoche. (Ud. se estará duchando a medianoche.)

3. Mis amigos y yo estaremos muriéndonos de sueño a las cuatro. (Mis amigos y yo nos estaremos muriendo de sueño a las cuatro.)
4. Pablo y Ramón estarán jugando videojuegos a las doce y media.
5. Yo estaré escuchando música a la una y media.
6. Tú estarás comiendo una pizza a las tres.
7. Uds. estarán enviándome un email a las cinco. (Uds. me estarán enviando un email a las cinco.)

H

1. Llevo doce años pintando retratos.
2. Llevo unos meses usando estos pinceles.
3. Llevo varios años dibujando con modelos.
4. Llevo treinta años dedicándome a la pintura.
5. Llevo un año vendiendo mis cuadros de paisajes por Internet.
6. Llevo poco tiempo interesándome en los murales.
7. Llevo nueve años trabajando en cerámica.
8. Llevo cinco años viviendo en Nueva York.

I

1. están animando
2. está robando
3. estamos viendo
4. está marcando
5. están saliendo
6. está regateando
7. están pidiéndoles
8. están entusiasmándose
9. están oyendo
10. está atrayendo

J

1. Estamos divirtiéndonos mucho. (Nos estamos divirtiendo mucho.)
2. Ud. estuvo trotando hasta que empezó a llover.
3. Siguen sirviendo la cena en el Hotel Palacio.
4. Voy conociendo Madrid.
5. Mateo y Victoria estarán jugando al tenis toda la tarde.
6. Pedro y yo seguimos leyendo.

K

Answers will vary.

11 The Subjunctive in Noun Clauses: Present and Present Perfect Subjunctive

A

1. Pero yo quiero que trabaje en el informe.
2. Pero yo quiero que consigas empleo.
3. Pero yo quiero que nos escriban.
4. Pero yo quiero que siga nuestros consejos.
5. Pero yo quiero que comamos fuera hoy.
6. Pero yo quiero que vuelvas temprano.
7. Pero yo quiero que duerman la siesta.
8. Pero yo quiero que pidamos taxi.
9. Pero yo quiero que abran la tienda hoy.
10. Pero yo quiero que entienda.
11. Pero yo quiero que piense en nosotros.
12. Pero yo quiero que envíe el paquete.
13. Pero yo quiero que cierres las ventanas.
14. Pero yo quiero que nos divirtamos.
15. Pero yo quiero que se gradúen este año.

B

1. Sí. Se alegra de que conozca a Pedro.
2. Sí. Se alegra de que tengamos un día libre.
3. Sí. Se alegra de que le traiga flores.
4. Sí. Se alegra de que me mude al centro.
5. Sí. Se alegra de que construyan una casa.
6. Sí. Se alegra de que salgan juntos.
7. Sí. Se alegra de que oigamos música clásica.
8. Sí. Se alegra de que hagamos un viaje.
9. Sí. Se alegra de que componga música.
10. Sí. Se alegra de que sea mañana.
11. Sí. Se alegra de que haya reunión la semana que viene.
12. Sí. Se alegra de que vayan a España.

C

1. realices
2. se acerquen
3. comience
4. dirija
5. saquen
6. recojamos
7. se dedique
8. explique
9. entregues
10. consiga
11. organicen
12. almuerce
13. convenza
14. apaguemos
15. venzan

D

1. digamos
2. aprenden
3. se gradúe
4. comiencen
5. te quejas
6. me matricule
7. vayáis
8. sale
9. tiene
10. podemos
11. sea
12. haya
13. están
14. hagas
15. sé
16. consigue

E

1. Laura espera perfeccionar su español.
2. Ricardo y Beti prefieren visitar la Catedral Metropolitana de la Ciudad de México.
3. Ud. debe conocer Taxco.
4. Pablo y yo deseamos ir a Puebla.
5. Tú prefieres hacer una excursión a la Ciudad Universitaria.
6. Yo siento no poder quedarme más tiempo en el Bosque de Chapultepec.
7. Uds. insisten en escaparse un par de días a Mérida.
8. Todos nosotros nos alegramos de estar en Oaxaca.

F

1. Laura espera que nosotros perfeccionemos nuestro español.
2. Ricardo y Beti prefieren que Ud. visite la Catedral Metropolitana de la Ciudad de México.
3. Ud. necesita que Leo conozca Taxco.
4. Pablo y yo deseamos que Uds. vayan a Puebla.
5. A ti te gusta que yo haga una excursión a la Ciudad Universitaria.
6. Yo siento que nosotros no podamos quedarnos más tiempo en el Bosque de Chapultepec.
7. Uds. insisten en que los cuates se escapen un par de días a Mérida.
8. Todos nosotros nos alegramos de que tú estés en Oaxaca.

G

1. Elena espera que sus cuñados tengan éxito.
2. El señor Ayala les pide a sus suegros que vengan a verlos los domingos.
3. La madrina se alegra de que su ahijado saque buenas notas en el colegio.
4. Los padres quieren que sus hijos se ganen la vida.
5. A la señora Ayala le gusta que los bisabuelos sean felices en la tercera edad.

6. Yo le aconsejo a la nieta que se haga arquitecta.
7. Terencio les prohíbe a las ahijadas que vayan solas al extranjero.
8. Tú sientes que tu cuñado no esté contento con el nuevo empleo.
9. La suegra prefiere que los recién casados se muden con ella.
10. Uds. les ruegan a los padrinos que acepten su regalo.
11. Ricardo y yo necesitamos que los nietos nos den muchos besos y abrazos.
12. Los hijos no dejan que sus padres trabajen demasiado manteniéndolos.

H

1. te encuentres	12. debes
2. estamos	13. sé
3. puedas	14. vas
4. voy	15. vas
5. llegues	16. hay
6. pasen	17. se despierten
7. compren	18. puedo
8. traigan	19. tengo
9. hace	20. escribas
10. está	21. viene
11. llueve	

I

1. pero	6. sino que
2. sino	7. pero
3. pero	8. sino
4. sino	9. sino que
5. sino que	10. pero

J

1. Es malo que vean el desorden.
2. Es necesario que hagamos la limpieza del apartamento.
3. Es importante que Lupe friegue las cacerolas.
4. Es probable que Uds. recojan las cajas de pizza.
5. Más vale que sus padres traigan trapos y productos para la limpieza.
6. Es preciso que yo limpie el polvo.
7. Es dudoso que los papás se metan en todo esto.
8. Es posible que María y Diana guarden su ropa sucia en la cómoda.
9. Es mejor que tú quites las telarañas del techo.
10. ¡Qué lástima que no nos relajemos en todo el día!

K

1. No estoy seguro que Lorenzo siga enfermo.
2. Es obvio que Teresa y Jesús se quieren mucho.
3. No es cierto que Uds. tengan problemas con el coche.
4. Es que Julia llega el sábado.
5. No es seguro que Alejandro sea de origen ruso.
6. No es evidente que los niños estén aburridos.
7. No es que Carmen lo sepa todo.
8. Es cierto que Martín renuncia a su puesto.

L

1. Oye, Anita, insisto en que estudies para los exámenes finales.
2. Oye, Miguel, me sorprende que no trabajes en la librería.
3. Oye, Rebeca, más vale que escribas el informe para el proyecto.
4. Oye, Tomás, es útil que practiques el ruso.
5. Oye, Graciela, es importante que tomes apuntes en historia.
6. Oye, Alfredo, te ruego que hagas la tarea.
7. Oye, Carolina, espero que saques buenas notas.
8. Oye, Joaquín, te prohíbo que juegues al béisbol todo el día.

M

1. Es bueno que haya tantos adelantos tecnológicos.
2. Preferimos usar la energía nuclear aún más.
3. Todo el mundo se alegra (está contento) de tener la computadora.
4. Es una lástima que las guerras sigan estallando.
5. Sentimos que las ciudades tengan tanto crimen.
6. No queremos pagar tantos impuestos.
7. Es probable que la contaminación ambiental haga mucho daño.
8. Es obvio que la economía del mercado libre es la mejor.
9. Es necesario controlar la inflación y el desempleo.
10. Les aconsejamos a los líderes políticos que gasten el dinero con más responsabilidad.
11. Ojalá que haya elecciones libres en todos los países.
12. Nadie duda que el siglo veintiuno va a traer muchos cambios.

N

1. Clara siente que Uds. no hayan visto la exposición de arte.
2. Dudamos que hayáis escrito el contrato.
3. Me alegro de que Carlos se haya hecho ciudadano.
4. Esperan que hayas visto la nueva película policíaca.
5. Es una lástima que haya muerto el bisabuelo de Paco.
6. Es mejor que las chicas no hayan dicho nada.
7. Nos sorprende que haya habido un incendio en el metro.
8. No piensan que Luz se haya puesto brava.
9. No creen que le haya gustado el concierto.

O

1. Me alegro de que Julia y Paco se hayan casado.
2. Es bueno que hayamos visto esos sitios web.
3. Ellos dudan que los Tigres hayan ganado el campeonato de fútbol.
4. Esperamos que Fernando se haya hecho rico.
5. ¿Le sorprende que la familia Núñez se haya mudado?
6. Ana no piensa que los chicos hayan roto la ventana.

P

Answers will vary.

12 The Imperfect Subjunctive and Past Perfect Subjunctive; Conditional Sentences

A

1. se diera / se diese
2. encontrara / encontrase
3. se pusieran / se pusiesen
4. supiéramos / supiésemos
5. hubiera / hubiese
6. siguieras / siguieses
7. durmiera / durmiese
8. viera / viese
9. se reunieran / se reuniesen
10. oyéramos / oyésemos
11. dijerais / dijeseis
12. fueran / fuesen
13. construyeran / construyesen
14. trajeras / trajeses
15. se fuera / se fuese

B

1. Felipe les sugirió que fueran a una discoteca.
2. Felipe esperaba que Angélica bailara con él y nadie más.
3. Teodoro también deseaba que Angélica saliera con él.
4. Angélica temía que los chicos tuvieran celos.
5. Era posible que Felipe y Teodoro se pelearan por Angélica.
6. Felipe no creía que fuera una buena idea ir a la discoteca.
7. Felipe le propuso a Angélica que vieran una película.
8. A Angélica le agradaba que Felipe y Teodoro la quisieran, ¡pero ella estaba enamorada de Julio!

C

1. hubiera
2. fuera
3. pudiera
4. se llevara
5. cayera
6. aprobaran
7. quisiera

D

1. fueran
2. diera
3. saliera
4. acompañara
5. jugara
6. trataran
7. condujera

E

1. me hiciera
2. siguiéramos
3. tuviéramos
4. trabajara
5. nos casáramos
6. fuéramos
7. nos dedicáramos
8. nos ayudáramos
9. vivieran

F

1. cortaras
2. descongelaras
3. regaras
4. hicieras
5. bañaras
6. pusieras
7. guardaras
8. sacaras
9. repararas

G

1. sacara
2. mintiera
3. rompiera
4. tuviera
5. hiciera
6. invitaran
7. tomara
8. fueran
9. fuera

H

1. Ojalá que yo fuera de vacaciones en julio.
2. Ojalá que Uds. recibieran una beca.
3. Ojalá que Diana no se quejara de todo.

4. Ojalá que nuestro equipo ganara el campeonato.
5. Ojalá que Bernardo y Marta no discutieran tanto.
6. Ojalá que tú no te preocuparas por nada.
7. Ojalá que tú y yo pudiéramos asistir al congreso en San Diego.
8. Ojalá que vosotros nos invitarais a vuestra hacienda.

I

1. Era bueno que Rebeca hubiera llegado a ser arquitecta.
2. Nos gustó que las hermanas Cela hubieran hecho un viaje a Santo Domingo.
3. Me extrañó que Uds. se hubieran quedado tanto tiempo.
4. Era necesario que tú hubieras comprado una computadora nueva.
5. Era importante que yo hubiera conocido Roma.
6. Todos se alegraron de que Juan y yo nos hubiéramos comprometido.

J

1. Tú esperabas que ellos hubieran tenido éxito.
2. Ellos temían que alguien me lo hubiera dicho.
3. Sentíamos que Ud. no hubiera oído lo que pasó.
4. Sarita dudaba que hubiéramos vuelto del campo.
5. Me alegraba de que hubiera hecho calor y sol.
6. Ojalá que Uds. nos lo hubieran dicho lo antes posible.

K

1. puedo / visitaré
2. ofrecen / aceptará
3. saldremos / tenemos
4. llama / diré
5. pones / harán
6. Habrá / hace
7. tendrás / comes
8. preguntan / sabrán
9. vendremos / hay

L

1. tuviera / haría
2. vendrían / invitáramos
3. vería / hubiera
4. ganara / se compraría
5. hiciera / saldríamos

6. dormiría / se sintiera
7. pudieras / resolverías
8. saldríais / fuera
9. supieran / dirían

M

1. encontrara / me casaría
2. besara / dejaría / me convertiría
3. hubiera / notaría
4. vinieran / comería
5. mintiera / crecería
6. diera / se despertaría
7. tuviera / tendría
8. soplara / derrumbaría

N

1. fuera / gustaría
2. hicieran / irían
3. pudieran / se quedarían
4. pasáramos / tomaríamos
5. visitaras / probarías
6. quisiera / conocería

O

1. hubieran preguntado / habríamos/ hubiéramos dicho
2. habría/hubiera devuelto / hubiera visto
3. se hubiera hecho / habría/hubiera estado
4. habríamos/hubiéramos llamado / hubiéramos sabido
5. hubiera jugado / habría/hubiera roto
6. hubieras leído / habrías/hubieras entendido

P

1. Pablo habría/hubiera asistido al teatro si hubiera vivido en la ciudad.
2. Amelia habría/hubiera ordeñado las vacas si hubiera nacido en una finca.
3. Pablo se habría/hubiera puesto más nervioso si hubiera oído tanto ruido todos los días.
4. Amelia habría/hubiera respirado aire no contaminado si hubiera vivido en el campo.
5. Pablo habría/hubiera tomado el metro y los taxis si hubiera trabajado en la ciudad.
6. Amelia habría/hubiera aprendido a montar a caballo si hubiera pasado su vida en el campo.
7. Pablo habría/hubiera comprado toda la comida en el supermercado si hubiera hecho la compra en la ciudad.
8. Amelia habría/hubiera comido frutas y legumbres muy frescas si se hubiera criado en el campo.

9. Pablo habría/hubiera llevado un traje, camisa y corbata si se hubiera ganado la vida trabajando en una empresa.
10. Amelia habría/hubiera usado un sombrero de paja si hubiera cultivado la tierra.

Q

1. hubiera terminado / habría/hubiera podido
2. hubiera planeado / habría/hubiera perdido
3. hubiera hecho / habría/hubiera bailado
4. hubiera gastado / habría/hubiera disfrutado
5. hubiera manejado / me habría/hubiera atrasado
6. se hubieran divertido / se habrían/hubieran quedado
7. se hubiera acostado / habría/hubiera tenido

R

1. Si Victoria hubiera tenido la llave, habría/hubiera abierto la maleta.
2. Si Uds. hicieran un viaje este verano, ¿adónde irían?
3. Si Pedro hubiera tenido más cuidado, no se le habría perdido su celular.
4. Si Ud. dobla a la derecha en la esquina, verá el museo.
5. Si ellos dieran buenos consejos, yo les haría caso.
6. Si hubieras navegado más en la red, habrías/hubieras encontrado el sitio web.

S

1. fuera
2. vivieran
3. tuviera
4. pensara
5. supiera
6. oyeras
7. dolieran
8. comprendierais

T

1. hubieran comido
2. hubiera visto
3. hubiera sido
4. te hubieras divertido
5. se hubiera hecho
6. hubiera podido

U

Answers will vary.

13 The Subjunctive: Adverb and Adjective Clauses

A

1. manden
2. aconseje
3. llueva
4. haya
5. quieras
6. sea
7. prefiera
8. digamos
9. vaya

B

1. Elena y Mario salieron del banco antes de que nosotros entráramos en la zapatería.
2. Ud. encontró la tienda de mascotas antes de que yo volviera de la farmacia.
3. Uds. compraron los sellos en el supermercado antes de que Miguel pudiera ir al correo.
4. Fernando y yo estacionamos en el centro comercial antes de que tú llegaras al cine.
5. Yo saqué la ropa de la tintorería antes de que Juana tuviera su cita en la peluquería.
6. Tú fuiste a la joyería antes de que Arturo y Bárbara buscaran una librería.
7. Vosotros llegasteis a la gasolinera antes de que Pedro y yo regresáramos de la tienda de cómputo.

C

1. sepa
2. vino
3. necesiten
4. pudiera
5. invitemos
6. entramos
7. diera
8. terminó
9. vuelvas
10. tuviera

D

1. Los llamaré cuando llegue al aeropuerto.
2. Vamos a ver el partido de fútbol hasta que empiece a llover.
3. Consuelo puso la mesa una hora antes de que llegaran sus amigos.
4. Hicieron cola en la taquilla después que almorzaron (después de almorzar).
5. Ud. no quería ir de compras sin que nosotros fuéramos también.
6. Háganlo como ellos quieran.
7. Aunque hace frío debemos dar un paseo.
8. Te presto el libro para que no tengas que sacarlo de la biblioteca.
9. Carlos va a estudiar para su examen antes de jugar al tenis (antes que juegue al tenis).

E

1. Tú quieres un apartamento que tenga dos baños.
2. Mateo necesita un apartamento donde haya aire acondicionado.
3. Javier y yo buscamos un apartamento que esté cerca de la universidad.
4. Uds. necesitan un apartamento que no cueste un ojo de la cara.
5. Yo quiero un apartamento que no necesite renovación.
6. Pepe y Leo desean un apartamento que sea moderno y fácil de limpiar.
7. Octavio busca un apartamento que dé a una calle poco transitada.
8. Ud. necesita un apartamento donde quepan todos los fiesteros.

F

1. sepa
2. pueda
3. comprenda
4. me divierta
5. sea
6. tenga

G

1. reúna
2. sea
3. quieras
4. vaya
5. tenga
6. se enamore

H

1. diera
2. se esforzara
3. permitiera
4. compartiera
5. invirtiera
6. fuera
7. pudiera
8. hubiera
9. dejara

I

1. Mario y Carmen buscan una casa que tenga nueve cuartos.
2. No hay ninguna comida que le guste.
3. Yo quería un amigo/una amiga que me acompañara a los museos.
4. ¿No conoce Ud. a nadie que llegue antes de las tres?
5. Rosa preparará el plato que escojamos.
6. Necesitaban un secretario/una secretaria que trabajara los sábados.
7. Tomaremos la clase con el profesor/ la profesora que enseñe mejor.
8. Yo tomaré el tren a la hora que llegue.
9. Roberto buscaba un sitio web que tuviera todos los datos necesarios.
10. Nos quedaremos en el hotel que les guste.

11. No había ningún restaurante italiano que estuviera abierto a la una de la mañana.
12. Buscan a los programadores que trabajan los fines de semana.

J

Answers will vary.

14 Commands

A

1. Añada las patatas y cebollas peladas y picadas.
2. Cocine a fuego lento.
3. Espolvoree con sal.
4. Bata los huevos.
5. Ponga los huevos en la sartén.
6. Haga dorar los huevos.
7. Déle la vuelta a la tortilla.
8. No deje que se pegue la tortilla.
9. Sirva en una fuente.

B

1. Asistan a la reunión semanal en la oficina del director.
2. Traigan la computadora.
3. Creen una base de datos.
4. Envíen el correo electrónico.
5. Sigan los consejos del gerente.
6. Actualicen el sitio web.
7. Lean el manual sobre el programa de gráficas.
8. Hagan copias de seguridad.

C

1. Sí, búsquelo. No, no lo busque.
2. Sí, fírmela. No, no la firme.
3. Sí, llénelo. No, no lo llene.
4. Sí, démelo en pesos. No, no me lo dé en pesos.
5. Sí, úsela. No, no la use.
6. Sí, calcúlemelos. No, no me los calcule.
7. Sí, ciérrela. No, no la cierre.
8. Sí, cóbremelos. No, no me los cobre.
9. Sí, pruébela. No, no la pruebe.

D

1. Demos un paseo por la zona de la Plaza de Armas. / Vamos a dar un paseo por la zona de la Plaza de Armas.
2. Vamos de compras en el Jirón de la Unión.
3. Conozcamos la Universidad de San Marcos. / Vamos a conocer la Universidad de San Marcos.

4. Hagamos una excursión a Machu Picchu. / Vamos a hacer una excursión a Machu Picchu.
5. Visitemos la catedral y unas iglesias de Cuzco. / Vamos a visitar la catedral y unas iglesias de cuzco.
6. Quedémonos en Miraflores. / Vamos a quedarnos en Miraflores.
7. Sentémonos en el Malecón. / Vamos a sentarnos en el Malecón.

E
1. Cómo no. Démoselos. / Cómo no. Vamos a dárselos.
2. Cómo no. Saquémoslos. / Cómo no. Vamos a sacarlos.
3. Cómo no. Vamos al museo por la tarde.
4. Cómo no. Caminemos por el parque. / Cómo no. Vamos a caminar por el parque.
5. Cómo no. Inscribámonos en la clase de computación. / Cómo no. Vamos a inscribirnos en la clase de computación.
6. Cómo no. Juguemos al tenis. / Cómo no. Vamos a jugar al tenis.
7. Cómo no. Conozcámoslo. / Cómo no. Vamos a conocerlo.
8. Cómo no. Enseñémoselo. / Cómo no. Vamos a enseñárselo.
9. Cómo no. Tumbémonos en la playa. / Cómo no. Vamos a tumbarnos en la playa.

F
1. Haced la torta, pero no le pongáis el glaseado.
2. Abrid las botellas de vino, pero no cortéis las rebanadas de naranja.
3. Sacad los platitos para las tapas, pero no preparéis el chorizo.
4. Poned la mesa, pero no coloquéis los claveles.
5. Salid a comprar aceitunas, pero no vayáis al supermercado.
6. Removed la sangría, pero no la sirváis en este jarro.
7. Invitad a Pilar, pero no le digáis nada a Consuelo.
8. Traed discos compactos, pero no traigáis vídeos.

G
1. Sed pacientes.
2. Idos.
3. Decid la verdad.
4. No seáis desagradables.

5. No os enojéis.
6. No salgáis todavía.
7. Asistid a la conferencia.
8. Tocad el piano.
9. Acostaos temprano.
10. Buscadla en Facebook.

H
1. Da un paseo todos los días.
2. Haz ejercicio.
3. Toma una infusión de manzanilla.
4. Tranquilízate escuchando música.
5. No te pongas pesimista.
6. Sal a divertirte.
7. Reúnete con tus amigos.
8. No te preocupes por tonterías.
9. Búscate otro novio más compasivo.

I
1. Pórtate bien.
2. No hagas payasadas.
3. No seas terco.
4. Deja al perro en paz.
5. Recoge las migas de las galletas.
6. No derrames el perfume de tu mamá.
7. Hazme caso.
8. No te encierres en el baño.
9. Ven acá inmediatamente.
10. No toques la computadora.

J
1. Tito, date prisa.
2. Tito, no te lastimes.
3. Tito, no te cortes el dedo.
4. Tito, ten cuidado.
5. Tito, no te rompas el pie.
6. Tito, no enciendas los fósforos.
7. Tito, conduce más lentamente.
8. Tito, ponte una armadura.

K
1. déjelo
2. te mojes
3. déle
4. juegues
5. hágale
6. te quites
7. tráigalo
8. ven
9. sal

L
1. Sí, dáselos.
2. Sí, mándenoslos. (Sí, mándanoslos.)
3. Sí, entréguenmelo.
4. Sí, pónmelo.
5. Sí, prepáreselos. (Sí, prepárarselos.)
6. Sí, sírvanselo.
7. Sí, explícamela.
8. Sí, díselos.
9. Sí, enséñenselas. (Sí, enseñémoselas.)

M

1. No, no se los des.
2. No, no nos los mande. (No, no nos los mandes.)
3. No, no me la entreguen.
4. No, no me lo pongas.
5. No, no se los prepare. (No, no se los prepares.)
6. No, no se lo sirvan.
7. No, no me la expliques.
8. No, no se los digas.
9. No, no se las enseñen. (No, no se las enseñemos.)

N

1. Que los lea Manolo.
2. Que las dibujen Terencio y Elena.
3. Que los observe Paulina.
4. Que los hagan los otros.
5. Que las investigue Samuel.
6. Que las limpien mis compañeros.
7. Que lo escriba Federico.

O

1. Que se lo dé ella.
2. Que se vayan.
3. Que se las mande él.
4. Que no se te pierda la cartera.
5. Que vean nuestras fotos en Facebook.
6. Que no se les acaben los tacos.

P

1. Cortarlos a tiritas.
2. Añadir el vino.
3. Dejarlo evaporar.
4. Partirlos en trozos.
5. Tapar las papas.
6. Secar los tomates.
7. Añadirlas a la salsa.
8. Removerlo.
9. Ponerla en una fuente.
10. Cocerlo a fuego lento.

Q

1. Hagan el favor de ir a la biblioteca.
2. Tengan la bondad de aprender los diálogos de memoria.
3. Favor de traer el diccionario.
4. Tengan la bondad de matricularse si no lo han hecho todavía.
5. Háganme el favor de comprar el libro de texto y el cuaderno de trabajo.
6. Favor de apuntarse en esta lista.

7. Hagan el favor de buscar sitios web en español.
8. Tengan la bondad de ver películas en español.

R

1. llamar	5. dirigirse
2. Enviar (Mandar)	6. adjuntar
3. escribir	7. ponerse en contacto
4. presentarse	8. concertar

S

Answers will vary.

15 The Infinitive

A

1. Los españoles quisieron celebrar el santo del rey.
2. Uds. siempre procuraban ir de vacaciones en la Semana Santa.
3. Paco no pudo salir con su novia el Día de los Enamorados.
4. Sueles hacer una barbacoa el Día de la Independencia.
5. Raúl y Pepita no consiguieron asistir a la Misa del Gallo este año.
6. Los niñitos esperaban recibir muchos regalos lindos el Día de Reyes.
7. No resuelves gastar bromas el Día de los Inocentes.
8. Debe haber unos desfiles el Día de la Raza.
9. Decidimos traerles flores y bombones a los tíos por el Año Nuevo.

B

1. Sabían nadar muy bien.
2. Ud. mereció ganar más plata.
3. Logré terminar el proyecto.
4. Felipe teme estar solo en la casa.
5. Se prohíbe salir por esa puerta.
6. Han preferido tocar un vals.
7. Hacíamos limpiar la casa.
8. ¿No quisisteis escuchar estos discos?
9. Impiden buscar los datos en ese sitio web.
10. Desea encontrar a sus amigos en Facebook.

C

1. a	8. de
2. en	9. con
3. en	10. a
4. a	11. de
5. de	12. con
6. a	13. de
7. en (por)	14. que

D

1. Nos acostumbrábamos a cenar a las nueve de la noche.
2. ¿Por qué demoraron (tardaron) tanto en llamarnos?
3. Esteban se negó a prestarle dinero a Diego.
4. Trate de pagar con una tarjeta de crédito.
5. Vuelvan a cantar esa canción.
6. Voy a asistir a la conferencia.
7. Silvia amenazó con irse inmediatamente.
8. Ellos sueñan con hacerse millonarios.

E

1. Pedro llegó a hacerse presidente de la empresa.
2. Consuelo necesita escribir su tesis.
3. Tratamos de escribir un blog.
4. El profesor ordenó cerrar los libros.
5. Uds. se arrepintieron de perderse la boda.
6. Yo no me acordé de recoger los pasteles.
7. ¿Cómo es que comenzaste a hacer el presupuesto a las dos de la mañana?
8. No se permitía entrar en las salas de escultura.
9. Están vacilando en invertir dinero en la compañía.

F

1. Te llamaremos antes de salir.
2. Viajaron a Ponce en carro sin parar.
3. Niños, acuéstense después de cepillarse los dientes.
4. Bernardo debe leer un libro en vez de mirar la televisión.
5. Voy a estar en mi oficina hasta volver a casa.
6. Elena va a patinar con tal que Daniel patine también.
7. Invíteles en caso de verlos.
8. Cuando llegamos (Al llegar) a la fiesta, empezamos (nos pusimos) a bailar.

G

1. Mis padres toman sus vitaminas al desayunar.
2. Pablo y yo trotamos al salir de la escuela.
3. Al salir del trabajo, Teresa y Laura van al gimnasio.
4. Tú levantas pesas al despertarte.
5. Vosotros camináis al terminar de almorzar.
6. Al salir a comer, pido comida sana.

7. Elena me llama al llegar a la piscina.
8. Al terminar un maratón, me tomo una botella de agua con electrolitos.

H

1. Los empleados se quejan al exigir demasiado el señor Montalbán.
2. Al ver un problema grande, el señor Montalbán convoca una reunión.
3. Los empleados se ponen gruñones al recibir el aviso de la reunión.
4. En la reunión, todo el mundo se calló al entrar el señor Montalbán.
5. El señor Montalbán se puso muy serio al dirigirse a sus empleados.
6. Al irse el señor Montalbán, todos empezaron a chismear.

I

1. Sí, los oí ladrar.
2. Sí, lo oí maullar.
3. Sí, los oí despegar y aterrizar.
4. Sí, las oí susurrar.
5. Sí, los oí gritar.
6. Sí, la oí roncar.

J

1. Los vimos trotar.
2. Os vimos hacer ejercicio.
3. Lo vimos entrar en la discoteca.
4. La vimos dictar una conferencia.
5. Los vimos hablar por celular.
6. Te vimos escanear los documentos.
7. La vimos salir de la tienda por departamentos.

K

1. que	3. para
2. para	4. que

L

1. X	3. X
2. de	4. de

II　Nouns and Their Modifiers; Pronouns

16　Nouns and Articles

A

1. el	5. el
2. el	6. la
3. el	7. la
4. la	8. el

9. la
10. el
11. la
12. el
13. la
14. el
15. la
16. la
17. el
18. el
19. la
20. el
21. la
22. el
23. la
24. el
25. el
26. el

B

1. la profesora
2. la reina
3. la artista
4. la abogada
5. la princesa
6. la gobernadora
7. la representante
8. la policía
9. la emperatriz
10. la actriz
11. la estadista
12. la holandesa
13. la cliente
14. la atleta
15. la programadora
16. la bailarina

C

1. El señor Galíndez se va en viaje de negocios el martes y volverá el jueves.
2. No ponga la sartén en el lavaplatos.
3. El inglés y el francés son las lenguas oficiales de Canadá.
4. Mozart nació el veintisiete de enero de mil setecientos cincuenta y seis.
5. Mis colores favoritos son el verde y el azul.
6. Vamos a recoger (Recojamos) manzanas de ese manzano.
7. El ave nacional de los Estados Unidos es el águila calva.
8. ¿Les gustó más el crucero en el Mediterráneo o en el Caribe?
9. El leer es tan agradable.
10. Un frente tropical llegará mañana.
11. Vamos a invertir (Invertiremos) nuestro capital en una compañía multinacional.
12. ¿Cómo se llaman los personajes de la novela?
13. Al cámara se le perdió su cámara.
14. En la película que vimos, los ángeles salvaron al bebé.
15. Los testigos hablaron con la víctima del accidente.

D

1. los guantes
2. los lavaplatos
3. las religiones
4. los orígenes
5. las reuniones
6. los colores
7. las amistades
8. los reyes
9. las voces
10. los martes

11. los irlandeses
12. los paréntesis
13. los señores Sánchez
14. las luces
15. los tés
16. los israelíes

E

1. las vacas
2. los orangutanes
3. los elefantes
4. los avestruces
5. los leones
6. los castores
7. los loros
8. los cóndores
9. los delfines
10. los gorriones
11. los faisanes
12. las panteras
13. los tigres
14. las ovejas
15. los monos
16. los camellos

F

1. Lucía pide guisantes.
2. Yo prefiero espárragos.
3. Tú ordenas papas.
4. Claudia y Jesús quieren chiles.
5. Nosotros tenemos ganas de comer aguacates.
6. Ud. y Luis piden frijoles.
7. Ud. quiere palomitas de maíz.
8. Vosotros coméis camarones.

G

1. los pianos
2. las flautas
3. las violas
4. los clarinetes
5. los violonchelos
6. los violines
7. las trompetas
8. los trombones
9. las arpas
10. los oboes
11. los tambores
12. las tubas

H

1. la / las / aceitunas
2. el / los / ensayos
3. el / las / aguas
4. el / los / árboles
5. el / los / dulces
6. la / las / demoras
7. la / las / sales
8. el / los / pasaportes
9. el / los / volcanes
10. la / las / actividades
11. el / los / salvavidas
12. el / los / orígenes
13. la / las / fotos
14. el / los / meses
15. la / las / serpientes
16. el / los / sillones
17. la / las / mieles
18. el / los / lápices
19. el / los / franceses
20. la / las / veces

21. el / los / tenedores
22. la / las / pirámides
23. la / las / raíces
24. el / los / sacapuntas
25. la / las / naciones
26. el / los / pintores
27. el / los / jardines
28. el / los / jugadores
29. el / los / esquíes (esquís)
30. el / los / panes

I

1. los ojos
2. las mejillas
3. las manos
4. los dedos
5. los labios
6. los dientes
7. el pelo
8. el cuello
9. las orejas

J

1. X	9. Las / la
2. el	10. El
3. el	11. X
4. X	12. la
5. X	13. Los / la
6. las	14. la
7. X	15. La / la
8. el	16. el

K

1. La familia Sánchez va a la Florida en la primavera.
2. Florencia se puso las medias.
3. Dénos los libros de latín.
4. A Juli y a Nicolás les encanta nadar.
5. ¿Qué hicieron los turistas en el mar?
6. Los gemelos se lavaron la cara.
7. Elías sabe portugués, habla italiano, lee ruso y aprende alemán.
8. El baile fue el sábado. Comenzó a las nueve y media de la noche.
9. La novela fue escrita en polaco y traducida al griego.

L

1. X / X	5. X
2. X	6. X
3. X / X	7. X / X
4. los	8. X

M

1. El	13. un
2. un (al)	14. el
3. X	15. los (unos)
4. lo	16. al
5. del	17. las
6. Lo	18. la
7. del	19. unas
8. las	20. Un
9. X	21. lo
10. X	22. la
11. las	23. el
12. el	24. un

N

1. un / unos / mares
2. un / unos / ángeles
3. un / unas / hachas
4. un / unos / comedores
5. un / unos / olores
6. un / unos / oboes
7. un / unas / áreas
8. una / unas / mochilas
9. un / unos / jóvenes OR una / unas / jóvenes
10. un / unos / nadadores
11. un / unos / papeles
12. una / unas / leyes
13. un / unos / menús
14. un / unos / cereales
15. un / unos / buzones
16. un / unos / irlandeses
17. un / unas / almas
18. un / unos / paraguas
19. un / unos / camarones
20. un / unos / garajes
21. una / unas / voces
22. un / unos / desfiles
23. una / unas / naciones
24. un / unos / lavaplatos
25. un / unos / lemas
26. una / unas / sucursales
27. un / unos / ascensores
28. un / unas / hablas
29. una / unas / postales
30. un / unas / aguas

O

1. un	7. unos
2. unas	8. una
3. unos	9. unos
4. un	10. una
5. unas	11. un
6. una	12. una

P

1. X	7. X
2. un	8. X
3. X / X	9. un
4. X / X	10. X
5. X	11. X
6. un	12. X

Q

1. Concepción y Simón fueron al puesto de periódicos.
2. Yo fui al ayuntamiento.
3. Domingo y Brígida fueron al supermercado.
4. Ud. fue a la heladería.
5. Lourdes fue a la iglesia.
6. Vosotros fuisteis a la farmacia.
7. Nosotros fuimos a la estación de tren.
8. Tú fuiste al centro comercial.

R

1. Tú y yo volvimos del banco.
2. Mercedes y Julio salieron del cine.
3. Yo regresé de la librería.
4. Uds. volvieron de la tienda de zapatos.
5. Pedro salió del apartamento.
6. Tú regresaste de la galería de arte.
7. Vosotros salisteis del museo de ciencias naturales.
8. Ud. volvió del aeropuerto.

S

1. ¿De quién es el almacén? Es del señor Acosta.
2. ¿De quién son los peines? Son de Adela y Matilde.
3. ¿De quién es el equipaje? Es de los turistas.
4. ¿De quién son los discos compactos? Son del pianista.
5. ¿De quién es este llavero? Es de la empleada.
6. ¿De quién son las sartenes? Son del cocinero.
7. ¿De quién son las raquetas? Son de estas tenistas.
8. ¿De quién es el reloj? Es del doctor Villanueva.

T

1. la florería del señor Valle
2. la oficina del presidente
3. los discos de la programadora
4. el horario de la dentista
5. los empleados del doctor Arriaga
6. los sitios web del diseñador
7. las conferencias de la profesora Salas
8. el proyecto del ingeniero

9. los hijos de los señores Manrique
10. el informe de la jefa

U

Answers will vary.

17 Adjectives

A

1. Están felices.
2. Estoy contento.
3. Se encuentra nerviosa.
4. Se siente deprimido.
5. Se encuentran tristes.
6. Estamos cansadas.
7. Se sienten enfermos.
8. Estamos preocupados.
9. Está aburrida.

B

1. Paco cree que Jacobo es listo.
2. La señora Alvarado piensa que Luisa es encantadora.
3. El profesor de cálculo encuentra a los hermanos inteligentes y trabajadores.
4. Nieves cree que Jacobo es sincero.
5. El señor Alvarado dice que Luisa es graciosa y generosa.
6. Las profesoras de computación encuentran a Jacobo serio y responsable.
7. Los hijos de los Alvarado creen que Luisa es independiente y simpática.
8. Todo el mundo dice que Jacobo y Luisa son buena gente y corteses.

C

1. arrogante
2. molesto
3. tacaños
4. tontos
5. mentirosa
6. desleales
7. engañosos

D

1. roja
2. amarillos
3. marrones
4. negros
5. azules / anaranjadas / verdes
6. blanco
7. negro
8. rosada
9. morados / grises

E

1. mejor día
2. algunos discos compactos
3. muchos días
4. poemas renacentistas
5. energía nuclear
6. ambas clases
7. ojos castaños
8. suficiente plata
9. vino tinto
10. cuántas horas
11. peor decisión
12. teorías políticas

F

1. ¡Qué absurda situación!
2. ¡Qué clima tan perfecto!
3. ¡Qué partido más emocionante!
4. ¡Qué paella tan rica!
5. ¡Qué hermosos zapatos!
6. ¡Qué ideas más estupendas!
7. ¡Qué problemas más complicados!
8. ¡Qué frescas legumbres!
9. ¡Qué cariñosos niños!
10. ¡Qué reunión tan animada!

G

1. primer
2. mala
3. grandes
4. buen
5. tercera
6. algún
7. ningún
8. San
9. buenas
10. gran
11. ninguna
12. algunas
13. Cualquier
14. Santa
15. primeros
16. tercer
17. mal

H

1. mismo dentista
2. ciudad antigua
3. cosa cierta
4. medio portugués / medio mexicano
5. gran soldado
6. funcionario cualquiera
7. dramaturgo mismo
8. pura agua
9. persona única
10. Cierta empresa
11. hombres pobres
12. vieja casa
13. varios libros / mismo tema
14. cualquier regalo
15. únicos pianistas
16. pobre viuda

I

1. Sí, es ruso.
2. Sí, son canadienses.
3. Sí, es israelí.
4. Sí, es costarricense.
5. Sí, es guatemalteco.
6. Sí, son belgas.
7. Sí, es japonés.
8. Sí, es india.
9. Sí, son egipcias.
10. Sí, es inglesa.
11. Sí, es surcoreano.
12. Sí, son franceses.

J

1. Yo soy de origen polaco.
2. Teodoro e Irene son de origen salvadoreño.
3. Uds. son de origen libanés.
4. Gabriel es de origen vietnamita.
5. Adela y Rosa son de origen iraní.
6. Estanislao y Sofía son de origen griego.
7. Tú eres de origen nicaragüense.
8. Ud. y yo somos de origen taiwanés.
9. Gualterio es de origen húngaro.
10. Vosotros sois de origen inglés.

K

1. buenos
2. españoles
3. recogidas
4. ingleses
5. blancos
6. frescos
7. grises
8. rebajados
9. minerales
10. nuevos
11. magníficas
12. negros
13. caros
14. creativos

L

1. Federico Felino es el mejor director de cine joven.
2. *El tango rojo* es su primer film doblado.
3. Será una gran película extranjera.
4. Tiene algunas escenas románticas.
5. Se oye un diálogo bueno.
6. Hay diferentes efectos fotográficos.
7. Escribieron un guión inteligente.
8. Trabajaron en el film algunos intérpretes principales.
9. Hay algunos subtítulos bien traducidos.
10. La película tiene un argumento interesante.
11. La película ganará un importante premio cinematográfico.

M

1. frita / fritos
2. hecho / hecha
3. muertas / muertos
4. comida / comidas
5. metido / metidos
6. pagada / pagadas
7. dormido / dormido
8. hechas / hecha

N

1. está echada
2. está parado
3. están sentados
4. está asomada
5. están arrodillados
6. están tirados
7. está inclinada

O

1. Ya está bañado.
2. Ya están afeitados.
3. Ya está maquillada.
4. Ya estamos vestidos/vestidas.
5. Ya estoy peinado/peinada.
6. Ya estamos duchados/duchadas.
7. Ya estoy arreglado/arreglada.

P

1. Ya están puestos.
2. Ya está servida.
3. Ya está preparado.
4. Ya están rotos.
5. Ya está cortado.
6. Ya está hecha.
7. Ya están fritas.
8. Ya están pelados.

Q

1. Me gusta más la instrumental. / Me gusta más la vocal.
2. Prefiero los serios. / Prefiero los cómicos.
3. Prefiero comer en el chino. / Prefiero comer en el francés.
4. Me gustan más los azules. / Me gustan más los marrones.
5. Prefiero el moderno. / Prefiero el viejo.
6. Me gusta más la particular. / Me gusta más la estatal.
7. Prefiero las norteamericanas. / Prefiero las extranjeras.
8. Quiero vivir en la grande. / Quiero vivir en la pequeña.
9. Me interesan más las de ciencias políticas. / Me interesan más las de ciencias naturales.

R

1. Luisa es más astuta que Ana. / Ana es menos astuta que Luisa.
2. El museo de historia natural es mejor que el de arte. / El museo de arte es peor que el de historia natural.
3. Yo soy más inteligente que mi novio. / Mi novio es menos inteligente que yo.
4. Tu cuarto es más hermoso que el de Elena. / El cuarto de Elena es menos hermoso que el tuyo.
5. La película francesa es más aburrida que la inglesa. / La película inglesa es menos aburrida que la francesa.
6. Los cantantes son más talentosos que los bailarines. / Los bailarines son menos talentosos que los cantantes.
7. Las blusas de seda son más elegantes que las de algodón. / Las blusas de algodón son menos elegantes que las de seda.
8. Tu hermana es mayor que tu hermano. / Tu hermano es menor que tu hermana.

S

1. José habló más francamente que Consuelo. / Consuelo habló menos francamente que José. / José habló tan francamente como Consuelo.
2. Los enfermeros trabajaron más cuidadosamente que los médicos. / Los médicos trabajaron menos cuidadosamente que los enfermeros. / Los enfermeros trabajaron tan cuidadosamente como los médicos.
3. Virginia resolvió los problemas más fácilmente que Cristina. / Cristina resolvió los problemas menos fácilmente que Virginia. / Virginia resolvió los problemas tan fácilmente como Cristina.

T

1. La obra de teatro es tan divertida como la película.
2. Las clases de física son tan fáciles como las clases de cálculo.
3. Los documentales son tan artísticos como los reportajes.
4. Los platos griegos son tan sabrosos como los platos húngaros.
5. Esta actriz es tan célebre como ese actor.
6. El arroz es tan bueno como el maíz.
7. El príncipe es tan valiente como el rey.
8. Francisca es tan trabajadora como su hermana María.
9. La inflación actual es tan baja como la inflación de hace tres años.

U

1. Alejandro manda tanto correo electrónico como Felipe.
2. Miriam tiene tanta paciencia como Catalina.
3. Ellos pasan tantas horas en línea como nosotros.
4. Ella come tanta comida rápida como tú.
5. Sus amigos ven tantos programas de realidad como Uds.
6. Los asesores demuestran tanto interés en el proyecto como vosotros.
7. A él le queda tanto dinero como a ti.
8. Yo conozco tantos clubes de jazz como Marcos.

V

1. Juan Pablo es el estudiante más aplicado.
2. Daniel y Arturo son los estudiantes menos obedientes.
3. Silvia es la estudiante más simpática.
4. Irene y María son las estudiantes menos trabajadoras.
5. Verónica es la estudiante más inteligente.
6. Diana y Esteban son los estudiantes más habladores.
7. Sergio es el estudiante más encantador.
8. Rosa y Jacinto son los estudiantes menos preparados.

W

1. Sí. Es interesantísima.
2. Sí. Es viejísimo.
3. Sí. Son hermosísimas.
4. Sí. Es grandísimo.
5. Sí. Parece ferocísimo.
6. Sí. Son simpatiquísimos.
7. Sí. Son larguísimas.
8. Sí. Es bellísimo.

X

1. Allí se encuentra la plaza más imponente de la ciudad.
2. Aquí ven la catedral más antigua del estado.
3. En frente hay la universidad más conocida del país.
4. Ésta es la calle más larga de la ciudad.
5. En esta calle hay las tiendas más hermosas de la zona.
6. Allí está la tienda de comestibles más estimada del barrio.
7. Delante de nosotros hay el hotel más internacional del país.

8. En este barrio se encuentran los restaurantes más concurridos de la ciudad.
9. Aquí ven el teatro más viejo de la ciudad.
10. Pronto veremos el estadio más grande de la región.

Y

1. Es el poema más conocido de la literatura europea.
2. Es la obra de teatro más presentada del año.
3. Es la comedia más aplaudida del teatro nacional.
4. Es la novela más vendida de la literatura moderna.
5. Es la tragedia más estimada de nuestro teatro.
6. Es el poeta más respetado de su siglo.
7. Es el novelista más leído del mundo.
8. Es el dramaturgo más apreciado de nuestra época.

Z

1. Yo leo más que Ud.
2. Ellos saben menos que nosotros.
3. Ignacio se queja tanto como su mujer.
4. Yo tengo más discos compactos que Federico.
5. Eva ve menos películas que Margarita.
6. Nosotros hacemos tantos viajes como ellos.
7. Nosotros tenemos más de diez mil libros en nuestra biblioteca.
8. El partido de fútbol fue más emocionante de lo que esperaban.
9. Ruíz es el mejor programador de la compañía.
10. Ésta es la playa más hermosa del país.
11. Vosotros vivís en el barrio más elegante de la ciudad.
12. A ella le gustó la pelicula más que a nosotros.
13. Rolando navega en la red más que nadie.
14. Uds. se reúnen más que nunca.

AA
Answers will vary.

18 Demonstratives and Possessives

A

1. Estos libros de texto están bien escritos. / Esos libros de texto están bien escritos. / Aquellos libros de texto están bien escritos.

2. Compré este compás anteayer. / Compré ese compás anteayer. / Compré aquel compás anteayer.
3. Consultaré este mapa. / Consultaré ese mapa. / Consultaré aquel mapa.
4. Prefiero esta tarjeta de memoria. / Prefiero esa tarjeta de memoria. / Prefiero aquella tarjeta de memoria.
5. Este lápiz no tiene borrador. / Ese lápiz no tiene borrador. / Aquel lápiz no tiene borrador.
6. Me gusta este diccionario de español. / Me gusta ese diccionario de español. / Me gusta aquel diccionario de español.
7. Estos bolígrafos no sirven. / Esos bolígrafos no sirven. / Aquellos bolígrafos no sirven.
8. Encontré estas reglas en el escritorio. / Encontré esas reglas en el escritorio. / Encontré aquellas reglas en el escritorio.
9. Estas enciclopedias están en línea. / Esas enciclopedias están en línea. / Aquellas enciclopedias están en línea.

B

1. este
2. Ese
3. este
4. aquel
5. estas
6. ese / esas / aquella
7. Esta / ese
8. estas / esos / Este / esta / ese / aquel / esa
9. Esto

C

1. Me gustó ésa más que aquélla. (Me gustó aquélla más que ésa.)
2. Me gustaron aquéllos más que éstos. (Me gustaron éstos más que aquéllos.)
3. Me gustó éste más que ése. (Me gustó ése más que éste.)
4. Me gustaron ésas más que aquéllas. (Me gustaron aquéllas más que ésas.)
5. Me gustó éste más que ése. (Me gustó ése más que éste.)
6. Me gustaron éstos más que aquéllos. (Me gustaron aquéllos más que éstos.)
7. Me gustó ésta más que ésa. (Me gustó ésa más que ésta.)

D

1. No, no es suyo. Será de Martina.
2. No, no son suyas. Serán de nosotros.
3. No, no es suyo. Será de Enrique.
4. No, no son suyos. Serán de Uds.
5. No, no son suyas. Serán tuyas.
6. No, no es suya. Será de la profesora Márquez.
7. No, no es nuestro. Será de ellos.

E

1. las maletas tuyas
2. el equipaje de mano nuestro
3. las tarjetas de crédito suyas
4. la bolsa de viaje suya
5. los maletines nuestros
6. la mochila suya
7. el pasaporte mío
8. las visas suyas
9. los billetes electrónicos tuyos
10. la computadora portátil vuestra

F

1. ¡Pero el mío es más moderno que el tuyo!
2. ¡Pero el mío es más nuevo que el tuyo!
3. ¡Pero la mía es más simpática que la tuya!
4. ¡Pero la mía es más rápida que la tuya!
5. ¡Pero las mías son más interesantes que las tuyas!
6. ¡Pero las mías son mejores que las tuyas!
7. ¡Pero el mío es más inteligente que el tuyo!

G

1. Los suyos estarán en el estante.
2. El mío estará en mi cartera.
3. Las suyas estarán en la cómoda.
4. Los nuestros estarán en la gaveta.
5. La nuestra (La suya) estará en el escritorio.
6. Los nuestros estarán en el baño.
7. La mía estará encima del piano.

H

1. No, no se salen con la suya.
2. No, no se sale con la suya.
3. Sí, me salgo con la mía.
4. No, no se sale con la suya.
5. No, no nos salimos con la nuestra.
6. Sí, me salgo con la mía.
7. Sí, nos salimos con la nuestra.
8. Sí, se salen con la suya.

I

1. Esto de la compañía es difícil de comprender.
2. Eso de nuestro viaje tiene que resolverse.
3. Vamos a tener que hablar de eso de comprar un coche nuevo.
4. Un viejo amigo mío llega el sábado.
5. ¿Cómo está tu familia? (¿Cómo están los tuyos?)
6. Esperamos que gane nuestro equipo. (Esperamos que ganen los nuestros.)
7. Lo suyo es traer las flores.
8. Lo mío es hacer copias.

J

Answers will vary.

19 Personal Pronouns: Subject, Object, Prepositional

A

1. nosotros	6. Ud., ella
2. Ud., él	7. vosotros, vosotras
3. vosotras	8. tú
4. Uds., ellos, ellas	9. Uds., ellas
5. yo	10. Ud., ella

B

1. Yo trabajo de lunes a viernes, pero tú trabajas los fines de semana.
2. Nosotros estudiamos en una universidad particular, pero Uds. estudian en una universidad estatal.
3. Ellas viven en pleno centro, pero Ud. vive en las afueras.
4. Tú vas de compras el sábado, pero nosotros vamos de compras el jueves.
5. Él es abogado, pero yo soy profesor.
6. Ud. desayuna fuerte, pero ella desayuna poco.
7. Ellos escuchan música clásica, pero vosotros escucháis rock.

C

1. para él	8. de vosotros
2. contigo	9. para ellas
3. según tú	10. por ti
4. por nosotros	11. menos tú
5. salvo yo	12. como yo
6. sobre Ud.	13. en ella
7. conmigo	14. entre tú y yo

D

1. Sí, vivo cerca de ellas.
2. Sí, trabajaba en ella.
3. Sí, logramos hablar sobre ellos.
4. Sí, pagué un dineral por él.
5. Sí, salí con ellos.
6. Sí, hay mucho trabajo para ella.
7. Sí, se casó con él.
8. Sí, felicité a los jugadores por ella.

E

1. No, con ellas, no.	5. No, para ellos, no.
2. No, con él, no.	6. No, por él, no.
3. No, para ella, no.	7. No, con ellos, no.
4. No, por ella, no.	8. No, para ti, no.

F

1. X	11. a
2. a	12. X
3. X	13. X
4. al	14. al
5. a	15. a
6. A	16. X
7. a	17. a
8. X	18. al
9. X	19. X
10. X	20. A

G

1. a	6. a
2. a	7. A / a / a
3. a	8. a
4. a	9. a
5. a	10. a

H

1. Pida otra botella de vino.
2. Aprovechemos (Vamos a aprovechar) esta venta (liquidación).
3. Mira el hermoso mar.
4. Voy a esperarlos hasta las tres.
5. Busca a sus hermanos.
6. ¿Pagaron sus padres los muebles?
7. Escuchemos la orquesta.

I

1. No, no lo cambié. / Voy a cambiarlo.
2. No, no lo reparé. / Voy a repararlo.
3. No, no las pedí. / Voy a pedirlas.
4. No, no las llevé. / Voy a llevarlas.
5. No, no lo usé. / Voy a usarlo.
6. No, no los puse. / Voy a ponerlos.
7. No, no lo arreglé. / Voy a arreglarlo.
8. No, no lo instalé. / Voy a instalarlo.

J

1. Piensa comprarlo. / Lo piensa comprar.
2. Tiene que llenarlo. / Lo tiene que llenar.
3. Trata de leerlas. / Las trata de leer.
4. Prefiere conducirlo. / Lo prefiere conducir.
5. Debe cargarla. / La debe cargar.
6. Teme tenerlo. / Lo teme tener.
7. Procura evitarlas. / Las procura evitar.
8. Necesita cerrarlo. / Lo necesita cerrar.

K

1. la conozco
2. los comprendo
3. la llamo
4. las busco
5. lo llevo
6. las espero
7. lo ayudo
8. los veo

L

1. Márquelos. / No los marque.
2. Llámalo. / No lo llames.
3. Recójanlos. / No los recojan.
4. Sáltelas. / No las salte.
5. Hazla. / No la hagas.
6. Mírenla. / No la miren.
7. Láncela. / No la lance.
8. Felicítalo. / No lo felicites.
9. Levántenlas. / No las levanten.

M

1. Sí, lo he visto.
2. No, no los he visto.
3. Sí, la hemos visto.
4. No, no los he visto.
5. No, no las he visto.
6. Sí, las hemos visto.
7. Sí, lo he visto.
8. No, no la he visto.

N

1. Los arquitectos están empleándolo. / Los arquitectos lo están empleando.
2. Los constructores van cubriéndola. / Los constructores la van cubriendo.
3. Los dibujantes están dibujándolas. / Los dibujantes las están dibujando.
4. Los maestros de obras están echándolos. / Los maestros de obras los están echando.
5. Los frailes y las monjas siguen rezándolas. / Los frailes y las monjas las siguen rezando.
6. Los trabajadores siguen colocándolos. / Los trabajadores los siguen colocando.
7. Los albañiles van trayéndolas. / Los albañiles las van trayendo.
8. Los obreros están poniéndola. / Los obreros la están poniendo.

O

1. Tu celular lo puse en tu mesa de trabajo.
2. A mis primos los llevé al colegio.
3. Tu tablet lo dejé en el jardín.
4. A mis padres los vi en la sala.
5. Tus libros los coloqué en tu oficina.
6. Las cartas que escribiste las eché al correo.
7. Tu abrigo lo colgué en el armario.
8. Las galletas que compraste las comí.

P

1. Te traje los refrescos.
2. Nos dieron flores.
3. Me mandó una tarjeta postal.
4. Le dijeron los precios.
5. Le ofrecimos el escritorio.
6. Le preguntó la hora.
7. Os expliqué mis ideas.
8. Les recordaron el cumpleaños de Leo.

Q

1. A nosotros / a Uds.
2. a mí / a ti
3. a él / a ella
4. A ti / a ellos
5. A vosotros / a nosotros
6. A ellas / a Ud.

R

1. A tres jóvenes les suspenden el permiso de manejar.
2. Los políticos nos ocultan los problemas económicos del país.
3. Al pueblo le exigen más sacrificios.
4. Nuestro país le va a comprar (va a comprarle) barcos a España.
5. El gobierno les quita la visa a tres extranjeros.

S

1. Le encantan esos perfumes.
2. Nos interesan estas novelas.
3. Les quedan unos exámenes.
4. Te entusiasman las comedias.
5. Os importan las ideas.
6. Me hacen falta unas guías.
7. Les fascinan estas materias.
8. Le faltan unos cuadernos.

T

1. Nos van a importar sus problemas.
2. No les va a quedar mucho dinero.
3. Le va a encantar visitar a sus abuelos.
4. No les va a sobrar comida.

5. Os va a convenir viajar en tren.
6. Te van a fascinar esos cuadros.
7. Me van a entusiasmar sus obras.
8. No le van a interesar esos programas.

U

1. A él.	5. Nosotros sí.
2. Ellos.	6. A Ud.
3. A ella no.	7. A mí sí.
4. Yo no.	8. Ellas sí.

V

1. (A mí) Me gustaría hacer un viaje a España.
2. (A mí) Me encantaría visitar a mis parientes en Chile y Argentina.
3. (A mí) Me interesaría ir de camping en Nuevo México o Arizona.
4. Y (a mí) me fascinaría ver la nueva moda italiana.
5. (A mí) Me entusiasmaría hacer deportes acuáticos.
6. Nos conviene tomar una decisión lo antes posible.
7. Nos sobran sugerencias. ¡Echemos suertes!
8. ¡Me toca a mí primero!

W

1. Se nos acabó	5. se te rompieron
2. Se le perdieron	6. se les ocurrió
3. Se me olvidó	7. se les cayeron
4. Se os quedó	

X

1. Que no se les olvide asistir a la conferencia.
2. Que no se le pierdan los anteojos.
3. Que no se le acabe la paciencia.
4. Que no se os queden los cheques.
5. Que no se le rompan las estatuillas de porcelana.
6. Que no se te ocurran tales cosas.
7. Que no se les caiga la torta de chocolate.

Y

1. ¿Se le perdió la cartera? / No, se me había quedado en casa.
2. Se les acaban (están acabando) los pasteles en la pastelería. / ¿No se te ocurrió comprarlos esta mañana?
3. ¡Tengan cuidado! ¡Se les van a caer las tazas! / ¡Ya se nos rompieron dos!
4. Se le olvidó recoger (buscar) a Tere y a Leo. / ¿No se le ocurrió que esperaban toda la noche?

Z

1. Me los dijeron.
2. Se los hemos puesto.
3. Está explicándosela. (Se la está explicando.)
4. Os lo muestro.
5. ¿Te la darían?
6. Se los cuentas.
7. Nos las ha hecho.
8. Devuélvamelo.
9. Me las estaban enseñando. (Estaban enseñándomelas.)
10. ¿A quién se lo vendiste?
11. Os la había escrito.
12. ¿Nos los prestarás?
13. Apréndansela de memoria.
14. ¿Estáis preguntándoselo? (¿Se lo estáis preguntando?)
15. Se la pusieron.
16. Se los preparó.
17. Estará bajándomelo. (Me lo estará bajando.)
18. Vendámosela.
19. Estuvimos trayéndoselos. (Se los estuvimos trayendo.)
20. Te la apagaré.

AA

1. Van a traérmela. / Me la van a traer.
2. Acaba de decírtelo. / Te lo acaba de decir.
3. Vamos a hacérselos. / Se los vamos a hacer.
4. Acabo de ponéroslas. / Os las acabo de poner.
5. Va a mostrárselo. / Se lo va a mostrar.
6. Acabáis de comprárnosla. / Nos la acabáis de comprar.
7. Vas a contármelos. / Me los vas a contar.
8. Acabo de arreglárselas. / Se las acabo de arreglar.
9. Van a subírtela. / Te la van a subir.
10. Acabamos de dároslo. / Os lo acabamos de dar.
11. Vamos a describírselo. / Se lo vamos a describir.
12. Acabo de ofrecérsela. / Se la acabo de ofrecer.
13. Va a limpiártelos. / Te los va a limpiar.
14. Acabo de encontrárselas. / Se las acabo de encontrar.
15. Van a pedírmela. / Me la van a pedir.
16. Acabas de buscárnoslo. / Nos lo acabas de buscar.

17. Vamos a llevároslos. / Os los vamos a llevar.
18. Acaba de servírselas. / Se las acaba de servir.
19. Vais a devolvérselo. / Se lo vais a devolver.
20. Acabo de cantártela. / Te la acabo de cantar.

BB

1. Papi, dámelos. / Sí, hijita, te los doy.
2. Mami, cómpramelos. / Sí, hijita, te los compro.
3. Juan, préstamela. / Sí, hermanita, te la presto.
4. Amparo, enséñamelo. / Sí, hermanita, te lo enseño.
5. Abuelo, regálamelo. / Sí, hijita, te lo regalo.
6. Elvira, sírvemelo. / Sí, hermanita, te lo sirvo.
7. Tía, pónmelas. / Sí, hijita, te las pongo.
8. Abuela, tráemelas. / Sí, hijita, te las traigo.

CC

1. a. Fernando gave it to her (him, them, you).
   b. She (He, You) gave it to Fernando.
2. a. The consultants told it to you (her, him, them).
   b. You (They) told it to the consultants.
3. a. The analyst lent them to you (her, him, them).
   b. He (You, She) lent them to the analyst.
4. a. My colleagues asked her (him, them, you) for them.
   b. They (You) asked my colleagues for them.
5. a. Laura returned it to you (him, her, them).
   b. He (She, You) returned it to Laura.

DD

1. —¿Sabes si las tiendas están abiertas?
   —No te lo sabría decir. (No sabría decírtelo.)
2. No sé cómo Raúl se las arregla/se las compone/se las apaña. Cree que todo el mundo se la tiene jurada. (Cree que todos se la tienen jurada.)
3. Cualquier estudiante que se porte mal tendrá que vérselas conmigo.
4. —¿Son ingenieros Ramón y Sergio?
   —No, no lo son. Son programadores.
   —Creo que son muy inteligentes.
   —Sí, lo son.
5. Pedrito no se pudo poner el abrigo, así es que se lo puse yo.
6. —¿Debo pedirles sus apuntes de historia a Alicia y a Pedro?
   —Pídeselos a él. No se los pidas a ella.
7. —Javier, mándame los informes, por favor.
   —Consuelo, te los mandé la semana pasada.
   —Lo siento. Se me perdieron.

EE

Answers will vary.

20 Relative Pronouns

A

1. Veo al médico que tiene su consulta en aquel edificio.
2. Quiero ver la película que se rodó en Perú.
3. Me gustan más las revistas que se publican en Asunción.
4. Prefiero el restaurante que sirve comida del Caribe.
5. Voy a la peluquería que está en la calle del Conde.
6. Queremos comprar los libros que nos recomendó el profesor.
7. Uso la computadora que me regalaron mis padres.
8. Hablábamos con esa secretaria que contratamos la semana pasada.
9. Repara mi coche el mecánico que conoce mi vecino.
10. Estoy leyendo el email que me mandó Silvia ayer.

B

1. La profesora que todos los estudiantes admiran. / La profesora que enseña francés y español. / La profesora que acaba de casarse. / La profesora que conocen mis padres.
2. La casa que compraron Juana y Rafael. / La casa que tiene patio y piscina. / La casa que construyeron en 2018. / La casa que es de ladrillos.
3. El regalo que mis hermanos y yo recibimos hace dos días. / El regalo que nos mandaron mis tíos. / El regalo que te enseñé ayer. / El regalo que nos gustó tanto.
4. El restaurante que nuestros amigos abrieron el año pasado. / El restaurante que sirve comida española. / El restaurante que tiene manteles rojos. / El restaurante que frecuentan muchos artistas.
5. El senador que eligieron el año pasado. / El senador que prometió reducir los impuestos. / El senador que es casado con una arquitecta. / El senador que era jefe de una empresa.

C

1. El señor Mora, quien se encarga de los archivos, es secretario general de la universidad.
2. El profesor Uriarte, quién asistió a un congreso en la UNAM, enseña química.
3. Los estudiantes, quienes se gradúan en junio, tienen que entregar una tesis.
4. La doctora Arrieta, quien figura en el tribunal de exámenes, tiene dos ayudantes de laboratorio.
5. Estos decanos, quienes planean el programa, trabajan en la facultad de ingeniería.
6. El rector de la universidad, quien dicta conferencias de ciencias políticas, es abogado.
7. Algunos estudiantes de medicina fueron a hablar con el profesor Quijano, quien estaba ya en el salón de actos.
8. La profesora Arenas, quien hace investigaciones de biología, se jubila el año que viene.

D

1. Mis primos a quienes vi en Caracas hace dos años están de vacaciones en los Estados Unidos.
2. La pintora a quien vieron en la exposición sólo pinta acuarelas.
3. La muchacha a quien le di un regalo ayer me dio las gracias hoy.
4. Los amigos a quienes llamamos a la una de la mañana no quisieron salir.
5. Los vecinos a quienes buscábamos se habían mudado.
6. La dependienta a quien Ud. conoció el año pasado ya no trabaja en esta tienda.
7. El señor a quien encontraste en la calle es mi profesor de cálculo.

E

1. a quien	5. quienes
2. quien	6. a quien
3. quienes	7. a quien
4. a quienes	8. quien

F

1. los que	5. lo que
2. lo que	6. el que (la que)
3. la que (el que)	7. las que
4. lo que	

G

1. los cuales	5. lo cual
2. lo cual	6. el cual (la cual)
3. la cual (el cual)	7. las cuales
4. lo cual	

H

1. debajo de las cuales hay varias líneas de metro / debajo de las que hay varias líneas de metro
2. cerca de la cual vivimos / cerca de la que vivimos
3. enfrente del cual hay un restaurante / enfrente del que hay un restaurante
4. con quienes solemos pasar los domingos aquí / con los cuales solemos pasar los domingos aquí / con los que solemos pasar los domingos aquí
5. en medio de la cual hay una exposición de arte / en medio de la que hay una exposición de arte
6. detrás de los cuales hay un mercado al aire libre / detrás de los que hay un mercado al aire libre
7. hacia el cual caminamos ahora es muy antiguo / hacia el que caminamos ahora es muy antiguo
8. al otro lado del cual se encuentran unas tiendas elegantes / al otro lado del que se encuentran unas tiendas elegantes

I

1. en que	5. en el que
2. en el que	6. en los que
3. en que	7. en que
4. en que	8. en las que

J

1. The benefit concert was an event through which the university received a lot of money.
2. A new skyscraper has been built from which there are fabulous views of the city.
3. These are the books according to which Professor Sorolla reached his conclusions.
4. I always remember the Greek ruins we walked among.
5. A hotel opened next to where a mall will open.
6. Let's get together at the engineering school across from where we met.
7. There's the fountain in front of which we fell in love.

8. What's the name of the company Antonio works for?
9. Do you know which ideas the researchers based their theories on?

K

1. cuyas	5. cuyo
2. cuyos	6. cuyas
3. cuyo	7. cuya
4. cuya	8. cuyos

L

1. Now you know the reason why I got angry.
2. We used to live in a neighborhood where there were many stores.
3. There to the right is the door through which the actors enter and leave.
4. I don't understand the reasons why the union declared the strike.
5. The kids didn't tell me where they were going.
6. They're the hours during which Miguel surfs the web.
7. Here's the newspaper stand behind which Sergio and Sol agreed to see each other.
8. I'll introduce you to the young man whose father was my marketing professor.
9. Jaime didn't invite us to his party, which surprised us.

M

Answers will vary.

III Other Elements of the Sentence

21 Adverbs

A

1. alegremente	14. violentamente
2. descuidadamente	15. perspicazmente
3. cruelmente	16. burlonamente
4. artísticamente	17. comercialmente
5. normalmente	18. sagazmente
6. abiertamente	19. honradamente
7. francamente	20. humildemente
8. nerviosamente	21. difícilmente
9. evidentemente	22. admirablemente
10. responsablemente	23. estupendamente
11. débilmente	24. afectuosamente
12. verdaderamente	25. vulgarmente
13. torpemente	

B

1. Sí, habló orgullosamente.
2. Sí, habló sinceramente.
3. Sí, hablaron tristemente.
4. Sí, hablé furiosamente.
5. Sí, habló malhumoradamente.
6. Sí, hablamos avergonzadamente.
7. Sí, hablé distraídamente.
8. Sí, habló incoherentemente.
9. Sí, hablamos felizmente.

C

1. Pronunciaron mal las frases.
2. Trabajaron muy responsablemente.
3. Las cosas andaban bien.
4. Quiero que mis hijos vivan felizmente.
5. Su última película fue muy interesante.
6. El niño miraba a sus padres inocentemente.
7. Patricia encontró esos problemas sumamente difíciles.
8. Salgan de la casa muy rápidamente.
9. Encontramos el proyecto totalmente ridículo.
10. Estamos súper ocupados esta semana.
11. Carlos estaba medio dormido.

D

1. Martín y Fernando trabajan inteligentemente.
2. Lola canta maravillosamente.
3. Carmen y Pilar escriben hábilmente.
4. Rafa conduce prudentemente.
5. Lucas estudia diligentemente.
6. Marcos pinta divinamente.
7. Carla y Pedro viajan frecuentemente.
8. Alfonso juega enérgicamente.

E

1. con inteligencia	9. con lealtad
2. con armonía	10. con suavidad
3. con elegancia	11. con fuerza
4. con diligencia	12. con felicidad
5. con delicadeza	13. con tristeza
6. con cariño	14. con calor
7. con alegría	15. con claridad
8. con ligereza	16. con violencia

F

1. ¿Ya fue al supermercado? / Todavía no. No me he vestido todavía.
2. Vuelvo en seguida. / Ven acá ahora mismo.
3. Mariana no puede encontrar a su gato por ningún lado. / ¡Mire en lo alto! (¡Mire arriba!) El gato está en el árbol.

4. ¿Están los chicos por aquí? / Estarán en la casa. / ¿Sabes si están arriba o abajo? / Estarán escondidos detrás de algún mueble.
5. ¿Está lejos la tienda de cómputo? / No, está cerca. Y hay una maravillosa heladería al lado.

G

1. elegante y cuidadosamente
2. lenta y suavemente
3. cariñosa y calurosamente
4. oportuna y apasionadamente
5. ligera y perezosamente
6. fiel y lealmente
7. sabia y astutamente
8. deprimida y tristemente

H

1. Él escribe más sarcásticamente que tú.
2. Tú analizas el artículo menos críticamente que yo.
3. Ellos lo hacen tan fácilmente como nosotros.
4. Ana habla más francamente que Lucía.
5. Este niño juega menos alegremente que aquél.
6. Ella se expresa tan lógicamente como tú.
7. Nosotros mandamos los emails más frecuentemente que ellos.
8. Vosotros nos recibís tan afectuosamente como Pablo y Lucero.

I

Answers will vary.

22 Prepositions

A

1. a	6. a
2. X	7. A
3. a	8. X
4. X	9. a
5. al / a	

B

1. Escribí el informe a doble espacio.
2. A su llegada a medianoche se acostó.
3. El bebé anda a gatas.
4. Me encanta la ropa que está hecha a mano.
5. Los niños comieron todas las galletas a escondidas.
6. El centro comercial queda a siete millas de mi casa.

C

1. de
2. X
3. X
4. del
5. X
6. de
7. de
8. de

D

1. Me regalaron una pulsera de oro y unos pendientes de plata.
2. Bernardo es alto y ancho de espaldas.
3. ¿Quieres trabajar de día o de noche?
4. La pobre de su tía está de luto.
5. Se pusieron de rodillas.

E

1. I recognized her (you) by her (your) voice.
2. They sold it to me for $2,000.
3. The value has gone up by 15%.
4. The workers are against the strike.
5. They got together at the Segovia café.

F

1. Pensamos ir en avión.
2. Los recogeré en el aeropuerto.
3. Miguel es más alto que Juan en una cabeza.
4. ¿Dices esto en serio o en broma?
5. Saldrán en una hora.

G

1. con leche
2. con llave
3. con cuerda
4. con un apretón
5. con caramelos
6. con esfuerzo

H

1. del	12. en
2. Con	13. a
3. a	14. a
4. en	15. en
5. en	16. de
6. con	17. a
7. de	18. de
8. a	19. de
9. de	20. de
10. con	21. Al
11. con	22. Al

I

1. Para ganar dinero.
2. Para aprender mucho.
3. Para ayudar a mis papás.
4. Para demostrarle mi cariño.
5. Para perfeccionarlo.
6. Para ser buen ciudadano.
7. Para llevar una vida moral y feliz.

J

1. Para pasado mañana.
2. Para la semana entrante.
3. Para el martes.
4. Para finales del semestre.
5. Para el mes próximo.
6. Para las cinco de la tarde.
7. Para el fin de semana.

K

1. Fui al almacén por un par de zapatos.
2. La felicitamos por su cumpleaños.
3. Me duele (la espalda) por jugar al tenis por cuatro horas.
4. No lo terminó por pereza.
5. Los veremos por la tarde.
6. Salieron por el puente más céntrico.
7. Iremos por salchicha y queso.
8. Tendré que hacerla por escrito.
9. Darán un paseo por el bulevar Alameda.
10. Voy a pasar por Micaela y Angustias.

L

1. Por la fotografía.
2. Por el argumento.
3. Por la dirección.
4. Por el guión.
5. Por el escenario.
6. Por la música.
7. Por los efectos especiales.
8. Por el diálogo.

M

1. para / por / por / por
2. para / por
3. Para / Por
4. por / para / Para / por / para
5. Para / para / por
6. por / Para / por / para
7. por / Para
8. por / Por / Por / por
9. por / por

N

1. I'm an American on both sides.
2. We'll go with you earlier just in case.

3. They praise the composer to the skies.
4. Ricardo must have called for a reason.
5. Three times eight is twenty-four.
6. Mortadelo and Filemón are two of a kind.
7. "I'll love you forever," don Quijote said to Dulcinea.

O

1. Beatriz fue por los panecillos. Pagó treinta dólares por ellos.
2. Carlos y Leo fueron por los refrescos. Pagaron cincuenta y cinco dólares por ellos.
3. Paula y yo fuimos por las servilletas. Pagamos siete dólares por ellas.
4. Tú fuiste por los fiambres. Pagaste cien dólares por ellos.
5. Yo fui por la torta. Pagué dieciocho dólares por ella.
6. Uds. fueron por el vino. Pagaron cuarenta y tres dólares por él.
7. Ud. fue por la fruta. Pagó veintidós dólares por ella.
8. Vosotros fuisteis por los quesos. Pagasteis sesenta y un dólares por ellos.

P

1. Mi tarea está (queda) sin terminar.
2. Puse (Coloqué) un libro sobre otro (encima de otro).
3. Lo vi salir hacia atrás.
4. Vivió durante muchos años entre los indígenas.
5. Hace calor hasta en la sierra.
6. Los inmigrantes sienten amor hacia su nuevo país.
7. Nos siguieron desde la puerta del cine.
8. Leo un libro sobre Puerto Rico.

Q

1. c	11. c
2. c	12. c
3. c	13. c
4. a	14. a
5. a	15. a
6. b	16. b
7. a	17. a
8. b	18. c
9. b	19. c
10. a	20. c

R

Answers will vary.

23 Interrogative Words and Question Formation

A
1. ¿De qué se quejaba?
2. ¿En qué se interesan?
3. ¿De qué se jacta?
4. ¿Con quién se casará?
5. ¿En qué se metieron?
6. ¿En qué se fija?
7. ¿De qué se ríe?
8. ¿De quién se enamoró?
9. ¿Con quién soñó?

B
1. ¿De dónde es? (¿Cuál es su nacionalidad?)
2. ¿Qué es? (¿Cuál es su profesión?)
3. ¿Para quién trabaja?
4. ¿Dónde vive?
5. ¿Con quién es casado?
6. ¿Cuántos hijos tiene?
7. ¿Dónde nació? (¿En qué país nació?)
8. ¿De qué origen es? (¿De dónde son sus abuelos?)
9. ¿Cuándo se mudó al Canadá? (¿Cuántos años tenía cuando se mudó al Canadá? OR ¿Adónde se mudó cuando tenía cuatro años?)
10. ¿Qué estudia? (¿Dónde estudia?)
11. ¿Cuándo terminará sus estudios?
12. ¿Dónde vive? (¿Con quiénes vive?)
13. ¿Qué ganó?
14. ¿Qué es?
15. ¿Por quién fue condecorado? (¿Quién lo condecoró?)
16. ¿Cuántas bicicletas tiene?
17. ¿Cuál de sus bicicletas le gusta más? (¿De dónde es la bicicleta que le gusta más? OR ¿De qué color es la bicicleta que le gusta más?)
18. ¿Qué quiere hacer?
19. ¿Adónde irá de vacaciones? (¿Para qué irá al Caribe?)
20. ¿A quiénes llevará? (¿Cuántas hijas tiene?)

C
1. ¿Dónde?
2. ¿Cuántas?
3. ¿Cuántos?
4. ¿Cuántos?
5. ¿A quién?
6. ¿Cuánto?
7. ¿De qué?
8. ¿Cuál?
9. ¿Cómo? / ¿Con qué?
10. ¿Cómo? / ¿En qué?
11. ¿A qué hora? / ¿Adónde?
12. ¿Cuándo? / ¿Adónde?

D
1. Cuántas
2. Cuáles
3. Quién
4. Cómo
5. Cuántos
6. Por qué
7. Dónde
8. Qué
9. A qué
10. De quién
11. Qué
12. Dónde
13. De qué
14. Cuál
15. Adónde
16. quién
17. Cómo / Qué
18. Qué / Por qué
19. Por qué

E
1. Dónde
2. Qué
3. Cuándo (A qué hora)
4. Cuál
5. Quién
6. Adónde
7. De dónde
8. Cuántos
9. Cuánto

F
1. ¿De parte de quién?
2. ¿Dónde queda la casa? / ¿En qué calle queda la casa?
3. ¿De quién es el coche?
4. ¿De qué color es?
5. ¿A quién vas a llevar?
6. ¿A qué hora llegarán?
7. ¿Cuántos años tienes?
8. ¿A quiénes piensas ver?
9. ¿Cuándo será? / ¿Qué día será?
10. ¿Quiénes llegan?
11. ¿Cuánta plata gastaste? / ¿Cuánto gastaste?
12. ¿Qué tiempo hace?
13. ¿Cómo se encuentran?
14. ¿Hasta cuándo te quedas? / ¿Hasta qué día te quedas?
15. ¿Cuál quieres?
16. ¿De qué origen es?

G
1. ¿Cuándo vamos a comprar los boletos/billetes (sacar las entradas) para la obra de teatro?
2. ¿Qué te parece si vamos mañana? ¿Dónde queda la taquilla?
3. En la avenida Pamplona. ¿Cuántos boletos necesitamos (nos hacen falta)?
4. Seis. ¿Cuánto cuestan (valen)?

5. Cincuenta dólares cada uno. ¿Quién los paga?
6. Cada persona pagará el billete suyo. ¿Qué día vamos?
7. El jueves. ¿A qué hora empieza la función?
8. A las ocho. ¿A quién invitas?
9. ¡A nadie! ¡El billete es muy caro! (¡El billete cuesta muy caro!) ¿Cómo llegamos?
10. En coche o en tren (metro).

H
1. ¿Cuánto tiene el río Iguazú de largo?
2. ¿Qué longitud tiene el río Amazonas?
3. ¿Cuánto mide el río Mississippi de largo?
4. ¿A qué altura está el lago Titicaca?
5. ¿Cuánto tiene el desierto de Atacama de largo?
6. ¿Qué altura tiene el monte McKinley?
7. ¿Cuánto mide la cumbre Aconcagua de alto?

I

1. Cuál	5. Cómo
2. Qué	6. Cuál
3. Cómo	7. Qué
4. Cuál	

J
1. ¿Para quién son estas rosas?
2. ¿Sobre qué hablaron los ingenieros?
3. ¿En qué oficina trabaja Celeste?
4. ¿Con cuántas personas fue Alberto?
5. ¿De quiénes son los celulares?
6. ¿Hacia dónde caminaba Daniel?
7. ¿Por dónde entró Jeremías?
8. ¿Con quién soñó?
9. ¿En qué se metieron?
10. ¿De dónde vienen?

K
1. ¿Aprenden Gustavo y Juana francés?
2. ¿Trabaja Pepe en una tienda de deportes?
3. ¿Toca Ud. el piano?
4. ¿Se han vestido los niños?
5. ¿Jugará Cristóbal al béisbol?
6. ¿Se matriculó Elena anteayer?
7. ¿Deben Uds. quedarse unos días más?
8. ¿Está Ramona a dieta?

L
1. ¿Son traviesos estos niños?
2. ¿Son bonitas las margaritas?
3. ¿Estaba descompuesto el televisor?
4. ¿Está abierto el museo?
5. ¿Es italiana la revista?

6. ¿Fueron robadas las joyas?
7. ¿Están rotos los pantalones?
8. ¿Es buena esta marca?
9. ¿Fue impresionante el espectáculo?
10. ¿Están ricas las chuletas de cordero?

M
1. No, Pedro no. Los trae Memo.
2. No, Domingo y Toni no. Lo compran Manolo y Juan.
3. No, Dora no. Las va a preparar Leonor.
4. No, Jorge no. Los traerá Miguel.
5. No, Carmen no. Piensa llevarlas Marcos.
6. No, nosotros no. Los harán Olivia y Nacho.
7. No, ellos no. Las sirves tú.
8. No, Mari no. Quiero comprarla yo.

N
1. Felipe me preguntó qué haría en la tarde.
2. Isabel me preguntó con quiénes había salido (salí).
3. Carlos me preguntó por qué no quería jugar al baloncesto.
4. Sol me preguntó a qué hora había vuelto (volví) a casa.
5. Claudio me preguntó para cuándo necesitaba escribir el informe.
6. Mi hermana me preguntó cuándo la llevaba a una discoteca.
7. Mis colegas me preguntaron por qué no los invitaba a tomar una copa.
8. El director me preguntó quien hizo (había hecho) el presupuesto.
9. Yo me pregunté a mí mismo por qué me había levantado (me levanté) de la cama.

O
Answers will vary.

24 Negative and Indefinite Words

A
1. No, no fui nunca (jamás).
2. No, no aprendimos chino tampoco.
3. No, no ha llamado nadie.
4. No, no va a tomar álgebra nunca más.
5. No leeré ni la novela ni el guión de la película.
6. No, no renunció al puesto ningún jefe (ninguno).
7. No, no conoció a nadie.
8. No, no queda ninguno (ningún durazno).
9. No, no limpio la casa los sábados nunca.
10. No, no he visto a ninguna.

B

1. No queda nada de la comida.
2. No hay refrescos tampoco.
3. No bailan ni los chicos ni las chicas.
4. No se acerca ninguno de los chicos para hablarme.
5. No canta bien ningún cantante.
6. No tiene ganas nadie de quedarse.
7. No dan fiestas divertidas nunca.

C

1. ¡Qué va! Nadie te regaló dos millones de dólares.
2. ¡Qué va! Ninguna chica dice que eres un Adonis.
3. ¡Qué va! Nunca (Jamás) sacas un diez en tus exámenes.
4. ¡Qué va! Los reyes de España no te mandaron nada.
5. ¡Qué va! Tú tampoco vas a la luna.
6. ¡Qué va! Conchita no va a salir contigo nunca más.
7. ¡Qué va! Tus padres no te van a regalar ni un Rolls-Royce ni un Lamborghini.

D

1. nada / nadie
2. En la vida / Nunca
3. nada / algo
4. nunca
5. sino también
6. casi nada
7. alguien
8. nunca acabar
9. de nada
10. nadie
11. no solamente (sólo) / sino también
12. ninguna

E

1. I can't stand her at all.
2. I know you from somewhere.
3. They're going to see each other at the usual time.
4. They don't call her charming for nothing.
5. If Isabel told you that, there must be a reason.
6. All the time and all the plans came to nothing.
7. When all is said and done, all the arguing was useless.
8. What you're saying has nothing to do with the present situation.

F

1. a
2. b
3. b
4. a
5. b
6. a
7. a
8. b
9. a
10. b

G

1. No por nada renunció a su puesto.
2. Llamarán en cualquier momento.
3. Caminamos todo el día por toda la ciudad.
4. Cualquiera podría ayudarnos con el trabajo.
5. Toda avenida está embotellada (Todas las avenidas están embotelladas) en las horas punta.
6. Hay ruinas romanas por toda España.

H

1. Aunque te querré para siempre, tengo que decir: "¡hasta nunca!"
2. Más vale algo que nada. (Algo es algo.)
3. ¡Nada de ir a Marte antes de graduarte!
4. ¡Y aquí acaba el cuento de nunca acabar!
5. De algo lo (la) conozco. Será alguien.
6. ¡Haz lo que quieras! ¡Ve adonde quieras! ¡Yo no te olvidaré nunca jamás!
7. ¿Este final? ¿Ese final? ¡Yo estoy contento/a con cualquiera de los dos!
8. Nada más. ¡Mañana es otro día!

I

Answers will vary.

25 Numbers; Dates; Time

A

1. cien grapadoras
2. mil ochocientos veintiún teléfonos celulares
3. mil quinientos cuarenta y nueve rotuladores, plumas y bolígrafos
4. setecientas cincuenta y una cajas de gomas, grapas y sujetapapeles
5. cuatrocientos sesenta y siete cartuchos de tinta
6. novecientos nueve calendarios y lápices
7. mil sobres y etiquetas
8. mil trescientas ochenta y una cámaras digitales

B

1. (España) cuarenta y siete millones cuatrocientos ochenta y seis mil novecientos treinta y cinco habitantes / cuarenta y dos millones cuatrocientos mil setecientos cincuenta y seis usuarios de Internet
2. (México) ciento veintiocho millones novecientos setenta y dos mil cuatrocientos treinta y nueve habitantes / noventa y dos millones diez mil usuarios de Internet
3. (Panamá) cuatro millones trescientos cincuenta y un mil doscientos sesenta y siete

habitantes / dos millones trescientos setenta
y un mil ochocientos cincuenta y dos
usuarios de Internet

4. (Costa Rica) cinco millones ciento cincuenta
y tres mil novecientos cincuenta y siete
habitantes / tres millones quinientos once
mil quinientos cuarenta y nueve usuarios
de Internet

5. (Guatemala) diecisiete millones seiscientos
ocho mil cuatrocientos ochenta y tres
habitantes / once millones setecientos
cincuenta mil usuarios de Internet

6. (Puerto Rico) tres millones doscientos
cincuenta y seis mil veintiocho habitantes /
dos millones seiscientos sesenta y cuatro mil
novecientos veintiocho usuarios de Internet

7. (la República Dominicana) once millones
ciento diecisiete mil ochocientos setenta
y tres habitantes / seis millones novecientos
noventa y siete mil cuatrocientos setenta
y dos usuarios de Internet

8. (Colombia) cincuenta y un millones
quinientos dieciséis mil quinientos sesenta y
dos habitantes / treinta millones quinientos
cuarenta y ocho mil doscientos cincuenta y
dos usuarios de Internet

9. (Argentina) cuarenta y cinco millones
doscientos setenta y seis mil setecientos
ochenta habitantes / treinta y tres millones
quinientos sesenta y un mil ochocientos
setenta y seis usuarios de Internet

10. (Uruguay) tres millones cuatrocientos
veintiséis mil doscientos sesenta habitantes /
dos millones trescientos sesenta mil
doscientos sesenta y nueve usuarios de
Internet

11. (Chile) diecinueve millones cuatrocientos
noventa y tres mil ciento ochenta y cuatro
habitantes / catorce millones ochocientos
sesenta y cuatro mil cuatrocientos cincuenta
y seis usuarios de Internet

12. (Perú) treinta y tres millones setecientos
quince mil cuatrocientos setenta y un
habitantes / quince millones seiscientos
setenta y cuatro mil doscientos cuarenta
y un usuarios de Internet

C

1. Silvia y Adela viven en el piso doce.
2. Carlos vive en el quinto piso.
3. Yo vivo en el primer piso.
4. José Miguel vive en el noveno piso.
5. Ana María vive en el décimo piso.

6. Patricio vive en el cuarto piso.
7. Lucía vive en el tercer piso.
8. Daniela vive en el piso catorce.

D

1. dos mil diez / mil novecientos treinta y seis
2. mil novecientos noventa / mil novecientos
catorce / mil novecientos noventa y ocho
3. mil novecientos ochenta y nueve /
mil novecientos dieciséis / dos mil dos
4. mil novecientos ochenta y dos /
mil novecientos veintiocho / dos mil catorce
5. mil novecientos setenta y siete /
mil ochocientos noventa y ocho /
mil novecientos ochenta y cuatro
6. mil novecientos setenta y uno /
mil novecientos cuatro / mil novecientos
setenta y tres
7. mil novecientos sesenta y siete /
mil ochocientos noventa y nueve /
mil novecientos setenta y cuatro
8. mil novecientos cincuenta y seis /
mil ochocientos ochenta y uno /
mil novecientos cincuenta y ocho
9. mil novecientos cuarenta y cinco /
mil ochocientos ochenta y nueve /
mil novecientos cincuenta y siete
10. mil novecientos veintidós / mil ochocientos
sesenta y seis / mil novecientos cincuenta
y cuatro
11. mil novecientos cuatro / mil ochocientos
treinta y tres / mil novecientos catorce

E

1. del diez al dieciséis de octubre de mil
setecientos ochenta / veintidós mil muertos
2. del diecinueve al veinte de septiembre de
mil novecientos setenta y cuatro / ocho mil
muertos
3. del ocho al veintiuno de noviembre de mil
novecientos noventa y cuatro / mil ciento
cuarenta y cinco muertos
4. del veintidós de octubre al cinco de
noviembre de mil novecientos noventa
y ocho / once mil muertos
5. del trece al veintiocho de septiembre de dos
mil cuatro / tres mil veinticinco muertos
6. del veintitrés al treinta de agosto de dos mil
cinco / mil ochocientos treinta y seis
muertos
7. del veinte al veintiuno de septiembre de dos
mil diecisiete / dos mil novecientos setenta
y cinco

F

1. Los turistas salen para visitar Santo Domingo de Silos el sábado a las dieciséis.
2. Los viajeros llegan a Burgos donde se hospedan en un hotel el sábado a las veinte.
3. Los turistas salen en autocar para visitar el Monasterio de las Huelgas el domingo a las diez treinta.
4. Los turistas visitan la Catedral de Burgos el domingo a las dieciséis treinta.
5. Los viajeros salen para Madrid el domingo a las dieciocho treinta y nueve.
6. Los viajeros llegan a la estación Madrid-Chamartín el domingo a las veintiuna cincuenta y cinco.

G

1. $174 + 89 = 263$; doscientos sesenta y tres
2. $603 - 281 = 322$; trescientos veintidós
3. $49 \times 5 = 245$; doscientos cuarenta y cinco
4. $1284 \div 4 = 321$; trescientos veintiuno
5. $80 \times 3/4 = 60$; sesenta
6. $\$80.000 \times .25 = \$20.000$; veinte mil dólares

H

Answers will vary.

IV Idiomatic Usage

26 Idioms, Expressions, and Proverbs

A

1. éxito
2. pies ni cabeza
3. en la punta de la lengua
4. pelo de tonto
5. los huesos molidos
6. suerte (buena estrella)
7. malas pulgas
8. ojos de lince
9. mala cara / los nervios de punta
10. vergüenza / líos

B

1. Amparo se lo tomó con calma.
2. Los García tomaron a pecho la muerte del vecino.
3. Pedro tomó a broma (risa) las diabluras de su hijo.
4. La profesora tomó a mal lo que le dijo Marianela.
5. Paco tomó partido por Juan Carlos en la discusión.

C

1. estar hecho polvo
2. estar calado (mojado) hasta los huesos OR estar hecho una sopa
3. estar sin blanca
4. estar hecho una fiera
5. estar a sus anchas (estar como el pez en el agua)

D

1. de menos
2. flores
3. se las echaba
4. chispas
5. la bronca

E

1. (la) lata / guerra
2. por vencidos
3. el golpe de gracia
4. rienda suelta
5. por sentado

F

1. hacer las paces
2. hacerse rica / hacer su agosto
3. hacer un papel
4. hacer la vista gorda
5. hacer de las suyas

G

1. va sobre ruedas
2. Quedamos en
3. Se llevan como el perro y el gato.
4. llevarte un chasco
5. lleva la contraria
6. llevar a cabo
7. quedé boquiabierto
8. se quedó con el día y la noche / se quedó sin blanca

H

1. d
2. e
3. b
4. h
5. a
6. g
7. f

I

1. c
2. a
3. c
4. b
5. b

J

1. f
2. h
3. c
4. i
5. d
6. e
7. a
8. g

K

1. g	5. j
2. e	6. c
3. i	7. f
4. a	8. b

L

1. g	5. i
2. d	6. c
3. a	7. j
4. b	8. e

M

1. b	4. c
2. a	5. c
3. a	

N

1. la mona / mona: You can't make a silk purse out of a sow's ear.
2. pájaro: A bird in the hand is worth two in the bush.
3. perro: Nonsense! Don't give me that!
4. gato / liebre: Don't get taken in.
5. El sapo / la sapa: Beauty is in the eye of the beholder.
6. peces: big shots
7. caballo: Don't look a gift horse in the mouth.
8. gato: There's something fishy.
9. la gallina: He killed the goose that laid the golden eggs.
10. pájaros: It's good that we killed two birds with one stone.
11. mirlo: His plan was an impossible dream.
12. lobo: Without realizing it, he walked into the lion's den.
13. gallina: She got goose bumps.
14. el perro / el gato: What a twosome! They're always fighting.
15. lince: She has eyes like a hawk.
16. pájaros: He has bats in the belfry.

27 Word Formation and Diminutives

A

1. formar	5. grabar
2. programar	6. presentar
3. dominar	7. obligar
4. preparar	8. complicar

B

1. el comportamiento	6. el planteamiento
2. el encarcelamiento	7. el tratamiento
3. el consentimiento	8. el nombramiento
4. el movimiento	9. el crecimiento
5. el pensamiento	10. el sufrimiento

C

1. saborear / to savor
2. gotear / to drip, leak
3. golpear / to hit, beat
4. teclear / to run one's fingers over the keys, strike the keys repeatedly
5. hojear / to leaf through
6. zapatear / to stamp one's feet
7. patear / to kick

D

1. encasillar
2. el engrasamiento / grease / to grease
3. ensañar
4. embotellar / el embotellamiento
5. el emparejamiento
6. el enfrentamiento

E

1. e	5. c
2. f	6. b
3. h	7. d
4. g	8. a

F

1. to flower, bloom	4. to moisten
2. to strengthen	5. humidifier
3. to strengthen	

G

1. endurecer	6. ennegrecer
2. embellecer	7. enrojecer
3. enflaquecer	8. enronquecer
4. ennoblecer	9. ensordecer
5. enloquecer	

H

1. pastry chef
2. spoonful
3. hat shop
4. coffee pot
5. salad bowl
6. pencil case
7. silly thing OR silly remark
8. boatload
9. slam of a door
10. stepdaughter
11. salt shaker
12. party lover

I

1. la vocecita
2. la cartita
3. el trajecito
4. el pececito
5. el cuentecito
6. la piernecita
7. el caballito
8. el bosquecito
9. el dolorcito
10. la cabecita
11. el laguito
12. suavecito
13. el vientecito
14. el juguito
15. el carrito
16. fuertecito
17. chiquito
18. nuevecito
19. fresquito
20. la lucecita

28 ¡Ojo! Common Errors and Pitfalls

A

1. dejar
2. salir / deje
3. te vayas / dejes
4. se fue / dejó
5. salió
6. deja / salir
7. salió
8. salieron
9. dejan

B

1. conoce
2. conocen
3. Sabe
4. conozco
5. sabe

C

1. oídos
2. la oreja
3. buen oído
4. la oreja
5. oído

D

1. Nos quedan dos semanas en Puerto Rico.
2. Quédate con el dinero. No me hace falta.
3. Me he quedado sin salidas.
4. Se quedaron con una familia mexicana.
5. Les quedan tres oraciones por traducir.
6. Quedó sordo a causa de (por) la explosión.
7. ¿Dónde queda el correo, por favor?
8. Paula y yo quedamos en ir al cine.

E

1. ¿Quién rompió mi periódico? (¿Quién me rompió el periódico?)
2. Mi silla está rota.
3. La radio está descompuesta.
4. Tengo el abrigo roto. (Mi abrigo está roto.)
5. Espero que no se nos descomponga el coche.
6. No comprendemos por qué rompió a llorar.
7. No te rompas la chaqueta.

8. Elena rompió con su novio.
9. El enemigo rompió el fuego.
10. Quien rompe paga.

F

1. Marqué mal. (Marqué un número equivocado.)
2. Se ha equivocado de tren.
3. ¿Qué le pasa al celular?
4. No es el momento adecuado.
5. Leí mal el título.
6. Tienes los guantes al revés.
7. Tiene un puesto que no le conviene.
8. La definición está mal (es inexacta OR es incorrecta).
9. Hice mal en no creerlo.
10. Sumó mal.

G

1. se perdió
2. falta
3. perder
4. erró el tiro (falló el blanco)
5. no entendí (no oí OR no comprendí)
6. falla
7. faltan
8. echo de menos (extraño)
9. desaparecidos

V Review

29 Review Exercises

A

1. escribo
2. trabaja
3. viven
4. comprendes
5. esperamos
6. estudia
7. comen
8. aprende

B

1. salgo
2. conozco
3. hago
4. doy
5. voy
6. sé
7. tengo
8. vengo

C

1. somos
2. están
3. es
4. estoy
5. son
6. es
7. están
8. soy
9. está
10. eres
11. estamos
12. está
13. es
14. Son

D

1. Mis padres vuelven el viernes.
2. Beatriz pide postre con el café.
3. Uds. pueden comprar boletos en línea.
4. Yo pienso en el futuro.
5. Llueve toda la semana.
6. ¿Tú quieres acompañarnos?
7. Nosotros empezamos a navegar en la red.
8. Ud. sirve unos platos riquísimos.

E

1. compré
2. corrió
3. recibiste
4. vendieron
5. encantaron
6. comencé
7. leyó
8. jugué
9. vistió
10. durmieron
11. busqué
12. sirvió

F

1. dije
2. trajeron
3. hiciste
4. supimos
5. tuvo
6. fueron
7. pudo
8. quisieron
9. vinimos
10. estuve

G

1. practicábamos
2. Eran
3. quería
4. tenían
5. vivías
6. veían
7. estaba
8. Había
9. iba
10. navegábamos

H

1. Llovía / volvimos
2. cenaba / sonó
3. ponía / llegaron
4. Era / empecé
5. oyó / dormía
6. dije / iba
7. Había / despegó
8. Pasó / dabas
9. conocimos / éramos
10. escribió / pensaba
11. tomábamos / pidió
12. estaban / murió

I

1. Imprimiré estos documentos.
2. Brindaremos por su salud.
3. ¿Prenderás la tele?
4. La reunión comenzará a las dos.
5. Me pondré la camisa blanca.
6. Los actores se divertirán mucho.
7. Te probarás los zapatos nuevos, ¿no?
8. Saldremos para la oficina en media hora.
9. Diego se graduará el año que viene.
10. Yo volveré el miércoles.
11. ¿Qué habrá en la bolsa?
12. La boda será en el hotel Plaza.

J

1. Mateo vendrá la semana próxima.
2. Todos Uds. no cabrán en el carro.
3. ¿Tus amigos no te dirán la verdad?
4. Haremos escala en Madrid.
5. Me reuniré con todo el equipo.
6. El anillo valdrá una fortuna.
7. Nos veremos el domingo.
8. ¿Te aprovecharás de las ofertas?
9. Mis colegas lo sabrán todo.
10. Yo me arreglaré.

K

1. analizarían
2. compartiría
3. gustaría
4. podríamos
5. Habría
6. estarías
7. Haría
8. interesaría
9. tendría
10. diríamos

L

1. Nos quedamos en la ciudad.
2. Se acuesta a las once.
3. Se lavan las manos.
4. Me pruebo la chaqueta.
5. Nos pusimos de pie.
6. Se divirtieron en el baile.
7. Se cortó el pelo.
8. Te despertaste temprano.
9. Despídase de ellos. / No se despida de ellos.
10. Acuéstense. / No se acuesten.
11. Vete. / No te vayas.
12. Vistámonos. / No nos vistamos.
13. Ríase. / No se ría.
14. Acérquense. / No se acerquen.
15. Duérmete. / No te duermas.
16. Pongámonoslo. / No nos lo pongamos.

M

1. El presupuesto fue elaborado por el asesor.
2. Los platos principales fueron preparados por la cocinera.
3. La mesa fue puesta por Nora y Jaime.
4. Los emails fueron escritos por esos secretarios.
5. El software fue creado por una programadora.
6. Todos los problemas fueron resueltos por Andrés.

7. Mi computadora fue reparada por un técnico.
8. Unos gerentes fueron enviados a Buenos Aires por la compañía.

N
1. Se firman los contratos.
2. Se trabaja de lunes a jueves.
3. Se alquilan apartamentos.
4. Se habla inglés.
5. Se llega en tren.
6. Se venden flores.
7. Se pagan los impuestos.
8. Se sirve comida vegetariana.
9. Se calculan los gastos.
10. Se sale por aquella puerta.
11. Se visita la ciudad vieja.
12. Se hacen copias.

O
1. El viajero ha llegado a la puerta de embarque.
2. ¿Has bebido té o café?
3. ¿Qué ha ocurrido?
4. Los profesores han entendido la teoría.
5. Alfonso ha abierto los ficheros.
6. Ha habido mucho tráfico últimamente.
7. Rebeca se ha maquillado la cara.
8. No hemos visto a nadie.
9. El niño se los ha puesto.
10. No se lo he dicho a nadie.
11. Los gerentes no han podido entregarle el informe a su jefe.
12. Te la hemos devuelto.

P
1. La cantante ha grabado la canción. / La canción está grabada.
2. Yo he subido los archivos. / Los archivos están subidos.
3. Los contadores han pagado las cuentas. / Las cuentas están pagadas.
4. El niño ha tirado sus juguetes. / Sus juguetes están tirados.
5. Nosotros hemos desarrollado el plan de negocios. / El plan de negocios está desarrollado.
6. El presidente ha tomado una decisión. / Una decisión está tomada.
7. Alonso ha vendido su carro. / Su carro está vendido.
8. Uds. han prendido la tele. / La tele está prendida.

Q
1. Tú habías regresado a la oficina.
2. Nosotros nos habíamos mudado.
3. Yo había buscado al nuevo diseñador.
4. El auxiliar de vuelo se había puesto el cinturón de seguridad.
5. Ellos no habían oído la noticia.
6. Uds. le habían pedido más plata.
7. Yo había apagado las luces.
8. ¿Los muchachos se lo habían leído?

R
1. Estoy hablando con mis amigos.
2. Estamos comiendo al aire libre.
3. Está nevando hoy.
4. ¿Estás imprimiendo el contrato?
5. El avión está aterrizando.
6. Te estás despertando. / Estás despertándote.
7. Nosotros se lo estamos sirviendo. / Nosotros estamos sirviéndoselo.
8. Yo se las estoy trayendo. / Yo estoy trayéndoselas.

S
1. asistan
2. entienda
3. te tranquilices
4. practique
5. sean
6. tengamos
7. te pongas
8. hagan
9. nos divirtamos
10. diga

T
1. vengamos
2. se lleven
3. sea
4. se molesta
5. apoyes
6. hacen
7. sepa
8. está

U
1. Es importante que Ud. disfrute de la vida.
2. Es bueno que nosotros leamos las obras maestras de la literatura universal.
3. Es posible que ellos se gradúen en enero.
4. Es imprescindible que Uds. coman sano.
5. Es útil que ella traiga la computadora.
6. Es triste que tú estés lejos de la familia.
7. Es bueno que tú y yo llevemos una vida tranquila.
8. Es necesario que yo me aproveche de esta oportunidad.

V
1. Nos alegramos de que Mario haya escrito otra novela.
2. Es mejor que no hayamos dicho nada.

3. Me sorprende que no te hayan devuelto el dinero.
4. ¿Dudas que haya habido muchos problemas políticos?
5. Espero que hayas tenido mucha suerte.
6. Sienten que al futbolista se le haya roto el pie.

W

1. se hiciera	5. consiguiera
2. pasáramos	6. pudiéramos
3. vieran	7. fuéramos
4. fuera	8. salieras

X

1. Trabaje los lunes. / No trabaje los lunes.
2. Escríbalo. / No lo escriba.
3. Léalos. / No los lea.
4. Vaya a la clase. / No vaya a la clase.
5. Pruébesela. / No se la pruebe.
6. Salgan ahora mismo. / No salgan ahora mismo.
7. Dénselas. / No se las den.
8. Explíquenmelas. / No me las expliquen.
9. Devuélvanselo. / No se lo devuelvan.
10. Lávensela. / No se la laven.
11. Sé amable. / No seas amable.
12. Ven conmigo. / No vengas conmigo.
13. Sal a las cuatro. / No salgas a las cuatro.
14. Háznosla. / No nos la hagas.
15. Póntelo. / No te lo pongas.
16. Vamos de compras. / No vayamos de compras.
17. Relajémonos. / No nos relajemos.
18. Sirvámoselo. / No se lo sirvamos.
19. Quitémonoslas. / No nos las quitemos.
20. Cepillémonoslos. / No nos los cepillemos.

Y

1. Me gustan estos museos.
2. Nos interesa mucho la arqueología.
3. Les importa el medio ambiente.
4. ¿Les cayó mal ese tipo?
5. ¿Te entusiasmaron los espectáculos?
6. Nos encantaría hacer un viaje.
7. Le tocó a él.
8. Le hace falta decidirse.

Z

1. Se le perdió la mochila.
2. Se me quedó el paraguas en la oficina.
3. Se les descompuso el carro.
4. Se le rompieron las gafas oscuras.
5. Se les acabó la energía.
6. Se te cayeron los vasos.
7. Se nos ocurrió algo.
8. Se le olvidó el cumpleaños de su hermana.

Index

About the Authors

Ronni L. Gordon, PhD, is a prominent author of foreign language textbooks and multimedia instructional materials, including more than 40 titles in Spanish and other languages. She has taught Spanish language and Spanish American literature and coordinated Spanish language programs at Harvard University, Boston University, and Cornell University. A foreign language consultant, she has read for the National Endowment for the Humanities, presented at the United States Department of Education, and consulted on states' K–12 academic standards for world languages. She has presented at conferences on foreign language pedagogy and Spanish American literature, as one of the first scholars to give a college course on Spanish American women writers, and has been acknowledged by Uruguay's Ministerio de Educación y Cultura for her promotion of Uruguayan culture. As chairwoman of the Board of Directors of Dolce Suono Ensemble, an acclaimed chamber music organization, she focuses on Latino community engagement through concerts and education outreach as part of its award-winning "Música en tus Manos" (Music in Your Hands) project. Committed to excellence in education for all students, she and co-author David Stillman founded the Committee for Quality Education, an organization devoted to the improvement of academic standards in the public schools of Brookline, Massachusetts, where she was an elected member of Town Meeting.

David M. Stillman, PhD, is a well-known author of foreign language textbooks and multimedia instructional materials, with a bibliography that includes titles in Spanish, French, Italian, and German. He taught Spanish, French, Italian, and Hebrew at the College of New Jersey, where he was instrumental in the creation of a linguistics major and coordinated an innovative program of student-led oral proficiency classes. He taught in and coordinated foreign language programs at Boston University, Harvard University, and Cornell University. He has consulted on states' K–12 academic standards for world languages, presented at national and regional conventions of language educators, and has been appointed to national committees devoted to the improvement of teacher training. He founded and was president of Multilingua, a company that provided foreign language instruction and translation services to the business community and English language instruction to immigrant communities. He was also founding president of Mediatheque, Inc., a company that provided authoring and editorial services to major publishing houses.

Lennon—some of them shocking even today. . . . Norman says he sought to portray Lennon candidly as 'both a massive influence on twentieth-century culture and an ultimately adorable human being,' and, tabloid headlines aside, he has succeeded."

—*USA Today*

"It sharpens what we know about Lennon at just about every turn. . . . Norman pushes beyond the clichés in exploring how the books and poems Lennon loved as a child reemerged in both his songs and his prose. And he cracks the mystery of the affair Lennon admitted writing about in 'Norwegian Wood.' . . . Devotees will relish the new information, while casual readers will find a familiar story told more truly than ever before."

—*Rolling Stone*

"Fascinating. . . . Mr. Norman, author of the well-regarded *Shout! The Beatles in Their Generation*, provides enormously detailed accounts of John's childhood in middle-class Liverpool and his life-long insecurities; the birth, rise, and contentious death of the Beatles; and the Yoko years. . . . Mr. Norman's meticulous research includes Aunt Mimi's papers and interviews with Ms. Ono, Beatles producer George Martin, and Mr. McCartney. Each is positively represented. . . . But in the end, neither Ms. Ono nor Mr. McCartney seemed pleased with Mr. Norman's book. The reader should have no such problems."

—*Dallas Morning News*

"A highlight is the way Norman weaves in the intricate compositions Lennon wrote with his partner of approximately twelve years, Paul McCartney. . . . He writes an intimate look at the fine balance between creativity, friendship, and competing ambitions that defined their relationship. This book also draws on a great many sources, including the many people in John's life, from the famous to the forgotten. The information gleaned from Lennon's many family members in Liverpool adds interesting elements as well to create a rich portrait of Lennon, (many) warts and all. . . . Overall, this a moving tale of the formation of a complicated personality who touched the world, lifted it up, and made it better."

—*Pittsburgh Post-Gazette*

"It's this level of detail that makes Norman's 822 pages such compulsive reading."

—Bloomberg News

"More moving and less plausible than most fiction, Lennon's life is one of the great twentieth-century fables, and it's told here definitively by a major Beatles scholar. Even as Lennon went from young tough to global pop star to hippie prophet, he never ceased to be a shattered, motherless little boy. When have so many ever followed anyone so lost? A."

—*Time*

"Reading this book brings the John Lennon I knew vividly back to life."

—Bill Harry, founder of *Mersey Beat*

"The most explosive rock story of the year. . . . There is always an arresting new fact around the corner. . . . *John Lennon: The Life* may be a warts-and-all kind of biography but it's also respectful and affectionate. . . . This is the best Lennon book so far."

—*The Word* (UK)

"This extensive, thoroughly researched biography traces the life of John Lennon, who, nearly thirty years after his murder, remains one of the most intriguing and respected figures in popular music. Novelist and biographer Norman, who recounted the story of the Beatles in *Shout!*, focuses here on Lennon's life outside his legendary band. . . . Lennon's treatment of his discarded first wife and long-suffering, seafaring father are examined in rich detail, shedding new light on his complex personality. . . . Exclusive new commentary from Yoko Ono, Paul McCartney, and sundry confidants and family members provides fresh insight."

—Library Journal

"To Norman's credit, the reader comes away from the multifaceted John Lennon feeling like he almost knew him—and that he probably wouldn't have liked him if he did. . . . The music . . . is where Norman—author of the definitive 1981 Beatle biography *Shout! The Beatles in Their Generation*—shines. In extravagant sentences, Norman revels in the single dimension of his subject that he unequivocally loves and appreciates. Such enthusiasm could be grating, but Norman's is refreshing and heartening. . . . Norman's reconciliations of man and music comprise the most interesting passages."

—NPR.org

"In *John Lennon: The Life* by Philip Norman, the author of the acclaimed 1981 Beatles biography *Shout!* uncovers new details about the rock icon's psychologically scarred childhood, his possessiveness (which nearly drove Yoko away), the $50 million offer for the Beatles to reunite ('I'd stand on me head in the corner for that kind of money,' said Lennon), and his poignant efforts to reconcile with the father he believed deserted him."

—AARP Magazine